D0758496

*H*ANDBOOK OF
ORGANIZATIONAL
AND MANAGERIAL
*W*ISDOM

To Kim, Jake, and Danny, who inspire me with their love and lives, as well as the countless others who have contributed to my ongoing search for wisdom.

—EHK

To my father, Francis E. "Buck" Bailey, who was always my hero, in his life and in his death, and who every single day I understand as more wise that I ever grasped.

—JRB

HANDBOOK OF
ORGANIZATIONAL
AND MANAGERIAL
WISDOM

EDITED BY
ERIC H. KESSLER
Pace University

JAMES R. BAILEY
George Washington University

Foreword by Karl E. Weick

SAGE Publications
Los Angeles • London • New Delhi • Singapore

For information:

Sage Publications, Inc.
2455 Teller Road
Thousand Oaks, California 91320
E-mail: order@sagepub.com

Sage Publications Ltd.
1 Oliver's Yard
55 City Road
London EC1Y 1SP
United Kingdom

Sage Publications India Pvt. Ltd.
B 1/I 1 Mohan Cooperative Industrial Area
Mathura Road, New Delhi 110 044
India

Sage Publications Asia-Pacific Pte. Ltd.
33 Pekin Street #02-01
Far East Square
Singapore 048763

Printed in the United States of America

Library of Congress Cataloging-in-Publication Data

Handbook of organizational and managerial wisdom / editors, Eric H. Kessler, James R. Bailey.
      p. cm.
Includes bibliographical references and index.
ISBN 978-1-4129-1561-8 (cloth)
    1. Decision making. 2. Wisdom. 3. Management. 4. Organizational sociology. I. Kessler, Eric H. II. Bailey, James Russell, 1963–
HD30.23.H355 2007
302.3'5—dc22   2006102691

This book is printed on acid-free paper.

07   08   09   10   11   10   9   8   7   6   5   4   3   2   1

Acquisitions Editor:	Al Bruckner
Editorial Assistant:	MaryAnn Vail
Production Editor:	Diane S. Foster
Copy Editor:	D. J. Peck
Typesetter:	C&M Digitals (P) Ltd.
Proofreader:	Scott Oney
Cover Designer:	Janet Foulger
Marketing Manager:	Nichole M. Angress

Contents

Foreword _____

Karl E. Weick

In November 2002, a renowned organizational consultant made the following comment to me: "I refuse to play the expert role. Playing the expert role leads to arguments and people pitting facts against facts. I play the sage role. When they ask a question, I tell a story."

If one examines the word *sage* in a synonym dictionary (*Merriam-Webster Dictionary of Synonyms*, 1984), here is what the entry says: Sage characterizes a person "who is eminently wise, being a philosopher by temperament and experience. The term commonly suggests a habit of profound reflection upon men and events and an ability to reach conclusions of universal as well as immediate value, and has been applied chiefly to persons and utterances that are venerated for their wisdom and good counsel" (p. 889). Is that what organizations are looking for when they hire this consultant? Why does it seem like there are no sages internal to the organization?

And if an organization feels that it has few individuals or teams who are "eminently wise," then what kinds of people does it think it has? More important, what kinds of relationships does it make possible? Here is where it gets interesting because the antonym for the word *wise* is not the word *foolish,* as one might expect (Sternberg, 2005), but rather the word *simple* (*Merriam-Webster Dictionary of Synonyms,* 1984, p. 889). Simple, simplify, and simplification are the essence of organizing, suggesting that wisdom might well undermine organizing. The intention to simplify shows up in discussions of mindlessness, routines, normalizing, maxims for action (e.g., "keep it simple, stupid"), requisite variety, organizing principles (Turner, 1978), and generalizing as the cornerstone of organizing (Tsoukas, 2005). If simplifying is an imperative in organizational life, then wisdom should be both rare and difficult to implement. By this line of thinking, organizations that exhibit a "reluctance to simplify" (e.g., high-reliability organizations as described by Weick, Sutcliffe, & Obstfeld, 1999) would be the surprising sites of wise action as well as the sites of nonsimple organizational forms. Furthermore, reliability may be the site for wisdom in organizing, just as efficiency may be the site for its antithesis.

It is possibilities such as these that surface when one reflects on wisdom using this handbook as the pretext for reflection. People who study managing and organizing are already working with notions of wisdom, albeit usually without awareness that this is the case. Wisdom is wrapped around many of the durable themes in organizational theory. For example, uncertainty reduction is a hallmark of organizational studies, and Brugman (2000) described wisdom as expertise in, and acceptance of, uncertainty. Judgment is a prominent theme in organizational theory (e.g., Bazerman, 2005) as well as in discussions of wisdom. The richness of this juxtaposition was suggested by Cooperrider and Srivastva (1998) when they argued, "Wisdom is not a permanent trait but [rather] a dynamic process of subtle *judging* and knowing that must always be readjusted, restructured, and rebuilt" (p. 5, italics added). Gioia's definition of wisdom in this volume (Chapter 13) places judgment in a central position when he treats wisdom as "the acquired ability to create viable realities from equivocal circumstances and to use informed judgment to negotiate prudent courses of action through the realities created." As Gioia goes on to say, judgment is expressed in informed sensemaking and learned sensegiving.

Further points of provocative contact between wisdom and organizing were apparent when Taranto (1989) argued that wisdom "involves a recognition of and response to human limitations" (p. 15). This contact is exemplified by a view of wisdom that has already had a significant impact on organizational studies (e.g., Pfeffer & Sutton, 2006; Weick, 1998, 2000), namely, Meacham's (1990) proposal that wisdom is an attitude that balances knowledge and ignorance:

> The essence of wisdom . . . lies not in what is known but rather in the manner in which that knowledge is held and in how that knowledge is put to use. To be wise is not to know particular facts but [rather] to know without excessive confidence or excessive cautiousness . . . to both accumulate knowledge while remaining suspicious of it, and recognizing that much remains unknown, is to be wise. . . . The essence of wisdom is in knowing that one does not know, in the appreciation that knowledge is fallible, in the balance between knowing and doubting. (pp. 185, 187, 210)

Students of organization already know something about Meacham's version of wisdom because they have used a parallel idea called "bounded rationality." The interesting thing about bounded rationality is that some organizational members recognize and respond to these limitations on rationality, but most do not. Again, high-reliability organizations become an intriguing site for organizational studies because they are notable for their preoccupation with small failures that are signs of potentially larger system problems. As Reason (1997) noted, failures are inevitable, so the question is whether organizational forms allow people to spot and contain them. The implied answer is *yes* if wisdom is cultivated or *no* if wisdom is discouraged.

Several other juxtapositions of wisdom and organizing resonate, but in a more challenging manner. For example, in organizations in the Western world, wisdom and knowledge are treated as synonymous (Takahashi & Overton, 2005, p. 36). This means that wise action involves an extensive knowledge database, analysis, cognition, and sufficient information processing skill to use the database. Thus, studies of knowledge management, in this context, should serve as gateways to wisdom, and the findings should suggest organizational substitutes for wisdom. But that is true only if one adopts a very narrow view of wisdom. The narrowness becomes clear in the context of Birren and Fisher's (1990) definition of wisdom:

> Wisdom is the *integration of the affective, conative, and cognitive* aspects of human abilities in response to life's tasks and problems. Wisdom is a balance between opposing valences of intense emotion and detachment, action and inaction, and knowledge and doubts. It tends to increase with experience and therefore age, but it is not exclusively found in old age. (p. 326, italics in original)

In the Birren and Fisher description, wisdom involves more than cognition, more than analysis, more than organizational tasks, more than resolved oppositions, and more than stable forms. The crucial question now becomes the following: What properties of organizing and organizations in the West preclude affective and conative influence, synthesis, work on life tasks, balancing of oppositions, and the necessity to reaccomplish dynamic balancing?

A further challenge lies in the reliance of organizations on texts, language, and representations rather than on direct undistracted attention (Weick & Sutcliffe, 2006). In the words of artist Robert Irwin, "Seeing is forgetting the name of the thing one sees" (Weschler, 1982). The complexities of organizing can be knowable but unnameable, although this possibility is missed by those who focus on representations (for an elaboration of this point, see Chia & Holt [Chapter 22] in this volume). English words in particular can be troublesome in the pursuit of wisdom because, as Paget (1988) made clear, "English is an adjectival language, and for this reason, a difficult language in which to portray action happening. . . . English is also an abstract language and often far removed from the subtle details of human communication, the details that make it possible to understand what is being said" (p. 146). What all of this suggests is that a closer look at wisdom may improve the clarity with which we think about organizing. As an example of thinking differently, consider Taylor and Van Every's (2000) argument that when people communicate,

> they arrive at a situation in which both subjects and their objects are constituted and thus turned into a site of organization. As they construct their situation, they also give it discursive form and a kind of

cognitive as well as lived reality, in that they now can talk about what they are living. We see the role of language in this realization as providing the surface on which organization can be read. (pp. 38–39)

Conversations provide the site and texts provide the surface of what will have become an instance of organizing. Multiple conversations, with

their distributed–segmented partial-images of a complex environment, can, through interaction, synthetically construct a representation of it that works, one which, in its interactive complexity, outstrips the capacity of any single individual in the network to represent and discriminate events. . . . Out of the interconnections, there emerges a representation of the world that none of those involved individually possessed or could possess. (p. 207)

The distributed representation is subsymbolic. Efforts to formulate it

in a conventional language of symbols is the motivation for the emergence of organizational macro-actors. These actors speak in the name of the group as a whole and thus represent it, both by giving it a voice and by interpreting back to it in symbolic form what it collectively knows, at the subsymbolic level of cognition. (pp. 140–141)

To intuit these operations, to value the development of integrated sensory modalities that grasp these operations, to avoid overt intellectualizing that masks these operations, to see synthesis as reality, and to see shortcomings in synthesis as inevitable is to interweave organizing and wisdom.

To wade into the topic of wisdom is to see organizing differently. To wade into this volume is to see wisdom differently. Both forms of effort embody a wonderful moment of wisdom itself, as Lao Tzu saw clearly (cited in Muller, 1999, p. 134):

In pursuit of knowledge, every day something is acquired;
In pursuit of wisdom, every day something is dropped.

To acquire the messages of this volume is to know. To then drop the messages of this volume and move on is to live.

References

Bazerman, M. H. (2005). *Judgment in managerial decision making.* New York: John Wiley.

Birren, J. E., & Fisher, L. M. (1990). Conceptualizing wisdom: The primacy of affect–cognition relations. In R. J. Sternberg (Ed.), *Wisdom: Its nature, origins, and development* (pp. 317–332). New York: Cambridge University Press.

Brugman, G. (2000). *Wisdom: Source of narrative coherence and eudaimonia*. Delft, Netherlands: Uitgeverij Eberon.

Cooperrider, D. L., & Srivastva, S. (1998). An invitation to organizational wisdom and executive change. In S. Srivastva & D. L. Cooperrider (Eds.), *Organizational wisdom and executive courage* (pp. 1–22). San Francisco: New Lexington Press.

Meacham, J. A. (1990). The loss of wisdom. In R. J. Sternberg (Ed.), *Wisdom: Its nature, origins, and development* (pp. 181–211). New York: Cambridge University Press.

Merriam-Webster dictionary of synonyms: A dictionary of discriminated synonyms with antonyms and analogous and contrasted words. (1984). New York: Merriam-Webster.

Muller, W. (1999). *Sabbath: Restoring the sacred rhythm of rest*. New York: Bantam Books.

Paget, M. (1988). *The unity of mistakes: A phenomenological interpretation of medical work*. Philadelphia: Temple University Press.

Pfeffer, J., & Sutton, R. I. (2006). *Hard facts, dangerous half-truths, and total nonsense*. Boston: Harvard Business School Press.

Reason, J. (1997). *Managing the risks of organizational accidents*. Aldershot, UK: Ashgate.

Sternberg, R. J. (2005). Foolishness. In R. J. Sternberg & J. Jordan (Eds.), *A handbook of wisdom: Psychological perspectives* (pp. 331–352). New York: Cambridge University Press.

Takahashi, M., & Overton, W. F. (2005). Cultural foundations of wisdom: An integrated developmental approach. In R. J. Sternberg & J. Jordan (Eds.), *A handbook of wisdom: Psychological perspectives* (pp. 32–60). New York: Cambridge University Press.

Taranto, M. A. (1989). Facets of wisdom: A theoretical analysis. *International Journal of Aging and Human Development, 29*, 1–21.

Taylor, J. R., & Van Every, E. J. (2000). *The emergent organization: Communication as its site and surface*. Mahwah, NJ: Lawrence Erlbaum.

Tsoukas, H. (2005). *Complex knowledge: Studies in organizational epistemology*. Oxford, UK: Oxford University Press.

Turner, B. (1978). *Man-made disasters*. London: Wykeham.

Weick, K. E. (1998). The attitude of wisdom: Ambivalence as the optimal compromise. In S. Srivastva & D. Cooperrider (Eds.), *Organizational wisdom and executive courage* (pp. 40–64). San Francisco: New Lexington Press.

Weick, K. E. (2000). Quality improvement: A sensemaking perspective. In R. E. Cole & W. R. Scott (Eds.), *The quality movement and organization theory* (pp. 155–172). Thousand Oaks, CA: Sage.

Weick, K. E., & Sutcliffe, K. M. (2006). Mindfulness and the quality of organizational attention. *Organization Science, 17*, 514–524.

Weick, K. E., Sutcliffe, K. M., & Obstfeld, D. (1999). Organizing for high reliability: Processes of collective mindfulness. In B. Staw & R. Sutton (Eds.), *Research in organizational behavior* (Vol. 21, pp. 81–123). Greenwich, CT: JAI.

Weschler, L. (1982). *Seeing is forgetting the name of the thing one sees: A life of contemporary artist Robert Irwin*. Berkeley: University of California Press.

Introduction

Understanding, Applying, and Developing Organizational and Managerial Wisdom

Eric H. Kessler
James R. Bailey

The daily lives of most of us are full of things that keep us very busy and preoccupied. But every now and then we find ourselves drawing back and wondering what it's all about. And then, perhaps, we may start asking fundamental questions that normally we do not stop to ask. . . . This can happen with regard to any aspect of life. . . . People can subject any field of human activity to fundamental questioning like this . . . which is a way of saying that there can be a philosophy of anything.

—Bryan MaGee, 1998

Philosophy is essentially the completion of science in the synthesis of wisdom.

—Will Durant, 1961

Wisdom is among the most complex and profound concepts in our vernacular. It represents the epitome of human development and conduct yet remains stubbornly enigmatic. Notwithstanding this duality—or perhaps as a result of it—wisdom has been the subject of constant inquiry across every age of our history and every culture of our construction. It characterizes the most enlightened and successful people and collectives. Philosophers and religious thinkers, scientists and scholars, and authors and artists alike have attempted to crystallize its character. Yet wisdom defies a universally accepted definition or comprehensively applicable model. Thus, one might rightly conclude that there is nothing as simultaneously important and mysterious as wisdom.

In this handbook, we examine wisdom as applied to the ubiquitous social structure of the organization and its management. This is no small undertaking given that one would be hard-pressed to conceive of human life untouched by formal organizations, the proper stewardship of which forms the academic and professional fields of management and where rigorous treatment of wisdom is just beginning to emerge. Whereas wisdom is frequently alluded to, indirectly referenced, or casually conceived in this growing area, our charge here is to progress meaningfully toward a systematic and deep consideration of its application to professional pursuits. Toward this end, we have commissioned some of the brightest minds in the field to confront the problem of defining what organizational and managerial wisdom (OMW) is, how to best apply it, and how to develop it. The contributions herein are profound and well intentioned, but our objective is not to put the issue to rest. To the contrary, the content of this handbook represents less a conclusion than an introduction, less a final word than an opening argument, and less a comprehensive model than a structured exploration. None of us would be so bold (or unwise) as to claim an exclusive channel into the ideal of OMW, but together we seek to construct what it might look like.

In this introductory chapter of the *Handbook of Organizational and Managerial Wisdom,* we sketch the rationale for this inquiry, construct objectives and structure, preview the book's contributions, and suggest a common ground for understanding, applying, and developing wisdom in the practice of organization management. The introductory chapter is organized as follows: (a) Wisdom, (b) Organizational and Managerial Wisdom, (c) *Handbook of Organizational and Managerial Wisdom,* and (d) Insights From the *Handbook of Organizational and Managerial Wisdom.*

Wisdom

> *Until . . . political greatness and wisdom meet in one, and those commoner natures who pursue either to the exclusion of the other are compelled to stand aside, cities will never have rest from their evils—no, nor the human race, as I believe—and then only will this our State have a possibility of life and behold the light of day.*
>
> —Plato, *The Republic* (Book V)

> *Totally ignored in mainstream scientific inquiry for decades, wisdom is beginning to return to the place of reverence that it held in ancient schools of intellectual study.*
>
> —Robert Sternberg and Jennifer Jordan, 2005

Volumes upon volumes have been written about wisdom. Indeed, considerations of its nature can be traced back more than 5,000 years (*Encyclopedia Britannica,* 2006). Although we do not pretend to resolve the question, it is necessary to delineate some essential characteristics so that we might go about this exploration of wisdom's organizational and managerial manifestations.

Wisdom Is Important

There is perhaps nothing more important for orienting and conducting human affairs than wisdom. It is an ideal to be emulated because it yields immeasurable returns, as conveyed through memorable adages such as that wisdom "outweighs any wealth" (Sophocles), is "organized life" (Immanuel Kant), "is the principal thing" (Proverbs 4:7), and is "sacred communication" (Victor Hugo). That wisdom is absolutely critical in the conceptualization and execution of one's life and work is self-evident. Therefore, the first principle we adopt here is that wisdom is an important—some might even say critical—subject of inquiry.

The wisdom ideal has been represented in myriad ways (see the following section) and has been equated with sages, scholars, and deity. Yet one thing remains constant throughout the ages: Wisdom represents the highest stages of development attainable by humans and their most desirable patterns of behavior (Baltes & Staudinger, 2000; Rice, 1958). Birren and Fisher (1990) explained wisdom's placement at the pinnacle of existence by tracing the evolution of the term. The concept is generally used to represent the best of a context or an age. Its etymology even suggests a place on the top of a hierarchy of attributes, an amalgam of superior human qualities to enable esteemed action. Thus, wisdom facilitates more successful cognition and volition, more penetrating understanding and affect, and more effective action and decision making.

We would also argue that life—personal or professional—is more meaningful with wisdom, partly because it allows one to extract more meaning from life. Thus, wisdom is terminally important as well as instrumentally important. Just as the folksy admonition to "stop and smell the roses" advises taking time for one to absorb and appreciate the world more completely—to take notice of the details and differences in things— so too does delaying managerial dictates allow others to assume responsibility, that is, to sense the discretion and autonomy required of professional identity. The benefits are real and considerable, and in the long run they are more effective and efficient. Wisdom, then, becomes something to pursue not just for its own sake or immediate functionality but also because it lightens the load so frequently bemoaned by making it sublimely easier to bear.

Wisdom Is Complex and Multifaceted

To consider the meaning and fundamental nature of wisdom is no simple endeavor. It is ironic that Socrates told us that the beginning of wisdom is the definition of terms in that turning this starting point on itself begets an intriguing tautology. There have been countless conceptualizations of the construct, and one is hard-pressed to decipher which ones are true if indeed it can be said that any can be true inasmuch as the concept transcends time and location. Therefore, the second principle that we adopt in compiling this handbook is that wisdom covers an astonishingly broad and diverse collection of attributes and actions.

There are as many dictionary definitions of wisdom as there are dictionaries. The term is often vaguely defined as being wise or related to insight or judgment. *Wisdom* is seen both as a noun, inferring that it can be possessed to varying degrees, and as a verb, a process of understanding and acting on the world. A brief review from a plethora of sources includes the following definitions of wisdom: (a) the quality of being wise, or the body of knowledge and experience that develops within a specified society or period (*Oxford English Dictionary*, 2006); (b) the ability to make correct judgments and decisions (*Wikipedia*, 2006); (c) accumulated philosophical or scientific learning (*Merriam-Webster Online Dictionary*, 2006); (d) the ability to make sensible decisions and judgments based on personal knowledge and experience (*Encarta*, 2006); (e) possessing or showing the ability to make good judgments, based on a deep understanding and experience of life (*Cambridge Dictionaries Online*, 2006); (f) the quality of being wise; the faculty of making the best use of knowledge, experience, understanding, etc.; good judgment, sagacity (*Webster's New Twentieth Century Dictionary*, 1961); and (g) the ability to discern or judge what is true, right, or lasting; insight; common sense, good judgment (*American Heritage Dictionary of the English Language*, 2006).

Turning to philosophical dictionaries, yet another genre of responses to the question of "What is wisdom?" emerges. Philosophically, the ancient Greek "φιλοσοφια" (*philosophia*) is roughly translatable as "love of wisdom." Thus, we are philosophers when we earnestly and passionately pursue the meaning and practice of what is wise. This love entails the most general and abstract features of the world and categories with which we think—mind, matter, reason, proof, truth, and the like, which are in turn the topic of inquiry. Perhaps "the shortest definition, and it is quite a good one, is that philosophy is thinking about thinking . . . reflective thought" (Honderich, 1995, p. 666). The disciplinary philosophy of (say) history, physics, or law seeks not so much to solve specific questions as to examine those elements that structure thinking about specific questions and to lay bare their foundations and presuppositions. According to the *Cambridge Dictionary of Philosophy* (Audi, 1999), wisdom represents "an understanding of the highest principles of things that function as a guide for living a truly exemplary human life." The *HarperCollins Dictionary of Philosophy*

(Angeles, 1992) defines the term in a related manner, as representing "prudent judgment as to how to use knowledge in the everyday affairs of life; the correct perception of the best ends in life, the best means to their attainment, and the practical intelligence to successfully apply those means." These definitions rely heavily on—and indeed attempt to synthesize—Plato's concern for ideal forms and Aristotle's distinction between the intellectual *sophia* (theoretically deep understanding of reality) and the applied *phronesis* (practically skilled judgment and behavioral alacrity).

Religious traditions bring yet another framework to the wisdom concept. For example, fear of God is the beginning of wisdom in Judaism, and in Islam Allah is said to be full of wisdom. Devotion and virtue are central themes in Christian writings, where wisdom (prudence) stands with justice, fortitude, and moderation as one of the four cardinal virtues. Wisdom is seen here as an intellectual virtue of knowing truth and believing the ultimate cause. Buddhist and Hindu writings take a more multidimensional view; Buddhism differentiates good wisdom from evil wisdom and conventional wisdom from ultimate wisdom, and Hinduism accepts several wisdoms such as oneness, awareness, infinity, eternity, balance, faith, and holiness. Confucian thought sees wisdom as more in line with respect as per the idea that "to give one's self earnestly to the duties due to men, and, while respecting spiritual beings, to keep aloof from them, may be called wisdom." Taoist doctrine tends to see wisdom as learned, particularly through introspection.

Obviously, the pursuit of wisdom has a long and varied history. A select representation of its lineage as sketched by Birren and Svensson (2005) is presented in Table I.1.

Insofar as the contributors to this handbook consider the organizational and managerial manifestations of wisdom, we focus on human, as opposed to theological, conceptions. Yet even within this sphere, the perceptive reader will notice a gap between the study of wisdom during the Enlightenment and that during our current time. Indeed, some scholars have concluded that wisdom had practically "dropped off the scholarly map" until its recent resurgence. This is corroborated by the absence of the term in philosophical, psychological, and related encyclopedias during this neglected period (Robinson, 1990).

Scientific attention to wisdom was, until fairly recently, almost nonexistent. According to Trowbridge (2005), systematic research into wisdom is scant but growing. He concluded that during the 1980s only 5 studies were conducted, whereas during the first half of the 2000s he found an increased—but still miniscule—16 studies, although few of these are seen as substantial theoretical or empirical undertakings. This notwithstanding, one can discern at least three distinct genres of rigorous inquiry that in turn yield potentially useful frameworks for understanding wisdom. We characterize these as the integrative approach of Ardelt, the developmental approach of Baltes and his colleagues, and the balance approach of Sternberg.

Table I.1   Select Definitions of Wisdom

Sumerian	Wisdom as practical advice for daily living
Egyptian	Wisdom as precepts for good behavior
Greek	*Socrates:* Wisdom as what we need to know to live the good and just life; we can be lovers of wisdom but never truly wise *Plato:* Wisdom as the discernment of the meaning of life and the nature of the world *Aristotle:* Wisdom as both practical (prudence) and speculative (highest form of knowledge)
Hebrew	Wisdom as divine enlightenment; revelation of truth from God; guides to behavior
Christian	Wisdom as a gift from God; moral perfection; first principles
Hindu	Wisdom as a vast intuitive understanding of the nature of life and death
Buddhist	Wisdom lies in stilling all desires; knowing something truly
Taoist	Wisdom is in obedience to nature and refusal to interfere in the natural course of things
Confucian	Wisdom begins in the individual moral order and continues into proper social and political order
Renaissance	*Montaigne:* Wisdom in living life in accordance with nature and being aware of one's ignorance *Bacon:* Wisdom as knowledge gained through inductive reasoning and systematic scientific inquiry
Enlightenment	*Descartes:* Wisdom as cognitive knowing through reflection, reason, and ethical deliberation *Locke:* Wisdom as knowing God and primary qualities through meditation and reason *Kant:* Wisdom can be loved but not attained in accordance with the categorical imperative; act only on the maxim whereby one can at the same time will that it should become a universal law *Schopenhauer:* Wisdom as an objective view of the world through awareness of and freedom from desires
Psychological and empirical sciences	*Dewey:* Wisdom is found in deferring action based on knowledge *Erikson:* Wisdom as the mastery of ego integrity versus despair *Baltes and colleagues:* Wisdom as an expert knowledge system in the domain; fundamental life pragmatics *Sternberg and colleagues:* Wisdom as metacognitive—the integration of the affective, conative, and cognitive aspects of human abilities in response to life's tasks and problems *Meacham:* Wisdom as maintaining a position between knowledge and doubting (similar to Weick) *Bruman:* Wisdom as expertise in uncertainty

SOURCE: Adapted from Birren and Svensson (2005).

Ardelt (2000, 2004) proposed that wisdom is essentially an *integrative* dynamic resulting from the synthesis of cognitive (knowing and comprehending), reflective (perspective and introspection), and affective (compassion and empathy) dimensions. Wisdom, as compared with knowledge, ultimately involves a deeper and more fundamental understanding of the world and one's place in it.

Baltes and colleagues (Baltes & Staudinger, 2000; Baltes & Kunzmann, 2004), in what has been termed the *Berlin Wisdom Paradigm,* proposed that wisdom is essentially a *developmental* dynamic that emerges from several antecedent conditions and includes performance along a variety of criteria. Personal, domain-specific, and contextual factors form the enabling foundations for wisdom, which in turn is manifested in individual and collective progression. As such, wisdom can be enhanced through experience and structured intervention. Ultimately, Baltes and colleagues see wisdom as an evolving metaheuristic to orchestrate mind and virtue in the fundamental pragmatics of life.

Sternberg (1990, 2003a, 2003b) proposed that wisdom is essentially a *balancing* dynamic that involves the reconciliation of several related yet distinct cognitive factors. As per Jordan and Sternberg's description in Chapter 1 of this handbook, "wisdom is the ability to use one's successful intelligence, creativity, and knowledge, as mediated by personal values, to reach a common good by balancing intrapersonal, interpersonal, and extrapersonal interests over the short and long terms to adapt to, shape, and select environments." Therefore, wisdom involves both individual and systemic balancing that ultimately—when combined with intelligence and creativity (i.e., the WICS model)—is oriented toward effective leadership and positive contributions to the common good.

Other efforts supplement what we see as these primary streams. For example, McKee and Barber (1999) contended that wisdom's range of conceptualizations—theoretical, practical, divine, secular, scientific, and so on—ultimately converge to indicate the ability to see truly, or through life's illusions.. Seligman and Csikszentmihalyi (2000) introduced the idea of positive psychology and its promise for unlocking our understanding of the elements that make life worth living—including wisdom. Srivastava and Cooperrider (1998) connected the concept with courage and sensemaking.

More recently, Sternberg and Jordan's (2005) edited book celebrates the revival of serious scholarly interest in wisdom, announcing its "return to the place of reverence that it held in ancient schools of intellectual study." Indeed, their volume represents a most impressive and systematic effort to understand the concept. Incorporating psychological, historical, philosophical, and other perspectives, it is a critically important contribution to our understanding of the wisdom concept. As valuable as it is, Sternberg and Jordan's contribution differs from our handbook in significant ways. First, their contributors tend to look at the extremely complex concept of wisdom altogether—in toto. Whereas they focus on wisdom as a whole, we consider its various facets and manifestations to synthesize insights. Second, they examine wisdom proper and do not explicitly address it to the context of professional pursuits. Alternatively, our handbook is centered on the practical implications of wisdom in the business of organizations and their management.

Finally, we would be remiss—in a section on the complexity of wisdom—if we did not note how differently wisdom is conceived across cultures. Cultural differences alone justify a multivolume series. Acknowledging this, Takahashi and Overton (2005) observed that "wisdom is not a unitary but a multidimensional construct and is defined differently across various populations" (p. 38). In the West wisdom is conceived more along the cognitive dimension, and in the East it is conceived more along the affective dimension (Takahashi & Bordia, 2000). For example, Mahayana Buddhism includes the concept of *prajna,* the ultimate wisdom, inaccessible to human experience but partially revealed through nirvana and emptiness (Flesher, 2006). This notion of contingency is well represented throughout the contributions in this handbook, particularly in focal treatments of international culture (Chapter 14) and comparative analysis of East–West perspectives (Chapter 22).

Wisdom Is Preeminent to Knowledge

To be wise means more than merely to be knowledgeable. Surely, we all have witnessed our share of intelligent yet foolish individuals. Knowledge might be necessary, but it is certainly not sufficient for wisdom. As famously lamented by the poet T. S. Eliot in *The Rock,* "Where is the wisdom we have lost in knowledge? Where is the knowledge we have lost in information?" (Eliot, 1934). We offer the following reconciliation. Data are raw facts. One memorizes them to impress other people or to score well on game shows. Information is meaningful and useful data. One gives form and function to numbers to make sense of them. Knowledge is clear understanding of information. One analyzes and synthesizes information to truly comprehend it. Wisdom is something more—deeper, broader, apparent, contradictory, evident, lucid and nebulous, experienced and naive, all at the same time. If one's goal is to live better—whatever way one may define that—more data, more information, or more knowledge neither unequivocally nor universally leads to personal happiness (Van Doren, 1991) or firm success (Schrage, 2001). Therefore, the third principle that we adopt in compiling this handbook is that wisdom is superordinate to just knowing; indeed, it comprises something entirely different.

Wisdom is clearly differentiated from knowledge. Philosophically, the concepts are quite distinct. Knowledge involves holding justified true belief, whereas wisdom uses this knowledge in the conduct of sound and serene judgment (Edwards, 1972). This distinction is fairly consistent with Eastern thought, where in Confucianism the wise know and walk along The Way

(Tao) and in Buddhism the wise live life consistent with enlightened realization (nirvana). Western thinkers lean toward a pragmatic vision of wisdom as "value added." Aristotle (1984), in his *Nicomachean Ethics*, spoke of "practical" wisdom as the ability to deliberate well about what is good and expedient. In *Critique of Practical Reason*, Kant (1778/1997) described a state of true wisdom as the practical end of the existence of humans on the earth. James's (1909/1995) *Pragmatism* subjected ideas to the criterion of usefulness and spoke of their "cash value." Even in *War and Peace*, Tolstoy (ca. 1865/1994) talked of wisdom being found not in science but rather through explaining humans' place in the entirety of it all. Jonas Salk, in *The Survival of the Wisest* (Salk, 1973), wrote that "importance is attached to the notion that wisdom is of practical value" for human survival and for the maintenance and enhancement of the quality of life.

Again, knowledge might be necessary but certainly is not sufficient for wisdom. Scientific knowledge can tell us how to do things but not whether they ought to be done. Take, for example, the fundamental questions posed by the movie *Jurassic Park*—not only "can we?" but also "should we?" This harkens back to J. Robert Oppenheimer's reflection on, and Harry Truman's decision regarding, the use of the atomic bomb in World War II. Knowledge gives us the means, but wisdom provides the context and direction.

Knowledge can also be a double-edged sword that retards wisdom. Productively, it provides the raw materials from which to reflect on and derive global principles and meanings and was the foundation for the Enlightenment and all of the advances it bestowed. Destructively, knowledge can inhibit our pursuit of wisdom if it acts to obscure perspective, just as individual intelligence can make us resistant to positive change, inhibit our creativity, and close our minds. On the level of the firm or organization, knowledge can have similar effects, turning our competencies into crippling rigidities (Leonard, 1995). Moreover, Roger Shattuck, in his wonderful *Forbidden Knowledge* (1996), provided an amazingly lucid analysis of how knowledge can be twisted to darker, more prurient ends. Instructions for the assembly of explosive devices or graphic depictions of human depravity used to be hard to come by. But in the information-saturated environment that is enabled by modern technology, this brand of knowledge is readily acceptable. But is it good and prudent? There is darkness in the world, and because knowledge can be put to its purposes, one should never forget that knowledge, like freedom, is purchased at a cost.

This schism is also evident in efforts investigating whether and how information technology (IT) systems can model wisdom in organizations (Courtney, Haynes, & Paradice, 2005; Turban, Leidner, McLean, & Wetherbe, 2005). This begs the "art versus science" debate and the perennial issue of artificial intelligence (artificial wisdom?). Society visits here regularly, especially when ushered by technological advances. The "man versus machine" context (Deep Blue beat Kasparov at chess?!) is reflected in popular culture's musings about the rise of computers and is evidenced in science fiction literature and cinematic productions such as *The Terminator* and *The Matrix*. From a scientific perspective, it is clear that programmable systems are increasingly sophisticated entities, but there is no evidence that they are serious competition for knowledge, much less wisdom. Issues such as values, a primary basis for human decisions and actions, and emotion, a primary engine of human events and the source of all our pleasure, are hardly ever discussed in artificial intelligence contexts. As always, technology and knowledge are but tools that serve explicit or implicit masters.

A perfectly apt summation of this point comes from perhaps the greatest scientific mind of the modern era. Albert Einstein told us,

> Convictions which are necessary and determinant for our conduct and judgments cannot be found solely along this solid scientific way. . . . The scientific method can teach us nothing else beyond how facts are related to, and conditioned by, each other. . . . Knowledge of what *is* does not open the door directly to what *should be*. One can have the clearest and most complete knowledge of what is, and yet not be able to deduct from that what should be the goal of our human aspirations. Objective knowledge provides us with powerful instruments for the achievement of certain ends, but the ultimate goal itself and the longing to reach it must come from another source. . . . The knowledge of truth as such is wonderful, but it is so little capable of acting as a guide that it cannot prove even the justification and the value of aspiration toward that very knowledge of truth. Here we face, therefore, the limits of the purely rational conception of our existence. . . . Intelligence makes clear to us the interrelation of means and ends, but mere thinking cannot make clear these fundamental ends and valuations. (Einstein, 1939/1954, pp. 41–42)

Wisdom Is Elusive

Not everyone is wise; in fact, a very select few have approximated this ideal. The same is true of organizations, both public and private, as a considerable proportion of unwise institutions line the ash can of history. Therefore, the fourth principle that we adopt in compiling this handbook is that the achievement of wisdom is difficult insofar as it is simultaneously a rare commodity and an arduous process, it represents a cumulative phenomenon, and it is lamentably yet inherently incomplete.

The phrase "common sense ain't common" is attributed to American folk wit Will Rogers. If "common" refers to a commodity and "sense" refers to good judgment, it is safe to say that Rogers was ribbing the rarity of wisdom as the exception rather than the rule. Why is wisdom so rare? So elusive? If it is a central human calling, as we have described, and the better minds of our species have devoted themselves to its study or attainment of knowledge, why is this thing so difficult to understand and acquire? If it were so integral to the human experience, why wouldn't it be, like procreation, a frequent result of pleasurable attempts? And surely, if age is the hardiest measure of adaptability, why isn't wisdom incumbent on one's advanced years? Simply stated, why would something so central be so elusive?

The answer is infinitely more prosaic than the question. The human tendency is to conjure a guru whose status, insight, or bravery in the face of a great cause we can never hope to repeat. Buddha, Gandhi, Jesus, Lincoln, King, and Mandela are just a few of the giants who became our standard. But this approach has its risks. To be sure, seeking perfection propels humanity, but in our day-to-day affairs it is an impossible comparison that, almost inevitably, invites disappointment. Just like in the leadership literature, the mystique of wisdom clouds judgment, perhaps preventing us from seeing and practicing it in the small but enormously significant ways that make a true difference in our everyday lives.

Conversely, the adjectives applied to business leaders—the erstwhile "captains of industry"—are colorfully evocative of action and confidence—decisive, assured, certain, definitive, determined, firm, forceful, imperious, intent, preemptory, resolute, and strong-minded. Flattering descriptions, to be sure, but it is curious that "wise," or some variation thereof, is seldom attributed to businesspeople (except on occasion when, e.g., a depreciated acquisition boosts stock prices, and even then only post hoc). Were Jack Welch, Anita Roddick, Robert Johnson, or Richard Branson ever described as wise in the popular press or in an academic case study? Innovative, focused, and inspirational, maybe, but not wise. Why is this? Is the action-oriented language of business such that it simply cannot accommodate the concept of wisdom, or does it simply employ a separate, but equally expressive, vocabulary with an equally valid semantic? Who is to say that the creation of an airline when most other airlines were performing abysmally, or the creation of cosmetics composed of organic materials when that market was flooded by competitors, was not wise? Indeed, it is consistent with Plato's ideas in *The Republic* that those dominated by the intellectual are best fit as philosopher kings, those dominated by the emotional are best fit as soldiers, and those dominated by appetite and ambition are best fit for commerce and trade. But in international relations, troop deployment, and entrepreneurial ventures, there is nothing in Plato's categorization to prevent the king, the soldier, and the businessperson, respectively, from being wise in their cogitation or conduct.

If wisdom is elusive, certainly part of the reason is that it is arduous; that is, it is difficult to obtain. Anything that is valuable and difficult to acquire usually is rare. Diamonds do not, after all, grow on trees. And wisdom does not happen overnight. If a century of social science has taught us anything, it is that humans tend to be impulsive creatures drawn to immediate gratification. Everybody plays checkers, but the skilled chess player is unusual.

Jack Kerouac can opine about the journey or collective quest, but most of us also yearn for the destination. A few quotes should illustrate the arduous nature of wisdom:

- Albert Einstein—"Wisdom is not a product of schooling but of the life-long attempt to acquire it."
- Socrates—"Wisdom begins in wonder."
- Confucius—"By three methods we may learn wisdom: first, by reflection, which is noblest; second, by imitation, which is easiest; and third, by experience, which is the bitterest."
- Lucius Annaeus Seneca—"No man was ever wise by chance."
- Benjamin Franklin—"The doors of wisdom are never shut."
- William James—"The art of being wise is the art of knowing what to overlook."
- Francis Bacon—"A prudent question is one-half of wisdom."
- Goethe (Faust)—"The last result of wisdom stamps it true: He only earns his freedom and existence who daily conquers them anew."

Part of the reason why wisdom is elusive and rare is that it is cumulative. Cumulative means over time, and over time means patience, and patience once again flies in the face of the human tendency—not to put too fine a point on it—to "want it now." Delay of gratification and impulse control are in short supply despite childhood assurances that "good things come to those who wait." Evolution is slow, whereas life is short and, if Hobbes is to be believed, nasty and brutish as well. These are not ideal conditions for wisdom to flourish.

Experience, then, becomes a key element of the wisdom equation. But there is such a thing as precociousness—those who are "wise beyond their years." Similarly, there are those who have been everywhere and done everything but who repeat the same mistakes over and over as if they are encountering the world for the first time. Wisdom, then, is not exclusively a prisoner of the past, just as the past is no guarantee of wisdom. Experience, like knowledge, is a necessary but not sufficient condition of wisdom. Wisdom is not such experience per se but is more derivative of the attitude brought to experience (Gandhi, 1927/2006). This is nicely illustrated by the following quotes:

- Abraham Lincoln—"I do not think much of a man who is not wiser today than he was yesterday."
- George Santayana—"The wisest mind has something yet to learn."
- Japanese proverb—"You are wise to climb Mt. Fuji, but a fool to do it twice."
- Cato the Elder—"Wise men learn more from fools than fools [learn] from the wise."

- Thomas Jefferson—"I hope our wisdom will grow with our power and teach us that the less we use our power the greater it will be."
- George Bernard Shaw—"We are made wise not by the recollection of our past, but by the responsibility for our future."

If wisdom is elusive because it is rare, and it is rare because it is difficult to obtain, and it is difficult to obtain because it is cumulative, it stands to reason that—to exacerbate matters further—wisdom is inherently incomplete. Once something is known, absorbed, and thoughtfully engaged, that something changes. Any parent who has tried to comfort a distressed child should be able to relate; what works today often fails tomorrow. Or, to illustrate in a different arena, a cosmological wisdom derived from intimate knowledge of Newtonian physics must, at the very least, be updated in light of Einstein's quantum reasoning and perhaps explorations of string and M-theories (Hawking, 2001). Similarly, in the focal domain, a wisdom of human nature extracted from decades in the food and beverage industry might benefit from reexamination when applied to the securities industry. And all rules might go out the window when an industry experiences competitive, technological, or other disruptions and undergoes radical paradigmatic transformation. If the proposition that wisdom is cumulative is accepted, by definition it is constantly maturing, transforming, and accumulating. Therefore, we should not pretend to its mastery and instead should acknowledge the imperfect art and provisional perspective—consistent with Wittgenstein's (1921/2001) ladder and the idea of disposable theories—that encapsulate the necessary humility in our search for wisdom, as suggested by the following quotations:

- Socrates—"The only true wisdom is in knowing you know nothing."
- Proverb—"The wisest man is he who does not believe he is wise."
- William Shakespeare—"The fool doth think he is wise, but the wise man knows himself to be a fool."
- Bertrand Russell—"The whole problem with the world is that fools and fanatics are always so certain of themselves, but wiser people [are] so full of doubts."
- Mohandas Gandhi—"It is unwise to be too sure of one's own wisdom. It is healthy to be reminded that the strongest might weaken and the wisest might err."
- Ralph Waldo Emerson—"Wisdom is like electricity. There is no permanently wise man, but men capable of wisdom, who, being put into certain company, or other favorable conditions, become wise for a short time, as glasses rubbed acquire electric power for a while."
- Lord Chesterfield—"In seeking wisdom thou art wise; in imagining that thou hast attained it—thou art a fool."
- Johann Wolfgang von Goethe—"With wisdom grows doubt."

In this section, we have put forth that wisdom is important, complex, preeminent, and elusive—qualities that are magnified when transported to the professional domain.

Organizational and Managerial Wisdom

It's easy to be a holy man on top of a mountain.

—W. Somerset Maugham, 1946

Precisely at a time when we sense the need for wisdom is higher than ever, it appears, paradoxically, to be less and less available. . . . Wisdom is the pivotal force behind organizational greatness.

—Srivastava and Cooperrider, 1998

Perhaps it is relatively easier to dispense wisdom from the stark surrounds of the mountaintop or the reflective rituals of the cloister. To be removed from humanity's swell and unfettered by its investment surely aids sagacity. But few of us are so fortunate. We live instead in a bustling, bristling web of relationships, perspectives, and objectives, all of which require resolution to lead to solution, all the more so for those in the thick of the business world, where very genuine consequences attend even the smallest of decisions. Yet this is where the action is, or at least where we spend a large part of our time. As Srivastava and Cooperrider (1998) suggested, wisdom's supply and demand curve especially favors the former. In the following, we consider the characterization, application, and development of wisdom as embedded in the context of organizational and managerial dynamics.

Organizations and Management Are Ubiquitous

For better or worse, we live in a world of organizations. Our time is spent interacting with them, our lives are spent serving and being served by them, and our very existence depends on them. They are both pervasive and important.

From the moment of conception, we are inextricably linked with organizations. Most of us are born in hospitals—bureaucracies par excellence. From there we transfer home, where the social configuration—including hierarchy, division of labor, unity of command, seniority, and other familiar concepts—is the bedrock for nearly all organizational designs. The food and shelter, clothing and furnishings, and services and utilities on which we unconsciously rely all are products of organizations. Many of us also commonly experience some form of religious observance. Whether Catholic, Protestant, Judaic,

Muslim, Hindu, or any other variety, religion tends to be "organized" by codified methods of worship and endorsed paths to salvation, enlightenment, or whatever the end state might be. From home we shuffle off to school, a bureaucracy where disciplinary and status divisions abound and where the authority of the teacher and the principal are all-encompassing. From this gauntlet the majority of us emerge to take a post in a private or public, for profit or nonprofit firm and commence to repeat the cycle. As we do so, every good we consume, every road we traverse, and every relationship we form is governed by a few fundamental rules derived from ancient patterns and rebound today. There just is no escaping the ubiquity of organizations.

Given the pervasive nature of organizations, the question becomes one of whether they, or their elements, can display wisdom. Whereas in this introductory chapter we have already entertained the dilemma of the wise individual, it is yet another matter to consider whether groups can be deemed more or less wise. There is in fact much evidence that groups are on the whole more capable of wisdom than are individuals. If properly managed—and this is a big *if*—interacting individuals can leverage diverse competencies and perspectives to produce results superior to those of the individual. Technically, we might designate these groups as "teams," attach labels such as "synergy," and seek guidance about their enactment in the works of Hackman (2002, *Leading Teams*) and Katzenback and Smith (2003, *The Wisdom of Teams*). On the flip side, groups can be profoundly unwise, making poor decisions and harming their membership, as noted in the insights of Janis (1972) and others.

Although they are often large and complex, organizations are composed of interdependent individuals who have at least mildly aligned goals. Unfortunately, the headlines are replete with so many foolish and malicious cases by both bigger and smaller entities that we can also confidently assert the negative—that organizations are capable of being "unwise." Semantics are important here because some people might interpret wisdom as profitability (e.g., Google), survival (the Catholic Church), environmental impact (The Body Shop), or a host of other criteria. Nevertheless, there are better and worse performers on any of these scales; thus, we can infer that there are relatively wiser and less wise organizations.

One could also consider whether strategies can be deemed wise. Again, notwithstanding the definition of terms, one might sort out approaches that have worked better than others. This can be done in a plethora of strategic spheres such as government (democracy), economics (capitalism), and business (empowerment). Of course, the previous examples are hotly debated depending on one's political, financial, and managerial predilections. Is profitability the ultimate metric, or is it perhaps one's larger systemic impact or one's principles of conduct? That is to say, conceptions of the wise strategy can vary by the criteria and perspective employed. Thus, judgments are not as objective as the scientist might prefer, but they are nonetheless amenable to some form of assessment.

Organizations and Management Are in Need of Wisdom

Whereas every generation thinks that its challenges are unique, the world, particularly that of organizations and management, is as much in need of wisdom now as ever before. Examples of organizational idiocy are so legion that it is impossible to recount them here, but be they blunders of strategic, moral, or human stripe, the question remains: Why is this happening? Are organizations and their managers becoming less intelligent, or is the business context becoming more difficult? No less an astute observer than Scott Adams of *Dilbert* fame contends that it is a synthesis of the two, that "people are idiots," and that "change makes us stupider, relatively speaking. Change adds new information to the universe. . . . Our knowledge—as a percentage of all the things that can be known—goes down a tick every time something changes" (Adams, 1996, p. 198).

We cannot speak to Adams's (1996) conjecture about human intelligence (although there is ample evidence to support it), but his remarks about change are right on the mark. This managerial and organizational "idiocy" is manifested by deep-seated prejudices and fallacies—as per Francis Bacon's idols of the tribe, cave, marketplace, and theater—that underlie human social behavior and hence are difficult to remedy (Kessler, 2001). Adaptation and intervention, if possible, take time. For individuals, groups, and organizations, responding to new conditions necessitates a "learning curve" where performance often dips below previously established baselines. The plotted progress curve would look something like an EKG, only with an overall cumulative pattern (hopefully).

If new conditions require adaptation, and adaptation requires a period of adjustment during which performance is far from peak, we could assume that wisdom would quicken the path of the learning curve. Considering the rapid changes in the nature of work—the accelerated pace of technological innovation, the growing complexity of internal and external environments, the fierce competitiveness brought on by globalization, the increasing workforce diversity, and the emergence of knowledge work and strategic human resources as core competencies—it is fair to say that modern organizations are in a constant state of adaptation. The old Chinese adage, "May you live in interesting times," is both a curse and a blessing.

From sage to scripture, in working and in living, wisdom *initiates and guides* change. As such, it is the apex of intellectual and moral judgment, the reconciliation of oneself with a greater spiritual force, the ability to achieve, and the path toward true understanding and happiness. Jordan and Sternberg, in Chapter 1 of this handbook, put it as follows: "It could be argued that the most important factor in an organization's success is wisdom." Indeed, one of the most strikingly consistent observations of this handbook's contributors is that there is a gap between where we are in terms of wise organization and management and where we could be.

We Are Not Trained, nor Do We Train, for Wisdom

It is peculiarly ironic that the terminal degree in our field, doctor of philosophy (Ph.D.), does not generally require even cursory study of philosophy. Surely, doctoral-granting institutions, in bestowing an august title such as *lover of wisdom,* should incorporate the topic into the curriculum. With this deficit in mind, it is hardly surprising that the academic literature is dominated by narrowly defined constructs and elaborate statistical manipulations that unintentionally eschew cross-disciplinary and "big picture" inquiries. Moreover, there is a vocal stream lamenting the poor preparation that future managers and leaders receive through master's of business administration (MBA) programs (Ghoshal, 2005; Mintzberg, 2004; Pfeffer & Fong, 2002). In a similar vein, Small (2004) argued that management development programs are insufficiently based on wisdom-related principles. If one is not trained for wisdom, wisdom cannot be expected.

Harkening back to an earlier discussion, our professional training and socialization is grounded more in a tradition of information and knowledge than in the concepts of wisdom and truth. In our unholy determination to represent even the most nuanced forms of human social experience in mathematical terms, social science was caught unaware by many of the watershed events of the latter half of the 20th century such as the fall of the Soviet Union and the emergence of demagogic nationalism. These events were fueled by ethnic passion and religious fervor that our instrumentation was too blunt to detect. The situation is exacerbated in organization and management studies. As a practical discipline, we are obliged to follow practice, and two of the most powerfully emergent practices of the past few decades are information technology and knowledge management. The valence against a serious consideration of wisdom is fierce. To counter with productive weight, we believe that the time is right within the academic realm to reconceptualize knowledge creation and dissemination within the rubric of wisdom.

As for knowledge creation, in his seminal work, Ernest Boyer, president of the Carnegie Foundation for the Advancement of Teaching, complained that the professoriate had moved to privilege research above its other two missions, teaching and service (Boyer, 1990). He observed that research is solidly entrenched at the top of the academic hierarchy, whereas teaching is merely the communication of that research to others. Boyer argues this shift is due to a narrowing definition of scholarship among the nation's most prestigious universities. In an effort to move beyond this constricted conception, Boyer argued that universities must rethink what it means to be a scholar and must embrace a more expansive definition of the construct. Rather than viewing scholarship as merely "research," Boyer offered four forms: discovery, integration, application, and teaching. The fundamental idea is to balance research endeavors so as to more fully represent the range of purposes for which knowledge is created and to which it is put.

The *scholarship of discovery* is the most easily grasped because it refers to what academics describe as research. Pursuit of this form of scholarship is generally considered to be the essence of the professional academy—researching issues from novel viewpoints; the ability to create knowledge for its own sake; and the capacity to examine questions without specific limit. The scholarship of discovery has thrust universities to the forefront of knowledge generation and insight about the human condition, both of which are preconditions to wisdom. Numerous Nobel Prize winners, literary stars, and patent holders populate the faculties of first-class institutions and contribute both to the intellectual vibrancy of academic culture and to a stream of financial support that cyclically sustains high-caliber research and holds tuition at an affordable level.

The *scholarship of integration* refers to research activities that "make connections across the disciplines" (Boyer, 1990, p. 18). Here, knowledge developed through discovery is extended to comparable knowledge derived from other disciplines and paradigms. This is "interdisciplinary" in that the scholarship of integration is about connecting the boundaries of a particular field or tradition to relatable ideas and theories in other traditions or putting them in a larger perspective to infuse broader meaning. Boyer (1990) reported the results of a survey across faculty at many different types of academic institutions, finding that 85% of faculty at research institutions believed that multidisciplinary work had significant value and importance in giving research streams within a discipline a larger meaning and context. As discussed previously, integration of diverse streams of inquiry is integral to any concept of wisdom.

The *scholarship of application* is consistent with our premise that wisdom inheres in action as much as in intent. Here researchers investigate ways in which the scholarship of discovery and integration can be applied to real-world problems. This form directs the consequences of research to specific practical issues, and conversely uses the practical issues themselves to direct research. This third form of scholarship is a genuine attempt to apply the findings from discovery and integration to significant practical or social problems and to create and sustain the agenda for future discovery and integration that is informed from this application. In this sense it facilitates the transition of knowledge to wisdom.

The last form is the *scholarship of teaching*, which emphasizes dissemination of knowledge derived through the other three forms, and, as such, can be thematically conceived as imparting wisdom. Teaching educates and entices future practitioners and scholars. Faculty who both understand their field and its nuances and are capable of finding creative and engaging ways of communicating that knowledge to others are true scholars of teaching, in the best of ancient Greek traditions. Effective teaching is a communicative and communal act. Good teachers must be intellectually engaged and active learners. But they also must be able to transform and extend their own learning so that they are able to stimulate others to think, understand, and explore.

Once knowledge is created, how it is structured and delivered—that is, taught and disseminated—has profound impact on how it is cognitively integrated and behaviorally executed. This is where Boyer's scholarship of teaching is most significantly observed. As distinguished from training, effective education strives to achieve multiple high-level learning objectives. For instance, memorizing a concept or formula may be important, but it serves mainly as a platform on which to construct more complex understanding. Practically applying principles, structuring meaningful data, and evaluating alternative courses of action all require a superior level of cognitive integration. It is, then, the charter of educational institutions broadly, and business schools especially, to provide instructional experiences that develop mastery of higher order conceptualizations that approximate the wisdom concept more closely.

The most broadly developed scheme for benchmarking knowledge dissemination is Bloom's (1956) *Taxonomy of Educational Objectives*. This model depicts various levels of instructional sophistication that form the basis of pedagogy. The first, and most foundational, levels of educational objectives include *knowledge* and *comprehension*, which indicate, respectively, a memory for and understanding of concepts, formulas, events, and the like. Managers demonstrate knowledge, for example, by recalling performance metrics. In contrast, comprehension is the ability to grasp the meaning of material. A development professional may explain a promotion scheme to demonstrate successful comprehension of advancement opportunities. These first two levels refer to "understanding" a thing as it is, whereas the next three objectives reflect an ability to "transform" that thing through functional purpose. *Application* is the ability to transform knowledge to action in new and concrete situations, for example, when a manager uses goal-setting theory to motivate an alienated employee. *Analysis,* or the ability to deconstruct knowledge into its component parts to establish a total structure, takes place when a leader articulates and appreciates the unstated norms that govern an organizational culture. *Synthesis* is the ability to reconstruct elements into a new whole. This involves detailed knowledge as well as the conception of unique connections. An example would be redesigning a reporting relationship to transfer information and objectives more efficiently. Bloom's final and most sophisticated cognitive skill, *evaluation,* is judging the value of information for a given purpose. Evaluation integrates the first five levels while intertwining tacit knowledge and opinion. Managers use evaluation when determining a strategic course of action from several options.

We submit that, educationally, wisdom is the seamless mastery of all six of Bloom's (1956) levels. Thus, to instill and nurture wisdom, pedagogical methods of knowledge dissemination should intentionally integrate these learning objectives. Taking students—be they undergraduates or executives—through an instructional journal that connects knowledge to comprehension to application to analysis to synthesis to evaluation represents a cogent path toward wisdom. Unfortunately, most formal instruction focuses on knowledge and comprehension, leaving application, analysis, synthesis, and evaluation to that greatest of teachers—experience. A careful treatment of the reasons for this state of affairs is beyond the scope of this introductory chapter. However, if schools of business and management become serious about imparting wisdom, a wholesale reformation will be at hand, including curricular redesign and commensurate shifts in internal reward systems that align individual incentives with institutional missions.

The premise of this section is that academics, as stewards of knowledge, are not normally trained in, nor do they train for, wisdom. For this, we offer two ameliorants. The first is to reconceptualize the scholarly endeavor in a manner that is more compatible with wisdom and the range of human purposes, and the second is to tend more carefully to the levels of mastery that are communicated by our pedagogy. These activities may be directed at a wide variety of audiences—to those who will become practitioners, those who will become purveyors of the four forms of scholarship, or those who simply seek to become wiser and more broadly educated. Engaging effectively in this scholarship requires more than effective transmission of knowledge, but as Boyer (1990) emphasized, it requires actively participating in the examination and evaluation of those knowledge dissemination activities so as to improve the very practice of the scholarship of teaching itself.

We Must Consider Organizational and Managerial Wisdom

We are organizational philosophers when we apply the inquiry of the wise to the management of people, groups, structures, and strategies. By extension, organizational action at all levels and in all domains cannot be understood properly, much less investigated, disseminated, or performed properly, without considering wisdom adequately.

Let us assume for a moment that our field, organizational and managerial (OM) studies, can be conceptualized as a body of thought concerned with the function and management of social systems at both micro and macro levels of analysis (Astley & Van de Ven, 1983). It is essentially derived from social sciences such as psychology, sociology, anthropology, political science, industrial engineering, general systems theory, decision theory, economics, mathematics, and practitioner experience (Koontz, 1980). OM studies are dynamic disciplines marked by progressive evolutionary phases, the practitioners of which consider a wide variety of issues such as scientific management, bureaucracy, industrial and economic forces, neoclassical and human relations models, power and politics, decision-making models, structural contingency theory, communication and network relationships, open systems and ecological factors, and postmodern conceptions of the firm (cf. Clegg, Hardy, & Nord, 1996; Perrow, 1973; Scott, 1961). OM studies investigate these issues on various levels of analysis, including the individual, the interpersonal, the organizational, and the strategic (Scott, 1987).

It is often said that the more things change, the more they remain the same. As already described, the context-specific answers generated by OM studies are derivative of the general questions, issues, and debates raised long ago in philosophy. Consider, for example, the following lines of inquiry. How can we be internally consistent in our thoughts and actions? How should governance mechanisms be constructed? What is an appropriate code of behavior? How does one motivate and lead people? What are the sources and limits to knowledge resources? These questions are fundamentally philosophical but become managerially relevant when applied to the domain of organizations. Thus, it is incumbent on us to consider the arguments and insights of history's greatest thinkers to properly reflect on how wisdom might be applied to OM studies. Indeed, a philosophical approach to exploring organizational theory informs fundamental concepts, explains divergence of theories, and helps to formulate policies and practices.

There have been several attempts to marry philosophy with its business application. For instance, Hartman (1988) surveyed the conceptual foundations of organizational theory, attempting to ground it in an underlying logic and fundamental questions, charging that a discipline can "free itself from philosophy" only when it develops a precise vocabulary and agreed-on rules and evaluative criteria. Indeed, our field is far from such a consensus (Pfeffer, 1993). Another effort to relate OM studies to the infrastructure of philosophy was undertaken by Burrell and Morgan (1979), who observed that the enduring sociological debates could be understood dimensionally via objectivism versus subjectivism as well as regulation versus radicalism. Morgan (1986) continued this analysis in his metaphor-based attempt to categorize organizational theories into different "frames," many of which were linked to philosophical roots. Others, such as Badaracco (1992), have attempted to develop ideas on business ethics based in philosophy and manifested in OM studies.

In our field, the opposite of OMW might be seen as simplicity or folly. To the issue of simplicity, Weick (1993) spoke of wisdom at the intersection of knowing and ignorance. Here the wise are seen as embracing the complexity of organizational life rather than obscuring it, simultaneously drawing from and ignoring lessons from the past and, as such, improving adaptability. To the issue of folly, Kerr (1975) maintained that perverse reward systems can motivate people to act in a manner diametrically opposed to what is desired and deemed strategically important. Ghoshal (2005) described the folly in which pursuing academic credibility via rigorous research has led business theory to adopt a set of assumptions about human nature that provide intellectual justification for a class of behaviors that sours the corporate ethical climate. Jones (2005) argued that ethical lapses are directly traceable to a lack of wisdom-based paradigms for business structures and practices. In the pop culture domain, we can also highlight Adams's *Dilbert* comic strip as a compendium of folly at work.

In a general sense, Gandhi told us that finding a truthful way to solutions requires constant testing—that "the way a person behaves is more important than what he achieves." Thus, individuals become wise through their cumulative experiences and reflection in an organization, industry, and career. Confucius similarly reminded us that only the wisest and the very stupidest cannot change—that "the superior man thinks of virtue; the small man thinks of comfort. The proper man understands equity; the small man profits." Thus, individuals become wise when they are open-minded enough to be guided by principle. More specific to our field, Malan and Kriger (1998) defined *managerial* wisdom as "the ability to detect those fine nuances between what is right and what is not . . . the ability to capture the meaning of several often contradictory signals and stimuli, to interpret them in a holistic and integrative manner, to learn from them, and to act on them" (p. 249). According to Vaill (1996), this type of wisdom can be seen in managers and organizations navigating permanent "white water" without losing their sense of purpose and direction. And as reported by Engardio (2006), ancient lessons such as in the Bhagavad-Gita are being increasingly applied to conceptualize more holistic approaches to corporate strategy and leadership. Together, these insights blend wisdom with implementation—the abstract with the impact.

In this section, we have put forth that organization and management are ubiquitous yet often in need of wisdom and, moreover, that scholars and practitioners are not trained for wisdom per se yet must rightly consider it to do their jobs properly. Driven by a pronounced lack of wise management practices in organizations, research in this domain is increasing. However, what does exist is diffuse and ill connected. The need to consider wisdom is clear, as is the need to organize that consideration systemically. In short, the moment is ripe for a *Handbook of Organizational and Managerial Wisdom*.

Handbook of Organizational and Managerial Wisdom

> *A philosophy of a discipline such as history, physics, or law seeks not so much to solve historical, physical, or legal questions as to study the concepts that structure such thinking and to lay bare their foundations and presuppositions. In this sense philosophy is what happens when a practice becomes self-conscious.*
>
> —*Oxford Dictionary of Philosophy*, 1996

> *Organizational theorists bite off too little too precisely, and we've tried to encourage them to tackle bigger slices of reality. And if poetry, appreciation, and the artistry of inquiry need to be coupled with science to produce those bigger bites, so be it.*
>
> —Karl Weick, 1979

Wisdom is inherently action oriented. To paraphrase Gandhi, the wise both know and have the courage to do what is right. Conversely, Confucius observed that to see what is right and not do it is cowardice. Thus, the wise not only talk the walk but also walk the talk. Organizing and managing are action oriented as well but are not requisitely wise. As we have noted, wisdom in these domains is more the exception than the rule. The opening quotations suggest this is so because we do not look sufficiently inward to surface foundational assumptions or sufficiently outward to appreciate overarching context. The purpose of this handbook is to provide a venue for both through the prism of wisdom.

The *Handbook of Organizational and Managerial Wisdom* is structured according to primary levels of analysis—individual, interpersonal, organizational, and strategic—and thematically around the five primary philosophical branches: logic, ethics, aesthetics, epistemology, and metaphysics. It integrates the insights of some of the field's most respected thinkers to further our understanding of this emerging domain, consider how it might be applied practically to real organizations, and explore how it might be fostered and developed.

Levels of Organizational and Managerial Wisdom

Consider the following:

Joseph Wiseman, chief executive officer. How should he reason? How might he act? What do he and his employees, customers, and the like really want? What does he know, and what can he be expected to know? What is his fundamental purpose?

Team Illuminati. How can the team members synergize? How should they negotiate interactions? What role do emotional and social factors play in their relationships? What impact does diversity have on their dynamics? Is their existence essentially and/or rightly unequal and power driven?

Philos Enterprises. How should the firm be structured? How should it be led? What is the best way to approach change? What is the best way to design for learning? In what way will globalization affect its processes and objectives?

Wisestrat Consultants. How might the consultants facilitate an effective or even enlightened policy? How should they advise the client to interact with their context? What is the best way to construct human resource systems? What is the best way to create and leverage resources? Can education and development truly convey any of these insights?

After pondering these questions and their associated implications, take one more moment to consider the following. What people would you then consider wise? What teams, companies and institutions, or strategies? Why? From a contextual perspective, the lattice of these levels can be visually depicted as in Figure I.1 and constitutes one dimension of this handbook's organizational scheme.

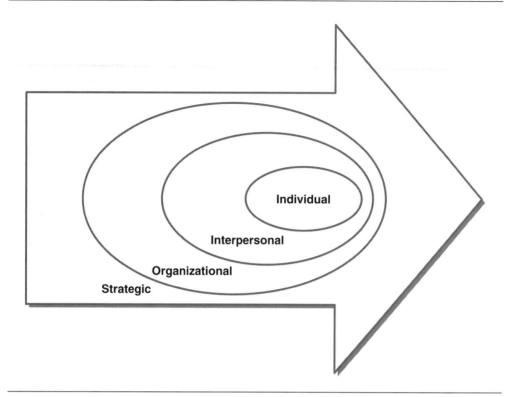

Figure I.1   Levels of Inquiry Explored in the Handbook

Individual Inquiry. Organizations do not behave. Neither do nations, societies, industries, cultures, or families. Individuals behave. People are the fundamental unit of analysis because all of these other entities exist only in the abstract—reifications, if you will. Individuals are, ultimately, responsible for the whole of human history because events are made, not discovered. Thus, organization management phenomena can always be traced to the people who occupy the space. It is their judgments that create the organizational logic, their morals that create the organizational ethic, their values that create the organizational design, their interpretations that create the organizational knowledge, and their reflection that creates the organizational reality.

Interpersonal Inquiry. One cannot explain a collective by summing the parts. The interpersonal cannot be amalgamated with units. Collective dynamics, such as groupthink, risky shift, social loafing, contagion, and social facilitation, are but some of the unique impacts that highlight the complex interdependencies between people and ultimately create positive synergy or process loss. Therefore, a reasonable understanding of organization management must augment individual examination with interpersonal analysis, adding to the mix factors such as negotiated decisions, social exchanges, collective sensemaking, cultural diversity, and power and influence.

Organizational Inquiry. It is axiomatic in the social sciences that behavior is influenced by its context. No person acts in a vacuum. Rather, a host of environmental features, such as the nature of the activity, involved others, and assumed or assigned roles, have a profound impact on how one acts at any given moment. In this way, organizations are created systems that furnish the fundamental situation in which individual behavior is executed. For example, even the most creative individuals may fail to produce innovative outcomes if bogged down by boundless bureaucracy and disempowered by autocratic managers. Therefore, we must also consider judgment and teams within the context of organizational systems, virtue and negotiation within the context of organizational leadership, values and exchanges within the context of organizational development, sensemaking and diversity within the context of organizational learning, and reflection and influence within the context of organizational globalization.

Strategic Inquiry. It is difficult to understand a phenomenon if one does not consider its intention, direction, and relationship to broader systems. Strategy is the amalgam of all these things, incorporating the how and the why as well as the present and the future. Strategic dynamics are essential for properly exploring the wisdom of organizations and management. It follows that judgment, teams, and structures can be better understood by adding business policy (section on logic); virtue, negotiation, and leadership can be better understood by adding environmental interface (section on ethics); values, social exchange, and development can be better understood by adding human resource management (section on aesthetics); sensemaking, diversity, and learning can be better understood by adding innovation (section on epistemology); and reflection, influence, and globalization can be better understood by adding education (section on metaphysics).

Altogether, we put forth in this handbook that there can be more or less wise individuals, interactions, organizations, and strategies engaged in the practice of organization management and that, therefore, we seek to explore the nature, application, and source of this variability.

Domains of Organizational and Managerial Wisdom

According to the *Columbia Encyclopedia* (2005), philosophy (i.e., the love and pursuit of wisdom) can be defined as the "study of the ultimate reality, causes, and principles underlying being and thinking." To this end, philosophical inquiry traditionally is divided into several branches or approaches. *Logic* is concerned with the laws of valid reasoning, *ethics* deals with problems of right conduct, *aesthetics* attempts to determine the nature of beauty and the criteria of artistic judgment, *epistemology* investigates the nature of knowledge and the process of knowing, and *metaphysics* inquires into the nature and ultimate significance of the universe. These branches are neither comprehensive nor independent, but they are useful for discerning fundamental questions and, as such, constitute a second dimension of this handbook's organizational scheme (Figure I.2). The following discussion draws from several sources (Craig, 1998; Durant, 1961; *Encyclopedia Britannica* [http://concise.britan nica.com]; Scruton, 1996; Solomon & Higgins, 1997; *Wikipedia* [http://en .wikipedia.org]) to discuss these domains of inquiry.

Logic. *Logic,* from ancient Greek for "the word," is at its foundation the study of inference and argument. More broadly, it investigates ideal methods of thought by asking questions about what constitutes sound reasoning and what can be construed as rational. Great thinkers such as Aristotle, John Stuart Mill, David Hume, Gottlob Frege, and Bertrand Russell have taken up this challenge. Most recently, logic has been applied to matters concerning computer and information systems as well as artificial intelligence. The central property of logic is "soundness" or internal fidelity. If the parts of an argument (propositions or premises) are noncontradictory and systematically lead to the end goal (conclusions or inferences), reasoning is said to be rational (sound). A person, a practice, an entity, or an approach can be said to be logical, or by extension rational, when its objectives follow from its parts in an internally consistent manner. Thus, individual logic

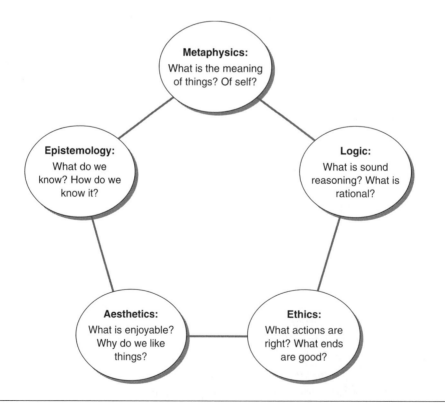

Figure I.2   Philosophical Branches of Thought Considered in this Handbook

relates to sound judgment, interpersonal logic relates to sound interactions and dynamics, organizational logic relates to sound institutionalized context, and strategic logic relates to sound policy formulation and implementation. For example, consider the syllogistic reasoning embedded in the following: Premise 1 (heavyweight project leaders are most appropriate for radical innovation) combined with Premise 2 (this nanotechnology initiative is a radical project) would suggest a conclusion (we should put a heavyweight leader in charge of the nanotechnology project). The rigorous and purpose-driven elements of logic are apparent. Of course, logical decisions at one level must be combined with, and embedded within, a larger system to produce desired results. Even people with good judgment must work within team structures, design contexts, and strategic frameworks. The parts should inductively suggest the whole, and the whole should deductively suggest the parts. Logic simultaneously operates at and reconciles the micro, meso, and macro.

Ethics. Ethics is concerned with ideal conduct, the nature of ultimate value, and the moral standards by which human action can be judged. Its study investigates what actions are "right" and what ends are "good," thereby deriving a method or code by which people should live. Great thinkers such as Plato, Immanuel Kant, Thomas Hobbes, Jeremy Bentham, G. E. Moore, and A. J. Ayer have taken up the challenge of investigating ethics, and the study of the subject also has a rich history in nearly all major world religious traditions. Perhaps the most widespread understanding of the field is synchronous with what is commonly referred to as a normative approach to ethics, which is concerned primarily with the questions of proper conduct. Here are debates about what should and should not be done. Arguments can use a variety of vehicles, such as the scientific (ethics is derived), the theological (ethics is divine), the economic (ethics is systemic), and the professional and political (ethics is applied). Specific to the scope of our handbook, we suggest that individual ethics relates to personal virtue, interpersonal ethics relates to negotiated interaction, organizational ethics relates to proper leadership, and strategic ethics relates to principled synthesis with embedded and overlapping systems. A particularly interesting ethical debate involves whether there is one true ethical standard or relative standards that are dependent on time and context. This translates in a business domain to the question of whether there is a single set of ethical criteria for all organizations or whether such criteria are moderated by differences in culture and industry. Carried further is the related issue as to where criteria should be applied: the individual (e.g., Hobbes), the institution (e.g., Hegel), the society (e.g., Mill), or the greater purpose (e.g., Anselm). The application of ethics to organization management must, then, consider multiple analytic levels. Indeed, there is much fodder for discussion, as cases abound regarding ethics and business issues such as bribery, deception, creative accounting, layoffs and takeovers, discrimination, insider trading, environmental impact, and stakeholder rights.

Aesthetics. *Aesthetics* is the study of ideal form or beauty, including the character of tastes and preferences. Etymologically, it derives from the ancient Greek term for perception. It is concerned with questions such as what is enjoyable and why, linking design and art to objects, structures, experiences, and language. Thus, we can say that to some extent individual aesthetics relates to personal values and interests, interpersonal aesthetics relates to empathy and exchange, organizational aesthetics relates to change and development, and strategic aesthetics relates to human resource systems and practice. When approaching organizational and managerial aesthetics, we acknowledge the open debate as to whether there are objective universal tastes (cf. Maslow) or in fact subjective considerations that locate beauty in the proverbial "eye of the beholder." As organizations and their activities are increasingly framed in terms of artistic-related conceptualizations (e.g., in the emergence of design-based approaches), the concept of aesthetics is receiving more interest. Analogies between the expressive endeavors and organizations are plentiful and include management as performance and prose, teamwork as symphony, structural context as architecture, and leadership and strategy as art form.

Epistemology. *Epistemology* focuses on the origin, nature, and limits of human knowledge, both a priori (theory) and a posteriori (empiricism). It is concerned with what we know and how we know it as well as the question of whether knowledge is even possible. Insofar as we can know, *knowledge,* as opposed to speculation or opinion, is justified true belief. This definition dates back to Plato and can be traced through the writings of Russell and Wittgenstein. Epistemology considers whether all knowledge is gathered through the senses or if there is any real a priori knowledge and whether knowledge is the product of reasoned thought or if there are other sources such as experience and mysticism. Ideas on the nature of knowledge and subsequent epistemological systems abound. Hence, we are forced to confront and reconcile diverse frameworks such as idealism, positivism, and pragmatism, as well as a plethora of other competing models, for explaining knowledge phenomena. Focusing the epistemological lens on the subject at hand, we can say that to some extent individual epistemology relates to a person's sensemaking process, interpersonal epistemology relates to diversity and the synthesis of knowledge frameworks, organizational epistemology relates to a process of institutionalizing knowledge and learning, and strategic epistemology relates to innovation and the creation and application of new knowledge.

Metaphysics. *Metaphysics* is the study of ultimate reality and what constitutes the structure and content of what exists as real. It considers categories and natures of things, their interrelation, and their manifestation in complex systems. In so doing, it confronts mind and body, cause and effect, what it means to exist and be a person, and one's relation to the larger world. A fair consideration of metaphysics must acknowledge the multifarious approaches to understanding reality and existence. Metaphysical problems include those of an ontological (existence), theological (divine), and cosmological (universal principles) nature. As it is often put, metaphysics asks the really big questions such as "who am I?," "what is reality?," and "for what purpose do I exist?" Mirrored questions in the realm of organization management are equally germane, such as "why does and how should this team [or firm or strategy] exist?" Thus, we can say that to some extent individual metaphysics relates to personal reflection, interpersonal metaphysics relates to influence and power relationships, organizational metaphysics relates to global and intercultural mind-sets, and strategic metaphysics relates to pedagogy and education.

Altogether, we put forth in this handbook that organization management processes can be more or less wise in the domains of logic, ethics, aesthetics, epistemology, and metaphysics; as such, we seek to explore the nature, application, and source of this variability.

Contributions to the Handbook

Of course, the full richness of OMW can be better appreciated by experiencing these manifestations of the phenomena more specifically and directly. To this end, the 22 original contributions were commissioned for the *Handbook of Organizational and Managerial Wisdom*. Together, they offer a veritable smorgasbord of wisdom to be savored and digested. Bon appétité.

Part I: **LOGIC**	1. Individual Logic *Wisdom in Organizations: A Balance Theory Analysis*	Jennifer Jordan Robert J. Sternberg

Part I covers organizational and managerial logic.

In Chapter 1, titled "Wisdom in Organizations: A Balance Theory Analysis," Jennifer Jordan and Robert J. Sternberg address individual logic by considering judgment. Jordan is a postdoctoral research fellow at Dartmouth College. Sternberg is dean of the School of Arts and Sciences at Tufts University, former director of the PACE (Psychology of Abilities, Competencies, and Expertise) Center at Yale University, and past president of the American Psychological Association. Using Johnson & Johnson as a case study, Jordan and Sternberg integrate their interests to address the impact that leaders' intelligence and creativity can have on their organizations. They present the balance theory of wisdom to explain how James Burke used his intelligence and creativity to manage competing interests and help Johnson & Johnson recover from the Tylenol poisoning dilemma. Jordan and Sternberg then draw similarities between the balance theory and judgment, calling particular attention to enhancing one's character through knowing when to act versus when to observe and knowing when to incorporate personal values versus when to disregard them. The authors integrate logic, emphasizing a wise leader's ability to consider multiple points of view and focus on the impact of time. Yet Jordan and Sternberg are quick to point out that wisdom is all too often not present. If a leader has both intelligence and creativity, he or she can still fail to be wise based on an inability to act on these skills or an unwillingness to incorporate good judgment into his or her actions. The authors argue that this inability or unwillingness comes from a number of factors (dubbed fallacies), including an egocentric attitude—the belief that one is omnipotent, omniscient, or invulnerable—and reliance on unrealistic optimism. These fallacies are used in the Johnson & Johnson examples to explain why Burke succeeded in dealing with the Tylenol dilemma, whereas Ralph Larsen failed when facing medical stent problems. Ultimately, Jordan and Sternberg detail a number of means that leaders can use to foster wisdom within their organizations. They conclude that "wise decision making can be developed. We have a way. We need only the will."

Part I: **LOGIC**	2. Interpersonal Logic *Team Wisdom: Definition, Dynamics, and Applications*	Tjai M. Nielsen Amy C. Edmondson Eric Sundstrom

In Chapter 2, titled "Team Wisdom: Definition, Dynamics, and Applications," Tjai M. Nielsen, Amy C. Edmondson, and Eric Sundstrom address interpersonal logic by considering teams. Nielsen is an assistant professor of management at George Washington University. Edmondson is the Novartis Professor of Leadership and Management at Harvard University. Sundstrom is a professor of psychology at the University of Tennessee as well as an evaluator for the National Science Foundation. Building on a shared interest in groups or teams, the authors develop a framework for understanding team wisdom. Such a concept is achieved when teams become effective at recognizing and managing the multitude of tensions underlying teamwork. These tensions are predominantly related to team boundaries (distinguishing the team from its surrounding environment), temporal scope (dividing time between varying goals and purposes), and multiple priorities (prioritizing the importance of competing tasks). Nielsen, Edmondson, and Sundstrom argue that wisdom can be developed within teams when managers work with the rest of the team to enhance member attributes, establish team norms, and acknowledge that conflict may arise. Conflict can be generated from choices regarding the self versus the team, internal versus external demands, and short-term versus long-term goals. The authors provide examples of conflicts arising from these issues in a variety of team types before concluding with a practical discussion of how to address tension and develop wisdom in teams.

Part I: **LOGIC**	3. Organizational Logic *Institutionalizing Wisdom in* *Organizations*	Paul R. Lawrence

Paul R. Lawrence addresses organizational logic by considering institutionalization and systems in Chapter 3, titled "Institutionalizing Wisdom in Organizations." Lawrence is the Wallace Brett Donham Professor of Organizational Behavior (Emeritus) at the Harvard Business School. He uses his knowledge of organizational structure, environment, and design to detail how the U.S. government and human brain function to foster wisdom within their subjects. First, Lawrence uses the U.S. Constitution as an example to facilitate a discussion about how this imparting of wisdom is accomplished. He draws on the competing forces of passion and reason as conceptualized by the Founding Fathers to emphasize the inner dichotomy present in every individual. Passions are described as the emotional urges that drive individuals to satisfy impulses. Reason is seen as the regulator of passion and the gateway to virtue (the placement of public good over individual gain). The government functions to provide the checks and balances necessary to tilt the dichotomy in favor of virtue within its subjects. Lawrence then turns to the drives underlying both passion and reason, exploring them from a neurological point of view. Returning to the concerns raised by the Founding Fathers, Lawrence argues that there are often conflicting drives that generate emotions. These emotions are examined and possibly censored by reason. Lawrence then presents mental models that accomplish this task, and the process of decision making in the brain is detailed using these drives. Similar to the regulation of emotions by reason seen in the human mind, Lawrence views the government as a balancing force that supports wise behavior in its subjects through an emphasis on dialogue and logic—the system of checks and balances. Finally, Lawrence concludes by commenting on the current prevalence of special interest factionalism within the U.S. government as caused by the involvement of corporations.

Part I: **LOGIC**	4. Strategic Logic *Toward a Wisdom-Based* *Approach to Strategic Management*	Paul E. Bierly III Robert W. Kolodinsky

In Chapter 4, titled "Toward a Wisdom-Based Approach to Strategic Management," Paul E. Bierly, III and Robert W. Kolodinsky address strategic logic by considering business policy. Bierly is the Zane Showker Professor of Management and director of the Center for Entrepreneurship at James Madison University. Kolodinsky is an assistant professor at the same institution. After presenting an overview of strategic management, Bierly and Kolodinsky outline several shortcomings to the simplified view of the world on which most strategic decisions rely. As a solution to these shortcomings, the authors present varying levels of wisdom, beginning with executive wisdom. For Bierly and Kolodinsky, executive wisdom is composed of five components: (a) judgment, (b) accumulation of knowledge, (c) deep reflection about one's own and others' past experiences, (d) actions performed for the "common good," and (e) moral maturity. They elaborate on this framework by examining the associated concepts of knowledge, experience, maturity, discipline, and generativity. These concepts are guided by spirituality and lead to a number of beneficial outcomes such as enlightenment. Bierly and Kolodinsky expand the concept of executive wisdom from here to the more complex notion of organizational wisdom, noting that this complexity stems from the multitude of levels involved in such a concept. Furthermore, the authors point out, at this level knowledge accumulation is a far more complex amalgamation; however, leaders can help to foster this form of wisdom through advocating and supporting organizational spirituality and balance. Bierly and Kolodinsky close with a discussion of how to foster the spirituality and balance necessary for wisdom as well as the positive outcomes that can result from wisdom.

Part II: **ETHICS**	5. Individual Ethics *The Virtue of Prudence*	Jean M. Bartunek Jordi Trullen

Part II covers organizational and managerial ethics.

Chapter 5, titled "The Virtue of Prudence," is where Jean M. Bartunek and Jordi Trullen address individual ethics by considering virtue. Bartunek is the Robert A. and Evelyn J. Ferris Chair and professor of organizational studies at Boston College as well as a fellow and past president of the Academy of Management. Trullen is a doctoral candidate in organizational studies at the same institution. Their combined interests in wisdom and spirituality led Bartunek and Trullen to the notion of prudence; however, before directly addressing that issue, the authors raise the concept of *virtue*. An individual concept that relates to a strong moral character and commitment to the environment beyond individual gain, virtue is equated with individuals performing at their best. Bartunek and Trullen then introduce prudence as the link between intellectual and moral virtue. The authors detail the situational nature of prudence as they explore how it arises in response to specific stimulants. When individuals must make decisions in complex situations, prudence is particularly visible because many competing factors must be evaluated, weighed, and acted on. The results are rarely the linear and rational decisions often emphasized by academics. The tripartite brain is evoked as the authors find wise individuals from those who can integrate their cognition, affection, and conation. Bartunek and Trullen argue that individuals develop this integration through experience. They provide several cases to illustrate the acquisition and impact of wisdom in organizations and conclude by speculating on the effect that academic work can have on fostering wisdom.

Part II: ETHICS	6. Interpersonal Ethics *The Wise Negotiator*	Roy J. Lewicki

Chapter 6, titled "The Wise Negotiator," is where Roy J. Lewicki addresses interpersonal ethics by considering negotiation. Lewicki is the Dean's Distinguished Teaching Professor of Management and Human Resources at The Ohio State University and founding editor of *Academy of Management Learning and Education*. Relying on his extensive experience in the field, Lewicki introduces wisdom by emphasizing how, in negotiations, the concept has become synonymous with competitiveness and domination. However, wisdom is not found in bending ethical principles to advance a self-serving path. Using many common themes from Jordan and Sternberg's definition of wisdom in Chapter 1, Lewicki argues that wise negotiators embrace the ethical and moral foundations of negotiation and try to act as truthfully as possible to establish a fair and lasting relationship with their counterparts. He then presents a series of 10 actionable principles for wise negotiators, namely that they (1) recognize opportunities to negotiate (even when such opportunities are not obvious), (2) eschew an exclusive reliance on a competitive approach, (3) prepare thoroughly, (4) accept the perceptual biases that can enter into the process, (5) commit to interpersonal relationships, (6) listen actively throughout the process, (7) accept the influence that the context has on events, (8) are aware of but do not emphasize the power they have, (9) appreciate cultural differences, and (10) maintain personal integrity. These principles are explored in-depth and operationalized in negotiation settings.

Part II: ETHICS	7. Organizational Ethics *Acting Wisely While Facing Ethical Dilemmas in Leadership*	Jay Conger Robert Hooijberg

In Chapter 7, titled "Acting Wisely While Facing Ethical Dilemmas in Leadership," Jay Conger and Robert Hooijberg address organizational ethics by considering leadership. Conger holds the Henry Kravis Research Chair Professorship of Leadership at Claremont McKenna College, is a visiting professor of organizational behavior at the London Business School, and is a senior research scientist at the Center for Effective Organizations at the University of Southern California. Hooijberg is a professor of organizational behavior at the International Institute for Management

Development (IMD) in Lausanne, Switzerland. Beginning their chapter with a case, Conger and Hooijberg emphasize that the practicality of applying wisdom is often lost in the theoretical conceptualization of it. A myriad of connections between wisdom and action are presented to emphasize the multileveled and situational aspects of the term. The authors settle on *wise action* as adaptive behaviors that are based on intelligence and experience to bring about a common good in both the short and long term beyond the mere benefit of the decider. To make this concept of wisdom more applicable, Conger and Hooijberg present and analyze two cases. In so doing, the authors convey that wise decisions are not always the most popular ones. They see wise decisions as often emphasizing values and priorities, but with a commitment to compromising, improving, and accepting uncertainty. Conger and Hooijberg then expand the discussion to address how the organization itself can support wise action by providing a moral compass and establishing an emphasis on core values. However, most important is an organization's willingness to look beyond financial reward and allow its managers to make potentially unpopular decisions. They argue that, in so doing, managers are encouraged to break down the barriers to wisdom rather than eschew it for short-term benefits.

Part II: ETHICS	8. Strategic Ethics *Strategy, Wisdom, and Stakeholder Theory: A Pragmatic and Entrepreneurial View of Stakeholder Strategy*	R. Edward Freeman Laura Dunham John McVea

In Chapter 8, "Strategy, Wisdom, and Stakeholder Theory: A Pragmatic and Entrepreneurial View of Stakeholder Strategy," R. Edward Freeman, Laura Dunham, and John McVea address strategic ethics by considering the environment. Freeman is the Elis and Signe Olsson Professor of Business Administration and director of the Olsson Center for Applied Ethics at the University of Virginia. Dunham and McVea both are assistant professors in the Schulze School of Entrepreneurship at the University of St. Thomas. Using their shared interest in strategy, they integrate wisdom into the strategy-making process through the construct of stakeholder theory. The authors raise a philosophical impasse between means and ends that underlies this theory, giving rise to practical and ethical shortcomings. They present pragmatism and managerial wisdom to revisit this theory and deal with these shortcomings, integrating these two concepts into the stakeholder approach through an emphasis on perception, deliberation, experimental action, and reflection. Freeman, Dunham, and McVea explore these skills in greater depth to demonstrate the potential benefits of such practical wisdom. To orient managers toward practical wisdom, they call on researchers and educators to focus on the preceding skills. In so doing, practitioners of stakeholder theory become adept at solving ethical dilemmas, using human intelligence, and approaching complex problems realistically.

Part III: AESTHETICS	9. Individual Aesthetics *Self-Interest*	Russell Cropanzano Jordan Stein Barry M. Goldman

Part III covers organizational and managerial aesthetics.

In Chapter 9, titled "Self-Interest," Russell Cropanzano, Jordan Stein, and Barry M. Goldman address individual aesthetics by considering the self-interest drive. Cropanzano is the Brien Lesk Professor of Organizational Behavior at the University of Arizona's Eller College of Management, a fellow in the Society for Industrial/Organizational Psychology, and editor of *Journal of Management*. Stein is a doctoral candidate, and Goldman is an assistant professor, at the same institution. Implying that wisdom is obtained through understanding the root motivation of individuals, the authors delve into a discussion of self-interest. By reviewing the historical foundation that motivation theory has established, they present self-interest as the primary motivating factor. Three fundamental concerns—material interests, interpersonal interests, and moral principles—are explored to reveal that their roots are far more complex then a mere reliance on self-interest. Concepts such as values, altruism, empathy, principles, and justice are also explored to reveal possible foundations in self-interest. Yet Cropanzano, Stein, and Goldman show that every concept represents far more than a desire for self-enhancement. Subsequently, they explore emotions to raise the question of whether these are simply reflections of self-interest or are indicative of other factors. Given the results presented, the authors argue that the current definition of self-interest does not take into consideration all of the potentially relevant factors that it influences; therefore, they offer a broader definition. Despite this, the authors undermine this broader definition through a discussion of the practical value of such a conceptualization. Concluding with a discussion of ethics and morals, they raise the question of whether self-interest is fundamentally negative or if it can have beneficial outcomes in the domain of organization management.

Part III: AESTHETICS	10. Interpersonal Aesthetics *Emotional and Social Intelligence Competencies Are Wisdom in Practice*	Richard E. Boyatzis

In Chapter 10, titled "Emotional and Social Intelligence Competencies Are Wisdom in Practice," Richard E. Boyatzis addresses interpersonal aesthetics by considering emotion. Boyatzis is a professor in the Departments of

Organizational Behavior and Psychology at Case Western Reserve University and an adjunct professor in human resources at ESADE in Barcelona, Spain. He presents three overarching rules of wisdom obtained from the ancient Greeks: "know thyself," "nothing too much," and "treat others as you wish to be treated." Boyatzis integrates these rules into five key theories, driving the understanding of aesthetics to establish their timelessness and global relevance. He presents emotional and social intelligence (ESI) both as a means to practicing and as a result of being familiar with these overarching rules, stating that through exhibiting ESI one is actually practicing the act of wisdom. As a result, Boyatzis describes the set of competencies and abilities underlying ESI and outlines how it has been operationalized and measured. The self-knowledge that leads to both ESI and wisdom can be obtained by progressing through five discontinuities: (a) who you want to be versus who you are, (b) how others see you versus how you see yourself, (c) your desired future versus your probable future, (d) whether you act toward a desirable future or maintain stability, and (e) whether you rely on reference groups or rely exclusively on yourself. Boyatzis elaborates on these discontinuities to create a five-step progression that leads an individual toward the interconnected concepts of ESI and wisdom.

Part III: AESTHETICS	11. Organizational Aesthetics *Aesthetics and Wisdom in the Practice of Organizational Development*	W. Warner Burke

In Chapter 11, titled "Aesthetics and Wisdom in the Practice of Organization Development," W. Warner Burke addresses organizational aesthetics by considering organization development. Burke holds the Edward Lee Thorndike Professorship of Psychology and Education at Teachers College, Columbia University, is codirector of the Eisenhower Leader Development M.A. program for the U.S. Military Academy at West Point, and is a past editor of both *Organizational Dynamics* and *Academy of Management Executive*. Fusing his lifetime of experience in organizational development (OD) with a practice-based approach toward wisdom leads Burke to three recommendations when attempting a wise OD initiative, namely to (a) take the time to develop relevant knowledge, (b) reflect on previous practices, and (c) know when and how to apply the knowledge obtained. Exploring the increasingly elaborate definitions and outcomes associated with OD, Burke emphasizes the wealth of knowledge available to those designing a change. Integrating culture into the discussion, Burke details 11 characteristics of a culturally wise OD initiative. He also introduces a systems perspective and describes wise OD as an initiative embracing the underlying systemic nature of most manifest problems and committed to truly changing them. This discussion gives rise to several examples of what unwise OD resembles. In turn, these examples give way to three basic processes that must be embraced in a wise OD process: conflict resolution, trusting the process, and leader coaching. Burke provides a thorough case example to emphasize the need for a coherent mission statement and to detail how this is accomplished. Ultimately, he concludes this case by emphasizing that a commitment to wise OD often takes a great deal of time and does not always yield wise results. However, truly wise OD can yield a positive and beautiful change that aids the organization in realizing its potential and fosters a more positive environment.

Part III: AESTHETICS	12. Strategic Aesthetics *Wisdom and Human Resource Management*	Angelo S. DeNisi Carrie A. Belsito

Chapter 12, titled "Wisdom and Human Resource Management," is where Angelo S. DeNisi and Carrie A. Belsito address strategic aesthetics by considering human resource management (HRM). DeNisi is a professor of organizational behavior and dean of the A.B. Freeman School of Business at Tulane University and a past editor of *Academy of Management Journal*. Belsito is a lecturer and doctoral candidate at Texas A&M University. From their interests in HRM and strategy, the authors build wisdom into an HRM system to develop a sustainable strategic advantage. This system is achieved through maintaining the delicate balance between the financial goals of the organization and the personal goals of employees. Arguing that the traditional system has been far more focused on the prior, DeNisi and Belsito outline the history of strategic HRD. Fundamentally, they argue that this overreliance on financial performance has stemmed from the incorrect belief in a bipolar relationship between the two variables. Exposing the independence actually present in this relationship, the authors assert that wise strategic HRM results in a focus on practices that maximize both variables. They discuss how to accomplish this mutual maximization, covering relevant issues such as selection, compensation, training and development, performance appraisal systems, and union–management relations. Through this integration, not only does the firm improve its performance; employees become more motivated and committed as well. Finally, the authors conclude with a discussion of the relevance of manager education to the process of a wise strategic HRD system.

Part IV: EPISTEMOLOGY	13. Individual Epistemology *Interpretive Wisdom*	Dennis A. Gioia

Part IV covers organizational and managerial epistemology.

In Chapter 13, titled "Interpretive Wisdom," Dennis Gioia addresses individual epistemology by considering sensemaking. Gioia is a professor in the Department of Organizational Behavior at Pennsylvania State University. Gioia begins by presenting a piece of art to emphasize how interpretations about an objective object can differ. This difference is further exacerbated when one attempts to infer meaning from the piece of art. The author expands this discussion by giving a musical example of multiple perspectives being generated around the Beatles' *Sergeant Pepper's Lonely Hearts Club Band*. Sensemaking is introduced to characterize both examples in which individuals make their own interpretations of information. Expanding the sensemaking process to include interpersonal interactions, Gioia emphasizes how two individuals conversing with one another embody very different realities. Through these examples, he builds his case that perception is the only reality and that wisdom is obtained by embracing this notion and acting with this awareness in mind. The constructionist approach on which this argument rests is detailed and elaborated through five interrelated conceptions about the world, namely that (a) it is constructed, (b) it is interpreted, (c) it is collectively constructed, (d) it is relative, and (e) it is treated as objective. The concept of wisdom is again raised as the ability to create viable realities based on experiences and to use informed judgment to act prudently in these realities. As a result, sensemaking—and the awareness that sensemaking is always occurring—is essential to wisdom. Gioia concludes with a discussion of the misgivings that he faced when asked to write about wisdom and a personal experience that gave rise to a mental approach oriented to both sensemaking and sensegiving.

Part IV: EPISTEMOLOGY	14. Interpersonal Epistemology *Wisdom, Culture, and Organizations*	P. Christopher Earley Lynn R. Offermann

In Chapter 14, titled "Wisdom, Culture, and Organizations," P. Christopher Earley and Lynn R. Offermann address interpersonal epistemology by considering cultural diversity. Earley is the dean and Cycle and Carriage Professor at the National University of Singapore Business School and is a professor of organizational behavior at the London Business School. Offermann is a professor of industrial/organizational psychology at George Washington University and a fellow in the Society for Industrial/Organizational Psychology, the American Psychological Association, and the Association for Psychological Science. Beginning by detailing an auspicious task, Earley and Offermann attempt to disentangle the more universal aspects of wisdom (etic wisdom) from the more culture-specific aspects of it (emic wisdom). They introduce cultural intelligence as a fundamental tool to accomplishing this task. The concept of culture itself is distinguished from associated constructs to distill an essential core construct that is used to explore the moral foundations of wisdom. The authors then expand this discussion to a more extensive comparison of wisdom and intelligence as it differs across cultures. Four distinguishing dimensions are presented: (a) cognitive capability, (b) the application of cognitive competencies to issues encountered in life, (c) interpersonal capacities, and (d) demeanor with those considered wise. Earley and Offermann conclude by combining their areas of interest to develop a coherent analysis of the application of culture-based wisdom in organizations. This analysis generates an exploration of a number of areas, including cultural training, leadership, multinational/multicultural teams, and multinational organizations. Within these areas, relationships are explored, motivational elements are addressed, the benefits and disadvantages of global homogenization are raised, and the individual is connected to the overall organization.

Part IV: **EPISTEMOLOGY**	15. Organizational Epistemology *Interpersonal Relations in Organizations and the Emergence of Wisdom*	Peter B. Vaill

In Chapter 15, titled "Interpersonal Relations in Organizations and the Emergence of Wisdom," Peter B. Vaill addresses organizational epistemology by considering learning. Vaill is a professor of management at Antioch University. Beginning with a poem emphasizing the escalating complexity of achieving shared understanding in a field relying on increasingly specialized expertise, Vaill presents three premises, namely that (a) wisdom is needed in all organizational action, (b) wisdom is a social phenomenon, and (c) wisdom results from interrelated external and internal sources. Through a discussion of these premises, Vaill sees scientific wisdom as ineffective in organizations; instead, he shows wisdom as arising from relationships that do not necessarily involve wise individuals. In contrast, Vaill argues that wisdom arises based on the social choices that individuals make. Given the social nature of wisdom, Vaill goes on to introduce the "error of the third kind" to explain how wisdom is often prevented from arising in interaction. He presents *from within* wisdom as a means of overcoming the decline in the value of meetings by cultivating wisdom-generating relationships in a group context. To foster this environment, groups must deal with what Vaill has dubbed the "permanent white water" of unexpected problems and continual change. He presents seven hypotheses to help solve this problem and, in so doing, to increase group wisdom. At this point, Vaill introduces a case to explain how wisdom can emerge from relationships. Aiding this emergence is an interpersonal focus on acceptance, empathy, and congruence.

Ultimately, Vaill explains these terms and brings them into the organization to help create a clear pathway to wisdom.

Part IV: EPISTEMOLOGY	16. Strategic Epistemology *Innovation and* *Organizational Wisdom*	Arnoud De Meyer

In Chapter 16, titled "Innovation and Organizational Wisdom," Arnoud De Meyer addresses strategic epistemology by considering innovation. De Meyer is professor of management studies at Cambridge University and director of the Judge Business School, a fellow of Jesus College, and a former Akzo Nobel Fellow in Strategic Management and professor of technology management at INSEAD. Relying on his career involved in innovative management processes, De Meyer presents the relationship between innovation and wisdom as more complex than the traditional belief that the former arises out of the latter. To accomplish this, he defines innovation and applies it in the organizational environment. Subsequently, De Meyer details how wisdom is manifested in practice by showing how in organizations it is split into organizational and user components. Arguing that innovation arises from the wise organization's ability to accumulate and integrate knowledge, De Meyer moves on to a discussion of five actions designed to create and mobilize organizational wisdom: (a) creating credibility, (b) stimulating diversity, (c) focusing on communication and cooperation, (d) developing an extended network, and (e) investing in procedures and tools. De Meyer brings the discussion down to the component level by exploring how organizations can access the user wisdom of their employees. The author then addresses the possibility that wisdom can actually function to hinder innovation through the creation and operation of defense mechanisms and the calcification of ways of thinking. As a result, De Meyer concludes with a discussion of how to use wisdom to assess whether innovation is beneficial and how to maintain a wise and agile organizational environment.

Part V: METAPHYSICS	17. Individual Metaphysics *The Getting of Wisdom:* *Self-Conduct, Personal* *Identity, and Wisdom* *Across the Life Span*	Nigel Nicholson

Part V covers organizational and managerial metaphysics.

In Chapter 17, titled "The Getting of Wisdom: Self-Conduct, Personal Identity, and Wisdom Across the Life Span," Nigel Nicholson addresses individual metaphysics by considering reflection. Nicholson, a professor of organizational behavior at the London Business School, emphasizes unique ways of looking at problems and fostering learning. He uses a Darwinian approach to argue that wisdom is a complex system of learning that is formed by unique self- and social insight. Insight of this nature generates effective judgments that help to guide individuals through an increasingly complex world. These insights can be generated in three domains: human affairs, interpersonal relationships, and self-conduct. One gains insight by experiencing the world, understanding how to read and survive with others, and controlling oneself and one's impulses. Nicholson expands on these three areas before detailing how one can gain wisdom in them throughout life. Finally, he uses biography to address how wisdom is not exhibited by constantly resisting destiny (a function of upbringing that gives individuals the tendency to act in set ways); instead, wisdom is the knowledge of when it is valuable to fight destiny and when it is more efficient to go along with it. Thus, through a commitment to learning and creativity, one develops the potentiality to observe one's destiny and to know when it is more valuable to make judgments based on it and when it is best to fight it and make independent judgments.

Part V: METAPHYSICS	18. Interpersonal Metaphysics "We Live in a Political World": The Paradox of Managerial Wisdom	Tyrone S. Pitsis Stewart R. Clegg

In Chapter 18, titled "'We Live in a Political World': The Paradox of Managerial Wisdom," Tyrone S. Pitsis and Stewart R. Clegg address interpersonal metaphysics by considering influence. Pitsis is a senior research associate at the University of Technology, Sydney. Clegg is director of the Innovative Collaborations Alliances and Networks (ICAN) and a professor of management at the same institution and also holds chairs at Aston University, the University of Maastricht, and Vrije Universiteit. Defined as the willingness to pursue knowledge about what is accepted as social reality, wisdom is really about knowing what one does not know. However, upper level managers traditionally have imprisoned wisdom within organizations. Rather than acting in a wise manner, they have been trained to create routines and processes to limit the reflection that is the foundation of both wisdom and ethics. This limits the true value of wisdom because it greatly hinders its social construction. With their lack of focus on dialogue, orientation to amassing control, and focus on practice, Pitsis and Clegg incorporate the works of Ghoshal, Weick, Mintzberg, and Pfeffer to argue that managers often see wisdom as opposing their purpose. This discussion is expanded to an analysis of why management learning literature has not fostered wisdom within its readers. Emphasizing the economic and hierarchical model in which management is currently ensconced, the authors argue that wisdom can be fostered by a turn to shared power. This is a possibility only through a commitment to "heterarchy" and positive organizational scholarship. Pitsis and Clegg explore these two concepts to uncover how they foster wisdom throughout the organization.

Part V: METAPHYSICS	19. Organizational Metaphysics *Global Wisdom and the Audacity of Hope*	Nancy J. Adler

In Chapter 19, titled "Global Wisdom and the Audacity of Hope," Nancy J. Adler addresses organizational metaphysics by considering international management. Adler is a professor of organizational behavior in the Faculty of Management at McGill University and a fellow of the Academy of Management, the Academy of International Business, and the Royal Society of Canada. Embracing a view of pragmatic wisdom and a focus on globalization, Adler uses her extensive experience in these areas to explain how wisdom moves from understanding to action. Global wisdom is substantiated through a discussion of the possibilities of change, hope, and courage in today's world. The presence of these factors is essential because it is through hope and courage that wisdom is translated from understanding to action. Adler presents the organization Uniterra as an international initiative designed to foster the hope-based courageous actions that constitute the application of wisdom. Its progression from an idea to a reality is examined thoroughly, providing an effective case study of a wisdom-based progression from understanding to action. Adler elaborates on this progression by focusing on the organization's partnering with the following factors: each other, oneself, generosity, expertise, the unknown, the world, structure, challenges, and success. The end result of this process is a partnering with hope. Uniterra is seen as an organization emphasizing the power of partnering wisdom and hope in a world that often sees negative outcomes from this pairing. Instead, Uniterra has succeeded in unifying experience with idealism to become a trailblazer in how to foster wisdom as a means to developing a successful organization.

Part V: METAPHYSICS	20. Strategic Metaphysics *Can Wisdom Be Taught?*	Cynthia V. Fukami

In Chapter 20, titled "Can Wisdom Be Taught?," Cynthia V. Fukami addresses strategic metaphysics by considering management education. Fukami is a professor of management at the University of Denver and a fellow of the Carnegie Foundation for the Advancement of Teaching. Relying on her interest in teaching effectiveness and scholarship, Fukami argues that wisdom is the bridge between theory and practice and is of fundamental importance in management education. Management educators have been quick to emphasize the imparting of knowledge in the classroom while the application of this knowledge is left to the students. Arguing that education has not relied enough on professors as role models, Fukami suggests that a gap between knowing and doing has evolved. Through encouraging individuals to apply their knowledge appropriately in various scenarios, wisdom can be operationalized as situation recognition. Fukami goes on to detail several root causes behind the lack of wisdom in education, namely the low status of teaching, a focus on teaching rather than on learning, a focus on quantity rather than on quality, highly competitive classrooms, poor acknowledgment of students as whole individuals, ignorance of tacit knowledge, and a shift in schools to hiring researchers rather than practitioners. Many of these problems have been brought to the forefront recently by the recognition that teaching is an integral part of faculty scholarship. Furthermore, the literature on pedagogy in management education is already present and merely needs to be used to foster a wiser teaching environment. Fukami details several pedagogies intended to help professors bring wisdom into the classroom and transfer it to the practice of organization management, such as a focus on cooperation, out-of-classroom activities, practical experience, team teaching, and values. Although Fukami concludes that wisdom cannot fundamentally be taught, she argues that it can be fostered through effective teaching.

Part VI: SYNTHESIZING COMMENTARY	21. *Wisdom: Objectivism as the Proper Philosophy for Living on Earth*	Edwin A. Locke

Part VI presents synthesizing commentaries that employ particular lenses to reconcile the levels and schools of thought into more overarching explorations of OMW. As such, the following chapters present two contrasting approaches.

In Chapter 21, titled "Wisdom: Objectivism as the Proper Philosophy for Living on Earth," Edwin A. Locke offers a synthesis of OMW by using the lens of objectivism. Locke is Dean's Professor of Leadership and Motivation (Emeritus) in the R. H. Smith School of Business at the University of Maryland as well as a fellow of the American Psychological Society, the American Psychological Association, and the Academy of Management. With a heavy reliance on the philosophy of Ayn Rand, Locke explores the philosophy that underlies wisdom, namely metaphysics, epistemology, ethics, politics, and aesthetics. In metaphysics, Locke addresses the basic axioms of existence, identity, and consciousness. Moving on to epistemology, Locke outlines his basic premise of the fundamental importance of objectivism and the impact that it has on concept formation and causality. Shifting to ethics, Locke outlines the potential costs of ethical behavior for organizations before going on to address the benefits that an objective code of ethics has over dominant approaches such as skepticism and religious dogmatism. Virtue is also integrated into the ethical framework through six types, as outlined by Rand: honesty, integrity, independence, productiveness, justice, and pride. Locke's discussion of ethics concludes with an analysis of who should fundamentally benefit from ethics and morals. Moving on to politics, Locke outlines a number of principles that individuals should use to function together as a society. Power and rights are also integrated into politics, and the implications of objectivism for these components are explored, yielding an orientation toward laissez-faire capitalism. Locke outlines the implications of laissez-faire capitalism for the business world through exploring 10 commonly discussed business issues. Concluding with aesthetics, he tackles the function of art and beauty from an objectivist viewpoint. Locke sums up with an argument that the embracing of an objective outlook yields a rational world, making wisdom inherently obtainable.

Part VI: SYNTHESIZING COMMENTARY	22. *Wisdom as Learned Ignorance: Integrating East–West Perspectives*	Robert Chia Robin Holt

In Chapter 22, titled "Wisdom as Learned Ignorance: Integrating East–West Perspectives," Robert Chia and Robin Holt offer a synthesis of OMW by using the lens of the East–West dichotomy. Chia is a professor of management at the University of Aberdeen Business School. Holt is a professor of management at the Leeds University Business School. Using their extensive philosophical backgrounds, Chia and Holt argue that wisdom is actually a process of learned ignorance or unlearning rather than the accumulation of knowledge and information. In fact, extensive knowledge is shown to impede one's ability to learn from practical experience, an outcome that limits the potential for wisdom. Humans are seen as constantly striving to fill the void caused by ignorance rather than reflecting on it, a tendency that fundamentally drives humanity further from Socrates's belief that wisdom is knowing what one does not know. Chia and Holt take the reader on a journey through Western philosophy, showing how the pure Socratic notion of wisdom has been compromised throughout history. They return to the concept of learned ignorance through an emphasis on Eastern philosophy. Outlined through a review of East–West thinkers, Chia and Holt show Eastern thinking as fundamentally comfortable with the emptiness that Western thinking seeks to eliminate so aggressively. They bring the concept of this comfort with emptiness into organizations to detail the potential for "performative extravagance," which arises when individuals are willing to abandon orthodox thinking and fundamentally alter how things are done. The authors wrap up their discussion by exploring how to foster wisdom in the workplace. Ultimately, Chia and Holt conclude by raising the innately paradoxical task of writing a book about wisdom, and they present several methods to ease such a contradiction.

In this section, we have surveyed the structure and content of our contributors' contributions to the challenge of finding the nexus of wisdom and organization management. In the final section, we attempt to synthesize their insights, and add some of our own, to help crystallize and facilitate the development of this most important area of inquiry.

Insights From the *Handbook of Organizational and Managerial Wisdom*

Our approach to creating this handbook was to embrace the inherent complexity of wisdom and consider its various forms and manifestations within the context of organizing and managing. This being said, the challenge remains as to how these pieces might fit together or, to use a different analogy, how the pixels produce the picture. In this final section, we explore the combined insights that emerge from our consideration of the topic. To review, we present a grid delineated by level and perspective, with the final two chapters attempting synthesis using two distinct lenses (Table I.2).

A recurrent theme in wisdom lore is that it is unwise to consider oneself wise. This paradox is usually resolved by acknowledging one's limitations and seeking counsel from others, and that is the approach adopted in this synopsis. Rather than a priori profess a superordinate definition of wisdom, we reflect on the offerings of our esteemed colleagues—each of whom was chosen specifically for his or her expertise in a particular content and analytic domain—and attempt to develop integrative insights. To this end, our objective within is the trifurcate quest for edification, application, and development. Thus, we entertain the following questions, processed through the experts but filtered through our own personal predilections and perspectives:

Objective 1: What is the *essence* of organizational and managerial wisdom?

Objective 2: What are the best practices for *applying* organizational and managerial wisdom?

Objective 3: What are ways for *developing* organizational and managerial wisdom?

Objective 1: Understanding the Essence of Organizational and Managerial Wisdom

Given the enormity of defining organizational and managerial wisdom, we employ the spirit of successive approximation. First, we synthesize conceptions across common *content domains* to understand OMW through the spectrum of logic, ethics, aesthetics, epistemology, and metaphysics. The

Table I.2   Organizational Schema of the Handbook

Introduction					
	Logic	*Ethics*	*Aesthetics*	*Epistemology*	*Metaphysics*
Individual	1	5	9	13	17
Interpersonal	2	6	10	14	18
Organizational	3	7	11	15	19
Strategic	4	8	12	16	20
Synthesizing Commentary: 21–22					

product of such an endeavor is reconciliations of component OMW dimensions. Similarly, we synthesize conceptions across *analytic levels* to understand wisdom in the individual, interpersonal, organizational, and strategic domains. The product will be reconciliations of component OMW agents. Considering these conceptualizations alongside means for implementation and development, we then return to explore whether there is perhaps a metaconceptualization of OMW to be had.

Content Domains

What is organizational and managerial logic, ethics, aesthetics, epistemology, and metaphysics? A synthesis of the relevant contributions to the handbook yields the following (Table I.3).

Organizational and managerial logic is sound and balanced judgment (individual), integrated within a team framework that manages inherent tensions (interpersonal) and is institutionalized in a structure of checks and balances (organizational), used to leverage collective knowledge so as to maximize organizational and societal effectiveness (strategic). Here the components, dynamics, design, and orientation of the system are seen as inherently sound. Each part is balanced and reconciled within its larger context to function effectively and efficiently. That is, each element makes sense in both the "micro" self and the "macro" scheme. The essence of organizational and managerial logic, then, is that of a finely tuned machine.

Organizational and managerial ethics is prudent behavior (individual), integrated within ethically negotiated relationships (interpersonal) and viability-enhancing leadership (organizational), used to discern the most appropriate action for achieving joint value in a multiplicity of complex stakeholder relationships and uncertain situations (strategic). Here the components, dynamics, design, and orientation of the system are seen as inherently moral. Each part is grounded in and supportive of its larger context. That is, each element is firmly based in a set of fundamental principles. The

Table I.3   Domains and Levels of Organizational and Managerial Wisdom

Question 1: What Is Organizational and Managerial Wisdom?	
Domains	
Logic	Sound and balanced judgment (individual), integrated within a team framework that manages inherent tensions (interpersonal) and is institutionalized in a structure of checks and balances (organizational), used to leverage collective knowledge so as to maximize organizational and societal effectiveness (strategic)
Ethics	Prudent behavior (individual), integrated within ethically negotiated relationships (interpersonal) and viability-enhancing leadership (organizational), used to discern the most appropriate action for achieving joint value in a multiplicity of complex stakeholder relationships and uncertain situations (strategic)
Aesthetics	Mitigated facilitation of self-interests (individual), integrated within socially and emotionally intelligent interactions (interpersonal) and behaviorally grounded change processes (organizational), used to seek a synergy between financial and personal well-being (strategic)
Epistemology	Informed sensemaking and sensegiving (individual), integrated within multicultural contexts and views (interpersonal) and emergent in accepting, empathic, and congruent understanding (organizational), used to facilitate and properly orient the creative transformation function (strategic)
Metaphysics	Reflective and farsighted understanding (individual), integrated within intersubjectively created and collaboratively formed relationships (interpersonal) and a vision that inspires courage and hope of making a positive difference (organizational), used to marry knowing and doing (strategic)
Levels	
Individual	The wise actor is characterized by sound and balanced judgment (logical), prudent behavior (ethical), mitigated facilitation of self-interests (aesthetic), informed sensemaking and sensegiving (epistemological), and reflective and farsighted understanding (metaphysical)
Interpersonal	The wise team is characterized by managed tensions (logical), morally negotiated relationships (ethical), socially and emotionally intelligent interactions (aesthetic), multiculturally reconciled contexts and views (epistemological), and intersubjectively created and collaboratively formed relationships (metaphysical)
Organizational	The wise organization is characterized by institutionalized structure of checks and balances (logical); viability-enhancing leadership (ethical); behaviorally grounded change processes (aesthetic); accepting, empathic, and congruent understanding (epistemological); and a vision that inspires courage and hope to make a positive difference (metaphysical)
Strategic	The wise strategy is characterized by leveraging collective knowledge to maximize organizational and societal effectiveness (logical), discerning the most appropriate action for achieving joint value in a multiplicity of complex stakeholder relationships and uncertain situations (ethical), seeking a balance between financial and personal well-being (aesthetic), improving and properly orienting the creative transformation function (epistemological), and combining knowing and doing (metaphysical)

essence of organizational and managerial ethics, then, is that of a well-intentioned agent.

Organizational and managerial aesthetics is mitigated facilitation of self-interests (individual), integrated within socially and emotionally intelligent interactions (interpersonal) and behaviorally grounded change processes (organizational), used to seek a synergy between financial and personal well-being (strategic). Here the components, dynamics, design, and orientation of the system are seen as inherently holistic. Each part is fulfilled and collaborative with its larger context. That is, each element is partner to the dance or brushstroke to the masterpiece. The essence of organizational and managerial aesthetics, then, is that of a mutually reinforcing relationship.

Organizational and managerial epistemology is informed sensemaking and sensegiving (individual), integrated within multicultural contexts and views (interpersonal) and emergent in accepting, empathic, and congruent understanding (organizational), used to facilitate and properly orient the creative transformation function (strategic). Here the components, dynamics, design, and orientation of the system are seen as inherently harmonious. Each part is active and interactive with its larger context. That is, each element is both creator of and created in a dynamic discernment. The essence of organizational and managerial epistemology, then, is that of an emergent comprehension.

Organizational and managerial metaphysics is reflective and farsighted understanding (individual), integrated within intersubjectively created and collaboratively formed relationships (interpersonal) and a vision that inspires courage and hope to make a positive difference (organizational), used to marry knowing and doing (strategic). Here the components, dynamics, design, and orientation of the system are seen as inherently valuable. Each part is important and contributory with its larger context. That is, each element is an end as well as a process. The essence of organizational and managerial metaphysics, then, is that of a meaningful journey.

Analytic Levels

What is wisdom across the individual, interpersonal, organizational, and strategic dynamics of organization management? A synthesis of the relevant contributions to the handbook yields the following (Table I.3).

The wise actor is characterized by sound and balanced judgment (logical), prudent behavior (ethical), mitigated facilitation of self-interests (aesthetic), informed sensemaking and sensegiving (epistemological), and reflective and farsighted understanding (metaphysical). The person who is the embodiment of individual wisdom within the domain of organization management is a complex and thoughtful contributor.

The wise team is characterized by managed tensions (logical), morally negotiated relationships (ethical), emotionally and socially intelligent interactions (aesthetic), multiculturally reconciled contexts and views (epistemological), and intersubjectively created and collaboratively formed relationships (metaphysical). The wise team, then, is the embodiment of interpersonal wisdom as a rich and supportive interaction.

The wise organization is characterized by an institutionalized structure of checks and balances (logical); viability-enhancing leadership (ethical); behaviorally grounded change processes (aesthetic); accepting, empathic, and congruent understanding (epistemological); and a vision that inspires courage and hope to make a positive difference (metaphysical). The embodiment of organizational-level wisdom, then, is that of an enabling and synergistic context.

The wise strategy is characterized by leveraging collective knowledge to maximize organizational and societal effectiveness (logical), discerning the most appropriate action for achieving joint value in a multiplicity of complex stakeholder relationships and uncertain situations (ethical), seeking a balance between financial and personal well-being (aesthetic), improving and properly orienting the creative transformation function (epistemological), and combining knowing and doing (metaphysical). The embodiment of strategic wisdom within the domain of organization management, then, is that of a productive and inclusive vision.

Objective 2: Delineation of Best Practices for Applying Organizational and Managerial Wisdom

Now that we have proposed a platform for understanding some of the manifestations of OMW across content domains and analytic levels, we turn to the second objective of the handbook. The intersection of wisdom and organization management is necessarily practically focused and application oriented; therefore, it is necessary to go beyond a discussion of the phenomena in the abstract. To generate useful guideposts for wise action, we must relate it to the professional function. In the following, we synthesize our coauthors' contributions to discern central tenets, and thereby best practices, for applying OMW.

The first best practice we identify for applying OMW is to "think." *Think* implies that the wisest individuals, teams, organizations, and strategies demonstrate *extraordinary intellectual prowess*. This is evidenced by characterizations of said actors as possessing highly developed intellectual capacity, keen insight, the ability for complex deliberation, deep cultural intelligence, and a broad knowledge base. Thus, wise actors in the professional domain are smart. They use their heads. They get it. They deploy their resources to process issues and figure things out.

The second best practice we identify for applying OMW is to "feel." By *feel*, we mean that the wisest individuals, teams, organizations, and strategies demonstrate *extraordinary emotive capacity*. This is evidenced by characterizations of said actors as possessing profound spirituality, a fundamental prudence, the courage to do what is right, empathy and understanding of others, and an openness to differences between peoples and contexts. Thus, wise actors in the professional domain are intimately connected. They use their hearts. They deploy their empathy and sensitivity to be in touch.

The third best practice we identify for applying OMW is to "synergize." To *synergize* implies that the wisest individuals, teams, organizations, and strategies demonstrate *extraordinary collaborative orientation*. This is evidenced by characterizations of said actors as possessing strong norms and systemic checks that balance, productive change, mutual collaboration, and collective coherence. Thus, wise actors in the professional domain are unified. They coordinate their efforts. They deploy their harmony and congruence to be on the same page and move to the same music.

The fourth best practice we identify for applying OMW is to "engage." Possessing the ability to *engage* implies that the wisest individuals, teams, organizations, and strategies demonstrate *extraordinary functional application*. This is evidenced by characterizations of said actors as possessing behavioral proactiveness, situational recognition, consistent experimentation, established networks, and practical experience. Thus, wise actors in the professional domain are active. They engage their world. They deploy their flexibility, energy, and acumen to adapt to their stage and cast.

The fifth best practice we identify for applying OMW is to "reflect." *Reflect* implies that the wisest individuals, teams, organizations, and strategies demonstrate *extraordinary introspective insight*. This is evidenced by characterizations of said actors as possessing contemplative understanding and appreciation of their values, needs, emotions, interpretations, and sense of being. Thus, wise actors in the professional domain are deep. They discover their identity. They deploy their insight and grounded base to realize and leverage the self.

The sixth best practice we identify for applying OMW is to "aspire." *Aspire* implies that the wisest individuals, teams, organizations, and strategies demonstrate *extraordinary principled objectives*. This is evidenced by characterizations of said actors as possessing a concern for the public good, striving for a common purpose, establishing sustainability, promoting humaneness, and addressing profound and meaningful issues. Thus, wise actors in the professional domain are well-intentioned. They channel their will in positive directions. They deploy their humanity and citizenry to make themselves and their world better.

Altogether, *the wise agent demonstrates a smart, connected, unified, active, deep, and good-intentioned approach in the practice of organization management,* as illustrated in Table I.4.

Objective 3: Exploration of Ways to Develop Organizational and Managerial Wisdom

We have so far explored the essence and deployment of wisdom within the domain of organization management in hopes of understanding the

Table I.4   Best Practices for Applying Organizational and Managerial Wisdom

Question 2: What Are the Best Practices for Applying Organizational and Managerial Wisdom?		
Best Application Practices	*Objective*	*Select Elements and Chapters*
To think The OMW actor is smart.	Extraordinary intellectual prowess	Intellectual capacity (1) Insight (6) Deliberation (8) Cultural intelligence (14) Knowledge base (16)
To feel The OMW actor is connected.	Extraordinary emotive capacity	Intuition (4) Prudence (5) Courage (7) Empathy (10) Openness (14)
To synergize The OMW actor is unified.	Extraordinary collaborative orientation	Norms (2) Checks and balances (3) Productive change (11) Mutual benefit (12) Coherence (15)
To engage The OMW actor is active.	Extraordinary functional application	Proactiveness (5) Recognition (6) Experimentation (8) Networks (16) Experience (20)
To reflect The OMW actor is deep.	Extraordinary introspective insight	Values (1) Needs (9) Emotions (10) Interpretations (13) Self (17)
To aspire The OMW actor is well-intentioned.	Extraordinary principled objectives	Public good (1) Common purpose (4) Sustainability (5) Humaneness (18) Meaningful issues (19)

NOTE: Chapter numbers are in parentheses.

concept. But understanding does not imply existence. Wisdom is not magically transported from mind to matter simply by attaining a conceptual or philosophical comprehension. The proper conditions need to be created. Thus, the previous sections are necessary but not sufficient treatments of the topic insofar as OMW must be developed.

The first best practice we identify for developing OMW is a "focus on attitude." This *focus on attitude* implies that it is possible to move toward the wisdom ideal through a consideration of orientation or the way one sees things. This is essentially a matter of defining one's worldview. A focus on attitude addresses the *what* issue: "What is your outlook?" Thus, insofar as attitude underlies wisdom, we need to develop the proper mind-set. This is a function of factors such as personal and collective schemas, approach, and definitions. As the contributors to this handbook suggest, a focus on attitude is put into practice via pedagogical and diffusive interventions aimed at crystallizing and fostering dialogue, acceptance, aesthetic regard, recognition, and positive vision.

The second best practice we identify for developing OMW is a "focus on awareness." This *focus on awareness* suggests that one can move toward the wisdom ideal through a consideration of identity. This is essentially a matter of discovering one's true nature. A focus on awareness can be seen to address the proverbial *who* issue: "Who are you?" Thus, insofar as awareness underlies wisdom, we need to develop the appropriate sense of self. Again, the contributors suggest that a focus on awareness is put into practice by pedagogical and diffusive interventions aimed at crystallizing and fostering spirituality, essential values, motivating interests, core ideals, and the practice of self-talk.

The third best practice we identify for developing OMW is a "focus on ability." When *focusing on ability,* one can move toward the wisdom ideal through a consideration of capability or the things one can do. This is essentially a matter of growing one's fundamental competencies. A focus on ability addresses the *why* issue: "Why can you in effect perform some functions and not others?" And insofar as ability underlies wisdom, we need to develop the appropriate capacity. Our contributors suggest that a focus on ability is put into practice via pedagogical and diffusive interventions aimed at crystallizing and fostering sound thought processes, relevant experience, broad education, specific training, and use of knowledge resources.

The fourth best practice we identify for developing OMW is a "focus on application." In *focusing on application,* one can move toward the wisdom ideal through a consideration of behavior or causal and networked relationships. This is essentially a matter of learning effective principles. A focus on application addresses the *how* issue: "How do things really work?" Thus, insofar as application underlies wisdom, we need to develop the appropriate practical orientation. As per the contributions to this handbook, a focus on application is put into practice via pedagogical and diffusive interventions aimed at crystallizing and fostering the practices of coaching, action and reflection, mentorship, intentional change, and engaged experimentation.

The fifth best practice we identify for developing OMW is a "focus on design." This *focus on design* implies that one can move toward the wisdom ideal through a consideration of arena or overarching framework. This is essentially a matter of building facilitative contexts. A focus on design addresses the *where* issue: "Where do you operate?" Thus, insofar as design underlies wisdom, we need to develop the appropriate systems. Our contributors find that a focus on design can be put into practice via pedagogical and diffusive interventions aimed at crystallizing and fostering team support, a balanced structure, inclusive stakeholder relationships, culture sensitivity and alacrity, and positive power dynamics. In sum, a development program for OMW would employ methods to develop appropriate attitude, awareness, ability, application, and design, as illustrated in Table I.5.

Final Thoughts

What, then, is our ultimate conceptualization of OMW? This is a fantastic question, and the reader will note that we have so far resisted answering it. Surely, the contributing authors would cry foul (as we required definitions in their content domain chapters). This notwithstanding, we acknowledge that wisdom in the practice of organization management, by its very nature, is resistant to a simple characterization or delineation. This is evident in its manifest complexity and elusiveness. The closest we might come to reconciling the contributions of the handbook is that OMW suggests the application of a deep understanding and fundamental capacity about *living well* to professional pursuits. Given its inherent action orientation, living well does not merely mean knowledge of the good life or how to achieve it; it also means the fostering and implementation of intellectual, spiritual, behavioral, and all related dynamics to lead the good life and enable it for others. Therefore, in the interest of fairness, we give our "two cents" on the matter in the following, humbly offered not as a universal definition but rather as a basis for exploration:

> **Organizational and managerial wisdom** is the application to professional pursuits of a deep understanding and fundamental capacity for living well. This includes the visioning, integration, and implementation of multifarious dimensions (within logical, ethical, aesthetic, epistemological, and metaphysical domains) as well as the development and enactment of multifarious elements (across individual, interpersonal, organizational, and strategic levels) to lead the good life and enable it for others.

But what exactly is *living well*? Another outstanding question. The term *living* implies existence. OMW specifies the domain of this existence. Individuals exist and live, as do their interpersonal relationships, their organizations, and their strategic objectives, movements, and causes. As such, there can be a wisdom, or lack thereof, in any domain and at each of

Table I.5   Ways for Developing Organizational and Managerial Wisdom

Question 3: What Are Ways for Developing Organizational and Managerial Wisdom?		
Best Development Practices	*Focus*	*Select Elements and Chapters*
Focus on attitude	Orientation: What is your outlook? Define worldview	Dialogue (5) Acceptance (7, 18) Aesthetic regard (8) Recognition (13) Positive vision (19)
Focus on awareness	Perception: Who are you? Discover true self	Spirituality (4) Values (7) Interests (9) Ideals (10) Self-talk (17)
Focus on ability	Capability: Why can you perform? Grow fundamental competencies	Thought processes (1) Experience (5) Education (12) Training (14) Knowledge (16)
Focus on application	Behavior: How do things work? Learn effective principles	Coaching (6, 11) Action/Reflection (7) Mentorship (8, 20) Intentional change (10) Experimentation (15)
Focus on design	Arena: Where do you operate? Build facilitative contexts	Support (2) Structure (3) Stakeholders (4) Culture (14) Power (18)

NOTE: Chapter numbers are in parentheses.

these levels. Yet the term *well* implies an implicit or explicit set of values and assumptions, a particular cultural or institutional context, and defined and delineated criteria. It also implies a province of thought such as logic and what is reasoned, ethics and what is good, aesthetics and what is beautiful, epistemology and what is understood, and metaphysics and what is meaningful. As such, there can be a wisdom, or lack thereof, in any culture or context as well as to any of these ends. This further implies that, just as our personal and professional lives are mystifyingly multifarious, so too must be our conception of OMW. With apologies to the Warren Commission, there is simply no "magic" OMW bullet.

It is useful to note that there are several basic tensions that underlie, and emerge from, this thinking. First, is there such a thing as a *universal* OMW? Or, as Earley and Offermann put it in Chapter 14, is OMW an emic or an etic? Said yet another way, is the solution to this dilemma derivative of an ecumenical or pluralist framework (cf. Bolman & Deal, 2006)? No matter how the question is phrased, the issue will haunt. We are of the position that even among the divergences in intellectual, cultural, spiritual, and religious traditions of the world, there is indeed a commonality that could be approximate. As such, we advocate approaching the issue from an Aristotelean contingency perspective while still aspiring to a Platonic synthesis. This is based on our conclusion that OMW has (a) a customized and relativistic element as well as (b) an equifinal and mutually reinforcing nature. It is customized and relativistic insofar as OMW often requires different means in different contexts. It is equifinal and mutually reinforcing insofar as OMW ultimately aspires to common or collaborative ends.

Second, is there a *feasible* OMW? That is to say, can we ever really attain this austere condition, or is it more accurate, and useful, to frame the concept as an ideal meant to inspire movement? For sure, there are many barriers in the pursuit of OMW, but there are also a plethora of rich opportunities to reduce impediments and empower potentialities. As such, we advocate approaching issues from an incrementalist and conditional perspective while aspiring to a paradigmatic transformation. Third, and in a related sense, is there a *perennial* OMW? Is OMW a noun, a state of being, something that is to be grasped, applied, and developed? Alternatively, is it a verb, an eternal process, a journey or quest that is to be experimented with, reflected on, and tried again? Or is it both of these, à la Xeno's paradoxical arrow and Einstein's mysterious light, which will forever and concurrently be and not be? As such, we advocate approaching the issue from a fluid perspective while aspiring to achieve the quintessential "aha" enlightened moment.

Within these tensions lays the central paradox of this handbook. To publish a "handbook" implies that there is a knowable, comprehensive, finite, and definitive conceptualization of the focal phenomena. But to say this is profoundly "unwise" because the wise know what they do not and cannot know. The purposeful, albeit somewhat quixotic, approach of this handbook, then, is to suggest a framework and set of insights but ultimately to leave the conceptualization of wisdom and its organizational and managerial manifestation unresolved. In the distinguished tradition of the Greek philosophical school, we offer systematically arranged domain-specific truths (Aristotle's lowercase "t" truth or, in this instance, lowercase "w" wisdom) in the hope of approximating a universal truth (Plato's uppercase

"T" Truth or, in this instance, uppercase "W" Wisdom). Our contributors have put forth their lowercase OMw's, and we have extracted central themes to approximate what an uppercase OMW might be, how it might appear, and from where it might arrive. In this sense, we reiterate the words of wisdom in Karl Weick's foreword to our handbook to recommend embracing rather than obscuring the inherent complexity of OMW. And similarly in the profound and mysterious tradition of our Eastern colleagues, we invite the reader to reflect on, infer, and apply his or her personal path(s) as appropriate.

We put forth that, in the domain of organizational and managerial activity, there is a both a Wisdom and many $w$isdoms to be realized and applied. Speaking to the issue of universality, we suggest that there are common elements found in all manifestations of the OMW concept. As illustrated in Figure I.3, there are varied overlaps with specific OMw's and overarching OMW, such as with the circles on the left. There are also interactions between multiple OMw approaches, such as with the circles on the right. *Therefore, the seeker and practitioner of OMW must simultaneously be a realist and an idealist, demonstrating a resilient flexibility (to engage wisdoms) while at the same time exhibiting a broad-mindedness and integrative—perhaps visionary—quality (in pursuing Wisdom).*

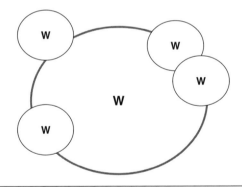

Figure I.3   Overlaps With and Interactions Between Organizational and Managerial Wisdom and $w$isdoms

Speaking to the issues of feasibility and eternality, we put forth that as a noun, OMW suggests a state or potential that can be greater or lesser and that can grow or decline. Simultaneously as a verb, OMW suggests a process of engagement, the effectiveness of which varies by circumstance and the maturity of which varies by stages. It stands to reason that potential will affect process, which in turn will alter potential. In other words, one's specific experiences and reflections can enact wisdoms that in turn might add to or detract from one's overall or general Wisdom at any given time. These characteristics and dynamics are illustrated in Figure I.4. *Therefore, to truly understand, practice, and develop OMW, we must see it as both snapshot and cinema, as the fundamental interplay between acquiring and using wisdom (and the virtual or vicious cycles that may result), and as the inseparable interaction of being and acting wise.*

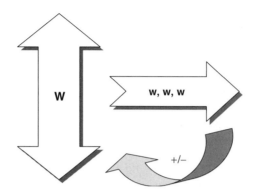

Figure I.4   Development and Use of Organizational and Managerial Wisdom and *w*isdoms

We close, as per Socrates, by restating the belief that we can at best be lovers of wisdom and devotees to its pursuit. OMW is represented across a complex array of dimensions and a dynamic interaction of actors. It is found in the abstract and the specific, can be facilitated and impeded, is more or less generalizable, and represents both a state and a process. As such, its application to professional pursuits is a central yet perennial objective. It is our hope that the *Handbook of Organizational and Managerial Wisdom* will both inspire and facilitate this most noble end.

References

Adams, S. (1996). *The Dilbert Principle*. New York: HarperCollins.

American Heritage dictionary of the English language (4th ed.). (2006). Boston: Houghton Mifflin.

Angeles, P. A. (1992). *HarperCollins dictionary of philosophy* (2nd ed.). New York: HarperCollins.

Ardelt, M. (2000). Intellectual versus wisdom-related knowledge: The case for a different kind of learning in the later years of life. *Educational Gerontology, 26,* 771–789.

Ardelt, M. (2004). Wisdom as expert knowledge system: A critical review of a contemporary operationalization of an ancient concept. *Human Development, 47,* 257–285.

Aristotle. (1984). *Nicomachean ethics* (D. Ross, Trans.). New York: Oxford University Press.

Astley, G., & Van de Ven, A. H. (1983). Central perspectives and debates in organization theory. *Administrative Science Quarterly, 28,* 245–273.

Audi, R. (Ed.). (1999). *Cambridge dictionary of philosophy* (2nd ed.). Cambridge, UK: Cambridge University Press.

Badaracco, J. (1992, Spring). Business ethics: Four shapers of executive responsibility. *California Management Review,* pp. 64–70.

Baltes, P. B., & Kunzmann, U. (2004). The two faces of wisdom: Wisdom as a general theory of knowledge and judgment about excellence in mind and virtue vs. wisdom as everyday realization in people and products. *Human Development, 47,* 290–299.

Baltes, P. B., & Staudinger, U. M. (2000). Wisdom: A metaheuristic (pragmatic) to orchestrate mind and virtue toward excellence. *American Psychologist, 55,* 122–136.

Birren, J. E., & Fisher, L. M. (1990). The elements of wisdom: Overview and integration. In R. J. Sternberg (Ed.), *Wisdom: Its nature, origins, and development* (pp. 317–332). New York: Cambridge University Press.

Birren, J. E., & Svensson, C. M. (2005). Wisdom in history. In R. J. Sternberg & J. Jordan (Eds.), *A handbook of wisdom: Psychological perspectives* (pp. 3–31). New York: Cambridge University Press.

Bloom, B. S. (Ed.). (1956). *Taxonomy of educational objectives: Vol. 1. Cognitive domain.* New York: Longman.

Bolman, L. G., & Deal, T. E. (2006). *The wizard and the warrior: Leading with passion and power.* San Francisco: Jossey-Bass.

Boyer, E. L. (1990). *Scholarship reconsidered: Priorities for the professoriate.* Princeton, NJ: Princeton University Press.

Burrell, G., & Morgan, G. (1979). *Sociological paradigms and organizational analysis.* London: Heinemann.

Cambridge dictionaries online. (2006). [Online]. Available: http://dictionary .cambridge.org

Clegg, S. R., Hardy, C., & Nord, W. R. (1996). *Handbook of organizational studies.* Thousand Oaks, CA: Sage.

Columbia encyclopedia (6th ed.). (2005). New York: Columbia University Press.

Courtney, J. F., Haynes, J. D., & Paradice, D. B. (2005). *Inquiring organizations: Moving from knowledge management to wisdom.* Hershey, PA: Idea Group.

Craig, E. (Ed.). (1998). *Routledge encyclopedia of philosophy.* London: Routledge.

Durant, W. (1961). *The story of philosophy: The lives and opinions of the greater philosophers.* New York: Washington Square Press.

Edwards, P. (1972). *The encyclopedia of philosophy.* New York: Macmillan/Free Press.

Einstein, A. (1954). May 19th address at Princeton Theological Seminary. In A. Einstein, *Ideas and opinions by Albert Einstein.* New York: Bonanza Books. (Original work published 1939)

Eliot, T. S. (1934). *The rock.* New York: Harcourt Brace.

Encarta. (2006). [Online]. Available: http://encarta.msn.com

Encyclopedia Britannica. (2006). [Online]. Available: www.britannica.com

Engardio, P. (2006, October 30). Karma Capitalism. *BusinessWeek, October 30:* pp. 84–91.

Flesher, P. V. M. (2006). *Buddhism glossary* [Online]. Available: http://uwacadweb .uwyo.edu/religionet

Gandhi, M. K. (2006). *The story of my experiments with truth.* Ahmedabad: Navajivan Publishing House. Original work published 1927.

Ghoshal, S. (2005). Bad management theories are destroying good management practice. *Academy of Management Learning & Education, 4,* 75–91.

Hackman, R. (2002). *Leading teams: Setting the stage for great performances.* Boston: Harvard Business School Press.

Hartman, E. M. (1988). *Conceptual foundations of organizational theory.* Cambridge, MA: Ballinger.

Hawking, S. (2001). *The universe in a nutshell.* New York: Bantam Books.

Honderich, T. (Ed.). (1995). *The Oxford companion to philosophy.* New York: Oxford University Press.

James, W. (1995). *Pragmatism.* New York: Dover. (Original work published 1909)

Janis, I. L. (1972). *Victims of groupthink.* Boston: Houghton Mifflin.

Jones, C. A. (2005). Wisdom paradigms for the enhancement of ethical and profitable business practices. *Journal of Business Ethics, 57,* 363–375.

Kant, I. (1997). *Critique of practical reason* (Cambridge Texts in the History of Philosophy). New York: Cambridge University Press. (Original work published 1778)

Katzenbach, J. R., & Smith, D. K. (2003). *The wisdom of teams: Creating the high-performance organization* (Collins Business Essentials). New York: HarperCollins.

Kerr, S. (1975). On the folly of rewarding "A" while hoping for "B." *Academy of Management Journal, 18,* 769–783.

Kessler, E. H. (2001). The idols of organizational theory: From Francis Bacon to the Dilbert Principle. *Journal of Management Inquiry, 10,* 285–297.

Koontz, H. (1980). The management theory jungle revisited. *Academy of Management Review, 5,* 175–187.

Leonard, D. (1995). *Wellsprings of knowledge.* Boston: Harvard Business School Press.

MaGee, B. (1998). *The story of philosophy: The essential guide to the history of Western philosophy.* London: DK Publishing.

Malan, L. C., & Kriger, M. P. (1998). Making sense of managerial wisdom. *Journal of Management Inquiry, 7,* 242–251.

Maugham, W. S. (1946). *The razor's edge.* Philadelphia: Blakiston.

McKee, P., & Barber, C. (1999). On defining wisdom. *International Journal of Aging & Human Development, 49,* 149–164.

Merriam-Webster online dictionary. (2006). [Online]. Available: www.m-w.com

Mintzberg, H. (2004). *Managers not MBAs: A hard look at the soft practice of managing and management development.* San Francisco: Berrett-Koehler.

Morgan, G. (1986). *Images of organization.* Newbury Park, CA: Sage.

Oxford dictionary of philosophy. (1996). Oxford, UK: Oxford University Press.

Oxford English dictionary. (2006). [Online]. Available: www.oed.com

Perrow, C. (1973). The short and glorious history of organizational theory. *Organizational Dynamics, 2*(1), 2–15.

Pfeffer, J. (1993). Barriers to the advancement of organizational science: Paradigm development as a dependent variable. *Academy of Management Review, 18,* 599–620.

Pfeffer, J., & Fong, C. T. (2002). The end of business schools? Less success than meets the eye. *Academy of Management Learning and Education, 1,* 78–95.

Plato. (1991). *The republic: The complete and unbridged Jowett translation.* Vintage: New York

Rice, E. F., Jr. (1958). *The Renaissance idea of wisdom.* Cambridge, MA: Harvard University Press.

Robinson, D. N. (1990). Wisdom through the ages. In R. J. Sternberg (Ed.), *Wisdom: Its nature, origins, and development* (pp. 12–24). New York: Cambridge University Press.

Salk, J. (1973). *The survival of the wisest.* New York: Harper & Row.

Schrage, M. (2001, December 10). But wait, there's more. *Fortune*, p. 276.

Scott, W. G. (1961). Organization theory: An overview and an appraisal. *Academy of Management Journal, 4*, 7–26.

Scott, W. R. (1987). *Organizations: Rational, natural, and open systems.* Englewood Cliffs, NJ: Prentice Hall.

Scruton, R. (1996). *Modern philosophy: An introduction and survey.* New York: Penguin.

Seligman, M. E. P., & Csikszentmihalyi, M. (2000). Happiness, excellence, and optimal human functioning. *American Psychologist, 55*, 5–183.

Shattuck, R. (1996). *Forbidden knowledge: From Prometheus to pornography.* New York: St. Martin's.

Small, M. W. (2004). Wisdom and not managerial wisdom: Do they have a place in management development programs? *Journal of Management Development, 23*, 751–763.

Solomon, R. C., & Higgins, K. M. (1997). *A passion for wisdom.* New York: Oxford University Press.

Srivastava, S., & Cooperrider, D. L. (Eds.). (1998). *Organizational wisdom and executive courage.* San Francisco: New Lexington Press.

Sternberg, R. J. (Ed.). (1990). *Wisdom: Its nature, origins, and development.* New York: Cambridge University Press.

Sternberg, R. J. (2003a). WICS: A model of leadership in organizations. *Academy of Management Learning and Education, 2*, 386–401.

Sternberg, R. J. (2003b). *Wisdom, intelligence, and creativity synthesized.* New York: Cambridge University Press.

Sternberg, R. J., & Jordan, J. (Eds.). (2005). *A handbook of wisdom: Psychological perspectives.* New York: Cambridge University Press.

Takahashi, M., & Bordia, P. (2000). The concept of wisdom: A cross-cultural comparison. *International Journal of Psychology, 35*, 1–9.

Takahashi, M., & Overton, W. F. (2005). Cultural foundations of wisdom: An integrated developmental approach. In R. J. Sternberg & J. Jordan, *A handbook of wisdom: Psychological perspectives* (pp. 32–60). New York: Cambridge University Press.

Tolstoy, L. (1994). *War and peace.* New York: Random House. (Original work published ca. 1865)

Trowbridge, R. H. (2005). *The scientific approach to wisdom.* Unpublished doctoral dissertation, Union Institute and University, Cincinnati, OH.

Turban, E., Leidner, D., McLean, E., & Wetherbe, J. (2005). *Information technology for management: Transforming organizations in the digital economy.* New York: John Wiley.

Vaill, P. B. (1996). *Learning as a way of being.* San Francisco: Jossey-Bass.

Van Doren, C. (1991). *A history of knowledge.* New York: Ballantine.

Webster's new twentieth century dictionary of the English language–unabridged (2nd ed.). (1961). New York: Publishers Guild.

Weick, K. E. (1979). *The social psychology of organizing.* New York: McGraw-Hill.

Weick, K. E. (1993). The collapse of sensemaking in organizations: The Mann Gulch disaster. *Administrative Science Quarterly, 38*, 628–652.

Wikipedia. (2006). [Online]. Available: http://wikipedia.org

Wittgenstein, L. (2001). *Tractatus logico philosophicus.* London: Routledge. (Original work published 1921)

PART I

Logic

1

Individual Logic

Wisdom in Organizations: A Balance Theory Analysis

Jennifer Jordan
Robert J. Sternberg

It could be argued that the most important factor in an organization's success is wisdom, particularly the wisdom of those within the organization's leadership ranks. An organization, whether it is a corporation, a government agency, or an academic institution, can go from being at the top of its game in an industry to struggling to scrape by—based solely on who is at the helm and this leader's ability to impart wise leadership on the organization. Similarly, but perhaps less drastic, an organization can make one wise decision followed by a less wise one based on how well its leaders are able to integrate the organization's values and prudently use the resources it has been allotted when making decisions. Johnson & Johnson (J&J) presents an example of this contrast.

Logic can be used as a basis for wisdom. Wisdom, as defined in this chapter (Sternberg, 1998, 2000, 2005b), involves an individual's ability to balance the interests of multiple constituencies in a manner that serves each constituency's needs and well-being over the long and short terms. To

AUTHORS' NOTE: Preparation of this chapter was supported by Contract MDA 903-92-K-0125 from the U.S. Army Research Institute and by Grant Award 31-1992-701 from the U.S. Department of Education, Institute for Educational Sciences, as administered by the Temple University Laboratory for Student Success. Grantees undertaking such projects are encouraged to express their professional judgment freely. This chapter, therefore, does not necessarily represent the position or policies of the U.S. Army Research Institute or the U.S. Department of Education, and no official endorsement should be inferred.

balance these interests, the information that the decision maker uses must be based in truth and logic. Without logic, it is impossible to be wise. In addition to examining what wisdom *is,* this chapter examines factors that can lead wisdom (and thus truth) to be lost or obscured in organizational and managerial contexts. We label these factors *fallacies of thinking* (Sternberg, 2002, 2003, 2005a), but they could just as well be considered *fallacies of informal logic* because of their direct and negative effects on the process of obtaining a logical outcome.

In this chapter, we use two anecdotes—both about crucial decision-making situations at the J&J corporation. These anecdotes are used to illustrate contrasting examples of wise and not-so-wise decision making within an organizational context. We then move from the examples into theory and describe the balance theory of wisdom (Sternberg, 1998, 2005a) and a related theory of foolishness (Sternberg, 2002, 2003).

Johnson & Johnson's Decision-Making Dilemmas

Founded in 1886 as a medical products company, J&J quickly defined itself as one of the most brilliantly managed and innovative pharmaceutical and medical supply companies in the world. In 1976, James Burke, the former vice president of product management, ascended the ranks and became J&J's chief executive officer (CEO). By 1981, the corporation was ranked 74th among the largest U.S. industrials. One of J&J's best-selling products during the early 1970s and 1980s was Tylenol. In 1974, this product accounted for 90% of the nearly $88 million market in acetaminophen-based, over-the-counter painkillers. By 1981, J&J's sales revenue from all Tylenol products was estimated at more than $400 million. This success was quickly put in jeopardy when, in the fall of 1982, four individuals died from ingesting cyanide-tainted Extra-Strength Tylenol capsules produced at J&J's Pennsylvania plant. Three other individuals later died from tainted capsules produced at other plants.

Burke's swift and responsible actions were credited for J&J's victorious emergence from this crisis. Specifically, Burke took two actions that came to be considered crucial in the resolution of this tragic situation. The first is that he and his colleagues were completely candid and forthright with the media. They did not try to sidestep the crucial and sometimes unflattering questions that were posed to them, and they did what they could to inform the public of any danger. The organizational leaders took these actions despite the fact that there was no evidence that any of the contamination took place either at a J&J plant or during the shipping process.

The second crucial action was that J&J made sweeping actions for the purpose of protecting the public. In light of pressures from regulatory agencies to do otherwise, Burke decided to pull all Tylenol capsules from the market and offered to exchange all capsule products for tablets, a decision that was estimated to have cost J&J millions of dollars. But Burke believed that this was the only responsible reaction.

Fast-forward 12 months after the poisonings. At the height of the hype, analysts predicted that J&J never would recover from this catastrophe. First, they claimed that J&J's funds were too depleted; it was estimated that the corporation lost $100 million over the course of this crisis. Second, it was believed that the public never again would place its trust in a company whose product was responsible for the deaths of seven innocent victims— even though the company itself was not found to be negligent in any way.

To the surprise of everyone, only 1 year after the incident, Tylenol had regained 85% of its precrisis market share. By the fall of 1983, the product held 30% of the $1.3 billion over-the-counter painkiller market and was continuing on this upward trend (Smith & Tedlow, 1989).

When Burke retired as CEO in 1989, the position was assumed by Ralph Larsen. Larsen and Burke shared many attributes (Deutsch, 1988; Hurstak & Pearson, 1992). Larsen liked the reigning J&J corporate culture as it was when he took the position, stating that "Jim [Burke] has created a culture based on intelligent risk taking, on not being afraid to fail, on getting everything on the table and arguing if you have to. I love it, and it works" (quoted in Deutsch, 1988, sec. 1, p. 6). A fellow J&J director was quoted as saying, "Ralph and Jim have identical values" (p. 6). Given these similarities, it is surprising that Larsen ignored customer interests, which Burke had placed in such high regard, when it came time to make an important decision as CEO.

In 1996, with Larsen as CEO, J&J's sales of the very popular Palmaz–Schatz medical stent accounted for approximately 10% of the company's total earnings. Despite its widespread use in the cardiovascular industry, the stent had problems. First, it came in only one size and was significantly more costly than competitors' products. Unlike Tylenol users, cardiologists—the main consumers of stents—typically did not adhere to the concept of brand loyalty. They ordinarily used whatever product was best for their patients and was sold at the lowest cost, regardless of the company producing it. Customers were beginning to loudly voice their dissatisfaction with the Palmaz–Schatz stent, but J&J did not seem alarmed by these complaints and did little to address customers' concerns.

Why? The most likely explanation is that J&J had become arrogant, fixated on its own success and relying on its past achievements. J&J was at the top of the stent market and did not perceive a threat coming from companies lower in the ranks. In late 1995, when J&J was still in its prime, it purchased Cordis, a small medical products company that was experienced in dealing with customers within this highly specialized industry. This merger was predicted to produce the "golden egg"—a stent so well designed that no other company could compete. With Cordis onboard, J&J likely felt impervious to the competition.

Unfortunately, J&J never allowed itself to realize the tremendous potential produced by this acquisition. One reason for J&J's poor performance following the acquisition was that it was very slow to integrate the two organizations. J&J failed to harness Cordis's strengths early enough—or ever. The final blow came when the Food and Drug Administration (FDA) approved a competitor's stent in 1997. This new product addressed customers' needs at a cost that was significantly less than that of J&J's Palmaz–Schatz. Within 1 year, J&J's stent sales were down 8%, and consequently J&J lost control over an industry it had captured so tightly just a few years earlier. The company's unwise decision making cost it its industry standing as well as a significant source of profits (Finkelstein, 2003).

Analyzing the Two Situations

Why had Burke brought J&J through the Tylenol poisonings with such grace and aplomb, whereas Larsen allowed J&J to lose its footing in the stent business? Was it because the former leader possessed more analytical intelligence than did the latter? Perhaps. But it appears more likely that it was not Larsen's lack of analytical intelligence that led to J&J's problems with the Palmaz–Schatz stent; rather, it was his (and his colleagues') inability to integrate wisdom with his analytical intelligence and creativity. It could also be seen as a failure of logic because Larsen failed to truthfully perceive and account for the competition and challenges that his product would face on the medical market.

These two J&J dilemmas are harnessed as a method for illustrating wise (and unwise) decision making in organizational settings. Specifically, this chapter employs Sternberg's (1998, 2000, 2005b) balance theory of wisdom as a framework for analyzing decision making in each of these situations and for analyzing wise decision making in organizations in general.

After defining the balance theory and illustrating how the J&J examples relate to its specific components, the chapter examines wise decision making within three traditional frameworks of ethics and two frameworks of reasoning. It also integrates the fallacies of thinking that lead smart individuals to exhibit unwise behavior. The chapter closes by presenting an argument for the importance of wise decision making in business and suggesting strategies for developing wisdom in organizational settings.

According to the balance theory (Sternberg, 1998, 2000, 2005b), wisdom is the ability to use one's successful intelligence, creativity, and knowledge, as mediated by personal values, to reach a common good by balancing intrapersonal, interpersonal, and extrapersonal interests over the short and long terms to adapt to, shape, and select environments.

The first and central component of the balance theory is the use of one's intelligence. Possessing wisdom is not just possessing vast amounts of analytical intelligence and practical knowledge but also knowing *what to do* with that knowledge. People can be extremely intelligent but still not wise. Both Burke and Larsen had the necessary intelligence and information required to carry out actions that could be beneficial for the entire organization, but only one (Burke) chose to apply this information in a way that balanced interests—moderating tendencies toward becoming focused too egocentrically on one's own interests. Wisdom is not solely about serving one's own interest but also about balancing various self-interests (intrapersonal) with the interests of others who are directly involved in the situation (interpersonal) and of other more external stakeholders (extrapersonal) such as one's city or country. Problems requiring wisdom always involve some element of these three potentially competing interests. Given the extensive area of needs, desires, and rights that these interests encompass when considered in concert, a decision must be made in the context of what the whole range of available options is.

In reference to the Tylenol poisonings, Burke had concerns about the multiple interests seemingly at odds with one another. In the best interest of the public, he wanted to conduct a national recall of the product; however, both the FDA and Federal Bureau of Investigation strongly advocated against this option. The regulatory agencies argued that a national recall would encourage other mentally unstable individuals to attempt similar poisoning plots solely to satisfy their desire to attract national attention. Burke was faced with the challenge of managing multiple competing interests—those of his own company (intrapersonal), those of the public (interpersonal), and those of the regulatory agencies (extrapersonal). In the end, he decided to do what he thought was in the service of his most important constituency, the public, while at the same time not disregarding the needs of the "others" involved. His decision to remove all capsules from the market led to significant proximal costs for J&J (it is estimated that J&J lost $100 million over the course of this crisis) but also led to distal gains for J&J. Burke's later cooperation with the FDA in the manufacture of safety-sealed bottles served the interests of the regulatory bodies (extrapersonal). But perhaps most important, his decision to recall all Tylenol capsules protected the safety of the public (interpersonal). He put the long-term common good of the public above the short-term good of himself or even, it seemed, his company.

Burke also applied his explicit and implicit knowledge. One way in which he did this was to collect the maximum information available so that he could make an informed decision. This procedure included conducting extensive surveys on consumer sentiment only hours after the poisonings began to receive national media coverage. This strategy allowed him to gauge how much trust had been lost. He also arranged multiple meetings with his colleagues to discuss the issue and debate multiple plans of action.

Last, the balance theory proposes that one must know when to *adapt, shape,* or *select* environments in reaction to a difficult dilemma. More specifically, one must consider how to adapt oneself or others to existing environments, shape environments to mold them into greater compatibility with oneself or others, or select new environments that are more conducive to meeting one's goals for the situation.

Burke's decision to pull all products from the market was an application of *shaping* the situation. He understood the issues involved, acknowledged all interests, and in the end decided that he needed to take the actions necessary to protect those who were most vulnerable to harm. How did he come to this decision? By applying the values on which J&J was founded—an application based in logic and truth.

In reference to Burke's focus on J&J's founding principles in resolving this crisis, he stated, "Everybody who puts something into this organization that builds that trust is enhancing the value long term of the business. I think that these values were here. We traded off them. We articulated them through the Credo. We spent a lot of time getting people to understand what we meant in the Credo" (quoted in Smith & Tedlow, 1989, p. 7). J&J's credo was not ambivalent about the organization's obligations. It stated, "We believe our first responsibility is to the doctors, nurses, and patients, to mothers and all others who use our products and services. . . . Everyone must be considered as an individual. . . . We are responsible to the communities in which we live and work and to the world community as well" (p. 22).

With a value system that targeted customers' needs so strongly and explicitly, how could J&J have so blatantly ignored complaints coming from doctors in the Palmaz–Schatz stent case? Clearly, J&J's exemplary leadership failed to see the warnings coming and thus failed to use logic as a basis of decision making. The leaders' proverbial eyes and ears were closed to the interests of the other parties involved—including those of their shareholders (extrapersonal). J&J had allowed its own hubris to corrupt its strengths.

We return to the discussion of wisdom and failures in wisdom later. But first, the balance theory is compared with theories of business ethics and general logic.

The Balance Theory and Traditional Theories of Ethics

The balance theory shares many characteristics with traditional theories of ethical reasoning. Most theories of ethical reasoning can be divided into three categories: deontological, teleological, and ontological (Newton & Schmidt, 2004).

Deontological Reasoning

Deontological reasoning, also known as nonconsequentialist reasoning, is based on the notion that every action has an underlying duty that one must observe to act ethically. A prescribed "duty" depends on a person's value system. Some values are universal (e.g., "murder is wrong"), whereas others are culturally specific (e.g., "it is wrong to commit adultery"). The balance theory captures this value-based component by acknowledging that the manner in which one decides to apply his or her knowledge and intelligence is based on a system of personal values.

Within the organizational domain, the application of personal values when making a decision that affects the entire organization is a controversial issue. It is questionable whether a manager has the right to apply his or her personal values to decisions that have consequences for the organization as a whole. For example, an upper level manager may confront the question of whether or not to allow same-sex partners to receive healthcare benefits similar to those given to opposite-sex spouses. In such a situation, should the manager allow his or her own beliefs about same-sex marriage to enter into the decision-making process? In the context of the balance theory, the answer is *yes*—with some qualifications. To partake in wise decision making, the manager must allow these personal values to enter into the process *so long as* the ultimate decision balances the interests of the multiple parties involved. These multiple interests must also include extrapersonal interests, which include the interests of the corporate community. For a manager's decision to qualify as wise, the manager would need to consider how his or her interests would set a precedent for the entire industry.

Teleological Reasoning

A form of consequentialist reasoning, teleological reasoning, states that an action should be judged as ethical based on the good that is derived from its outcome. The ethicality of a result is calculated by weighing the benefits that come from the decision in comparison with the costs that it consumes. The utilitarian theory of ethics, one of the most widely applied theories of ethics in business, is considered to be under the rubric of teleological reasoning. Utilitarianism proposes that any act should not be undertaken if it consumes greater good than it produces.

The balance theory captures this same spirit of balance by incorporating the *common good* into the decision-making process. For a decision to be considered wise, it must first pass a common good litmus test; that is, does it collectively benefit all stakeholders rather than just serving a few isolated interests?

In application to the business domain, the issue of a common good is particularly salient. Often a leader's downfall is witnessed in his or her focus on one or a few isolated parties at the enormous expense of other parties. For example, a manager may decide to expand a currently well-functioning business into a new industry—one in which the organization has little history or expertise. The venture can lead the company to sacrifice its strong reputation and value to shareholders and may even cause the organization to need to lay off a significant percentage of the current workforce to support the costs of the poor decision. Such a decision would not be considered ethical by the standards of teleological reasoning, or wise by the standards of the balance theory, because it was not undertaken with an understanding of how a balance could be achieved from the decision's outcome.

Ontological Reasoning

Ontological reasoning, also known as virtue-based reasoning, proposes that a decision is evaluated for its ethical content based on its service to instilling good character within the decision maker. Ontological reasoning holds central the notion that every time a person commits an act, the person is simultaneously defining his or her character. Thus, ontological reasoning is based not only on outcome but also on the process and on how this process contributes to the ethical development of the decision maker. This form of reasoning begins with the assumption that individuals strive to be virtuous and to have traits that maximize their ethical value in whatever domain they seek to excel. It asserts that a person will avoid committing a crime or another unethical action not because of the effect that the action will have on the good of the society but rather because it will soil the virtue of the individual who commits it and will thwart the person's progress in becoming a valuable member of society.

This theory of reasoning integrates the three components of the balance theory discussed earlier: personal values, common good, and balancing multiple interests. The balance theory proposes that an individual not only must hold values that are conducive to realizing a good outcome but also must seek an outcome that is beneficial to more than just himself or herself. In other words, the individual should seek an outcome that is virtuous.

In reference to ethical conduct in management, ontological reasoning considers the characteristics of the manager in the context of the way this individual interacts with the environment. A manager must strive to hold the values needed to lead a corporation successfully while at the same time working in an environment where those values are ideal for business development. A manager can meet his or her downfall when he or she tries to embody a management style that is suited for a different industry or type of workforce. The balance theory proposes that an individual cannot be successful unless he or she is able to fit skills with environmental demands. A manager who tries to control a large, culturally diverse organization in the same way he or she would control a small family business is destined to meet resistance and impede the progress of the organization.

The Balance Theory and Theories of Logic

The traditional ethics-based theories of deontological, teleological, and ontological reasoning can also be contrasted within frameworks of dialogical and dialectical reasoning.

Dialogical Reasoning

Dialogical reasoning is the consideration of multiple points of view when partaking in decision making. In terms of the balance theory of wisdom, it is the ability to look at intrapersonal, interpersonal, and extrapersonal interests and to balance these interests when making decisions. In reference to Burke's decision making that is described throughout this chapter, his decisions were based on what he thought would serve the company, the public, and the regulatory agencies that were affected by the crisis. In business, dialogical (and wise) reasoning suggests that a decision will always have the most favorable outcome when all stakeholders are considered.

Dialectical Reasoning

Dialectical reasoning integrates how the merits of an argument or outcome can change over time. It professes that a decision cannot be judged as good, or in this case as ethical, in a contextual vacuum; rather, a decision must be judged within the environment in which it exists and is being used. The balance theory addresses this method of logic by emphasizing the importance of both short- and long-term evaluation. A decision that may be prudent today might not be favorable in the future and vice versa. This proximal versus distal consideration is especially important to take into account within the organizational arena, which often emphasizes and rewards short-term, rather than long-term, outcomes. It could be argued that Burke would not have recalled all Tylenol products from the market had it not been for the specific and unique factors that were present, including the lack of clear evidence for how the cyanide had contaminated the capsules and the panic from consumers.

When Wisdom Fails

Not every business leader is likely to possess high levels of wisdom because such levels of wisdom are rare (Smith & Baltes, 1990). If one does not have wisdom but does have intelligence and creativity, can one still be an exceptional business leader? The answer, we suggest, is *no*. In fact, individuals who have high amounts of both intelligence and creativity may possess exceptional potential for leadership but will be incapable of demonstrating this potential through their actions (Sternberg, 2005a, 2005b). These individuals can be described as "charismatic," "innovative," or even "shrewd," but wisdom is required for a business leader to reach his or her maximum level of performance over the long term. The most dangerous individuals are perhaps those who possess the latter two components of the WICS (wisdom, intelligence, and creativity synthesized) model (Sternberg, 2005b), that is, those who are exceptionally intelligent and creative but who lack wisdom. These are the individuals who may use their own strengths to manipulate others. Smart people can do very foolish things (Sternberg, 2002, 2005a). Without wisdom, individuals are susceptible to committing at least one of five fallacies of thinking. These five fallacies are the fallacies of egocentrism, omnipotence, omniscience, invulnerability, and unrealistic optimism (Sternberg, 2002, 2003, 2005a). In the context of business, some of these fallacies apply more to organizational structures, whereas others are more relevant to individual managers.

Fallacy of Egocentrism

The *fallacy of egocentrism* is the belief that one is, and rightfully should be, the center of attention—the most important entity, which should receive priority in all decisions. In the context of organizational and managerial decision making, the fallacy of egocentrism can manifest itself in multiple ways. For example, a manager can become so fixated on or infatuated with a certain project or idea that he or she begins to ignore the larger picture and allows other more practical issues to fall by the wayside. Usually the execution of the project is to the leader's benefit—or so he or she believes.

An example of egocentrism in organizations can be found in a corporation's tendency to focus only on what those inside the organization think and believe. The more successful a corporation is, the more likely this mentality is to take hold. Why, after all, should a highly admired organization listen to criticism from the outside? The belief that an organization is "the best" can set it up for dangerous thinking and "groupthink" (Janis, 1972), causing those within it to ignore warnings of which they otherwise might have been cognizant. When faced with the Tylenol poisonings, Burke counteracted this tendency by immediately gauging public sentiment on trust and loyalty to the now tainted product.

Egocentric organizations can also fail to see and anticipate competition. A corporation that is more focused on its own performance than on the outside climate will shut its eyes to challenges that lie ahead, leaving it no leeway to make preparations. For example, J&J paid little attention to the small international stent producers that were beginning to flex their muscles in the American marketplace. As Larsen stated in response to problems among J&J's multiple consumer lines when he assumed the role as CEO, "We were arrogant. . . . We had leadership positions, and we were slow to respond to the competition" (quoted in Deutsch, 1988, sec. 1, p. 6).

Last, egocentric managers can fail to hear the complaints and suggestions of employees, just as egocentric organizations can fail to hear the complaints and requests of customers. There are many organizations that are good at producing what the market demands, but unless they are first receptive to these requests, they will often miss the mark and customers will go elsewhere. This fallacy of thinking could be attributed to why J&J failed to listen to the suggestions of its customers and to be prepared for the ensuing competition in the stent industry.

Fallacy of Omnipotence

The *fallacy of omnipotence* is the belief that one is all-powerful—able to direct others to follow one's every whim and wish. In the organizational context, this fallacy can manifest itself in the belief that the organization is capable of manipulating random or uncontrollable factors to work in its favor or in a leader's belief that he or she can direct outcomes of situations that are, in reality, determined by the confluence of many external factors beyond his or her control.

This fallacy can also manifest itself in a manager's attitude within the workplace. One of the most dangerous behaviors that can stymie wise decision making is a leader's portrayal that he or she is so powerful that followers are discouraged from voicing any open dissent. Wise decision making is based on a balanced presentation of the situation and the multiple interests involved. If a leader acts as though he or she is all-powerful, other perspectives will never be acknowledged or presented. In reference to J&J's problems in the stent industry, it is likely that the hierarchy of authority was so elaborate and confusing that customers' complaints were never able to reach the level of management responsible for making changes to the stent's design.

We are not arguing that an organization should not strive to be at the top of its industry; rather, we are arguing that this should not be the organization's explicit goal at the expense of responsibility to all stakeholders. This mind-set encourages organization personnel to adopt strategies that may focus only on short-term gain rather than on long-term sustained viability.

Fallacy of Omniscience

The *fallacy of omniscience* is the belief that one is all-knowing. A leader's downfall can result from a false belief that he or she knows more than do others around him or her—particularly more than the leaders of other competing organizations. For example, a leader may believe that his or her organization is capable of surpassing other larger competitors, even though none of the objective factors seems to support this notion. An omniscient mind-set can also give birth to an unreceptive manner of logic and decision making. Managers who believe that they know everything will not listen to or solicit criticisms from inside or outside the organization. They will not admit to and learn from mistakes. Why? Because they believe that there is nothing they can learn from others. They will also not actively seek out information to help them improve their organization because they do not believe that they can learn from others' successes or failures.

When Burke was making his decision as to how to proceed with the Tylenol poisonings, he first arranged and participated in a series of discussions—sometimes heated—with his subordinates so that a variety of opinions would be presented and acknowledged.

If one knows everything, he or she is incapable of making errors. For this reason, possessing the fallacy of omniscience makes one intolerant of others' errors. Managers or organizations that believe they know everything will cultivate an atmosphere where anything less than the appearance of (often shallow) perfection is met with contempt and penalty. This attitude sets an organization up for unwise decision-making processes. Wise decision making can result only from weighing all of the facts and acknowledging the main party's faults as well as its strengths—a strategy built on principles of logic.

Fallacy of Invulnerability

The *fallacy of invulnerability* is the belief that an individual or organization is not susceptible to any harm or ill effects—whether self- or externally inflicted. In business, a manager's downfall can originate from his or her belief that a product or strategy will not suffer the same fate that a similar strategy suffered when attempted by another organization. It may also manifest itself in an organization's determination to create maximum efficiency—even if this fast production rate is at the expense of the quality and safety of its products. An organization may be under the fallacious belief that it can manufacture a product faster than other companies and with fewer preshipment safety measures and not fall prey to any ill effects from these policies.

The fallacy of invulnerability can also manifest itself in an organization's belief that it can never fail—no matter how risky its ventures become. It is sometimes the most successful organizations that fall prey to such beliefs. If an organization's prior track record indicates only stellar performance, the organization is likely to believe that all future performance will conform to past results. It is often the underdogs in an industry that will rise to supremacy as a result of their more prudent plans and respect for the power of unforeseeable and unpredictable negative events. Remember that J&J held 90% of the market share in cardiovascular stents before it began its rapid descent (Finkelstein, 2003).

Fallacy of Unrealistic Optimism

The *fallacy of unrealistic optimism* is the belief that even the worst acts will result in favorable outcomes. In reference to organizational and managerial behavior, this fallacy can manifest itself in a leader's willingness to commit unethical and even illegal acts while believing that he or she will not be caught or punished for this behavior.

Even after an organization has made one or several poor judgments that are obvious to outside observers, managers who have succumbed to the fallacy of unrealistic optimism will never admit to failure and will claim that their actions were done for the organization's welfare. They may even claim that actions that were obvious blunders have yet to realize their positive potential for the organization. These managers are blind to their faulty behavior, thereby setting a pattern where they are unable to learn from their mistakes and to make better decisions in the future.

Having leaders in an organization hold and encourage a positive upbeat attitude is an advantageous asset; however, this perpetual "Pollyanna-ism" can lead a company to begin to ignore its shortcomings and to punish those who are messengers of less than cheerful, albeit realistic, news. Organizations need to stay hopeful and vibrant, but they can and should do so only if the organization's performance warrants such an attitude. Turning the other cheek and smiling can often be synonymous with ignoring vital information. As Finkelstein (2003) wrote in his book, *Why Smart Executives Fail,*

> Gradually, a relentlessly positive attitude will change the whole way the business runs. It becomes a company of yes-men. Employees might deliver whatever senior management asks for, but no one in the company will speak up if what is requested turns out to be the wrong thing. Company executives might keep things running smoothly, but they won't be able to introduce more disruptive innovations necessary to keep the company competitive over the long haul. (p. 177)

Mechanisms of the Five Fallacies of Thinking

These five fallacies exist on a continuum. Some managers and organizations have more susceptibility to each fallacy than do others, and it could be claimed that every manager or organization is susceptible to each of the fallacies to some degree. The five fallacies are not all-or-nothing constructs, but it is those who have the most susceptibility to them who are also most in danger of committing foolish harmful mistakes.

Organizational leaders may be even more susceptible to making foolish mistakes that sabotage their organization's success than are individuals in non-leadership positions. When one is at the helm of an organization, he or she is capable of exerting control over that domain, allowing these fallacies to be lived out within the walls of his or her small dominion (Finkelstein, 2003; Sternberg, 2002). The five fallacies are just that—cognitive constructions of reality. In truth, no mortal is ever all-powerful, but a corporate leader (without sufficient governance by a strong and assertive board of directors) can wield an unreasonable amount of control over the workings of the organization, creating a fiefdom rather than a democratic organization. Likewise, no one is ever invulnerable, but a corporate leader can create the appearance of invulnerability by building an insular series of protocols where information and criticism from the outside environment cannot penetrate the organization's existing strategy. Finally, no one is omniscient, but a corporate leader can appear to be omniscient and lead subordinates to believe that he or she is so by forging an alliance of advisers who supply the individual with an unending amount of information and by creating an environment where dissent is always punished and agreement is always praised.

The notion that one's own hubris can be the cause of one's demise is not entirely novel. The classic tragedy in Greek mythology often describes the fall of the once heroic protagonist because of a flaw in character that eventually proved to be fatal. For example, the myth of Icarus tells of the impetuous youth who was warned by his father not to fly too high because the sun would melt his wings made of wax and feathers. Fully absorbed in his exceptional ability to soar across the sky, Icarus ignores his father's warning and falls to his death in the sea. In a similar vein, the myth of Sisyphus tells of a man known for his great chicanery and cunning. After falsely believing that he could outwit the god Hades and evade his fate to stay in the underworld, Sisyphus is punished and made to spend the rest of his days eternally pushing a boulder uphill. The myths are fantasies, but their lessons are real.

The Importance of Wisdom in Organizational and Managerial Contexts

There are few important situations in business that do not require, or at least benefit from, the application of wisdom. Given this fact, it is surprising how little attention has been paid to cultivating it or explicitly seeking it in those in leadership positions in comparison with the other dimensions of the WICS model. Perhaps this is because the factors that produce the wise man or woman seem far more elusive than those that produce the analytically intelligent or creative man or woman. It may also be because the products of analytical intelligence and creativity are easier to quantify explicitly. An exceptionally intelligent individual in business may be one who displays skills in understanding market forces or who knows the history of an industry inside and out. And an exceptionally creative individual in business may be one who is able to generate innovative competitive strategies or new product ideas. However, what are the markers of an exceptionally wise individual in business? Investigations that report people's implicit theories of wisdom demonstrate that individuals believe that wise people are peaceful, understanding, empathetic, intuitive, able to learn from ideas and environments, perspicacious, and sagacious (Clayton & Birren, 1980; Sternberg, 1985)—all characteristics that are not highly likely to manifest themselves in a tangible product. The skills of wisdom prepare an individual to be labeled as an exceptional leader or as someone who defines an era within an organization, but they are not those that necessarily lead one to receive a high score on a measure of analytical intelligence.

Returning to the J&J examples highlighted earlier in this chapter, one should refrain from drawing the conclusions that Burke was a wise organizational leader, whereas Larsen was not. First, in this chapter we have considered each individual's behavior in response to only one isolated situation. We have not considered the leader's behavior, as well as the corporation's performance, during the leader's entire tenure at the organization. Second, just as there are many positive developments that came out of the Larsen administration, J&J did experience struggles during the time that Burke was at the helm. For example, the Tylenol poisonings that characterized Burke's time as CEO left an indelible dent on company finances for which Larsen then had to take responsibility (Smith & Tedlow, 1989).

In organizational management situations, it is difficult to classify an organization as being a "wise corporation" or a manager as being a "wise leader." Other than those exceptional organizations or individuals who take part in multiple egregious acts that eventually run a previously healthy organization into the ground, organizations and individuals set an inconsistent track record. Most leaders produce several exemplary and several not so admirable decisions throughout their histories or tenures. It is more accurate to examine organizations' and individuals' actions and to label them as including or discarding the tenets of wise and balanced (and thus logical) decision making than to make sweeping judgments that characterize their leadership.

In summary, recommended actions for promoting wisdom in organizations and management begin with promoting awareness of the fallacies of thinking. Unless a manager can harness tendencies toward believing that he or she is the center of attention, all-powerful, all-knowing, invulnerable, or unrealistically optimistic, the manager is likely to adopt these faulty and dangerous cognitions (Sternberg, 2002, 2005a). Organizations and individuals who are at the top of their games may be even more vulnerable to these fallacies than are those who are just beginning to create reputations in their industries.

Research Directions in Organizational and Managerial Wisdom

Effective promotion of wisdom within organizations also requires a sufficient understanding of wisdom in this context. The dearth of existing literature on the topic provides a bounty of possible areas of investigation. For example, this chapter has highlighted the need for research that answers the question of who has wisdom in organizations and how having wisdom within an organization's leadership ranks affects corporate outcomes. Research that examines managers' inclusion of the various dimensions of the balance theory in their decision making is also needed. How well do managers balance multiple interests? How well do they integrate both proximal and distal implications? One could also undertake a qualitative examination of managers' use of adaptation, shaping, or selection in response to difficult decisions.

Studying wisdom also illuminates questions about lacking wisdom. In other words, what is the role of the fallacies of thinking in organizational and managerial situations? A scale that measures a person's susceptibility to these fallacies already exists (Jordan, 2005); however, the fallacies' implications for decisions in organizational settings have yet to be examined.

Developing Wisdom for Organizational Settings

How does one develop wisdom for organizational settings? Ideally, wisdom-related skills would be developed in undergraduate and graduate business programs. They would also be developed through job-related experience. Here are some principles for developing wisdom in managerial settings:

1. *Dialogical thinking.* Dialogical thinking involves understanding single issues from multiple points of view. How do different stakeholders within an organization comprehend a managerial decision? How can the decision be communicated to various stakeholders so that they best understand the decision and, ideally, the rationale for it? Moreover, how do people in other organizations understand the decisions that are made? It is often important to maintain favorable relations with suppliers, distributors, and even competitors. Understanding their way of thinking is important. In case study teaching, the cases should be understood not just in terms of the readers' points of view but also in terms of all stakeholders' points of view.

2. *Dialectical thinking.* Dialectical thinking involves recognizing that what constitutes a good answer to a question can change over time. Managerial solutions that are wise at one time or in one place might not be wise at another time or in another place. Hence, decision makers must learn how to contextualize their decisions so as to optimize their decision making for a given time and place.

3. *Role modeling.* One method for teaching wise decision making is role modeling. One cannot develop wise thinking in others unless one serves as a role model for it. If managers make foolish decisions, they can expect that their subordinates will follow their example.

4. *Balance for a common good.* At the heart of the balance theory is balance that seeks the common good. Decision makers need to learn to weigh various factors and to achieve an outcome that represents the greatest good in common for all.

5. *Knowledge for good use.* Students today exist in an environment that often emphasizes knowledge for its own sake rather than knowledge for a common good. Ultimately, wisdom is about using knowledge well—not just about possessing it.

In sum, then, wise decision making can be developed. We have a way. We need only the will.

References

Clayton, V. P., & Birren, J. E. (1980). The development of wisdom across the life-span: A reexamination of an ancient topic. In P. B. Baltes & O. G. Brim, Jr. (Eds.), *Lifespan development and behavior* (pp. 103–135). New York: Academic Press.

Deutsch, C. H. (1988, October 30). Taking the reins from a legend. *New York Times*, sec. 1, p. 6.

Finkelstein, S. (2003). *Why smart executives fail*. New York: Portfolio Press.

Hurstak, J. M., & Pearson, A. E. (1992). *Johnson & Johnson in the 1990s*. Boston: Harvard Business School Press.

Janis, I. L. (1972). *Groupthink*. Boston: Houghton Mifflin.

Jordan, J. (2005). *Business experience and moral awareness: When less may be more*. Unpublished doctoral dissertation, Yale University.

Newton, L. H., & Schmidt, D. P. (2004). *Wake-up calls: Classic cases in business ethics*. Cincinnati, OH: Thomson South-Western.

Smith, J., & Baltes, P. B. (1990). Wisdom related knowledge: Age/cohort difference in response to life-planning problems. *Developmental Psychology, 26*, 494–505.

Smith, W. K., & Tedlow, R. S. (1989). *James Burke: A career in American business (A/B)*. Boston: Harvard Business School Press.

Sternberg, R. J. (1985). Implicit theories of intelligence, creativity, and wisdom. *Journal of Personality and Social Psychology, 49*, 607–627.

Sternberg, R. J. (1998). A balance theory of wisdom. *Review of General Psychology, 2*, 347–365.

Sternberg, R. J. (2000). Creativity is a decision. In B. Z. Presseisen (Ed.), *Teaching for intelligence: II. A collection of articles* (pp. 83–103). Arlington Heights, IL: Skylight Training and Publishing.

Sternberg, R. J. (2002). Smart people are not stupid, but they sure can be foolish: The imbalance theory of foolishness. In R. J. Sternberg (Ed.), *Why smart people can be so stupid* (pp. 232–242). New Haven, CT: Yale University Press.

Sternberg, R. J. (2003). WICS: A model of leadership in organizations. *Academy of Management: Learning and Education, 2*, 386–401.

Sternberg, R. J. (2005a). Foolishness. In R. J. Sternberg & J. Jordan (Eds.), *Handbook of wisdom: Psychological perspectives* (pp. 331–352). New York: Cambridge University Press.

Sternberg, R. J. (2005b). WICS: A model of positive educational leadership comprising wisdom, intelligence, and creativity synthesized. *Educational Psychology Review, 17*, 191–262.

2 Interpersonal Logic

Team Wisdom: Definition, Dynamics, and Applications

Tjai M. Nielsen
Amy C. Edmondson
Eric Sundstrom

The power of effective teamwork can result in amazing innovation, brilliant strategy, and saved lives. For example, new product development teams navigate disciplinary boundaries to develop breakthrough technologies, surgery teams learn new lifesaving techniques, and executive teams candidly share crucial strategic information with implications for improving market performance. Ineffective teamwork, in contrast, can lead to bankruptcy (consider Enron), accidents, and missed opportunities. For example, dysfunctional top management teams can let politics and disagreements consume their attention, leaving their organizations floundering in a competitive marketplace; poorly coordinated mountain expedition teams can allow a team member's death; and misaligned product development teams can waste money and time, missing crucial market windows. Teams that have developed wisdom are more likely to avoid these negative outcomes and achieve their goals.

This chapter focuses on wisdom manifested in *work teams*, defined here as groups of interdependent individuals who share responsibility for specific outcomes for their organizations (Sundstrom, DeMeuse, & Futrell, 1990). Understanding how wisdom applies in teams has particular urgency considering their ubiquity in today's organizations—at every level from executive teams to customer service and production teams, across disciplines from health care to engineering, in a seemingly endless variety of specific

21

applications such as surgery, intercontinental flights, and emergency rescue (Edmondson, 2002, 2003; Nielsen, Sundstrom, & Halfhill, 2002).

As described in previous sources and in other chapters of this volume, *wisdom* has been defined in varied ways. It entails perspectives and practices that promote effectiveness in challenging contexts such as articulating and questioning assumptions (Weick, 1993), applying accumulated knowledge and experience (Sutton & Hargadon, 1996), recognizing and acting in synchrony with the larger context (Csikszentmihalyi & Rathunde, 1990), balancing tensions among conflicting priorities (Sternberg, 1990), and managing trade-offs among multiple goals (Weick, 1993).

In exploring how wisdom applies to work teams, we begin by offering a definition of *team wisdom* that involves recognizing and managing the tensions inherent in teamwork. We then offer a framework outlining the dynamics of team wisdom. Subsequent sections apply the framework, starting with using it as a basis for organizing a review of current research relevant to team wisdom. Second, we apply our framework to identify how tensions inherent in teamwork affect six types of teams. Third, we identify potential ways of developing team wisdom. We conclude with a discussion of potential implications for current theory and research about work teams.

Wisdom may represent an essential quality in effective teams, particularly when teams face challenging tasks or contexts. This inference follows from a logical analysis that draws from the extensive literature of empirical studies, cases, and theories on many facets of teamwork that provides a solid foundation. Our analysis integrates previous research on teams with our own experience working in teams. We hope this integration contributes to the clarity with which we develop our ideas and to the ability of others to build on our work in the future.

Toward a Definition of Team Wisdom and Its Dynamics

Defining Team Wisdom

Team wisdom represents the capacity to recognize and effectively manage inherent tensions faced by teams in organizations. Tensions refer to the relationship between conflicting or competing demands. In this section, we identify three tensions in the team experience related to team boundaries, temporal scope, and multiple priorities and propose that team wisdom involves managing these tensions effectively.

In addition to recognizing tensions inherent in the effective execution of their work, teams and their members must make choices, sometimes facing thorny dilemmas in which two options at first seem equally undesirable. Thus, we conceptualize teams with wisdom as teams that are able to conceptually understand—and discuss—the tensions they face as well as to make difficult choices between competing options. Team wisdom is manifested as attitudes and actions through which team members make difficult choices to benefit the whole (team or organization). Benefiting the whole is about serving the greater good, whether that means the longer term interests of the individual members, team, or organization, or the longer term interests of customers or beneficiaries of the team's work. We discuss each tension in turn along with the ways in which wisdom can enhance team effectiveness.

Team Boundaries

Boundaries refer to discontinuities of behavior or environment that distinguish or separate a social system from its environment (Katz & Kahn, 1978). Team boundaries can take the form of physical space, membership, or even time. Some boundaries are temporary, such as those during a meeting in a conference room that ends with the team dispersing back to its other work locations. Boundaries may exist when a project team works from physically separated locations and communicates via e-mail and video conference. An important source of tension stems from what Katz and Kahn (1978) called "partial inclusion" in social systems; individuals who belong to a team usually also belong to other social entities—often including other teams in the same organization. Any one team claims only a share of each member's time and attention. Individuals generally face demands from multiple roles in the organization, community, and family. To address its mission, a team occasionally must achieve shared collective focus of its members' attention and effort toward the team's mission. This requires team members to suspend other interests and memberships and to focus on the team's work. In this instance, the team can be said to establish temporary boundaries from its surrounding social systems—boundaries that are of sufficient integrity to enable the team to perform but do not place excessive demands on team members.

Addressing the integrity of team boundaries requires that teams acknowledge and actively manage a tension between individual and team interests. This tension involves team members considering what is best for them versus what is best for the team and often needing to choose one over the other. For example, many team members face the dilemma of balancing work against family commitments. Wise teams understand the need for team members to balance their commitments and so provide a safe forum for discussing associated challenges (Edmondson & Detert, 2005).

In addition to membership and physical boundaries, teams exist as small social systems within a larger social system—the organization (itself a social system within an industry, within society, etc.). Teams with wisdom conduct fruitful and appropriate exchanges with external counterparts (Balkundi & Harrison, 2006; Sundstrom, 1999). For example, a management team demonstrates wisdom when its members exhibit awareness of the expectations of specific individual organizational constituents outside of the team while also serving the interests of the organization as a whole. This can create challenging relationship dynamics within the management team (Edmondson, Roberto, & Watkins, 2003). Thus, there is a tension between the organization's needs and individual constituents' needs, introducing very real trade-offs that must be managed in difficult decisions regarding the allocation of time and other resources. Moreover, the team must decide how much time and attention to focus on internal team relationships compared with maintaining necessary external contacts. Teams with wisdom understand the need to integrate with their contexts while investing in relationships inside the team.

Temporal Scope

Teams must also balance the allocation of members' focus and efforts between short-term tactical goals and longer term strategic purposes and capacity. A team that spends too much time addressing urgent, immediate pressures can lose sight of its ultimate mission, whereas a team that dwells too long on its strategy might miss important short-term deadlines (Nielsen & Halfhill, 2006).

Managing the inherent tension of temporal scope requires teams to make decisions and take action based on a short- or long-term approach. One fundamental dilemma resulting from this tension is a constant challenge for management teams—satisfying stakeholders with higher stock prices while also making strategic decisions that ensure long-term performance and viability. Wise teams concentrate on short-term results, but never at the expense of long-term performance and viability.

Multiple Priorities

A third tension inherent in teamwork is created by multiple priorities, such as delivering on speed and quality while also developing members' skills and knowledge. Setting priorities inevitably means making trade-offs in the team's time and effort. Most teams face pressures to produce output by a certain time, to meet standards of quality, to innovate, and to maintain or improve the team's ability to perform effectively into the future. Covey (1989), among others, pointed out the difficulty and importance of maintaining balance between production and capacity.

Teams can manage multiple demands by carefully choosing which attributes of performance or personal development matter to them most. For example, many new product development teams face competing demands from manufacturing, marketing, sales, and finance. Wise new product development teams prioritize these multiple aims by concentrating on the most appropriate issue given their context and circumstances. Some projects are best used to focus on developing state-of-the-art technologies, whereas others are better off getting to market quickly. But how do teams gain the wisdom necessary to manage these tensions successfully?

Dynamics of Team Wisdom: Proposed Model

Teams do not develop wisdom overnight. The process of developing wisdom is likely to be enabled by a strong foundation of sharing an overarching purpose or goal. Although it helps to have enabling conditions in place for a team, such as a compelling direction or a well-designed interdependent task (Hackman, 2002), wise teams can overcome difficulties. Managers who form, guide, support, and sometimes eventually disband a team can help teams and their leaders to develop wisdom. We propose that manager actions and an appropriate mix of team member attributes promote the development of team wisdom (Figure 2.1).

Appropriate manager actions coupled with certain team member attributes contribute to the ability of teams to establish effective norms related to exercising wisdom. This subsequently leads to teams that conduct better discussions, manage boundaries, perform effectively in the short term, and develop the capacity for excellence well into the future. Team member attributes, in turn, are influenced by manager actions that help to develop productive team norms. This framework occurs within, and is influenced by, the context of the organization within which the team operates. Multiple factors in an organization's context may impede or facilitate each component of this model. In the following subsections, we describe the model's specific components to elaborate our proposed explanation of how teams develop wisdom.

Manager Actions

Managers must define team boundaries and specify a team's role within its context. Defining boundaries helps to identify the team's role and facilitates the specification of life span and deliverables. Once a team's deadlines and deliverables are identified, specific priorities can be established in precise terms. Each of these manager actions contributes to managing the inherent tensions of teamwork. That is, when a manager defines a team's boundaries by establishing the reward structure, he or she is establishing parameters that will help the team to openly discuss individual issues relative to the team and successfully manage the integrity of team boundaries. One example of this at the individual level is managing individual and team interests simultaneously. Another precursor to developing team wisdom involves the attributes of team members.

Team Member Attributes

Individuals with self-awareness who know how to communicate effectively with others, how to recognize important needs in their environment, and how to think strategically and tactically will contribute to establishing team norms necessary for developing and sustaining team wisdom. As we do with manager actions, we identify team member attributes at four levels to link to inherent tensions in teamwork. For example, teams whose members

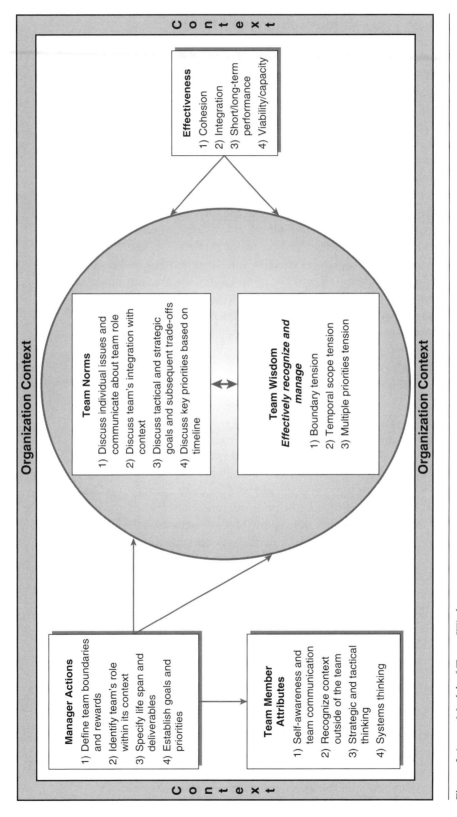

Figure 2.1 Model of Team Wisdom

can think strategically and tactically will be better able to discuss the trade-offs of different approaches and to more effectively manage the constant tension of balancing short- and long-term strategies. The proper mix of team member attributes and manager actions sets the stage for the development of effective team norms and wisdom.

Team Norms

We suggest that certain norms help teams to act with wisdom. Specifically, norms that support open discussion of individual and team issues, awareness of external constituents of the team, and explicit discussion of priorities are consistent with team wisdom. Such norms facilitate a team's ability to exercise wisdom by making difficult choices and acting consistently with those choices.

Team Wisdom

Management teams in particular must struggle with temporal scope—balancing a focus on short- and long-term results. Norms supporting the open discussion of performance trade-offs associated with different action options help teams to manage this tension more effectively. When teams discuss the trade-offs associated with specific strategies, they are better positioned to act on the most important shared priorities—a fundamental element of wisdom. Discussing and establishing priorities manifests wisdom by coping explicitly with the challenge of facing multiple priorities. Our model suggests that the relationship between norms and wisdom is bidirectional. Appropriate team norms promote the development of wisdom, which in turn helps to build and reinforce the norms.

The enablers, manager actions, attributes, and norms described above are not new but are reframed here using wisdom as a mechanism or lens that helps to explain why these factors translate into team effectiveness. Managers and researchers have identified these factors as predictors of team effectiveness previously, and here we build on this foundation by calling attention to the inherent tensions of teamwork and the difficult choices that teams frequently must face. Our intention is to focus researcher and practitioner attention on this central, but little discussed, aspect of organizational work teams and to suggest that wisdom is needed to help teams sort out their tensions, make difficult choices and take appropriate actions to act on their most important priorities.

Choice and Action

We propose that understanding the tensions of teamwork is a first step toward developing team wisdom. Having achieved understanding, however, teams then must make difficult choices, drawing on members' skills and backgrounds to do so, and using open and frank discussion to sort out criteria and trade-offs (Figure 2.2).

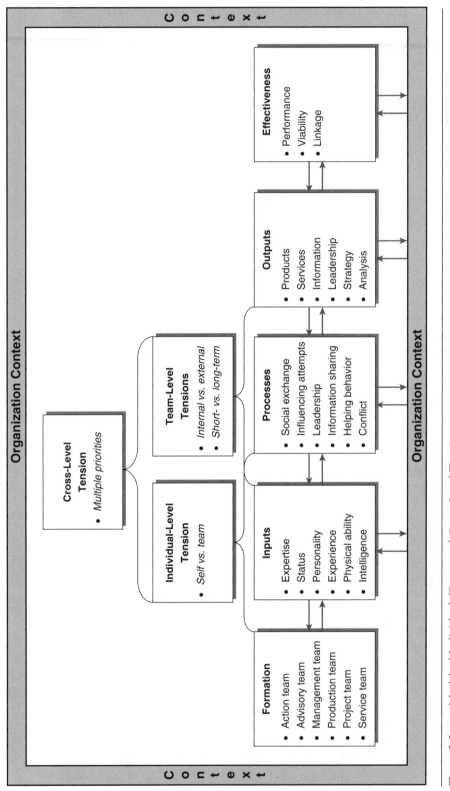

Figure 2.2   Model of Individual, Team, and Cross-Level Tensions

In some cases, the inherent tensions of teamwork give rise to tough choices between two, often equally undesirable options such as letting one's family down or letting the team down. We discuss four manifestations of the inherent tensions of teamwork: one at the individual level, two at the team level, and one that crosses levels. In each case, wisdom requires deliberate decisions, leading to action that serves one aim or constituent while ignoring another.

At the individual level, team members need to choose between their own interests and those of the team. Teams share responsibility for balancing a focus on internal and external demands and to balance short- and long-term approaches when pursuing goals and making decisions. Team members and teams must also have the ability to make difficult choices in order to manage their multiple priorities. We posit that teams with greater levels of wisdom will manage these tensions more effectively. In the following section, we apply the team wisdom framework, review related research, and provide case study examples that illustrate wisdom in action.

Choosing Between Self and Team

Prior research has shown that individual team members who develop teamwork skills are more effective in a team context (Stevens & Campion, 1994). For example, researchers have studied the importance of members' ability to manage interpersonal relationships successfully and the ability to manage conflict effectively (Hackman & Morris, 1975; Perkins & Abramis, 1990). It makes sense that these abilities are important individual elements contributing to more effective teams, but less is known about the conditions under which individuals are willing to put team goals ahead of individual goals.

Individuals who are members of work teams belong to other groups as well. Team members may have kids, spouses, partners, and friends who compete for their time. This contributes to the challenge of maintaining the integrity of the team boundary. In some cases, individual team members must sacrifice their own needs and goals for the good of the team, and individuals who recognize what is best for the team and willingly behave in a manner that supports the team are invaluable (Hackman, 1987). However, sacrificing individual goals for those of the team goes against core psychological drivers motivating self-preservation and promotion (Kramer, 1989). Thus, in many cases, self-interest takes priority over group interest. Simple examples include a team member leaving work at the normal time when his or her team has an important deadline approaching, an individual taking credit for work done by the team, and a team member pursuing a promotion with the knowledge that his or her team is in the middle of an important project. More complex examples might involve a top management team member arguing vehemently for resources for his or her part of the organization (e.g., marketing) when in fact those resources would be better used by another part of the company (e.g., operations), resulting in greater benefit for the organization as a whole, and a professional athlete rejecting a slight decrease in salary so that his or her team can hire more talent. Teams in individualistic societies such as the United States and Australia are likely to have more difficulty in managing this tension than are teams in more collectivistic societies such as Japan and Korea (Sosik & Jung, 2002). Individualistic organizational cultures place a premium on self-interest and thus can make teamwork difficult (Chatman & Spataro, 2005; Early, 1994).

Case Study

A minimally invasive technique for performing cardiac surgery (MICS) was introduced and adopted by the Mountain Medical Center, a pseudonym (Edmondson, 2002). The Mountain Medical Center's team leader was a young ambitious surgeon eager to establish his reputation. Despite his individualistic orientation, he also recognized that MICS represented a paradigm shift for the operating room team, such that the surgeon needed to become more of a "partner" and less of a "boss" if the team was to learn to use the new technology. Thus, the surgeon made an effort to change his own behavior from that of order giver to that of team member and worked to empower and inspire other team members. His effort worked. Other team members were enthusiastic and willing to invest in the effort of learning a new technique. Other team members noted that communication was "much more intensive" and that "there's a free and open environment with input from everybody." Beyond the operating room, nurses began to reframe their roles from those of skilled technicians who used their hands to support surgeons' work to those of involved thinkers who read the medical literature. The Mountain Medical Center went on to become one of the most successful implementers of MICS among all customers of the new technology.

The surgical team at the Mountain Medical Center demonstrates several elements of wisdom. First, due to the safe and open environment partially created by the team leader, team members were able to balance their own personal interests with those of the team. Team members were able to put some of their own needs on hold temporarily and fully commit to team goals during the transition phase. Second, the team recognized the pressure and desire to get results immediately and decided explicitly to remain patient with the need to learn all of the necessary techniques and information. They moved forward very methodically with learning as their initial measure of success. The Mountain Medical Center surgical team concentrated on key short-term goals that enabled long-term success.

Choosing Between Internal and External Demands

Many teams of varying types must balance their focus on internal versus external demands (Ancona, 1990; Ancona & Caldwell, 1992). In particular, management and project teams provide good examples of teams facing this tension on a regular basis. Management team members have significant responsibilities outside of their teams such as leading their respective parts of the company and dealing with business partners outside of the organization (e.g., suppliers, customers, stock analysts) (Edmondson et al., 2003). These teams must manage these external relationships to stay effectively integrated with their external context. Project team members also may operate as representatives of different functional areas, perhaps working as liaisons between the project team and their functional area. Both management and project team members must balance the goals of integrating with the external context and fostering internal relationships and communication. This is a collective or team-level challenge that the team, rather than individual members, must face.

Case Study

In 1981, Fannie Mae was losing $1 million every business day, with underwater mortgage loans totaling $56 billion. The company was in serious trouble, putting a significant amount of pressure on David Maxwell and his top management team (Collins, 2001). Many outside the company believed there was nothing that could be done to save the company short of government intervention to freeze interest rates. However, Maxwell and his team were confident that they could turn things around. They decided to lessen their exposure to interest rates by creating sophisticated mortgage finance instruments (Collins, 2001). Analysts criticized this approach: "When you've got $56 billion worth of loans in place and underwater, talking about new programs is a joke" (p. 82). But even in the face of unrelenting external pressure, Maxwell and his team remained motivated and focused on their game plan. Thus, in this case, they chose an internal focus over external events—a display of wisdom driven by the team's confidence that its focused actions would pay off. Over time, the Fannie Mae team created a high-performance culture and generated stock returns nearly eight times the market average over 15 years.

Another example from the healthcare industry involves a surgical team from a small community hospital located between two large cities. This team also decided to adopt the new cardiac surgery technology discussed earlier in this chapter (see also Edmondson, 2002). Despite having many of the same enabling conditions in place as did the Mountain Medical Center team (talented team members and necessary resources), this team proved to be unsuccessful at implementing the new technology. The team leader presented the goal of learning the new technology as driven by an effort to maintain the hospital's image and ability to compete with hospitals in large cities nearby. The team members did not find this a compelling goal, and their department's use of the new technology eventually became nonexistent (Edmondson, 2002). In this example, the team leader's external focus was not helpful to the goal of motivating internal effort on learning. The focus on how the hospital and team would be perceived by the medical community, with little energy being spent on internal functional and relationship issues, represented a poor choice and an unwise allocation of effort.

Choosing Between Short- and Long-Term Goals

We propose that teams that consciously determine which outcomes are most critical to their success are displaying wisdom and are more likely to succeed than are those that fail to consider and make such decisions. Consider a project team tasked with producing a report on the training progress of safety personnel. This team could decide that the short-term outcome of delivering the report as quickly as possible is most critical.

Conversely, this team could decide that the long-term outcome of quality, comprehensiveness, and accuracy is most important, thereby increasing the timeline for delivery. Deciding which outcome best serves the organization will influence the team's ability to determine how it will accomplish its task. In this case, if half of the team is short-term focused and the other half is long-term focused, results are likely to be poor for the entire team.

In another example, management teams often struggle to decide whether to deliver on short- or long-term results. A short-term approach might yield modest positive results and boost an organization's stock price, whereas a long-term strategy might hurt the stock price in the short term but result in more significant financial gains in the future. Managing this tension by determining the most appropriate strategy collectively based on current conditions is essential for management teams to be effective. Teams with wisdom wrestle with these trade-offs explicitly with careful consideration given to the current context of the business.

Case Study

General Electric's (GE's) top management team experienced a period of significant transition when Jack Welch stepped down as chief executive officer (CEO) in 2001 and handed the reins to Jeff Immelt. This transition was watched carefully by the business community, with much prognostication about how Immelt would perform compared with the legendary Welch. The pressure to perform was intense. Nevertheless, Immelt and his team decided to pursue a strategy focusing on long-term performance over short-term results. They made many decisions designed to improve and support GE's performance for years to come. Performance results declined initially but improved significantly during subsequent years. GE's top management team was able to avoid external pressures and pursue a long-term focus through decisions it thought would improve GE's results well into the future. The Immelt/GE story demonstrates the kind of deliberate choice and action that constitute team wisdom in a challenging environment.

Choosing Among Multiple Priorities

The need to balance speed with quality is just one dimension of the multiple priorities tension. Teams face a variety of demands and must be able to prioritize which ones merit their time. This work is done at both the individual and team levels and requires coordination to ensure that priorities are aligned. Deciding the issues that are most critical to the success of the team and organization is challenging and, if not done effectively, can have debilitating effects on team effectiveness.

The need to manage multiple priorities is common to many work teams. New product development teams (NPDTs) are responsible for coming up with a viable product and then developing, designing, manufacturing, marketing, and selling it. Each of these demands may seem urgent, but teams must be able to step back, reflect, discuss, and determine what area should be their top priority at any given time. Wise NPDTs consider strategic organizational priorities and other issues central to their success to help them decide how to allocate their time and resources.

Management teams also face multiple demands such as satisfying shareholders, maintaining company morale, maximizing profitability, and improving their organization's reputation. Teams lacking wisdom will often focus on what is urgent but not necessarily important. For example, choosing a short-term strategy to increase stock price in an effort to satisfy shareholders is often considered urgent but could hurt long-term performance. Wise management teams candidly discuss the implications of each option to sort out trade-offs and goals. Another challenge for management teams is putting aside the time necessary for their own development. The importance of individual and team development is often overshadowed by the urgency of day-to-day problems. Wise management teams understand the importance of development, choose to make it a priority, and willingly sacrifice attention to other priorities.

Case Study

Mount Everest is the tallest mountain on Earth, and reaching its peak is the ultimate goal of many mountaineers and nonmountaineers alike. The margin for error when attempting to summit the world's tallest mountains is perilously thin. Staying alive requires adhering strictly to preset guidelines and often requires making excruciating choices. In 1996, two Mount Everest climbing expeditions were led by a pair of the top mountaineers in the world, Rob Hall and Scott Fischer. During their attempt on the summit, both Hall and Fischer failed to emphasize and enforce a time limit for aborting summit attempts. This partially contributed to the continuation of the climb well past the designated turnaround time. Hall, Fischer, and several of their clients lost their lives that day and the next day. Considering the amount of time and effort invested, there is little doubt that the choice between possibly reaching the summit and turning back is incredibly tough. Wise teams, however, understand that such a dilemma is possible and prepare for it by discussing trade-offs and deciding what their most important priorities should be. If Hall's and Fischer's teams had explicitly discussed and identified returning safely as their first priority, it is likely that they would have made different decisions that would have increased their chances of survival (Kayes, 2004; Roberto, 2002).

These examples demonstrate the benefits of having wisdom and the costs when it is lacking. Teams should understand the tensions involved with teamwork and should be prepared to make the tough choices that will contribute most to their effectiveness. However, some teams, due to their tasks and responsibilities, will be more prone to specific tensions. In the following section, we focus on which tensions deserve the most consideration from specific types of teams.

Difficult Choices and Team Type

The classification of different types of work groups aids in understanding team effectiveness in various contexts. Sundstrom, McIntyre, Halfhill, and Richards (2000), building on earlier typologies, identified six types of work teams: (a) action teams, (b) advisory teams, (c) management teams, (d) production teams, (e) project teams, and (f) service teams. We suggest that certain teams, based on their primary tasks and responsibilities, will experience certain tensions more consistently and face the difficult choices that follow (Table 2.1). We highlight those dynamics in the following subsections.

Table 2.1   Relevant Individual, Team, and Cross-Level Tensions Based on Team Type

	Team Type					
	Action	*Advisory*	*Management*	*Production*	*Project*	*Service*
Individual-level tension						
Self vs. team	*	*	* *	*	*	*
Team-level tensions						
Internal vs. external	* *	*	* *	*	* *	*
Short- vs. long-term	*	*	* *	*	* *	*
Cross-level tension						
Multiple demands	* *	* *	* *	*	* *	*

NOTE: * = minor for specific team type; * * = significant for specific team type.

Action Teams

These teams (e.g., search-and-rescue teams, terrorist response units, surgery teams) have complex tasks and varying degrees of autonomy in how they do their work. They consist of individual experts and support staff who conduct complex, time-limited performance events involving audiences, adversaries, and/or challenging environments. Action teams must focus on the multiple priorities tension because during any given performance event they are faced with many important tasks. They are forced to make difficult choices between tasks that seem equally urgent. For example, a terrorist response unit is called to a subway bombing in a large city. After assessing the scene, team members learn that there are many seriously injured passengers, the terrorists may still be nearby, and additional unexploded devices exist. This team must decide what to do first, knowing that each option has attendant undesirable consequences.

Advisory Teams

These teams (e.g., task forces) have tasks of varying complexity and have varying degrees of autonomy regarding how they do their work. They consist of different employees, sometimes from multiple levels within the organization, who solve problems and recommend solutions. Advisory team members come from different organizational units and are often part of more than one team. This highlights the relevance of the team boundary tension. Consider an advisory team formed to create a vision statement that best represents the organization. Should team members represent the part of the organization for which they usually work, or should they ignore those ties and focus on the goals of the advisory team? A wise team recognizes this tension and openly discusses its impact on the task at hand. This better enables advisory team members to collectively choose to engage in the work of the team while not feeling as if they are being disloyal.

Management Teams

These teams (e.g., senior leadership) complete complex tasks and have a high degree of autonomy regarding how they do their work. They consist of senior managers who coordinate work units through joint planning, policymaking, budgeting, staffing, and logistics. Management teams face each of the three tensions we have discussed so far. Because they engage in complex work and have a high degree of autonomy, it is essential for management teams to determine collectively whether they will implement short- or long-term strategies or some combination. If not, they may focus on work that is not aligned with an overarching outcome. The wisdom of Immelt and his senior team at GE was their understanding and discussion of the significant trade-offs associated with a long-term strategy (e.g., criticism, decrease in stock price) and their willingness to make the tough choices necessary to make that strategy successful. Just as it is essential for management teams to concentrate on the temporal scope tension, it is also vital to collectively prioritize the multiple demands on their time. Management teams must prioritize issues requiring their time and must determine, based on benefits to the organization, what course to pursue. A third tension frequently faced by management teams involves balancing their focus on internal issues (e.g., relationships) and external issues (e.g., managing their part of the business). Executives on these teams experience a constant tug-of-war between issues inside and outside their teams. The wisdom of Maxwell and his team at Fannie Mae manifested in understanding this tension and remaining willing to ignore external forces outside the team so as to concentrate on executing their strategy.

Production Teams

These teams (e.g., car assembly teams, paper mill work crews) complete relatively simple tasks and have minimal autonomy in deciding how they do their work. They consist of frontline employees who repeatedly produce tangible outputs for their organization. Production team members regularly face choices between their own interests and those of the team. Each team member is responsible for a particular function and is prone to making decisions based on his or her own interests. However, these choices are somewhat constrained by the fact that production teams are typically involved in additive tasks and are less able to highlight or manipulate their contributions without hurting team performance.

Project Teams. These teams (e.g., new product development teams) engage in tasks of varying complexity and usually have a high degree of autonomy in how they approach their work. They consist of members who tend to come from different departments and/or functional areas. Collectively prioritizing key objectives for project teams can be difficult because each member may have his or her own focus depending on the member's functional area. Project teams are often responsible for designing, engineering, manufacturing, marketing, and staying on budget. Similar to management teams, project team members must often choose whether to focus on the work of the project team (i.e., internal) or on their normal work responsibilities (i.e., external).

Service Teams. These teams (e.g., airline attendant teams, retail sales teams) have a relatively lower degree of task complexity (due to repetition) and a low degree of control over how they do their work. They consist of employees who cooperate to conduct repeated transactions with customers. Service teams frequently face choices related to internal and external issues. For example, most retail sales teams are very focused on their customers and concentrate much of their effort in this direction. However, if this comes at the expense of paying attention to internal issues such as communicating and maintaining relationships, their effectiveness will suffer.

The inherent tensions of teamwork may manifest in ways that affect teams differently depending on the unique dynamics of their task. Teams with wisdom will understand these tensions and will deliberately choose to focus on one aim or deliverable at the expense of another. But what steps can teams take to increase their chances of developing wisdom and increasing their overall effectiveness? Wisdom is not acquired overnight; it is the result of accumulated experience and specific effort. In the next section, we discuss methods that may help a team to develop wisdom.

Developing Team Wisdom: Practical Guidelines _____

Fostering team wisdom requires attention to key steps at multiple stages of a team's maturation. We suggest a series of manager actions that directly and indirectly support and enforce norms related to increased levels of team wisdom. These actions focus on formation, support, development, and disbandment.

Forming. The formation of a team obviously is a key first step but is often given little attention regarding future performance. There are three key areas on which managers must focus when forming teams: (a) creating "real teams"; (b) focusing on including members with appropriate knowledge, skills, and abilities (KSAs); and (c) establishing a charter defining purpose, deliverables, resources, timeline, and the leader's role. First, to create real teams, clear boundaries that distinguish members from nonmembers must be established, team members must be interdependent and share responsibility for a common outcome (Sundstrom et al., 1990), and membership must be moderately stable so that members learn how to work together (Hackman, 2002). Teams that are formed in name only will quickly dissolve into groups of individuals working toward unique goals. Second, selecting people for work in teams is different from hiring people for individual work because team members share responsibility for the completion of team tasks, with each member having specific roles and responsibilities. Team members depend on each other to make unique contributions according to their specific mix of KSAs. Managers must focus on creating teams with individuals who will perform well collectively (Borman, Hanson, & Hedge, 1997). Focusing on composition will contribute to developing norms of active communication and open discussion of individual and team issues—key to the development of wisdom (Halfhill, Nielsen, Sundstrom, & Weilbaecher, 2005). Third, managers should focus on creating a team charter that clearly identifies the team's purpose, deliverables, current resources, and timeline as well as the expectations of its leader. Teams with effective charters are better at identifying key priorities, more able to discuss the trade-offs associated with multiple priorities, and better at making tough choices that improve effectiveness. Even when teams are formed with these elements in mind, they require support from the organization.

Supporting. Once a team is formed, it must be appropriately supported to be successful and enhance its ability to develop wisdom (Sundstrom, 1999). Training, measurement and feedback, reward systems, information systems, and physical facilities are five essential types of support necessary for promoting the development of team wisdom. These support systems are necessary for achieving sustained success but are also directly related to the formation of important team norms. The ability to discuss tactical and strategic goals—a key team norm related to wisdom—is difficult when a team does not have in place measurement systems that provide important feedback about performance. Moreover, tough choices are made more difficult without quality information. Another important support mechanism involves reward and information systems that help to identify and define key boundary conditions. For example, the ability for team members to consciously prioritize team goals over individual ones—a key choice frequently faced by team members—is related to the reward structure and its inclusion of team-based rewards.

Support systems such as training are related to sustaining the development of teams and their members. In addition to implementing support mechanisms, managers must emphasize individual and team development.

Developing. To develop the norms related to wisdom, teams must be focused squarely on their own development. This can occur through coaching, facilitation, training, and exposure to developmental experiences (Nielsen & Halfhill, 2006). Managers who provide and support these activities contribute indirectly to the formation of developmental norms. For example, the ability to give and receive feedback effectively contributes to establishing feedback loops. Feedback loops facilitate candid team discussion—necessary for determining priorities and making subsequent choices. Managers who concentrate on implementing and reinforcing peer and leader coaching instill the importance and maintenance of feedback loops. This type of environment enables team members to share their perspectives on team goals more effectively, improving the ability of teams to analyze multiple options and determine the attendant trade-offs. There are situations where teams clearly are not performing effectively. These situations call for managers to consider reforming or disbanding the teams.

Disbanding. When teams are not performing well and appear unlikely to perform at even moderate levels of effectiveness, the development of wisdom is beyond reach. Situations of this ilk require managers to take more drastic action such as disbanding the team. This creates options of reforming a new team with a different mix of member traits or developing specific organizational support systems prior to reformation. The possibility of disbanding may also serve as a key motivator for team members. A manager's decision to reform a team should depend on his or her ability to fix or resolve the root cause of the team's problem(s). For example, if key organizational support systems are not in place, reforming a team—even with highly skilled members—will likely be futile. Disbanding is a topic not often discussed in research on teams, but it is one option that may contribute to the development of team wisdom.

Conclusions

Our review and exploration of team wisdom suggest one broad conclusion and six narrower ones. The broad conclusion concerns our application of a logic model of wisdom to teams as an instance of its application to interpersonal relationships, as seen in other chapters of this volume (e.g., see the chapters by Jordan and Sternberg [Chapter 1], Lawrence [Chapter 3], and Bierly and Kolodinsky [Chapter 4]). Consistent with those chapters, we arrived at the same general conclusion: A logical approach to wisdom in teams offers both a perspective for understanding why teams succeed or fail and a practical framework to guide actions likely to promote their success. Applying the logic model suggests the following conclusions about team wisdom.

1. *Team wisdom is easier to recognize than to practice.* Our first specific conclusion echoes those of chapters in this volume on other forms of wisdom: Recognizing team wisdom comes much more easily than does demonstrating it in practice. Like other forms of expertise, team wisdom has many deep inherent complexities that make it difficult to carry out or even to fully understand from seeing others practice it.

Both the difficulty and complexity of team wisdom stem from the dynamic interplay among its three components—boundaries, temporal scope, and multiple priorities—all of which can change over time. Team wisdom calls, first, for recognizing the complexities of teamwork and, second, for making choices among multiple opposing influences that present a continuing series of interrelated tensions. Demonstrating team wisdom means navigating the tension through a series of wise choices involving trade-offs among desirable and undesirable alternatives. Like other delicate balancing acts, team wisdom is harder than it looks—and unfortunately, its best practitioners make it appear most deceptively simple.

The inherent difficulty of team wisdom suggests a priority for future research: Identify the specific knowledge and skills required for its practice. As outlined in our model in this chapter, the knowledge and skill inherent in team wisdom go far beyond the basic interpersonal skills of teamwork (e.g., Stevens & Campion, 1994) and call for gathering and synthesizing information about the team's performance in context, assessing members' individual capabilities, analyzing the resulting interdependencies, and so on (Kozlowski & Ilgen, 2006). Current research has only begun to address the wide range of knowledge and skills potentially required for team wisdom among managers, leaders, and team members.

2. *Team wisdom is contingent on context.* A second specific conclusion reinforces a point that is repeated more often than it is heeded in the literature on work team effectiveness: A team's success depends critically on how it manages relationships with the context in which it is embedded (Kozlowski & Ilgen, 2006; Nielsen, Sundstrom, & Halfhill, 2005; Sundstrom, 1999). As described in this chapter, many of a team's inherent tensions involve relationships with the host organization and/or external counterparts. Prior research points to differences among kinds of teams in the features of context most critical to their success. We hope that future research places a high priority on analyzing and characterizing the interplay between teams and their contexts.

3. *Team wisdom requires managers to play a key role.* A third conclusion concerns the role of team managers, largely invisible in empirical research on team effectiveness yet described in management books as essential to the success of team-based organizations (e.g., Collins, 2001). We conclude that team effectiveness depends on the extent to which managers apply team wisdom as they form, develop, support, and disband teams. Managers arguably have the primary role. A team often begins with a manager's decision to form, or not to form, a team in the first place—rarely examined in the existing research on teams. It continues with the necessity of meshing each team with its organizational context over its life span— also rarely examined in research.

4. *Team wisdom requires a longitudinal perspective.* A fourth conclusion echoes an often-repeated mantra of team research: Team wisdom depends on a longitudinal perspective that takes account of development over time (Nielsen et al., 2005). Research on team effectiveness has only occasionally adopted a longitudinal approach and instead has generally used a cross-sectional approach, sometimes addressing teams at only one point in time or for just a brief period. Longitudinal research, of course, takes longer and costs more. Hackman's (1990) case studies helped to steer research toward the temporal perspective inherent in team wisdom.

5. *Team wisdom is rare and sporadic.* The difficult, complex, manager-driven, context-embedded, temporal nature of team effectiveness implies a fifth conclusion: Team wisdom occurs only rarely and sporadically when the necessary ingredients converge. Unfortunately, a team that fails to navigate any one of the inherent tensions of teamwork will likely flounder. Only a few rare teams succeed in managing all of their critical dilemmas. Uncommon sporadic success at demonstrating team wisdom could help to explain why empirical research has found such a variety of weak, situation-specific correlates of team effectiveness.

6. *Team wisdom is amenable to development.* A sixth conclusion reflects optimism: Available evidence suggests that those involved with teams— managers, leaders, and members—can learn and develop the knowledge and skills required for team wisdom and can use them to foster team effectiveness in today's organizations, in particular when forming, developing, supporting, and disbanding teams. In doing this, they may face a steep learning curve involving a complex array of factors, including those outlined in our model. But with careful attention to these factors, team leaders and members can help their teams to develop wisdom.

References

Ancona, D. G. (1990). Outward bound: Strategies for team survival in an organization. *Academy of Management Journal, 33,* 334–365.

Ancona, D. G., & Caldwell, D. F. (1992). Bridging the boundary: External activity and performance in organizational teams. *Administrative Science Quarterly, 37,* 634–665.

Balkundi, P., & Harrison, D. (2006). Ties, leaders, and time in teams: Strong inference about network structure's effects on team viability and performance. *Academy of Management Journal, 49,* 49–68.

Borman, W. C., Hanson, M. A., & Hedge, J. W. (1997). Personnel selection. *Annual Review of Psychology, 48,* 299–337.

Chatman, J. A., & Spataro, S. E. (2005). Using self-categorization theory to understand relational demography-based variations in people's responsiveness to organizational culture. *Academy of Management Journal, 48,* 321–331.

Collins, J. C. (2001). *Good to great: Why some companies make the leap and others don't.* New York: HarperCollins.

Covey, S. R. (1989). *The seven habits of highly effective people: Restoring the character ethic.* New York: Simon & Schuster.

Csikszentmihalyi, M., & Rathunde, K. (1990). The psychology of wisdom: An evolutionary interpretation. In R. Sternberg (Ed.), *Wisdom: Its nature, origins, and development* (1st ed., pp. 25–51). New York: Cambridge University Press.

Early, P. C. (1994). Self or group? Cultural effects of training on self-efficacy and performance. *Administrative Science Quarterly, 37,* 89–117.

Edmondson, A. C. (2002). The local and variegated nature of learning in organizations: A group level perspective. *Organization Science, 13*(2), 128–146.

Edmondson, A. C. (2003). Speaking up in the operating room: How team leaders promote learning in interdisciplinary action teams. *Journal of Management Studies, 40,* 1419–1452.

Edmondson, A. C., & Detert, J. R. (2005). The role of speaking up in work life balancing. In E. E. Kossek & S. J. Lambert (Eds.), *Work and life integration: Organizational, cultural, and individual perspectives* (pp. 401–427). Mahwah, NJ: Lawrence Erlbaum.

Edmondson, A. C., Roberto, M. A., & Watkins, M. D. (2003). A dynamic model of top management team effectiveness: Managing unstructured task streams. *Leadership Quarterly, 14,* 297–325.

Hackman, J. R. (1987). The design of work teams. In J. Lorsch (Ed.), *Handbook of organizational behavior* (pp. 315–342). Englewood Cliffs, NJ: Prentice Hall.

Hackman, J. R. (Ed.). (1990). *Groups that work (and those that don't): Creating conditions for effective teamwork.* San Francisco: Jossey-Bass.

Hackman, J. R. (2002). *Leading teams: Setting the stage for great performances.* Boston: Harvard Business School Press.

Hackman, J. R., & Morris, C. G. (1975). Group tasks, group interaction process, and group performance effectiveness: A review and proposed integration. In L. Berkowitz (Ed.), *Advances in experimental social psychology* (Vol. 8, pp. 45–99). New York: Academic Press.

Halfhill, T., Nielsen, T. M., Sundstrom, E., & Weilbaecher, A. (2005). Group personality composition and performance in military service teams. *Military Psychology, 17*(1), 41–54.

Katz, D., & Kahn, R. L. (1978). *The social psychology of organizations* (2nd ed.). New York: John Wiley.

Kayes, D. C. (2004). The 1996 Mount Everest climbing disaster: The breakdown of learning in teams. *Human Relations, 57,* 1263–1284.

Kozlowski, S. W. J., & Ilgen, D. R. (2006). Enhancing the effectiveness of work groups and teams. *Psychological Science in the Public Interest, 7*(3), 77–124.

Kramer, P. D. (1989). *Moments of engagement: Intimate psychotherapy in a technological age.* New York: Viking.

Nielsen, T. M., & Halfhill, T. (2006). A strategic contingency model of team leadership. In C. Cooper (Ed.), *Inspiring leaders* (pp. 191–211). London: Taylor & Francis.

Nielsen, T. M., Sundstrom, E., & Halfhill, T. (2002, April). Organizational citizenship behavior and work team performance: A field study. In T. M. Nielsen (Chair), *Work group composition and effectiveness: Personality, diversity, and citizenship.* Symposium conducted at the 2002 Society for Industrial and Organizational Psychology Conference, Toronto, Ontario, Canada.

Nielsen, T. M., Sundstrom, E., & Halfhill, T. (2005). Group dynamics and effectiveness: Five years of applied research. In S. A. Wheelan (Ed.), *Handbook of group research and practice* (pp. 285–311). Thousand Oaks, CA: Sage.

Perkins, A. L., & Abramis, D. J. (1990). Midwest Federal Correctional Institution. In J. R. Hackman (Ed.), *Groups that work (and those that don't): Creating conditions for effective teamwork* (pp. 309–329). San Francisco: Jossey-Bass.

Roberto, M. A. (2002). Lessons from Everest: The interaction of cognitive bias, psychological safety, and system complexity. *California Management Review, 45*(1), 136–158.

Sosik, J. J., & Jung, D. I. (2002). Work-group characteristics and performance in collectivistic and individualistic cultures. *Journal of Social Psychology, 142,* 5–23.

Sternberg, R. J. (Ed.). (1990). *Wisdom: Its nature, origins, and development.* New York: Cambridge University Press.

Stevens, M. J., & Campion, M. A. (1994). The knowledge, skill, and ability requirements for teamwork: Implications for human resource management. *Journal of Management, 20,* 503–530.

Sundstrom, E. (1999). Challenges of supporting work team effectiveness. In E. Sundstrom & Associates (Eds.), *Supporting work team effectiveness: Best management practices for fostering high performance* (pp. 3–23). San Francisco: Jossey-Bass.

Sundstrom, E., DeMeuse, K. P., & Futrell, D. (1990). Work teams: Applications and effectiveness. *American Psychologist, 45,* 120–133.

Sundstrom, E., McIntyre, M., Halfhill, T. R., & Richards, H. (2000). Work groups: From the Hawthorne Studies to work teams of the 1990s and beyond. *Group Dynamics, 4,* 44–67.

Sutton, R. I., & Hargadon, A. (1996). Brainstorming groups in context: Effectiveness in a product design firm. *Administrative Science Quarterly, 41,* 685–718.

Weick, K. E. (1993). The collapse of sensemaking in organizations: The Mann Gulch disaster. *Administrative Science Quarterly, 38,* 628–652.

3

Organizational Logic

Institutionalizing Wisdom in Organizations

Paul R. Lawrence

What a challenging theme! When I first started teaching many years ago, the wisest teacher I knew operated on the adage that wisdom cannot be taught. Why should I abandon his good advice now at my advanced years? But obviously I have done so. My excuse is that I did get two insights that just might make this most difficult topic a bit more manageable. First, I wondered what would happen if I dug into some of the details on how the Founding Fathers thought out the organizational design built into the U.S. Constitution. Perhaps that just might lead the way to some degree of understanding about institutionalizing wisdom in organizations. Second, I wondered whether analyzing the newer neuroscience findings of how the human brain works to produce wise adaptive decisions would also help. So this is essentially what I propose to do.

The Wisdom of the U.S. Constitution

Looking back across the 220 years since the Constitutional Convention met in Philadelphia, it is now clear that the U.S. Constitution was a truly significant turning point in all human history. The writers of the Constitution created an institutional framework of a radically new kind of government for a powerful, rapidly growing nation. Americans wanted a self-governed

AUTHOR'S NOTE: The author gratefully acknowledges the important help he received from Fred Dalzell in doing the historical research for this chapter.

nation—of the people, by the people, and for the people. They wanted to create a workable humane republic. They were aware of Montesquieu's judgment that the republican form of government would work only for small nations, smaller than the United States. All traditional governments for larger nations at that time, and all those of earlier times that the writers knew about, stood on three foundational pillars: the monarch, the aristocracy, and the established church. These institutions were considered as essential for "civilization" and social order among the masses. The Founding Fathers saw, from their own observations of Europe, that these three pillars supported governments that consistently oppressed the many for the benefit of the elite few. They were in total agreement that they wanted to abandon all three of these pillars in their new government. This was a truly radical thought. But how could it be done? They assembled a diverse set of experienced men from across the states, set aside the time needed, and went to work, long day after long day. After all of the intense discussion and debate, they were able to reach a true consensus of the final result.

Did they develop any guiding premises? Did they employ a central organizing principle? Did they have a clear idea about the functions of government, about the limits of government, or about the necessity of government? Did they know what major hazards were to be avoided? And most important, did they share a model of man, of human nature? It turned out that they worked out answers to all of these questions. And we are fortunate that they left us with an amazingly complete record not only of their conclusions in the document itself but also of the thought process by which they reached their conclusions. The *Federalist Papers* are the heart of this record, supported by numerous supplementary notes, letters, and the like.

The Founding Fathers had a strong sense of the importance of the moment, the importance of their undertaking. Both the federalist supporters of the new Constitution and the antifederalist opponents saw themselves as having been thrust into a situation fraught with unique and far-reaching consequences. They had been given an opportunity to plan a government out of whole cloth. It was a very rare greenfield project, and the participants perceived that they were making history. As Simeon Baldwin, a Connecticut lawyer and federalist, said,

> Revolutions in government have in general been the tumultuous exchange of one tyrant for another. . . . Never before has the collected wisdom of a nation been permitted quietly to deliberate and determine upon the form of government best adapted to the genius, views, and circumstances of the citizens. Never before have the people of any nation been permitted candidly to examine and then deliberately to adopt or reject the constitution proposed.[1]

The Founders saw the challenge clearly, and they approached the assignment with trepidation. Patrick Henry warned,

You ought to be extremely cautious, watchful jealous of your liberty, for instead of securing your rights you may lose them forever. If a wrong step now be made, the republic may be lost forever . . . and tyranny must and will arise. . . . We are wandering on the great ocean of human affairs. I see no landmark to guide us.[2]

Benjamin Franklin, in response to the question of what kind of government had been created, replied, "A republic, if you can keep it."

Looking back on their accomplishment, James Madison said,

Why is the experiment of an extended republic to be rejected merely because it may compromise what is new? Is it not the glory of the people of America, that, whilst they have paid a decent regard to the opinions of former times and other nations, they have not [allowed] a blind veneration for antiquity, for customs to overrule the suggestions of their own good sense and the lessons of their own experience? Posterity will be indebted for the possession and the world for the example of the numerous innovations displayed on the American theatre in favor of private rights and public happiness. . . . Happily for America, happily we trust for the whole human race, they have pursued a new and more noble course. . . . They reared the fabrics of government which have no model on the face of the globe.[3]

So the Founders were conscious of working without a lot of useful building materials that European states had used to structure government. What did they have left to work with? The Founders hoped to use the raw forces, the "passions" of what they knew of human nature, and bend these human drives to the work of managing and upholding republican government.

The Founders started on the premise that government was absolutely essential if humans were going to live together in peace and prosperity. They talked with each other a great deal about the nature of humans, and they were by no means utopians. They were distrustful of human nature and warned that a constant hunger for power and wealth drove people to become tyrants. It was because of such human passions and the subsequent impulsive behavior of a few that the Founders firmly believed that people truly needed government to enable a peaceful and productive life for the many. As John Jay said, "Nothing is more certain than the indispensable necessity of Government, and it is equally undeniable that whenever and however it is instituted, the people must cede to it some of their natural rights in order to vest it with requisite powers."[4] But the Founders also feared anarchy as much as they did tyranny. To them, "freedom" and "liberty" were never total, never license, but always relative to the despotism they saw in Europe.

Madison said, "What is government itself but the greatest of all reflections on human nature?"[5] In other words, if government is to work, it must reflect human nature. The Founders delved deeply into what they referred to as human nature. They needed to figure out what "being human" meant. What were the ultimate motives or drives that made people tick? They recognized that they would need to tap into and properly regulate these forces if they hoped to fashion a functional government.

This phrase "human nature" appears 15 times in the *Federalist Papers.* This is a touchstone concept. And so was the equivalent concept of "passions," a word that appears no less than 68 times in the text. Generally speaking, it carried a negative connotation for the Founders. Passions in the *Federalist Papers* are frequently violent, fleeting, and dangerous political impulses. The concept is a foil to "reason," which the Founders upheld as the basis of sound and sober government undertaking the public interest. Madison imagined a scenario in which scheming parties would take control of the government: "The PASSIONS, therefore, not the REASON of the public, would sit in judgment. . . . The passions ought to be controlled and regulated by the government."[6]

The passion about which the Founding Fathers worried the most was the one they called "ambition," a word that appears 47 times in the *Federalist Papers.* Ambition was invariably used in a negative sense—as an impulse to be checked. So, for example, Alexander Hamilton warned against "the ambitious enterprise and vainglorious pursuits of a monarchy" and the "ambitious intrigues of . . . Executive magistrates."[7] And Madison warned against "the intrigues of the ambitious or the bribes of the rich."[8]

Above all, the Founders feared the prospect of concentrated political power. Drawing on their deepest political instincts, they tried to create institutions of government that dispersed, rather than consolidated, power. The federalists held this conviction firmly, and in the Constitution they tried to create a structure of government that would contain and channel this drive of personal ambition into publicly constructive paths. Hamilton said,

> Men are ambitious. Has it not . . . invariably been found that momentary passions and immediate interests have a more active and imperious control over human conduct than general or remote considerations of policy, utility, or justice? . . . Have we not already seen enough of the fallacy and extravagance of those idle theories, which have amused us with promises of an exemption from the imperfections, weaknesses, and evils incident to society in every shape? Is it not time to awake from the deceitful dream of a golden age and to adopt as a practical maxim for the direction of our political conduct that we as well as other inhabitants of the globe are yet remote from the happy empire of perfect wisdom and perfect virtue?[9]

Hamilton chose to emphasize that even in America there were clever people who would strive to seize the reins of power and become the absolute ruler of the nation.

As Madison observed,

If men were angels, no government would be necessary. . . . In framing a government, which is to be administered by men over men, the great difficulty lies in this: You must first enable the government to control the governed, and in the next place oblige it to control itself. A dependence on the people is, no doubt, the primary control on the government; but experience has taught mankind the necessity of auxiliary precautions.[10]

Yet the Founders did not think that human nature was irretrievably grasping and corrupt. People, they insisted, were capable of displaying wisdom, virtue, and public spirit. The passion they looked to as a check on ambition was called "virtue." This term for a more benevolent dimension of human nature appears 23 times in the *Federalist Papers*. In general, the term signifies a public-mindedness and an instinct to act for the common good. In other words, people become "virtuous" as they put aside particular selfish interests in a search for the public good. Their virtue amounted to an instinct to bond broadly with others and act for the common good. And the Founders searched earnestly for ways to structure government so as to tap into this drive.

Take, for example, one of Madison's remarks at the Virginia ratifying convention. He was replying to antifederalist George Mason's prediction that federal congressional representatives would do everything they could to acquire and eventually abuse power under the new government. Madison conceded that it would be a mistake to "place unlimited confidence in them and expect nothing but the most exalted integrity and sublime virtue," yet he insisted that citizens would be capable of finding, recognizing, and electing virtuous representatives: "I go on this great republican principle that the people will have virtue and intelligence to select men of virtue and wisdom. Is there no virtue among us? If there be not, we are in a wretched situation. No theoretical checks, no form of government, can render us secure."[11]

Madison also made essentially the same point in writing,

As there is a degree of depravity in mankind which requires a certain degree of circumspection and distrust, so there are other qualities in human nature which justify a certain portion of esteem and confidence. Republican government presupposes the existence of these qualities in a higher degree than any other form. Were the pictures drawn by some among us faithful likenesses of the human character, the inference would be that there is not sufficient virtue among men for self-government and that nothing less than the chains of despotism can restrain them from destroying and devouring one another.[12]

Madison concluded, "The aim of every political constitution is, or ought to be, first, to obtain for rulers men who possess most wisdom to discern and most virtue to pursue the common good of the society, and in the next place, to take the most effectual precautions for keeping them virtuous whilst they continue to hold their public trust."[13]

Thus, the most basic point that the federalists clung to was the idea that the American people—and hence people generally—under the right political, social, and economic circumstances were capable of self-government. A confluence of circumstances, the Founders believed, had equipped Americans for republican government. Madison declared

> It is evident that no other form [than republican government] would be reconcilable with the genius of the people of America, with the fundamental principles of the Revolution, or with that honorable determination which animates every [advocate] of freedom to rest all their political experiments on the capacity of mankind for self-government.[14]

The government created by the Constitution was anything but streamlined. In fact, it was designed to be intricate, complicated, and studded with process and procedure. It forced all important issues into open and extended dialogue. It tried to outlaw secret closed-door deals. Even though it grew out of an effort to centralize power in a new national government, the Constitution reflected political instincts that warned against concentrating the awesome power of government itself in a few hands. The Founders worked carefully to prevent consolidation of authority in the hands of any single person or dominant office. So how specifically did they do this?

The one organizing algorithm, the one design mechanism, that the Founders relied on consistently in creating the constitutional structure can be summed up by the phrase "checks and balances"—or, more completely, checking the impulsive drives of human nature in some officials by the balancing effect of the drives of others. These checks and balances are built into every provision of the Constitution. Baldwin summed it up: "In this beautiful graduation, we find all those checks which are necessary for the stability of republican government."[15] Hamilton stated most bluntly the reason for using checks and balances so carefully:

> An *elective despotism* was not the government we fought for, but one which should not only be founded on free principles, but in which the powers of government should be so divided and balanced among several bodies of magistracy, as that no one could transcend their legal limits without being effectively checked and restrained by the others.[16] (italics in original)

All of this occurred in an effort to institutionalize wisdom into the essential, but dangerously powerful, organization of government.

The Wisdom of the Brain

Now I must make a significant digression. This is to point out the amazing similarity of the Founders' design principle—the checks and balances of the drives of human nature—to what contemporary science hypothesizes about how the human brain works, again by checks and balances of drives.

What follows is my summary of the recent work, primarily of neuroscientists but also of many other kinds of behavioral scientists, that I have assembled in detail in my book *Being Human: A Neo-Darwinian Theory of Human Behavior,* which is currently moving toward publication. This book draws heavily on a 2002 book I did with Nitin Nohria, *Driven: How Human Nature Shapes Our Choices.* This earlier book posited that humans have evolved four unconscious drives or ultimate motives. These drives are manifested in our consciousness as emotions or intuitive senses. We concluded that all people have a persistent drive to acquire (dA) objects and experiences that improve their status relative to others. In other words, they are motivated in part by self-interest as defined by neoclassical economics. But humans also have their other drives that are ultimate and independent in the sense that fulfilling one does not fulfill the others. They have a drive to bond (dB) with others and with collectives in long-term relationships of mutually caring commitment; they have a drive to comprehend (dC) and make sense of the world and of themselves; and they have a drive to defend (dD) themselves, their love ones, their beliefs, and their resources from harm. All four of these primary drives have been established in the human brain by means of Darwinian evolutionary mechanisms because the existence of these drives improved the odds that the genes of their carriers would be passed on to subsequent generations.

In *Driven,* Nohria and I recognized that all four of these drives were in play as humans decided on courses of action in complex circumstances, but we did not have an explanation as to how the brain worked out the combining of the drives into a coherent plan of action. This is the major step taken now by the second book, *Being Human,* which pulls together the work primarily of neuroscientists on the functions of the prefrontal cortex. This part of the brain is known as the executive center and has dense two-way connections with the limbic area, the locus of the drives.

In describing the role of the prefrontal cortex, I draw heavily on Rita Carter's description in her book *Mapping the Mind* and link this with my description of the functions of the drives in the limbic area. Carter summarized the overall role of the prefrontal cortex:

The prefrontal cortex is given over to man's most impressive achievements—juggling with concepts, planning and predicting the future, selecting thoughts and perceptions for attention and ignoring others, binding perceptions into a unified whole, and, most important, endowing those perceptions with meaning. . . . This is the only part of the brain that is free from the constant labor of sensory processing. It does not concern itself with the mundane tasks in life such as walking around, driving a car, making a cup of coffee, or taking in the sensory perceptions from an unremarkable environment. When something untoward occurs . . . the prefrontal cortex springs into life and we are jettisoned into full consciousness as though from a tunnel into blazing sunshine.[17]

I argue that these "untoward" events are signals from the limbic area that two or more of our drives have been activated by sense organ signals and are rapidly signaling, in conflicted ways, for the attention of the prefrontal cortex. This is what turns on our full, high-level consciousness. These emotionally loaded signals enter the module of the prefrontal cortex known as the ventromedial cortex. To quote Carter again,

> This [ventromedial module] is where emotions are experienced and meaning [is] bestowed on our perceptions. This is the brain's emotional control center. . . . The connections between this region and the limbic system beneath it are very dense, closely binding the conscious mind with the unconscious, and this configuration is probably what gives it its special status; it is, if you like, the part that best incorporates the whole of our being, making sense of our perceptions and binding them into a meaningful whole. . . . It makes sense of our existence.[18]

Carter did not call the ventromedial module the seat of the soul, but from this description it seems to me to be a candidate. Antonio Damasio, a prominent neuroscientist, was more explicit about this issue in his book, *Descartes' Error:* "Feelings form the base for what humans have described for millennia as the human soul or spirit."[19]

The ventromedial module sits alongside the orbitofrontal module, the second of four special prefrontal cortex modules that work tightly together to perform the brain's executive function. This module, according to Carter, "inhibits inappropriate actions, freeing us from the tyranny of our urges and allowing us to defer immediate reward in favor of long-term advantage."[20] In this sense, the orbitofrontal module seems to evaluate these conflicting emotional markers and initiate a downward checking with the limbic area concerning the prefrontal cortex's tentative attempts to generate balanced action plans. As Carter suggested,

> The orbito-frontal cortex has rich neural connections to the unconscious brain where drives and emotions are generated. The down signals from the cortex inhibit reflex clutching and grabbing, and if you take away that control—as happens sometimes in frontal lobe injury—the unconscious retakes the body. . . . Orbito-frontal cortex seems, then, to be the area of the brain that bestows a quality we may refer to as free will.[21]

This module seems to have the capacity to discipline the emotional centers to defer an impulse on behalf of other essential impulses—a will to accept the pain of giving something up for a greater good or a lesser evil. It seems to be the "check" of the check-and-balance system. It also seems to be the final chooser of the brain, not in the sense of actually making the choices but rather in the sense that it counts the votes from the limbic area and announces the decision.

Just above this module lies the dorsolateral module. Here is where, according to Carter, "things are held 'in mind' and manipulated to form plans and concepts."[22] This is where tentative plans can be mentally juggled. It is the center of what has been called the "working memory." It is the focal point of consciousness. Various action scenarios that are imagined can be fed back through the lower modules to the limbic area for multiple readings on their ability to fulfill the several drives. The dorsolateral module works very closely with the fourth module, which has actually been in full operation since the conflict of drives was first sensed by the ventromedial module.

That fourth module is the anterior cingulate cortex, which Carter maintained "helps focus attention and 'tune in' to one's own thoughts."[23] It is this module that is in constant close touch with other parts of the cortex where the various memories and skills are held. It is the module that calls the entire cortex to attention to focus on the critical issue at hand. It can call up the relevant representations and bring them into the juggling process going on in the dorsolateral module next door. To quote Carter again, "This part of the brain lights up when [the brain] does something of its own volition—it is one of the areas which seems to contain the 'I' we all feel we have inside us."[24] It seems to be the site of the self-concept, the place that pulls together elements that are called personality, personal character, and competencies.

Figure 3.1, which has been adapted from Carter, summarizes the hypothesized functions and the interrelations of the four critical modules of the prefrontal cortex.

The next step in understanding the decision-making process is spelled out in Figure 3.2. This schematic diagram can be read as follows, starting from the bottom left corner. Current environmental information passes to the sensory areas of the brain through the sense organs. This information may be in the form of cultural cues (e.g., the raised eyebrow of an elder), observations of well-known things (e.g., a coveted sports car), or observations about a new situation (e.g., the cultural practices of an unfamiliar human group). Although our examples will deal with visual information processed through the eyes, the model applies equally to information processed through the ears, nose, skin, and so on. The signals from the sensory areas are passed through the limbic system, where the four drives reside. Here these signals are evaluated by the drive modules and pick up

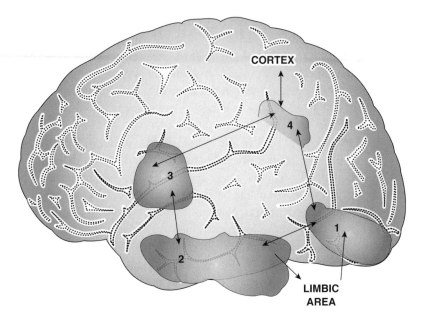

1. VENTROMEDIAL CORTEX

   Where emotions are experienced and meaning is bestowed on our perceptions. Tightly linked to the limbic area and possible location of the soul.

2. ORBITOFRONTAL CORTEX

   Inhibits inappropriate actions. Where emotional impulses check each other and willful choices are made. Tightly linked to the limbic area and possible location of the will.

3. DORSOLATERAL CORTEX

   Working memory where all signals are held "in mind" and manipulated to form tentative plans and concepts. Possible focus of consciousness.

4. ANTERIOR CINGULATE CORTEX

   Helps to focus attention and tap into cortex for relevant representations, cultural memes, and skills. Possible location of the self-concept.

Figure 3.1   Modules of the Prefrontal Cortex and Their Functions

SOURCE: Adapted from Carter, *Mapping the Mind*, p. 182.

emotional markers depending on which of the four drives they activate. Any sensory signal may be loaded with more than one emotional marker such as when the sight of the coveted sports car triggers the dA module to load the signal with a positive evaluation while also triggering the dB module to load it with a negative evaluation arising from a sense of bonded obligation to save money and stay safe for the sake of one's family.

These emotionally marked signals are then processed in the prefrontal cortex. The prefrontal cortex has the cognitive capacities to generate potential courses of action that might satisfy the drives. This process is supported

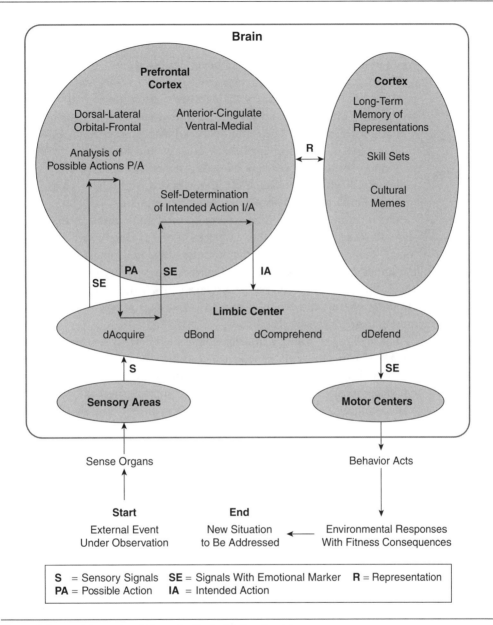

Figure 3.2   Schematic of How the Brain Makes Decisions

by long-term personal memories, skill sets, and cultural memes summoned as representations from the rest of the cortex.

Once a tentative action (e.g., to postpone buying the sports car) is chosen through the exercise of human will, this signal is fed back through the limbic center to test whether the proposal is at least tolerable to the four drives. If it is satisfactory, even though less than optimal to all of the drives, it will pick up the emotional energy provided by the drives. These energized signals are then relayed to motor centers that control the muscles and other bodily parts. The resulting actions are what we recognize as deliberately intended human behavior (e.g., walking away from the show-room in which the tempting car is being displayed).

These actions in turn generate environmental responses with survival consequences (e.g., a spouse's loving appreciation along with a lingering regret from forgoing the sports car), a new situation with which the indi-vidual must now deal. The impulse/check/balance process has now played itself out. All of this can happen very quickly, and such cycles are repeated over and over in our everyday lives. We always have mixed emotions and real conflicts of interest facing off in our brains, and this is what forces us to make hard choices. This is what makes us human.

The third and final step in explaining the brain's decision making is to show how the four drives serve as checks of one another by way of the "dia-logue" that proceeds between the modules of the prefrontal cortex and with the limbic area. This is shown in Figure 3.3, where each drive's ability to check the other three drives is displayed in a simplified form. It is this checking process that enables humans to sustain a very dynamic balance among their four powerful drives.

The analogy of riding a unicycle might help here by its obvious require-ment for balancing skills. One can succumb to the pull of gravity in any of the four directions: right, left, forward, and backward. Furthermore, the balancing must go on all the time; a rider can never succeed on the basis of a single impulsive action for more than a very brief time. Also, to stay still

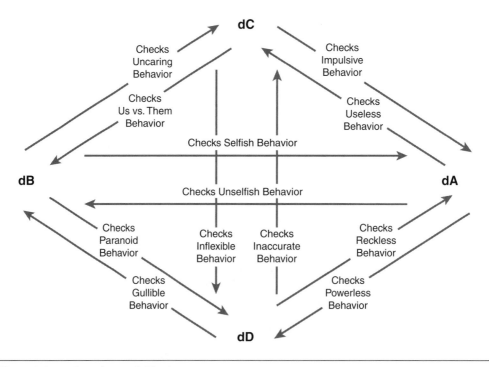

Figure 3.3   Impulses and Checks

is to fall; one must move forward to remain upright, continually compensating for each misstep with a move in the opposite direction. It takes extensive practice to develop one's unicycle skill, but it can be done. This is also true of keeping on track in one's own life, and this balancing act proceeds in the prefrontal cortex. Neuroscientists tell us that the last part of our developing brain to become fully functional is the prefrontal cortex—around the early 20s. This is why younger people need loving guidance. But once it is mature, this high-quality brain system works amazingly well to produce wise adaptive behavior. It is a personal governance system, but it is not foolproof—as the Founding Fathers well knew. Humans need governments to support and reinforce individuals in acting in a wise balanced manner. Steven Pinker, in his book *The Blank Slate,* offered a revealing example in this regard:

> As a young teenager in proudly peaceable Canada during the romantic 1960s, I was a true believer in Bakunin's anarchism. I laughed off my parents' argument that, if the government ever laid down its arms, all hell would break loose. Our competing predictions were put to the test at 8:00 A.M. on October 17, 1969, when the Montreal police went on strike. By 11:20 A.M. the first bank was robbed. By noon most downtown stores had closed because of looting. Within a few more hours taxi drivers burned down the garage of a limousine service that competed with them for airport customers, a rooftop sniper killed a provincial police officer, rioters broke into several hotels and restaurants, and a doctor slew a burglar in his suburban home. By the end of the day, six banks had been robbed, a hundred shops had been looted, twelve fires had been set, forty carloads of storefront glass had been broken, and three million dollars in property damage had been inflicted before city authorities had to call in the army and, of course, the Mounties to restore order. This decisive empirical test left my politics in tatters.[25]

So Pinker learned that humans really need to supplement their built-in check-and-balance mental system with that of government if they are to live together in peace and prosperity.

The Parallels Between the Wisdom of the Brain and the Wisdom of the Constitution

Now that we have described the check-and-balance system of the brain, we need to reexamine in somewhat more detail how this process was built into the Constitution. As we have seen, the Founders worked carefully to prevent consolidation of power in the hands of any single individual, dominant office, or institution. The phrase "checks and balances," used over and over in creating the constitutional structure, sums up the one organizing algorithm, the one design mechanism, on which the Founders relied consistently for this purpose. This counterbalancing was carried out by denying ultimate power to any one body and thereby forcing decisions to be made by reasoned debate. This is where dialogue that relies on logic is forced onto center stage to resolve the inevitable conflicts. This was the royal road—the only road—to wisdom in public affairs. Each governmental element was positioned as a check on the other governmental elements so as to sustain a dynamic balance.

The Founders poised the voting rights of the people as a check on the entire governmental apparatus, even as the government and its laws were to check the impulsive behavior of the people. Each branch of government—legislative, judicial, or executive—was designed to balance any rash and hasty actions by the other branches. The president commanded the military, whereas Congress funded it. The House was given the power to bring articles of impeachment, whereas the Senate had the power to try them. The federal right to levy taxes, incur debts, and regulate foreign and interstate commerce served to check the individual states, whereas the states explicitly retained all other rights not conferred on the federal government.

The president was given the power to negotiate treaties, whereas the Senate had the power to ratify them. Hamilton stated explicitly that the goal was to disperse the power of treaty making:

> The security essentially intended by the Constitution against corruption and treachery in the formation of treaties is to be sought for in the numbers and characters of those who are to make them. The JOINT AGENCY of the Chief Magistrate of the Union, and of two thirds of the members of a body selected by the collective wisdom of the legislatures of the several States, is designed to be the pledge for the fidelity of the national councils in this particular.[26]

Another example—and this was a major innovation—was the principle of an independent judiciary. In a traditional government, the judges were under the control of the monarch. Even Britain, whose laws at the time were enacted by Parliament, left the enforcement and interpretation of the law to judges serving at the pleasure of the monarch. This left the ordinary citizen subject to the judgments of men beholden to the monarch, who was himself largely above the law. Under the leadership of John Adams, Massachusetts took the initiative in establishing the principle of the independent judiciary in its state constitution, and the U.S. Constitution writers followed this example.

Religion posed a unique problem that resulted in a unique solution. Although Americans were certain that they could do without a monarchy and an aristocracy, they had no intention of doing without the third traditional pillar of governance—religion. But how was religion to be checked? With what could it be balanced? There was no answer, and for perhaps the first time in history a government explicitly denied itself the right to name an established religion. This was by no means an obvious step at the time—even in America. Six of the colonies had records of recognizing an established church. But they were different churches. In Virginia and other southern colonies, it was the Anglican Church; in Massachusetts and Connecticut, it was the Congregational Church; and in Pennsylvania, it was the Quaker Church. The separation of church and state was first hotly debated in Virginia, but under Thomas Jefferson's leadership it was enacted into law in 1785, and other colonies quickly followed. The leaders of all the colonies had come to realize that to establish any one church would make it impossible to unite the states. This did not mean that these men did not share a belief in a divine creator. Some of them may have been agnostics, but it is very unlikely that any of them were atheists. A number of them were in fact Deists, a faith that emerged from the Enlightenment and expressed a belief in a divine creator of the universe but eschewed more specific doctrines.

The final masterstroke of the system of checks and balances was the Bill of Rights, which was not added until 1790 but which has become, in most Americans' minds, the very heart of the Constitution. The Bill of Rights explicitly named those rights of the people on which the government had no right to infringe. It became a linchpin of legitimacy for this new kind of government, unique in being defined not only by what government could do but equally by what it could not do.

Baldwin summed it up:

> By the Constitution of the United States, all the essential rights of freemen and the dignity of individual States are secured. The people have the mediate or immediate election of their rulers—to the people they are amenable for their conduct and can constitutionally be removed by the frequency of election. While the voice of the people is heard in the House of Representatives, the independent sovereignty of the several States will be guarded by the wisdom of the Senate, and the disinterested penetration of the President will balance the influence and prevent the encroachments of each. In this beautiful gradation we find all those checks which are necessary for the stability of republican government and the due deliberation of the most perfect legislature.[27]

The U.S. Constitution remains the preeminent example in human history of a social invention that truly embodied wisdom in a large-scale human institution. Its parallels with the design of the human brain are truly amazing. Translating the Founders' language into the terms of the *Being Human* book, "human nature" is our innate features of the brain. More specifically, the Founders' "passions" and "impulses" are our innate drives: their "ambition" is our drive to acquire, their "virtue" is our drive: to bond, their "reason" is our drive to comprehend, and their "wisdom" is our state of dynamic balance. For the Founders, impulses are checked by counterimpulses in others and by the process of dialogue. In the brain, impulsive drives are checked by other drives and by the neural exchanges, the dialogue among the prefrontal modules and the limbic drives. Amazingly, the Founders created a government that, in essence, serves the American people as a prefrontal cortex in relation to the limbic drives. What an insightful design—if we can keep it.

As the Founders finished their work, they still had two big worries about the future of the country. The first was the continuing existence of the institution of slavery. They knew that slavery was a major contradiction to the nation's founding premises and was a horribly cruel fact of American life that needed to be eliminated. They also knew that this could not be done at that time while still getting the new government under way. They knew, for example, that the expression "United States of America" still called for a plural verb form. The United States of America did not have first call on the loyalty of most of its citizens; the individual states did. It took some 70 years for the loyalty to the Union to build up to the point where the federal government could face up to the slavery issue. This precipitated the horrendous crisis of the Civil War and its aftermath.

The second major worry of the Founders going forward was the "factionalism" of political parties or special interests. They feared that some faction might seize the powerful reins of government for some narrow special interest. Madison again spoke to the issue: "By a faction, I understand a number of citizens who are united and actuated by some common impulse of passion, or of interest, adverse to the rights of other citizens, or to the permanent and aggregate interests of the community."[28] He warned that the problem would not be solved easily: "The latent causes of faction are . . . sown in the nature of man."[29] Madison argued in particular that this was true because people were actuated by powerful "acquisitive instincts."

Madison recognized that societies would inevitably fractionate into special interests:

> Those who hold and those who are without property have ever formed distinct interests in society. Those who are creditors, and those who are debtors, fall under a like discrimination. A landed interest, a manufacturing interest, a mercantile interest, a moneyed interest, with many lesser interests, grow up of necessity in civilized nations and divide them into different classes, actuated by different sentiments and views. The regulation of these various and interfering interests forms the principal task of modern legislation and involves the spirit of party and faction in the necessary and ordinary operations of the government.[30]

Although Madison recognized the inevitability of such special interests, he believed strongly that no one of them should ever be allowed to dominate government.

Relevant Questions Concerning the Building of Wisdom Into Corporate Governance

In regard to the current status of this hazard of special interest factionalism, I can only raise some pointed questions. But first I should point out just a few relevant facts. At the time the Constitution was written, there were no corporations that were set up as legal entities as we know them today. These new institutions have, over the years, grown into massive organizations that have concentrated power in a few hands. Consider the corporations that we know and constantly study. We all know that corporations can be tremendous engines of innovation and efficient producers of vast goods and services for the benefit of all. But we can also not duck the fact that corporations do, from time to time, go off the constructive path and use their great power to exploit the many for the benefit of the very few at the top who are serving only their narrow self-interests. Think of the robber barons of only a century ago and of the recent leaderships of Enron, Tyco, WorldCom, and the like. The abuses of corporate power can take any combination of six forms: (a) the abuse of employees, (b) the abuse of small stockholders, (c) the abuse of consumers, (d) the abuse of suppliers, (e) the abuse of the natural environment, and (f) the corruption of government. Enron seems to have engaged in all six forms of these abuses.

Now for the tough questions. Do corporations have checks and balances permanently built into their top-level governance mechanisms? Would it be possible to build into corporation governance checks and balances, comparable to those in the Constitution, that would keep corporations on the constructive path for the common good? What would they look like? Have corporations ever gone through a constitutional convention process similar to the one that created the Constitution? Does more organizational design work need to be done before corporations can be considered as self-governing institutions, trusted to act wisely in regard to both the public good and private rights? What might be the role of national government in specifying the required governance structures in all corporate charters and in monitoring the ongoing compliance with these rules and procedures?

I believe that such questions about corporations are calling out for our attention, and I have made a start toward this process in the application chapters of *Being Human*. I base my suggestions not only on the newer understandings of how the human brain makes decisions but also on the premise that we still have much to learn from our Founding Fathers about how to institutionalize wisdom.

Notes

1. Baldwin, Simeon, *The Debate on the Constitution: Federalist and Antifederalist Speeches, Articles, and Letters During the Struggle Over Ratification,*

Vol. 2: *January to August 1788*. Bernard Bailyn, ed. New York: Library of America, 1993, pp. 520–521.

   2. Henry, Patrick, *Debate on the Constitution,* p. 596.

   3. Madison, James, *The Federalist Papers*. New York: Bantam Books, 1982, No. 14.

   4. Jay, John, *Federalist Papers,* No. 2.

   5. Madison, *Federalist Papers,* No. 51.

   6. Ibid., No. 49.

   7. Hamilton, Alexander, *Federalist Papers,* No. 34.

   8. Madison, *Federalist Papers,* No. 57.

   9. Hamilton, *Federalist Papers,* No. 6.

   10. Madison, *Federalist Papers,* No. 51.

   11. Madison, quoted in Bernard Bailyn, *Faces of Revolution: Personalities and Themes in the Struggle for American Independence*. New York: Knopf, 1990, p. 260.

   12. Madison, *Federalist Papers,* No. 55.

   13. Ibid., No. 57.

   14. Ibid., No. 39.

   15. Baldwin, *Debate on the Constitution.*

   16. Hamilton, *Federalist Papers,* No. 48.

   17. Carter, Rita, *Mapping the Mind*. Berkeley: University of California Press, 1998, p. 182.

   18. Ibid., p. 187.

   19. Damasio, Antonio, *Descartes' Error*. New York: Avon Books, 1994, p. xvi.

   20. Carter, *Mapping the Mind,* p. 197.

   21. Ibid.

   22. Ibid., p. 182.

   23. Ibid.

   24. Ibid., p. 195.

   25. Pinker, Steven, *The Blank Slate*. New York: Viking, 2002, p. 331.

   26. Hamilton, *Federalist Papers,* No. 66.

   27. Baldwin, *Debate on the Constitution,* p. 521.

   28. Madison, *Federalist Papers,* No. 10, p. 43.

   29. Ibid., p. 44.

   30. Ibid.

4

Strategic Logic

Toward a Wisdom-Based
Approach to Strategic Management

Paul E. Bierly, III
Robert W. Kolodinsky

W isdom is a fascinating and captivating concept. For thousands of years, philosophers and theologians have pondered its meaning and value, commonly attributing great reverence and awe to those few possessing it. Probably because of the confusion about the term and the ambiguity of its meaning, wisdom has remained mostly absent from the mainstream management literature, with the most notable exceptions being work from authors of chapters in this book. In particular, the field of strategic management has not sufficiently included the concept of wisdom in theoretical frameworks or empirical studies. However, as many have yearned for a better understanding of organizational knowledge and have struggled to successfully apply the knowledge-based view of the firm to strategy, we believe that the time has arrived to consider the importance of wisdom in organizational settings.

The purpose of this chapter is an initial attempt to explain through logic why the field of strategic management must finally consider ways to include the concept of wisdom in its theory development and managerial advice. The first step of our journey is to identify several major shortcomings of the field of strategic management. Second, we focus on the role of top managers and discuss the concept of *executive wisdom*, briefly outlining its antecedents and consequences. Third, we shift the unit of analysis to the organization and discuss *organizational wisdom* and how it can influence strategic management. This includes a discussion about how leadership and organizational culture are important mechanisms for enabling the development of organizational wisdom. We conclude by discussing research and managerial implications of developing a wisdom-based approach to strategic management.

Review and Critique of
Strategic Management Research _____

The field of strategic management has evolved rapidly over the past 25 years, being influenced by researchers in a variety of academic disciplines. Michael Porter pioneered the concept of business strategy by applying his expertise in industrial organization economics to analyze the determinants of firm profitability (Porter, 1980, 1985). This approach to strategy focused on finding an optimal position, or a niche, in an attractive industry setting and on defending the position by using either a low-cost or differentiation generic strategy. He stressed the need for internal consistency of strategic actions, organizational design, control systems, human resource systems, and organizational culture to support the chosen generic strategy.

During the 1990s, the resource-based view of strategic management became the most popular school of strategy, shifting the primary focus of strategy toward the internal resources of the firm. The resource-based view provides a theoretical framework to determine which resources and capabilities will provide sustainable competitive advantages and lead to above-average rates of return (Barney, 1991; Grant, 1991; Mahoney & Pandian, 1992; Peteraf, 1993; Wernerfelt, 1984). Resources include a firm's tangible, intangible, and human resources, whereas capabilities refer to a firm's ability to apply its resources to the undertaking of productive activities (Grant, 1991). Generally speaking, resources and capabilities will be sources of sustainable competitive advantages only if they are rare, valuable, inimitable, and nonsubstitutable (Barney, 1991). Resources and capabilities have causal ambiguity and are difficult to imitate if they are more tacit, complex, and specific (Lippman & Rumelt, 1982; Reed & DeFillippi, 1990).

The dynamic capabilities approach to strategy, which also became popular during the 1990s, is similar to the resource-based view concerning most of the underlying theory but takes a more dynamic perspective and places more emphasis on learning and innovation (Nelson, 1991; Nelson & Winter, 1982; Prahalad & Hamel, 1990; Teece, Pisano, & Shuen, 1997). This approach to strategy is more appropriate in fast cycle markets (Williams, 1992) that have also been called Schumpeterian markets, hypercompetition (D'Aveni, 1994), and high-velocity industries (Brown & Eisenhardt, 1997). In these types of environments, a specific resource or capability usually produces a competitive advantage for only a relatively short period of time. Competitors respond quickly by either imitation or development of their own improved products. Thus, they argue, the true sources of durable rents are organizational capabilities that enable firms to innovate at a faster rate. This shifts the focus from the stock of technological capabilities to the flow of technological capabilities and gamesmanship among competitors.

Recently, the knowledge-based view of the firm was introduced as an extension of both resource-based theory and the dynamic capabilities approach. The underlying assumption of this approach is that knowledge is the principal productive resource of the organization (Grant, 1996a, 1996b; Kogut & Zander, 1992; Leonard-Barton, 1995; Nonaka, 1994). Following a traditional epistemology, knowledge can be defined as "justified true belief" (Nonaka, 1994). Others have argued against such a positivistic approach, claiming that one's perception of knowledge depends on the interpretive context and experience (Spender, 1996; Tsoukas, 1996). They view the organization as a distributed knowledge system (Tsoukas, 1996) or as a knowledge-based activity system (Spender, 1996). Both approaches stress the importance of identifying different types of knowledge and the relationship between individual and social knowledge. The two main types of knowledge are explicit knowledge, which is articulable and codifiable, and tacit knowledge, which is not articulable or codifiable and is generally gained through experience (Polanyi, 1966). Tacit knowledge is more difficult to transfer and integrate with other knowledge in the organization, but it is also more difficult for competitors to imitate (Kogut & Zander, 1992). Thus, tacit knowledge, as compared with explicit knowledge, can be a more viable source of sustainable competitive advantages and, consequently, above-normal rents.

Each of these schools of strategy has a common set of shortcomings. Throughout the rest of this chapter, we argue that a wisdom-based approach to strategy is a viable platform for overcoming each of the following shortcomings.

Organizational Purpose

Most organizations lack a meaningful purpose for their existence that promotes passion in the workforce. Current approaches to strategy assume that the primary goal of strategic management is to maximize either profitability or shareholder value. They fail to fully consider the firm's impact on society, its responsibility to act for the "common good," and how such system-wide stakeholder approaches can result in positive, long-term reputational and financial effects. Often researchers acknowledge multiple purposes of the firm but largely disregard them when they simplify the firm's goals to make analyses manageable (Grant, 2005). However, current approaches to organizational strategy are commonly devoid of a meaningful purpose for organizations' existence. If the only purpose for workers is to make money for their organization, their work life and mission lack meaning beyond material ends—clearly not the primary motivation of most

U.S. workers, who want autonomy, time with family, recognition, and other intrinsic satisfiers (e.g., de Graaf, 2004; Giacalone & Jurkiewicz, 2003). Moreover, firms today are so focused on "beating the competition" (or even just surviving) that they are not striving to be the best they can be, nor are they truly focused on positively influencing society and the common good.

Complexity and Judgment

The current analytical processes of strategy focus on resources, capabilities, and managing knowledge but do not focus enough on judgment, intuition, and the complexity of the decision-making process. To produce a specific quantifiable solution, strategists too often base their analyses on simplifications, often not considering very important but abstract concepts such as morality, justice, value-based culture, social responsibility, their role in the environment, and their symbiotic relationships with others. Rational, data-driven strategies may appear to be appropriate and sufficient in such a bounded rationality setting, but too often they are revealed to be incomplete in a real-world environment, resulting in suboptimal outcomes. For example, an underlying principle of these current approaches is that maximizing a firm's knowledge base or technological capabilities will lead to a sustainable competitive advantage and organizational success. We argue that strategy is less about maximizing a stock of knowledge or physical assets and is more about principle-centered judgments about the proper use of these assets. In this sense, the "logic" behind decisions and actions in complex organizational environments must rely on more than simplified, profit-focused, and data-driven algorithms and models. Intuition, morality, and the impact on the common good must also be considered to maximize organizational effectiveness.

Multilevel Analysis

Current strategy approaches tend to assume that strategy is a firm-level concept and do not fully appreciate the complexity of multilevel analysis. They do not appropriately consider the role of the individual, the role of the top management team, and the relationships between individuals in the firm. While it is beyond the scope of this paper to include detailed descriptions of all the levels, we focus on (arguably) the two most critical: executive-level wisdom and organizational-level wisdom.

Executive Wisdom

General Model

The primary purpose of this chapter is to discuss the relationship between organizational wisdom and strategic management, using logic to

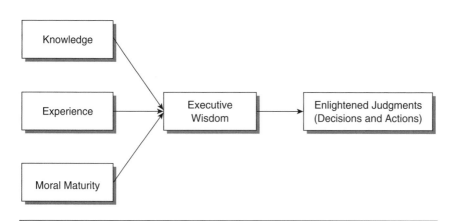

Figure 4.1   A Framework of Executive Wisdom

justify our assertions. However, before tackling the complexity of wisdom at the organizational level, we need a basic understanding of individual-level wisdom within the context of an organization, which we refer to as *executive wisdom* (Figure 4.1). In particular, we focus on the top managers[1] involved in the strategic management of a firm and their unique role in setting business policy. A starting point is the dictionary definition of wisdom: "the faculty of making the best use of knowledge, experience, and understanding by exercising good judgment" (Merriam-Webster, 1961). To this basic definition, we add—and stress—key components of wisdom so that the concept can be applied to top managers in an organizational setting. Implicit throughout our assertions is that wisdom is indeed rare among top managers and in organizational strategy making.

First, at the core of the concept of wisdom is the notion of judgment. Executive wisdom incorporates both decision making and action. It involves making the best decisions as well as the implementation of those decisions; wisdom is an action-oriented construct (Bierly, Kessler, & Christensen, 2000).

Second, the accumulation of knowledge is a prerequisite to executive wisdom. To make a wise decision, a top manager must know about and understand each situation requiring a decision or an action, including the degree to which it is important and urgent. Moreover, to the degree appropriate for each situation, the gathering of data to support decision making is wise. Increasing knowledge, or learning, is critical to enhancing wisdom.

Third, executive wisdom involves deep reflection on one's own and others' past experiences. Others have discussed how reflectiveness is an important component of wisdom (Beyer & Nino, 1998; Bierly et al., 2000; Weick, 1998). Understanding each strategic decision in the context of previous experiences enables executives to rely on intuition based on tacit knowledge.

Fourth, the primary outcome of executive wisdom is beyond what is best for the individual top manager or even for the firm; it involves what is best for the common good. Eastern thought, such as the teachings of Confucius and the core beliefs of Buddhism, stress the importance of harmony with one's environment as being a key component of wisdom. Thus, wisdom requires the subjugation of self-interest and ego in strategic decision making; it sensitively considers the impact on all stakeholders.

Finally, we argue that one's moral maturity is a critical component of wisdom by providing a foundation for discerning right from wrong and for providing the rationale as to why individuals value the needs of others and act in a moral and just manner. A common source of moral maturity, faith, often fuels an individual's moral passion and courage to act wisely.

Individual Knowledge

Knowledge involves both knowing how, which is generally more tacit knowledge, and knowing about, which is more explicit knowledge (Grant, 1996a, 1996b). Knowledge implies a deep understanding of information concerning a topic, and increasing one's knowledge provides the potential for enhancing wisdom. However, as we explain later, knowledge is necessary but not sufficient to attain wisdom (e.g., Sternberg, 2003).

Certainly, executives would be wise to gather and retain as much relevant internal and external data as is feasibly possible. Such information is requisite to becoming informed and certainly aids decision making. Indeed, attempts at making strategic decisions without data on competitors, economic forces, and other market dynamics—as well as without intimate knowledge about one's own distinct competencies, strengths, and weaknesses—would be unwise and likely would result in disastrous consequences.

However, relying too much on explicit knowledge, or believing that one has all of the pertinent knowledge about a topic, often leads to judgments and actions that are unwise. Weick (1998) explained this issue with particular insight. He described wisdom as an attitude toward one's beliefs, values, information, and knowledge that balances overconfident knowing and overly cautious doubt (see also Meacham, 1990). Even though the world is mostly unknowable and unpredictable, decisions must still be made and actions must still be taken based on incomplete information. Weick argued that a key element of wisdom is the awareness of constraints and contingencies about a given situation such that one takes action knowing that his or her knowing is fallible. In other words, a key part of wisdom is the knowledge that one does not know it all.

Weick (1998) argued that an absence of wisdom occurs when there is a lack of balance between overconfident knowing and doubt. Wisdom falters when the overconfident executive believes that what he does not know is unimportant. The executive may become too attached to old comfortable ideas and may modify the interpretation of new inputs to fit such ideas. Because strategic decisions are very visible and important, top managers feel added pressure to justify them. Weick claimed that this type of justification and commitment to a specific course of action is the enemy of wisdom because it minimizes doubt. Wisdom involves questioning the validity of knowledge and decreasing attachment and bias toward any specific option.

Perhaps just as important, wisdom is not attainable if one lacks knowledge and is excessively cautious. Not knowing enough about a situation can create too much doubt and a lack of confidence to act. Continual inaction exacerbates the problem as opportunities to learn through experience are thwarted. In fact, experience is integral to gaining and applying executive wisdom.

Experience

The education, training, and "life experiences" of top managers can help them along the path to wisdom. Experience can aid in understanding the broader context of issues, seeing how new knowledge can be integrated into existing knowledge, and assigning value to different types of knowledge. Experience is particularly important in understanding and being able to apply tacit knowledge (Nonaka, 1994; Polanyi, 1966; Spender, 1996).

Experiential learning theory provides a model of how learning might be maximized through a cycle of concrete experience to observations and reflection, followed by the formation of abstractions and generalization that are then applied in new situations (Kolb, 1984). Similarly, Malan and Kriger (1998) maintained that wisdom develops from a process of progressively finer discernment of variability in the environment. That is, interactions with the environment (experience) lead to the ability to discern variability, which in turn leads to learning and ultimately wisdom. At its core, experience gives individuals the ability to assess the relative salience of events, detect changing patterns, judge the importance of developments, and make confident decisions—particularly in situations of incomplete information. Importantly, for experience to influence wisdom, executives must reflect, either consciously or subconsciously, on their past.

Experience also fuels the accumulation and reliability of intuition in the strategic decision-making process, and this can be viewed as an important component of wisdom. Chester Barnard, back in 1938, observed that many decisions by executives did not follow a rational analytic process but instead relied on intuition and judgment through a "nonrational" decision-making process (Barnard, 1938). Polanyi's (1966) work on tacit knowledge and "personal knowing" helped scientists in a variety of disciplines to understand the importance of experience, imagination, and "gut feelings" in facilitating decision making. Polanyi argued convincingly that unwillingness to rely on one's personal (tacit) knowledge and intuition was a root cause of many theoretical and experimental failures. Intuition is particularly valuable when time pressures do not allow decisions to be made in a systematic analytic manner.

At this point in the discussion, we think that it is important to note that intuition is largely distinct from emotion. Intuition draws on executives' experience, training, and prior learning by rapidly applying nonexplicit "chunks" or patterns of information stored in memory to a specific situation (Simon, 1987). Intuition produces rapid solutions using recognition cues based on professional judgment. Alternatively, decisions based on emotion can be considered as "irrational" in the sense that they are based not on knowledge accrued through experience but rather on individuals' current feelings and biases. Making decisions based on intuition can be surprisingly effective, but decisions based on emotion usually are poor ones (Klein, 2003).

Herbert Simon illustrated the effectiveness of intuition in decision making by analyzing the behavior of chess masters (Simon, 1987). These experts can play as many as 50 games simultaneously, taking only seconds to decide each move, and maintain a high level of play. They do not have time to carefully analyze each move. Instead, they use their experience to rapidly evaluate patterns and clusters of pieces on the board and then quickly make wise strategic moves. Their nearly automatic decisions are based on cues of opportunism and dangers associated with the different patterns. They do not consciously evaluate alternatives; rather, they rely on their intuition to such an extent that they cannot articulate how they have made decisions. In addition, chess masters have amazing recall of pieces after glancing at a board during a normal game. However, if pieces are placed on a board randomly, their recall is no better than that of a novice; their intuition does not help them because there are no meaningful patterns among the pieces.

We are not advocating that executives should forgo a formal analysis of strategy and rely only on intuition. Formal analyses should be performed as data and time permit. However, intuition can be a powerful tool to supplement the rational decision-making process. Indeed, using both explicit and tacit knowledge has been found to be a more effective decision-making strategy than using either one in isolation (e.g., Blattberg & Hoch, 1990).

Top managers can improve rapid decision making and become wiser by better using intuition in the following ways. First, they should acknowledge the importance of intuition in decision making and embrace its use. A common problem is the postponement of a decision because a formal rational analysis that "justifies" the decision cannot be conducted. Some organizational cultures may unwittingly stigmatize intuition. This seems unwarranted. Second, managers should remember that intuition is based on one's own training and experience and not simply on broader emotion. Traditional decision-making aids, such as having someone play the role of a devil's advocate, may assist in determining whether the intuitive decision is appropriate (Sadler-Smith & Shefy, 2004). Third, they should provide constructive feedback to decision makers using intuition so that they can better learn from an honest interpretation of their actions (Hogarth, 2001). Feedback also helps to improve confidence in executives who are hesitant to rely on intuition. Fourth, managers should integrate intuition and the use of imagery. Sadler-Smith and Shefy (2004) and Hogarth (2001) argued that imagery can improve intuition because many executives have problems in putting insights into words. A visual image can be used to express a richer, more tacit understanding of relationships and concepts.

Moral Maturity

To make wise judgments, it is essential that top managers understand the moral implications of the choices they make and how such choices affect the entire organizational system and the common good. Morality refers to "a system of principles and judgments shared by cultural, religious, and philosophical concepts and beliefs by which humans subjectively determine whether given actions are right or wrong" (www.wikipedia.org). It can be viewed further as ethical motives (www.wordnet.princeton.edu) and as "goodness according to a recognized code of conduct" (www.business words.com). Viewed as the highest level of moral development, moral maturity refers to "the ability to stand outside the situation and justify one's actions in terms of universal moral principles" (Dreyfus, 1990). Universal principles—integrity, compassion, responsibility, forgiveness, honesty, justice, trust, and so on (Covey, 1990; Lennick & Kiel, 2005)—are the unchanging, proven "natural laws and governing social values that have gradually come through every great society, every responsible civilization, over the centuries" (Covey, 1990, p. 69). Developing one's moral maturity, which can be viewed as progressing further along Kohlberg's (1969, 1983) stages of moral development, is foundationally vital to being wise because less focus is on self-interests and more focus is on others' needs. Thus, wisdom requires, using Kohlberg's terminology, transitioning from the conventional level to the postconventional level. The conventional level is characterized by seeking the approval of others (Stage 3) and by conformity to the law and obligations of duty (Stage 4). Stage 5, at the postconventional level, is the "social contract" stage where an individual becomes a "truly autonomous moral entity" (Thompson, 2000, p. 121, cited in Senske, 2004, p. 46) who takes a genuine interest in the welfare of others and believes that all individuals should be afforded basic rights and have democratic processes available to them. According to Mathieson and Miree (2003), "postconventional reasoning is a sign of moral maturity" (p. 464). Kohlberg (1983) suggested that less than 20% of the American population reaches this level. Kohlberg and others (e.g., Fowler, 1981) proposed a sixth stage—"principled conscience"—reserved for those few transformational leaders who model respect for universal principles and who live with a "felt participation in a power that unifies and transforms the world" (Fowler, 1981, pp. 200–201, cited in Senske, 2004, p. 46).

Hence, we suggest that moral maturity requires modeling universal principles and reaching the postconventional level of moral development. Only when top managers move beyond self-interests and conformity to truly caring about others can they begin to manifest true wisdom. However, although we assert that being a postconventional individual is vital to achieving wisdom, it is also necessary to have threshold levels of knowledge and experience. As such, reaching higher levels of moral maturity is a necessary but not sufficient condition for becoming wise. Three important components that bolster one's moral maturity—and indeed one's wisdom—are discipline, generativity, and spirituality. We briefly discuss these issues next in the context of strategic management.

Discipline

Disciplined top managers have a greater likelihood of becoming morally mature than do their less disciplined counterparts. Discipline can be viewed as "any training intended to produce a specific character or pattern of behavior, especially training that produces moral or mental development in a particular direction" (www.wordiq.com). Covey (1990) defined discipline as "the ability to make and keep promises and to honor commitments" (p. 73). Inherent in both of these definitions is the consideration of the moral impact on others. Furthermore, discipline implies the intentional constraint of thoughts and activities primarily to those that are most salient and that further one's objectives. In the current context, becoming disciplined implies a focus on, and proactive attention to, the most significant and impactful organizational issues. To the degree that such discipline results in decisions and behaviors deemed to be moral, moral maturity is fostered.

In the context of organizational strategy, executives need discipline to maximize the effectiveness of their strategic decision making and actions. Given the high-velocity pace of many organizational environments today, top managers do not have the luxury of letting much time pass without attending to the most critical strategic issues influencing their organization (Brown & Eisenhardt, 1997). The ability and willingness to stay focused and on task in a largely undistracted manner is a hallmark of becoming an effective executive. In Covey's (1989) terms, the most highly effective people "put first things first" and spend greater amounts of time on tasks that are important but not yet urgent. Compared with their less disciplined counterparts who are constantly in crisis mode, executives with the discipline to focus extensive amounts of time on scanning, planning, and understanding environmental threats and opportunities—and pondering alternatives with deep reflection of past decisions and experiences—are more likely to make wise strategic decisions. Moreover, top managers who regularly spend time on building their knowledge base and expertise while actively seeking relevant experiences are most likely to recognize trends, combat threats, and visualize opportunities that aid strategic decision making.

Furthermore, wise executives are fully aware of the impact their strategic decisions have on both internal and external stakeholders, and they willingly constrain such judgments to only those that fit within a framework of moral acceptability. Morally mature executives have an "internal moral compass" that points "true north"—"the magnetic principle of respect for people and property" (Covey, 1990, p. 94). Such morally mature restraint, fostered by discipline, best serves the common good in both the short and long term. In sum, discipline facilitates morally mature strategic judgments in wise executives.

Generativity

Wise, morally mature executives are concerned about the long-term impact their judgments have on salient stakeholders and take action to ensure that their judgments indeed have the intended altruistic impact. Generativity, Erikson's seventh stage of psychosocial development, refers to the genuine concern that some people have for generating things that help future generations (Erikson, 1950) and for "making a difference and leaving something of value behind" (Izzo & Klein, 1998, p. 63; see also Klein & Izzo, 1998). Covey (2004) offered further validation of the importance of generativity, with the following four basic needs of people: to live, to love, to learn, and to leave a legacy.

Unfortunately, driven by short-term pressure to maximize profits and satisfy shareholders, as well as by the desire for personal wealth enhancement, too few executives appear to concern themselves with the long-term system-wide effects of their commonly self-serving decisions. The strategic choices they make indeed have powerful effects, but too often the only positive effect is financial, while people—workers and their families as well as other community members—are left to deal with the adverse vestiges of the decisions of a few. The harmful impact of executive decisions related to the space shuttle *Challenger* (Morton Thiokol and NASA), to wildlife in and near Alaska (Exxon), to health and safety in Bhopal, India (Union Carbide), and to retirement benefits and the careers of thousands of workers (e.g., Enron, WorldCom, Adelphia, Tyco, Global Crossings) are but a few examples of choices made that failed to adequately account for the impact on others—and clearly indicate moral immaturity and unwise strategic thinking on the part of such executives.

Alternatively, wise executives are concerned about the long-term impact their judgments have on salient stakeholders. Such top managers are keenly aware of the generative impact their decisions have and make decisions that clearly show concern for future generations. These morally mature individuals recognize that strategic organizational decisions indeed influence more than the bottom line; they affect multitudes of internal and external stakeholders, often in significant and powerful ways. For example, the executive decision that Aaron Feuerstein of Malden Mills made to rebuild his

Massachusetts-based clothing plant after a devastating fire, rather than transfer operations overseas to a considerably cheaper labor pool, positively and directly influenced not only each of the plant's workers, who received compensation even during the rebuilding effort, but also the whole community, which continued to rely on Malden Mills for a significant portion of its employment and economic well-being (Lennick & Kiel, 2005). This willingness to put concern for people over money, and to generate strategic decisions that influence people positively in the long run, is a key characteristic of morally mature—and wise—executives.

Spirituality

Perhaps the most common and enduring path to moral maturity is through spiritual means. Spirituality can be viewed in a variety of ways, including belief in and a relationship with a higher power that ultimately affects human behavior (Armstrong, 1996); a "basic feeling of being connected with one's complete self, others, and the entire universe" (Mitroff & Denton, 1999, p. 83); and an "animating force that inspires one toward purposes that are beyond one's self and that give one's life meaning and direction" (McKnight, 1984, p. 142).

For most Americans, spirituality involves religion, belief in God, and the constraint of behaviors based on one's belief in what God desires for one's life. Although a recent poll indicated that 50% of Americans believe that one can be moral without faith in God (http://pewforum.org), other polls revealed that 6 of 10 Americans believe that religion is "very important in their lives," with just 10% regarding themselves as neither religious nor spiritual (Gallup Organization, 2002–2003). Hence, the most common path to spirituality in America appears to be through one's faith. According to Fowler (1981), adults can develop through up to four stages of faith, with the highest (and most rare) level being "universalizing faith"—the stage where the center of concern shifts from self to others. This central focus is analogous to Kohlberg's postconventional level, where (in the current context) executives understand the interconnected consequences of their strategic decisions.

We suggest that morally mature executives, whether religious or not, have the potential for wisdom that manifests in decisions and actions that benefit the common good. However, a question that is left unanswered is why an individual would do this. What is the rational logic for an individual to consider the best interests of others along with, and possibly more than, self-interests? Why do some individuals make "right" moral decisions when other options may appear to benefit them more, at least in the short term?

We argue that, for most Americans, an individual's faith is a common driving force of this type of behavior and wisdom. Faith in a higher power (i.e., God) commonly provides a foundation for living a moral and compassionate life and provides a rationale for differentiating between right and wrong. Indeed, the Bible repeatedly describes wisdom as being attainable only as a gift from God (e.g., 1 Kings 4:29 [Tyndale House, 1991]). Furthermore, faith provides a sense of meaning and direction to one's life. Individuals make the right decisions because they want to honor and please God. Although the foregoing argument follows Christian beliefs, similar arguments certainly can be made within the belief structures of other religions given that nearly all major religions, including Christianity, Buddhism, Confucianism, Hinduism, Islam, and Judaism, follow a variation of one fundamental law: "Love your neighbor and treat your neighbor as you would wish to be treated" (Marcic, 1997). Understanding one's relationship with the environment and understanding why it is important to treat others with integrity, compassion, and justice are central tenets of all major religions.

Certainly, having faith helps top managers to become more morally mature in that faith helps individuals to move their focus away from selfish interests and more to the well-being of others. Moreover, faith helps to keep individuals from making poor ethical choices—critical to postconventional thinking. Still, having faith does not guarantee wisdom. However, when faith is combined with discipline, generativity, and moral maturity (along with knowledge and experience), a top manager has the powerful ingredients to becoming wise.

In summary, business executives would be well served to understand the spiritual realities of their environments—their own spiritual needs, the needs of workers and the communities in which they work, and the interrelatedness of strategic decisions affecting salient stakeholders. Given the increasingly obvious reality that we all are part of a global community and are affected by the decisions of powerful individuals (e.g., business executives; politicians), the size of an organization's salient stakeholders grows ever larger. Executives who are willing to constrain decisional alternatives to those that reduce harm and consider the common good ultimately will be judged as wiser than those who make only the most financially expedient decisions. Executives who understand the needs and concerns of human spirituality are more likely to render judgments that take this understanding into account and thus will more likely reflect moral maturity—and wisdom.

Outcomes of Executive Wisdom

As we have argued, knowledge, experience, and moral maturity commonly accelerated by faith combine to fuel executive wisdom. Using intentionally accumulated explicit knowledge helps top managers to gather the data necessary to make informed decisions. Relying on experience, a source of tacit knowledge, facilitates use of one's intuition—that deep form of knowing that is difficult to make explicit but nonetheless has been shown to be extremely valuable to decision making (Polanyi, 1966; Simon, 1987). Combining moral maturity with knowledge and experience provides the top manager with a principles-centered moral framework against which the costs and benefits of one's decisions may be measured. With this model, the judgments made by individual executives are sifted through a three-layered filter prior to final decision making. The results of this filtering process are judgments that are informed, that feel good deep in one's gut, and that fully consider the primary stakeholders affected by such decisions or actions. Moreover, using this model in strategy making enables a top manager to better affect positive change for the long term. Indeed, one true measure of wisdom is to leave a legacy of right thinking that continues to influence the judgments of others long after one has departed. Mother Teresa, Mahatma Gandhi, Martin Luther King, Jr., and Jesus Christ are but a few great moral leaders whose positive legacies transcend their lives.

We suggest that the primary and overarching outcome of executive wisdom is enlightened judgments. By enlightened, we mean that the consequences of one's decisions and actions are considered in the full light of how such judgments affect self, others, the organization, and society at large. Enlightened judgments reflect executive integrity, courage, and careful concern for the common good. Such actions therefore transcend an executive's self-interests and center more on the needs of others. When enlightened judgments by top managers become the norm in an organization, workers respond with increased motivation and productivity as they come to recognize that management is taking into account their needs and values. Moreover, staffing issues tend to take care of themselves as fewer workers tend to leave an organization that clearly cares for them and outside candidates clamor to join such a unique firm. When outside stakeholders come to recognize that an organization's management team makes decisions with great concern for them as well, positive reputational effects accrue. All of these issues help the bottom line.

In sum, executive wisdom leads to enlightened judgments that result in positive long-term financial effects. Now we turn our attention away from individual-level wisdom and toward the organizational level.

Organizational Wisdom and Strategic Management

Need for Multilevel Analysis

An important consideration in the study of strategic management is that while the field deals with firm-level resources and capabilities, the decisions about the development and deployment of those resources are generally done by a small group, namely the top management team, or a single individual, such as the chief executive officer. A major weakness in the strategic management literature is that few studies of strategy analyze multiple levels, and this results in potential misspecification because most theory building is done at the firm level, whereas most measurement is of individuals, usually via surveys (Currall & Inkpen, 2002). Organizational theorists have suggested that a multilevel analysis could greatly enrich the understanding of complex organizational activities (Klein, Tosi, & Cannella, 1999); hence, the discussion of wisdom should span multiple levels of analysis. We believe this is especially appropriate because the concept of organizational wisdom is a complex concept that is best understood by first appreciating the key concepts of executive wisdom and then extending the discussion to include firm-level decision making and organizational wisdom. The final strategic decision is a firm-level action, but the decision typically is made by either a specific individual or a small group of executives. It would be a mistake either to focus on the firm and not address the importance of the individuals' wisdom or to focus on the individual level and not address the importance of the firm's culture, knowledge base, learning mechanisms, political processes, and established routines.

Whereas executive wisdom is associated with an individual, organizational wisdom is about decisions and actions of the organization as a single entity. Organizational wisdom is the exercising of good moral judgment by an organization that makes the best collective use of knowledge and experience of individuals and knowledge stored in the organizational memory as the organization strives to maximize organizational effectiveness and, simultaneously, to make a positive impact on society. Thus, organizational wisdom involves the process of choosing and applying knowledge from many sources throughout the organization. For the organization to act wisely, strategic decision makers must be able and willing to access knowledge from remote sources. Furthermore, the organization must have several key attributes; it must be designed, have an information technology (IT) system, and have a culture to facilitate the collection, transfer, and integration of individuals' and institutional knowledge. A specific strategic decision may be made by either a single executive or a group of executives, but the implementation of the decision may be done by different, often lower level, managers. Thus, not only must knowledge be transferred up to the strategic decision makers; it also must be transferred down to the managers that carry out the action.

Organizational Knowledge and Learning

Just as we argued that the accumulation of individual knowledge is a prerequisite for executive wisdom, the development of organizational knowledge is a prerequisite for organizational wisdom. Each firm's knowledge base is composed of the firm's intellectual capital, which can be viewed as the tangible and intangible knowledge, experience, and skills of employees in the organization (Bierly & Chakrabarti, 1996). According to Simon (1991), all knowledge is initially created or acquired by individuals. Individual learning is a prerequisite to organizational learning. After an individual learns, knowledge is first passed on to other "close" individuals who share similar interpretation frameworks or what Brown and Duguid (1991) referred to as a community-of-practice. This social context of knowledge transfer between individuals is an extremely important part of the organizational learning process (March, 1991). Besides having the ability to create or interpret new ideas from outside sources, expert individuals must also have the social skills to pass the knowledge to others. Whereas explicit knowledge may be passed easily from one individual to another, tacit knowledge may require informal and difficult methods such as the use of stories or metaphors (Brown & Duguid, 1991). Importantly, the collective knowledge of the group often is much more than the sum of the individuals' knowledge. Synergies exist between individuals as the knowledge is integrated and reinterpreted by others (Spender, 1994). Group norms can be used to store certain types of knowledge and pass them on to others.

Organizational knowledge can be viewed as the integration of group knowledge, mainly through middle-level managers (Nonaka, 1994). Generally speaking, organizational knowledge refers to knowledge that has diffused throughout the entire organization. However, in reality this is rarely the case because not all individuals have the ability to interpret and understand the new knowledge. Although it may be difficult to transfer knowledge to other work groups and there may be limited incentive to do so, it usually is critical to transfer knowledge up through an organization to the key strategic decision makers who allocate resources. Once knowledge has reached the top of the organization, it then can become institutionalized and form the basis for new organizational rules, procedures, and routines—the means by which the knowledge is stored within the organization. It is at this point that other individuals can be socialized to the new organizational beliefs (March, 1991). This process of mutual individual and collective learning typically is continuous. In addition, as the knowledge is transferred up and down the organization, the knowledge spirals and expands through different conversion modes, including the conversion of tacit knowledge to explicit knowledge and vice versa (Nonaka, 1994). Over time, the knowledge becomes embedded in routines (Nelson & Winter, 1982), and after employees come and go throughout the organization, the organization's knowledge base becomes distinct from the aggregate knowledge of individuals at a specific point in time. Hedlund (1994) developed an N-form organizational structure to facilitate knowledge integration, and Sanchez and Mahoney (1996) illustrated the importance of modularity with respect to product and organizational design to facilitate knowledge management.

When dealing with only explicit simple knowledge, the challenge is to obtain and manage the flow of information effectively, primarily through the use of IT. A common problem in strategic decision making is to not use information that is readily available. This may occur if key organizational members are not involved in the decision-making process, an effective IT system is not in place to collect the information, or the decision maker fails to use resources available to him or her. IT problems within organizations are well known and have become increasingly popular topics (Bossidy & Charan, 2004).

However, political and interpersonal issues and group dynamics also affect the organization's ability to manage its knowledge base and its potential for organizational wisdom. When a group of individuals makes a strategic decision, the information management challenge is not limited to an individual but rather involves the collective mind of the group. Experts may be biased in how they present information to others. Each group member may have a different perspective on the situation and different individual goals. Power struggles, which may include hoarding information from adversaries, may infect the overall decision-making process (Allison, 1971; Pfeffer, 1981).

Concerning organizational wisdom, one of the most important ways to improve the decisions of a collective mind is to improve heedfulness, defined as acting carefully, purposefully, and attentively (Weick & Roberts, 1993). One of the best ways to improve heedfulness at the organizational level is to help structure the views and opinions of the organization's members according to relevant criteria. Therefore, the careful consideration and development of a consistent template, essentially an intended categorization schema for evaluating strategic decisions, may be a useful way for firms to help guide their executives' thinking. Developing an intended categorization schema in advance is helpful because it can be done in a systematic manner without the pressure that usually surrounds strategic decisions. In addition, developing it in advance allows time for debate and dissent that otherwise might not occur.

Organizational Spirituality and the Role of Leadership

The concepts of organizational and executive wisdom certainly are interrelated. Earlier, we focused on top managers making wise decisions. This is a component of organizational wisdom because top managers often represent and act for the organization. However, top managers also develop organizational wisdom by the way they influence the actions of others. Specifically, their leadership and development of a corporate culture help to provide guidance for all employees to make decisions based on core values that promote organizational wisdom, such as an appropriate focus on morality, ethics, and concern for others.

According to Covey (1990), "Wisdom suggests a sage perspective on life, a sense of balance, a keen understanding of how the various parts and principles apply and relate to each other. It embraces judgment, discernment, and comprehension. It is a oneness, an integrated wholeness" (p. 22). We suggest that an understanding of values, principles, wholeness, and community—that is, spirituality—and a sense of balance all are critical to wise organizational leadership and strategy making.

Sadly, too few organizational leaders understand these concepts, and even fewer act on them. Consider the recent catastrophic effects from poor leadership judgments at Enron, WorldCom, Adelphia, Tyco, Arthur Andersen, and even the Roman Catholic Church. In each of these cases, a failure to provide moral leadership resulted in immeasurable suffering to millions (Senske, 2004). In the following section, we discuss the relationship of wisdom to organizational spirituality and highlight the critical role that leadership plays in enacting change. After that, we look at the importance of balance in strategic decision making.

Wisdom, Culture, and Organizational Spirituality

In his chapter on organizational greatness, Khandwalla (1998) suggested that the dominant paradigm of corporate performance excellence is to win in the competitive domain. Unfortunately, those who strive solely to win too often find themselves degenerating "into winning at all costs—costs to others as well as organizational stakeholders" (p. 168). He offered nine alternative paths to organizational greatness, including adopting a stakeholder orientation, attending to one's corporate social responsibilities, behaving ethically no matter what the costs, and behaving altruistically. Khandwalla suggested one path as most elusive—that of organizational spirituality—which he described as "the effort to dissolve interpersonal strife by recognizing the spiritual fraternity of all beings and to mitigate interpersonal stress by seeing work as worship, a divine calling, an offering to God" (p. 168).

Certainly, to make wise judgments, organizational leaders must understand the importance of organizational spirituality—both internally and externally. For our purposes, we suggest that organizational spirituality encompasses a wide range of issues, including transcendence of self-interest, integrity, and unity; a sense of purpose, truth, and trust; fairness and ethical mindfulness; the notion of social responsibility; gratitude; and altruism (e.g., Giacalone & Jurkiewicz, 2003; Khandwalla, 1998). Actions by organizational leaders that provide positive examples to others and further provide appropriate reward systems will more likely lead to institutionalization of these core values throughout the organization, creating a values-based and principles-centered culture.

There is a growing recognition, among both practitioners and academicians, that workers of all kinds and at all levels have spiritual needs that can be met at work (e.g., Giacalone & Jurkiewicz, 2003; Mitroff & Denton, 1999). According to Pfeffer (2003), workers value at least four primary spiritual dimensions from their workplaces:

(1) interesting work that permits them to learn, develop, and have a sense of competence or mastery, (2) meaningful work that provides some feeling of purpose, (3) a sense of connection and positive social relations with their coworkers, and (4) the ability to live an integrated life, so that one's work role and other roles are not inherently in conflict and so that a person's work role does not conflict with his or her essential nature and who the person is as a human being. (p. 32)

Fry (2003), in discussing his spiritual theory of leadership, suggested that organizational leaders should try to address workers' need for meaning and purpose, need for relationships and connectedness, need for growth and development, and self-esteem. Similarly, Ashmos and Duchon (2000) suggested that workplace spirituality involves a recognition that workers have an "inner life," want meaningful work, and want to work for an organization that serves these desires while also providing a sense of community.

To the degree that organizational leaders focus on meeting these spiritual needs, they have the opportunity to build a workplace that demonstrates to workers that the whole person matters—not just work tasks and financial performance. Such people-centered caring promotes "fit" and trust, freeing workers to maximize their value at work and hence their performance (e.g., Pfeffer, 2003). Moreover, attending to spirituality helps organizational leaders to foster a culture that gives workers a sense of purpose and an underlying feeling of unity (Khandwalla, 1998).

Wise organizational leaders develop people-focused strategies that center on addressing these spiritual needs of their workers. These "spiritual organizational leaders" focus their efforts on building and sustaining trust-based relationships and on serving others effectively. As both servant leaders (e.g., Autry, 2001; Greenleaf, 1977) and principle-centered leaders (Covey, 1990), these wise individuals understand that putting people first—understanding and addressing worker values, motivations, and need for meaning and purpose in one's work—ultimately trumps a profit-centered focus in the long term. Indeed, there is strong and growing evidence suggesting that organizations that focus on both people-centered values and high-commitment management practices—that is, practices that focus on satisfying the intrinsic values and motivations of workers—substantially outperform firms focused more on profits than on people (Burton & O'Reilly, 2000; Pfeffer, 2003). Moreover, organizations that concentrate on worker values are in a better position to be "built to last" (Collins & Porras, 1994).

Wisdom and Balance

In strategy making, wise organizational leaders delicately balance the needs and interests of a wide variety of stakeholders to achieve long-term sustained competitive advantage and to positively influence the common good. This notion of corporations as sensitive and responsible community members is not new. Henry Ford, Sr., founder of Ford Motor Company, said, "For a long time people believed that the only purpose of industry is to make a profit. They are wrong. Its purpose is to serve the general welfare" (Donaldson, 1982, p. 57). In the management literature, one can find several common good-related theories and frameworks, including works related to stakeholders (Freeman, Wicks, & Parmar, 2004; Jensen, 2002), corporate social responsibility (McWilliams & Siegel, 2001), and other-centered leadership (e.g., Covey, 1990; Greenleaf, 1977)—all providing some measure of validation of these concerns.[2]

Sternberg's (2000, 2003) balance theory of wisdom is helpful in this context. The balance theory of wisdom suggests that wise organizational leaders "skillfully balance interests of various kinds, including their own, those of their followers, and those of the organization for which they are responsible" (Sternberg, 2003, p. 395). The balance theory of wisdom "specifies the processes (balancing of interests and of responses to environmental contexts) in relation to the goal of wisdom (achievement of a common good)" (Sternberg, 2000, p. 638). Wisdom, more than just expert knowledge and know-how, is "relevant to the attainment of particular goals people value, not just any goals, but rather, a balance of responses to the environment—adapting, shaping, and selecting—so as to achieve a common good for all relevant stakeholders" (p. 638). Sternberg defined wisdom in this context as

> the application of tacit knowledge as mediated by values toward the goal of achieving a common good through a balance among multiple [1] *interests:* (a) intrapersonal, (b) interpersonal, and (c) extrapersonal in order to achieve a balance among [2] *responses to environmental contexts:* (a) adaptation to existing environmental contexts, (b) shaping of existing environmental contexts, and (c) selection of new environmental contexts. (p. 637, italics in original)

Although profit maximization and shareholder value are important concerns, organizations that focus on the common good—in their product or service offerings, in their treatment of workers, in the way the community benefits from the organizations—create goodwill and positive synergies that help them to outperform firms focused mainly on financial ends (e.g., Becker & Huselid, 1998; Collins & Porras, 1994; Pfeffer, 2003). Hence, we suggest that it is unwise to focus organizational strategies solely on profit maximization or shareholder value; ultimately, most stakeholders (including external shareholders) are people who want to feel connected to an organization in ways other than simply financial performance. For example, witness the interest and growth of investment in mutual funds focused on socially responsible firms.

To the degree that leadership is focused on issues such as profits over relationships, performance over people and society, extrinsic over intrinsic values and motivations, money more than principles, short-term performance more than long-term effectiveness, and what is best for self versus what is best for the common good, leadership will fail to make wise decisions and judgments. Moreover, such materially focused leaders typically behave in ways that reflect their short-term selfish desires and fail to act as principled role models that help workers to develop in ways that serve their spiritual needs. Profit-focused leaders unwittingly send the message to stakeholders that money is more important that people. Spiritual organizational leaders send the message that a people-oriented focus, rather than a money-oriented one, is the best strategy for long-term sustained competitive advantage and organizational effectiveness.

Outcomes of Organizational Wisdom

A wisdom-based approach to strategic management is superior to a profit-based approach to strategic management because the former maximizes both organizational effectiveness and the organization's impact on society. We argue that the advantage of a wisdom-based approach is not just that it has a dual focus but also that there are synergies by focusing on both common good and profits; in the long run, a wisdom-based approach will be more successful than a profit-based one. Figure 4.2 outlines different approaches to strategy based on two important dimensions: the extent to which organizations focus on increasing shareholder wealth and the degree of focus on making an impact on society.

A humanitarian approach, Quadrant 1 in Figure 4.2, strives to make an impact on society but does not focus on, and likely neglects, making profits. These firms approach strategy in a manner similar to that of as many non-profit organizations, such as relief organizations (e.g., CARE, Mercy Corps). Generally speaking, this approach is not sustainable in the long term for a for-profit organization. Without an appropriate focus on organizational effectiveness, these types of organizations frequently become inefficient. Suppliers and partners may be reluctant to work with them, fearing that the "causes" of such organizations become more important than fair dealings with suppliers and partners. An example of a company in this category was AES Corporation, an energy firm. AES instituted a decentralized decision-making process that gave local leaders an extraordinary level of independence. They

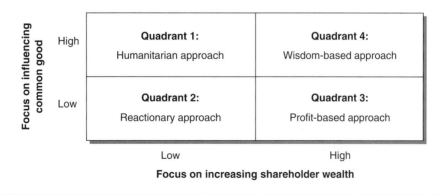

Figure 4.2   Classifying Different Top Management Approaches to Strategic Management

pushed the limits by developing management systems designed for employees to have fun, build trust, and enhance social responsibility to such an extent that a *Wall Street Journal* article described them as "empowerment gone mad" (Markels, 1995). A few years ago, when their industry ran into difficult times, they were not able to operate efficiently and encountered substantial losses. Recently, they have focused more on synergies across units and on becoming more centralized while trying to maintain their core values.

Quadrant 2 in Figure 4.2 represents reactionary organizations—firms that lack a focus either on influencing the common good or on increasing shareholder value. Essentially, these firms do not have a clear strategy and tend to "muddle through" in efforts to compete in their industry. They tend to be reactionary to changes in the environment or to competitive challenges by competitors. They initiate strategic attacks only infrequently, and they do not actively attempt to shape their competitive environment. Worker morale is usually very low because there is a lack of a sense of purpose and there are unpleasant working conditions. For these reasons, most firms in Quadrant 2 fail. Kmart largely fits the description of a reactionary organization.

Profit-based approaches, Quadrant 3 in Figure 4.2, are the current mainstream approaches to strategy we discussed and critiqued at the beginning of this chapter. Several of their disadvantages were mentioned earlier, including a failure to appreciate the responsibility of firms to influence society and the need to act for the common good. These approaches to strategy are focused primarily on satisfying the demands of the shareholders, who typically desire short-term profitability. Often drastic actions to maximize short-term profits cut too much organizational muscle and cause "corporate anorexia" that is damaging to long-term profits (Hamel & Prahalad, 1994). For example, reductions in research and development expenditures critical to the success of the firm initially boost short-term profits but could be devastating to the long-term strategic position of the firm. A related shortcoming of these approaches to strategy is that the needs of people in the organization are subservient to profitability metrics. People in the organization are not treated as the most important resources (even though they frequently are told they are); instead, they frequently are targeted as an expense that can be further trimmed to nudge up short-term profits. Examples of firms in Quadrant 3 include those that have encountered major problems due to a lack of moral maturity (e.g., Adelphia, Arthur Andersen, Enron, Tyco, WorldCom) and those that have muddled through with mediocre results due in part to low productivity of the uninspired workforce (e.g., General Motors, American Airlines).

A wisdom-based approach, Quadrant 4 in Figure 4.2, focuses not only on financial reward and organizational success but also on true caring for workers and all stakeholders and improvement of society. The results of a wisdom-based approach, as fostered by spiritual organizational leaders, include employee respond characterized by increased commitment, loyalty, and motivation, all leading to greater productivity and reduced organizational withdrawal. Potential job candidates find such an organization an attractive and energizing place to work, allowing the organization to hire superior employees. Customers have a stronger attachment and loyalty to a wisdom-based organization, respecting it for trying to improve the common good. The long-term sustained health of the organization is better ensured by a wisdom-based approach because both internal and external stakeholders, including suppliers and alliance partners, value the relationship-building model fostered by this approach. Reputational advantages will also accrue, based in part on a proactive posture to be involved in one's community and to be ethically and socially responsible. For these reasons, we argue that organizations following a wisdom-based approach to strategy will be more successful in the long run than will organizations focusing only on being profitable.

Although probably no firm exhibits all of the virtues that are associated with a wisdom-based approach to strategic management, there are examples of firms that generally fit in Quadrant 4. An excellent example of a company that consistently has been in Quadrant 4 is Johnson & Johnson, which has long had a reputation of being a company based on core values of integrity and caring for others. From the early years of Robert Wood Johnson to the more recent years of James E. Burke and Ralph S. Larsen, Johnson & Johnson has benefited from strong spiritual leadership to enable the development of a value-based culture. The company's credo, a one-page statement of its values written by Johnson, provides managers with guidance on how to faithfully balance the demands of its four constituencies: customers, employees, communities, and shareholders. Burke's handling of the famous Tylenol recall case by following the principles of the credo was one example of many actions that helped to develop the company's culture. Thus, Johnson & Johnson has been successful at maintaining high levels of profit and making an impact on society over many years.

Conclusion

We have outlined the core concepts toward the development of a wisdom-based approach to strategic management. This approach overcomes the three major shortcomings of the current mainstream approaches to strategic management that we listed at the beginning of this chapter. First, a wisdom-based approach is based on the organization having a meaningful purpose for its existence beyond just maximizing profits—making a lasting impact on society. Focusing on the common good, instead of only on self-interests, is a much more powerful purpose that can promote passion in the workforce. Second, a wisdom-based approach better addresses the complexity of the strategic management decision-making process. It extends the focus of analysis from resources and tangible assets to include the understanding and judgments of the strategic decision makers. The complexities of the knowledge-based view concerning tacit and explicit knowledge are incorporated into the wisdom-based approach, but it also includes the role of moral maturity of top managers. Third, the wisdom-based approach to strategic management does not assume that strategy analysis remains at the firm level. It forces analysts to appreciate the complexity of multilevel analysis by considering the role of individuals and their relationships, the top management team, and the organization as a single entity.

However, the process of changing the strategic direction of an established firm and developing a wisdom-based approach to strategy is not an easy journey. It requires top managers to have strong convictions and moral maturity. They must have passion to make an impact on society and appreciate the significance of leaving a legacy. Executives cannot be arrogant or selfish; instead, they must seek out and embrace the wisdom of the many employees throughout their organization. Top managers must have the humility to admit that they do not have all of the answers. As stated in the Bible, "When pride comes, then comes disgrace; but wisdom is with the humble" (Proverbs 11:2 [Tyndale House, 1991]).

The development of a wisdom-based approach to strategic management also has several interesting research implications for academic scholars. First, it encourages researchers to redefine success in organizations by looking beyond routine organizational performance parameters and to develop ways to measure the impact an organization has on society. Second, it guides researchers to refocus on the strategic management process to better understand how decisions are made. It encourages the use of multilevel analyses, which would be very beneficial. Third, it forces researchers to challenge positivistic approaches to strategy. Attempts to study executive and organizational wisdom force researchers to appreciate different interpretive contexts and experiences. Clearly, research in organizational wisdom will be a very challenging endeavor. However, successful contributions in this area could have tremendous ramifications for organizations and society. It is hoped that academic researchers will have the courage to challenge the norms of the strategic management field and embrace the complexity associated with the research issues inherent in studying organizational wisdom.

Notes

1. In this chapter, we use the terms *executive* and *top manager* interchangeably, with both meant to be largely distinct from the term *manager,* which refers more broadly to a wider range of organizational responsibilities that can include first-level supervisory tasks and day-to-day operational activities. In this chapter, our focus is on those organizational members (executives or top managers) who are focused more on strategic macro-level decisions and actions.

2. Although there have been some notable stumbles (e.g., Ford Pinto safety issues, Ford Explorer rollover problems, development of highly profitable but gas-guzzling large sport utility vehicles), for most of the past century Ford has been successful in being profitable and taking positive actions to benefit society, including efforts to minimize adverse effects on the environment. It remains to be seen whether Ford's latest environment-friendly strategy will help the company return to prominence.

References

Allison, G. T. (1971). *Essence of decision making: Explaining the Cuban missile crisis.* Boston: Little, Brown.

Armstrong, T. D. (1996). Exploring spirituality: The development of the Armstrong Measure of Spirituality. In R. Jones (Ed.), *Handbook of tests and measurements for Black populations* (pp. 105–115). Hampton, VA: Cobb & Henry.

Ashmos, D. P., & Duchon, D. (2000). Spirituality at work: A conceptualization and measure. *Journal of Management Inquiry, 9*(2), 134–145.

Autry, J. (2001). *The servant leader: How to build a creative team, develop great morale, and improve bottom-line performance.* New York: Prima/Random House.

Barnard, C. I. (1938). *The functions of the executive.* Cambridge, MA: Harvard University Press.

Barney, J. (1991). Firm resources and sustained competitive advantage. *Journal of Management, 17,* 99–119.

Becker, B., & Huselid, M. (1998). High performance work systems and firm performance: A synthesis of research and managerial implications. In G. Ferris (Ed.), *Research in personnel and human resource management* (pp. 53–101). Stamford, CT: JAI.

Beyer, J. M., & Nino, D. (1998). Facing the future: Backing courage with wisdom. In S. Srivastva & D. L. Cooperrider (Eds.), *Organizational wisdom and executive courage* (pp. 65–97). San Francisco: New Lexington.

Bierly, P., & Chakrabarti, A. K. (1996). Generic knowledge strategies in the U.S. pharmaceutical industry. *Strategic Management Journal, 17,* 123–135. (Winter special issue)

Bierly, P. E., Kessler, E. H., & Christensen, E. W. (2000). Organizational learning, knowledge, and wisdom. *Journal of Organization Change Management, 13,* 596–618.

Blattberg, R. C., & Hoch, S. J. (1990). Database models and managerial intuition: 50% model + 50% manager. *Management Science, 36,* 887–900.

Bossidy, L., & Charan, R. (2004). *Confronting reality: Doing what matters to get things right.* New York: Crown Business.

Brown, J. S., & Duguid, P. (1991). Organizational learning and communities-of-practice: Toward a unified view of working, learning, and innovation. *Organization Science, 2,* 40–57.

Brown, S. L., & Eisenhardt, K. M. (1997). The art of continuous change: Linking complexity theory and time-paced evolution in relentlessly shifting organizations. *Administrative Science Quarterly, 42,* 1–34.

Burton, M. D., & O'Reilly, C. A. (2000, August). *The impact of high commitment values and practices on technology start-ups.* Paper presented at the annual meeting of the Academy of Management, Toronto, Canada.

Collins, J. C., & Porras, J. I. (1994). *Built to last: Successful habits of visionary companies*. New York: Harper Business.

Covey, S. R. (1989). *The seven habits of highly effective people*. New York: Simon & Schuster.

Covey, S. R. (1990). *Principle-centered leadership*. New York: Simon & Schuster.

Covey, S. R. (2004). *The 8th habit: From effectiveness to greatness*. New York: Free Press.

Currall, S. C., & Inkpen, A. C. (2002). A multilevel approach to trust in joint ventures. *Journal of International Business Studies, 33*, 479–495.

D'Aveni, R. A. (1994). *Hypercompetition: Managing the dynamics of strategic maneuvering*. New York: Free Press.

de Graaf, J. (2004, December 20). *Time for bread and roses* [Online]. Available: www.alternet.org/story/20786

Donaldson, T. (1982). *Corporations and morality*. Englewood Cliffs, NJ: Prentice Hall.

Dreyfus, H. L. (1990). *What is moral maturity? A phenomenological account of the development of ethical expertise* [Online]. Available: http://ist-socrates.berkeley.edu/~hdreyfus/rtf/Moral_Maturity_8_90.rtf

Erikson, E. H. (1950). *Childhood and society*. New York: Norton.

Fowler, J. W. (1981). *Stages of faith*. San Francisco: Harper & Row.

Freeman, R. E., Wicks, A. C., & Parmar, B. (2004). Stakeholder theory and "The Corporate Objective Revisited." *Organization Science, 15*, 364–369.

Fry, L. W. (2003). Toward a theory of spiritual leadership. *Leadership Quarterly, 14*, 693–727.

Gallup Organization. (2002–2003). *Religion "very important" to most Americans* [Online]. Available: www.galluppoll.com/content/?ci=20539&pg=1

Giacalone, R. A., & Jurkiewicz, C. L. (2003). *Handbook of workplace spirituality and organizational performance*. Armonk, NY: M. E. Sharpe.

Grant, R. M. (1991). The resource-based theory of competitive advantage. *California Management Review, 33*(3), 114–135.

Grant, R. M. (1996a). Prospering in dynamically-competitive environments: Organizational capability as knowledge integration. *Organization Science, 7*, 375–387.

Grant, R. M. (1996b). Toward a knowledge-based theory of the firm. *Strategic Management Journal, 17*, 109–121. (Winter special issue)

Grant, R. M. (2005). *Contemporary strategy analysis*. Malden, MA: Blackwell.

Greenleaf, R. (1977). *Servant leadership*. Mahwah, NJ: Paulist.

Hamel, G. M., & Prahalad, C. K. (1994). *Competing for the future*. Boston: Harvard Business School Press.

Hedlund, G. (1994). A model of knowledge management and N-form corporation. *Strategic Management Journal, 15*, 73–90. (Summer special issue)

Hogarth, R. M. (2001). *Educating intuition*. Chicago: University of Chicago Press.

Izzo, J., & Klein, E. (1998). The changing values of workers: Organizations must respond with soul. *Healthcare Forum Journal, 41*(3), 62–65.

Jensen, M. C. (2002). Value maximization, stakeholder theory, and the corporate objective function. *Business Ethics Quarterly, 12*, 235–256.

Khandwalla, P. N. (1998). Thorny glory: Toward organizational greatness. In S. Srivastva & D. L. Cooperrider (Eds.), *Organizational wisdom and executive courage* (pp. 157–204). San Francisco: New Lexington.

Klein, E., & Izzo, J. (1998). *Awakening corporate soul: Four paths to unleash the power of people at work*. New York: Fairwinds.

Klein, G. (2003). *Intuition at work: Why developing your gut instincts will make you better at what you do.* New York: Currency Doubleday.

Klein, K. J., Tosi, H., & Cannella, A. A. (1999). Multilevel theory building: Benefits, barriers, and new developments. *Academy of Management Review, 24,* 243–248.

Kogut, B., & Zander, U. (1992). Knowledge of the firm, combinative capabilities, and the replication of technology. *Organization Science, 3,* 383–397.

Kohlberg, L. (1969). *Stages in the development of moral thought and action.* New York: Holt, Rinehart & Winston.

Kohlberg, L. (1983). *The psychology of moral development.* New York: Harper & Row.

Kolb, D. (1984). *Experiential learning: Experience as the source of learning and development.* Englewood Cliffs, NJ: Prentice Hall.

Lennick, D., & Kiel, F. (2005). *Moral intelligence: Enhancing business performance and leadership success.* Upper Saddle River, NJ: Wharton Business Press.

Leonard-Barton, D. (1995). *Wellsprings of knowledge.* Boston: Harvard Business School Press.

Lippman, S. A., & Rumelt, R. P. (1982). Uncertain imitability: An analysis of inter-firm differences in efficiency under competition. *Bell Journal of Economics, 13,* 418–438.

Mahoney, J. T., & Pandian, J. R. (1992). The resource-based view within the conversation of strategic management. *Strategic Management Journal, 13,* 363–380.

Malan, L. C., & Kriger, M. P. (1998). Making sense of managerial wisdom. *Journal of Management Inquiry, 7,* 242–251.

March, J. G. (1991). Exploration and exploitation in organizational learning. *Organization Science, 2,* 71–87.

Marcic, D. (1997). *Managing with the wisdom of love.* San Francisco: Jossey-Bass.

Markels, A. (1995, July 3). Team approach: A power producer is intent on giving power to its people. *The Wall Street Journal,* p. A1.

Mathieson, K., & Miree, C. E. (2003). Illuminating the invisible: IT and self-discovery in the workplace. In R. A. Giacalone & C. L. Jurkiewicz (Eds.), *Handbook of workplace spirituality and organizational performance* (pp. 461–474). Armonk, NY: M. E. Sharpe.

McKnight, R. (1984). Spirituality in the workplace: Empowerment and purpose. In J. D. Adams (Ed.), *Transforming work: A collection of organizational transformation readings* (pp. 138–153). Alexandria, VA: Miles River.

McWilliams, A., & Siegel, D. (2001). Corporate social responsibility: A theory of the firm perspective. *Academy of Management Review, 26,* 117–127.

Meacham, J. A. (1990). The loss of wisdom. In R. J. Sternberg (Ed.), *Wisdom: Its nature, origins, and development* (pp. 181–211). New York: Cambridge University Press.

Merriam-Webster. (1961). *Webster's new twentieth-century dictionary of the English language, unabridged.* New York: Author.

Mitroff, I., & Denton, E. (1999). A study of spirituality in the workplace. *Sloan Management Review, 40*(4), 83–92.

Nelson, R. R. (1991). Why do firms differ, and how does it matter? *Strategic Management Journal, 12,* 61–74.

Nelson, R., & Winter, S. (1982). *An evolutionary theory of economic change.* Cambridge, MA: Harvard University Press.

Nonaka, I. (1994). A dynamic theory of organizational knowledge creation. *Organization Science, 5,* 14–37.

Peteraf, M. A. (1993). The cornerstones of competitive advantage: A resource-based view. *Strategic Management Journal, 14,* 179–191.

Pfeffer, J. (1981). *Power in organizations.* Marshfield, MA: Pitman.

Pfeffer, J. (2003). Business and the spirit: Management practices that sustain values. In R. A. Giacalone & C. L. Jurkiewicz (Eds.), *Handbook of workplace spirituality and organizational performance* (pp. 29–45). Armonk, NY: M. E. Sharpe.

Polanyi, M. (1966). *The tacit dimension.* London: Routledge & Kegan Paul.

Porter, M. (1980). *Competitive strategy.* New York: Free Press.

Porter, M. (1985). *Competitive advantage.* New York: Free Press.

Prahalad, C. K., & Hamel, G. (1990). The core competence of the corporation. *Harvard Business Review, 68*(3), 79–91.

Reed, R., & DeFillippi, R. J. (1990). Casual ambiguity, barriers to imitation, and sustainable competitive advantage. *Academy of Management Review, 15,* 88–102.

Sadler-Smith, E., & Shefy, E. (2004). The intuitive executive: Understanding and applying "gut feel" in decision-making. *Academy of Management Executive, 18*(4), 76–91.

Sanchez, R., & Mahoney, J. T. (1996). Modularity, flexibility, and knowledge management in product and organization design. *Strategic Management Journal, 17,* 63–76. (Winter special issue)

Senske, K. (2004). *Personal values: God's game plan for life.* Minneapolis, MN: Augsburg Books.

Simon, H. A. (1987). Making management decisions: The role of intuition and emotion. *Academy of Management Executive, 1*(1), 57–64.

Simon, H. A. (1991). Bounded rationality and organizational learning. *Organization Science, 2,* 125–134.

Spender, J. C. (1994). Organizational knowledge, collective practice, and Penrose rents. *International Business Review, 3,* 353–367.

Spender, J. C. (1996). Making knowledge the basis of a dynamic theory of the firm. *Strategic Management Journal, 17,* 45–62. (Winter special issue)

Sternberg, R. J. (2000). Intelligence and wisdom. In R. J. Sternberg (Ed.), *Handbook of intelligence* (pp. 631–649). New York: Cambridge University Press.

Sternberg, R. J. (2003). *Wisdom, intelligence, and creativity synthesized.* New York: Cambridge University Press.

Teece, D. J., Pisano, G., & Shuen, G. (1997). Dynamic capabilities and strategic management. *Strategic Management Journal, 18,* 509–533.

Thompson, C. M. (2000). *The congruent life: Following the inward path to fulfilling work and inspired leadership.* San Francisco: Jossey-Bass.

Tsoukas, H. (1996). The firm as a distributed knowledge system: A constructionist approach. *Strategic Management Journal, 17,* 11–25. (Winter special issue)

Tyndale House. (1991). *Life application Bible.* Wheaton, IL: Author.

Weick, K. E. (1998). The attitude of wisdom: Ambivalence as the optimal compromise. In S. Srivastva & D. L. Cooperrider (Eds.), *Organizational wisdom and executive courage* (pp. 40–64). San Francisco: New Lexington.

Weick, K. E., & Roberts, K. H. (1993). Collective mind in organizations: Heedful interrelating on flight decks. *Administrative Science Quarterly, 38,* 357–381.

Wernerfelt, B. (1984). A resource-based view of the firm. *Strategic Management Journal, 5,* 171–181.

Williams, J. R. (1992). How sustainable is your competitive advantage? *California Management Review, 34*(3), 29–51.

PART II

Ethics

5

Individual Ethics

The Virtue of Prudence

Jean M. Bartunek
Jordi Trullen

I n this chapter, we focus on practical wisdom, a characteristic proper to individuals. Practical wisdom is also called *phronesis* (Aristotle's term) or prudence (the term introduced by Thomas Aquinas that is in most use by those focusing on virtue). We do so from social science, philosophical, and theological perspectives on virtue. Practical wisdom or prudence lies in the interstices of intellectual and moral virtues—of the theoretical and the practical domains. Hence, it is very important for both management theory and management practice.

Social science findings are often of limited use when dealing with real-life problems (Flyvbjerg, 2001), and many human decisions deal with moral dilemmas. Prudence is directly pertinent to such problems and dilemmas (Statler & Roos, 2006) and responds to ambiguities in a way that traditional management science often cannot.

We begin by describing the concept of virtue and introducing some types of virtues. We situate wisdom and then practical wisdom/prudence within this discussion. We then consider examples of prudence and make some recommendations about how it may be developed.

Virtues and Practical Wisdom

There is growing attention to virtue on the part of social scientists, especially those concerned with positive psychology or positive organizational science.

AUTHORS' NOTE: We are grateful to James Bailey, James Keenan, and Eric Kessler for their helpful suggestions.

For example, Peterson and Seligman (2003) recently authored a handbook of character strengths and virtues. There was also a special issue on virtuousness in the journal *American Behavioral Scientist* (Fowers & Tjeltveit, 2003). In the introduction to that issue, Fowers and Tjeltveit (2003) suggested that although virtue is a relatively timeless topic, having been taken up in many forms during various historical eras, it is particularly timely during a period that has been convulsed by widespread corporate fraud, terrorism, and war.

Virtue ethics, an intimately related topic, has also received considerable attention recently (e.g., Fowers, 2003; McCloskey, 2006; Meara & Day, 2003; Richardson, 2003). Scholars who emphasize the importance of virtue ethics argue that, contrary to the utilitarian and Kantian approaches that have informed much modern ethical thought and that focus primarily on reason and decision making in particular situations, it is the overall quality— the overall virtuousness—of the person making ethical decisions that is most important. Thus, developing virtue in a person over the long run is particularly important for fostering ethical decisions in particular circumstances.

The Meaning of Virtue and Virtuousness

Cameron and his colleagues (Cameron, 2003; Cameron, Bright, & Caza, 2004) treated the topic of virtue from a positive organizational scholarship perspective. They associated virtuousness with what individuals and organizations strive to be when they are at their very best. They suggested that virtuous organizations enable and support virtuous activities—transcendent elevating behavior—on the part of their members. Virtuousness is associated with moral goodness, with humans' individual flourishing and moral character, and with social betterment beyond mere self-interested benefit. In fact, concern for others is a basic characteristic of prudence. Prudence includes "the ability of an agent to comprehend the distinctive nature of the other and adjust her conduct by potentially breaking the rule to satisfy the exception" (Durand & Calori, 2006, p. 99).

Cameron and his colleagues' discussion did not focus on the meanings of the particular virtues, although it alluded to them, and their depiction of virtue as transcendent elevating behavior was fairly general (Cameron, 2003; Cameron et al., 2004). More specific definitions are required, and referring to Aristotle's original definition is the appropriate place to begin.

In his *Nichomachean Ethics,* Aristotle (ca. 350 BC/2002) defined virtue as a disposition to experience passions (desires) and to perform actions in ways that lie between excess and deficiency. This is nearly a quantitative concept. Virtue is situated between too much and too little; it is present at the right time, on the right occasion, and toward the right people.

Aristotle (ca. 350 BC/2002) also claimed that human happiness consists in a life of virtuous activity; this is a primary reason why virtue is so important.

Happiness for Aristotle is not understandable without the idea of virtuous action even when this means to restrain desire or endure pain. Therefore, virtuous acts bring happiness even when they involve struggle. This is, of course, a different kind of happiness from mere hedonism (Waterman, 1993).

Based on the work of Aristotle and its later development by Thomas Aquinas, Keenan (1995) defined the task of virtue as "the acquisition and development of practices that perfect the agent into becoming a moral person while acting morally well" (p. 711). In other words, being a virtuous person occurs only if one is acting virtuously, and each of our major decisions moves us in the direction of being more virtuous or not. Virtue is in an evolving spiral with virtuous behavior; it presupposes excellence of character and fosters it. This does not mean that everyone who performs one prudent act has an excellent character. It does mean, however, that character helps to foster prudence and that prudence fosters character over the long run. This same idea is present in contemporary educational philosophy. For example, Dewey (1956) argued persuasively about the principle of continuity of experience; any experience a person faces in life modifies the person's character, and this modification affects the quality of future experiences. It does so in two ways: by affecting positive or negative attitudes toward another similar experience in the future and by modifying the person's skills or abilities to be able to grasp a new and more complex experience in the future.

Fowers and Tjeltveit (2003), speaking from a psychological perspective, added that virtuousness is learned as part of a community and that society helps to define what is worthwhile and admirable. From a virtue ethics perspective, the individual's good is always tied up with the communal good. Individuals can truly flourish only in a setting that provides adequate safety, freedom, chances for meaningful activity and self-expression, and the possibility of friendship. Thus, virtue is not solely an individual trait or accomplishment, and what virtue means in one communal context might not be identical to what it means in other contexts.

In fact, as Tsoukas and Cummings (1997) pointed out, Aristotle's conception of virtuousness is linked with a teleological view of the universe where individuals and objects are defined primarily in terms of the purposes or roles they have in society. Hence, virtuous behavior cannot be understood in a social vacuum; rather, it depends on the context in which the person is located. "A teleological understanding of human beings conceives of them not as ahistorical selves or abstract individuals (this is a much later modern invention) but as persons defined by their social, cultural and historical circumstances" (p. 670). Hence, discussing prudence involves bringing in the idea of a person's community, with all its shared conventions, norms, and standards.

In summary, there are several important aspects of virtue to consider. One is that although individual acts may reflect virtue, it is the individual person—the whole of the individual person—who is virtuous or not. Second, virtuous behavior, in theory and intent at least, makes people happy. Third, virtuousness occurs only within the context of a larger community in particular historical circumstances.

Types of Virtues

Multiple categories of virtues exist, for example, theological virtues and virtues associated with particular professions such as compassion for medical personnel, hospitality, and thoughtfulness for academics (Meara & Day, 2003). One category scheme developed by Aristotle (ca. 350 BC/2002) that is particularly important for our purposes includes intellectual and moral virtues. Aristotle divided the intellectual virtues into the theoretical or *speculative* virtues—understanding, knowledge, and wisdom—that are ordered to knowing for its own sake and the *practical* virtues that have either doing (prudence) or making (art) as their end.

Briefly, *understanding* perfects the intellect in its grasp of true principles, the *sciences* perfect the intellect in its grasp of the truths derived from those principles, and *wisdom* perfects the intellect in its grasp of the highest causes. Thus, within Aristotle's framework, wisdom is one of the intellectual virtues. It is oriented toward truth on a theoretical plane and is linked with understanding and science.

However, the presence of the intellectual virtues, including wisdom, does not guarantee their virtuous use. For example, a social scientist may deliberately misread the listed significance of a statistical test in a computer printout, thereby being deceitful about the results of a statistical analysis, or the social scientist may fail to cite particular references, thereby giving the impression of having composed something that someone else created.

For their proper use, the intellectual virtues require the virtues centered on practical activities—on things made and actions performed. *Art* is concerned with bringing something into existence and is illustrated in contemporary design approaches (e.g., Boland & Collopy, 2004). *Prudence* is concerned with deliberating well about what is good and advantageous to oneself, others, and life as a whole. It includes both a disposition and an ability to take action concerning human goods.

For Aristotle (ca. 350 BC/2002), prudence was also a moral virtue along with *temperance, courage,* and *justice.* He emphasized that the moral virtues, in contrast to the intellectual virtues, make their possessor a good person; the moral virtues cannot be used for evil purposes. For example, some people might disagree about whether acting courageously in a particular situation is good, but that does not diminish the courage shown.

The Importance of Prudence Virtues

Prudence is the link—the bridging virtue (Peterson & Seligman, 2003)—between the intellectual and moral virtues. Aristotle (350 BC/2002) insisted that "it is not possible to possess excellence in the primary sense without [prudence]" (p. 189) because prudence is the capacity to pursue what is worthwhile in a way fitting to a specific situation. Unlike the intellectual virtues, practical wisdom, or prudence, cannot be misused for evil purposes because it is closely aligned with and drives the moral virtues. It is the (sole) virtue able both to recognize the intended ends of people's natural leanings and to bring them to realization through virtuous activity; it determines what it means to act justly, temperately, and courageously in specific situations. It strives for the mean in the sense of optimal moderation between extremes of behavior (neither impulsive, rash, ill-considered, impetuous behavior nor rigid, brittle, stubborn, inflexibly rule-governed behavior) (cf. Peterson & Seligman, 2003).

The material presented here makes evident how practically important prudence is. From a philosophical perspective, it has been recognized as crucial for millennia. It is only recently, however, that in the name of prudence, phronesis, or practical wisdom, is beginning to be included in management writing (e.g., Clegg & Ross-Smith, 2003; Durand & Calori, 2006; Oliver & Roos, 2005).

But prudence is crucial in management, as three illustrations of prudence, or the lack thereof, make evident. Antonio Fazio, the governor of the Bank of Italy, has acted in several ways that have been reported to be clearly unethical and imprudent (e.g., "Please Go," 2005), including his resistance to banking reforms after the Parmalat scandal and his inappropriate intervention in bids to purchase Banca Antonveneta. Alberto Vilar ("The Man," 2003), cofounder of the U.S. fund management firm Amerindo, demonstrated a more subtle lack of prudence. He made several large philanthropic pledges that he was not able to meet, and as a result some of the recipients of his pledges needed to retract public commitments they had made. On the other hand, Robert Stiller and Green Mountain Coffee provide an illustration of prudent action ("Q&A," 2002). Green Mountain Coffee has been heavily involved with fair trade coffee in different parts of the world, especially in South America (e.g., Spragins, 2003). They are doing this partly to foster sustainability. Stiller described his motives as follows: "We help the farmers grow better coffee. We help the local environment which also helps our product. We help the community. If we have a stronger community with more services it will help our employees as well as others" ("Q&A," 2002, p. 13).

In this chapter, we hope to rectify the comparative lack of attention paid to prudence in management and organizational literature. Within the context of the crucial emphasis of prudence on seeking the good, we discuss prudence as including (a) emphasis on a specific situation rather than on general laws; (b) attention to conflicting, complex, and sometimes contradictory pulls of a situation, including decision making and action when there are not clear parameters; (c) responses as whole people, including emotions, actions, and character; and (d) importance of learning through experience.

Prudence in Management

Emphasis on a Specific Situation
Rather Than on General Laws

Prudence applies to specific situations; it cannot be expressed adequately in general laws. Just as the Greek notion of Kairos referred to understanding the right time to take some particular action (Bartunek & Necochea, 2000), prudence requires sensitivity to the right action for a particular occasion. This is an important point and a crucial distinction between the work of Aristotle and many other philosophers. McCloskey (2006), for example, described how some philosophers, such as Kant and Bentham, focused on virtue as a type of general rule applicable to all situations. But Aristotle was concerned that knowing general abstract rules often does not help someone to act in a specific situation.

Fowers (2003) argued that prudent action begins in the capacity to discern what is at stake in a given situation for the ends people seek and on a practiced acuity in focusing on the most relevant of the multiple elements of a situation in such a way that its appropriate concerns are activated. Nelson (2003) emphasized that prudent judgment needs to be sensitive to the vagaries of particular changing situations: "Anything capable of [complete] expression in sets of equations or comparable theoretical forms would be too regular, too predictable, to count as prudence" (p. 229). Similarly, Tsoukas and Cummings (1997) argued, "When facing practical matters, whether one is acting wisely or not depends on one's readiness not just to calculate the timeless demands of intellectual formulae, but also to take decisions *pros ton kairon*—that is, as the occasion requires" (p. 667). Thus, for example, philanthropic efforts that assume resources the philanthropist expects to gain, as in the case of Vilar ("The Man," 2003), are not sensitive to the right action for a particular occasion.

The kinds of situations that call forth prudent responses include tragic situations such as terrorist attacks for which it is impossible to prepare (e.g., Dutton, Frost, Worline, Lilius, & Kanov, 2002). They may include occasions in which managers must create "necessary evils" through which they cause harm to others, which they ought to do in a way that enables organizational members to handle them as well as possible (e.g., Frost, 2003; Molinsky & Margolis, 2005). They also include situations in which ethical behavior might not be of immediate benefit to the person, as in the case of Fazio and the Bank of Italy ("Please Go," 2005).

Prudence is also a matter of everyday affairs; common daily problems often require it. Gosling and Mintzberg (2003) argued that companies need "down-to-earth" managers with good knowledge of the self, of one's relationships and their context, and of how to undertake action sensibly in addition to analytical thinking skills. In a brief letter to those with masters of business administration (MBAs), Mintzberg and Sacks (2004) argued that management depends considerably on craft and art and that these are acquired by experience. Management requires attention to small details, to local contexts, and to different worldviews (Gosling & Mintzberg, 2003).

The ability to take action that responds appropriately to a particular situation may be seen in the actions of expert professionals (Schön, 1983). Halverson (2004) illustrated such knowledge on the part of effective school administrators who rely on their sense of the local situations to determine, for example, which teachers would be best for dealing with specific concerns that arise. Stiller and Green Mountain Coffee seem to be demonstrating it with regard to coffee growing in poor parts of the world ("Q&A," 2002). Schön's (1983) experts have a repertoire of known situations and knowledge of how to deal with them. These guiding principles (Oliver & Roos, 2005) are mainly tacit and are acquired from experience and from repeatedly hearing other experts' stories about dealing with similar situations (Orr, 1996). This does not mean that people who act prudently ignore general laws. Rather, as Flyvbjerg (2001) suggested, prudence involves the capacity to flip back and forth between the requirements of a local situation and more general laws applicable to many situations.

Attention to Conflicting, Complex, and Sometimes Contradictory Pulls of a Situation, Including Decision Making and Action When There Are Not Clear Parameters

In many situations that decision makers face, there is not one clear good decision. There are multiple considerations, and some of these are contradictory; pursuing one aim may undermine or compromise efforts to attain others. Prudence is associated with recognizing the contradictory characteristics of a situation (Hariman, 2003) and, to the extent possible and appropriate, achieving its multiple and contradictory objectives. In fact, prudence is most likely to be called for in situations that are conflicting, complex, and contradictory. In situations that are unambiguous, it is much easier to determine the best way to act.

In his definition of practical wisdom, Sternberg (1998) referred to the need to balance interpersonal and extrapersonal interests, over both the short and long terms, as well as to achieve a balance among adapting to existing environments, shaping them, and selecting new environments. Durand and Calori (2006) asserted that prudence includes the capacity to truly distinguish the concerns of the self from the concerns of others. Prudence involves the ability to deal with complexity on multiple levels, including distinguishing between one's own and others' interests and attending to multiple aims and interests.

There have been similar discussions by others. Russell (1995) argued that wisdom lies in the "capacity to take account of all the important factors in a problem and to attach to each its due weight" (p. 160), even in very complex and contradictory situations, and Weick (2003) suggested that to act with wisdom is to be wary of simplicity and to both acknowledge and doubt what is known. People who exemplify prudence are able to deal with multiple goals and to hold and combine them in ways that are productive as well as possible in a given situation. Peterson and Seligman (2003) described prudent individuals as capable of harmonizing "the multiple goals and interests that motivate them, forming these into a stable, coherent, and unconflicted form of life" (p. 478). Baltes and Kunzmann (2004) showed that wisdom's functional consequences involve praxis-related behaviors: judgment, advice, and commentary in difficult and uncertain matters of life and life conduct. They also argued that achieving a coordination of the personal and common good is fundamental to wisdom.

This type of decision making differs considerably from the types of research-based prescriptions that academics are often most able to make. The findings of academic studies often lead to primarily linear sets of prescriptions, although these may sometimes include explicitly articulated contingencies (e.g., the path–goal theory of leadership). However, what we have been discussing are situations in which straightforward prescriptions are inadequate for guiding behavior.

When analyzing the reflection-in-action patterns of successful professionals, Schön (1983) realized that part of their artistry consisted in their seemingly effortless ability "to hold several ways of looking at things at once without disrupting the flow of inquiry" (p. 130). Thus, in one of his examples, an architecture student has a problem that involves apparently conflicting elements. On the one hand, there is the shape of the building she wants to create; on the other hand, the shape of the ground where the building is supposed to fit but does not seem to do so. Schön showed how the teacher—the expert architect—starts trying out different small changes in the design through several mental "what if" experiments. Some of these experiments seem to "work" somewhat, and some do not. The mental experiments are justified by the eventual discovery that a particular new geometry "works slightly with the contours"; yields pleasant nooks, views, and soft back areas; and evokes in the situation the potential for a new coherence (p. 95).

Schön's (1983) description suggested several ideas for how prudent behavior in complex situations may be enacted. First, when there are multiple goals or when essential elements conflict, people who are prudent try out new designs or frames to see what happens. This is similar to contemporary design approaches proposing that people try out various solutions to problems rather than assuming that one is completely correct, especially on the first try (e.g., Romme, 2003; van Aken, 2004). Second, Schön showed how the expert is able to try out new designs by relaxing the requisite of fitting the building on the slope completely. When multiple goals or values are present, the expert has the ability to temporarily weaken some goals and give priority to others to see what happens. Third, it is important to have an overarching value, that is, a recognition of the good appropriate to this situation that guides experimentation with the different ideas.

The ability to see situations in new ways that allow the combination of multiple conflicting goals is useful not only in dealing with professional practice problems but also, and perhaps more important, in dealing with other humans. Russell (1995) emphasized this in the following example:

> Consider the case of two men, Mr. A and Mr. B, who hate each other and, through mutual hatred, bring each other to destruction. Suppose you go to Mr. A and say, "Why do you hate Mr. B?" He will no doubt give you an appalling list of Mr. B's vices, partly true, partly false. And now suppose you go to Mr. B. He will give you an exactly similar list of Mr. A's vices with an equal admixture of truth and falsehood. Suppose you now come back to Mr. A and say, "You will be surprised to learn that Mr. B says the same things about you as you say about him," and you go to Mr. B and make a similar speech. The first effect, no doubt, will be to increase their mutual hatred, since each will be so horrified by the other's injustice. But perhaps, if you have sufficient patience and sufficient persuasiveness, you may succeed in convincing each that the other has only the normal share of human wickedness, and that their enmity is harmful to both. If you can do this, you will have instilled some fragment of wisdom. (p. 161)

Responses to Complex Situations as Whole People, Including Emotions, Actions, and Character

The previous two sections considered characteristics of situations in which prudence is called for and illustrations of what prudence might mean in such situations. As we noted earlier, however, it is important to consider the person as well as individual acts.

Some psychologists have advocated that what distinguishes wise individuals from others is their ability to integrate aspects of cognition, affection, and conation in their judgments (Orwoll & Perlmutter, 1990; Pascual-Leone, 1990). For Aristotle and others, prudence, or practical wisdom, is embodied in character. Durand and Calori (2006) focused on people who are practically wise, that is, who do not just act wise in one particular situation. In other words, prudence involves not solely intellectual or cognitive approaches to a particular situation; it includes emotions and character as well. An assumption of some philosophers (e.g., Plato) that reason is sufficient for ethical decision making is highly questionable (McCloskey, 2006). It ignores multiple other dimensions of human experience that affect behavior.

Fowers (2003) emphasized that emotional responses are central to virtue, and this is particularly the case with regard to the moral sensibilities required for prudence. Experiencing the feelings that are appropriate in a given situation is a mark of virtue. Consistent with his emphasis on virtue as the "mean," Aristotle (ca. 350 BC/2002) stated that emotions may be felt both too much and too little—and in both cases not well. But to feel them at the right times, with reference to the right objects, toward the right people, with the right motive, and in the right way, is what is both intermediate and best, and this is characteristic of virtue (see also Fowers, 2003). This is particularly important when we are assessing a complex situation (e.g., Seo, Barrett, & Bartunek, 2004); emotions will have strong impacts on our judgment about it.

Intellect and emotions are necessary, but not sufficient, for prudence. Durand and Calori (2006) presented a lengthy discussion of people who are practically wise. The characteristics of such people include the ability to comprehend the distinct nature of other people and to act accordingly. Practically wise people are also characterized by moral exemplarity and reciprocity; that is, they are able to recognize others' judgments as of value and subsume their own goals and actions under others' abilities to accept them.

Importance of Learning From Experience

People are not born with prudence. As Halverson (2004) noted, the skills associated with prudence need to be learned and practiced, and only then will they become habits manifested in action.

Developing excellence of character includes, as noted earlier, complex understanding, affective awareness, and strength of character. These require considerable experience. But experience alone is not enough. Excellence of character also requires a self-reflective capacity through which agents can consider the degree to which they are acting for the right reasons (Fowers, 2003). These kinds of learning may be facilitated by mentoring (e.g., Baltes & Kunzmann, 2004) from someone already skilled in the virtue. They may also be facilitated by hearing stories of situations where practical wisdom is lived out, accompanied by descriptions of carefully developed guiding principles (McCloskey, 2006; Oliver & Roos, 2005).

Stories and the academic use of them in case studies may be helpful in learning prudence. However, Sternberg (1998) noted that training that goes beyond case studies may be necessary; case studies do not require the student to be emotionally involved with the situation, a feature that is needed for practical wisdom to be acquired and practiced.

Statler, Roos, and Victor's (2006) work with the Center for Catastrophe Preparedness and Response (CCPR) illustrates this very well. The CCPR was created at New York University as a response to the 9/11 catastrophe in 2001. Its mandate was to analyze best practices in preparedness and response and to develop case studies and training materials for emergency personnel nationwide. The authors showed how the CCPR soon realized that, despite the fact that the detailed analysis of the causes of past events such as 9/11 were relevant to prevent the occurrence of future ones, training aimed at increasing preparedness in the eventuality of a future catastrophe of the same magnitude also needed a more integrated approach with real simulations. These would require decisions made on the spot and under emotional pressure. Experiential learning, whether direct or virtual, is particularly valuable for developing prudence.

Best Practices for, and Illustrations of, Practical Wisdom in Action

We have proposed that prudence has at least four important features, namely that (a) it responds to the demands of a complex situation; (b) it is activated when there are conflicting, complex, and sometimes contradictory pulls; (c) it includes the whole person, including intellect, emotions, actions, and personal character; and (d) it is learned (or not) over time. Here we provide some examples that are pertinent to each of these features.

We have already referred to some of Schön's (1983) illustrations of prudence in practice. We use a more extended example here. Schön described how Dean Wilson, a traditionally trained industrial systems engineer, tried to use some of his knowledge on process flow models to tackle the issue of malnourishment while working at a university in Colombia. His original use of the process flow model, where he conducted analyses using the model to convince others, was a failure. After this experience, Wilson "began to conceive of the nutrient flow model not as a general technique of diagnosis for use by outside experts but as a framework of analysis with which community residents could set and solve their own problems of malnourishment" (p. 195). He then started teaching the basic logic of nutrient flow models and the logic of experimenting to a group of high school students so that they could bring these same ideas into their communities.

In this brief example, Wilson adapted his abstract knowledge to a particular context that was very far from the traditional contexts to which he had been accustomed, and he did so through an original framing of the problem he was addressing. Rather than imposing his knowledge on others, he taught them the necessary skills to apply the knowledge themselves. His work illustrates reciprocity, one of the characteristics of prudence (Durand & Calori, 2006). He showed sensitivity to the community problems beyond his own self-interest.

Schön (1983) also gave an example of nonprudent behavior. He described a town planner whose job was to review proposals submitted by private developers. Schön provided the discussion that the town planner had with one of these developers who wanted to remodel an apartment building he owned. In the discussion, the town planner tried by all means to force the developer to accept all of the conditions that the town planner had in mind but that he never disclosed in the conversation. The town planner's role was supposed to be based on giving advice, but he was concerned only with maintaining his reputation and trying to make as few concessions as possible to the developer. If the town planner had wanted to act prudently, he would have attempted to work with the developer to balance the developer's legitimate claims and the city's regulations and needs. However, he did not do this.

Durand and Calori (2006) provided two additional contrasting examples of prudence in their comparisons of how executives of two major American airlines, United Airlines and Southwest Airlines, reacted in the aftermath of the 9/11 catastrophe. Southwest, faithful to its policy of no layoffs, started a program collectively organized by employees in which workers worked and contributed to a pool of hours for free so that no one was forced to leave the company. In contrast, United paid $35 million to three retiring executives and laid off 12,000 employees. United's chief executive officer declared that 9/11 allowed the airline to downsize in ways that would have been impossible otherwise. Durand and Calori noted that whereas Southwest's response illustrated reciprocity and moral exemplarity, United's response did not. Southwest recovered in less than a year, whereas United declared bankruptcy in 2003. Implicitly, Durand and Calori suggested that acting prudently may bring benefits in the long term, even if doing so may be more risky in the short term.

Flyvbjerg (2001, 2002) offered another example of prudence. His example is based on his own research on a major urban renewal project in Aalborg, Denmark. The project was intended to remodel the historic city center and make it solely pedestrian, radically improving environmental protection and enhancing public transport. Flyvbjerg's research indicated that the plan had a good chance of accomplishing these aims. However, the local aldermen privately opposed the project, fearing that it would reduce shopping in the area. When Flyvbjerg took initiative to challenge the aldermen publicly, they in turn challenged the ability of his data to support his claims. He submitted his data for scrutiny to the aldermen, who soon apologized. Flyvbjerg (2001) argued that researchers who are striving to be prudent sometimes need to take sides on the part of those with less power in a situation if the situation demands it.

In both the airline and Aalborg examples, one or more people acting prudently tried to attend to the different interests and pulls of their situations in creative ways that aimed at fostering the overall good of their communities. In neither case did being aware of the complexity of the situation lead to inaction. Rather, it involved taking appropriate action based on values of solidarity and common good.

Acting prudently is not without risks. Flyvbjerg (2001) described how the aldermen tried to publicly discredit his work. In Wilson's case (Schön, 1983), the community valued his teaching methods positively until his students started questioning a mayor's policy initiative. At that point, the local coffee planters started complaining about what was being taught to the students and tried to stop Wilson's work.

These actions and the responses they elicit help to highlight the moral dimension of prudence. In conversation, prudence is often linked with terms such as *realistic, personal cautiousness,* and *social conformity.* People sometimes use the term to rationalize inaction or to justify flagrant self-interest or rank careerism. These meanings are not, however, consistent with prudence as a virtue and as a crucial link between the intellectual and moral virtues.

We finish this section with another example from a business case. Statler and Roos (2006) discussed the consultant facilitation of two retreats in a multinational company that was attempting to start a major strategic change initiative. The objectives of the change were to increase coordination among different departments and to achieve a more global vision among country managers that shifted from a self-centered focus on sales to a general management perspective.

Although a strategic reorientation was much needed and the will to try to change self-interested behaviors into more interpersonal ones was very much in line with prudence, the change was not successful. Statler and Roos (2006) argued that although the change purpose was practically wise, the way in which it was carried out was not: "It was a top-down effort, designed by consultants who did not work for the organization, and presented to the . . . employees just like all other strategic efforts: something that they had to comply with and support sooner rather than later." This example shows that a good purpose for a change is not enough to consider it as practically wise; how actions are carried out is a crucial component.

_____ Additional Thoughts on Acquiring Prudence

In our previous discussion, we suggested several ways a person can develop prudence. The most cited source of practical wisdom is reflected-on experience. In addition, dialogue and discussion of case studies, narratives of prudent behaviors, and experiential learning all are appropriate (Clegg & Ross-Smith, 2003; McCloskey, 2006; Sternberg, 2001). We build a bit on that discussion here.

Aristotle (ca. 350 BC/2002) considered that only aged people could be wise. In the *Nichomachean Ethics,* he stated that "the objects of wisdom also include particulars, which come to be known through experience, and a young person is not an experienced one; for it is quantity of time that provides experience" (p. 183).

Since Aristotle, it has been more recognized that not all experiences are truly educative in terms of prudence and that age alone does not guarantee its development. Psychologists point to the quality of experiences and, more important, to how the individual faces these experiences as being more important for wisdom than age alone. Peterson and Seligman (2003), for example, noted that "studies have largely failed to find age-related differences in self-ratings of wisdom among individuals . . . or in wisdom-related performance"; rather, the development of perspective in individuals "is a function . . . of life experiences and how people respond to them" (p. 189).

The idea that the type of experience is key to prudence finds grounding also in the works of Dewey (1956) and Schön (1983). According to Dewey (1956), only those experiences that lead to growth are truly educative (or, in our context, conducive to prudence). Dewey's criterion for whether an experience is conducive to learning or not is how the following question is answered: "Does this form of growth create conditions for further growth, or does it set up conditions that shut off the person who has grown in this direction from the occasions, stimuli, and opportunities for continuing growth in new directions?" (p. 36). Dewey used the example of a burglar. It is clear that one can grow as a burglar, but this will shut off growth as a person in other directions.

Even practitioners who exhibit artistry in how they deal with situations engage in continuous learning. In his analysis of practitioners' interactions with novices in search of advice, Schön (1983) showed that expert practitioners have a "repertoire of examples, images, understandings, and actions" (p. 140) that allow them to see a unique case as something both familiar and unfamiliar at the same time. To some extent, experts approach problems by seeing them as situations already present in their repertoires, even though each situation has some unique features that will add to their existing repertoires. Schön stated, "Reflection-in-action in a unique case may be generalized to other cases, not by giving rise to general principles, but by contributing to the practitioner's repertoire of exemplary themes and guiding principles (Oliver & Roos, 2005) from which, in the subsequent cases of his practice, he may compose new variations" (p. 140).

The fact that experts have been in touch with many different kinds of unique situations in the past gives them a special sensitivity for seeing old patterns in unique cases and for quickly associating certain responses with them. To develop practical wisdom, novices should approach as many unique cases as possible to build their own repertoires. They also need to be free to creatively experiment with solutions to problems that are based on analogous experiences they have had in the past.

Dewey (1956) suggested that it is the obligation of more mature or wise individuals to use their greater insight in organizing the experiences of those they mentor. This does not mean an imposition of the personal values and goals of the mentor; rather, it means the provision of some structure and guidance so that apprentices develop their own professional personalities, so to speak. Such an approach to mentoring is an illustration of prudence.

Prudence and Academic Work

Can the work of academics help other people to develop practical wisdom? Most knowledge linked to prudence is tacit (Sternberg, 1998), and most knowledge produced by academics is a combination of different types of explicit knowledge, even including writing for practitioner journals (Rynes, Bartunek, & Daft, 2001). Thus, it is possible to conclude that academia has little to offer, as it stands, for practical wisdom. Nelson (2003), for example, argued that few academic accounts generate the narrative drive to probe the details of plausible characters in complicated settings and that, rather, stories do a better job of this. Detective stories in particular provide models of navigating complex situations in narrative form.

For prudence to be addressed adequately in management research, it would be helpful for academics to pay more attention to the work of practitioners so as to understand how they approach the dilemmas they encounter. Oliver and Roos's (2005) article is a good illustration of this, as is Schön's (1983) work. In addition, if academics want to pay more research attention to how prudence may be manifested in practice, it might be necessary to expand on some of the language traditionally used in scientific publications. Prudence is evoked in messy situations, and attempts to portray it as a clear-cut construct that can be easily generalized and operationalized in such settings are limited in their impacts on practice. More ethnographic research that contributes thick descriptions (e.g., Oliver & Roos, 2005) may be particularly useful. Moreover, skillful understanding of situational nuances may be something that managers can help researchers to learn.

Finally, what about our own actions as management scholars? Flyvbjerg (2001) suggested that social scientists are, on average, no more astute or ethical than anyone else. What might it mean for us as academics to act with practical wisdom in our own profession, especially our own teaching, instead of limiting ourselves to studying what practical wisdom means for others? Meara and Day (2003) discussed this issue for psychology professors. They commented, "The subject matter of psychology is often not only uncertain but also personal and thus very meaningful to students. What is said or written can be easily misunderstood, inappropriately overgeneralized to others, or mistakenly singularized to self" (p. 467). They described several approaches that professors should take to teaching, including being careful about the strategies they take to present sensitive subjects and tactfully answering questions that deal with misunderstandings. Meara and Day also described boundary issues of which psychology professors should be aware. For example, in discussions of mental illness, they should take care that students are not revealing personal or family information in a way that may prove to be embarrassing.

We management professors also end up dealing with delicate topics in our classrooms. We may deal with issues about which students as persons feel very sensitive, perhaps especially in diversity classes. We may deal with sensitive issues about the organizations or occupations in which students or their family members work, or groups in which they are carrying out projects. Professors' awareness of the kinds of classroom situations that call for prudence and attempts to handle such complex situations with prudence may help to make us more sensitive to the prudent activity of others.

In addition to how we act in class, as management researchers we may be called to deal with values issues in our own research. These might have to do with, among other things, what we choose to study, the perspective we take on what we are studying, and what we do with the findings of our research.

Flyvbjerg (2001) provided one template for researchers who want to be aware of the practical wisdom of their own research. This template includes asking three key questions (p. 364):

1. Where are we going?

2. Is this development desirable?

3. What, if anything, should we do about it?

These questions direct researchers not to conduct value neutral research but rather to focus their work on values and attention to what is desirable, with the hope that one outcome of the research can "increase the capacity of employees and managers to think and act in value-rational terms" (p. 367).

Conclusion

In this chapter, we have considered prudence within a context of virtue. Treating it in this way has made evident that wisdom, especially wisdom expressed in action, has a moral dimension, something that many discussions of wisdom ignore. This moral dimension is crucial for giving guidance to wisdom considered solely as an intellectual trait.

In other words, wisdom has a practical side, one that goes by the name of prudence. It is important for practitioners and academics alike, not only for work and research purposes but also as a guide for how to live.

References

Aristotle. (2002). *Nichomachean ethics* (C. Rowe, Trans.). Oxford, UK: Oxford University Press. (Original work written ca. 350 BC)

Baltes, P., & Kunzmann, U. (2004). The two faces of wisdom: Wisdom as a general theory of knowledge and judgment about excellence in mind and virtue vs. wisdom as everyday realization in people and products. *Human Development, 47,* 290–299.

Bartunek, J., & Necochea, R. (2000). Old insights and new times: Kairos, Inca cosmology, and their contributions to contemporary management inquiry. *Journal of Management Inquiry, 9,* 103–113.

Boland, R., & Collopy, F. (Eds.). (2004). *Managing as designing.* Stanford, CA: Stanford University Press.

Cameron, K. S. (2003). Organizational virtuousness and performance. In K. S. Cameron, J. E. Dutton, & R. E. Quinn (Eds.), *Positive organizational scholarship* (pp. 48–65). San Francisco: Berrett-Koehler.

Cameron, K. S., Bright, D., & Caza, A. (2004). Exploring the relationships between organizational virtuousness and performance. *American Behavioral Scientist, 47*, 766–790.

Clegg, S. R., & Ross-Smith, A. (2003). Revising the boundaries: Management education and learning in a postpositivist world. *Academy of Management Learning and Education, 2*, 85–98.

Dewey, J. (1956). *Experience and education.* New York: Macmillan.

Durand, R., & Calori, R. (2006). Sameness, otherness: Enriching organizational change theories with philosophical considerations on the same and the other. *Academy of Management Review, 31*, 93–114.

Dutton, J. E., Frost, P., Worline, M. C., Lilius, J. M., & Kanov, J. M. (2002, January). Leading in times of trauma. *Harvard Business Review, 80*, 54–62.

Flyvbjerg, B. (2001). *Making social science matter.* Cambridge, UK: Cambridge University Press.

Flyvbjerg, B. (2002). Bringing power to planning research: One researcher's praxis story. *Journal of Planning Education and Research, 21*, 353–366.

Fowers, B. J. (2003). Reason and human finitude. *American Behavioral Scientist, 47*, 415–426.

Fowers, B. J., & Tjeltveit, A. C. (2003). Virtue obscured and retrieved. *American Behavioral Scientist, 47*, 387–394.

Frost, P. J. (2003). *Toxic emotions at work: How compassionate managers handle pain and conflict.* Boston: Harvard Business School Press.

Gosling, J., & Mintzberg, H. (2003, November). The five minds of a manager. *Harvard Business Review, 81*, 54–64.

Halverson, R. (2004). Assessing, documenting, and communicating practical wisdom. *American Journal of Education, 111*, 90–121.

Hariman, R. (Ed.). (2003). *Prudence: Classical virtue, postmodern practice.* University Park: Pennsylvania State University Press.

Keenan, J. F. (1995). Proposing cardinal virtues. *Theological Studies, 56*, 709–729.

The man who gave too much. (2003, September 13). *The Economist*, p. 60.

McCloskey, D. (2006). *The bourgeois virtues: Ethics for an age of commerce.* Chicago: University of Chicago Press.

Meara, N. M., & Day, J. D. (2003). Possibilities and challenges for academic psychology. *American Behavioral Scientist, 47*, 459–478.

Mintzberg, H., & Sacks, D. (2004, June). The MBA menace. *Fast Company*, pp. 31–32.

Molinsky, A., & Margolis, J. (2005). Necessary evils and interpersonal sensitivity in organizations. *Academy of Management Review, 30*, 245–268.

Nelson, J. S. (2003). Prudence as republican politics in American popular culture. In R. Hariman (Ed.), *Prudence: Classical virtue, postmodern practice* (pp. 229–257). University Park: Pennsylvania State University Press.

Oliver, D., & Roos, J. (2005). Decision-making in high-velocity environments: The importance of guiding principles. *Organization Studies, 26*, 889–913.

Orr, J. (1996). *Talking about machines: An ethnography of a modern job.* Ithaca, NY: ILR Press.

Orwoll, L., & Perlmutter, M. (1990). The study of wise persons: Integrating a personality perspective. In R. J. Sternberg (Ed.), *Wisdom: Its nature, origins, and development* (pp. 160–177). Cambridge, UK: Cambridge University Press.

Pascual-Leone, J. (1990). An essay on wisdom: Toward organismic processes that make it possible. In R. J. Sternberg (Ed.), *Wisdom: Its nature, origins, and development* (pp. 244–278). Cambridge, UK: Cambridge University Press.

Peterson, C., & Seligman, M. E. P. (2003). *Character strengths and virtues: A handbook and classification.* Washington, DC: American Psychological Association.

Please go, Mr. Fazio. (2005, August 13). *The Economist,* pp. 13–14.

Q&A: Robert Stiller and Green Mountain Coffee. (2002, January 10). *Vermont Business Magazine,* pp. 10–17.

Richardson, F. C. (2003). Virtue, ethics, dialogue, and reverence. *American Behavioral Scientist, 47,* 442–458.

Romme, A. G. L. (2003). Making a difference: Organization as design. *Organization Science, 14,* 558–573.

Russell, B. (1995). *Portraits from memory and other essays.* Nottingham, UK: Spokesman.

Rynes, S., Bartunek, J. M., & Daft, R. L. (2001). Across the great divide: Knowledge creation and transfer between practitioners and academics. *Academy of Management Journal, 44,* 340–355.

Schön, D. A. (1983). *The reflective practitioner.* New York: Basic Books.

Seo, M., Barrett, L. F., & Bartunek, J. M. (2004). The role of affective experience in work motivation. *Academy of Management Review, 29,* 423–439.

Spragins, E. (2003, July 1). The three-peat: A Vermont coffee wholesaler is one of only four companies that have made the list three years in a row. *Fortune Small Business,* pp. 68–69. Available: http://money.cnn.com/magazines/fsb/fsb_archive/2003/07/01/347341/index.htm

Statler, M., & Roos, J. (2006). Reframing strategic preparedness: An essay on practical wisdom. *International Journal of Management Concepts and Philosophy, 2,* 99–117.

Statler, M., Roos, J., & Victor, B. (2006). Illustrating the need for practical wisdom. *International Journal of Management Concepts and Philosophy, 2,* 1–30.

Sternberg, R. J. (1998). A balance theory of wisdom. *Review of General Psychology, 2,* 347–365.

Sternberg, R. J. (2001). Why schools should teach for wisdom: The balance theory of wisdom in educational settings. *Educational Psychologist, 36,* 227–245.

Tsoukas, H., & Cummings, S. (1997). Marginalization and recovery: The emergence of neo-Aristotelian themes in management theory. *Organization Studies, 18,* 655–683.

van Aken, J. E. (2004). Management research based on the paradigm of the design sciences: The quest for field-tested and grounded technological rules. *Journal of Management Studies, 41,* 219–247.

Waterman, A. S. (1993). Two conceptions of happiness: Contracts of personal expressiveness (eudaimonian) and hedonic enjoyment. *Journal of Personality and Social Psychology, 64,* 678–691.

Weick, K. E. (2003). Positive organizing foreshadowed in organizational tragedies. In K. S. Cameron, J. E. Dutton, & R. E. Quinn (Eds.), *Positive organizational scholarship: Foundations of a new discipline* (pp. 66–80). San Francisco: Berrett-Koehler.

6

Interpersonal Ethics

The Wise Negotiator

Roy J. Lewicki

Writing a chapter on negotiation for a handbook of wisdom is an interesting challenge. Negotiation is normally not an area where people "search" for wisdom. In fact, most people assume that the best way to negotiate can be inferred from "tough" negotiators who they know intimately—the grandmother who negotiated a great price when she sold the family homestead, the father who negotiated a good price on a new SUV, or the labor leader who brags on television about his negotiating skills in securing a new union contract. The "wisdom" we often gain about how to negotiate is based on what we think we can learn from those who have boasted about their success. However, these success stories are often reflective of a competitive negotiating style in which the storyteller claims great economic victory; what is less clear is how that victory was achieved and what costs the other party may have incurred at the expense of the victor's domination.

There is actually a great deal of wisdom to be learned about the negotiation process. This wisdom is reflected in those who negotiate "for a living" (Benoliel, 2005; Saunders, 1999), those who write about the negotiation process (Fisher, Ury, & Patton, 1991; Shell, 1999), and those who summarize the extensive research that has been done on negotiations over the past 40 years (e.g., Lewicki, Saunders, & Barry, 2006). The purpose of this chapter is to summarize that wisdom for the reader. As with many tidbits of "wisdom," some points may be exceedingly obvious, whereas other points may be very nonobvious. In offering this wisdom, I seek to enlighten the reader to some of the intricacies of the negotiation process and offer advice not only on how to do negotiation well but also on how to become a wise negotiator.

The Ethical Grounding of the Wise Negotiator

Many of the other chapters in this volume grapple with the important question of defining wisdom and setting its context. For example, Jordan and Sternberg (this volume) suggest that wisdom is

> the ability to use one's successful intelligence, creativity, and knowledge, as mediated by personal values, to reach a common good by balancing intrapersonal, interpersonal, and extrapersonal interests over the short and long terms to adapt to, shape, and select environments. (chap. 1, based on Sternberg, 1998)

As I point out in this chapter, this definition could also stand as a definition of wise negotiating—reaching "a common good by balancing intrapersonal, interpersonal, and extrapersonal interests over the short and long terms." Much of what I offer in this chapter addresses the intelligence, creativity, and knowledge components, so it is important here to begin by establishing the ethical/values foundation for that development.

Crampton and Dees (1993) noted that "in an ideal world, people would simply do the right thing simply because it is right" (p. 361). However, in our less-than-ideal world, a number of pressures make morally "right" decisions more complex. People often do not agree about what the right thing is. Moreover, even when they do agree, moral standards and ideals—their obligations to others—conflict with concerns for personal self-interest. This gap between the demands of "doing the right thing" (ethics) and the pressures for the protection and advancement of self-interest (opportunism) creates problems for individuals and societies. At the individual level, there may be incentives to either pursue opportunism or constrain desperation. Problems of opportunism arise "when individuals willingly violate ethical norms in order to pursue opportunities for private gain" (p. 361). Problems of desperation arise when individuals also willingly violate norms, intending to avoid personal loss. Philosophers use the phrase "weakness of the will" to explain situations in which educated and moral individuals are tempted to compromise their ethical standards.

In interpersonal situations, the tensions between opportunism and desperation are magnified by a second problem: the parties' expectations for trust and fair play. If a party can expect that the other is trustworthy and will not engage in opportunistic behavior that will abuse or violate that trust, it is "safe" to behave ethically (for one review of trust dynamics see Lewicki, 2006b). Conversely, if a party is suspicious of the other party, he or she will expect that the other party will engage in opportunistic tactics to profit from the situation, and hence it may be necessary to engage in comparable "defensive" tactics, if only to ensure that the other party does not gain advantage. Parallel dynamics are likely to occur with regard to perceptions of whether the other party will follow the implicit rules of "fair play," given that judgments of fairness and justice closely parallel judgments of trust and trustworthiness (for one review, see Lewicki, Wiethoff, & Tomlinson, 2005).

Negotiation is an interesting context in which to observe the interplay and tensions between prescriptive rules for how one "ought" to behave and the pressures of opportunism, desperation, and maximization of self-interest. Lax and Sebenius (1986) defined negotiation as "a process of potentially opportunistic interaction by which two or more parties, with some apparent conflict, seek to do better through jointly decided action than they could otherwise" (p. 11). Lewicki and colleagues (2006) defined a negotiation situation as having the following parameters:

1. There are two or more parties who are interdependent.

2. There is a conflict of interest between the parties.

3. The parties attempt to use one or more forms of influence to obtain a larger share of the "object of interest" in the conflict than they could achieve if they simply accepted what the other side would give them voluntarily.

4. The parties expect that there will be some modification or change in their influence strategies through a process of "give-and-take," or concession making, as they develop an agreement to resolve their conflict of interest.

These definitional components infer that in their efforts to define and achieve a resolution to their conflict, as well as to maximize their own outcomes, each party must make the best possible case for his or her preferred solution and will also likely to attempt to move his or her opponent away from the opponent's preferred solution.[1] Thus, in this context, the conditions are ripe (a) for one or both parties to seek solutions that maximize private gain and act opportunistically, (b) for one or both parties to be concerned about the possibility of private loss and hence behave desperately, (c) for one or both parties to not trust the other party, and/or (d) for one or both parties to not expect that the other party will be committed to complying with the rules of fair play. Hence, negotiation is a rich social context in which to study ethical decision making.

Ethicists are not the only ones to note that negotiation offers an interesting context in which to study ethical conduct. The noted social psychologist Harold Kelley (1966), in his early research on negotiation, observed that effective negotiation requires the actor to resolve several key "dilemmas." Two of his fundamental dilemmas, those of honesty and openness, are central to the question of ethical decision making in negotiation:

> Inasmuch as information must at least appear to be exchanged in order that bargaining activity remain viable, each party is confronted with the problem of deciding how frank or deceitful to be. Being completely frank

may commit one to a position from which it is difficult to move at a later time. Moreover, to be frank in the face of a deceptive or exploitative other is to risk exploitation by him. There are thus real advantages to be gained by concealing information that could be turned against oneself at a later time. . . . On the other hand, each party must be able to convince the other that he is being honest and open about his position. . . . To sustain the bargaining relationship, each party must select a middle course between the extremes of complete openness toward, and total deception of, the other. Each must be able to convince the other of his integrity while not at the same time endangering his bargaining position. (Kelley, 1966, p. 60)

According to this view, therefore, negotiators *always* must address, in one manner or another, a decision about how open and honest they can "afford" to be. A negotiator cannot be completely honest and open without disclosing all of his or her confidential information and perhaps giving away his or her power to influence or persuade the other; in contrast, a negotiator cannot be completely silent about his or her preferences and still achieve an agreement or be completely deceptive about his or her intentions and still maintain some modicum of an effective relationship with the other party. These two dilemmas are the ethical Scylla and Charybdis of negotiation: to avoid complete honesty and not give away one's negotiating power but also to avoid complete dishonesty and preclude the ability of the parties to reach agreement or to work together in the future.

Research on how negotiators view what is ethically appropriate conduct reveals some remarkable consensus (e.g., Barry, Fulmer, & Long, 2000; Lewicki & Robinson, 1998). As noted earlier, the ethical decisions in negotiation are largely about standards of truth telling and lying—how honest and candid a negotiator should be. Thus, the emphasis is on what negotiators say (what they communicate), or the intentions they communicate, rather than on what they actually do (although there has been some attention given to the consequences of actually cheating, stealing, or taking advantage of the other party). Moreover, although there is no universally accepted "ethical code" among negotiators across political, economic, professional, or cultural lines, the research shows that most negotiators agree that by acting in a completely ethical manner on truth telling—that is, simply "telling the truth" at all times—one puts oneself in a competitively disadvantageous position. The social customs and rules of negotiation dictate that a certain amount of less-than-complete candor and trust is necessary to be maximally effective, even when negotiating with a close friend or business partner. If I want to sell my used car to my good friend, and the car is worth $12,000, it is not considered inappropriate for me to ask for $13,000. I am not violating standards of honesty by asking for more than I hope to receive and by pointing out all of the excellent features of the car while minimizing the dents, rattles, and pesky oil drip. Moreover, if I did ask for only $12,000, my friend would probably assume that I *was* asking for more than it was worth—by virtue of this being a "typical negotiation"—and would counteroffer at $11,000 or less. Successful (and wise) negotiators must know how to steer their way through these dilemmas. The aforementioned studies have shown that most negotiators agree that a subset of tactics framed as "traditional competitive bargaining" (e.g., not disclosing one's bottom line, making an inflated opening offer) and "emotional manipulation" (e.g., faking anger, fear, disappointment, elation, and/or satisfaction) are seen as generally acceptable in most negotiations across the board, whereas more serious distortions of the truth (e.g., making misrepresentations, bluffing, making empty promises, spying on the opponent, defaming the opponent's reputation) are seen as more ethically marginal and questionable (Barry et al., 2000; Lewicki & Robinson, 1998; for a more complete review of this research, cf. Lewicki et al., 2006).

In the principles outlined in the next section, I specify the conduct of the wise negotiator. From my perspective, the wise negotiator eschews utilitarian reasoning and embraces a commitment to act consistent with the best standards of truth telling; a commitment to build and maintain a strong, trusting, and enduring relationship with the other negotiator; and a commitment to embrace and follow the fairness norms of the community in which the negotiation is occurring. At the same time, the wise negotiator also recognizes that effective negotiation may occasionally legitimate a certain degree of exaggeration about what one desires, a certain degree of puffery about the virtues and benefits of proposals and agreements, and a certain degree of less-than-complete candor about what constitutes a minimally acceptable deal. The wise negotiator also holds an initial view of "trust but verify" of his or her opponent until the other party's behavior proves that suspicion is not warranted (Lewicki, 2006a). This balance among efficacy, honesty, and integrity is a difficult one to learn. But as I hope to demonstrate, it is absolutely critical to the wise negotiator's success.

The Top 10 Principles of the Wise Negotiator

Given this broad grounding in the broad ethical boundaries of honesty, candor, and trust, I now offer a series of major operating principles for managing one's negotiations effectively. I set out these principles as a "Top 10" list and use them as the subheadings to organize the remainder of the chapter. The principles are also summarized in Table 6.1.

Principle 1: The wise negotiator recognizes opportunities to negotiate and pursues negotiation strategies even when it would seem that others accept the world as it is

Probably one of the most striking findings from recent research on negotiation is that many people do not recognize opportunities to negotiate and

Table 6.1   The Top 10 Principles of the Wise Negotiator

1. The wise negotiator recognizes opportunities to negotiate and pursues negotiation strategies even when it would seem that others accept the world as it is.

2. The wise negotiator understands that there is more than one strategy in negotiation and that which strategy to pursue is also a matter of active choice.

3. The wise negotiator prepares thoroughly for negotiation.

4. The wise negotiator understands that perceptions and decision making in negotiation are fraught with numerous biases.

5. The wise negotiator understands that building and sustaining strong and positive interpersonal relationships is critical to successful deal making and that constructing those relationships requires skills in building trust, managing fairness, and acting ethically.

6. The wise negotiator listens at least as much as (if not more than) he or she talks.

7. The wise negotiator understands that much of what happens in negotiation is dictated by the context.

8. The wise negotiator knows how to use power appropriately.

9. The wise negotiator knows that although negotiation is universal around the world, cultures approach negotiation differently, and he or she understands these cultural differences.

10. The wise negotiator cultivates a reputation for integrity and continues to learn from his or her experience.

do not pursue negotiation strategies even when they might be a highly effective way to have their needs met. Negotiation opportunities are available to us every time we need to depend on and work with other people to achieve our objectives. Examples abound. Two cars head for the same parking space near the entrance of a crowded shopping mall; only one can park in that space, whereas the other must then park much farther away. Two friends agree to spend Saturday night together but cannot agree on what film to see or where to eat dinner first. One arrives a day after the deadline to apply for season tickets to one's favorite sporting event and must convince the clerk to accept the application. One gets settled in a hotel room and discovers that the bed is old and uncomfortable but does not complain to the front desk. One applies for a new job, is accepted by the organization, and immediately accepts the first salary offer placed on the table. All of these are examples of negotiation opportunities, yet there are two remarkable findings from recent research:

A. Many people do not recognize them as opportunities to negotiate—that is, a chance to exert influence so as to increase the likelihood of getting what they want.

B. Many people do not ask—that is, initiate an offer or make a counteroffer—in hopes of achieving a better outcome.

There may be a variety of reasons for such responses. One is that people do not know that negotiation is an option. That is, they think they are "required" to accept—pleasantly or even grudgingly—what the other party is offering or what is left. A second reason is that people are uncomfortable in negotiating; they do not think they know how to quote an opening offer, decide on a fair price, engage in friendly banter, or assert their preferences. Finally, many people think that to ask for more, or for something else, would be seen as rude, pushy, or even obnoxious; negotiation is not an expected part of the relationship. This informal "rule" may be assumed by the receiving side (i.e., she offered me coffee; I would really prefer tea, but it would be rude to ask), or it may even be broadly assumed as part of the culture. For example, in the U.S. culture, most people assume that even at a yard sale, flea market, craft sale, or secondhand shop, a stated price (on a price tag or sticker) is what the seller is asking for the item. I have watched numerous people in the United States simply pay the price rather than offer a lower price. In contrast, in exactly the same environments in other cultures, people aggressively negotiate for the same items. If one tried negotiating a discount on a bag of oranges or a dozen eggs in a U.S. supermarket, the attempt would be met with bizarre stares and sometimes rude responses, whereas this practice might be common in the market square in many cultures around the world.

There is no question that cultural norms do influence what is negotiable and how culture shapes the negotiation process, and I have more to say about this later in the chapter. But the disposition to not negotiate is quite strong—even when negotiation might be desirable and acceptable. Linda Babcock conducted a series of simple and ingenious studies at Carnegie Mellon University. She examined the starting salaries of graduates from the master of business administration (MBA) program who were entering the corporate world. The starting salaries for male graduates were, on average, 7.6% ($4,000) higher than those for female graduates. One might interpret this as simple gender discrimination by the employers until one examined the negotiating behavior of the graduates. Only 7% of the women graduates, compared with 57% of the male graduates, had asked for more money than they originally were offered. Moreover, those who *had* asked for more money increased their starting salaries by roughly $4,000—nearly the exact difference between the average posted starting salaries. Moreover, Babcock's analysis helps us to understand the power of asking for more when tracked over time. Suppose that a man and a woman start the same job at the same age and that the man asks for and receives a 7% increase. Now assume that they receive the same raises every year (e.g., 5%) for the remainders of their careers. Babcock showed that with the same raises, the woman would need to work 9 years longer to earn the same total income. If the man also negotiates raises as well as he did starting salary, the magnitude of the discrepancy grows even more dramatically as they approach retirement. The financial costs of *not* negotiating, compounded over time, can be profound (Babcock & Laschever, 2003).

The wise negotiator sees opportunities to negotiate rather than simply accept the other party's opening offer, terms, or conditions. Whether one chooses to negotiate still rests completely in his or her hands, but to recognize the choice, and act on it as one considers appropriate, gives the wise negotiator significantly more power in many relationships.

Principle 2: The wise negotiator understands that there is more than one strategy in negotiation and that which strategy to pursue is also a matter of active choice

Contrary to the advice of most mass market books on negotiation, there is not a single best way to negotiate. Some of these books advocate a competitive or "win–lose" strategy, whereas others advocate a more cooperative or "win–win" strategy. The wise negotiator understands that there are multiple strategies that can be pursued in negotiation. Savage, Blair, and Sorenson (1989) proposed an effective model for the choice of a negotiation strategy. According to this model, a negotiator's unilateral choice of strategy is reflected in the answers to two simple questions:

A. How much concern does the negotiator have for achieving the substantive outcomes at stake in this negotiation (substantive goals)?

B. How much concern does the negotiator have for the current and future quality of the relationship with the other party (relationship goals)?

The answers to these questions result in the mix of alternative strategies presented in Figure 6.1.

The power of the dual concerns model lies in requiring the negotiator to determine the relative importance and priority of the two questions about the outcome and the relationship with the other negotiator. Figure 6.1 suggests at least four types of initial strategies for negotiators based on the answers: competition, collaboration, accommodation, and avoidance.

A strong interest in achieving only substantive outcomes—getting this deal or winning this negotiation with little or no regard for the effect on the relationship or on subsequent exchanges with the other party—tends to support a competition strategy (in the lower left-hand corner of Figure 6.1). Tactics such as threats, bluffs, and strong-willed determination are consistent with this

		Substantive Outcome Important?	
		Yes	No
Relationship Outcome Important?	Yes	Collaboration	Accommodation
	No	Competition	Avoidance

Figure 6.1   The Dual Concerns Model

approach. A strong interest in achieving only the relationship goals—building, preserving, or enhancing a good relationship with the other party—suggests an accommodation strategy (in the upper right-hand corner of the figure). If both substance and relationship are important, the negotiator should pursue a collaborative (integrative) strategy. Finally, if achieving neither substantive outcomes nor an enhanced relationship is important, the negotiator might be best served by avoiding the negotiations altogether. Each of these different strategic approaches also has different implications for negotiation planning and preparation (outlined in the next section). The wise negotiator knows how to use all of these strategies and is able to select the strategy that best matches his or her objectives. (For a complete elaboration of these strategic approaches, see also Lewicki & Hiam, 2007; Lewicki et al., 2006.)

Principle 3: The wise negotiator prepares thoroughly for negotiation

The wise negotiator recognizes that the most important work in negotiation is accomplished before the parties get to the table rather than at the table. Breakdowns in this wisdom are most conspicuous among American negotiators, who are notoriously poor at planning for a negotiation; for the most part, they fail to recognize that the competitive advantage in negotiation is gained through effective planning and preparation rather than through tricks and tactics at the bargaining table.

Effective preparation requires, at a minimum, that the negotiator define four key points to lay out the appropriate bargaining range (cf. Walton & McKersie, 1965):

A. *A target point or goal.* This is the objective that the negotiator would like to achieve, that is, the place where he would like to see the negotiation end.

B. *An opening bid.* This is the place where the negotiator will make the first offer or counteroffer. It is usually the point at which the negotiator would achieve all of his or her goals if the other party were to say *yes.* Opening bids are usually framed with the negotiator allowing some "distance" between the opening bid and the target point so that he or she can make concessions during the give-and-take of negotiation and still achieve the target point by the time the negotiation has ended.

C. *A walkaway point or bottom line.* This is the place where the negotiator should drop out of the negotiation. The bottom line is the minimum settlement that the negotiator will accept; if the offer is below that, the negotiator should walk away and find some alternative way to get his or her needs met.

D. *An alternative.* Alternatives are other deals that a negotiator can make with some other party in some other transaction. I say more about alternatives later in the chapter.

Let me offer an example. Suppose that a person wants to sell his late model car. He surfs the Web and finds that the make, model, and year of his car has a market value of $12,000. He decides that this is the target value he will set for selling his car. To sell it for $12,000, he decides to advertise it for $13,000. This allows him $1,000 to make in price concessions during negotiations and still achieve his target (refer back to our discussion of exaggeration and ethics at the beginning of the chapter). He then decides that the lowest offer he will take for the car is $11,500; if someone offers him less than this, he will keep the car and not sell it. Finally, he decides that if he cannot sell it within a month, he will take it down to the local used car lot that has offered him $11,000. This would not be a good deal, but at least he would get rid of the car and not need to worry about advertising or showing it anymore.

The purpose of this planning is to give the negotiator the tools to create a clear map of where to start and end negotiations. In the competitive and tense progress of complex give-and-take, many negotiators lose track of how to define a starting point, how to keep track of their progress, and how many concessions they should make before they stop. As a result, they are far more likely to make mistakes common to many naive negotiators:

- Setting an opening offer that is either too extreme (and hence causing the other party to see the offer as outrageous) or too modest (and hence not allowing enough room for making concessions as one moves toward the target)
- Making concessions that are too large or too small (a wise negotiator starts with larger concessions and decreases their size and frequency as he or she approaches the target point)
- Allowing oneself to be pressured to move past one's walkaway point, usually because one is unwilling to walk away without a deal or has no viable alternative

For many negotiations, designating the four key points described earlier would constitute more planning than is usually done by unprepared or untrained negotiators. But without this planning, negotiators are more disposed either to make concessions too slowly or too quickly, or to not know when a deal is unacceptable and walk away.

These four points define the minimum level of planning. Negotiation planning might be made more complex in two ways. First, the negotiator might consider what the other party's key points (target and walkaway) are likely to be. This would allow the negotiator to anticipate where the other party would like to begin and end negotiations and hence to determine how tense or competitive the negotiation will be.

Finally, the wise negotiator considers the other party's personality and style in the upcoming negotiation. Often, the negotiator is so wrapped up in considering his or her own point of view that he or she does not think enough about the other party. Who is this person? What does one know about the other party's point of view, needs, or concerns? How do those needs or concerns match one's own? Can one expect the other party to approach the situation competitively or cooperatively? Does one have a long-term relationship that he or she wants to either establish or maintain? If the negotiator does not know the answers to these questions, he or she should be spending more time learning about the other party or preparing to ask questions of the other to learn more about the other. Too often, the unwise negotiator assumes that the other party's needs and interests mirror his or her own; as a result, the negotiator may assume that there is more direct conflict in their preferences than really exists or may miss opportunities to construct trade-offs, compromises, or collaborative agreements (cf. Lewicki et al., 2006).

Principle 4: The wise negotiator understands that perceptions and decision making in negotiation are fraught with numerous biases

In Chapter 1 of this volume, Jordan and Sternberg outline five "fallacies" that inhibit people's capacity to act wisely: egocentrism, omnipotence, omniscience, invulnerability, and unrealistic optimism. Extensive research has been done on how these biases affect perceptions and judgments in negotiation (Bazerman & Neale, 1992; Lewicki et al., 2006; Thompson, 2005). Although all of these fallacies can affect negotiators, several have been shown to have a particularly powerful effect on negotiators:

- *Irrational Escalation of Commitment.* Negotiators often make a commitment to a course of action—that is, to pursue a particular negotiation target—and then stick with that commitment even in the face of dramatic evidence that the course of action is likely to fail and should be abandoned (Brockner, 1992). Two negotiators irrationally committed to pursuing their objectives, each seeking to pressure the other to back down, can escalate a conflict to intractability and pay very high costs just to sustain that commitment. Examples include engaging in price wars, investing money to repair a car that should simply be sold or abandoned, and conducting military escalation.

- *Belief in a Mythical Fixed Pie.* As noted in the previous section, negotiators often assume that the other party wants the same thing as they do. Negotiators compound this fallacy by also assuming that there are insufficient resources to meet both parties' needs and hence that collaborative settlements and mutually beneficial trade-offs are not available (e.g., Thompson & Hastie, 1990). As a result, parties often fail to search for mutually beneficial integrative agreements (Pinkley, Griffith, & Northcraft, 1995).

- *Anchoring and Adjustment.* Once negotiators choose a "standard" (i.e., an initial offer or intended goal), and regardless of how carefully or haphazardly it is chosen, the standard tends to act as an "anchor" (i.e., a real and valid benchmark against which one judges all other offers and possible settlements). For example, Neale and Northcraft (1991) found that real estate appraisers, who should be making "independent" judgments about the value of a property, were heavily influenced by the asking price for the property, regardless of its actual value. Negotiators are hesitant to give up these anchoring judgments, even in the face of information suggesting that they have become invalid benchmarks for judging progress or finding an appropriate settlement (e.g., Ritov, 1996).

- *Availability of Information.* Information that is more available, easier to retrieve, or "packaged" more colorfully and vividly in its presentation is far more likely to be believed regardless of its accuracy. People may be persuaded by a colorful graph or pie chart without even asking whether the statistics on which that chart was drawn are accurate and valid.

- *Overconfidence.* Negotiators tend to believe that their ability to be correct is far greater than is actually the case. This can lead negotiators to strongly support positions or possible settlements that are incorrect or inappropriate and, similarly, can lead negotiators to discount the worth or validity of others' judgments (Kramer, Newton, & Pommerenke, 1993; Lim, 1997).

This is only a partial list. Many other authors (e.g., Hammond, Keeney, & Raiffa, 1998; Russo & Schoemaker, 1989) have documented other judgment biases and their impact on negotiation and decision making. Managing the impact of these perceptual and cognitive biases is equally challenging. Several studies have shown that simply informing people about these biases had little effect on their ability to avoid or manage the bias (Babcock & Loewenstein, 1997; Foreman & Murnighan, 1996). More research is necessary to understand how parties can systematically control the impact of these biases on their judgments.

Principle 5: The wise negotiator understands that building and sustaining strong and positive interpersonal relationships is critical to successful deal making, and that constructing those relationships requires skills in building trust, managing fairness, and acting ethically

As I noted in the introduction to the dual concerns model (Figure 6.1), negotiators are interested in achieving strong collaborative agreements. Creating these collaborative agreements requires pursuing an integrative negotiation strategy *and* working to build and manage a strong personal relationship with the other party. Although relationship building is a very complex process, two interrelated components are critical for negotiators: building trust and managing fairness.

First, trust is the glue that holds relationships together. Parties who trust each other have a very easy time in negotiation; they are open and share information readily (Butler, 1999); they believe what the other party says and do not doubt the credibility of what they are hearing; they are more optimistic about the progress and future of the negotiation; and they are more willing to do "business on a handshake," meaning that although the deal should be in writing, each party trusts that the other will live up to both the letter and spirit of their negotiated agreement (see also Lewicki, 2006a).

Building and sustaining trust is a complex process, and many researchers have devoted significant time to understanding the key components and dynamics of trust (cf. Lewicki et al., 2006, chap. 10). I can only briefly summarize that work here by mentioning a few key points:

- Many people approach new relationships with a surprising amount of trust given that they know almost nothing about the other party (Meyerson, Weick, & Kramer, 1996). This initial goodwill can be used to start the relationship off on a strong foot.
- People trust others who appear to be trustworthy—primarily by their demonstration of high ability, benevolence, and integrity. Ability is demonstrated by acting competently and professionally; benevolence is demonstrated by treating the other party nicely and courteously; and integrity is demonstrated by telling the truth, maintaining confidentialities, and keeping one's word to follow through on commitments (Mayer, Davis, & Schoorman, 1995). Thus, people can build trust in the other party by acting that way themselves.
- Trustors focus primarily on the risks of being trusted (i.e., how vulnerable they are), whereas those being trusted focus on the benefits to be received from the trust. Thus, trustors and the trusted often focus on different things, and each is often not sensitive to how the other party is evaluating the situation. If trustors feel highly vulnerable, they are less likely to take risks or share information. Trust building may be facilitated greatly by having the negotiators explicitly discuss the

perceived benefits and vulnerabilities as well as ways to manage these so that both parties can be satisfied (Malhotra, 2004). These dynamics are likely to be more extreme in competitive bargaining situations, where each party expects the other to behave competitively and take advantage. Competition decreases openness and honesty and also decreases the ability of each party to understand the other's perspective. Thus, information sharing and reciprocity decrease as trust declines (Malhotra, 2003).

- Trust is built and sustained faster by face-to-face negotiations and when parties negotiate personally for themselves rather than being represented by agents, lawyers, or representatives (Naquin & Paulson, 2003; Song, 2004).

These points may seem obvious and self-evident. But it is surprising how many negotiations deteriorate from initial assumptions of the other party's trustworthiness and credibility to ultimately result in distrust, loss of credibility, lack of information sharing, and proposals that seek either to benefit oneself at the expense of the other party or to worry excessively about self-protection rather than to maximize joint gain. Trust is hard to build and easy to destroy; parties need to monitor their own actions carefully to cultivate and create trust and to work quickly to repair it if it has been broken. The wise negotiator pays great attention to how his or her actions are being viewed and judged by the other so as to not act in ways that can diminish trust and all the benefits that accrue with it.

Second, the wise negotiator is also sensitive to concerns about fairness—that all parties in a negotiated agreement believe they are being treated fairly and are acting in ways to ensure that others are being treated fairly. Like trust, there are many components of fair treatment, although there is considerably less research on the subject. Here are several key observations:

- Negotiators are most likely concerned about several forms of fairness—whether the proposed outcome distribution is fair (distributive justice), whether the process used to determine the outcome is fair (procedural justice), and whether the other party in the negotiation treated one with courtesy and respect (interactional justice). These forms of justice are interrelated in that unfair treatment in one form can lead to perceptions of unfairness in other forms (Bies & Moag, 1986; Deutsch, 1985; Greenberg, 1986).
- Outcome fairness (distributive justice) is often achieved by the parties getting equal outcomes. Thus, when two negotiators agree to "split the difference" (the midpoint in between their opening offers), the outcome is often seen as fairer than if they "hard-bargain" to try to obtain a bigger share. In distributive justice terms, this is an "equality" settlement; however, there may be times when a settlement based on "equity" (one party rightfully deserves more than the other) or "need" (one party has

clear legitimate needs for a larger share) may also be seen as fair (Benton & Druckman, 1974; Deutsch, 1985).

- Establishment of some objective standards for determining what is fair has a positive impact on negotiations and satisfaction with the outcome. If parties know in advance what would be a fair settlement, they are much more satisfied with a deal that is close to that fairness standard. Using objective standards to determine what is fair has been a hallmark recommendation for those pursuing integrative negotiation (Fisher et al., 1991).

- Process fairness (procedural justice) is usually achieved by allowing all parties in negotiation opportunities to have input, to tell their sides of the story, and to believe that they had an impact on shaping the agreement. Involvement in the process of helping to shape a negotiation strategy increases commitment to that strategy and willingness to pursue it (Jones & Worchel, 1992).

- Interactional fairness is achieved by treating other people well. This recommendation is consistent with my earlier comments about trust. When the other party practices deception, is not candid, acts rudely, asks improper questions, makes discriminatory comments, and takes precipitous and provocative actions without justification, negotiators are much less likely to feel well treated, are less likely to believe that outcome and process are fair, and are less likely to trust each other (Bies & Moag, 1986).

Principle 6: The wise negotiator listens at least as much as (if not more than) he or she talks

Many people think that negotiation is about defining a position and arguing for that position assertively until the other party surrenders or backs down. But negotiation is very much about listening to the other party. Those who have studied listening have identified several forms of listening behavior (Athos & Gabarro, 1978; Gordon, 1977):

- *Passive Listening.* This involves receiving the other party's message but providing no feedback to the message sender about the accuracy or completeness of reception or understanding. If the other negotiator is very talkative, a good listener simply allows the other to talk so as to learn more about the other's position, arguments, perceptions, emotions, and underlying needs and interests.

- *Acknowledgment.* This requires the receiver to occasionally indicate that the message is being received by nodding the head, maintaining eye contact, offering verbal indicators such as "mm-hmm" and "un-huh," and so on. These responses offer encouragement to the speaker to keep talking, but they may be misinterpreted by the speaker as "agreement" with the content of the message rather than just acknowledgment that the speaker has been heard.

- *Active Listening.* Here the receiver paraphrases or restates the sender's message in the receiver's own words, as in the following example:
  Speaker: I thought our last negotiating session accomplished nothing!
  Listener: So you were disappointed by the discussion last week.
  Speaker: Yes, I thought we got hung up in some really irrelevant issues.
  Listener: Can you help me to understand which issues you thought were irrelevant?

In negotiation, the purpose of active listening is not to agree with the other party; rather, the purpose is to get the other to speak more fully about his or her feelings, priorities, and perspectives so that the listener can understand them more completely (Gordon, 1977).

Listening carefully is critical. First, careful listening helps one to understand better what the other negotiator wants. By this understanding, the negotiator can then determine whether it is possible to meet those wants. Second, careful listening can also help one to understand underlying needs and emotions—safety, security, protection, vulnerability, and so on. Finally, from a strictly tactical point of view, the more the other party talks, the more likely he or she may be to give out unintended information— settlement points, acceptable alternatives, and so on. Some "talkers" are uncomfortable with silence and will start talking just to fill the quiet space; the smart listener just sits back and waits for the other to say too much.

The wise negotiator also asks questions to keep the other party talking. A number of authors have written about the importance of asking good questions (Deep & Sussman, 1993; Nierenberg, 1976). Negotiators should learn how to ask "open" questions—those phrased to evoke more complete descriptions and more information from the speaker about his or her reasons, rationales, assumptions, and so on. Examples of open questions or phrases include "Why?," "Why not?," "Help me understand . . . ," and "Tell me more about . . . "

Principle 7: The wise negotiator understands that much of what happens in negotiation is dictated by the context

By *context*, I mean the environment that surrounds the negotiation. In negotiation, as in many other interpersonal encounters, people tend to overdetermine the degree to which they can influence and control the outcomes that occur, and they tend to underestimate the extent to which other factors will influence how a negotiation will evolve, proceed, and so on. Some of the most important context factors that influence negotiation include the following:

- *Are negotiators representing their own interests, or are there "agents" who have been hired to represent them?* An agent might be an attorney, an accountant, a salesperson, or just a friend. Negotiators who represent themselves are often caught up in the emotional aspects of the planning and the give-and-take; agents are often more dispassionate but usually lack the full authority to negotiate a deal without the principal's approval. Thus, agents usually follow a different set of negotiating rules than do principals. Agents usually argue for someone else's negotiating interests and priorities rather than their own; they may also be compensated and rewarded quite differently. Moreover, some of these negotiations draw lots of public and media attention to the negotiators. These dynamics make the negotiations much more public and change how the negotiators behave. Thus, for example, negotiators representing union and management in a big transit strike that has crippled a city are likely to face a much more complex set of social pressures and dynamics than will a single employer and employee negotiating a compensation package for the following year (Cutcher-Gershenfeld & Watkins, 1999; Lewicki et al., 2006).

- *Are there multiple groups of negotiators who may be choosing to form a strategic relationship?* The negotiation may even become more socially complex if the agent is representing a group of people who have a unique interest or agenda (e.g., a board, a group of owners) or if there are multiple groups that may be seeking ways to work together by forming an alliance or partnership. For example, negotiations among public interest groups, voting blocks, and so on are often about ways to band together to influence legislation, public policy, and the like either by pushing it forward or by blocking it. Thus, political negotiations are often about forming coalitions—determining who will support whom and what kinds of payoff will be given for that support. Coalition negotiations can be very different from simple buyer–seller transactions (Murnighan, 1986; Murnighan & Brass, 1991).

- *What is the negotiating problem?* The nature of the "problem" itself will shape the context. Is the negotiator buying or selling a commodity (e.g., a car, a house)? Is the negotiator working out a long-term business agreement such as a strategic alliance or partnership? Is the negotiator trying to solve a problem in his or her relationship, such as the fact that one party's messiness gets in the way of the other party's need to keep things clean and orderly? These are clearly different problems, and the type of problem will dramatically shape the nature of the give-and-take (Lewicki et al., 2006).

- *Are there general rules, operating procedures, "standards," or benchmarks in a particular industry that shape the negotiation?* For example, when negotiating the sale of a piece of real estate (e.g., a home, a small business), there are general laws and rules for the way most real estate transactions proceed (e.g., laws regarding what must be disclosed or not disclosed, laws regarding how appraisals influence the sale/purchase price). There may be different standards, rules, and procedures for negotiating a plea agreement in a lawsuit, negotiating a labor contract, and buying a software business. A negotiator new to a particular context should become familiar with the general rules, standards, and procedures for doing transactions in that context, so that he or she can plan and prepare appropriately (Lewicki & Hiam, 2007).

- *Is there an established long-term relationship between the parties that is to be maintained or strengthened, or do the parties intend to establish one?* Finally, I return to one of the defining characteristics of the "choice" matrix presented at the beginning of this chapter. If the parties are negotiating within a long-term relationship, their desire to preserve or strengthen that relationship will significantly determine how aggressively they negotiate on the merits of the negotiation problem/issue (Greenhalgh, 2001).

Principle 8: The wise negotiator knows how to use power appropriately

Power comes in many forms and shapes. I briefly mention only a few of the most clear and obvious ways in which negotiators gain or maintain power:

- *Better or More Complete Information.* Information is the primary source of power for a negotiator. The negotiator who is better informed, has done the "homework" I have talked about in this chapter, and is able to put together compelling and persuasive arguments is more likely to persuade the other party. That same base of information may also allow this negotiator to accumulate great expertise, which will give him or her great credibility when he or she speaks to an issue. Finally, the wise negotiator also has developed the ability to put information together to be effectively persuasive, that is, to use the information to construct an effective persuasive message. (cf. Cialdini, 2001).
- *Personality and Individual Differences.* Some individuals are simply more disposed to want power. This disposition can be affected by their cognitive orientation (i.e., the way they define power ideologically), their motivations (i.e., individual differences in the desire to seek and hold power) (McClelland, 1975), their general dispositions to use power in the context of being more cooperative or competitive with others, and their moral orientation to power (i.e., the degree to which they embrace egalitarianism or power sharing vs. more hierarchical or "entitled" social values).
- *Organizational Position.* Power based on position in an organization is usually manifested in two ways. First, position in an organization conveys legitimacy; this is the power that goes with the particular "box" in an organizational chart. A president has power because he occupies the top box in a formal organization, and people who are part of that organization recognize that they must comply with the orders/requests/decisions as part of that position. Second, that position also often

commands control over important resources—money, raw materials, labor, time, equipment, and so on. These resources are often used as rewards to those who follow orders or have the personal approval of the president, or they can be withdrawn or withheld as punishments for those who do not follow orders or who lose the personal approval of the president (Raven, 1993).

- *Relationships.* Power is also derived from the strength of the relationship a negotiator has with the other negotiator. A strong and positive set of common experiences, a good reputation, mutual respect, common group membership, similar status, and so on all can be called on to generate high amounts of trust and have significant influence in moving a negotiation in the right direction. In contrast, the absence of a good relationship, a questionable reputation, disrespect, and lack of trust clearly will be difficult obstacles to overcome in securing a productive negotiation outcome (Lewicki et al., 2006).

- *BATNAs.* The popular negotiation book *Getting to Yes* (Fisher et al., 1991) suggested that negotiators should evaluate the quality of any given agreement by comparing it with their best alternative to this negotiated agreement (BATNA). Alternatives are what the negotiator can do if he or she does *not* consummate the deal in front of him or her. Thus, a recruit trying to decide whether to take a $70,000 starting salary offer from a firm will compare that offer with other offers. If the recruit has no other offers, he or she will either stay in his or her present job (or stay unemployed) or take the $70,000 starting salary offer. However, if the recruit has one or more other offers, he or she will compare this offer and all its features—salary, job duties, work location, commute time, promotion opportunities, and the like—with those other offers. The better the alternatives, the more power the negotiator has to try to improve the firm's current offer. As noted earlier, an alternative is different from a walkaway; a walkaway point simply tells the negotiator when this deal is no longer worth it under any circumstances, whereas an alternative provides the opportunity for the negotiator to "horse-trade" deals against each other so as to improve one or both offers.

Principle 9: The wise negotiator knows that although negotiation is universal around the world, cultures approach negotiation differently, and he or she understands these cultural differences

During the past 25 years, a great deal has been learned about the way in which both the environmental context and the immediate context can shape and affect negotiation processes (Gelfand & Dyer, 2000). The environmental context includes elements over which neither negotiator can have much control. These include different political and legal structures as one goes from one country to another, the degree to which governments control business operations, political instability, different economic systems and fluctuating currencies, cultural orientations that favor capitalistic versus socialistic values, and differences in cultural orientations that can dramatically shape how negotiations evolve, who takes part, how decisions are made, and so on (Salacuse, 1988). The more immediate context of the negotiation is shaped by factors such as which parties have more bargaining power, the type of interdependence between the parties, the level of intensity of the conflict, the past relationship between the negotiating parties, the role of key stakeholders, and a variety of other factors identified earlier in this chapter (Phatak & Habib, 1996). In managerial negotiation, culture tends to shape how the parties define what the negotiation is about, whether the process is perceived as distributive or integrative, who is selected as a negotiator, the protocol that is followed, how the parties communicate, the importance of time, how much risk parties are willing to take, whether negotiation emphasizes individuals or groups, how concluding agreements are shaped, and how much emotion is displayed openly in the process (Foster, 1992; Hendon & Hendon, 1990; Moran & Stripp, 1991). From the length and complexity of this list, it should be clear that the wise negotiator should prepare carefully for a cross-cultural negotiation, particularly emphasizing how the cultural background of his or her opponent, and/or the culture in which the negotiation will occur, might differ from his or her own background and might affect the way negotiations may evolve.

Principle 10: The wise negotiator cultivates a reputation for integrity and continues to learn from his or her experience

Finally, the wise negotiator acts in a way that develops and sustains a reputation for integrity. A negotiator's reputation—particularly a positive one for acting fairly, honestly, and with integrity—is one of his or her greatest sources of power and competitive advantage. When a negotiator is known for telling the truth, acting fairly, keeping confidences, following through, and doing what the negotiator says he or she will do, others are delighted to deal with him or her. The negotiator can do business with anyone, often on a simple handshake and offering his or her word. In contrast, negotiators with the opposite reputation find it far more difficult to do business, and those deals are often encumbered with complex formal contracts, restrictive covenants, and complex legal procedures. One should cultivate and covet a reputation for integrity; it will be one's greatest asset (Ferris, Blas, Douglas, Kolodinsky, & Treadway, 2005).

Similarly, the wise negotiator must continue to learn from his or her own experience. Although differences in culture, background, and personality affect the way people will approach a negotiation, success is ultimately determined by skills in preparation and execution. And those skills are learned and rehearsed through repeated practice and coaching. The masters of any sport—golf, tennis, basketball, and so on—constantly work with their coaches to hone their skills, study their opponents, and prepare for engagements, and they debrief after engagements to identify areas for future practice and strengthening. Negotiation skills are no different. Experienced negotiators are constant learners (cf. the profiles compiled by Benoliel, 2005). If one wishes to be a master negotiator, one should also learn to be a perpetual "student" of the game and should continue to find ways to learn and benefit from his or her experience.

Summary

In this chapter, I have attempted to sketch out the parameters for wisdom in negotiation. This wisdom is derived from an understanding of the ethical and moral grounding of negotiation as a process, from extensive psychological research on effective negotiation practices, and from training thousands of students of the game at the undergraduate, master's, and executive levels. In this limited space, I could only sketch out these principles in rough tones. I encourage the would-be negotiator to read further and be coached regularly by others. Take my advice and negotiate wisely!

Note

1. Admittedly, these definitions presume negotiation to be a competitive distributive process. Other authors (e.g., Fisher et al., 1991; Pruitt, 1981) have defined negotiation in more cooperative, integrative terms. However, research has shown consistently (e.g., Thompson & Hastie, 1990) that parties approach negotiation with the expectation that the interests of the other will be completely opposed; therefore, we should presume that a more distributively-oriented definition is appropriate. Parties with an established relationship and foreknowledge of the other's intentions and style may legitimately presume a more integrative process—one in which, presumably, the ethical appropriateness of certain tactics is more clearly understood.

References

Athos, A. G., & Gabarro, J. J. (1978). *Interpersonal behavior: Communication and understanding in relationships.* Englewood Cliffs, NJ: Prentice Hall.

Babcock, L., & Laschever, S. (2003). *Women don't ask.* Princeton, NJ: Princeton University Press.

Babcock, L., & Loewenstein, G. (1997). Explaining bargaining impasse: The role of self-serving biases. *Journal of Economic Perspectives, 11,* 109–126.

Barry, B., Fulmer, I. S., & Long, A. (2000, August). *Ethically marginal bargaining tactics: Sanction, efficacy, and performance.* Paper presented at the annual meeting of the Academy of Management, Toronto, Canada.

Bazerman, M. H., & Neale, M. A. (1992). *Negotiating rationally.* New York: Free Press.

Benoliel, M. (2005). *Done deal: Insights from the world's best negotiators.* Avon, MA: Platinum.

Benton, A. A., & Druckman, D. (1974). Constituents' bargaining orientation and intergroup negotiations. *Journal of Applied Social Psychology, 4,* 141–150.

Bies, R., & Moag, J. (1986). Interactional justice: Communication criteria of fairness. In R. J. Lewicki, B. H. Sheppard, & M. H. Bazerman (Eds.), *Research on negotiation in organizations* (Vol. 1, pp. 43–55). Greenwich, CT: JAI.

Brockner, J. (1992). The escalation of commitment to a failing course of action: Toward theoretical progress. *Academy of Management Review, 17,* 39–61.

Butler, J. (1999). Trust, expectations, information sharing, climate of trust, and negotiation effectiveness and efficiency. *Group & Organization Management, 24,* 217–238.

Cialdini, R. B. (2001). *Influence: Science and practice* (4th ed.). Boston: Allyn & Bacon.

Crampton, P. C., & Dees, J. G. (1993). Promoting honesty in negotiation: An exercise in practical ethics. *Business Ethics Quarterly, 3,* 359–394.

Cutcher-Gershenfeld, J., & Watkins, M. (1999). Toward a theory of representation in negotiation. In R. H. Mnookin & L. E. Susskind (Eds.), *Negotiating on behalf of others* (pp. 23–51). Thousand Oaks, CA: Sage.

Deep, S., & Sussman, L. (1993). *What to ask when you don't know what to say: 555 powerful questions to use for getting your way at work.* Englewood Cliffs, NJ: Prentice Hall.

Deutsch, M. (1985). *Distributive justice: A social–psychological perspective.* New Haven, CT: Yale University Press.

Ferris, G. R., Blas, F. R., Douglas, C., Kolodinsky, R. W., & Treadway, D. C. (2005). Personal reputation in organizations. In J. Greenberg (Ed.), *Organizational behavior: The state of the science* (pp. 211–246). Mahwah, NJ: Lawrence Erlbaum.

Fisher, R., Ury, W., & Patton, B. (1991). *Getting to yes* (2nd ed.). Boston: Houghton Mifflin.

Foreman, P., & Murnighan, J. K. (1996). Learning to avoid the winner's curse. *Organizational Behavior and Human Decision Processes, 67,* 170–180.

Foster, D. A. (1992). *Bargaining across borders: How to negotiate business successfully anywhere in the world.* New York: McGraw-Hill.

Gelfand, M. J., & Dyer, N. (2000). A cultural perspective on negotiation: Progress, pitfalls, and prospects. *Applied Psychology: An International Review, 49,* 62–99.

Gordon, T. (1977). *Leader effectiveness training.* New York: Wyden Books.

Greenberg, J. (1986). Organizational performance appraisal procedures: What makes them fair? In R. J. Lewicki, B. H. Sheppard, & M. H. Bazerman (Eds.), *Research on negotiation in organizations* (Vol. 1, pp. 25–42). Greenwich, CT: JAI.

Greenhalgh, L. (2001). *Managing strategic relationships.* New York: Free Press.

Hammond, J. S., Keeney, R. L., & Raiffa, H. (1998). The hidden traps in decision making. *Harvard Business Review, 76*(5), 47–58.

Hendon, D. W., & Hendon, R. A. (1990). *World-class negotiating: Dealmaking in the global marketplace.* New York: John Wiley.

Jones, M., & Worchel, S. (1992). Representatives in negotiation: "Internal" variables that affect "external" negotiations. *Basic & Applied Social Psychology, 13,* 323–336.

Kelley, H. H. (1966). A classroom study of the dilemmas in interpersonal negotiation. In K. Archibald (Ed.), *Strategic interaction and conflict: Original papers and discussion* (pp. 49–73). Berkeley, CA: Institute of International Studies.

Kramer, R. M., Newton, E., & Pommerenke, P. L. (1993). Self-enhancement biases and negotiator judgment: Effects of self-esteem and mood. *Organizational Behavior and Human Decision Processes, 56,* 110–133.

Lax, D., & Sebenius, J. (1986). *The manager as negotiator: Bargaining for cooperative and competitive gain.* New York: Free Press.

Lewicki, R. J. (2006a). Trust and negotiation. In A. Schneider & C. Honeyman (Eds.), *The negotiator's fieldbook* (pp. 191–202). Chicago: American Bar Association.

Lewicki, R. J. (2006b). Trust, trust development, and trust repair. In M. Deutsch & P. Coleman (Eds.), *Theory and practice of conflict resolution* (2nd ed., pp. 92–119). San Francisco: Jossey-Bass.

Lewicki, R. J., & Hiam, A. (2007). *Mastering business negotiations.* San Francisco: Jossey-Bass.

Lewicki, R. J., & Robinson, R. (1998). A factor-analytic study of negotiator ethics. *Journal of Business Ethics, 18,* 211–228.

Lewicki, R. J., Saunders, D., & Barry, B. (2006). *Negotiation* (5th ed.). Burr Ridge, IL: McGraw-Hill/Irwin.

Lewicki, R. J., Wiethoff, C., & Tomlinson, E. (2005). What is the role of trust in organizational justice? In J. Greenberg & J. Colquitt (Eds.), *Handbook of organizational justice: Fundamental questions about fairness in the workplace* (pp. 247–270). Mahwah, NJ: Lawrence Erlbaum.

Lim, R. G. (1997). Overconfidence in negotiation revisited. *International Journal of Conflict Management, 8,* 52–70.

Malhotra, D. K. (2003). Reciprocity in the context of trust: The differing perspective of trustors and trusted parties. *Dissertation Abstracts, 63*(11-B).

Malhotra, D. K. (2004). Trust and reciprocity decisions: The differing perspectives of trustors and trusted parties. *Organizational Behavior and Human Decision Processes, 94*(2), 61–73.

Mayer, R. C., Davis, J. H., & Schoorman, F. D. (1995). An integrative model of organizational trust. *Academy of Management Review, 20,* 709–734.

McClelland, D. C. (1975). *Power: The inner experience.* New York: Irvington.

McClelland, D. C., & Burnham, D. H. (1976). Power is the great motivator. *Harvard Business Review, 43*(2), 100–110.

Meyerson, D., Weick, K. E., & Kramer, R. M. (1996). Swift trust and temporary groups. In R. M. Kramer & T. R. Tyler (Eds.), *Trust in organizations: Frontiers of theory and research* (pp. 165–190). Thousand Oaks, CA: Sage.

Moran, R. T., & Stripp, W. G. (1991). *Dynamics of successful international business negotiations.* Houston, TX: Gulf Publishing.

Murnighan, J. K. (1986). Organizational coalitions: Structural contingencies and the formation process. In R. J. Lewicki, B. H. Sheppard, & M. H. Bazerman (Eds.), *Research on negotiation in organizations* (Vol. 1, pp. 155–173). Greenwich, CT: JAI.

Murnighan, J. K., & Brass, D. J. (1991). Intraorganizational coalitions. In M. H. Bazerman, R. J. Lewicki, & B. H. Sheppard (Eds.), *Research on negotiation in organizations: The handbook of negotiation research* (Vol. 3, pp. 283–306). Greenwich, CT: JAI.

Naquin, C. E., & Paulson, G. D. (2003). Online bargaining and interpersonal trust. *Journal of Applied Psychology, 88*, 113–120.

Neale, M. A., & Northcraft, G. B. (1991). Behavioral negotiation theory: A framework for conceptualizing dyadic bargaining. In L. Cummings & B. Staw (Eds.), *Research in organizational behavior* (Vol. 13, pp. 147–190). Greenwich, CT: JAI.

Nierenberg, G. (1976). *The complete negotiator.* New York: Nierenberg & Zeif.

Phatak, A. V., & Habib, M. H. (1996). The dynamics of international business negotiations. *Business Horizons, 39*, 30–38.

Pinkley, R. L., Griffith, T. L., & Northcraft, G. B. (1995). "Fixed pie" a la mode: Information availability, information processing, and the negotiation of suboptimal agreements. *Organizational Behavior and Human Decision Processes, 62*, 101–112.

Pruitt, D. (1981). *Negotiation behavior.* New York: Academic Press.

Raven, B. (1993). The bases of power: Origins and recent developments. *Journal of Social Issues, 49*, 227–251.

Ritov, I. (1996). Anchoring in a simulated competitive market negotiation. *Organizational Behavior and Human Decision Processes, 67*, 16–25.

Russo, J. E., & Schoemaker, P. J. H. (1989). *Decision traps: The ten barriers to brilliant decision making and how to overcome them.* New York: Simon & Schuster.

Salacuse, J. W. (1988). Making deals in strange places: A beginner's guide to international business negotiations. *Negotiation Journal, 4*, 5–13.

Saunders, H. (1999). *A public peace process: Sustained dialogue to transform racial and ethnic conflicts.* New York: St. Martin's.

Savage, G. T., Blair, J. D., & Sorenson, R. L. (1989). Consider both relationships and substance when negotiating strategically. *Academy of Management Executive, 3*(1), 37–48.

Shell, G. R. (1999). *Bargaining for advantage.* New York: Viking.

Song, F. (2004). *Trust and reciprocity: The differing norms of individuals and group representatives.* Unpublished manuscript, University of Guelph.

Sternberg, R. J. (1998). A balance theory of wisdom. *Review of General Psychology, 2*, 347–365.

Thompson, L. (2005). *The mind and heart of the negotiator* (3rd ed.). Englewood Cliffs, NJ: Prentice Hall.

Thompson, L., & Hastie, R. (1990). Social perception in negotiation. *Organizational Behavior and Human Decision Processes, 47*, 98–123.

Walton, R., & McKersie, R. (1965). *A behavioral theory of labor negotiation.* New York: McGraw-Hill.

7

Organizational Ethics

Acting Wisely While Facing Ethical Dilemmas in Leadership

Jay Conger
Robert Hooijberg

You have supervised the building of a water treatment plant in a South American country, the plant is ready, 300 people will be directly and indirectly employed as a consequence of the opening of the plant, and the only thing holding it up is the final approval of the secretary of utilities. Although all permits have been filed and all audits have been completed, he has yet to sign the official papers permitting the opening of the plant. It becomes clear that what really stands in the way of opening the plant is the appropriate payoff to the secretary of utilities. Although the laws of the land prohibit bribes, it does seem to be common practice in this country.

Although wisdom seems like a wonderful quality to have, its application is rarely straightforward given the complexities of most leadership decisions. In this chapter, we explore the challenges of applying wisdom and offer practical advice about acting wisely in the face of ethical dilemmas such as those mentioned in the opening vignette. Although leadership researchers exhort leaders to act wisely and ethically (e.g., Gardner, 1990; Rost, 1991; Turner, Barling, Epitropaki, Butcher, & Milner, 2002) and even see acting with moral purpose as an essential component of transformational leadership (e.g., Burns, 1978; Shamir, House, & Arthur, 1993), leaders in organizations face dilemmas where wise and morally correct solutions do not readily present themselves. This is especially true under the social entity model of the organization—where multiple stakeholders are considered—but is also true under today's shareholder model.

In this chapter, we explore how existing frameworks of wisdom can provide assistance to "ordinary" leaders in solving the real-life ethical dilemmas they face. Take the case of the leader in the opening vignette. What is the wise course of action for him? Should he just say *no* to providing bribes? Although this is a principled statement, it also means that many people will not get paid and many others will not get water. On the other hand, if he does provide a bribe, he could get himself and his company in trouble for violating the laws of his home country. Which of these two possible solutions has a higher ethical value? Although this case may seem extreme to some, it seems familiar to many others. It certainly seems familiar to readers in the sense that every year leaders face ethical dilemmas to which there are no easy answers and no obvious wise decisions.

In this chapter, we offer a definition of wisdom along with practical guidelines for acting wisely in the face of ethical dilemmas. We begin by adapting Sternberg's definition of wisdom to leadership contexts by focusing on its enhancement of an organization's viability over time. We then apply our adapted definition to two case studies. These cases illustrate the complexity of ethical dilemmas and the role of wisdom in making the "right" decision. Throughout the chapter, we draw attention to the fact that individual leaders will find it difficult to find wise solutions for many of the ethical dilemmas they face. Although we do not have easy recipes to assist individual leaders in finding wise solutions, we do provide individual and organizational guidelines that can enhance the percentage of wise decisions leaders make in the face of ethical dilemmas.

What Is Wisdom in Leadership?

One of the great challenges in applying the term *wisdom* to leadership is simply the wide variety of perspectives and therefore definitions of the term. Wisdom is multidimensional and situational. In *Wisdom: Its Nature, Origins, and Development* (Sternberg, 1990), a group of psychologists illustrated the sheer variety of perspectives for thinking about wisdom and its sources. For example, Orwell and Perlmutter (1990) suggested that wise individuals not only are smart but also have a highly developed personality structure. Their personality enables them to transcend narcissistic personal needs, thoughts, and feelings and to reach a level of constructive detachment. At the same time, wise individuals are empathic, exceptionally understanding, and open to change. In contrast to this personality perspective, Arlin (1990) offered another frame on wisdom. For Arlin, wisdom is "the art of problem finding." He suggested that we cannot understand wisdom simply by looking at the results of specific decisions or solutions; rather, to reach wise decisions, we must first formulate the right questions to ask in any important decision. Other authors from Sternberg's (1990) edited volume suggested that personality and decision-making approaches in themselves are not enough to create wisdom; rather, context is a critical variable that determines whether or not to qualify actions or decisions as wise. For example, Meacham (1990) pointed out that many life experiences (including overaccumulation of information, success, and power) or climates (such as today's atmosphere of rapid technological and cultural change) can be extremely threatening and damaging to wisdom. Only a "wisdom atmosphere of supportive interpersonal relations" caters to building the personal strength necessary to "engage in confident and wise action even when in situations of doubt." In other words, for wisdom to be present, it is not enough to have the right disposition or proper processes for decision making. Wisdom is the product of an environment promoting wise actions.

This array of perspectives highlights the multiple dimensions of wisdom. It is truly multifaceted and multileveled. There is the individual decision maker. His or her personality and experience play a critical role in wisdom. It is difficult to imagine a power-hungry and highly narcissistic individual making wise decisions. It is also hard to imagine someone acting wisely without a depth of appropriate experiences on which to draw. But having the "right" personality and base of experience is not enough. The individual must also rely on sophisticated and objective processes of decision making. For example, a wise decision is made by asking the right kinds of questions, involving knowledgeable others, seeking a genuine breadth of perspectives on the issue, sourcing rich and reliable information pertinent to the decision, considering both the means and the ends, and weighing in a balanced fashion the interests and concerns of the multiple constituencies involved in the decision. Finally, it is difficult to act wisely in an environment that is highly discouraging of wisdom. An organization's leaders, rewards, processes, and culture must promote and reward wise decisions. Therefore, wisdom is the outcome of personality, experience, decision-making processes, and a highly supportive organizational environment.

Given these sources of, and contributors to, wisdom, how might we best define wisdom in a leadership situation? We prefer Sternberg's notion of wisdom. According to Sternberg (2005), people are wise to the extent that they use their intelligence and experience to seek a common good over both the short and long terms. They do so by balancing their own interests with those of other people and those of larger entities (e.g., family, community, nation). Wise people are also perceptive and highly adaptive. They can adapt to new environments, change their environments, or select new environments to achieve positive outcomes for multiple constituencies. Ideally, they are able to detach themselves from the influence of environments or climates that are not supportive of making wise decisions.

In the leadership world, therefore, wise decisions are those that are made carefully with a breadth of information and perspective and with great consideration of the multiple constituencies influenced by the decisions. Their aim is always to enhance the viability of their organization over time—a viability shaped and determined by multiple stakeholders. The ultimate proof of a wise decision, therefore, is that it enhances the long-term viability of an organization and also balances effectively and positively the needs of the fullest possible range of stakeholders. In many cases, however, this may mean that wisdom results in constructive compromises rather than clear and clean ethical solutions given that stakeholders themselves may hold widely diverging stances on a single issue.

That said, wisdom is more easily defined than implemented in organizations given the multitude of ethical dilemmas they face. With an increasing emphasis on both short- and long-term goals, and with a growing number of active and vocal stakeholders, making wise leadership decisions has become far more difficult. For example, how does a leader balance short- and long-term interests, especially when, at an individual level, not achieving short-term targets can make meeting long-term targets irrelevant? How much self-interest can a leader afford? Is it wise for leaders to make a decision that is beneficial for the organization but detrimental to their own careers? How and when do leaders balance the need for cost-cutting with long-standing commitments to their workforce?

The academic literatures on leadership, ethics, and wisdom offer practicing leaders few truly useful tools to answer thorny questions such as these. Most of the tools and competencies of wisdom provided by researchers on the topic tend to be generic. For example, Bluck and Glück (2005), Weick (1998), and Bigelow (1992) together offered the following set of critical elements for making wise leadership decisions (all of which are personal dimensions):

- Cognitive ability (e.g., intelligence, a rich store of relevant knowledge, expertise in the domain of the issue at hand)
- Insight (e.g., reasoning and problem-solving ability, cognitive meta-control, an understanding of systemic relationships)
- An adequate understanding of the limits to one's knowledge
- Reflective attitude (e.g., learning from insights, learning from mistakes)
- Concern for others (e.g., understanding, fair, open to learning from others)
- Real-world skills (e.g., communications, judgment, problem-solving skills)
- Appropriate values

Although we can see the utility of these types of knowledge, skills, abilities, and values, they still beg the question of how to apply them to real-life situations. For example, concern for others could lead to the deployment of organizational resources to retain employees longer than economic conditions warrant. This could result in even more individuals losing their jobs than would have occurred if a leader had taken action more swiftly. This is a common trade-off that leaders face. The trade-off, however, becomes more difficult to judge if we change the variables slightly. What if a manager believes that his or her business has hit a temporary slump and that economic conditions will pick up soon? If the manager lays off staff and the economy picks up, will he or she have the ability to rehire quickly enough? This raises issues regarding the manager's confidence about future events and the amount of risk taking with which he or she feels comfortable. Although Weick (1998) indicated correctly that both overconfidence and overcautiousness can lead to bad decision making, he did not provide a clear handle on how to find the right balance between confidence and caution. These are some of the challenges of applying the research on wisdom to acting wisely in a leadership setting.

_____ Real-Life Leadership Problems and Wisdom

To make the discussion and potential learning more tangible, we examine two concrete cases where the focal leaders face ethical dilemmas. We invite the reader to examine the cases and to think about what our preceding discussion would lead the reader to do in these situations.

Dealing With Richard Millar

In 1997, Rebecca Olson had just become chief executive officer (CEO) of St. Clement's Hospital in Omaha, Nebraska.[1] Many people were surprised when Olson got the job because her management experience consisted of 8 years as vice president of a chain of small "doc-in-the-box" clinics owned by a large health maintenance organization (HMO). Moreover, unlike all of her predecessors, Olson was not Catholic.

Clearly, the St. Clement's board had taken a calculated risk in hiring Olson. The board members had quickly agreed on the problems facing the hospital but had difficulty in deciding who was the right person to address them. The hospital had been losing market share for years, and several similar facilities had been forced to close their doors. Managed care had led to high turnover among the hospital's doctors, nurses, and administrators, and patient complaints were rising quickly. Olson's supporters on the board believed that she would bring energy, intensity, and creative new approaches to delivering medical care. Others on the board, believing that the financially fragile hospital needed a leader who knew the institution inside out, supported an inside candidate. Eventually, the board agreed to hire Olson.

A few days after Olson started work, the board chairman told her about a troubling personnel issue. Melanie Wermert, a clerical employee with physical infirmities, was about to file a complaint with the state employment agency accusing the hospital's vice president of operations, Richard Millar, of sexual harassment and discrimination. Olson had met Millar just a few weeks earlier, had a pleasant conversation with him, and remembered his confidence and quiet charm. Millar, a tall, distinguished-looking man in his mid-50s, had worked at St. Clement's for 25 years. He had held nearly every important nonmedical position, including community affairs director and head of accounting. Millar came from a prominent Omaha family and was the inside candidate supported by the cautious board members. Until the board announced its choice of Olson, most of the hospital staff believed that Millar would be the next CEO.

As soon as the board chairman left her office, Olson let her anger bubble to the surface. The chairman and a few others had known about the charges for several weeks but had waited until now to tell Olson. Even worse, the chairman confessed that he had discussed the matter with the previous CEO, who had decided not to get involved because he would not have been able to see the issue through to its conclusion. Olson thought that this was simply a cop-out. She also realized that she identified very strongly with Wermert, even though the two women had never met. Like Wermert, Olson was physically disabled. She walked with a pronounced limp, the result of a freak sledding accident when she was a teenager.

Because Olson had handled several other harassment complaints at past jobs, she understood the problem in front of her. The hospital's reputation, already hurt by financial problems, could suffer from a scandal. If the state commission found that harassment had occurred, it could penalize the hospital and the victim could file suit. Olson's handling of the situation would also color her initial relationship with the hospital staff, its board, and the local community (if the matter became public).

Olson began working on the problem immediately. Fortunately, the hospital had a process for investigating harassment charges, and she set these wheels in motion. In interviews with the hospital's outside counsel, Wermert repeated her charges and a coworker revealed that Wermert had told her about the incident shortly after it happened. In other interviews, rumors surfaced that Millar had harassed another woman at the hospital, but she had moved out of state and could not be located. The hospital's lawyer also told Olson that he suspected his investigation was being impeded because some people were intimidated by Millar. He also heard allegations that Millar had recently bullied two employees into leaving their jobs because Millar disliked them.

As Olson heard more about Millar's vindictive character, she found, to her surprise, that she was growing wary of him, even though this was the last thing that anyone who knew her would have expected. As a child, Olson played sports year-round and, because she played so aggressively, was injured frequently. After the sledding accident, when she could no longer compete in sports, she turned her high school and college studies into intense competitive events. Some of her medical school professors were tough and blunt, but she was proud that none of them had intimidated her. As a leader, Olson was viewed as direct, forceful, and sometimes harsh. Over the years, she had received several performance reviews suggesting that she "tone down" her style, but she had not paid much attention to this advice.

Millar's tranquility alarmed Olson. She assumed that he knew something about the charges against him because he had friends all around the hospital. But Olson saw Millar several times a day, often spending an hour or two in meetings with him, and he always seemed calm and relaxed. One afternoon, she even watched him trying to make small talk with one of his alleged victims. The woman sat rigidly and looked past Millar while he smiled and leaned against the side of her desk. This gave Olson the creeps. Millar did not seem to care what he had done or whether he was being investigated. He seemed to think that he was bulletproof.

The lawyer's report left Olson with little doubt that Millar deserved to be fired. In fact, Olson's gut reaction was that Millar not only should be fired but also should be dragged out of his office and thrown into the street. She did not want him to get away with his reprehensible behavior, and she believed that it belonged on his permanent record. In addition, firing Millar would also meet the principal demand of the woman who had charged him with harassment. The accuser had indicated that she would not go to the state board if the hospital fired Millar, and this would avoid a lot of ugly publicity.

Looking at this case, what action should Olson take? Given the severity of the problem and its impact on the organization's reputation, as well as on Olson's reputation, it is critical that Olson make a wise decision in this case. Leadership scholar Burns (1978) argued that transformational leaders do not water down their values and moral ideals. However, Olson faces a difficult ethical dilemma where we cannot clearly see what values and moral ideals she should uphold. Should the ethical solution focus on punishing the supposed sexual harasser? Should the ethical solution focus on saving the hospital from potential financial ruin? Should the ethical solution focus on Olson's personal values and principles? If Olson followed Burns's advice, what would that mean for her own career? What implications would that have for the employees of the hospital and the community in which it operates?

When we share this case in executive education classes, many participants feel that Millar should be fired. Others feel that concrete evidence does not exist and, therefore, that further due process and research into the legalities of the situation need to take place before further steps can be taken.

After extensive discussions with the board and the accuser, Olson ultimately wrote a letter of resignation for Millar. She and the board chairman called in Millar and told him that they wanted him to sign the letter of resignation stating that he was resigning "for personal reasons." They offered him a severance package and asked him to sign a letter stating that he would not discuss the case with anyone. Millar accepted and left the hospital, and Olson could focus on putting the hospital's affairs back in order.

When we share this outcome with participants in our executive education programs, they express disappointment with Olson's actions. Some feel disappointed that Millar did not need to pay for his harassing behaviors. Others feel disappointed because they think that due process has been given short shrift. Others feel disappointed because the woman who Millar harassed did not get justice.

However, if we look at our original definition of wise decisions, we see that Olson met all the elements of that definition. She met the needs of a broad range of stakeholders—the accuser, the board of the hospital, the employees of the hospital, and (one might argue) the larger community. She balanced short- and long-term interests of the hospital and also herself. Still, like many participants in our executive education classes, the final outcome does not leave us feeling satisfied. Did Olson make a wise decision in terms of protecting the hospital's viability? Absolutely. Did Olson do a good job in balancing the interests of a broad range of stakeholders? Absolutely. So, why do we do not feel better?

In organizations, ethical dilemmas do not have obvious solutions; most solutions will not please all stakeholders, most solutions will feel like compromises, and the long-term implications of solutions are unclear at best. In addition, making wise decisions will not necessarily leave the decision maker feeling good or gain immediate appreciation from others. Olson might have felt better personally if she had fired Millar, and that decision might even have gotten her respect and appreciation from at least a subset of the involved stakeholders. It could, however, have exposed the hospital to a nasty and very public legal battle on Millar's part. We realize, then, that this particular case and the emotions it involves do not exactly represent an invitation to leaders to make wise decisions. What, then, should entice leaders to make wise decisions, and what knowledge, skills, and attitudes will help them to make wise decisions?

Before we turn to this question, we invite the reader to look at another case of a leader facing an ethical dilemma.

The Case for Absolute Quality

Peter Dickson had recently accepted the presidency of a start-up venture within one of the world's largest automobile manufacturers. The parent organization decided to create a new venture that would focus on new vehicle and engine designs for specific consumer segments. The company was reluctant to put the new venture under its existing operations for fear that the venture's vehicle designs would produce only incremental improvements on the company's existing product line. Competition had become particularly fierce in the industry, and the company wanted to maintain its already strong leadership position with an entirely new generation of vehicles. It was decided that a stand-alone venture would greatly increase the probability of truly innovative designs to meet the demands of certain high-growth market segments.

With this mandate in hand from the parent organization, Dickson felt that it was imperative from the first day of the venture to devise a set of guiding core values. In a 2-day retreat, Dickson and his executive team crafted the values they felt were most appropriate given the venture's mission and strategy. One of the values that the team debated at length was the issue of product "quality." Most of the executive team felt that quality was no longer a distinguishing factor within the industry. In other words, it was difficult to compete on quality because industry quality standards were already so high. Given this situation, the group decided that a core value of "absolute quality" would be the only way to distinguish the venture's product from its industry peers on this dimension. Therefore, absolute quality became one of the venture's five core values.

Sometime later, during the early weeks of production of the first model car, Dickson received a phone call from one of his leaders. The tone on the line was anxious and urgent. As Dickson listened carefully, he learned that the supplier for the vehicles' radiator fluid had inadvertently shipped the wrong fluid. This particular fluid contained a corrosive chemical that would permanently damage the radiators over time. Already, 1,000 cars had been manufactured and shipped to dealers. All of the radiators in these cars contained the contaminated fluid.

Immediately after the call, Dickson called his executive team together for an emergency meeting. He explained what had happened to the radiators and canvassed the group as to how the company should respond. There was unanimous agreement that the company needed to recall all 1,000 automobiles immediately. One executive raised the question of whether simply replacing the radiator was sufficient given the need to build customer and dealer goodwill. Several executives, however, pointed out that the fluid probably had not had time to do any damage beyond the inner wall of the radiator itself. Simply replacing the radiators would be costly and a reasonable remedy in itself. A debate ensued. Dickson encouraged the group to consider as many options as possible before reaching a final decision.

One executive commented that customers should be given the choice of either full reimbursement or a completely new car. At this point, Dickson raised the issue of the venture's core value of absolute quality. What actions would such a value lead the executive team to take in this situation? And how broadly should absolute quality be defined? Should it go beyond the quality of the product and to the quality of the customer experience overall? Several executives concurred that the situation demanded the offer of a full refund if they were to define quality to include the customer experience. Customers should then be given the option of buying a new car with a significant discount. Others weighed in on the costs of such actions. They felt that this was a very costly choice for the organization. Their industry peers would never go to such lengths.

As the team members debated their predicament, it became clearer to everyone that the core value of absolute quality meant they would need to take an action beyond the norms set by the industry. The competition would simply recall the cars, replace the radiators, and hand them back to the owners. The new venture would need to do something different. One executive suggested that it might be important to make an even bolder statement to the public and to the organization. Why not destroy all of the recalled cars in a symbolic commitment to absolute quality and then give customers the option of either a new car or a full refund? It would be an expensive decision but a critical one for building goodwill among customers and for showing the executive team's commitment to the value of absolute quality. This idea generated a great deal of debate. One camp pointed out that destroying the cars would be foolish because most of the vehicle components were untouched by the problem. The debate raged on. But everyone felt that a decision needed to be made—and soon. The new venture's future was already at a critical juncture during the earliest days of its life.

Looking at this case, what action should Dickson and his team take? Given the severity of the problem and its impact on the organization's reputation, it is of course critical that Dickson make a wise decision. When we discuss this case in executive education classes, most participants feel that replacing the radiators is the optimal decision. After all, the mixup in the radiator fluid was not the fault of the venture; rather, it was the fault of the supplier. Going beyond this solution would be very costly. Others feel that to build customer goodwill, the company must offer the purchaser the option of either a full refund on the car or a replacement radiator.

So what did Dickson and his team do? After extensive discussions with his executives, as well as with executives at the parent organization, Dickson decided to recall all 1,000 cars. Every owner was given the choice of either a completely new vehicle or a full refund. If the owner opted for a replacement car, he or she was given a full 20% discount on the vehicle price. The owner was also provided with 3 years worth of free service on the vehicle. Dealers were provided with replacement cars at no charge along with subsidies for the 3 years of free service. The 1,000 vehicles were indeed destroyed despite the fact that the corrosive fluid in the radiators had not penetrated the radiator walls in a single vehicle. In other words, no car had suffered damage beyond the interior of the radiator.

When we share this outcome with participants in our executive education programs, they express genuine surprise with Dickson's actions. They
are disappointed that Dickson and his team chose the costliest possible outcome. They are often shocked that the company destroyed 1,000 new cars
that had only a single defective component in each. It appears to many to
be an unwise decision.

If we look at our earlier definition of wise actions, we see that Dickson's
decision and actions meet many of the elements of that definition. He met
the needs of the stakeholders most influenced by the corrosive fluid—the
customers and the dealers. Although in the short run the costs were higher,
the decision built tremendous goodwill with customers and dealers. It
established in a concrete fashion the company's core value of absolute quality. Internal stakeholders—the employees within the organization—were so
impressed with the decision that they themselves set higher internal standards on quality. As a result, overall quality within the operations, which
was already high, climbed steadily after the decision was made. The media
learned of the decision to destroy the cars and filmed the event when cars
were crushed. The news stories paradoxically generated extremely positive
publicity about a car company that had taken the concern for quality to a
remarkable standard. Sales of the new venture did not dip after the event
but rather climbed steadily thereafter. In this case, Dickson and his team
chose what was the costliest solution in the short term, but by doing so they
actually enhanced the long-term viability of the organization. They simultaneously reinforced one of the organization's most important values for all
of the stakeholders to see, and in this case they demonstrated its power in
terms of branding and competitive advantage. This outcome in turn met the
needs of the parent organization and its shareholders over the longer term
as well. Although some readers will feel uncomfortable about the costliness
of the solution, Dickson saw it as a critical investment rather than as a cost.

Making Wise Decisions

We believe that making wise decisions when facing ethical dilemmas requires
that leaders have the courage to balance short-term demands and pressures
with the long-term implications of their decisions. Leaders must be acutely
aware of the "tyranny of small steps." Small steps here are the short-term
decisions that meet the immediate needs of a narrow group of stakeholders,
but over time they erode the organization's values, credibility, and viability.
Because the immediate negative consequences of small steps appear to be
minor, they are made repeatedly. This phenomenon was most apparent in
the case of the Enron Corporation, where the executive team committed to
its egregious off-balance sheet partnerships one by one over an extended
period of time. The impact of the initial partnerships was limited, but their
cumulative impact led to the company's downfall. In contrast, Peter Dickson

and his colleagues did not give in to the pressure of the short-term need to minimize the costs of the recall; rather, they interpreted a core value in a manner that strengthened it powerfully and enhanced the viability of their organization over the long term.

At the same time, leaders must balance their determination to stand by their values, goals, and priorities with their ability to compromise and show tolerance for uncertainty. This fits well with what Weick (1998) referred to as the "attitude of wisdom," which he defined as a careful balancing of knowing and doubting: "It is a dynamic process in which people make sense of information differently depending on which side of the knowing–doubting scale they find themselves" (p. 57). According to Weick, those who maintain a healthy balance between feeling confident about what they know and doubting whether they really have all of the necessary information will have a greater likelihood of acting wisely than will those who either feel completely confident in what they know or doubt all of the information they have. Feeling completely confident can result in arrogance and resistance to taking in new information. Doubting all information can result in overcautiousness and lack of action. One of Weick's interesting suggestions for the development of wisdom is people's *willingness to improvise* as in the case of Rebecca Olson. This makes sense because wise decisions will need to be made in situations for which no clear-cut, ethically sound solutions exist; action needs to be taken, new knowledge gets created, and decisions need to be made.

The willingness to improvise also acknowledges that leaders do not have, and will not have, all of the information and knowledge they need. This in turn leads to the suggestion that leaders must gather information and insights from as broad a group of stakeholders as possible so as to enlarge their portfolio of potential options. With a wider set of potential actions, they can weigh the costs and benefits of each option and, hopefully, arrive at a decision that meets the criteria of our definition of wise actions.

Leaders will also find themselves to be more able to make wise decisions as they move to a longer term strategic perspective (Bigelow, 1992), as they learn more deeply from experience, and as they go through a value and orientation shift from a focus on self-interest to a focus on the breadth of constituents they must serve. All of this needs to be balanced with the leader's personal set of core values and interests. By this, we mean that leaders should not make decisions separate from their own moral principles and their own careers and livelihoods. If leaders make decisions that are not in accordance with their values, they will reduce their own effectiveness and self-confidence in the long run. The same holds for their careers. If they do not pay sufficient attention to their own careers, they will not be able to contribute effectively for a long time.

Although all of this sounds quite logical, why do we still find many examples of unwise decisions in the face of ethical dilemmas? There are numerous reasons. For example, unwise decisions are often the product of being overly decisive, serving solely one's personal needs, paying excessive attention to either short- or long-term concerns, paying too much attention to a single stakeholder, or having distracting psychological beliefs. We discuss some of these reasons in the next section.

Barriers to Wisdom in Leadership

It is clear that the rewards for wise leadership decisions are neither automatic nor immediately forthcoming in many organizations today. This is partly because, as McNamee (1998) indicated, wisdom resides in relationships rather than in individuals. Wisdom, she asserted, does not exist separate from those judging it. The difficulty is that many of those doing the judging still value strong decisive actions over more balanced wise actions. Often, the term *decisive action* can mean acting quickly without a genuine investigation of the issue or without a real understanding of the interests of a broader set of stakeholders. For example, there is one interest group that dominates today in the management world—the ever powerful pull of the financial community and its demands for short-term profitability. Many management decisions, especially at the executive level, consider all too narrowly the financial community's influence on the near-term value of the company's stock value. Investments toward the future viability of the organization are traded off for short-term equity valuation gains. Other times, self-serving needs for wealth guide executives' actions and result in unwise decisions that seriously harm the viability of the very organizations they are leading. As Sternberg (2004) pointed out, leaders in all walks of life have failed to act with wisdom when they ignored the broader interests of others. He cited Sigmund Freud, the "father of psychiatry," who lost many of his own followers because of his insistence that they rigidly follow his system of psychoanalysis. Napoleon's disastrous invasion of Russia was motivated more by his personal ego needs than by France's need to have Russia in its empire.

From our focus on individual leaders, we are particularly concerned about the personal or psychological barriers to dealing wisely with ethical dilemmas. Sternberg (2003) identified five personal beliefs that are critical hurdles to wisdom. Each of these hinders decision makers from gathering accurate and diverse information and from considering the broad range of stakeholders often influenced by a critical decision. The first barrier is the *unrealistic optimism fallacy*. This occurs when decision makers see themselves as much smarter and more effective than the colleagues around them. These decision makers in turn come to believe that they can do or accomplish whatever they wish. The second psychological hurdle is called the *egocentrism fallacy*. This barrier to wisdom occurs when individuals believe that the world revolves, or at least should revolve, around them. This leads them to act in ways that benefit themselves regardless of how that behavior affects others. The third hurdle to personal wisdom is the *omniscience fallacy*. In this case, decision makers believe that they know all there is to know and therefore do not need to listen to the advice and counsel of others. Fourth among the hurdles is the *omnipotence fallacy*, where individuals feel that they are all-powerful—that their intelligence, education, and experience somehow make them unique. The last of the barriers is called the *invulnerability fallacy*. Under this state of being, individuals come to believe that they can do whatever they want and that others will never be able to hurt or expose them; in other words, they can get away with anything because they are so clever.

All five of these personal beliefs move decision makers' attention away from the organization's long-term viability. They will not adequately survey the needs of all stakeholders and will not adequately balance the short- and long-term needs of their organization.

To see the influence of personal beliefs, leaders must cultivate a level of self-awareness and humility. They must also find advisers who are willing to challenge them personally. The burden for wise actions, however, should not be placed solely on the shoulders of individuals. Organizations can and should do a lot to guide their leaders and employees toward wise actions.

Organizational Support for Wise Actions

Beyer and Niño (1998) noted that certain types of organizational culture support leaders in acting wisely. They concluded that those companies that provide a moral compass are more likely to find leaders acting wisely than are organizations that reinforce individual opportunism, playing politics, and finger pointing.

Some companies go one step further and codify their core values in a corporate credo. Johnson & Johnson is a good example of one company that codified its values clearly and powerfully in its operations. Its credo was formulated under the leadership of Robert Wood Johnson, son of the founder, who argued a half century ago that "every act of business has social consequences." The company credo highlights the responsibilities of the company to the broadest range of possible stakeholders—from doctors, nurses, and patients, to employees, to communities, to shareholders. Interestingly, shareholders are last on the list. The Johnson & Johnson credo provided the top management of the company with clear guidelines for action when the Tylenol scandal broke. The scandal involved the deaths of seven individuals who had taken Extra-Strength Tylenol capsules that were later discovered to have been contaminated with cyanide. Guided by the credo's mandate that the first responsibility of the company was toward its customers, Johnson & Johnson promptly removed all Tylenol products from the store shelves across the United States at great financial cost to the company (an estimated $100 million). This decision balanced the various interests of stakeholders as well as short- and long-term interests. Investigations by law enforcement agencies would later show that the poisonings were the work of outsiders at some point in the distribution of the product rather than due to the company's internal production process. Over the long run, the company regained whatever share of the market had been lost by the incident, and the Tylenol brand suffered no long-term harm. The credo fostered a wise set of actions.

Other companies encourage wise decisions only after being pressured externally. For example, Nike formulated clear rules and guidelines regarding the minimum age of its workers in different countries, minimum working conditions in its factories, and rights to unionization only after receiving bad publicity about having child laborers in its overseas factories. Although in this case these rules and guidelines do not necessarily lead to wise actions, they do reduce the number of unwise actions.

Organizational support for making wise decisions in the face of ethical dilemmas can come in the form of clear norms, as in the case of Johnson & Johnson's credo, or in the form of rules and regulations, as in the case of Nike. However, Enron had an ethical code of conduct and still ended up making unwise decisions. To make norms and rules come alive, we find that it is critical that leaders regularly discuss key ethical dilemmas in an open and honest way. This helps leaders throughout the organization to understand what the organization's norms and rules mean for them in their jobs with their ethical dilemmas.

We witnessed one such example in a Dutch temporary employment agency. The salespeople found themselves confronted with racial discrimination issues when they visited customers. Certain customers would comment, "We need someone with [such and such] skills for 2 months, but please do not send us a colored one." This caused a lot of discomfort among the salespeople, who wanted to please their customers and make the sales but did not want to be discriminatory in their actions. In discussions with senior executives, the company provided its salespeople with the following standard response: "We will send you the most competent person we have." If a person of color was sent and the company protested, the customer was told that the employment agency would not work with that customer again.

Norms, credos, and rules are created by the senior executives of a company—and usually with good intentions. In many cases, however, they do not provide clear solutions for the ethical dilemmas faced by leaders further down in the organization. A culture that supports and even encourages open and honest dialogue around these ethical dilemmas is essential for making decisions that enhance the long-term viability of an organization. In addition, the organization's senior leadership must model ethical decision making. There must be rewards for ethical behavior and punishments for unethical conduct. The heroes of ethical decision making must be widely publicized. Finally, training and scenario exercises must be provided to assist employees in identifying the types of ethical dilemmas they may face along with processes to help them make the most appropriate decisions.

_____ Implications for Research, Teaching, and Practice

Research

The key question that we continue to find difficult to answer is why one person acts wisely in the face of ethical dilemmas, whereas another person does not. What made Rebecca Olson and Peter Dickson choose the wise paths, whereas others might have chosen to favor one stakeholder group more strongly than others? Will we find the differentiating factors in individual differences, or do we need to look at the organizational context?

In terms of individual differences, it may be worthwhile to explore the relationship between the Big Five personality traits (e.g., Goldberg, 1993; John, 1990; John & Srivastava, 1999) and wise decisions as well as variables such as tolerance of ambiguity (e.g., Chen & Hooijberg, 2000). Here we would expect that, for example, neuroticism would correlate negatively with making wise decisions because those high on neuroticism tend to be more emotionally reactive. We would expect conscientiousness and tolerance for ambiguity to correlate positively with making wise decisions because those high on conscientiousness tend to control their impulses better and those high on tolerance for ambiguity tend to be more comfortable in seeking diverse inputs. We would expect that those who do not react emotionally, control their initial impulses, and seek out diverse points of view are more likely to arrive at wise decisions. They would more naturally balance short- and long-term interests, as well as the interests of multiple stakeholders, and therefore strive to ensure the long-term viability of the organizations for which they work.

Even if individual characteristics explain part of the differences in the extent to which individuals seek out wise actions as we have defined them, what organizational variables influence wise actions the most? We have mentioned norms, rules, and dialogue. In addition to those variables, one might look at the influence of corporate values, the actions of senior leaders, reward systems, formal mechanisms for whistle-blowing, the presence or absence of an ombudsman role, how actively the board participates in the ethical governance of the organization, and how much the organization centralizes decision making versus encourages an upward flow of information.

Teaching

We find that the case method works well to engage students and participants in thinking and discussing ethical dilemmas, wisdom, and leadership because it allows them to understand the complexities involved in ethical decision making. Because the ethical dilemmas do not have easy answers, engagement and dialogue will foster a deeper understanding of the issues involved. Participants can appreciate the balancing acts in which one needs to engage and the personal and organizational characteristics that are necessary to make wise decisions.

When engaging participants and students in these types of discussion, participants must be prepared to face disillusionment with the outcomes of the cases. Many of those who come through our master of business administration (MBA) and executive programs still have an image of leadership that includes strong forceful action. This image conflicts with the constructive compromises that lie at the heart of wise decisions.

Practice

The best practical advice we can give is that leaders keep our definition of wisdom handy. Kurt Lewin once remarked that there is nothing as practical as a good theory, and that certainly applies here. That is, when we face ethical dilemmas, we consider as wise decisions those that are made carefully with a breadth of information and perspective and with great consideration of the multiple constituencies to the decisions. We consider decisions as wise when their outcomes enhance the *viability* of the organization over time—viability that is shaped and determined by multiple stakeholders. Therefore, the ultimate proof of a wise decision is that it enhances the long-term viability of an organization and also balances effectively and positively the needs of the fullest possible range of stakeholders, including the needs and drives of the decision maker. In many cases, however, this may mean that wisdom results in constructive compromises given that stakeholders themselves may hold widely diverging stances on a single issue. To make such wise decisions, then, leaders face a paradox. They need courage to stand up for what they believe is right, and need to have a strong set of core values so that they know what is right, while simultaneously being humble about what they know, seeking the involvement of others in thinking through the ethical dilemmas, and being willing and able to make constructive compromises.

Conclusion

Both individual leaders and organizations can do much to prevent unwise actions and to increase the probability of making wise decisions. Leaders can, by using our definition of wise action, reflect on what constitutes wise actions for the particular ethical and thorny dilemmas they face. To do so, they must constantly remind themselves of what kinds of actions will contribute to the long-term viability and adaptability of their organizations. That said, the reward for wise action ultimately lies in a sense of self-acceptance or moral well-being on the part of leaders who know they have done their work wisely. The moral well-being comes both from knowing they have adhered to a core set of constructive values and from having contributed to the larger good beyond narrow self-interests.

Note

1. This case study is adapted from Badaracco's (2002) *Leading Quietly* (pp. 12–15).

References

Arlin, P. K. (1990). Wisdom: The art of problem finding. In R. J. Sternberg (Ed.), *Wisdom: Its nature, origins, and development* (pp. 230–243). New York: Cambridge University Press.

Badaracco, J. L. (2002). *Leading quietly: An unorthodox guide to doing the right thing*. Boston: Harvard Business School Press.

Beyer, J. M., & Niño, D. (1998). Facing the future: Backing courage with wisdom. In S. Srivastava & D. L. Cooperrider (Eds.), *Organizational wisdom and courage* (pp. 65–97). San Francisco: New Lexington.

Bigelow, J. (1992). Developing leadership wisdom. *Journal of Management Inquiry, 1*(2), 143–153.

Bluck, S., & Glück, J. (2005). From the inside out: People's implicit theories of wisdom. In R. J. Sternberg & J. Jordan (Eds.), *A handbook of wisdom: Psychological perspectives* (pp. 84–109). New York: Cambridge University Press.

Burns, J. M. (1978). *Leadership*. New York: Harper & Row.

Chen, C., & Hooijberg, R. (2000). Ambiguity intolerance and valuing diversity in the workplace. *Journal of Applied Social Psychology, 30*, 2392–2408.

Gardner, J. (1990). *On leadership*. New York: Free Press.

Goldberg, L. R. (1993). The structure of phenotypic personality traits. *American Psychologist, 48*, 26–34.

John, O. P. (1990). The "Big Five" factor taxonomy: Dimensions of personality in the natural language and in questionnaires. In L. A. Pervin (Ed.), *Handbook of personality: Theory and research* (pp. 66–100). New York: Guilford.

John, O. P., & Srivastava, S. (1999). The Big-Five trait taxonomy: History, measurement, and theoretical perspectives. In L. A. Pervin & O. P. John (Eds.), *Handbook of personality: Theory and research* (Vol. 2, pp. 102–138). New York: Guilford.

McNamee, S. (1998). Reinscribing organizational wisdom and courage: The relationally engaged organization. In S. Srivastava & D. L. Cooperrider (Eds.), *Organizational wisdom and courage* (pp. 101–117). San Francisco: New Lexington.

Meacham, J. A. (1990). The loss of wisdom. In R. J. Sternberg (Ed.), *Wisdom: Its nature, origins, and development* (pp. 181–211). New York: Cambridge University Press.

Orwell, L., & Perlmutter, M. (1990). The study of wise persons: Integrating a personality perspective. In R. J. Sternberg (Ed.), *Wisdom: Its nature, origins, and development* (pp. 160–177). New York: Cambridge University Press.

Rost, J. (1991). *Leadership for the twenty-first century.* New York: Praeger.

Shamir, B., House, R. J., & Arthur, M. B. (1993). The motivational effects of charismatic leadership: A self-concept based theory. *Organization Science, 4,* 577–594.

Sternberg, R. J. (Ed.). (1990). *Wisdom: Its nature, origins, and development.* Cambridge, UK: Cambridge University Press.

Sternberg, R. J. (2003). *Why smart people can be so stupid.* New Haven, CT: Yale University Press.

Sternberg, R. J. (2004). What is wisdom and how can we develop it? *Annals of the American Academy of Political and Social Science, 591,* 164–174.

Sternberg, R. J. (2005). Foolishness. In R. J. Sternberg & J. Jordan (Eds.), *A handbook of wisdom: Psychological perspectives* (pp. 331–352). New York: Cambridge University Press.

Turner, N., Barling, J., Epitropaki, O., Butcher, V., & Milner, C. (2002). Transformational leadership and moral reasoning. *Journal of Applied Psychology, 87,* 304–311.

Weick, K. E. (1998). The attitude of wisdom: Ambivalence as the optimal compromise. In S. Srivastava & D. L. Cooperrider (Eds.), *Organizational wisdom and courage* (pp. 40–64). San Francisco: New Lexington.

8

Strategic Ethics

*Strategy, Wisdom,
and Stakeholder Theory:
A Pragmatic and Entrepreneurial
View of Stakeholder Strategy*

R. Edward Freeman
Laura Dunham
John McVea

The process of strategy making remains complicated by the challenges of dynamic change in volatile markets (Hamel, 1996; Liedtka, 1998; Liedtka & Rosenblum, 1996; Mintzberg, 1978; Mintzberg & Waters, 1985) as well as the need to incorporate an ethical dimension (Hosmer, 1994) in a way that is useful to practitioners (e.g., Markoczy, Floyd, & Baldridge, 2004). Stakeholder theory has been offered as an approach to strategy making that both enables flexible and responsive strategic action in turbulent markets (Freeman, 1984) and explicitly addresses morals and values as a central feature of strategic management (Phillips, Freeman, & Wicks, 2003). However, we believe that stakeholder theory's potential as a source of managerial guidance remains unfulfilled. Although stakeholder theory has been eagerly embraced by business ethics scholars, it has yet to have as great an impact on the strategic management literature, to say nothing of actual practice. Much of this has to do with criticism regarding both normative and practical issues around its implementation. In this chapter, we examine the promise of a new conceptualization of stakeholder management that we believe can help to dissolve some of these problems from an ethical and entrepreneurial perspective.

Stakeholder theory has become a multifaceted set of ideas with many meanings. In a number of places, some authors of these ideas have tried to explain, summarize, differentiate, and integrate the strands of the theory (see especially Donaldson & Preston, 1995; Freeman, 1994; Freeman & McVea, 2001; Freeman, Wicks, Parmar, & McVea, 2004; Jones & Wicks, 1999; Phillips, 1997; Phillips et al., 2003). Our task is not to repeat or contribute to these efforts. Rather, we want to suggest that we can see one strand of stakeholder theory—the one that Freeman (1984), building on others, crystallized as an approach to strategic management—as connected to an idea of wisdom. The idea of wisdom that we explore is Aristotle's concept of practical wisdom as it has been, or could have been, developed by pragmatist thinkers such as John Dewey, Richard Rorty, Hilary Putnam, and Martha Nussbaum. Our approach, stakeholder management as an exercise of "practical wisdom," returns stakeholder theory to its pragmatic roots, enabling us to adopt an explicitly creative, aesthetic, and adaptive perspective that is well suited to the dynamic and entrepreneurial challenges of today's strategic environment and is fully embedded with ethical focus. Using the stakeholder idea to see strategic management as practical wisdom rescues stakeholder theory from its potential to degenerate into "it means whatever you want it to mean." Furthermore, it yields a conception of strategic management that solves a problem: How can we think about value creation in a global, changing, complex business environment?

Our argument proceeds as follows. We begin the chapter by identifying those normative and practical issues that have limited acceptance and application of stakeholder theory as a tool for strategically sound and ethically satisfying decision making within a business context. We then develop a pragmatist approach to stakeholder theory and identify the central role of management wisdom. We go on to articulate a managerial conception of practical wisdom that places ethics at its core, and we close with suggested strategies for cultivating this critical capacity.

The Stakeholder Approach to Innovative Strategy _____

Strategic management is often considered as the most practical and instrumental of the management fields (Segal-Horn, 2004). It is an integrative and practical subject where the rubber hits the road, that is, where the ideal and theoretical solutions of disciplines such as finance, marketing, and operations are pulled together and compromised into a coherent plan of action. As such, the philosophical foundations of the strategy process have received modest attention from scholars.[1] We propose that this amoral approach is both ethically misguided and detrimental to the process of strategic thinking and the theory of strategy. Strategy obviously is deeply embedded with moral consequences and considerations. However, in this chapter we propose that, perhaps less obviously, it is only through the integration of skills that are irreducibly philosophical, such as management wisdom, that managers can release strategy from the "new paradigm" swings and roundabouts that have dominated strategy academia over recent decades (Ghoshal, 2005). In this section, we focus on the contribution that stakeholder theory can make to the challenges of developing innovative strategies in dynamic and entrepreneurial environments faced by today's practitioners. In particular, we develop the argument that management wisdom can play a critical role in enabling the stakeholder approach to avoid several intellectual and practical cul-de-sacs while retaining its ability to provide a creative, holistic, and enduring framework for innovative strategic thinking.

The common thread to what has become known as stakeholder theory is something like "managing the business in consideration of its effects on all stakeholders." In its original formulation, the stakeholder approach had two main objectives. First, it was focused explicitly on the field of strategic management and was developed as a practical tool to help business strategists constructively plot strategic paths through increasingly dynamic and uncertain environments. Second, it aimed at providing a lasting, flexible, and holistic strategy framework, allowing practitioners to break the faddish cycle of developing and adopting new frameworks every time environmental shifts create a new type of challenge (Freeman & McVea, 2001).

An unintended consequence of this conceptual flexibility has been the development of a theory compatible with many different senses of "purpose" for the firm. As a result, the stakeholder approach has been adopted and adapted by a broad range of theorists with diverse perspectives both on the nature of the strategy process and on the role of the firm itself (for notable examples, see Bowie, 1999; Clarkson, 1995; Hendry, 2001; Hill & Jones, 1992; Langtry, 1994; Phillips, 1997; Phillips et al., 2003; Sternberg, 1996). In particular, the stakeholder approach has been shown to be compatible with both utilitarian and Kantian conceptions of the firm, resulting in a vigorous debate between theorists in both camps over which conception is the correct one. The ongoing debate between these competing interpretations of the stakeholder approach has had two major consequences. First, the emphasis on determining the "best" philosophical foundations of stakeholder theory has resulted in a distancing of the stakeholder project from the practical challenges of strategic decision making by actual practitioners. Second, it has resulted in a predictable philosophical impasse that mirrors a centuries-old dialogue between the competing teleological and deontological approaches to moral inquiry. Indeed, many of the most frequent objections to the stakeholder approach can be traced directly back to this philosophical divide. On the one hand, critics of utilitarianism offer the "impossibility critique"—that stakeholder analysis constitutes an infinite, and thus uncompletable, task (Marcoux, 2003; Sundaram & Inkpen, 2004). On the other hand, others point out that "stakeholder theory provides no moral significance independent of Kant's or someone else's ethics"

(Soule, 2002, p. 115) and thus is, on its own, toothless and incapable of guiding decisions. Theorists on all sides have had the advantage of an ample pool of well-rehearsed criticisms and countercriticisms from the philosophy literature on which to draw. Meanwhile, as John Dewey might have put it, the world continues to turn and the practical challenges of how to develop good stakeholder strategies remain mostly neglected.[2]

However, there is, we believe, an alternative approach that can help us to avoid these philosophical cul-de-sacs and, at the same time, reconnect stakeholder theory with managerial practice. This alternative requires us, first, to apply the perspective of the American pragmatists to the task at hand and, second, to extend our pragmatist interpretation of stakeholder theory through a conception of practical wisdom that can serve as a model for making strategic stakeholder decisions. The pragmatist approach, represented here primarily by the work of Dewey, suggests that we need not focus so much attention on a philosophical battle about whether utilitarian or Kantian foundations are actually correct. The separation of consequences from motives that is central to these arguments not only is a philosophical mistake but also is a symptom of a larger error in attempting to consider ultimate ends of innovative strategy separately from the practical means. For the pragmatist, ends and means are inextricably linked. Indeed, it is only through the interaction between means and ends that rational and intelligent progress can be made. To separate these elements of progress would be to deny, for example, that the consequences of our decisions for stakeholders theory might actually influence the strategic objective of the enterprise. Thus, hewing to a strictly Kantian or utilitarian interpretation of stakeholder risks overlooking a very crucial and creative dimension of the strategy process. However, the history of philosophy has demonstrated how difficult it can be to bring means and ends together in the abstract.[3] Therefore, in this chapter we follow the lead of the American pragmatists in proposing that the tensions between means and ends (or between consequences and motives) can be meaningfully resolved only at the practical level, within the context of a real concrete problem, embedded in a real network of stakeholders—those with real "names and faces" (McVea & Freeman, 2005). For such strategies to emerge, however, the stakeholder strategist needs to develop an understanding of decision making as driven by a sense of practical wisdom that accepts the messy tangle of means and ends embedded in each decision context and cultivates the capacity to carefully deliberate among them toward decisions that fruitfully meet the needs of all affected stakeholders.

In the next section, we develop this pragmatist approach with the aim of illustrating how it helps to address some of the normative and practical problems of stakeholder theory as currently received. Later in the chapter, we propose that to make this conception of stakeholder strategy operational, we need to take seriously the role of management wisdom in driving ethically sound and strategically effective decision making.

The Pragmatist Alternative

In this section, we propose an approach to stakeholder strategy that avoids competing arguments about whether ends or means should hold sway in strategic thinking. In place of this tension, we offer a view of stakeholder strategy as a continuous process of experimental inquiry through the application of practical wisdom. We believe that such an approach can address the original problem that the stakeholder approach was trying to address—making innovative strategic decisions in dynamic and entrepreneurial environments. It is important to point out that the pragmatist approach we propose does not attempt to challenge or disprove Kantian or utilitarian underpinnings of the stakeholder approach. Rather, it simply challenges their philosophical status as ultimate or absolute foundations of the stakeholder approach. In this section, we make the case for a pragmatist alternative, first, by contrasting it with these Kantian and utilitarian approaches and, second, by describing how a pragmatist interpretation can enrich these traditional views.

Enriching the Kantian View

Kantian stakeholder theory has been framed around the need to provide justification for paying attention to stakeholders through the strategy process while also attempting to establish the principles for how conflicts and tensions between stakeholders should be resolved. We see two major difficulties in thinking about the stakeholder approach in this way. First, it emphasizes strategic abstractions at the expense of the challenges of practice. Second, it can lead to truncated strategic inquiry and an underestimation of the potential for creative and innovative solutions.

The first difficulty is rooted in the sharp distinction posed by the Kantian perspective when arguing that we, as decision makers, should be guided in our actions by what is right rather than by what is good. As such, this version of the stakeholder approach makes an authoritative claim about what is intrinsically, as opposed to contextually, moral (Bowie, 1999; Phillips, 1997). However, from the pragmatist perspective, it is this very separation of the right from the good, and of motive from consequence, that can lead the stakeholder strategist into difficulties and can lead stakeholder theory into abstraction. In making this distinction, the Kantian stakeholder approach encourages us, as managers, to view good strategy as requiring access to philosophical conceptions that are separate from our business lives, our experiences, and our professional skills. From a Kantian perspective, strategic goals must preexist, and indeed transcend, the challenges of the particular concrete situation facing the decision maker. In arguing the existence of such ultimate ends, a Kantian stakeholder approach encourages us to reject our practical intuitions and judgments about the situations we face, to attempt to blind ourselves from the concrete relations we have with particular stakeholders, and to instead seek access to ends that predate the strategic challenges at hand. As such, the very nature of this conception of the stakeholder approach separates strategic goals from the task of developing innovative strategies. Even where clarity over strategic foundations and principles is reached, there often remains a disconnect for the practitioner over how such principles should actually be applied within specific strategies. This disconnect between the practical matters at hand and the abstract strategic objectives that the Kantian stakeholder approach seems to place on the strategist is, we believe, one of the fundamental reasons for the failure of stakeholder theory to flourish as an innovative strategy framework in the field. After all, for the practitioner in the field, what precise guidance do "maximize value creation" and "justice as fairness" actually give to the practical task of developing an innovative strategy?

The second unfortunate consequence of the Kantian stakeholder approach also flows from the view that the strategy process has ends or objectives that predate the current strategic situation. As such, the major challenge of stakeholder strategy is to determine how these a priori objectives can be best met. However, for the pragmatist, separating the means and ends of strategic thinking in this way represents a terrible foreshortening of inquiry and a neglect of some important aspects of creative intelligence. Means and ends are not separate; rather, they are codependent and operate in a reciprocal fashion. Although it is tempting to think independently about strategic objectives and strategic plans, to do so is to risk losing sight of how they relate to each other. In other words, we can come to understand how much we truly value our strategic objectives only when we reflect on how we value (or dislike) the means and consequences through which we plan to achieve those objectives. Stakeholder managers, for example, may value highly the goal of being first to market with a new product until they realize that the goal can be attained only by taking shortcuts in research and development, or in design and manufacturing, that will result in a substandard product. Thus, although we might initially approach a situation with some "ends in view," practical experience suggests that we should think of these as only temporary objectives that strongly influence, and in turn are influenced by, the means (stakeholder strategies) through which we consider achieving them. Hence, the point of strategic thinking is not simply to draw up plans to achieve an overriding a priori goal. An integral and reciprocal part of the task is to determine what goals, in light of all the stakeholder means imaginable, are truly of value. A Kantian stakeholder approach cannot accommodate such flexibility.

It is important to note that proposing a pragmatist alternative does not constitute a complete rejection of Kantian logic. A practically wise practitioner of the stakeholder approach would indeed act in ways that are compatible with treating stakeholders as ends rather than means and would recognize the practical value of using the categorical imperative (Kant,

1785/1990) as a tool for thinking through issues. However, it is in the moral motivations that the two perspectives differ. For the pragmatist, there is no need to propose a separate moral motivation derived from duty to obey the moral law. Rather, through careful deliberation over the most fruitful means and ends in any particular situation, it becomes clear to the practically wise strategist that good stakeholder management is integral to the practice of good management. Specificity about the good, and about the appropriate action for achieving the good, emerges from the particularities of each situation:[4] "The good consists of friendship, family and political relations, economic utilization of mechanical resources, science, art, in all their complex and variegated forms and elements. There is no separate moral good, no separate empty and rival good will" (Dewey & Tufts, 1908, p. 273). Thus, the pragmatist alternative enables us to conceive of stakeholder management as neither guided nor constrained by philosophical abstractions but rather focused on the practice of good management within particular and concrete circumstances and on the development of managers as wise and reflective practitioners.

Having distinguished the pragmatist alternative from popular Kantian conceptions of the stakeholder approach, in the next subsection we compare it with a utilitarian interpretation, again proposing how this common interpretation can be enriched by the pragmatist alternative.

Enriching the Utilitarian Perspective

In contrast to the tension between a Kantian conception of stakeholder theory and the practical challenges of making strategic decisions, a utilitarian stakeholder approach is quite compatible with many familiar tools and techniques of management theory. Indeed, utilitarianism's close cousin, cost–benefit analysis, is a central building block of much of both finance and management decision theories. However, we propose that, despite its greater familiarity to practitioners, there are a number of equally unfortunate consequences of thinking about stakeholder management from a purely utilitarian perspective. In an important argument, Putnam (2000) proposed that Dewey's central pragmatist insight consists of two amendments to utilitarianism—a deliberative amendment and an aesthetic amendment—that result in fundamentally changing the nature of the decision-making process.

The first amendment to utilitarianism is to emphasize the importance of the evaluative or deliberative nature of the decision-making process. This suggests that we need to correct for what could be called "casual utilitarianism." To follow the traditional Benthemite emphasis on "maximizing the greater good by summing pleasures or preferences" could be to interpret the "greater good" simplistically and misconstrue the meaning of what we value. Dewey, and John Stuart Mill before him, emphasized the importance of differentiating between things that we value and things that are truly valuable. To operate on the basis of what we currently value in a situation could allow us to drive our decisions from "casual" feelings and pleasures rather than to challenge ourselves to reflect carefully and determine what will really be of value to us in the future. It is important that we engage our intelligence and judgment in each situation, that is, use our "operational thinking" and drive our decision processes off what Rawls (1999) called "considered judgments" rather than focus on quantifying our intuitive pleasures. Hence, there is a thin, but critical, line between intuitive dogmatism and deliberative judgment—between intuitive decision making and reflective strategy. However, as Putnam (2000) pointed out, this observation could probably be considered as a friendly amendment. It seems that most reasonable utilitarians would concur that "the greatest amount of *intelligently evaluated* enjoyment on the part of the largest number possible" might be a more appropriate maxim.

However, the pragmatist perspective also has some unfriendly amendments to the utilitarian view that challenge the nature of, as well as the motivations for seeking, the common good through decision making. It is in applying these amendments that we believe pragmatism can liberate innovative strategy from the pursuit of calculative algorithms and the limitations of cost–benefit maximization. In pursuing the common good, utilitarians begin by considering the good, the pleasure, or the happiness they associate with particular objects and activities in the situation they face. "When happiness is conceived of as an aggregate of states of feeling, these are regarded as homogeneous in quality, different from one another only in intensity and duration" (Dewey & Tufts, 1908, p. 257). This ability to dissociate pleasure, or utility, into a pure homogeneous category separate from the context or character of the decision maker is what gives the utilitarian perspective much of its practical power. Given the ability to identify "pure utility," seeking the "greater good" can then be interpreted as a summing or maximizing of this characteristic. The costs and benefits as they accrue to each stakeholder can be established and cashed out against each other, and alternative courses of action can be evaluated, compared, and prioritized. Thus, optimal stakeholder strategies emerge, according to the utilitarian perspective.

However, there are grave dangers in applying this approach to developing real-world stakeholder strategies. First, and central to our utilitarian critique, is that what is of value does not consist only of feelings that are stimulated by an object or activity. What we consider to be good and valuable cannot be summarized solely by stimulated pleasures. For Dewey, what is truly of value is the satisfaction of a capacity or capability of a person, as confirmed by an object or experience. Hence, we value more than just how we feel about things; we also value the sort of persons we are and the characters we come to possess as we deal with those objects. Our "pleasurable feelings" in a particular situation are, at most, indicators that we are on the right path, or else they represent opportunities to grow and progress. They are not an ultimate measure of what we value. For example, we value good music not just because of the pleasurable feelings stimulated by the tingle in our ears but also because of the sense of pleasure we gain from developing our artistic discernment. We value a particular business strategy not just for the net effects it will have on stakeholders but also because it aids development of firm competency and contributes toward determining what sort of a business it will become. The critical point here is that the pleasures associated with the development of valuable personal characteristics obviously are not homogeneous in the same fashion as is proposed by the concept of utility. They are strongly characteristic of the context, institutions, and people involved. As MacIntyre (1981) observed,

> The pleasure-of-drinking-Guinness is not the pleasure-of-swimming-at-Crane's-beach, and the swimming and the drinking are not two different means for providing the same end state. . . . The happiness which belongs peculiarly to the way of life of the cloister is not the same happiness as that which belongs peculiarly to the military life. For different pleasures and different happiness's [sic] are to a large degree incommensurable; there are no scales of quality or quantity on which to weigh them. (p. 64)

Hence, according to Dewey and Tufts (1908), "Pure pleasure is a myth. Any pleasure is quantitatively unique, being precisely the harmony of one set of conditions with its appropriate activity" (p. 257). Therefore, it really makes no sense to talk of strategic decision making as the process of pursuing the common good by summing up pleasures (or benefits) and maximizing them. Stakeholder strategists must reach beyond universal measures, such as utility, net present value, risk-adjusted cash flow, and cost–benefit dollars, to fully capture the strategic potential of the decisions they face. Rather, we should think of strategy as the process of "constructing the good" and thus as a never-ending aesthetic activity focused on recognizing, blending, and harmonizing the multiple values at stake in any decision context.

> In short, the thing actually at stake in any serious deliberation is not a difference of quantity, but what kind of person one is to become, what sort of self is in the making, what kind of world is [in the] making. . . . To reduce all cases of judgment of action to the simplified, and comparatively unimportant, case of calculation of quantities is to miss the whole point of deliberation. (Dewey, 1969/1991, middle works, Vol. 14, p. 151)

Dewey's critique of utilitarian decision making illustrates some of the dangers and weaknesses of importing this interpretation of stakeholder management into the strategy process. Such an approach emphasizes costs and benefits that are extrinsic to the character of the decision maker and the organization, and it focuses decision making on a process of maximization of values that are not actually quantifiable. It does not emphasize reflection and deliberation through which what we initially value is transformed into what is truly valuable. It does not acknowledge the incommensurability of the values embedded in any decision context.

The interpretation of the stakeholder approach that we want to defend is one that emphasizes the qualitative nature of what is valuable strategically and thus one that replaces the metaphor and the practice of maximization with one of stakeholder congruence, harmony, and growth. It is an interpretation that moves the central focus of strategic thinking from "How can we maximize our competitive advantage" to "What sort of strategies can we imagine that will best fit the needs of our stakeholders to flourish?" or "What sort of a business do we want to become?" It should be pointed out that this is not to propose imposing solely softhearted or patronizing thinking into our strategy processes. Rather, as any parent knows, the sort of decision required to encourage children to flourish is often tough and demanding of them. However, the frame of mind of the decision maker is very different from one that focuses on maximizing the children's happiness.

Recent examples of corporate fraud and excess, such as the infamous Enron and Tyco cases, obviously are the result of a complex confluence of circumstances. However, we believe that a strict adherence to managing businesses by attempting to maximize according to a single dimension, often short-term shareholder returns, to the exclusion of a richer understanding of strategy certainly has contributed to these tragic situations. A focus on efficient and quantifiably measurable strategies rather than wise strategies has often resulted in strategic myopia. However, we believe that there may also be cause for some optimism with regard to viewing strategy more richly than as the process of maximizing a predetermined goal. Recent "stirrings" at Wal-Mart and McDonald's might suggest that some traditional managements are beginning to recognize the risky long-term strategic consequences of stubbornly holding to the maximization of a single principle. It turns out that developing long-term strategies based solely on "everyday lowest price" as a principle, regardless of other criteria stakeholders may value, may ultimately constrain and damage long-term strategic performance. Although far from the sort of fully fledged practical wisdom that we propose should guide strategic thinking, admissions that employee healthcare concerns, small community local planning concerns, or animal rights and organic farming concerns (in the case of McDonald's) might now legitimately have an influence on an increasingly more complex and messy corporate strategy process give us reason for hope.

Summary

To this point, we have identified what we see as the weaknesses in two major interpretations of stakeholder theory, weaknesses that we propose limit their effectiveness in helping real practitioners to develop ethically satisfying solutions to messy real-world problems. We have suggested how a pragmatic approach to stakeholder theory helps to address some of these concerns.

However, it could be argued that, in proposing this interpretation of the stakeholder approach to strategy, we have created as many problems as we have resolved. For sure, such critics might argue, we might have alleviated some of the abstraction problems of Kantianism, and we might have alleviated some of the quantitative excesses of utilitarian decision making. For sure, it is important to emphasize the creative and aesthetic aspects of crafting good business strategies, but pragmatism does not give us any guidance on how to complete this complex art, nor does it supply any limits or constraints about how it might be carried out. Indeed, critics might argue that, by challenging the utilitarian calculus, we have removed the one clear goal and the only concrete procedures and activities that actually give guidance and direction to stakeholder strategists trying to make decisions in a sea of turbulence.

It would then seem that we are faced with the dilemma of arguing that existing (perhaps flawed and incomplete, but at least constrained and focused) interpretations of stakeholder theory should be replaced by a practically more pleasing but intangible dream. Does a pragmatist interpretation of the stakeholder approach not just leave us grasping at clouds? Having asked the orchestra to rip up the music score, is it possible for it to improvise, or will cacophony ensue? Furthermore, wouldn't this aesthetic view of the stakeholder approach encourage managers, now untethered from abstract principles or overarching moral duties, to believe that they can devise strategies without any constraint—subject only to their imaginations?

It is at this point in the chapter that we attempt to move our argument from the destructive to the constructive. We believe that there can be a sustainable and independent stakeholder approach that is philosophically sound, practical, manageable and accessible to practitioners, and embedded with ethical focus. However, to achieve this, we must reach out for some help that is grounded in the ancient philosophical concept of practical wisdom.

Stakeholder Management as the Exercise of Practical Wisdom

In abandoning the "certainty of method" of the utilitarian interpretation, how do we respond to the criticism that stakeholder management is structureless, purposeless, unconstrained, and anarchic? We believe that there is a third way between management science and management expedience or between abstract ethical ideals and expedience—a pragmatist interpretation of stakeholder strategy that is grounded in practical wisdom. We believe that an emphasis on practical wisdom can liberate stakeholder strategy from the normative and practical issues that have limited its acceptance and implementation as a useful tool for strategic management and can guide us toward identifying those skills and capacities necessary for successfully adjudicating the difficult problems facing the stakeholder strategist. We believe that rearticulating stakeholder management as an exercise of practical wisdom enables us to set out a version of stakeholder theory that does the following:

- Recognizes the centrality of ethics to strategic management
- Embraces the indeterminacy and changeability of the kinds of problems facing strategy makers and operates within the context of uncertainty and ambiguity
- Imposes no particular "formula" for balancing, weighting, offsetting, or dividing stakeholder interests or rewards but allows the most appropriate approach to emerge from the particular situation
- Fully appreciates and addresses the incommensurability of values embedded within the options among which the manager must decide
- Enables our sense of the good to emerge from the concrete particulars of our lives

Accordingly, we set out to reconceptualize stakeholder management as an exercise of practical wisdom. On first blush, wisdom might seem to be an odd choice for rescuing stakeholder theory from its alleged vagaries. After all, wisdom itself is an esoteric topic, one that until recently was considered as a subject of concern only for philosophers and theologians (and rather ancient ones at that)—a set of scholars whose impact on management can be described as minimal at best. And yet the ancient and venerable concept of wisdom is one that has been with us throughout the ages, much studied, admired, and taught. Its resurgence as a topic of interest among cognitive and developmental psychologists (e.g., Baltes & Staudinger, 2000; Sternberg, 2003) suggests that this might be a good time to revisit the concept of wisdom and consider its applicability to a variety of human settings and problems, in this case the field of management study and the particular problem of stakeholder management.

In this section, we set out to articulate our own pragmatic view of practical wisdom in an attempt to demonstrate its accessibility as a subject of study and its rich usefulness as a decision-making capacity that can be cultivated by all managers and deployed effectively in the stakeholder management process. In so doing, we draw on one of the earliest and most enduring accounts of wisdom—Aristotle's (1984) conceptualization of *phronesis*, or practical wisdom—but update it by viewing it through a pragmatist lens and considering management wisdom as it might have been interpreted by thinkers such as Dewey, Putnam, and Nussbaum. Aristotle's ethics have been shown to be a rich source of insight into contemporary problems of business ethics (e.g., Duska, 1993; Hartman, 1996; Solomon, 1992). However, his concept of practical wisdom has yet to be fully explored within the context of business ethics. It is our hope to begin that project here. In this section, we define practical wisdom, identify some of the operations involved in implementing it, and suggest ways of cultivating it within the management context.

A Managerial Concept of Wisdom

Following Aristotle (1984), we define practical wisdom as the capacity to understand and act on what is both good and feasible for oneself and others in particular situations. The practically wise individual recognizes that choosing the right course of action in complex human situations cannot be reduced to the application of a general rule or scientific law. Rather, choosing wisely requires a grasp of the good that can be obtained in particular circumstances as well as a commitment to practical action that achieves that good. Thus, it requires being able to specify the ends that are appropriate and valuable within the particular context and to evaluate the specific means available for achieving that desired end. In its emphasis on fruitful action tailored to individual situations, practical wisdom avoids the abstractions of Kantian reasoning and the simplistic calculations of utilitarianism, and it fully embraces the rich complexity of the decision-making context.

For managers, then, practical wisdom entails, first, understanding the shared sense of value that binds them to their stakeholders, that is, the good they seek to achieve together. Wisdom, then, requires the ability to discern the most appropriate action for achieving that joint value in a multiplicity of complex and uncertain situations.

Such an account of managerial wisdom helps us to address a number of criticisms leveled at stakeholder theory. First, the concept of practical wisdom that is presented here integrates ethics into strategic decision making seamlessly and thoroughly. In contrast to deontological and utilitarian-based approaches, in which ethical considerations can be construed as operating outside the perceived bounds of the practical process of decision making, in the role of annoying or even confounding constraints on business action, our Aristotelian/pragmatist account of wisdom makes ethics fully constitutive of managerial decision making as wise managers seek to judge "rightly" in the face of complex problems so as to construct an innovative course of action that will support the achievement of good for all stakeholders. Intelligent or "clever" decisions—those that demonstrate expertise in achieving one's immediate goals—are sharply distinguished from wise decisions, which obtain only when that expertise has been used toward ascertaining what good can be achieved for all involved and then acting in ways consonant with that good (Sternberg, 2003).

Second, our account of managerial wisdom helps to move us past the means–end dichotomy that limits the usefulness of other interpretations of stakeholder theory. Practically wise managers recognize that each situation is an opportunity to specify appropriate and valuable ends that take into account the interests of all affected, to reflect on acceptable means for achieving those ends, and then to go back and revise and refine their sense of valuable ends in light of what they have learned about the means. In this way, managerial wisdom enables strategists to both acknowledge and respond meaningfully to the untidy tangle of means and ends that characterize real decision contexts and to incorporate a creative adaptive approach that frees them to find better, more innovative, and more ethically satisfying solutions to the problems they face.

Finally, such an account of wisdom fully embraces the messy complexity of the decision contexts in which managers operate while recognizing the need for action despite that complexity. Practical wisdom is rooted in the recognition that the act of choosing wisely can never be reduced to general rules that apply smoothly across circumstances because of the ever uncertain and idiosyncratic nature of human action. To attempt to do so is to subvert rationality because it does not allow one to fully appreciate and consider the very rich, complex, and nuanced dimensions of the problem at hand. Hence, wisdom requires an acute sensitivity to the features of the particular situation and an ability to choose a course of action that is most fitting to that situation and most likely to achieve or further flourishing. In this emphasis on the individuality of problems—on the need for the decision maker to discern what is important within that problem, to grasp the unique dimensions of it, and to shape solutions that are uniquely suited to it—a pragmatic account of practical wisdom directly addresses the kinds of decision-making contexts that regularly confront stakeholder strategists. Thus, stakeholder theory construed through the lens of practical wisdom is not defeated by the unpredictability and indeterminacy of human problems. Rather, stakeholder strategy as practical wisdom is well suited to the demands of decision making in dynamically changing and entrepreneurial business environments.

Implementing a Stakeholder Approach to Strategy as Practical Wisdom

Practical wisdom is not rooted in some elusive mystical operations accessible only to the rarefied few. Rather, it is rooted in a series of fairly prosaic practices and capabilities that can be cultivated and carried out by any thoughtful practitioner. Drawing on both Aristotelian and pragmatic accounts, we suggest that stakeholder management as an exercise of practical wisdom entails four key operations: perception, deliberation, experimental action, and reflection.

Perception

Because decision making and action in practical matters cannot be reduced to a process of applying general rules or set formulas, the development and exercise of practical wisdom rest on the sensitivity with which one is able to perceive and interpret the unique features of each situation. "Situational appreciation" (Wiggins, 1980, p. 237) is key here: to be practically wise, one must cultivate a "sort of complex responsiveness to the salient features of one's concrete situation" (Nussbaum, 1990, p. 55); one must become adept at reading situations. Aristotle spoke of those with practical wisdom having an "eye"—an acute and discriminating awareness of the particulars as well as an immediate and larger grasp of the sort of situation with which they are faced. This perceptive capacity enables one, first to recognize the opportunity or need for action and, second to know "how to construe the case, how to describe and classify what is before one" (Sherman, 1989, p. 40).

Such perception requires keen attention to the details of each situation—to what is new and different about this situation and, similarly, to what links this situation with others one has experienced; to the particular persons and relationships involved (McVea & Freeman, 2005); to the complex constellation of factors that have shaped and continue to influence the situation; and to the qualitative differences among the multitude of values embedded within the options facing the decision maker. Noticing, appreciating, and interpreting these details require more than one's intellectual involvement; they require the full engagement of one's emotional, imaginative, and moral capacities. Emotion provides a depth of knowledge to perception that is not possible through intellectual analysis alone. One cannot fully apprehend a particular value in all its richness and complexity unless one feels at an emotional level.

> [For the] agent who discerns intellectually that a friend is in need or that a loved one has died, but who fails to respond to these facts with appropriate sympathy or grief, . . . it seems right to say . . . that a part of discernment or perception is lacking. This person doesn't really, or doesn't fully, *see* what has happened, doesn't recognize it in a full-blooded way or take it in. (Nussbaum, 1990, p. 79)

Imagination also comes into play by enabling the practically wise individual to form clear and concrete mental images that sharpen his or her sense of the particulars of the case at hand, to play with multiple interpretations of those particulars, and to generate novel ways of responding to the situation (Noel, 1997).

Above all, perception is rooted in our moral sensibilities. Ultimately, if the purpose of choosing wisely is to aid us in achieving the good life, our perceptions about any situation are shaped by and focused on our sense of what is conducive to the good in that situation. "Moral perception helps us to sort the significant aspects from the insignificant in our circumstances. Significance always emerges in relation to our aims, and therefore clarity about what is good and noble is the source of our moral vision" (Fowers, 2003, p. 416). This is not to say that our aims are always clear; part of the deliberative task of the practically wise individual is the ongoing specification of good ends in any particular situation, a task made challenging by the array of competing and often inconsistent claims and concerns presented in a typical decision context. Rather, the point is that practical wisdom requires a moral compass as one sizes up the situation with which one is faced and sets out to seek the means and ends most conducive to human good and flourishing in that situation.

An example of such perception is found in the story of Mohammad Yunus and the process through which he came to found the Grameen Bank of Bangladesh and, in so doing, to pioneer the microcredit movement. Yunus's entrepreneurial journey was sparked by a set of perceptions about the poverty around him that were richly informed by his emotional, imaginative, and moral response to the situation. Although others around him—fellow professors, government officials, and business leaders—had become inured to the sight of so many living in abject poverty, Yunus was outraged. "While people were dying of hunger on the streets, I was teaching elegant theories of economics. I started hating myself for the arrogance of pretending I had answers. . . . We knew nothing about the poverty that surrounded us" (Yunus, quoted in Jolis, 1996, p. 1). The emotional discomfort he felt caused him to challenge his own habits of thinking. "People see what they are trained to see. It takes a serious attempt on one's part to take off the glasses one has been fitted with during student days. . . . I was lucky I could start seeing things differently than I was trained to see" (Yunus, 1998b, p. 3). Through intensive research efforts and immersion in the life of the local village, Yunus came to understand the drivers of local poverty and to form a unique and imaginative set of insights regarding the potential for women, historically overlooked and oppressed in Bangladeshi society, to become effective wage earners for their families if provided with access to credit. Sparked by his moral outrage at "the problem of poverty which humiliates and denigrates everything that a human being stands for," Yunus (1998a, p. 3) perceived the situation around him very differently from his peers and, in so doing, perceived a new opportunity to achieve human flourishing for many thousands who typically were denied it.

Deliberation

If choosing the right course of action cannot become systematized through application of general rules and principles, and therefore all action must be tailored to the unique features of individual situations, the quality of the decision maker's deliberation over possible action becomes critical to wise decision making. Although, as described earlier, the practically wise individual must cultivate the ability to read new situations quickly and discern the moral implications, these perceptive qualities rarely yield an immediate and robust response to the problem at hand. The decisions with which we are faced typically are too complex and variegated. Therefore, deliberation is required to make sure that all concerns and considerations are aired thoroughly, that good ends are specified for the particular situation, that all possible actions are considered and evaluated, and that the preferred response meets the needs of the situation effectively.

Dewey provided us with some insight into this process with his suggestion that intelligent deliberation entails a process he termed "dramatic rehearsal." It is a series of imaginary experiments carried out to discover what various modes of action and different end states are really like. It is the creation and mental rehearsal of alternative strategies for resolving a new problem, and it entails an active mental and emotional engagement with the characters and relationships of the real actors who would be affected by each of these strategies. The power of dramatic rehearsal is that it allows the decision maker to experience various possibilities that may or may not help to solve the problem at hand without committing that person to action and its subsequent consequences.

Such deliberation departs from more mainstream accounts of rational deliberation in a number of ways. First, in dramatic rehearsal, the stress is on imagining and choosing means that are in harmony with the stakeholder environment rather than focusing on those that optimize toward an established goal. In the case of dramatic rehearsal, goals emerge from the process. Alternative means of action are imagined in vivid, emotion-laden detail as possible future ways of living, and decision makers can evaluate each only by imagining what their lives would be like if they selected that course of action. The means that are imagined shape one's sense and valuing of the ends that would ensue; for example, an individual might value a particular end more or less based on his or her perception of the goodness or attractiveness of the means (Anderson, 2005). Hence, the ends themselves become clear only in the course of fleshing out possible strategies for action.

Second, dramatic rehearsal does not assume that we already have a fixed and absolute set of preferences or values. Indeed, one of the purposes of the deliberative process is to discover what we prefer or what is really of value. It is only through careful deliberation that we gain clarity about those objects we previously deemed to be of value; it is only through envisaging our lives as transformed by different possible courses of action meant to achieve that object that we come to understand more vividly the features and consequences related to that object. This in turn can either deepen or alter our initial prizing of that object (Anderson, 2005), thereby transforming our system of values in a way that reflects our capacity for continued growth. In this way, the formation of preferences and values is an integral and emergent part of the decision-making process.

Finally, in dramatic rehearsal, practically wise individuals both acknowledge and deeply appreciate the incommensurability of values embedded within the options they face (for a more thorough elaboration of themes that follow and are highlighted only briefly here, see Nussbaum, 1990, pp. 56–66). The practically wise person recognizes the intrinsic merits and qualitative differences of each of his or her options and rejects any notion that a uniform value applies and can be maximized. To make any attempt to determine some "pure utility" disassociated from the context or character of the decision maker, which could facilitate some easy comparison of options and an overall maximization of utility, would be to fail to fully grasp and deliberate richly on the situation. The decision maker's task, then, is to clearly discern the plurality of values among which he or she must choose and to grasp the distinctive nature of those values as embedded within each of the options. As in a Deweyan account, these values represent more than the pleasure or happiness generated by the option under consideration. These values reflect a unique human capacity or capability that is expressed or enhanced through the option. Thus, the option is chosen for the unique value intrinsic to it and not for any consequence of happiness or pleasure that is subsequent to its choice. Wise deliberation requires the decision maker to give each option its due by reflecting fully on its distinctive value and then, despite the rich array of competing values, to choose the option that addresses the situation most adequately. Maximization is simply not possible here; in selecting one option and the value inherent in it, the decision maker must forgo the others. And so the practically wise individual fully recognizes the difficulties and often tragic dimensions of the problems he or she faces. To long for a simpler utilitarian compass is to subvert rationality and to fail to do justice to the act of deciding.[5]

Such deliberation is captured nicely in a story told by John Mackey, founder and chief executive officer of Whole Foods, about his confrontation with an animal rights activist, Lauren Ornelas, at the company's 2003 annual shareholders meeting (Fishman, 2004). Ornelas, director of the animal rights organization Viva! USA, had taken the floor to chastise the company for selling ducks that had been raised in inhumane circumstances. Mackey was insulted by her aggressive approach and was dismissive of her claims given the company's highly lauded record on animal rights, and he eventually walked out of the meeting. However, following the meeting he agreed to continue the conversation through e-mails. He also began a process of research and deliberation to better understand the situation. "'I didn't understand why these people were so passionate about this issue,' he says. 'I perceived them as our enemies. Now, the best way to argue with your opponents is to completely understand their point of view'" (Mackey, quoted in Fishman, 2004, p. 70). He took 3 months to immerse himself deeply in the issue. "The more I read, the more I was interested in it. I said, damn, these people are right. This is terrible" (p. 70). Mackey also investigated his company's suppliers. Although the company already followed stringent criteria in selecting suppliers to ensure that only high-quality organic foods landed on their shelves, Mackey discovered that, for instance, the supplier of organic ducks sold by Whole Foods raised the ducks entirely in barns. The ducks were never allowed outside and had their bills trimmed to avoid injury to each other. "Most stunning to Mackey, 'they are not allowed to swim. Ever. Ducks who never get to swim'" (p. 70). Although Mackey had never intended to become involved in the issue of animal rights, his imaginative and emotional deliberation led him to conclude that "before being consumed by humans, animals should at least be allowed, in his words, 'to live out their fundamental animal nature'" (p. 70). Mackey

instituted a new set of practices at Whole Foods, using the company's buying power to pressure suppliers into better treatment of the animals they
raise. Although such measures raise Whole Foods' costs, Mackey's deliberative process exemplifies one that is focused less on optimization than
on imagining and choosing means that are in better harmony with the
company's ethos and its stakeholder environment. Furthermore, although
there may be short-term costs, the long-term strategic benefits of this sort
of approach to strategic thinking is better reflected in Whole Foods' long-
term performance, which boasts some of the highest growth and profitability figures in the entire grocery industry. Wise strategies are not just rich,
creative, and sensitive to stakeholder concerns; they also cause the business
to flourish.

Experimental Action

Despite the often painful difficulties of choosing among competing values, the practically wise individual does indeed act, but his or her action is
richly informed by the deliberative process. While inevitably making trade-
offs among competing values, the individual acts in ways that incorporate
recognition of each separate value that has been forgone. Nussbaum (1990)
provided an illuminating example:

> Suppose, for example, we are in agreement that on balance Truman
> was correct in choosing to bomb Hiroshima, that this was the best
> available exit to the horrible dilemma in which he and the nation had
> been placed by factors beyond their control. Still, it matters deeply
> whether the bombing is to be treated simply as the winning alternative,
> or, in addition, as a course of action that overrides a genuine moral
> value. It matters whether Truman takes this course with unswerving
> confidence in his own powers of reason, or with reluctance, remorse,
> and the belief that he is obligated to make whatever reparations can be
> made. Whether all his attention is directed toward picking the top
> point on a single ordered line, or whether he attends, as well, to the
> intrinsic ethical character of the claim that on balance is not preferred.
> The Aristotelian leader, cherishing each separate value and attaching
> to each the appropriate emotions and feelings of obligation, behaves in
> the second of these ways. (p. 65)

Because of his or her deliberations, the practically wise strategist recognizes the ongoing responsibility of carrying out the chosen strategy in such
a way as to address the other values that have been decided against in this
particular situation.

The practically wise strategist would also recognize that all action is
subject to review and revision. Because choosing the right course of action is
not a science guided by fixed laws and principles, practical wisdom requires

that decision makers acknowledge the fallibility of the judgments they apply. Although each act is preceded by careful deliberation, practical wisdom requires that decision makers approach each course of action as provisional, carrying out that action as enlightened trial and error subject to constant monitoring and evaluation. When a course of action fails to achieve the good or value sought, practical wisdom requires that the decision maker reassess all aspects of the problem at hand. It is not enough to merely try another course of action. Rather, the practically wise individual uses the information gathered from putting action into practice to reappraise the entire situation, including his or her original perception or reading of the circumstances and the various courses of action considered. Most important, however, practical wisdom requires that the decision maker use the results of action to continue evaluating and refining his or her sense of what is of ultimate value. Thus, it is not only our actions, but also our most deeply held convictions of what is truly valuable, that are subject to review and revision. In this way, action and its results allow us to continue to grow as humans and to continually make progress by regularly reimagining our lives and conceiving new and better ways to live. As when Mackey was forced to grapple with the issue of animal rights, practically wise stakeholder managers remain ambivalent enough about their own wisdom (Weick, 1979) to continually test their own beliefs and strive to learn and grow.

Reflection

Each of the preceding operations of practical wisdom is vitally dependent on the individual's capacity for, and commitment to, critical reflection. Reflection entails not only close attention and consideration of the details of each decision context but also an ongoing discipline in which managers examine and learn from the accumulation of experiences with which they are faced. Critical reflection requires practically wise managers to regularly question their own assumptions, preferences, and values; to be aware of the mental frameworks and schemas that govern their thinking processes; and to be willing to revise their interpretations of events and the meanings they hold. As Johnstone (1983) put it, practical wisdom in a Deweyan scheme

> must include the expansion of *mind*. This indicates not merely the addition of bits of information to memory, but a diversification, expansion, and integration of meanings, of "the sense things make," wherein actions and other events are understood not as isolated and simple occurrences, but in terms of their connections with one another. Growth of mind is growth in the integrity of experience so that what is apprehended constitutes a genuine universe, a unified system of events that "fit in" with one another. It is growth in awareness of the wholeness of experience. (p. 192)

It is through the regular exercise of critical reflection that the practically wise person achieves this integration and expansion of meaning. This in turn shapes the person's ability to read each situation with heightened perception, to deliberate with sensitivity and imagination, and to act adaptively and responsively.

Cultivating Practical Wisdom

To reinterpret stakeholder theory as an exercise in practical wisdom, as we have suggested, constitutes a call for a great deal of work by researchers, educators, and practitioners to establish conditions and requirements that would support such a perspective. Much work remains to be done. However, even at this preliminary stage, a number of observations can be made about some initial steps that should be taken to start moving us in the right direction. We close this section by offering some brief thoughts on two practical means for cultivating wisdom within the context of business strategy and business education: an embracing of the arts and an emphasis on the role of mentoring.

In considering how to cultivate practical wisdom, we take a prototypical Deweyan perspective by first considering the following question: Who is the wise stakeholder strategist? The wise stakeholder strategist is the entrepreneurial thinker who has developed the skills and character to construct innovative strategies that transcend the tensions between stakeholders and create harmonious progress through value creation and trade. As such, the stakeholder strategist has become adept at the creative, aesthetic, and empathetic dimensions of decision making. It should be clear by now that the exercise of practical wisdom requires the cultivation of a set of skills and capabilities that are not typically associated with the businessperson's repertoire. The cultivation of practical wisdom is not rooted in the kinds of rational analytical tools and techniques with which we typically seek to inculcate the businessperson or in the knowledge of particular immutable laws and principles that explain and govern organizational action and performance. Rather, practical wisdom must be viewed as a moral and aesthetic exercise. It requires the ongoing cultivation of imagination, empathy, sensitivity to detail, aesthetic regard for fit and harmony, and moral awareness. Aristotle and Dewey were in agreement that in cultivating the kind of character that embodies these characteristics, real learning comes only with actual experience. One must regularly choose and act with wisdom to become adept in the art of wisdom. Although this may seem tautological, it does point us toward some practical strategies. Experiential education remains an important tactic for the development of practical wisdom. In business schools, case studies remain a premier vehicle for exposing students to a wide variety of decision contexts and providing them with the opportunity to exercise their judgment and then reflect on the content and effectiveness of their approach. Using case studies to develop practical wisdom requires that the exploration of case studies include a strong emphasis on the inherent ethicality of each managerial decision. However, from this perspective, it is particularly important that case studies not simply be used as illustrations or exemplars for the application of abstract theory but rather to create a complex and open-ended experience for students and practitioners to experiment and develop the sort of wise skills and practices described here.

However, although case-based learning certainly moves us in the direction of developing wise practitioners, even in its most sophisticated form it has certain inevitable limitations. For instance, case discussion can reinforce a form of moral relativism, where the emphasis is on understanding all stakeholder perspectives, but without imposing the demand that the students creatively resolve the tensions among these different perspectives. Second, from a pragmatist perspective, the case method can take us only so far in providing a "real" experience. The art of constructing truly wise strategies to address these problems makes sense only from the perspective of being fully engaged in the context and the human relationships of the real situations. Although case studies bring students closer to reality, students are not really making decisions while enmeshed in real relationships with real stakeholders.

To address some of these limitations, a number of approaches have been developed involving the use of the arts (e.g., the widespread use of jazz as a metaphor for decentralized management, the reading of biographies and literature in leadership studies) to enrich students' imaginations and stimulate the sense of empathy and connectedness that is essential to good deliberation. However, what we are proposing requires more than simple exposure to the arts. To create an environment where practical wisdom flourishes requires that we move beyond art as a metaphor and fully embrace strategic thinking as a practical art in itself. A first step in doing this is to begin exploring the possibilities and benefits of incorporating greater engagement with the arts into the business curriculum. Real engagement with the arts, or aesthetically rich experiences (Statler, Roos, & Victor, 2005), feeds practical wisdom by integrating three dimensions of human experience: thinking, feeling, and acting. Aesthetically rich experiences feed the emotions (a critical source of ethical knowledge) (Nussbaum, 1990), stimulate the imagination, and promote a sense of "solidarity" (Rorty, 1989) or connectedness that is critical to forming an understanding of and commitment to the good of all affected by one's decisions. Two of the current authors have had good success in drawing on the craft of theater for a business school elective focused on creative collaboration. In the course, students are required to write, direct, and act in a number of plays. Based on student feedback, the experience is a powerful one. Students cite multiple benefits, including a heightened ability to see situations from multiple perspectives, a new feeling of empathy for individuals very different from themselves, an appreciation for and commitment to an ethic of generosity toward collaborators, and (most important) a reinvigorated sense of imagination and creativity.

A second important direction for the development of stakeholder strategy is to gain a deeper understanding of the role and activities of a mentor. Traditionally, we think of wisdom as something we "learn at the feet of the wise." Both Dewey and Aristotle would agree that this aspect of practical wisdom is critical. Dewey's "learning by doing" approach to education is firmly rooted in a commitment to mentorship, a connection that has not always been well understood by his critics. In fact, Dewey needed to spend a great deal of time and effort in trying to undo the common misinterpretation that learning by doing consists of merely following one's instincts and intuition. To the contrary, Dewey placed great importance on the role of the mentor as one who selected and guided the experience of the student. Learning the wisdom of becoming a creative stakeholder strategist requires us to work hand-in-glove with a mentor already established as being wise. Thus, to cultivate wisdom within the business context, we need to rediscover within master of business administration (MBA) programs the idea of strategic stakeholder management as an apprenticeship. Furthermore, as an apprenticeship, we need to discover ways of guiding and developing this process beyond the separate classroom setting and of integrating it into the routine activities of the business itself. Such an imperative suggests renewed attention to action learning and internships as vehicles for fostering wisdom. In addition, if wise stakeholder management addresses the question "What sort of business should we become?," it is critical that we also focus our research efforts on the question "How do businesses ensure that their decision makers have the opportunity to become wise?"

Implications

Reconceptualizing stakeholder management as an exercise of practical wisdom returns stakeholder theory to its pragmatic roots, enabling us to adopt an explicitly creative, aesthetic, and adaptive perspective on the strategic task. Practical wisdom becomes the linchpin in a process that allows us to avoid the abstractions of deontological ethics without necessarily falling into the arms of utilitarian empiricism. The problem with these traditional approaches is that they underuse human intelligence and thus underestimate our ability to be "radically novel" in solving our most difficult problems. Rather than seeking some external ethical principle or decision rule to solve thorny management problems, and rather than waiting for the scientific management types to deduce some eternal laws and principles to which managers must defer, practical wisdom requires that we fully engage our intelligence and judgment in each situation—that we cultivate our ability to read situations, to recognize the moral implications, and to imagine and deliberate our way toward ethically and practically satisfying solutions.

Thus, stakeholder management can be construed as a third way between science and expedience or between abstract ethical ideals and expedience. Stakeholder management instead becomes a practical art focused on the central strategic task of fit/harmony and collective good in multiple and highly differentiated decision contexts.

So construed, stakeholder theory can embrace the concrete particularity of idiosyncratic strategic problems. It can escape the trap of "normative justification" and admit the inextricable links between ends and means. Trying some means leads to a revision of ends, and success or failure to achieve certain ends leads to new means. This is Dewey's (and our) understanding of the way the social world works. We are not so concerned with demarcating the empirical from the normative, but we are engaged in the process of seeing what works. The decision maker in a strategic process is necessarily a pragmatist in our interpretation.

Much work remains to be done. There is more to learn about the development and application of practical wisdom. The emerging science on wisdom gives us cause for optimism. But recognition of the importance of wisdom can also help us to better focus the task of management research away from the Holy Grail of scientific laws and principles through which we can control business environments and managerial action and toward seeking a greater understanding of this very real and human capacity for wise deliberation and action.

Notes

1. A recent exception is Powell (2003).

2. There have, however, been a few notable exceptions that focused on the practice of stakeholder management: for example, Harrison and St. John (1996) and Kochan (2000).

3. For the latest attempt to show how this is difficult given the state of philosophy, see Putnam (2004).

4. Indeed, this is the way we read Phillips's (2003) work on the obligations of fairness—in the pragmatist's vein rather than in the Kantian one. In Phillips's view, fairness is just good management and vice versa.

5. Wiggins (1980) put it nicely when he stated that he suspects that those theorists looking for a scientific theory of rationality really want "a system of rules by which to spare themselves some of the agony of thinking and all the torment of feeling and understanding that is actually involved in reasoned deliberation" (p. 237).

References

Anderson, E. (2005). Dewey's moral philosophy. In E. N. Zalta (Ed.), *The Stanford encyclopedia of philosophy* [Online]. Available: http://plato.stanford.edu/archives/spr2005/entries/dewey-moral

Aristotle. (1984). *Nicomachean ethics* (D. Ross, Trans.). New York: Oxford University Press.

Baltes, P. B., & Staudinger, U. M. (2000). Wisdom: A metaheuristic (pragmatic) to orchestrate mind and virtue toward excellence. *American Psychologist, 55,* 122–136.

Bowie, N. (1999). *Business ethics: A Kantian perspective.* Malden, MA: Blackwell.

Clarkson, M. (1995). A stakeholder framework for analyzing and evaluating corporate social performance. *Academy of Management Review, 20,* 92–117.

Dewey, J. (1991). *The collected works of John Dewey, 1882–1953* (J. A. Boydston, Ed.). Carbondale: Southern Illinois University Press. (Original work published 1969)

Dewey, J., & Tufts, J. H. (1908). *Ethics.* New York: Henry Holt.

Donaldson, T., & Preston, L. (1995). The stakeholder theory of the corporation: Concepts, evidence, and implications. *Academy of Management Review, 20,* 85–91.

Duska, R. F. (1993). Aristotle: A pre-modern post-modern? Implications for business ethics. *Business Ethics Quarterly, 3,* 227–249.

Fishman, C. (2004, July). The anarchist's cookbook. *Fast Company,* pp. 70–78.

Fowers, B. J. (2003). Reason and human finitude: In praise of practical wisdom. *American Behavioral Scientist, 47,* 415–422.

Freeman, R. E. (1984). *Strategic management: A stakeholder approach.* Boston: Pitman.

Freeman, R. E. (1994). The politics of stakeholder theory. *Business Ethics Quarterly, 4,* 409–421.

Freeman, R. E., & McVea, J. (2001). A stakeholder approach to strategic management. In M. Hitt, R. E. Freeman, & J. Harrison (Eds.), *The Blackwell handbook of strategic management* (pp. 189–207). Oxford, UK: Basil Blackwell.

Freeman, R. E., Wicks, A., Parmar, B., & McVea, J. (2004). Stakeholder theory: The state of the art and future perspectives. *Politeia, 20,* 9–22.

Ghoshal, S. (2005). Bad management theories are destroying good management practices. *Academy of Management Learning and Education, 4*(1), 75–91.

Hamel, G. (1996). Strategy as revolution. *Harvard Business Review, 74*(4), 69–82.

Harrison, J. S., & St. John, C. H. (1996). Managing and partnering with external stakeholders. *Academy of Management Executive, 10*(2), 46–59.

Hartman, E. M. (1996). *Organizational ethics and the good life.* New York: Oxford University Press.

Hendry, J. (2001). Missing the target: Normative stakeholder theory. *Business Ethics Quarterly, 11,* 159–176.

Hill, W. L., & Jones, T. M. (1992). Stakeholder agency theory. *Journal of Management Studies, 29,* 131–154.

Hosmer, L. T. (1994). Strategic planning as if ethics mattered. *Strategic Management Journal, 15*(5), 17–34.

Johnstone, C. L. (1983). Dewey, ethics, and rhetoric: Toward a contemporary conception of practical wisdom. *Philosophy and Rhetoric, 16,* 185–207.

Jolis, A. (1996, May 5). The good banker. *Independent on Sunday Supplement.*

Jones, T. M., & Wicks, A. C. (1999). Convergent stakeholder theory. *Academy of Management Review, 24,* 206–221.

Kant, I. (1990). *Foundations of the metaphysics of morals* (L. W. Beck, Trans.). New York: Macmillan. (Original work published 1785)

Kochan, T. (2000). Towards a stakeholder theory of the firm: The Saturn partnership. *Organizational Science, 11,* 367–386.

Langtry, B. (1994). Stakeholders and the moral responsibilities of business. *Business Ethics Quarterly, 4,* 432–441.

Liedtka, J. M. (1998). Strategic thinking: Elements, outcomes, and implications for planning. *Long Range Planning, 31,* 120–130.

Liedtka, J. M., & Rosenblum, J. W. (1996). Shaping conversations: Making strategy, managing change. *California Management Review, 39,* 141–157.

MacIntyre, A. (1981). *After virtue.* Notre Dame, IN: Notre Dame University Press.

Marcoux, A. (2003). A fiduciary argument against stakeholder theory. *Business Ethics Quarterly, 13,* 1–14.

Markoczy, L., Floyd, S. W., & Baldridge, D. C. (2004). Are managers from Mars and academicians from Venus? Toward an understanding of the relationship between academic quality and practical relevance. *Strategic Management Journal, 25,* 1063–1074.

McVea, J. F., & Freeman, R. E. (2005). A names-and-faces approach to stakeholder management: How focusing on stakeholders as individuals can bring ethics and entrepreneurial strategy together. *Journal of Management Inquiry, 14,* 57–69.

Mintzberg, H. (1978). Patterns in strategy formation. *Management Science, 25,* 934–948.

Mintzberg, H., & Waters, J. (1985). Of strategies, deliberate and emergent. *Strategic Management Journal, 6,* 257–272.

Noel, J. (1997). Interpreting Aristotle's *Phantasia* and claiming its role within *phronesis. Philosophy of Education.* [Online]. Available: www.ed.uiuc.edu/EPS/PES-Yearbook/97_docs/noel.html

Nussbaum, M. C. (1990). *Love's knowledge.* Oxford, UK: Oxford University Press.

Phillips, R. A. (1997). Stakeholder theory and a principle of fairness. *Business Ethics Quarterly, 7,* 51–66.

Phillips, R. A. (2003). Stakeholder legitimacy. *Business Ethics Quarterly, 13,* 25–41.

Phillips, R. A., Freeman, R. E., & Wicks, A. C. (2003). What stakeholder theory is not. *Business Ethics Quarterly, 13,* 479–502.

Powell, T. C. (2003). Strategy without ontology. *Strategic Management Journal, 24,* 285–292.

Putnam, H. (2000). Dewey's central insight. *Convegno Internazionale John Dewey, Cosenza,* Italia, 10–13 abril.

Putnam, H. (2004). *Ethics without ontology.* Cambridge, MA: Harvard University Press.

Rawls, J. (1999). *A theory of justice* (Rev. ed.). Cambridge, MA: Belknap.

Rorty, R. (1989). *Contingency, irony, and solidarity.* Cambridge, UK: Cambridge University Press.

Segal-Horn, S. (2004). The modern roots of strategic management. *European Business Journal, 16*(4), 1.

Sherman, N. (1989). *The fabric of character: Aristotle's theory of virtue.* Oxford, UK: Oxford University Press.

Solomon, R. C. (1992). *Ethics and excellence*. Oxford, UK: Oxford University Press.

Soule, E. (2002). Managerial moral strategies: In search of a few good principles. *Academy of Management Review, 27*, 114–125.

Statler, M., Roos, J., & Victor, B. (2005). *Dear Prudence: An essay on practical wisdom in strategy making* [Online]. Available: http://64.233.167.104/search?q=cache:4KHFWwNcCZoJ:sw-mos.insead.edu.sg/workshop3/Papers/RossStatlerVictor.pdf+dear+prudence+strategy&hl=en

Sternberg, E. (1996). Stakeholder theory exposed. *Corporate Governance Quarterly, 2*(1), 4–18.

Sternberg, R. J. (2003). *Wisdom, intelligence, and creativity synthesized*. Cambridge, UK: Cambridge University Press.

Sundaram, A. K., & Inkpen, A. C. (2004). The corporate objective revisited. *Organization Science, 15*, 350–363.

Weick, K. (1979). *The social psychology of organizing*. Reading, MA: Addison-Wesley.

Wiggins, D. (1980). Deliberation and practical wisdom. In A. O. Rorty (Ed.), *Essays on Aristotle's ethics* (pp. 221–240). Berkeley: University of California Press.

Yunus, M. (1998a, October 31). Banker to the poor. *The Guardian* (London).

Yunus, M. (1998b, August 13). Commencement address, Brigham Young University, Provo, UT.

PART III

Aesthetics

9

Individual Aesthetics

Self-Interest

Russell Cropanzano
Jordan Stein
Barry M. Goldman

Well, every government lays down laws for its own advantage. . . . In laying down these laws they have made it plain that what is to their advantage is just. They punish him who departs from this as a law-breaker and an unjust man. And this, my good sir, is what I mean. In every city it is the same.

—Plato, *The Republic*, Book I

My good Thrasymachus, are you going to depart after throwing a speech like that at us, before you have thoroughly taught us or learnt yourself whether or not such things be?

—Plato, *The Republic*, Book I

With those lines from *The Republic*, Plato (ca. 360 BC/1935) confronted us with a classic challenge for scholars: Are humans motivated by anything short of personal gain? Thrasymachus expounded what he believed to be a fundamental insight into human social life. Stated generally, he implied that our varied motives and behaviors reduce to a single ultimate goal—self-interest. Socrates, on the other hand, went on to argue that there is more to the matter than this. Self-interest exists, but it is not alone. One of these thinkers has much to teach us, and we would do well to act on his insight. The posture by which we confront our social worlds will likely be one way if we concur with Thrasymachus and quite another way if we concur with Socrates. One of these individuals, either Thrasymachus or Socrates, was exceptionally wise.

But which one?

Philosophers and social scientists have pondered this matter for centuries. Various thinkers have accepted the doctrine of universal self-interest. These include scholars such as Thomas Hobbes, who presented a secular theory in support of monarchial privilege (Hobbes, 1651/1998), and Jeremy Bentham, who was a social reformer that supported the American Revolution (Bentham, 1789/1988). These thinkers and others came to advocate a theory of universal self-interest (philosophers sometimes term it "universal egoism" [Thompson, 2003]), maintaining that the ultimate motivation for human behavior is self-gain. But is acting solely in one's self-interest aesthetically pleasing for the individual?

Other thinkers, who did not necessarily accept the exclusivity of self-interest, paid a sort of inadvertent tribute to the idea. Consider, for example, the philosophy of St. Augustine (Augustine of Hippo, 397/1907). On one level, Augustine denied the exclusivity of self-interest. However, only divine intervention (grace) allowed us to overcome our self-seeking tendencies. Obviously, a philosophical view that requires the work of God to move beyond egoism is implicitly acknowledging the power of the self-interest model.

Another philosophical nod to the power of self-interest can be found in Machiavelli's *The Prince* (1513/1908). Contrary to some superficial readings of his work, Machiavelli did not assert that all people were egoistic or that egoism was necessarily a good thing (e.g., Thompson, 2003). As Holmes (1990) observed, Machiavelli advanced "a prudential maxim. It was prudent for the Prince to expect the worst" (p. 344, note 96). In other words, leaders must contend with a competitive social landscape in which self-seeking rivals often undermine worthwhile intentions (for a general discussion, see Badaracco, 1997). Even if one does not believe that egoism is the only human motive, one certainly must grant this point.

As the behavioral sciences emerged from philosophy during the 19th century, they carried the doctrine of universal self-interest with them. The principle is associated most famously with economics (e.g., Edgeworth, 1881), but it soon spread to other disciplines as well. By the 20th century, Freud (1920/1974) could safely assert that humans were motivated by the "pleasure principle" to seek things that made them feel good and to avoid those that made them feel bad, a proposition very similar to Bentham's belief. Among more mainstream psychologists, Campbell (1975) and Gergen (1969) suggested that egoism was the preeminent human motive in psychology. By the late 1970s, Hatfield, Walster, and Piliavin (1978) were able to state flatly, "The majority of scientists—[us] included—are fairly cynical. They interpret apparent altruism in cost–benefit terms, assuming that individuals . . . perform those acts that are rewarded . . . and . . . avoid those acts that are not. . . . Most often scientists attribute apparent altruism to more selfish motives" (pp. 128–129). This continues to the present day. For example, Gillespie and Greenberg (2005) suggested that "the only ultimate goal(s) of individuals [is/]are self-directed" (p. 205).

Universal self-interest has even crept into popular culture (Weaver, 1984), at least among college students (Miller, 1999). Miller and Ratner (1998, Study 1) found that undergraduate research participants rated economic incentives as more effective in persuading people to donate blood than they actually were. In four subsequent studies, Miller and Ratner demonstrated that participants often believe group membership to be a more important determinant of attitudes and behaviors than is actually the case. In a follow-up article, participants reported that they believed they would be evaluated unfavorably if they supported a cause that was unrelated to their own needs (Ratner & Miller, 2001, Studies 1 and 3), although this could be corrected by providing social standing (Study 4). Moreover, participants were indeed apt to become angry if they learned of an individual who supported a position that was inconsistent with that individual's personal interests (Study 2). Taken together, these findings suggest that a self-interested view of human nature is widely shared among Americans to the point where some may fear social sanction for violating this norm (Holmes, Miller, & Lerner, 2002).

At least in some professions, it appears that individuals are sometimes socialized to act in their self-interest. Marwell and Ames (1981) discovered that graduate-level economics students were more likely than non-economics majors to "free ride" in situations that call for personal donations to public goods. Specifically, the students with economics training contributed a modest 20% of their funds to the public pot. This was significantly less than the 49% average for the non-economics students. Moreover, in spite of their higher incomes, economists can be somewhat less generous than others in terms of their monetary donations to charities (Frank, Gilovich, & Regan, 2000).

In view of such findings, there is no doubt that the doctrine of universal self-interest has had a profound impact on our understanding of human behavior (Mansbridge, 1990; Miller, 1999). From the vantage point of the social sciences, where so few questions are settled, one prefers to relish agreement rather than revisit old dialogues. Still, it is worth mentioning that doubts have always accompanied the theory of universal egoism. Indeed, philosophical concerns were raised more than two centuries ago by Joseph Butler (Butler, 1726/1983). And neither the free marketer Adam Smith (Smith, 1759/1853) nor the skeptic David Hume (Hume, 1739/2000) was reconciled to universal egoism. During more recent years, the political philosopher John Rawls maintained that there are times when "principles . . . override considerations of prudence and self-interest" (Rawls, 1971, p. 135; for more general philosophical critiques, see Holley, 1999; Thompson, 2003).

During the past few decades, behavioral scientists have added a heady dose of empirical data to this philosophical skepticism. Interestingly, this inquiry seems to have progressed more or less independently within several disciplines. For example, within the management sciences, De Dreu (2006), Ferraro, Pfeffer, and Sutton (2005), and Folger (2001) questioned whether self-benefit is sufficient to explain all human behavior. Likewise, among social psychologists, Batson (1991, 1994, 1995, 1998) and Lerner (1975, 1982, 2003) were sharply critical of universal egoism. Camerer and Fehr (2006), Sen (1990), Simon (1990, 1993), and Frank (1988, 1990) criticized the (over)use of self-interest within economics. Mansbridge (1990) and Wilson (1993) voiced similar worries within political science. Even within the psychoanalytic tradition, Freud's reduction of all behavior to the pleasure principle was questioned by later scholars such as Becker (1973) and Frankl (1984).

As we will see, this and related research suggests that an interdisciplinary consensus is beginning to appear: Self-interest seems to be among the most important of human motives. But that is not the whole story. It also seems to be the case that there are other motives in addition to self-interest. Of course, as we will see, even this modest statement is somewhat contingent on the definition of self-interest employed by the scholars in question.

With these thoughts in mind, we have structured our inquiry as follows. First, we define self-interest. In so doing, we discuss consequences that follow from our definition. Afterward, we present an interdisciplinary examination of universal egoism. In the course of this review, we do not neglect the management sciences but also consider evidence from economics, social psychology, and philosophy.

The Aesthetics of Self-Interest

In keeping with previous work (e.g., Blackburn, 2001; Holley, 1999), we define self-interest as a motive or behavior that seeks to benefit the self. These desired rewards may be tangible and concrete, such as money, but they may also be intangible, such as community standing. Universal self-interest posits that the only human motive is self-interest (Thompson, 2003). Other putative motives ultimately are self-serving. Notice that this definition has a special feature to which we should call attention.

Self-interest, as we define it here, is based on the intentions of the actor. A behavior is self-interested if undertaken for the purpose of self-gain. This is so even when the intended benefits will not be forthcoming until some later date. For example, one might help others in the hope of receiving a reciprocal favor sometime in the future (Homans, 1974), or one might support a norm of equity with the hope that it will benefit the self in the long run (Elser, 1990; Hatfield et al., 1978; van Dijk & De Cremer, in press). Indeed, J. P. Morgan probably had this in mind when he remarked, "A man always has two reasons for doing anything—a good reason and the real reason" (cited in Fuller, 1980, p. 249).

In another respect, however, our treatment of self-interest is a bit different from Morgan's. Although the issue before us has important ethical and empirical implications, our hope is to treat egoism as an aesthetic phenomenon. When philosophers use the term *aesthetics,* they are concerned with what is beautiful, sublime, or at least tasteful. When we study aesthetics, we desire to understand why some things engender positive emotions, whereas others create despair, rage, or simple disinterest. From this vantage point, our current question reduces to whether humans ever want something beyond their own interests. By treating the matter aesthetically, we analyze whether or not self-interest is the only thing that people find intrinsically enjoyable or meaningful. Alternatively, we consider the possibility that humans sometimes see value in helping others (altruism) or in upholding valued moral beliefs (principlism).

This aesthetic treatment should also be distinguished by what it is not. This chapter is not a moral treatise. It would be a tidy thing to say that self-interest = bad and that altruism = good, but like most conceptual simplicities this one is at best misleading and at worst incorrect. One suspects that only the very wise can ascertain when self-interest is a vice masquerading as a virtue or is a virtue masquerading as a vice. For one thing, the actual consequences of an act might not align with its intended purpose; self-interest is not necessarily "bad," and self-sacrifice is not necessarily "good." For another thing, a beneficial act is not necessarily self-interested. Let us consider each possibility.

Smith (1776/1966) was famously aware of the potential misalignment between intentions and behavior. As he remarked in *An Inquiry Into the Nature and Causes of the Wealth of Nations,*

> It is not from the benevolence of the butcher, the brewer, or the baker, that we expect our dinner, but from their regard to their own interest. We address ourselves, not to their humanity but to their self-love, and never talk to them of our necessities but of their advantages. Nobody but a beggar chuses [chooses] to depend chiefly upon the benevolence of his fellow citizens. (Book I, chap. 2, p. 13)

In his remarks about the "invisible hand," Smith was not telling us that people are motivated only by self-interest. As his *Theory of Moral Sentiments* (Smith, 1759/1853) made clear, he recognized motives other than egoism (cf. Burnham, 1943, although Smith's thinking was not always consistent; for details, see Holmes, 1990). Rather, Smith's point was that the pursuit of self-interest often yields practical benefits for society. Conversely, it is conceivable that an act undertaken for selfless motives could have unintended negative ramifications for others. Expected benefits could fail to materialize, or even if they do, unforeseen costs could be so high as to render the act pernicious (cf. Sowell, 1987, 1996). This is a practical consideration to which we return near the end of this chapter.

There is another implication. Simply because an act brings personal rewards does not make it self-interested unless it was originally intended to provide personal benefits. A person might engage in a course of action for selfless reasons but bring about personal gains inadvertently. For example, research shows that "altruistic punishment" (retaliation for violation of group norms) can foster intragroup cooperation (Fehr & Gächter, 2002). Consequently, a team member who sanctions a harmdoer might benefit the group. In the long run, a more effective group could yield benefits for the individual who provided the punishment. Even so, this would not imply that the censure was administered for self-interested reasons unless it could also be shown that the person engaging in retaliation did so in anticipation of the personal rewards (cf. Batson, 1994; Ostrom, 1998; Turillo, Folger, Lavelle, Umphress, & Gee, 2002). This has methodological implications because it suggests a challenge for scholars determining when an act is self-interested and when it has some other motivation.

In this chapter, we need to return to our definition at various points and in various ways, sometimes tightening our assumptions and sometimes loosening them. We have little choice. Scholars have employed sundry definitions, and we both review and appreciate these different perspectives. We organize our review by examining three sets of human concerns: material interests, interpersonal interests, and moral principles. We then revisit some of the definitional issues. Throughout the chapter, we seek to minimize moral censure and approbation, emphasizing instead the aesthetic questions of what people desire and seek. We save the question of what we should be seeking for another day.

Self-Interest and Material Gain

Historically, self-interest has often been understood as a concern with personal material gain. This interpretation is usually associated with classical economics (e.g., Cox, 2003; Edgeworth, 1881; Sen, 1990). There can be little doubt that people care a good deal for their material and economic well-being. For example, research by Parco, Rapoport, and Stein (2002) and Rapoport, Stein, Parco, and Nicolas (2003) shows that the greater the monetary profit, the more effectively it can serve to influence individuals' decisions. Such research demonstrates that people seek material gain. However, our concern is not with the existence of self-interest (which everyone accepts) but rather with its putative universality. In this regard, most modern economists would agree that individuals are concerned with matters beyond their material well-being. For example, research suggests that individuals will sometimes forgo profit to improve interpersonal cooperation (Bolton & Ockenfels, 2000; Fehr & Gächter, 2000), increase distributive justice (Rabin, 1993), and sanction violators of social norms (Fehr & Gächter, 2002; Kahneman, Knetsch, & Thaler, 1986; Ostrom, 1998). Economists have reached these conclusions for a number of reasons (for additional substantiation, see Frank, 1988, 1990; Rabin, 1993; Sen, 1990; Simon, 1990, 1993), and we review more evidence as this chapter unfolds. For now, and in the interest of brevity, we review only one line of inquiry: research on the ultimatum bargaining game.

The Ultimatum Bargaining Game

During the past several years, researchers have used variations of the ultimatum bargaining game to determine when and why bargainers make certain decisions (Surowiecki, 2004). This game, developed by Güth, Schmittberger, and Schwarze (1982), is based on the allocation of a fixed amount of money between two individuals. One of the players takes on the role of allocator and can offer a portion of the money to the recipient if he or she so chooses. If the recipient accepts this offer, both players will receive the amounts specified by the allocator. However, if the recipient refuses the offer, both players walk away empty-handed. The idea behind this game is that if bargainers are self-interested, they should be concerned only with maximizing their share of the money. If this is true, the allocator could offer the recipient the smallest denomination possible and the recipient should accept this offer because even a little money is better than no money at all.

Relevant Findings: Recipient Effects

The surprising thing about the ultimatum bargaining game is the behavior of the recipient. Generally speaking, when offers are noticeably less that 50/50, recipients tend to behave "irrationally," turning down their meager earnings and leaving the experiment with nothing (Güth et al., 1982). These effects occur even on one-shot interactions with a stranger, where there is no opportunity to maximize long-term profit (Camerer & Thaler, 1995). Similar results have been documented in ultimatum bargaining game studies conducted all over the world (Henrich et al., 2001), including in Indonesia when the rejected earnings were equal to approximately 3 days' pay (Surowiecki, 2004). Neutral observers seem to share this disdain for inequitable allocations. It has been found that third parties will sacrifice a portion of their potential winnings to punish someone who has distributed money unfairly, and this occurs even when the observer does not know the wronged party (Kahneman et al., 1986; Ostrom, 1998). These findings are important. Although people care about how much they receive, they are also concerned with whether or not it is allocated justly. That is, they want a "fair share" as well as a "big share." A similar, albeit somewhat more complex, situation exists when we look at the behavior of allocators.

Relevant Findings: Allocator Effects

Generally speaking, the allocator tends to propose an equal distribution of money (e.g., Camerer & Thaler, 1995; Thaler, 1988; van Dijk & Tenbrunsel, 2005). However, in view of the recipient effects we have already discussed, the reason for this equitable behavior is not entirely clear. The allocator might feel morally obligated to be fair or else might simply be afraid that the recipient will reject the offer (van Dijk & De Cremer, in press). Indeed, there is evidence that the allocator often behaves self-interestedly, making a seemingly fair offer to avoid having it vetoed by the recipient (Kagel, Kim, & Moser, 1996). Given such findings, variations of the ultimatum bargaining game have been conducted to ascertain whether allocators can be influenced by something other than personal gain.

To illustrate these effects more clearly, we discuss the delta game (Suleiman, 1996). In the original version of the ultimatum bargaining game, the power level of both parties is more or less equal (cf. Molm, Quist, & Wisely, 1994). Specifically, the power of the allocator and the recipient are determined as a function of the extent to which either one is dependent on the other for scarce resources (Emerson, 1972a, 1972b). To vary the relative power levels, Suleiman (1996) used the delta game, in which the recipient's rejection of the offer does not necessarily mean that both parties receive nothing. If the recipient rejects a particular distribution, both individuals will receive an amount equal to the original offer multiplied by a factor, delta, of which both parties are aware. The delta factor is always between 0 and 1. Therefore, when delta equals 0, we have the original version of the ultimatum bargaining game. As delta moves closer to 1, the recipient loses power and the allocator becomes more powerful. Suleiman's findings indicate that as the allocator has more power, the recipient is more frequently offered a smaller portion of the money. This initially suggests that allocators are merely acting in their self-interest when they split the money in half in the original bargaining game (see also Kagel et al., 1996).

Yet our story is not complete given that research on powerless recipients (delta = 1) paints a different picture. When delta reaches 1, we have a variant of the ultimatum bargaining game that is equivalent to a dictator game. Just as in the original version of the ultimatum bargaining game, the game is played as a single round where the participants do not see each other. The game is very much as it sounds; the allocator can dictate that the recipient receives any amount of the money, and the recipient is powerless to refuse. What is interesting about the dictator game is that the allocation tends to approximate an equal 50/50 split of the money (Suleiman, 1996; van Dijk & Vermunt, 2000). Because the allocator has complete power and there is no chance that the offer will be refused, this action is not in the best economic interest of the allocator. In these experiments, it makes far more (financial) sense to exploit a powerless person than it does to share with the recipient. One possible explanation for these results is that powerful allocators are drawing on considerations other than their own earnings, such as their values. There is evidence that is consistent with this possibility.

Social Value Orientation

Van Lange (1999) suggested that there are three major social value orientations: prosocials, competitors, and individualists. *Prosocials* place value on equality and combined outcomes. In a negotiation setting, prosocials prefer to maximize the collective gain of all. *Competitors*, as the name suggests, want to ensure that they get more than the other party. *Individualists* are concerned primarily with their own outcomes. They seek as much as they can reasonably get. It is common for scholars to collapse competitors and individualists together. When this is done, they are referred to as "proself" (Van Lange & Kuhlman, 1994). This prosocial–proself distinction is important. According to evidence reviewed by van Dijk and De Cremer (in press), prosocial allocators tend to be concerned with fairness. Proself allocators, on the other hand, will behave fairly so long as doing so serves their long-term interests (for empirical evidence supporting these ideas, see Stouten, De Cremer, & van Dijk, 2005; van Dijk, De Cremer, & Handgraaf, 2004). This literature suggests that proself individuals are strongly motivated by instrumental considerations, whereas prosocial individuals also take into account additional concerns. One might say that some individuals rely more on self-interest than do others.

The Ultimatum Bargaining Game Among Other Primates

A curiosity of the ultimatum bargaining game is that the recipient need not even be human to feel a sense of injustice. Primatologists have found that some monkeys are sensitive to inequities in the ultimatum bargaining game (De Waal, 1996). Brosnan and De Waal (2003) observed that female capuchin monkeys are insulted by unequal treatment. In their study, they trained capuchins to give them pebbles in return for tasty cucumbers. The game was set up so that the monkeys worked in groups of two. With this arrangement, Brosnan and De Waal found that both monkeys traded pebbles for cucumbers approximately 95% of the time.

From our description so far, this experiment would appear to be a simple learning study. Brosnan and De Waal (2003) confused matters by introducing grapes into their capuchin trade system. The little economy promptly fell apart. Because capuchins prefer grapes to cucumbers, monkeys receiving the latter did not respond favorably when they observed their peers earning a grape. Indeed, the capuchins sometimes reacted by refusing to eat their cucumbers, and 40% of the time they stopped trading pebbles altogether. This bad situation was made worse when one monkey was given a grape without even making the pebble exchange. In this case, the unjustly treated capuchin often threw away its pebble and agreed to trade only 20% of the time. Simply put, the capuchins were willing to give up the less desirable food (i.e., cucumbers) to express their unhappiness with their partners' unearned treasures (i.e., grapes). This is not economically rational behavior, but it is very human.

Self-Interest and Material Benefit: Closing Thoughts

It appears that individual monetary reward is not the exclusive motive for all human conduct. Worse still, from the point of view of universal egoism, people sometimes prefer allocation decisions that take into account the needs of others (De Dreu, 2006; Tyler & Dawes, 1993) and conform to norms of fair play (van Dijk & Tenbrunsel, 2005). These findings suggest that we must take a closer look at the social psychology of altruism.

Self-Interest and Altruism

In many social situations, there is strong evidence that individuals are attentive to the needs of other people. Indeed, this claim has been verified by research throughout social psychology and organizational behavior. For example, research on altruism indicates that we sometimes (but not always) render assistance to others and that we do so even in the absence of payment (Elser, 1990; Ozinga, 1999). Likewise, Deutsch's (1973) theory of cooperation and competition and Pruitt and Rubin's (1986) dual concern theory suggest that individuals often take into account the needs of others when bargaining and settling conflicts. Research findings generally have been supportive of these two models (De Dreu, 2006; De Dreu & Steinel, in press; De Dreu, Weingart, & Kwon, 2000).

As interesting as these findings are, however, they do not necessarily contradict the doctrine of universal egoism (cf. Hatfield et al., 1978; Schroeder, Steel, Woodell, & Bembenek, 2003). Returning to our original definition, we can see that egoism is based on what is intended, not on actual consequences. If the person offering altruistic assistance was attempting to benefit personally, the act is self-interested. To draw conclusions concerning the doctrine of universal egoism, we must proceed through two steps. First, it would be useful to provide an alternative theoretical account that is not self-interested. Fortunately, such accounts have long existed. They tend to emphasize the role of human emotion in promoting prosocial behavior (cf. Lerner, 1982, 2003). Second, we must consider this non-egoistic model against various self-interested alternatives. These comparative tests will allow for stronger interferences.

Empathy–Altruism as an Alternative to Egoistic Models of Altruism

Even so devoted a capitalist as Smith (1759/1853) argued that individuals possess what he called "moral sentiments." According to Smith, here is how these sentiments motivate our behavior:

How selfish so ever man may be supposed, there are evidently some principles in his nature, which interest him in the fortune of others, and render their happiness necessary to him. Of this kind is pity and compassion, the emotion which we feel for the misery of others, when we either see it, or are made to conceive it in a very lively manner. (p. I.i.1.1)

Hume (1739/2000) made similar arguments. Interestingly, evolutionary psychologists and sociobiologists have long argued for this tendency (e.g., De Waal, 1996; Ozinga, 1999; Simon, 1990; Wilson, 1993; Wright, 1994).

It remains to state these ideas in a form that is experimentally testable. Social psychologists have done so by attending to the concept of empathy. Specifically, empathy occurs when an individual is able to take the perspective of another and imagine how that individual is affected by his or her situation (Stotland, 1969). Many scholars have argued that the ability to empathize with another person is an important mechanism for driving other-oriented actions (e.g., Batson, 1995; Hoffman, 1976). According to this empathy–altruism hypothesis (Batson, 1991, 1998, in press), feelings of empathy toward someone in need spur us to render assistance. Research evidence for this contention is generally strong (Batson, Duncan, Ackerman, Buckley, & Birch, 1981; Coke, Batson, & McDavis, 1978; Dovidio, Allen, & Schroeder, 1990; Fultz, Batson, Fortenbach, McCarthy, & Varney, 1986; Krebs, 1975; Toi & Batson, 1982; for a review, see Eisenberg & Miller, 1987), but we also consider whether the empathy–altruism model can survive a comparison test (Batson, 1995).

Egoistic Explanations for Helping

Following from the work of Batson (1995), we can distinguish three egoistic accounts of altruistic behavior:

- *Aversive-arousal reduction.* We help so as to reduce unpleasant mood states.
- *Empathy-specific punishment.* We help so as to avoid guilt or shame as well as to avoid social censure.
- *Empathy-specific reward.* We help so as to induce positive mood states.

To provide the reader with a detailed explanation of the posited egoistic motives for helping behavior, we now delineate the previous research in this arena.

Aversive-Arousal Reduction

The empathy–altruism model argues that empathic feelings cause us to focus on the needs of others. Our goal, therefore, is to help reduce their aversive state. The aversive-arousal reduction model is willing to accept the concept of empathy. However, it makes a different assumption about the nature of empathic arousal, and this leads to different conclusions about the role of self-interest. Specifically, proponents of aversive-arousal reduction suggest that witnessing the suffering of other people is emotionally unpleasant for observers (Hoffman, 1981). Because humans would prefer to feel good rather than to feel bad, individuals will engage in helping behavior with the goal of eliminating their negative affective state and not with the goal of helping the people in need (although helping is a side effect of reducing this stress). Prosocial behavior might be a socially useful consequence of arousal reduction, but it is not the ultimate goal of the action. Hence, aversive-arousal reduction can be said to pose a self-interested account of altruistic behavior.

There seems to be solid evidence that individuals render assistance so as to regulate their moods (Schaller & Cialdini, 1988). Consider an experiment by Manucia, Baumann, and Cialdini (1984). Using a mood induction technique, they induced undergraduate participants to feel sad. The participants were then given a chance to help another person. Those who believed that their mood was fixed by a drug were relatively unhelpful. On the other hand, those who presumably believed that their mood could be improved were relatively more helpful. These "altruists" (we use the word with irony here) were most accommodating when they believed that doing so would improve their feeling states.

Of course, the work of Manucia and colleagues (1984) supports the possibility that people prefer not to be in unpleasant moods. However, this finding does not rule out the possibility that other empathic motives might exist. This possibility was tested directly in a series of studies reviewed by Batson (1991). By various manipulations, some participants were made to experience empathy for a coworker who supposedly was receiving some harm; other participants also witnessed the harm but did not have the empathy induction. Even when offered a simple means of leaving the situation, individuals with empathic feelings were likely to render assistance. Indeed, when empathy was induced, people were helpful even when doing so was personally troublesome, for example, when it exposed them to electric shocks.

Interestingly, those experiencing only generalized distress tended to take the most expedient route to mood enhancement, helping if absolutely necessary but preferring to avail themselves of the opportunity to escape. These studies demonstrate that aversive-arousal reduction does indeed impel altruistic behavior. However, it is only one mechanism. This mood maintenance effect works when a person is high in general distress. Mood maintenance does not seem to motivate altruism when a person is high in empathic feelings toward the victim (Batson, 1987, 1991, in press; Batson et al., 1991). Empathy, on the other hand, motivates behavior in the manner anticipated by Smith (1759/1853s). If empathy were only a matter of regulating an unpleasant mood state, those participants who experienced an empathy induction would have benefited from departing the situation as well. Instead, empathic participants remained in the laboratory and, in some variations of the research paradigm, agreed to take electric shocks in the victim's place. This implies that empathy created a concern with the needs of another person and a desire to reduce that person's potential suffering, even if it created suffering for the research participants.

Empathy-Specific Punishment

Although we have seen that the aversive-arousal reduction model does not adequately explain empathic behavior, there are still other egoistic models that have yet to be discussed. In particular, the empathy-specific punishment model argues that individuals have learned through their upbringing that if they see someone in distress, they should help that person. To not help would be socially unacceptable and bring about feelings of guilt and shame (Batson, 1995). Therefore, we tend to consider the negative social ramifications associated with not helping the person in need. Consequently, the empathy-specific punishment model suggests that individuals help others out of an egoistic desire to circumvent being socially ostracized.

The most frequently used technique to test this idea has been to provide the participant with a justification for not engaging in helping behavior. Explicitly, if the only reason why the participant is engaging in helping behavior is to evade social punishment, providing the participant with a good reason for not helping should decrease the rate of helping behavior displayed. Therefore, this 2 (justification: low vs. high) × 2 (empathy: low vs. high) study design produces different cell-specific predictions based on whether one adopts the empathy–altruism model or the empathy-specific punishment model.

Specifically, Batson and colleagues (1988) reasoned that if participants think that most people before them have decided not to help, the participants should feel less social pressure to engage in helping behavior. In the low-justification condition, the experimenters told participants that two of seven people had agreed to help. In the high-justification condition, the experimenters told participants that five of seven people had agreed to help. In addition, empathy was induced in the same manner as in the aforementioned experiments. The results did not support the empathy-specific punishment explanation. Individuals helped whenever their empathy was high, supporting the empathy–altruism model. Participants also helped when they lacked a justification for not doing so. Thus, it is clear that we are not selfless. We do indeed take into account the opinions of others. However, that is not the only motive for altruistic behavior (Batson, 1995).

Empathy-Specific Reward

The empathy-specific reward model states that we help others so as to earn some reward for our actions. This model theorizes that individuals anticipate being rewarded for helping behavior. This expectation of gain provides an impetus to our actions. Therefore, it is an egoistic desire for reward, and not the altruistic motivation, that drives helping behavior.

To test the idea that helping is due to anticipated rewards, Batson and colleagues (1988) designed an experiment with the following three dependent variables: empathy (low vs. high), prior relief of victim's need (relief vs. no relief), and performance of the helping task (perform vs. not perform).

Participants were told that a fellow participant would receive electrical shocks. They were further told that they would have a "no-cost, no-risk" opportunity to assist the victim. Thus, there was a person in need, but there was a clear avenue by which assistance could be proffered. Notice, of course, that if one helps so as to improve one's own mood, this would be excellent news indeed. At no risk to themselves, participants could make themselves feel good.

At this point, the other independent variables were manipulated. Half of the participants were told that they no longer had the option to help the person in need. Also, half of those participants were subsequently told that plans had changed and that the other participant would no longer receive the shocks. Batson and colleagues' (1988) study poses an interesting challenge. If one is helping only to experience personal rewards (the empathy-specific reward hypothesis), losing one's low-cost opportunity to help a potential victim is bad news. The participant has been deprived of a chance to feel good. According to the empathy-specific reward model, one should feel less positive affect when harm is taken away spontaneously than when one can prevent the harm.

On the other hand, the empathy–altruism hypothesis makes quite different predictions. This model argues that when empathy is induced, one should feel good when the victim is unharmed regardless of how the harm is prevented. In other words, it should not matter whether the participant is the agent of assistance. Results again supported the empathy–altruism hypothesis and not the empathy-specific reward explanation. More specifically, individuals who reported high levels of empathy were just as happy when they helped the individual as they were when the individual found relief without their assistance. This relationship was not significant among low-empathy individuals (Batson et al., 1988).

Summary

Based on the aforementioned research, it appears that the egoistic explanations of helping behavior do not provide the only explanation for altruistic behavior. Most available research supports the empathy–altruism model (Batson, 1995, 1998, in press). When these findings are coupled with the economic research reviewed in the previous section, it becomes clear that the doctrine of universal self-interest has some rather serious problems. In the next section, we turn our attention to an additional line of inquiry. Although these studies are based on a somewhat different conceptual paradigm, we will see that they point us in a similar direction.

Principlism and Self-Interest

Heretofore, we have considered two ways in which the self-interest debate has been framed: in terms of economic gain and in terms of altruism. We

have further observed that individuals seek goals other than individual material benefit and that altruism is often motivated by empathy for victims. By
themselves, these findings call into question the possibility that all human
behavior can be reduced to self-interest. We now take up a third approach
to understanding this issue. As we will see, this perspective poses additional
challenges for the doctrine of universal egoism.

Certain ethical philosophers have long argued that there are rules by
which people can evaluate the morality of their conflict (Velasquez, 2001).
Certain actions are wrong to the extent that they violate these standards
(Gaus, 2001a, 2001b). In other words, the concept of principlism suggests
that many people have internalized codes of moral conduct. When these
standards are salient, they attempt to behave in accordance with them.
Various scholars have argued for principled decision making, particularly
with respect to social justice. Probably the two best-known frameworks are
Folger and colleagues' (Folger, 2001; Folger, Cropanzano, & Goldman,
2005) model of deontic justice and Lerner's (1975, 1982, 2003) research on
justice motivation. There is also scholarship suggesting that principled
motivations are common to whistle-blowers (Locke, Tirnauer, Roberson,
Goldman, & Weldon, 2001).

We caution that the term *principled,* as it is used here, is not a synonym for
good. Rather, it means only that individuals are motivated by internal moral
standards that they view as worthwhile for their own sake (Cropanzano,
Goldman, & Folger, 2003). Whether or not an observer shares those beliefs is
a different question entirely. Nor is *principled* a synonym for *moral.* There are
alternative approaches to morality that are every bit as sincere and meaningful, such as an ethic of compassion (Gilligan, 1982) and utilitarianism
(Bentham, 1789/1988).

Evidence for Principlism

The defining attribute of principlism is the use of internal standards,
such as fairness, in deciding how to treat other people. Various lines of
inquiry have been cited in support of this notion (cf. Cropanzano et al.,
2003; Folger, 2001; Lerner, 1975, 1982, 2003). We consider some of the
strong evidence here.

Research on Principlism

One early line of research was presented by Miller (1977), who hired
research participants to work for either $2/hour or $3/hour. In addition,
Miller either (a) allowed participants to keep the full amount, (b) deducted
$1/hour without a good reason, or (c) deducted $1/hour to provide support
to an underprivileged family. When $1 was taken from $2, work motivation dropped. This was so regardless of whether or not the deduction went
to the family. Presumably, a 50% pay cut was always seen as unfair. The
more interesting effect comes when $1 was deducted from $3. In this case,

individuals worked harder when the money went to support the family. Individuals were willing to forgo some of their earnings to help others so long as doing so was just. In other words, economic motives matter, but so do other considerations (cf. van Dijk & Tenbrunsel, 2005).

Meindl and Lerner (1983) approached this issue from a different perspective. They told participants that four of them would be working together to pilot test commercial games. These four participants were broken into two dyads: (a) the subject and a partner and (b) an experimental accomplice and a partner. In the critical conditions, the accomplice launched a verbal tirade against one of the following individuals: the subject, the subject's partner, or the accomplice's own partner. Participants were then told that they would need to work on a second task. This task could be either (a) a profitable test of another game or (b) a chance to confront the ill-behaved accomplice. In the former option, research participants would earn money; in the latter option, they would lose money. Results demonstrated that the participants preferred to lose money so as to avenge an insult to themselves or, even more strongly, to their partner. This occurred, moreover, even when the bogus partner would not know that the participant had punished the accomplice.

Another important study was reported by Kahneman and colleagues (1986), who instructed research participants to allocate $20 among anonymous strangers. These participants were further provided with a bogus story about how these two individuals had allocated money in a previous session. One of the potential recipients supposedly had tried to distribute funds unfairly to another person. That is, this unfair recipient had retained most of the research money for himself or herself. The other recipient had sought to allocate funds fairly. This fair recipient had sought an equal split for all. Before allocating the $20, participants were given one more piece of information. A participant who assigned more funds to the unfair recipient would receive $6, whereas a participant who assigned more funds to the fair recipient would receive $5. Contrary to notions of economic self-interest, Kahneman and colleagues found that individuals were willing to forgo $1 in earnings so as to avoid giving extra money to an unfair person.

Turillo and colleagues (2002) extended this earlier work by conducting four experiments using the dictator game described earlier. Essentially, a research participant was allowed to assign dollars to a fair or unfair recipient. If the participant denied money to an unfair person, the participant would lose some of his or her own earnings. Even so, experimental participants showed a strong propensity to punish wrongdoers. These findings were supportive even when the alleged victim was anonymous to the other research participant (Study 2) or when the victim was a member of a social group with which the participant did not identify (Study 4). Interestingly, participants were harsher when the alleged injustice was deliberate. This suggests that individuals were making judgments based on their understanding of the actor's intent.

Justice and Values

The work of Kahneman and colleagues (1986) and Turillo and colleagues (2002) is very much in the tradition of the economic research reviewed earlier (e.g., van Dijk & Vermunt, 2000). Still, research on principlism extends the economic tradition in one respect. Principlism suggests that there is an internal standard, such as an internalized norm or value, that acts as a guide to behavior. There are a number of studies that concern topics such as social motives, moral development, and other orientation (cf. De Dreu, 2006; De Dreu & Carnevale, 2003; De Dreu & Steinel, in press; De Dreu et al., 2000). A full accounting of this important literature is beyond the scope of this chapter. However, to give the reader a sense of this research, let us consider a few illustrative examples.

An experimental study by Rupp (2003) provides an excellent example of this point. Rupp replicated Turillo and colleagues' (2002) findings. However, she also measured moral maturity using the Socio–Moral Reflection Measure. Consistent with earlier work, research participants were willing to forgo money so as to punish a wrongdoer. However, this effect was moderated by participants' moral maturity. Those high in moral maturity tended to punish partners who had behaved unfairly previously (otherwise, they divided benefits evenly). Those low in moral maturity tended to make self-serving allocations. Justice is an option of which we do not always avail ourselves (van Dijk & De Cremer, in press; van Dijk & Tenbrunsel, 2005).

This is consistent with earlier research by Vecchio (1981) also investigating moral maturity and equity theory. Prior work in equity theory (e.g., Adams, 1965; Adams & Freedman, 1976) investigated the issue of overpayment. If workers are to be compensated equitably, overpayment is unfair because it increases costs to the employer. Adams (1963) reported that workers paid by units produced under a piece-rate pay system sometimes resolved inequity by reducing quantity (thereby earning less and "cheating" the employer out of less money) while simultaneously increasing the quality of each unit (thereby increasing its value). Vecchio (1981) was interested in the issue of whether the likelihood of responding to overpayment was related to worker moral development. He expected to find that among individuals working under a piece-rate system, those with higher moral maturity (measured with a shortened version of the Moral Judgment Scale), and who perceived themselves to receive an overpayment, would diminish their quantity and increase the quality of units produced relative to workers with lower levels of moral maturity. Results supported his predictions. In short, those with high moral maturity were likely to restore equity even to the point of reducing compensation.

Concluding Thoughts

The research tradition reviewed here is based on a simple idea. Participants are allowed to make an allocation decision and/or to respond to an allocation decision made by someone else. The doctrine of universal self-interest is called into question when individuals forgo personal economic gain in lieu of the following: (a) boosting the earnings of others (Dawes, van de Kragt, & Orbell, 1990; Tyler & Dawes, 1993), (b) making just allocations to powerless individuals (van Dijk & Tenbrunsel, 2005), or (c) censuring someone who has treated another person unfairly (Fehr & Gächter, 2002; Henrich et al., 2001; Kahneman et al., 1986). They did so even when they were anonymous and even when the alleged victim was not in their in-group (Turillo et al., 2002), and the effects were stronger for those high in moral maturity (Rupp, 2003). But the debate is not over. In the next subsection, we consider an alternative explanation.

Principlism as Self-Reward

There is another perspective we can take on principlism. According to various authors, individuals may reward themselves, or at least avoid self-punishment, for behaving in a morally upright fashion. Batson (1995), while not necessarily advocating this position, summarized it as follows: "One gains social and self-rewards of being seen and seeing oneself as a good person; even more plausible perhaps, one avoids the social and self-punishments of shame and guilt for failing to do the right thing. Any or all of these benefits could be the ultimate goal of wanting to uphold a moral principle" (p. 371). Likewise, Colquitt and Greenberg (2001) argued that people may act justly so as to "protect their self-images or avoid feelings of guilt" (p. 221). This is an intriguing concept.

Like many of the ideas in this chapter, this one is of a distinguished linege (Campbell, 1975). Freud (1930), for example, even posed a developmental model to articulate how this might occur. According to Freud, parents and society instruct children in the appropriate rules and standards of moral conduct. If training is sufficient, these guidelines are then internalized. Once the guidelines are internalized, people experience negative feelings (e.g., guilt, shame, low self-esteem) when they violate the standards, and they experience positive feelings (e.g., pride, high self-esteem) when they fulfill them. Through these self-reinforcing mechanisms, moral conduct is thereby maintained. Batson (1995) summarized the perspective well when he observed that it is "in our best personal interest to act morally" (p. 371). To have a point of reference, we term this conceptual orientation the self-reward perspective.

We caution that the word *reward* is used in a broad sense, so it refers to both pleasures gained and punishments avoided. We necessarily keep our analysis somewhat general. We will see that the self-reward approach is a general perspective, lacking a sizable body of research. Nevertheless, the model is worth considering. Not only is it quite plausible and consistent with other evidence, but it also has two special advantages for our current discussion. First, a close analysis of the self-reward model can serve to sharpen our understanding of self-interest as a concept. As we will see, egoistic and non-egoistic motives are sometimes tied together. Second, the self-reward model poses a particular framework for understanding the relationship between emotions and moral behaviors. There is an alternative approach that complements this model with a different perspective.

Self-Reward and Moral Behavior: Basic Tenets and Assumptions

The self-reward model operates through a sort of "pleasure principle" like that of Bentham (1789/1988) and Freud (1920/1974). The starting premise is that individuals seek to obviate bad feelings and facilitate positive ones. Generally speaking, the self-reward approach seems to stress the avoidance of the negative emotions that can be engendered when one fails to "live up to" one's own principles. We follow this emphasis on negative emotion in our comments below. That said, we caution that this perspective can easily be expanded to include the seeking of positive emotions and high self-regard. For example, an individual might help someone in need so as to experience pride and to engender a sense that he or she is a "good person." Of course, doing so will not change our conclusions in a major way.

Finally, we caution that the self-reward model has not, to our knowledge, been fully tested. Nevertheless, we believe that it is worth discussing because it is quite plausible and has, in any case, been proposed by several scholars. Besides, there is evidence that is broadly consistent with this model. There is a body of literature indicating that people use their anticipated feeling states when making decisions. If they anticipate regretting a course of action, they are less likely to choose it (e.g., Connolly, Ordóñez, & Coughlan, 1997; Connolly & Zeelenberg, 2002; Ordóñez & Connolly, 2000; Zeelenberg, van Dijk, & Manstead, 1998). Consequently, and for the sake of argument, we accept the theoretical propositions as if they had been confirmed empirically. Still, we do this for pedagogical purposes and caution strongly that more research on anticipatory guilt and shame is necessary (for a similar caveat, see Batson, 1995).

Having already accepted the possibility that individuals dispense self-reward and self-punishment, we have but one more consideration: Should behavior be considered self-interested if it is performed to receive a self-administered reward or to avoid a self-administered punishment? To answer this question, we must look closely at how self-reward works. Doing so will confront us with perhaps the most interesting intellectual questions of this chapter.

Self-Reward and Universal Self-Interest I: Why Feel Guilty?

In probing the self-reward model, it seems worthwhile to consider both proximal and distal goals. The proximal goal in the self-reward model would conform to our earlier definition of a self-interested action. That is, the intent of the individual is to regulate his or her emotional state (i.e., to reduce shame or guilt) and to buttress the self-image. In Batson's (1994) terms, this sort of mood management is "instrumental" (p. 604). That is, the putatively self-sacrificial behavior is a means by which another end is accomplished.

Of course, if we grant this possibility, it raises an inquiry about the distal goal. Why would a completely self-interested individual have so strong an aversion to injustice that ignoring mistreatment by another person causes guilt or shame? Moreover, why would an individual use justice as a relevant criterion for assessing his or her self-worth? These questions are especially relevant when one recalls that, in Turillo and colleagues' (2002) studies, there was no danger of being found out and no responsibility toward the victim.

To answer these questions, we can turn to the large body of research exploring the phenomenology of guilt and shame. These emotions occur when one accepts some measure of blame for an action that violates an internally held standard (Tangney, 1995; Tangney & Fischer, 1995). Because the responsibility is personally accepted, neither guilt nor shame requires an audience (although one is often present [Tangney, Miller, Flicker, & Barlow, 1996]). When the response of the audience is critical, one tends to experience the somewhat different emotion of embarrassment (Keltner & Anderson, 2000; Keltner & Buswell, 1997; Keltner, Young, & Buswell, 1997). Consequently, by acknowledging the emotions of shame and guilt, the self-reward model implicitly recognizes that people are motivated by some internalized benchmark for their behavior. In other words, the distal goal in the guilt reduction model would be to behave in accordance with some personally significant rule of conduct.

This issue becomes even clearer when one emphasizes self-regard rather than emotions. As we have seen, some variants of the self-reward model maintain that overlooking an injustice could threaten a person's self-esteem (Colquitt & Greenberg, 2001). However, this could occur only if behaving fairly were seen as a relevant criterion for self-judgment. That is, a person must accept justice as personally important before an injustice will damage his or her self-image. By extension, we can say that the self-reward model of justice is predicated on reactions that occur after individuals have already internalized a standard of conduct. Self-reward suggests a sort of egoistic model, but the "interest" involved has to do with maintaining a principled commitment to certain ethical norms.

To refer to guilt aversion or self-esteem threat as "self-interest" is technically correct because the actor is seeking a course of behavior on the basis of self-image enhancement and/or on anticipated emotional experience. However, the self-reward model does not support the claim to universal self-interest because it implies the existence of internalized moral standards. These standards have the power to influence a person's opinion of himself or herself as well as to elicit powerful negative emotions. In other words, the self-reward model involves more than self-interest. Specifically, it contains both egoistic and non-egoistic elements, and this is what makes it so interesting. In short, even if one were to accept the self-reward model as the only explanation for the results obtained in the works of Meindl and Lerner (1983), Turillo and colleagues (2002), and Kahneman and colleagues (1986)—and this is a position we do not hold—the doctrine of universal egoism would remain in jeopardy for two reasons.

First, and most critically, this approach to self-interest does not preclude the possibility that individuals hold and are committed to norms of moral conduct. The fact that one feels guilt or has diminished self-regard implies that a standard of good conduct was internalized and seen as relevant to one's self-appraisal. These types of bad feelings are apt to come from doing something that an individual believes he or she should not have done.

Second, the self-reward approach to self-interest need not imply moral hypocrisy. A person risks guilt because he or she is sincerely committed to treating others morally. The sincerity of one's standards engenders bad feelings when they are violated. Again we see that self-reward is an approach to self-interest that allows for genuine moral conduct. The model works because some individuals have internalized concerns that transcend their own well-being.

All told, the possibility that guilt reduction or self-esteem threat motivates moral behavior strikes us as plausible (Connolly et al., 1997; Connolly & Zeelenberg, 2002). This is an empirically interesting idea because it suggests an affective mechanism by which moral principles exert their behavior on human conduct. In the next subsection, we consider another approach by which emotions can engender moral conduct.

Self-Reward and Self-Interest II: Emotion and Principled Behavior

One of the fascinating aspects of the self-reward model is that it is a "pull" or anticipatory model of emotion. It suggests that individuals predict the emotions they are going to feel and then adjust their behavior so as to alter their future emotional states. In their discussions of retribution, some philosophers have termed such models "forward-looking" (Farrell, 1985) because these accounts of individual conduct emphasize the future benefits to be obtained through ethical action. As intriguing as this possibility may be, research suggests that the pull of the future is but one way in which emotions can produce principled moral conduct. Other theories have been termed "backward-looking" because they emphasize the emotional "push" that results from some stimulus condition (Holmgren, 1989).

Most psychological theories linking emotion to behavior are backward-looking. That is, they posit that behavior is impelled forward by the power of emotions rather than pulled forward by an analysis of future profits and losses (Folger et al., 2005; Goldberg, Lerner, & Tetlock, 1999). It seems that observing or experiencing an injustice is apt to elicit some emotion, and this response seems to spur action against the wrongdoer (e.g., Bies, 2001; Bies & Tripp, 2001, 2002; Bies, Tripp, & Kramer, 1997; Lerner, 1975; Lerner, Goldberg, & Tetlock, 1998; Mikula, Scherer, & Athenstaedt, 1998; Rozin, Lowery, Imada, & Haidt, 1999). A good example of this tradition can be found in research on anger. In one study, Goldman (2003) examined 583 former employees who had lost their jobs recently. Goldman found that anger was often a response to injustice and that, more relevant to the current argument, angry workers were more likely to seek legal redress.

Backward-looking models suggest that emotions prime behavior in a relatively automatic fashion that does not require detailed cognitive processing (Goldberg et al., 1999; Lerner, 1982). Indeed, this thinking is supported by the observation that realistic and emotion-provoking injustices rouse especially profound responses from observers (Lerner, 2003). The fact that strong emotions can push automatic responses poses even more problems for the doctrine of universal self-interest than do pull models. Emotion-driven responses suggest that people may be acting without an egoistic consideration of their costs and benefits.

It is noteworthy that in backward-looking theories principled behavior results from emotion and that emotion results from an event in the person's environment. These theories are not instrumental in the sense that they are not oriented toward future profit, including the hedonic benefit of mood maintenance. Rather, the emotions come with their own goals and predispositions, and these need not be self-interested ones (Folger et al., 2005; Goldberg et al., 1999; Lerner, 1975, 1982, 2003). More research surely is needed, but if evidence supports this mechanism, it would provide an additional argument against the theory of universal egoism. To better describe how backward-looking models work, we now turn our attention to research on revenge.

Emotion and Revenge

The term *revenge* has been defined as an "action in response to some perceived harm or wrongdoing by another party that is intended to inflict damage, injury, discomfort, or punishment on the party judged responsible" (Aquino, Tripp, & Bies, 2001, p. 53; see also Allred, 1999; Bies, 2001; Bies & Tripp, 1996, 2001, 2002). Research in the area of revenge suggests that it can be caused by both good and bad motivations and can have both good and bad consequences in organizations.

Tripp and Bies (1997) investigated the aspects of revenge that make it morally good or bad. In a qualitative study of workers, they concluded that there were several principles people use to assess acts of revenge. They reported that the actors judged their acts to be morally good if the acts restored the avenger's status or corrected the harmdoer's behavior. Moreover, avengers reported their acts as morally bad if the acts hurt innocent bystanders or invited further retaliation from the original harmdoer. Whether acts of revenge are good or bad in and of themselves, it is noteworthy that this research found strong associations between these acts and morality-based principles because it suggests that revenge may be a consequence of principlism.

A common theme of the organizational revenge literature is that revenge is associated with justice and, in particular, is triggered by injustice (e.g., Bies, 2001; Bies & Tripp, 2001, 2002; Bies et al., 1997). Experimental evidence supports this contention. For example, DaGloria and DeRidder (1977, 1979) found that norm violations prompted research participants to aggress against transgressors. Hence, this literature suggests that retribution is one way in which workers cope with, and respond to, injustice. This literature in part considers organizational practices, typically injustices, that precipitate or justify acts of revenge (McLean Parks, 1997). So what is the trigger for these revenge responses? Bies and Tripp (1996) argued that the catalyst is changes to the rules or criteria of decision making (including contract violations) or violations of norms. These norms, of course, are perceived by the avenger to be accepted standards of conduct.

The violation of these perceived standards seems to involve, to the avenger, an important violation of the "sense of injustice" that Cahn (1949) referred to as "the sympathetic reaction of outrage, horror, shock, resentment, and anger, those affections of the viscera and abnormal secretions of the adrenals that prepare the human animal to resist attack. Nature has thus equipped all men to regard injustice to another as personal aggression" (p. 24). It follows from our previous discussion of principlism that those with strong internalized standards of moral principles are more likely to have strong beliefs regarding duties and norms. As such, they should be more likely to have a more refined sense of injustice that, once violated, will more likely lead them to engage in revenge than is the case with those with less principled positions.

Implicit in the transformation of a perceived harm into a sense of injustice and revenge is the assignment of blame. This assignment of blame allows a harmful—but not necessarily intentional—act to be perceived as an intentional violation of a duty. This element of blameworthiness propels the victim to have moral justification for the act of revenge (Aquino et al., 2001). This morality for revenge seems to be important to avengers (Bies & Tripp, 2001, 2002) and serves to distinguish revenge from many other unprovoked harmful acts. Bies and Tripp (1996) reported that avengers justify their actions as morally right and in the service of justice.

Research by Reb, Goldman, Kray, and Cropanzano (2006) helps to illustrate the previous points. They studied various types of remedies that organizations can take to atone for perceived injustices. They presented two studies: one in the field and the other in the laboratory. Both studies found that when an injustice involved interpersonal mistreatment (i.e., interactional injustice), workers preferred a punitive remedy, presumably because it helped to restore individuals' sense of morality.

As we have seen, research on revenge suggests that it is pushed or propelled forward by one's emotional response to injustice in his or her environment. As Bies and Tripp (1996) suggested, it seems to be encouraged by a desire to restore a sense of fair play. Retribution, in other words, can be a principled response. Violations of principles create the emotion, and a hope of restoration prompts the behavior.

Some Final Thoughts Regarding Principlism

Even apart from empathy–altruism, the evidence for principlism poses a serious threat to the doctrine of universal self-interest. Experimental evidence has shown that individuals seem to act on their moral standards even when doing so costs them money and even when they do not have social ties to the victim (Kahneman et al., 1986; Turillo et al., 2002). The self-reward model provides one possible explanation for these effects. However, under closer scrutiny it appears that the self-reward model also presupposes that individuals have internalized some standards of appropriate conduct. Hence, support for self-reward does not buttress the model of universal egoism.

We also discussed evidence suggesting that individuals' emotions have the capacity to push principled behavior forward. These frameworks suggest that behavior can be motivated by goals other than self-gain. If future evidence supports these models, this would provide additional evidence suggesting that self-interest is not the only goal motivating human conduct. However, we emphasize that questioning universal self-interest is not the same thing as claiming that people always behave effectively. Instead, we reviewed evidence for retributive justice, suggesting that individuals are often motivated to seek revenge.

Self-Interest and Grand Unifying Pessimism

The doctrine of universal self-interest has not fared well during the past few decades. Nobel laureates have criticized it (Kahneman et al., 1986; Simon, 1990, 1993). Economists no longer maintain (if they ever did) that humans have only material concerns (e.g., Frank, 1988; Sen, 1990). Social psychologists have successfully tested models of altruism that rely on empathic concern rather than on mood maintenance and other forms of personal gain (e.g., Batson, 1991, 1994, 1995, 1998, in press; Ozinga, 1999). Other researchers have presented evidence, albeit of generally a more recent vintage, that individuals sometimes attempt to uphold moral principles such as justice (e.g., Cropanzano, Goldman, & Folger, 2003, 2005; Folger, 2001; Lerner, 1975, 1982, 2003). Given such considerations, one can see why behavioral scientists and philosophers have been moving away from this doctrine. In this section, we examine one last attempt to save the model of universal self-interest.

Considering an Alternative Definition of Self-Interest

Inconsistent empirical evidence is seldom enough to reject a well-known social scientific construct. Because many ideas are not delineated rigorously, it is often possible to expand their meanings. This may render problematic findings irrelevant, but at the expense of making one's definition less precise. This sort of semantic drift (cf. Holley, 1999; Holmes, 1990; Macaulay, 1978) seems to have occurred with regard to universal self-interest. Faced with evidence that egoism is not adequate to explain all human behavior, the definition of self-interest has simply become broader.

For example, when Dawes and colleagues (1990) and Tyler and Dawes (1993) wrote their critiques of universal egoism, they treated the doctrine economically. Self-interest was concerned with individual material gain. Dawes and colleagues observed that people also care about the rewards given to teammates even when this permanently diminishes the size of their own earnings. Given this, their findings opposed the belief in universal self-interest when self-interest was understood as economic advantage (for a similar analysis, see De Dreu, 2006). Without gainsaying these specific empirical findings, researchers redefined self-interest so that it included social considerations (e.g., Gillespie & Greenberg, 2005; Turillo et al., 2002). The conclusions of Dawes and colleagues were, in effect, defined out of the debate. This is not to say that a broader definition was inappropriate. Quite the contrary, we think that it makes a good deal of sense for scholars to consider both economic and social benefits. Still, it is difficult to interpret the research because scholars were trying to hit a moving target.

Regardless, even using this expanded definition, the doctrine of universal self-interest was questioned. As we have seen, research has found that people are often concerned with the way strangers are treated (Lerner, 1975, 1982, 2003) and will pay money so as to uphold a norm of fair play (Kahneman et al., 1986; Turillo et al., 2002). Hence, it seems unlikely that general social considerations provide a full accounting of human conduct. Confronted with this evidence, notions of self-interest have been broadened once more, so that self-interest now includes the good feelings that could result from helping others (e.g., Hoffman, 1981); however, it is unclear whether mood management originally was part of rational choice models (Miller, 1999).

In any case, mood maintenance models seem to be inadequate for explaining all altruistic behavior (Batson, 1994, 1995, 1998, in press). In other cases, such models imply the existence of moral standards (Cropanzano et al., 2005). Lacking these, individuals would have no reason to feel guilt or shame, nor would they need to lower their self-esteem. This may seem to settle the definitional matter, but in fact the meaning of self-interest can be expanded even more.

Grand Unifying Pessimism

Throughout this chapter, we have employed a straightforward definition of self-interest that was taken from previous social scientific and philosophical thinking. That is, we have maintained that an egoistic action or motive is said to exist when one's objective is self-benefit. An egoistic person may take into account the interests of others, but only as they serve his or her own objectives instrumentally. By this reckoning, if one is not seeking self-benefit, or if one is taking into account others' needs without seeking personal gain, one is not egoistic. Although this is consistent with the treatment of self-interest by most scholars and laypeople, another semantic approach is possible. Other scholars have considered a more expansive definition of egoism. Although this approach is distinct from our definition, it is worthy of careful consideration. We consider it here.

Overview of an Alternative Definition

When people choose to act in an altruistic or principled fashion, they have selected one course of action over some alternative. To enact any motives implies that a self wants some result. Consequently, one could claim that such putatively helpful individuals are acting in accordance with their own desires. They are doing what they want to do and are trying to bring about a state of affairs that they see as worthwhile. By extension, even if someone longs to help others or to uphold justice, he or she is still self-interested in this loose sense of pursuing a personally pleasing goal. Holley (1999) summarized the logic this way: A person must be motivated by self-interested desires because what moves her to act is always *her own* desires" (p. 42, italics in original). If, for example, an individual wants to help someone else, that individual sees helping as a good thing. The individual is behaving with his or her interests in mind.

The reader will readily see why this new definition is broader than the one we provided earlier. We treated self-interest as the pursuit of a goal that is self-beneficial. This new definition goes beyond that. Self-interest is now said to exist whenever one seeks to fulfill any objective or desire that one might hold (Holley, 1999). There is a simple reason for this. Once an individual decides that a goal or course of action is good, it is in his or her interest to fulfill that objective. The individual is acting as he or she thinks best. Even altruism and principled moral conduct are self-interested, because the actor desires to help others or to behave fairly. Blackburn (2001) termed this the theory of "grand unifying pessimism" (p. 35) because it proposes a single comprehensive (and none too sanguine, in Blackburn's view) explanation for all motivated human behavior.

Points of Clarification

It is worthwhile to note that this expansive conceptualization does not contradict any of the studies we have already reviewed. This broader characterization of egoism allows for situations in which people render altruistic assistance empathically (Batson, 1995, 1998, in press), seek just allocations of resources (Rabin, 1993; van Dijk & Tenbrunsel, 2005), and give up money so that unfair people are punished (Meindl & Lerner, 1983; Turillo et al., 2002). Indeed, this definition is so wide-ranging that it even allows for people to sincerely put others' needs before their own and to be genuinely dedicated to moral principles. For example, if an individual wants to help others, benevolence is desirable to that individual and so it is in his or her interest to be altruistic. Likewise, if an individual prefers justice to injustice, behaving fairly is in his or her interest, broadly defined. It is not that altruism and justice fail to occur, or even that kindness and principle are disingenuous. This definition allows one to accept a committed concern for others and/or the internalization of moral principles. However, this general approach to egoism considers them to be special types of self-interest. People are doing what they want to do. If one wants to be fair or helpful, so much the better, but these are interests nevertheless.

Alternative Viewpoints

To be sure, one can always define self-interest, or any other term, so broadly that it includes all possible human motives. For this reason, we would not say that this expanded definition is incorrect. It is simply a different understanding of an idea. Besides, redefining the term does not change any of the conclusions we have drawn so far. Doing so simply provides a different label. A better question is whether a general definition is more useful than a narrow one. In this regard, certain concerns have been raised about the broad understanding of egoism.

Risk of Tautology. Earlier in this chapter, we defined self-interest in terms of the type of outcome that a person was seeking to achieve. If one sought self-benefit, one was behaving self-interestedly. In this alternative understanding, only the presence of a personal desire is required to create an egoistic act. One can be altruistic, principled, or the like, but these all are treated as variants of self-interest. The broad definition is unconcerned with goal content. Blackburn (2001) observed that this "kidnaps the word 'self-interest' for *whatever* the agent is concerned about" (p. 36, italics in original). An act is made egoistic by the simple pursuit of a freely selected and personally desirable goal, not by whether the act in question benefits the self. In other words, we are not discussing what specifically motives an individual; we are only acknowledging that an individual is motivated (Butler, 1726/1983). Even if we adopted the broad definition, we would still require a theoretical account of why some individuals pursue some goals (e.g., personal financial gain) while others pursue different goals (e.g., altruistic helping).

This broad definition, while rendering universal self-interest impervious to empirical harm, has the effect of trivializing the idea (Turillo et al., 2002). Essentially, to say that one is self-interested is equivalent to saying, as Macaulay (1974) aptly put it, "A man had rather do what he had rather do" (p. 125). This is virtually true by definition. These problems occur because of a lack of specificity. The broad definition does not stipulate what it is that the person is seeking to accomplish, only that he or she is seeking something desirable. The term *self-interest* becomes a rough synonym for "doing what one wants" or "pursuing a personally attractive goal" (Holley, 1999; Rachels, 1986).

This is not an especially surprising or informative idea, and it leaves researchers in a difficult conceptual situation. To predict behavior, scholars would need to differentiate among different types of self-interest. For example, there would be the type of self-interest in which people seek to maximize personal gain, the type of self-interest in which people sacrifice personal gain so as to benefit others, and the type of self-interest in which people sacrifice personal gain so as to do what they think is morally right. It is not at all obvious that our understanding is improved by labeling the latter two examples as types of egoism rather than by simply naming the motives directly.

Conceptual Clarity. Scholarly inquiry and effective managerial practice require that people distinguish among different constructs. A manager who is sincerely concerned with treating his or her employees fairly is different from a manager who wishes to exploit employees to maximize his or her own profit. Calling both of these individuals self-interested is confusing and misleading. In this regard, Holley (1999) observed the following concern:

> If this distinction is erased by some definitional maneuver, nothing will have changed factually, but we may have more difficulty pointing to a difference that we sometimes judge to be important. The egoist wants to suggest that all these behaviors are alike in some sense, but focusing on the sense in which they are all alike can conceal differences that we might judge to be important. (p. 43)

In a similar vein, Simon (1993) lamented, "Neoclassical economics assumes that people maximize utility but postulates nothing about what utility is. With this only assumption, it is impossible to distinguish altruism from selfishness" (p. 158). Under the broad definition, anything that a person wants, even if one wants to help others and behave justly, is part of the utility function. Thus, seeking to maximize utility could mean a number of very different things.

A characterization that stimulates new research ideas and directs our thinking in important practical directions is relatively useful. On the other hand, a characterization that lumps together distinct ideas detracts from our ability to make important scholarly distinctions. Consider, for example, a case of whistle-blowing. A person who, guided by moral values, brings a case of fraud to enforcement authorities is behaving quite differently from one who hides illegal activity in the hope of personal profit. In trying to understand the whistle-blowing activity, maintaining that both of these individuals are guided by their self-interest is not as useful as recognizing the unique things driving their divergent behavioral choices (Cropanzano & Rupp, 2002).

Concluding Thoughts

The broad characterization of self-interest creates certain difficulties, even if it is not technically incorrect. For this reason, we have elected to retain our original definition. Self-interest exists when an action or goal is undertaken for the purpose of self-gain. Such a view seems to be consistent with that of most scholars (cf. Batson, 1995; Blackburn, 2001; Holmes, 1990). Nevertheless, we emphasize that the broad definition is not necessarily wrong so long as one is clear as to the meaning. We suspect that some of the debate among scholars has resulted from these different uses of the term *self-interest*.

Regardless, for current purposes, the most important issue is the underlying research findings, and these are not changed by a new appellation. The evidence reviewed here suggests that people feel empathic concern (Batson, 1995, 1998, in press) and care about moral principles (Folger, 2001; Lerner, 2003). Individuals will sometimes relinquish their own opportunities to help those in need (e.g., Miller, 1977), support their teammates (e.g., Dawes et al., 1990; Tyler & Dawes, 1993), behave fairly (van Dijk & Tenbrunsel, 2005), and punish injustice (e.g., Turillo et al., 2002). Expanding the definition of self-interest simply gives these phenomena a new moniker; it does not change their basic reality.

Conclusion

Given such a high standard of proof, the outcome of our review should not come as a surprise. Humans are complex animals. To reduce all that we do to any single motive was bound to be a difficult undertaking. Self-interest remains ubiquitous, but it does not seem to be universal unless it is defined very broadly. If future research supports these conclusions, scholars may be confronted with a new set of challenges. In particular, our aesthetic treatment of self-interest will give way to concerns that are moral, empirical, and practical. The doctrine of universal self-interest has been a simple and concise means of summarizing human motivation. Considering additional sources of human motivation will require more than adding a few simple constructs. It will also require reframing the way we ask certain questions. Before closing this chapter, we will try to illustrate this point with three questions: the moral question, the empirical question, and the practical question.

The Moral Question: When Is Self-Interest a Good Thing?

For this chapter, the question before us was whether universal egoism is sufficient to explain all human behavior. That is, we were analyzing a scientific *description* and not providing an ethical *prescription*. Absent additional evidence and argument, one should not assume that a selfless intention is morally superior to an egoistic one. Philosophical objectivists (e.g., Rand, 1961) and ethical egoists (e.g., Thompson, 2003) have suggested that people should be given wide latitude to seek individual gain. We suspect that even those who reject these philosophies would still agree that there is nothing intrinsically wrong with looking out for one's own interests. It seems worthwhile for people to seek comfortable and productive lives for themselves, and we should be careful to avoid blanket condemnations. The ethical debate should reside in how one's interests are understood (Holley, 1999), the extent to which others' needs should be considered (Blackburn, 2001), the circumstances in which other motives are a superior guide to behavior (Rachels, 1986; Weaver, 1984), and other such questions. These are complex matters, but this makes a healthy debate all the more important.

The Empirical Question: When and How Much Self-Interest?

To evaluate the doctrine of universal egoism, we examined the available data in an "either/or" fashion. We believe that self-interest is a very important human motive, but we wonder whether additional motives might also exist. The approach may soon be obsolete. If one accepts that egoism is one important motive among others, this recognition demands that we reflect on matters in a more nuanced fashion. Once we recognize that self-interest is not alone, this realization opens new opportunities for inquiry. In particular, researchers will want to examine when self-interest is especially important as well as the possibility that self-interest could work alongside other motives. Let us consider some recent examples of these types of investigations.

Self-Interest Versus Other Motives

Even if self-interest is not the only human motive, it remains a very important one (Rapoport et al., 2003). An important area of recent research examines when individuals base their decisions on egoistic considerations rather than on other motives. Foreshadowing this new look is a chapter by van Dijk and Tenbrunsel (2005), who agreed that both self-interest and fairness provide motives for human behavior. Hence, they discussed different situational factors that could cause one to seek either egoism or justice. In a like fashion, van Dijk and De Cremer (in press) agreed that some people take into account fairness when making allocation decisions. However, they added that decision makers can also use justice strategically so that it serves their instrumental concerns (van Dijk et al., 2004).

A similar regard for both self-interested and non-self-interested motives seems to be emerging in the behavior economics literature. For example, Camerer and Fehr (2006) discussed various aspects of partner behavior that could lead one to become more self-regarding or more other-regarding. This would seem to be an especially useful scholarly approach because it has the potential to increase our knowledge and thereby offer valuable advice to organizations. To the extent that scholars fail to appreciate the complexity of human motives, then, our practical recommendations could be similarly impoverished.

Self-Interest and Other Motives

Scholars have begun to consider how self-interest can complement other orientations. This research is quite promising, and we hope to see more in the future. For example, Margolis (1990) considered how individuals trade off concern for the self with concern for others. A similar program of study has been presented by De Dreu and colleagues (De Dreu, 2006; De Dreu & Steinel, in press; De Dreu et al., 2000), who recognized human complexity and attempted to understand how people make decisions that balance potentially competing motives. Along the same lines, Rocha and Ghoshal (2006) suggested that the traditional notion of universal egoism has limitations, but they argued that self-interested and non-self-interested motives can be integrated into a unified framework. Based on the venerable work of Aristotle, Rocha and Ghoshal (2006) maintained that humans have an "inclination . . . to strive for their own good and perfection" (p. 601). They termed this predilection "self-love," asserting that self-interest is only one part of self-love. The key difference, as we have noted throughout this chapter, is that self-interest takes account of only one's own concerns; others matter instrumentally for how they influence one's individual objectives. Self-love, on the other hand, includes cases where personal excellence is realized through non-self-interested goals such as selfless duty and altruism (for similar ideas, see Holley, 1999). These ideas fit nicely with our perspective because they recognize the existence of multiple motives. Rocha and Ghoshal (2006) argued, as we argue, that people sometimes see value in goals that benefit others. Of course, these ideas tend to be of recent origin, and more research is necessary.

The Practical Question: What Are Organizations to Do?

Earlier, we observed that self-interest should not be equated with immorality. Here we go further. Even if one does not consider self-interest to be ethically praiseworthy, it still would not necessarily follow that egoism produces bad policy. The thinking of Smith (1776/1966) and Sowell (1996) examined this important point of caution. Although we may pursue social good in a well-meaning fashion, we often do so with limited information. Our mistakes can lead to poor policy decisions. Individual self-interest can be a constructive, albeit sometimes unappreciated, motive (for discussions of this and related possibilities, see Bethell, 1998; Hayek, 1944; Sowell, 1987). In any case, it strikes us as worthwhile for organizations to meet the legitimate needs of employees though the provision of adequate pay, dignity, and respect (cf. O'Reilly & Pfeffer, 2000; Pfeffer, 1998).

That said, if there is more than only self-interest, organizations will likely want to find ways of meeting other human objectives. Ferraro and colleagues (2005) recently argued that the assumption of self-interest has influenced the practical advice that management scientists give to organizations. If humans have concerns beyond egoism, this suggests that our advice to date has been somewhat limited. Clearly, organizations will want to attend to other concerns such as promoting workplace fairness (e.g., Folger, 2001; Folger et al., 2005). More generally, research also attests to the effectiveness of transformational leaders who, among other things, rouse workers with charisma and inspirational motivation (e.g., Avolio, 1999; Bass, 1998). Similarly, Gardner and Laskin (1995) argued that great leaders need to be great storytellers who provide followers with a sense of meaning and purpose. Research of this kind could provide invaluable insights for future research and practice.

Closing Thoughts

We opened this chapter with Thrasymachus's famous challenge to Socrates. Stated generally, we asked whether there was anything beyond self-interest. We have examined this dialogue from six perspectives: philosophical (Bentham, 1789/1988; Blackburn, 2001; Butler, 1726/1983; Hobbes, 1651/1998; Holley, 1999; Rachels, 1986; Thompson, 2003), economic (Bethell, 1998; Bolton & Ockenfels, 2000; Camerer & Fehr, 2006; Camerer & Thaler, 1995; Cox, 2003; Fehr & Gächter, 2000, 2002; Frank, 1988, 1990), social psychological (Batson, 1991, 1994, 1995, 1998; DaGloria & DeRidder, 1977, 1979; Lerner, 1975, 1982, 2003), management science (Bies, 2001; Bies & Tripp, 1996, 2001, 2002; De Dreu, 2006; De Dreu et al., 2000; Turillo et al., 2002), political science (Burnham, 1943; Mansbridge, 1990; Wilson, 1993), and even biological (Brosnan De Waal, 2003; De Waal, 1996). Our journey has taken us back to ancient times (Augustine of Hippo, 397/1907; Plato, ca. 360 BC/1935), through the Enlightenment (Hume, 1739/2000; Smith, 1759/1853), and all the way to contemporary thought. Each time we turned over a stone, we found evidence for self-interest. To be sure, humans are egoistic creatures. However, people are not only egoistic. No single motive, even self-interest, is sufficient to account for all of our behavior.

References

Adams, J. S. (1963). Toward an understanding of inequity. *Journal of Abnormal and Social Psychology, 47,* 422–436.

Adams, J. S. (1965). Inequity in social exchange. In L. Berkowitz (Ed.), *Advances in experimental social psychology* (Vol. 2, pp. 267–299). New York: Academic Press.

Adams, J. S., & Freedman, S. (1976). Equity theory revisited: Comments and annotated bibliography. In L. Berkowitz (Ed.), *Advances in experimental social psychology* (Vol. 9, pp. 43–90). New York: Academic Press.

Allred, K. G. (1999). Anger driven retaliation: Toward an understanding of impassioned conflict in organizations. In R. J. Bies, R. J. Lewicki, & B. H. Sheppard (Eds.), *Research on negotiations in organizations* (Vol. 7, pp. 27–58). Greenwich, CT: JAI.

Aquino, K., Tripp, T., & Bies, R. (2001). How employees respond to personal offense: The effects of blame attribution, victim status, and offender status on revenge and reconciliation in the workplace. *Journal of Applied Psychology, 86,* 52–59.

Augustine of Hippo. (1907). *The confessions of St. Augustine.* London: J. M. Dent. (Original work written ca. 397)

Avolio, B. J. (1999). *Full leadership development: Building the vital forces in organizations.* Thousand Oaks, CA: Sage.

Badaracco, J. L., Jr. (1997). *Defining moments: When managers must choose between right and right.* Boston: Harvard Business School Press.

Bass, B. M. (1998). *Transformational leadership: Industrial, military, and educational impact.* Mahwah, NJ: Lawrence Erlbaum.

Batson, C. D. (1987). Prosocial motivation: Is it ever truly altruistic? In L. Berkowitz (Ed.), *Advances in experimental social psychology* (Vol. 20, pp. 65–122). San Diego: Academic Press.

Batson, C. D. (1991). *The altruism question: Toward a social–psychological answer.* Hillsdale, NJ: Lawrence Erlbaum.

Batson, C. D. (1994). Why act for the public good? Four answers. *Personality and Social Psychology Bulletin, 20,* 603–610.

Batson, C. D. (1995). Prosocial motivation: Why do we help others? In A. Tesser (Ed.), *Advanced social psychology* (pp. 332–381). Boston: McGraw-Hill.

Batson, C. D. (1998). Altruism and prosocial behavior. In D. T. Gilbert, S. Fiske, & G. Lindzey (Eds.), *The handbook of social psychology* (4th ed., Vol 2, pp. 282–316). New York: McGraw-Hill.

Batson, C. D. (in press). "Not all is self-interest after all": Economics of empathy-induced altruism. In D. De Cremer, M. Zeelenberg, & K. J. Murnighan (Eds.), *Social psychology and economics.* Mahwah, NJ: Lawrence Erlbaum.

Batson, C. D., Batson, J. G., Slingsby, J. K., Harrell, K. L., Peekna, H. M., & Todd, R. M. (1991). Empathic joy and the empathy–altruism hypothesis. *Journal of Personality and Social Psychology, 61,* 413–426.

Batson, D. C., Duncan, B., Ackerman, P., Buckley, T., & Birch, K. (1981). Is empathic emotion a source of altruistic motivation? *Journal of Personality and Social Psychology, 40,* 290–302.

Batson, D. C., Dyck, J. L., Brandt, J. R., Batson, J. G., Powell, A. L., McMaster, M. R., & Griffitt, D. (1988). Five studies testing two new egoistic alternatives to the empathy–altruism hypothesis. *Journal of Personality and Social Psychology, 55,* 52–77.

Becker, E. (1973). *The denial of death.* New York: Free Press.

Bentham, J. (1988). *An introduction to principle of morals and legislation.* Buffalo, NY: Prometheus Books. (Original work published 1789)

Bethell, T. (1998). *The noblest triumph: Property and prosperity through the ages.* New York: St. Martin's.

Bies, R. J. (2001). Interactional (in)justice: The sacred and the profane. In J. Greenberg & R. Cropanzano (Eds.), *Advances in organizational justice* (pp. 89–118). Stanford, CA: Stanford University Press.

Bies, R. J., & Tripp, T. M. (1996). Beyond distrust: "Getting even" and the need for revenge. In R. M. Kramer & T. Tyler (Eds.), *Trust in organizations* (pp. 246–260). Thousand Oaks, CA: Sage.

Bies, R. J., & Tripp, T. M. (2001). A passion for justice: The rationality and morality of revenge. In R. Cropanzano (Ed.), *Justice in the workplace* (pp. 197–208). Mahwah, NJ: Lawrence Erlbaum.

Bies, R. J., & Tripp, T. M. (2002). "Hot flashes, open wounds": Injustice and the tyranny of its emotions. In S. W. Gilliland, D. D. Steiner, & D. P. Skarlicki (Eds.), *Emerging perspectives on managing organizational justice* (pp. 203–221). Greenwich, CT: Information Age.

Bies, R. J., Tripp, T. M., & Kramer, R. M. (1997). At the breaking point: Cognitive and social dynamics of revenge in organizations. In R. A. Giacalone & J. Greenberg (Eds.), *Antisocial behavior in organizations* (pp. 18–36). Thousand Oaks, CA: Sage.

Blackburn, S. (2001). *Being good: A short introduction to ethics.* Oxford, UK: Oxford University Press.

Bolton, G., & Ockenfels, A. (2000). ERC: A theory of equity, reciprocity, and competition. *American Economic Review, 90,* 166–193.

Brosnan, S. F., & De Waal, F. B. M. (2003). Monkeys reject unequal pay. *Nature, 425,* 297–299.

Burnham, J. (1943). *The Machiavellians: Defenders of freedom.* London: Putnam.

Butler, J. (1983). *Five sermons preached at the Rolls Chapel and a dissertation upon the nature of virtue.* Indianapolis, IN: Hackett. (Original work published 1726)

Cahn, E. (1949). *The sense of injustice.* New York: New York University Press.

Camerer, C. F., & Fehr, E. (2006). When does "economic man" dominate social behavior? *Science, 311,* 47–52.

Camerer, C., & Thaler, R. H. (1995). Anomalies: Ultimatums, dictators, and manners. *Journal of Economic Perspectives, 9,* 209–219.

Campbell, D. T. (1975). On the conflicts between biological and social evolution and between psychology and moral tradition. *American Psychologist, 30,* 1103–1126.

Coke, J. S., Batson, C. D., & McDavis, K. (1978). Empathic mediation of helping: A two-stage model. *Journal of Personality and Social Psychology, 36,* 752–766.

Colquitt, J. A., & Greenberg, J. (2001). Doing justice to organizational justice: Forming and applying fairness judgments. In S. Gilliland, D. Steiner, &

D. Skarlicki (Eds.), *Theoretical and cultural perspectives on organizational justice* (pp. 217–242). Greenwich, CT: JAI.

Connolly, T., Ordóñez, L. D., & Coughlan, R. (1997). Regret and responsibility in the evaluation of decision outcomes. *Organizational Behavior and Human Decision Processes, 70,* 73–85.

Connolly, T., & Zeelenberg, M. (2002). Regret in decision making. *Psychological Science, 11,* 212–216.

Cox, J. C. (2003). How to identify trust and reciprocity. *Games and Economic Behavior, 46,* 260–281.

Cropanzano, R., Goldman, B. M., & Folger, R. (2003). Deontic justice: The role of moral principles in workplace fairness. *Journal of Organizational Behavior, 24,* 1019–1024.

Cropanzano, R., Goldman, B. M., & Folger, R. (2005). Self-interest: Defining and understanding a human motive. *Journal of Organizational Behavior, 26,* 985–991.

Cropanzano, R., & Rupp, D. E. (2002). Some reflections on the morality of organizational justice. In S. Gilliland, D. Steiner, & D. Skarlicki (Eds.), *Emerging perspectives on managing organizational justice* (pp. 225–278). Greenwich, CT: Information Age.

DaGloria, J., & DeRidder, R. (1977). Aggression in dyadic interaction. *European Journal of Social Psychology, 7,* 189–219.

DaGloria, J., & DeRidder, R. (1979). Sex differences in aggression: Are current notions misleading? *European Journal of Social Psychology, 9,* 49–66.

Dawes, R. M., van de Kragt, A. J. C., & Orbell, J. M. (1990). Cooperation for the benefit of us—Not me, or my conscience. In J. J. Mansbridge (Ed.), *Beyond self-interest* (pp. 97–110). Chicago: University of Chicago Press.

De Dreu, C. K. W. (2006). Rational self-interest and other orientation in organizational behavior: A critical approach and extension of Meglino and Korsgaard (2004). *Journal of Applied Psychology, 91,* 1245–1252.

De Dreu, C. K. W., & Carnevale, P. J. (2003). Motivational bases of information processing and strategy in conflict and negotiation. In M. P. Zanna (Ed.), *Advances in experimental social psychology* (Vol. 35, pp. 235–291). San Diego: Academic Press.

De Dreu, C. K. W., & Steinel, W. (in press). Social decision-making in fuzzy situations: Motivated, information-processing, and strategic choice. In D. De Cremer, M. Zeelenberg, & K. J. Murnighan (Eds.), *Social psychology and economics.* Mahwah, NJ: Lawrence Erlbaum.

De Dreu, C. K. W., Weingart, L. R., & Kwon, S. (2000). Influence of social motives on integrative negotiation: A meta-analytic review and test of two theories. *Journal of Personality and Social Psychology, 78,* 889–905.

Deutsch, M. (1973). *The resolution of conflict: Constructive and destructive processes.* New Haven, CT: Yale University Press.

De Waal, F. (1996). *Good-natured: The origins of right and wrong in humans and other animals.* Cambridge, MA: Harvard University Press.

Dovidio, J. F., Allen, J. L., & Schroeder, D. A. (1990). The specificity of empathy-induced helping: Evidence for altruistic motivation. *Journal of Personality and Social Psychology, 59,* 249–260.

Edgeworth, F. Y. (1881). *Mathematical psychics: An essay on the application of mathematics to the moral sciences.* London: C. K. Paul.

Eisenberg, N., & Miller, P. (1987). Empathy and prosocial behavior. *Psychological Bulletin, 101,* 91–119.

Elser, J. (1990). Selfishness and altruism. In J. J. Mansbridge (Ed.), *Beyond self-interest* (pp. 44–52). Chicago: University of Chicago Press.

Emerson, R. M. (1972a). Exchange theory: I. A psychological basis for social exchange. In J. Berger, M. Zelditch, Jr., & B. Anderson (Eds.), *Sociological theories in progress* (Vol. 2, pp. 38–57). Boston: Houghton Mifflin.

Emerson, R. M. (1972b). Exchange theory: II. A psychological basis for social exchange. In J. Berger, M. Zelditch, Jr., & B. Anderson (Eds.), *Sociological theories in progress* (Vol. 2, pp. 58–87). Boston: Houghton Mifflin.

Farrell, D. M. (1985). The justification of general deterrence. *Philosophical Review, 44,* 367–394.

Fehr, E., & Gächter, S. (2000). Cooperation and punishment in public goods experiments. *American Economic Review, 90,* 980–994.

Fehr, E., & Gächter, S. (2002). Altruistic punishment in humans. *Nature, 415,* 137–140.

Ferraro, F., Pfeffer, J., & Sutton, R. I. (2005). Economics language and assumptions: How theories can become self-fulfilling. *Academy of Management Review, 30,* 8–24.

Folger, R. (2001). Fairness as deonance. In S. W. Gilliland, D. D. Steiner, & D. P. Skarlicki (Eds.), *Research in social issues in management* (Vol. 1, pp. 3–33). Greenwich, CT: Information Age.

Folger, R., Cropanzano, R., & Goldman, B. (2005). Justice, accountability, and moral sentiment: The deontic response to "foul play" at work. In J. Greenberg & J. Colquitt (Eds.), *Handbook of organizational justice* (pp. 215–245). Mahwah, NJ: Lawrence Erlbaum.

Frank, R. H. (1988). *Passions within reason: The strategic role of the emotions.* New York: Norton.

Frank, R. H. (1990). A theory of moral sentiments. In J. J. Mansbridge (Ed.), *Beyond self-interest* (pp. 71–96). Chicago: University of Chicago Press.

Frank, R. H., Gilovich, T., & Regan, D. T. (2000). Does studying economics inhibit cooperation? In T. Connolly, H. R. Arkes, & K. R. Hammond (Eds.), *Judgement and decision making: An interdisciplinary reader* (2nd ed.). New York: Cambridge University Press.

Frankl, V. E. (1984). *Man's search for meaning: An introduction to logotherapy* (3rd ed.). New York: Simon & Schuster.

Freud, S. (1930). *Civilization and its discontents.* London: Hogarth.

Freud, S. (1974). *Beyond the pleasure principle.* New York: Norton. (Original work published 1920)

Fuller, E. (Ed.). (1980). *4800 wise-cracks, witty remarks, and epigrams for all occasions.* New York: Avenel.

Fultz, J., Batson, C. D., Fortenbach, V. A., McCarthy, P. M., & Varney, L. L. (1986). Social evaluation and the empathy–altruism hypothesis. *Journal of Personality and Social Psychology, 50,* 761–769.

Gardner, H., & Laskin, E. (1995). *Leading minds: Anatomy of leadership.* New York: HarperBooks.

Gaus, G. F. (2001a). What is deontology? I. Orthodox views. *Journal of Value Inquiry, 35,* 27–42.

Gaus, G. F. (2001b). What is deontology? II. Reasons to act. *Journal of Value Inquiry, 35,* 179–193.

Gergen, K. (1969). *The psychology of behavior exchange.* Menlo Park, CA: Addison-Wesley.

Gillespie, J. Z., & Greenberg, J. (2005). Are the goals of organizational justice self-interested? In J. Greenberg & J. A. Colquitt (Eds.), *Handbook of organizational justice* (pp. 179–213). Mahwah, NJ: Lawrence Erlbaum.

Gilligan, C. (1982). *In a different voice: Psychological theory and women's development.* Cambridge, MA: Harvard University Press.

Goldberg, J. H., Lerner, J. S., & Tetlock, P. E. (1999). Rage and reason: The psychology of the intuitive prosecutor. *European Journal of Social Psychology, 29,* 781–795.

Goldman, B. M. (2003). The application of referent cognitions theory to legal-claiming by terminated workers: The role of organizational justice and anger. *Journal of Management, 29,* 705–728.

Güth, W., Schmittberger, R., & Schwarze, B. (1982). An experimental analysis of ultimatum games. *Journal of Economic Behavior and Organizations, 3,* 367–388.

Hatfield, E., Walster, G. W., & Piliavin, J. A. (1978). Equity theory and helping relationships. In L. Wispe (Ed.), *Altruism, sympathy, and helping: Psychological and sociological perspectives* (pp. 115–139). New York: Academic Press.

Hayek, F. A. (1944). *The road to serfdom.* Chicago: University of Chicago Press.

Henrich, J., Boyd, R., Bowles, S., Camerer, C., Fehr, E., Gintis, H., & McElreath, R. (2001). In search of *Homo economicus:* Behavioral experiments in 15 small-scale societies. *American Economic Review, 91,* 73–78.

Hobbes, T. (1998). *The leviathan.* Oxford, UK: Oxford University Press. (Original work published 1651)

Hoffman, M. L. (1976). Empathy, role-taking, guilt, and development of altruistic motives. In T. Lickona (Ed.), *Moral development and behavior: Theory, research, and social issues* (pp. 124–143). New York: Holt, Rinehart & Winston.

Hoffman, M. L. (1981). The development of empathy. In J. P. Rushton & R. M. Sorentino (Eds.), *Altruism and helping behavior: Social, personality, and developmental perspectives* (pp. 41–63). Hillsdale, NJ: Lawrence Erlbaum.

Holley, D. M. (1999). *Self-interest and beyond.* St. Paul, MN: Paragon House.

Holmes, J. G., Miller, D. T., & Lerner, M. J. (2002). Committing altruism under the cloak of self-interest: The exchange fiction. *Journal of Experimental Social Psychology, 38,* 144–151.

Holmes, S. (1990). The secret history of self-interest. In J. J. Mansbridge (Ed.), *Beyond self-interest* (pp. 267–286). Chicago: University of Chicago Press.

Holmgren, M. H. (1989). The backward-looking component of weak retributivism. *Journal of Value Inquiry, 23,* 135–146.

Homans, G. C. (1974). *Social behavior: Its elementary forms* (Rev. ed.). New York: Harcourt Brace Jovanovich.

Hume, D. (2000). *Treatise of human nature.* Oxford, UK: Oxford University Press. (Original work published 1739)

Kagel, J. H., Kim, C., & Moser, D. (1996). Fairness in ultimatum games with asymmetric information and asymmetric payoffs. *Games and Economic Behavior, 13,* 100–111.

Kahneman, D., Knetsch, J. L., & Thaler, R. H. (1986). Fairness and the assumptions of economics. *Journal of Business, 59,* 285–300.

Keltner, D., & Anderson, C. (2000). Saving face for Darwin: The functions and uses of embarrassment. *Current Directions in Psychological Science, 9,* 187–191.

Keltner, D., & Buswell, B. (1997). Embarrassment: Its distinct form and appeasement functions. *Psychological Bulletin, 122,* 250–270.

Keltner, D., Young, R. C., & Buswell, B. N. (1997). Appeasement in human emotion, social practice, and personality. *Aggressive Behavior, 23,* 359–374.

Krebs, D. L. (1975). Empathy and altruism. *Journal of Personality and Social Psychology, 32,* 1134–1146.

Lerner, J. S., Goldberg, J., & Tetlock, P. (1998). Sober second thoughts: The effects of accountability, anger, and authoritarianism on attributions of responsibility. *Personality and Social Psychology Bulletin, 24,* 563–574.

Lerner, M. J. (1975). The justice motive in social behavior: Introduction. *Journal of Social Issues, 31*(3), 1–20.

Lerner, M. J. (1982). Justice motive in human relations and the economic model of man. In V. Derlega & J. Grzelak (Eds.), *Cooperation and helping behavior* (pp. 249–277). New York: Academic Press.

Lerner, M. J. (2003). The justice motive: Where social psychologists found it, how they lost it, and why they may not find it again. *Personality and Social Psychology Review, 7,* 388–389.

Locke, E., Tirnauer, D., Roberson, Q., Goldman, B., & Weldon, E. (2001). The importance of the individual in an age of groupism. In M. Turner (Ed.), *Groups at work: Advances in theory and research* (pp. 501–528). Mahwah, NJ: Lawrence Erlbaum.

Macaulay, T. (1978). Mill's essay on government: Utilitarian logic and politics. In J. Lively & J. Rees (Eds.), *Utilitarian logic and politics* (p. 124). Oxford, UK: Clarendon.

Machiavelli, N. (1908). *The prince.* New York: Everyman's Library. (Original work published 1513)

Mansbridge, J. J. (1990). The rise and fall of self-interest in the explanation of political life. In J. J. Mansbridge (Ed.), *Beyond self-interest* (pp. 3–22). Chicago: University of Chicago Press.

Manucia, G. K., Baumann, D. J., & Cialdini, R. B. (1984). Mood influences on helping: Direct effects or side effects? *Journal of Personality and Social Psychology, 46,* 357–364.

Margolis, H. (1990). Dual utilities and rational choice. In J. J. Mansbridge (Ed.), *Beyond self-interest* (pp. 239–253). Chicago: University of Chicago Press.

Marwell, G., & Ames, R. (1981). Economists free ride, does anyone else? Experiments on the provision of public goods. *Journal of Public Economics, 15,* 295–310.

McLean Parks, J. M. (1997). The fourth arm of justice: The art and science of revenge. In R. J. Lewicki, R. J. Bies, & B. H. Sheppard (Eds.), *Research on negotiation in organizations* (Vol. 6, pp. 113–144). Greenwich, CT: JAI.

Meindl, J., & Lerner, M. J. (1983). The heroic motive in interpersonal relations. *Journal of Experimental Social Psychology, 19,* 1–20.

Mikula, G., Scherer, K. R., & Athenstaedt, U. (1998). The role of injustice in the elicitation of differential emotional reactions. *Personality and Social Psychology Bulletin, 24,* 769–783.

Miller, D. T. (1977). Personal deserving and justice for others: An exploration of the justice motive. *Journal of Experimental Social Psychology, 13,* 1–13.

Miller, D. T. (1999). The norm of self-interest. *American Psychologist, 54,* 1053–1060.

Miller, D. T., & Ratner, R. K. (1998). The disparity between the actual and assumed power of self-interest. *Journal of Personality and Social Psychology, 74,* 53–62.

Molm, L. D., Quist, T. M., & Wisely, P. A. (1994). Imbalanced structures, unfair strategies: Power and justice in social exchange. *American Sociological Review, 59,* 98–121.

Ordóñez, L. D., & Connolly, T. (2000). Regret and responsibility: A reply to Zeelenberg et al. (1998). *Organizational Behavior and Human Decision Processes, 81,* 132–142.

O'Reilly, C. A., III, & Pfeffer, J. (2000). *Hidden value: How great companies achieve extraordinary results with ordinary people.* Boston: Harvard Business School Press.

Ostrom, E. (1998). A behavioral approach to the rational choice theory of collective action. *American Political Science Review, 92,* 1–22.

Ozinga, J. R. (1999). *Altruism.* Westport, CT: Greenwood.

Parco, J. E., Rapoport, A., & Stein, W. E. (2002). Effects of financial incentives on the breakdown of mutual trust. *Psychological Science, 13,* 292–297.

Pfeffer, J. (1998). *The human question: Building profits by putting people first.* Boston: Harvard Business School Press.

Plato. (1935). *The republic.* New York: Everyman's Library. (Original work written ca. 360 BC)

Pruitt, D. G., & Rubin, J. Z. (1986). *Social conflict: Escalation, stalemate, and settlement.* New York: Random House.

Rabin, M. (1993). Incorporating fairness into game theory and economics. *American Economic Review, 83,* 1281–1302.

Rachels, J. (1986). *Elements of moral philosophy.* New York: Random House.

Rand, A. (1961). *The virtue of selfishness: A new concept of egoism.* New York: New American Library.

Rapoport, A., Stein, W. E., Parco, J. E., & Nicolas, T. E. (2003). Equilibrium play and adaptive learning in a three-person centipede game. *Games and Economic Behavior, 43,* 239–265.

Ratner, R. K., & Miller, D. T. (2001). The norm of self-interest and its effects on social action. *Journal of Personality and Social Psychology, 81,* 5–16.

Rawls, J. (1971). *A theory of justice.* Cambridge, MA: Harvard University Press.

Reb, J., Goldman, B. M., Kray, L. J., & Cropanzano, R. (2006). Different wrongs, different remedies? Reactions to organizational remedies after procedural and interactional injustice. *Personnel Psychology, 59,* 31–64.

Rocha, H. O., & Ghoshal, S. (2006). Beyond self-interest revisited. *Journal of Management Studies, 43,* 585–619.

Rozin, P., Lowery, L., Imada, S., & Haidt, J. (1999). The CAD triad hypothesis: A mapping between three moral emotions (contempt, anger, disgust) and three moral codes (community, autonomy, divinity). *Journal of Personality and Social Psychology, 76,* 574–586.

Rupp, D. E. (2003, April). *Testing the moral violations component of fairness theory: Moral maturity as a moderator of the deontological effect.* Paper presented at the meeting of the Society for Industrial and Organizational Psychology, Orlando, FL.

Schaller, M., & Cialdini, R. B. (1988). The economics of empathic helping: Support for a mood-management motive. *Journal of Personality and Social Psychology, 24,* 163–181.

Schroeder, D. A., Steel, J. E., Woodell, A. J., & Bembenek, A. F. (2003). Justice within social dilemmas. *Personality and Social Psychology Review, 7,* 374–387.

Sen, A. K. (1990). Rational fools: A critique of the behavioral foundations of economic theory. In J. J. Mansbridge (Ed.), *Beyond self-interest* (pp. 25–43). Chicago: University of Chicago Press.

Simon, H. A. (1990). A mechanism for social selection and successful altruism. *Science, 250,* 1665–1668.

Simon, H. A. (1993). Altruism and economics. *American Economic Review, 83,* 156–161.

Smith, A. (1853). *A theory of moral sentiments.* London: Henry G. Bohn. (Original work published 1759)

Smith, A. (1966). *An inquiry into the nature and causes of the wealth of nations.* New Rochelle, NY: Arlington House. (Original work published 1776)

Sowell, T. (1987). *A conflict of visions: Ideological origins of political struggles.* New York: Quill.

Sowell, T. (1996). *Knowledge and decisions.* New York: Basic Books.

Stotland, E. (1969). Exploratory studies of empathy. In L. Berkowitz (Ed.), *Advances in experimental social psychology* (Vol. 4, pp. 271–313). New York: Academic Press.

Stouten, J., De Cremer, D., & van Dijk, E. (2005). All is well that ends well, at least for proselfs: Emotional reactions to equality violations as a function of social value orientation. *European Journal of Social Psychology, 35,* 767–783.

Suleiman, R. (1996). Expectations and fairness in a modified ultimatum game. *Journal of Economic Psychology, 17,* 531–554.

Surowiecki, J. (2004). *The wisdom of crowds: Why many are smarter than a few and how collective wisdom shapes business, economics, societies, and nations.* New York: Doubleday.

Tangney, J. P. (1995). Shame and guilt in interpersonal relationships. In J. P. Tangney & K. W. Fischer (Eds.), *Self-conscious emotions: Shame, guilt, embarrassment, and pride* (pp. 114–139). New York: John Wiley.

Tangney, J. P., & Fischer, K. W. (Eds.). (1995). *Self-conscious emotions: Shame, guilt, embarrassment, and pride.* New York: John Wiley.

Tangney, J. P., Miller, R. S., Flicker, L., & Barlow, D. H. (1996). Are shame, guilt, and embarrassment distinct emotions? *Journal of Personality and Social Psychology, 70,* 1256–1269.

Thaler, R. H. (1988). Anomalies: The ultimatum games. *Journal of Economic Perspectives, 2,* 195–206.

Thompson, M. (2003). *Ethics.* London: Teach Yourself.

Toi, M., & Batson, C. D. (1982). More evidence that empathy is a source of altruistic motivation. *Journal of Personality and Social Psychology, 43,* 281–292.

Tripp, T. M., & Bies, R. J. (1997). What's good about revenge? The avenger's perspective. In R. J. Lewicki, R. J. Bies, & B. H. Sheppard (Eds.), *Research on negotiation in organizations* (Vol. 6, pp. 145–160). Greenwich, CT: JAI.

Turillo, C. J., Folger, R., Lavelle, J. J., Umphress, E., & Gee, J. (2002). Is virtue its own reward? Self-sacrificial decisions for the sake of fairness. *Organizational Behavior and Human Decision Processes, 89,* 839–865.

Tyler, T. R., & Dawes, R. M. (1993). Fairness in groups: Comparing self-interest and social identity perspectives. In B. A. Mellers & J. Baron (Eds.), *Psychological perspectives on justice: Theory and applications* (pp. 87–108). New York: Cambridge University Press.

Van Dijk, E., & De Cremer, D. (in press). Tacit coordination and social dilemmas: On the importance of self-interest and fairness. In D. De Cremer, M. Zeelenberg, & K. J. Murnighan (Eds.), *Social psychology and economics*. Mahwah, NJ: Lawrence Erlbaum.

Van Dijk, E., De Cremer, D., & Handgraaf, M. J. J. (2004). Social value orientations and the strategic use of fairness in ultimatum bargaining. *Journal of Experimental Social Psychology, 40,* 697–707.

Van Dijk, E., & Tenbrunsel, A. (2005). The battle between self-interest and fairness: Evidence from ultimatum, dictator, and delta games. In S. W. Gilliland, D. D. Steiner, D. P. Skarlicki, & K. van den Bos (Eds.), *What motivates fairness in organizations?* (pp. 31–48). Greenwich, CT: Information Age.

Van Dijk, E., & Vermunt, R. (2000). Strategy and fairness in social decision making: Sometimes it pays to be powerless. *Journal of Experimental Social Psychology, 36,* 1–25.

Van Lange, P. A. M. (1999). The pursuit of joint outcomes and equality in outcomes: An integrative model of social value orientations. *Journal of Personality and Social Psychology, 77,* 337–349.

Van Lange, P. A. M., & Kuhlman, D. M. (1994). Social value orientations and impressions of partner's honesty and intelligence: A test of the morality effect. *Journal of Personality and Social Psychology, 67,* 126–141.

Vecchio, R. P. (1981). An individual-differences interpretation of the conflicting predictions generated by equity theory and expectancy theory. *Journal of Applied Psychology, 66,* 470–481.

Velasquez, M. G. (2001). *Business ethics: Concepts and cases* (5th ed.). Englewood Cliffs, NJ: Prentice Hall.

Weaver, R. M. (1984). *Ideas have consequences.* Chicago: University of Chicago Press.

Wilson, J. Q. (1993). *The moral sense.* New York: Free Press.

Wright, R. (1994). *The moral animal: The new science of evolutionary psychology.* New York: Pantheon Books.

Zeelenberg, M., van Dijk, W. W., & Manstead, S. R. (1998). Reconsidering the relation between regret and responsibility. *Organizational Behavior and Human Decision Processes, 74,* 254–272.

10 Interpersonal Aesthetics

Emotional and Social Intelligence Competencies Are Wisdom in Practice

Richard E. Boyatzis

As I pant up this vertiginous path, the glare from the bright Grecian sun in August is intense. The sun bakes you even before it burns you. Although it seems forever, I keep walking and wondering why I am doing this. The answer is that I am in search of wisdom. Up and up, the climb is to the temple of Apollo. To be accurate, I am not in search of wisdom as much as I am seeking to understand life's experiences and their meaning. For more than 2,500 years, people have come to hear the prognostications of the oracle of Delphi and to find some guidance.

On the way up, the path takes me by smaller temples and places for prayer. The entire mountainside seems like an invitation for contemplation. The inscriptions are philosophical guideposts. After a sip of water and a few minutes under the shade of a tree, it dawns on me. I am hearing from the oracle without needing to make a sacrifice, place gifts on temple ledges, or ask a question. It is a surprise as to how quickly my quest is fulfilled. The answers are here! They are listed like an FAQ[1] on the meaning of life. My Ancient Greek is a bit rusty, but three of them invade my consciousness for the next day:

1. Know thyself

2. Nothing in excess

3. Do unto others . . . (as you would wish them to do unto you)

In this chapter, I explain what I learned on this quest about the meaning of experience and how it relates to emotional and social intelligence (ESI) competencies—and even how they are developed. In this sense, ESI is wisdom in practice or application. The basis of the argument is three pieces of philosophical advice that appear to be universal. That is, they appear in most, if not all, religions and faiths of the world. Each one requires elements of ESI to enact. Furthermore, the sustainable development of ESI competencies follows the elements of intentional change theory that are, in themselves require these three pieces of wisdom to occur. But first, let us examine what we mean by wisdom.

Wisdom

Wisdom is a deep understanding of the nature of things. *Deep* means not just *how* it works or is but also *why* it works or is. According to the *American Heritage Dictionary of the English Language* (1969), wisdom is "1. understanding of what is true, right, or lasting; 2. common sense; sagacity; good judgment . . . ; 3. learning; erudition." *Webster's Seventh New Collegiate Dictionary* (1963) defined it as "1. a) accumulated philosophic or scientific learning: knowledge; b) ability to discern inner qualities and relationships: insight; c) good sense: judgment; 2. a wise attitude or course of action; 3. the teachings of ancient wise men."

Wisdom is this deep understanding of what is "true, right, or lasting" or the "accumulated . . . learning" of the past. As such, it is constructed on building block concepts of values and philosophy and then becomes the building blocks for future generations of thought. But throughout this amalgamation, these philosophical guideposts shine through. They seem timeless. They defy postmodernist contentions of infinite levels of cultural relativism. Like Taylor's (1991) "moral horizons of significance," the three inscriptions reverberate in my consciousness like a song you hear in the morning and hum all day. They seem to be human universals. Before looking at these three gems of wisdom, let us look at the context or human experience to which they apply.

The challenge of this chapter is to understand human experience. For this, one is drawn into the part of philosophy called *aesthetics*. Early in philosophical writing, aesthetics was the quest for understanding or knowledge. As fields of specialized knowledge emerged, the focus of many of the sciences differentiated themselves from this basic quest, while psychology remained more closely aligned to it. Baumgarten (1735/1954) is credited with the split from Descartes and his followers by his focus on sensory and perceptual cognition—the experience of "it." He proposed that aesthetic value was directly proportional to the clarity of the ideas being examined in understanding a person's experiences. In this sense, clarity of thought became a subordinate goal, integrating some elements of Confucian and

Daoist thought. The five key theories driving the understanding of aesthetics have been (a) hedonism, (b) catharsis, (c) Gestalt psychology, (d) scientific aesthetics, and (e) experiential justification for moral and aesthetic value judgments.

Hedonism examined pleasure-seeking drives and behavior in humans (Santayana, 1896) that have morphed into the intent of positive psychology (Seligman, 1991). Catharsis theory explored the need and paradox of being drawn to tragedy (Aristotle, 1932). Gestalt psychology emerged from the German word for the search for "patterns" and as a focus on a person's emotions as their reality (Arnheim, 1954). Munro (1928, 1970) is credited with the attempt to create a scientific approach to aesthetics. But aesthetics took its enduring framework from Immanuel Kant, who proposed that experience is the basis for nonscientific examination, especially in how it determines the basis for moral decision and judgments of aesthetic value (Kant, 1790/1987). Nearly in opposition to positivistic and empirical science, the human experience, he claimed, was the basis for knowledge and insight. All of these prominent authors in aesthetics contributed to how and why we may explore human experience for insight into human nature. To understand aspects of human experience, let us return to the three pieces of wisdom found at Delphi.

The first inscription was "Γνωθει σ'αυτον." It is roughly translated as "know yourself," although it is typically quoted as "know thyself." Often misattributed to Socrates, the source is one of the Seven Sages of Ancient Greece, Thales of Miletus (Diogenes Laertius, *Lives of Eminent Philosophers*, I.1, p. 40). This piece of wisdom is an invitation to continue self-exploration and reflection. It tells us to deepen our awareness and understanding of ourselves.

Knowing yourself invokes more than awareness, recognition, and understanding. It invites authenticity. To be better people, we are asked to know what is in our hearts, minds, and bodies; what drives us; and what we value. We are also asked, through this simple yet profound dictum, to be genuine and congruent. That is, how we act should reflect what we believe in and what we think. All of these should be consistent with our feelings and in tune with our bodies.

The second inscription is "Παν μετρον αριστον." It is roughly translated as "nothing too much," often referred to as "nothing in excess" or "everything in moderation." Little do most people know that one of the tenets of most diets comes from an inscription on the temple of Apollo. This phrase is also often attributed to Socrates, albeit incorrectly. It comes to us from Kleovoulos (Diogenes Laertius, *Lives of Eminent Philosophers*, I.6, p. 93) and his students, eventually passed on to Socrates, Plato, and Aristotle.

"Nothing too much" is an invitation to moderation. It allows us to dabble or try many things but asks us to keep them all in control and in the *correct* balance. It is not a conceptually rigid "thou shall . . ." or "thou shall not. . ." It is a gray area, subject to the interpretation of the person in the context of his or her specific situation, culture, and larger context. Of course, if you have in-depth self-knowledge, it is easier to make appropriate judgments as to how much is enough and what is too much, whether it be money, love, chocolate, coffee, or exercise.

The third inscription is "Α τοιζ αλλοιζ επιτιμομεν, αυτοι μεδρομεν." It roughly translates as "do unto others as you would wish them to do unto you." This piece of wisdom is also referred to as the "ethic of reciprocity."

Socrates said it, as have others. His Beatitude Archbishop Anastasios, of the Eastern Orthodox Church of Albania, summarized, with detailed references, how this "golden rule" has come to us in writing in most religions of the world. He described this in a speech at the 100th anniversary of the Titan Cement Company in Athens on October 24, 2002. The message appears in the *New Testament of the King James Bible* for Christians (in Matthew, 7:12, and Luke, 6:31) as part of the message from Jesus in his Sermon on the Mount. It also appears in Mosaic Law (*Talmud*, Shabbat 31a), the *Qur'an* (Hadith No. 13, sayings of the Prophet, from *Al-Nawawi's Forty Hadiths*), and Confucian thought (*Analects of Confucius*, 15:23) as well as in the writing of Buddhism (*Udana-Varga*, 5:18), Hinduism (*Mahabharata*, 5:1517), and most aboriginal religions. It predated Socrates, with the earliest attribution appearing from Ancient Egypt in *The Tale of the Eloquent Peasant* (*Ancient Egyptian*, 109–110, translated by R. B. Parkinson). This was followed by a reference in Zoroastrianism (*Dadistan-i-Dinik*, 94:5). Like this third inscription, the first two also appear repeatedly, in one form or another, in each of the religious writings just cited and others.

So it seems that these three phrases are wisdom, with a timeless and global message of meaning (Novak, 1994). To be honest, to date archeologists have not found tablets or frescoes with these actually inscribed on the walls of the temple of Apollo or at Delphi. But it is believed that they were common themes of discussions and have appeared in the writings of Socrates, Plato, and Aristotle. So I took some literary license for the imagery of discovery. Now let us examine how people can and do use this understanding. How they apply it can be said to be an expression of their ESI.

Emotional and Social Intelligence

"Emotional and social intelligence" is a convenient phrase with which to focus attention on the underlying emotional components of human talent. Early psychologists explored the concept of "social intelligence" (Thorndike during the 1920s and 1930s; cf. Goleman, 1995) as a single concept. Recent psychologists have described it in terms of multiple capabilities (Bar-On, 1992, 1997; Goleman, 1998). Gardner (1983) conceptualized this arena as constituting intrapersonal and interpersonal intelligence—two of his seven intelligences, with the others being bodily–kinesthetic, aesthetic, musical, logical–mathematical, and spatial. Salovey and Mayer (1990) first used the expression "emotional and social intelligence" in academic journals and described it in terms of four domains: knowing and handling one's own and others' emotions. Other conceptualizations have used labels such as "practical intelligence" and "successful intelligence" (Sternberg, 1996), which often blend the capabilities described by other psychologists with cognitive abilities and anchor the concepts around the consequence of the person's behavior, notably success or effectiveness.

Boyatzis and Sala (2004) contended that ESI, to be considered an intelligence, should be (a) related to differentiated neural circuitry and endocrine systems, (b) related to a set of alternate behavioral manifestations (allowing different expression in different settings), (c) related to life and job outcomes, and (d) sufficiently different from other personality constructs to which the concept adds value in understanding the human personality and behavior. Meanwhile, the measures of the concept, as a psychological construct, should satisfy the basic criteria for a sound measure, that is, show convergent and discriminant validity (American Psychological Association, 1997; Campbell & Fiske, 1959). This set of criteria is different from Mayer, Salovey, and Caruso's (1999) three standards for an intelligence (for a discussion of these differences, see Boyatzis & Sala, 2004).

The integrated concept of ESI offers more than a convenient framework for describing human dispositions; it offers a theoretical structure for the organization of personality and linking it to a theory of action and job performance. Goleman (1998) defined an "emotional competence" as a learned capability based on emotional and social intelligence that results in outstanding performance at work. In Goleman (2006), he went on to differentiate the emotional capabilities as distinct from the social ones. In other words, if a competency is an "underlying characteristic of the person that leads to or causes effective or superior performance" (Boyatzis, 1982, p. 14), an ESI competency is an ability to recognize, understand, and use emotional information about oneself or others that leads to or causes effective or superior performance (Boyatzis, 2006b).

A simpler definition of ESI is the intelligent use of one's emotions. This definition can be elaborated as how people handle themselves and their relationships (Goleman, Boyatzis, & McKee, 2002). The definition can be further expanded to say that ESI is a set of competencies, or abilities, in how a person (a) is aware of himself or herself, (b) is able to manage his or her own emotions, (c) is aware of others and their emotions, and (d) is able to deal with and manage his or her relationships using emotional awareness.

The behavioral manifestation of ESI is evident in how ESI competencies were found and how they are assessed. This is vital to understanding how a person can apply wisdom in general and the three philosophical guideposts we addressed at the beginning of this chapter.

Measurement of ESI Competencies

The assessment of ESI competencies began as a search for early identification of talent (McClelland, Baldwin, Bronfenbrenner, & Strodbeck, 1958). These were framed as abilities and thought to be part of the concept of personality (McClelland et al., 1958). During the early 1970s, this line of research focused on competencies (McClelland, 1973). By the late 1970s, as the research was quickly adapted as creating useful insight within practitioner communities, the "competency" label spread.

A related stream of research has emerged focusing on explaining and predicting effectiveness in various occupations, often with a primary emphasis on managers and leaders (Bray, Campbell, & Grant, 1974; Boyatzis, 1982; Luthans, Hodgetts, & Rosenkrantz, 1988; Kotter, 1982; McClelland, 1973; McClelland et al., 1958; Spencer & Spencer, 1993; Thornton & Byham, 1982). In this competency approach, specific capabilities were identified and validated against effectiveness measures, or they were discovered inductively and then articulated as competencies.

If a competency is defined as a single construct, the tendency to believe that more effective people have the vital ingredients for success invites the attribution of a halo effect. For example, Person A is effective; therefore, he or she has all of the right stuff such as brains, savvy, and style. Like the issue of finding the best "focal point" with which to look at something, the dilemma of finding the best level of detail in defining constructs with which to build a personality theory may ultimately be an issue of which focal point is chosen. With regard to ESI, we believe that the most helpful focal point allows the description and study of a variety of specific competencies, or abilities, that can be empirically and causally related to effectiveness and also describe the clusters within which these competencies are organized. But we must start with the competencies. The articulation of one overall ESI might be deceptive and suggest a close association with cognitive capability (i.e., traditionally defined intelligence or what psychologists often call g for general cognitive ability). The latter not only would be confusing but also would raise the question as to what one is calling ESI and whether it is nothing more than an element of previously defined intelligence or cognitive ability.

A competency is defined as a capability or an ability. It is a set of related but different sets of behavior organized around an underlying construct that we call the *intent*. The behaviors are alternate manifestations of the intent, as appropriate in various situations or times. For example, listening to someone and asking him or her questions are several behaviors. A person can demonstrate these behaviors for multiple reasons or to various intended ends. A person can ask questions and listen to someone to ingratiate himself or herself or to appear interested, thereby gaining standing in the other person's view. Or a person can ask questions and listen to someone because he or she is interested in understanding this other person, his or her priorities, or his or her thoughts in a situation. We would call the latter a demonstration of *empathy*. The underlying intent is to understand the person. Meanwhile, the former underlying reason for the questions is to gain standing or impact in the person's view, elements of what we may call demonstration of *influence*. Similarly, the underlying intent of a more subtle competency, such as emotional self-awareness, is self-insight and self-understanding.

The anchor for understanding the specific behaviors and specific intent relevant to the use of a competency in a situation emerges from predicting effectiveness. The construction of the specific competency is a matter of relating different behaviors that are considered as alternate manifestations of the same underlying construct. But they are organized primarily, or more accurately initially, by the similarity of the consequence of the use of these behaviors in social or work settings. For example, the competency called *empathy* can be observed by watching someone listen to others or by asking questions about his or her feelings and thoughts. If one is demonstrating empathy, the person would be undertaking these acts with the intent of trying to understand another person. On the other hand, someone could show these acts while cross-examining a witness in a criminal trial where the intent is to catch the witness in a lie, and this is also likely to be the demonstration of another competency—*influence*.

Building on and integrating a great deal of competency research, Goleman and colleagues (2002) presented a model of ESI with 18 competencies arrayed in four clusters (Boyatzis, 1982; Boyatzis & Sala, 2004; Goleman, 1998; Jacobs & McClelland, 1994; McClelland, 1998; Rosier, 1994–1997; Spencer & Spencer, 1993; Wolff, 2005). Shown in detail in Table 10.1, they are as follows:

Emotional intelligence competencies:

1. The *self-awareness* cluster contains emotional self-awareness, accurate self-assessment, and self-confidence.

2. The *self-management* cluster contains emotional self-control, achievement, initiative, transparency, adaptability, and optimism.

Social intelligence competencies:

3. The *social awareness* cluster contains empathy, service orientation, and organizational awareness.

4. The *relationship management* (or *social skills*) cluster contains inspirational leadership, influence, conflict management, change catalyst, developing others, teamwork, and collaboration.

Because of their behavioral manifestations, assessing ESI competencies requires observing a person's behavior. In fact, observations of the patterns of a person's behavior, or his or her habits, would be most useful. This can be done directly through videotaping a person at work, at play, or with family.

Table 10.1   Scales and Clusters of the Emotional Competency Inventory, Version 2 (ECI-2)

The **Self-Awareness** cluster concerns knowing one's internal states, preferences, resources, and intuitions. It contains three competencies:
  Emotional self-awareness: Recognizing one's emotions and their effects
  Accurate self-assessment: Knowing one's strengths and limits
  Self-confidence: Having a strong sense of one's self-worth and capabilities

The **Self-Management** cluster refers to managing one's internal states, impulses, and resources. It contains six competencies:
  Emotional self-control: Keeping disruptive emotions and impulses in check
  Transparency: Maintaining standards of honesty and integrity
  Adaptability: Being flexible in handling change
  Achievement orientation: Striving to improve or meeting a standard of excellence
  Initiative: Being ready to act on opportunities
  Optimism: Seeing the positive aspects of things and the future

The **Social Awareness** cluster refers to how people handle relationships and awareness of others' feelings, needs, and concerns. It contains three competencies:
  Empathy: Sensing others' feelings and perspectives and taking an active interest in their
    concerns
  Organizational awareness: Reading a group's emotional currents and power relationships
  Service orientation: Anticipating, recognizing, and meeting customers' needs

The **Relationship Management** (or **Social Skills**) cluster concerns the skill or adeptness at inducing desirable responses in others. It contains six competencies:
  Developing others: Sensing others' development needs and bolstering their abilities
  Inspirational leadership: Inspiring and guiding individuals and groups
  Influence: Wielding effective tactics of persuasion
  Change catalyst: Initiating or managing change
  Conflict management: Negotiating and resolving disagreements
  Teamwork and collaboration: Working with others toward shared goals and creating group
    synergy in pursuing collective goals

NOTE: The ECI-2 was replaced by the Emotional and Social Competency Inventory in 2007.

An alternative can be audiotaping critical incident reports of important events (Spencer & Spencer, 1993). Either of these approaches requires the application of valid "coding systems" applied with reliability (Boyatzis, 1998) to discern the use and frequency of the competencies. A popular vehicle for approximating observation by many is the 360-degree assessment used by many organizations. In the research, this is called multisource feedback assessment. In this approach, a person's behavior is described by others around him or her. These informants can include the person's boss, peers, subordinates, clients, customers, spouse, friends, and classmates, among others.

The importance of observing or describing patterns of a person's behavior is particularly relevant to wisdom and its enactment. For decades, research in social psychology has shown a low correlation, if any, between a person's explicit values and his or her behavior. There is a major association between a person's expressed values and his or her preferences and attitudes but not between those values and the person's behavior. Boyatzis, Murphy, and Wheeler (2000) contended that this was due to the assessment of specific values rather than to the person's operating philosophy—how the person determines value. Both concerns apply to the enactment of wisdom in terms of the values represented. A person may value "do unto others . . ." but might not act consistently with that belief. Likewise, the very nature of excessive attention to something, such as one's golf or bridge game, might not reflect the person's lack of belief in "nothing in excess." It may be that the person's pragmatic philosophy places the level considered as moderate versus excessive at a different point than does someone with a dominant humanistic philosophy.

Wisdom Is ESI in Practice

The search for wisdom, or the pursuit of living this wisdom, brings us to the intersection of the three phrases and a person's behavior. It is through a person's thoughts and actions that he or she engages in desired practices and aspires to be consistent with being a wise person or at least a good one. The competencies provide a framework for observing and interpreting how a person's behavior may foster wisdom, or the lack of them may indicate quite the opposite.

"Know thyself" is clearly an entreaty to the ESI competencies in the self-awareness cluster. These competencies are the beginning of the search for wisdom and the practice of living wisely. This calls for the emotional self-awareness competency as well as a candid sense of self evident in the accurate self-assessment competency. The self-confidence competency can help or hinder in the application of wisdom. It is sensitive to the second phrase—"nothing in excess." Too much self-confidence breeds arrogance, and too little results in distortion and subjugation of one's sense of self to others.

"Nothing in excess" invokes the ESI competencies in the self-management cluster. It is possible through emotional self-control, adaptability, optimism, initiative, transparency, and possibly even achievement orientation (the latter in the measurement of what is excessive and what is moderate). Of course, these competencies are difficult to use with the self-awareness competencies.

"Do unto others . . ." is just as clearly an invitation for a person to use the social awareness and relationship management clusters of ESI competencies. It is difficult to assess one's effect on others if one is not using social awareness competencies such as empathy, organizational awareness, and service orientation. Similarly, it is difficult to manage one's interactions with others, and therefore one's effect on them, without using competencies such as developing others, influence, inspirational leadership, conflict management, and teamwork and collaboration. In professional and executive roles, change catalyst becomes another important element in pursuit of the golden rule.

Therefore, the person pursuing wisdom will use ESI competencies. The person trying to live a wise and good life will use ESI competencies—and use them frequently. But what of the person who does not have these competencies as parts of his or her current behavioral habits? How can he or she develop them and then go on to practice wisdom?

Intentional Change

The development of ESI competencies would, with the rationale provided earlier, create the possibility that a person will achieve wisdom or, more likely, develop the practice of using wisdom in his or her actions. Development of ESI raises the possibility of being able to nurture the precursor to wisdom in practice in others. A series of longitudinal studies in the Weatherhead School of Management at Case Western Reserve University showed that ESI can be developed in adults and that the changes are sustainable for at least 7 years. The results of these studies are summarized in Figure 10.1 along with comparative data from other longitudinal studies of master of business administration (MBA) programs and training organizations (Boyatzis, 2006a; Boyatzis, Stubbs, & Taylor, 2002; Goleman et al., 2002). Evidence amassed from the Consortium for Research on Emotional Intelligence in Organizations revealed 15 model programs that had, like the Weatherhead School of Management MBA program, shown positive impact with scientifically credible studies (Cherniss & Adler, 2000). The consortium had scanned the existing scientific literature around the world for 50 years. The good news is that it could find programs that worked. The bad news is that there were so few. And the sobering news is that most of the programs had ceased to exist by the time the findings were published.

These studies have shown that adults learn what they want to learn. Other things, even if acquired temporarily (i.e., for a test), are soon forgotten (Specht & Sandlin, 1991). Students, children, patients, clients, and subordinates may act as if they care about learning something, go through the motions, but then proceed to disregard it or forget it—unless it is something they want to learn. This does not include changes induced, willingly or not, by chemical or hormonal changes in one's body. But even in such situations, the interpretation of the changes and behavioral comportment following them will be affected by the person's will, values, and motivations.

In this way, it appears that most, if not all, sustainable behavioral change is intentional. Intentional change is a desired change in an aspect of who you are (i.e., the real), who you want to be (i.e., the ideal), or both (Boyatzis, 2006a).

The role of the three tenets of wisdom that are the basis for this chapter are central to the process of sustainable change. Even the will to change comes from a degree of self-knowledge. An indication of the need for pursuit of self-awareness ("know thyself") comes in the observation that the need for change often arrives in a person's consciousness as a surprise. It would be impossible to engage in helping others develop their ESI competencies without using social awareness and relationship management

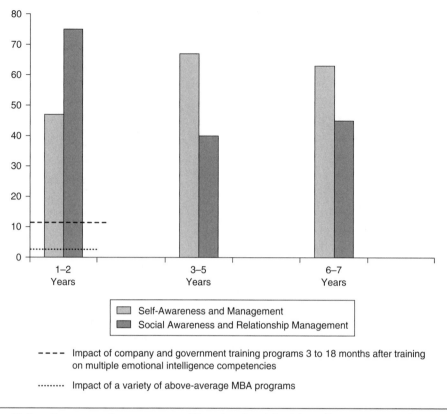

Figure 10.1   Percentage Improvement of Emotional and Social Intelligence From Behavioral
Measurement of Competencies of Different Groups of MBA Graduates Taking
LEAD

NOTE: For *n* values and descriptions of measures, see Boyatzis, Stubbs, and Taylor (2002). Comparison
references are listed in Goleman, Boyatzis, and McKee (2002).

competencies as well as practicing the wisdom of "do unto others . . ." It
appears as a discontinuous revelation, epiphany, or discovery (Boyatzis,
2006a). These wake-up calls are described as an emergence in complexity
theory (Goleman et al., 2002).

Change is a discontinuous process for most people. That is, it goes
through "fits and starts" or surprises. As shown in longitudinal studies of
sustainable change, the description and explanation of the process in this
chapter is organized around five points of discontinuity or discovery. The
process of experiencing these five discoveries is described in intentional
change theory (Boyatzis, 2006a), as shown in Figure 10.2.

The First Discontinuity: Catching
Your Dreams, Engaging Your Passion

The first discontinuity and potential starting point for the process of
intentional change is the discovery of who we want to be. Our Ideal Self is

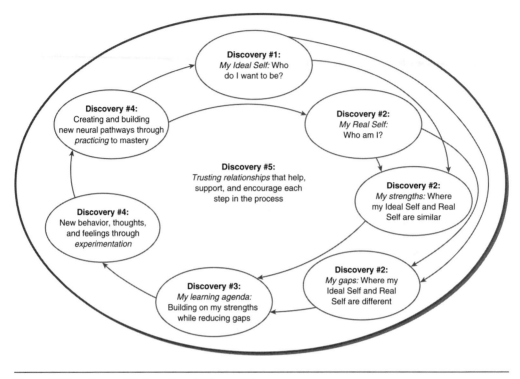

Figure 10.2   Boyatzis's Intentional Change Theory

an image of the person we want to be (Boyatzis & Akrivou-Naperksy, 2006). It emerges from our ego ideal, dreams, and aspirations. The past 20 years have revealed literature supporting the power of positive imaging or visioning in sports psychology, meditation and biofeedback research, and other psychophysiological research. It is believed that the potency of focusing one's thoughts on the desired end state or condition is driven by the emotional components of the brain (Goleman, 1995).

This research indicates that we can access and engage deep emotional commitment if we engage our passions and conceptually integrate our dreams in our Ideal Self image. It is an anomaly that we know the importance of consideration of the Ideal Self and yet often, when engaged in a change or learning process, skip over the clear formulation or articulation of our Ideal Self image. If a parent, spouse, boss, or teacher tells us something that should be different, that person is telling us about the person *he or she* wants us to be. As adults, we often allow ourselves to be anesthetized to our dreams and lose sight of our deeply felt Ideal Self.

Deep emotional commitment would be difficult, if possible at all, without "know thyself." It requires reflection and recognition of one's values, philosophy, passion and desired legacy, purpose or calling, and strengths. Beyond that piece of wisdom, any attempt to sort out one's dreams and passions involves a great deal of self-management. In this way, "nothing in excess" comes into play. So a person needs to be practicing wisdom in these two forms and the self-awareness and self-management clusters of ESI competencies to get the process of intentional change started in an effective way. Helping someone else to reach this discovery will require the social awareness and sensitivity inherent in "do unto others. . ."

The Second Discontinuity: Am I a Boiling Frog?

The first two pieces of wisdom addressed in this chapter are also the basis for the second discovery. Coaching or helping others with this second discovery is based, in part, on the third piece of wisdom addressed in this chapter. The awareness of the current self, the person who others see and with whom they interact, is elusive. Our mind protects us from potentially noxious or threatening input to our conscious realization about ourselves. These are ego defense mechanisms. They also conspire to delude us into an image of who we are that feeds on itself, becomes self-perpetuating, and eventually may become dysfunctional (Goleman, 1985).

The greatest challenge to an accurate current self-image (i.e., seeing ourselves as others see us and consistent with other internal states, beliefs, emotions, etc.) is the boiling frog syndrome. It is said that dropping a frog into a pot of boiling water will result in the frog jumping out immediately. But place a frog in a pot of cool water and gradually raise the temperature to boiling, and the frog will remain in the water until it is cooked.

Several factors contribute to our becoming boiling frogs. First, people around us might not let us see a change. They might not give us feedback or information about how they see it. Also, they may be victims of the boiling frog syndrome themselves as they adjust their perception on a daily basis. Second, enablers—those who forgive the change, are frightened of it, or do not care—may allow it to pass unnoticed.

To truly consider changing a part of ourselves, we must have a sense of what we value and want to keep. These areas in which our Real Self and Ideal Self are consistent or congruent can be considered as strengths. Likewise, considering what we want to preserve about ourselves involves admitting aspects of ourselves that we wish to change or adapt in some manner. Areas where our Real Self and Ideal Self are not consistent can be considered gaps or weaknesses.

All too often, people explore growth or development by focusing on the gaps or deficiencies. Organizational training programs and managers conducting annual reviews often make the same mistake. There is an assumption that we can "leave well enough alone" and get to the areas that need work. This arouses defensive stressful feelings, which in turn set off a neural circuit and hormones that decrease a person's ability to learn and stay focused (Boyatzis & McKee, 2005; Boyatzis, Smith, & Blaize, 2006; Howard, 2006). It is no wonder that many of these programs or procedures intended

to help a person develop result in the individual feeling battered, belea-
guered, and bruised—not helped, encouraged, motivated, or guided.

The Third Discontinuity: Mindfulness
Through a Learning Agenda

The third discontinuity in intentional change is to develop an agenda and
focus on the desired future. Whereas performance at work or happiness in life
may be the eventual consequence of these efforts, a learning agenda focuses
on development. A learning orientation arouses a positive belief in one's capability and the hope of improvement. This results in people setting personal
standards of performance rather than "normative" standards that merely
mimic what others have done (Beaubien & Payne, 1999). Meanwhile, a performance orientation evokes anxiety and doubts about whether or not people
can change (Chen, Gully, Whiteman, & Kilcullen, 2000).

As part of one of the longitudinal studies at the Weatherhead School of
Management, Leonard (1996) showed that MBA graduates who set goals
desiring to change on certain competencies changed significantly on those
competencies as compared with other MBAs. Previous goal-setting literature
had shown how goals affected certain changes on specific competencies
(Locke & Latham, 1990) but had not established evidence of behavioral
change on a comprehensive set of competencies that constitute ESI.

A major threat to effective goal setting and planning is that people are
already busy and cannot add anything else to their lives. In such cases, successful change occurs only if people can determine what to say *no* to and
stop so as to make room for new activities. Determining these goals and
actions requires a great deal of self-knowledge, but executing them requires
huge amounts of self-management—again, back to "know thyself" and
"nothing in excess."

Another potential threat to the development of a plan is one that calls for
people to engage in activities different from their preferred learning style or
learning flexibility (Boyatzis, 1994; Kolb, 1984). In such cases, people commit to activities or action steps in a plan that requires a learning style that is
not their preference or not within their flexibility. When this occurs, people
become demotivated and often stop the activities or become impatient and
decide that the goals are not worth the effort. Unintentionally, this is one of
many ways people may sabotage their change efforts before they get started.

The Fourth Discontinuity: Metamorphosis

As with the third discovery, the fourth discovery requires the same
emphasis and application of "know thyself," "nothing in excess," and "do
unto others. . ." The fourth discontinuity is to experiment and practice

desired changes. Acting on the plan and toward the goals involves numerous activities. These are often made in the context of experimenting with new behavior or rediscovering an ability used well in the past but not in people's current repertoire or habits. Typically following a period of experimentation, people practice the new behaviors in actual settings where they wish to use them, such as at work and at home. During this part of the process, intentional change begins to look like a "continuous improvement" process.

To develop or learn new behavior, people must find ways to learn more from current or ongoing experiences. That is, the experimentation and practice do not always require attending "courses" or a new activity. They may involve mindfulness—trying something different in a current setting, reflecting on what occurs, and experimenting further in this setting. Sometimes this part of the process requires finding and using opportunities to learn and change. People might not even think they have changed until they have tried new behavior in a work or "real-world" setting.

Dreyfus (1990) studied managers of scientists and engineers who were considered to be superior performers. Once Dreyfus documented that they used considerably more of certain abilities than did their less effective counterparts, she sought to establish how they developed some of those abilities. One of the distinguishing abilities was group management, also called team building. She found that many of these middle-aged managers had first experimented with team-building skills in high school and college, sports, clubs, and living groups. Later, when they became "bench scientists and engineers" working on problems in relative isolation, they still pursued using and practicing this ability in activities outside of work. They practiced team building and group management in social and community organizations, such as 4-H Clubs, and in professional associations (e.g., planning conferences).

The experimentation and practice are most effective when they occur in conditions where the person feels safe (Kolb & Boyatzis, 1970). This sense of psychological safety creates an atmosphere in which the person can try new behavior, perceptions, and thoughts with relatively less risk of shame, embarrassment, or serious consequences of failure. The challenge is to practice to the point of mastery, not merely to the point of comfort.

The Fifth Discontinuity: Relationships That Enable Us to Learn

Our relationships are an essential part of our environment. The most crucial relationships are often a part of groups that have particular importance to us. These relationships and groups give us a sense of identity, guide us as to what is appropriate and "good" behavior, and provide feedback on our behavior. In sociology, they are called reference groups. These relationships create a "context" within which we interpret our progress on desired changes, interpret our progress on the utility of new learning, and even contribute significant input to formulation of the ideal (Kram, 1996). These relationships cannot develop without practicing "do unto others . . ." and using the ESI competencies from the social awareness and relationship management clusters.

In this sense, our relationships are mediators, moderators, interpreters, sources of feedback, and sources of support and permission for change and learning. They may also be the most important source of protection from relapses or returning to our earlier forms of behavior. Wheeler (1999) analyzed the extent to which the MBA graduates worked on their goals in multiple "life spheres" (e.g., work, family, recreational groups). In a 2-year follow-up study of two of the graduating classes of part-time MBA students, Wheeler found those who worked on their goals and plans in multiple sets of relationships improved more than those who worked on goals in only one setting, such as work, or within one relationship.

In the studies of the impact of the year-long executive development program for doctors, lawyers, professors, engineers, and other professionals mentioned earlier, Ballou, Bowers, Boyatzis, and Kolb (1999) found that participants gained self-confidence during the program. Even at the beginning of the program, others would say that these participants were very high in self-confidence. It was a curious finding. The best explanation came from follow-up questions to the graduates of the program. They explained the evident increase in self-confidence as an increase in the confidence to change. Their existing reference groups (e.g., family, groups at work, professional groups, community groups) all had an investment in them staying the same, whereas the people wanted to change. The Professional Fellows Program allowed them to develop a new reference group that encouraged change.

Based on social identity, reference group, and (now) relational theories, our relationships both meditate and moderate our sense of who we are and who we want to be. We develop or elaborate our Ideal Self from these contexts. We label and interpret our Real Self from these contexts. We interpret and value strengths (i.e., aspects considered as our core that we wish to preserve) from these contexts. We interpret and value gaps (i.e., aspects considered as weaknesses or things that we wish to change) from these contexts.

Summary and Concluding Thoughts

This chapter has focused on two domains of wisdom: self and others in the human world. Three timeless and seemingly universal pieces of wisdom were examined: "know thyself," "nothing in excess," and "do unto others . . ." (as you would wish them to do unto you).

ESI was shown to be a set of competencies, or behavioral habits, in four clusters: self-awareness, self-management, social awareness, and relationship management. "Know thyself" is the application or practice of using the self-awareness competencies. "Nothing in excess" is the application or practice of using self-management competencies. "Do unto others . . ." is the application or practice of using the social awareness and relationship management competencies. Furthermore, the process of sustainable development of these ESI competencies was described through intentional change theory. Here again, effective development required the practice and application of "know thyself" and "nothing in excess." Helping others change required "do unto others. . ."

Wisdom and ESI are inexorably linked. Key elements of wisdom are manifest in a person's behavior by his or her use of ESI competencies. In other words, a person needs to be using ESI competencies to seek these three elements of wisdom or live consistent with them—that is, to live the wise or good life. To develop the ESI competencies, a person needs to apply these three pieces of wisdom. So we come full circle about wisdom and ESI. They are each the result of and the cause of the other. To be more specific, they are each one of the results of and one of the causes of the other. To be wise, a person should use his or her ESI. To want to use his or her ESI, a person must seek wisdom and want to live by it. Furthermore, to develop ESI, a person must apply this wisdom, but to apply the wisdom the person must be using his or her ESI. In this way, they are parts of the same thing. ESI is wisdom in practice.

Note

1. The abbreviation FAQ stands for frequently asked questions, often seen on websites.

References

American Heritage dictionary of the English language. (1969). Boston: Houghton Mifflin.

American Psychological Association, Public Affairs Office. (1997). *Intelligence: Knowns and unknowns.* Washington, DC: Author.

Aristotle. (1932). *Poetics in Aristotle in 23 volumes* (Vol. 23, W. H. Fyfe, Trans.). Cambridge, MA: Harvard University Press.

Arnheim, R. (1954). *Art and visual perception.* Berkeley: University of California Press.

Ballou, R., Bowers, D., Boyatzis, R. E., & Kolb, D. A. (1999). Fellowship in lifelong learning: An executive development program for advanced professionals. *Journal of Management Education, 23,* 338–354.

Bar-On, R. (1992). *The development of a concept and test of psychological well-being.* Unpublished manuscript, Tel Aviv University.

Bar-On, R. (1997). *Bar-On Emotional Quotient Inventory: Technical manual.* Toronto: Multi-Health Systems.

Baumgarten, A. (1954). *Reflections on poetry* (K. Aschenbrenner & W. B. Holther, Trans.). Berkeley: University of California Press. (Original work published 1735)

Beaubien, J. M., & Payne, S. C. (1999, April). *Individual goal orientation as a predictor of job and academic performance: A meta-analytic review and integration.* Paper presented at the meeting of the Society for Industrial and Organizational Psychology, Atlanta, GA.

Boyatzis, R. E. (1982). *The competent manager: A model for effective performance.* New York: John Wiley.

Boyatzis, R. E. (1994). Stimulating self-directed change: A required MBA course called managerial assessment and development. *Journal of Management Education, 18,* 304–323.

Boyatzis, R. E. (1998). *Transforming qualitative information: Thematic analysis and code development.* Thousand Oaks, CA: Sage.

Boyatzis, R. E. (2006a). Intentional change theory from a complexity perspective. *Journal of Management Development, 25,* 607–623.

Boyatzis, R. E. (2006b). Using tipping points of emotional intelligence and cognitive competencies to predict financial performance of leaders. *Psicothema, 17,* 124–131.

Boyatzis, R. E., & Akrivou-Naperksy, K. (2006). The ideal self as a driver of change. *Journal of Management Development, 25,* 625–642.

Boyatzis, R., & McKee, A. (2005). *Resonant leadership: Renewing yourself and connecting with others through mindfulness, hope, and compassion.* Boston: Harvard Business School Press.

Boyatzis, R. E., Murphy, A., & Wheeler, J. (2000). Philosophy as the missing link between values and behavior. *Psychological Reports, 86,* 47–64.

Boyatzis, R. E., & Sala, F. (2004). Assessing emotional intelligence competencies. In G. Geher (Ed.), *Measuring emotional intelligence* (pp. 147–180). New York: Nova Science.

Boyatzis, R. E., Smith, M., & Blaize, N. (2006). Sustaining leadership effectiveness through coaching and compassion: It's not what you think. *Academy of Management Learning and Education, 5*(1), 8–24.

Boyatzis, R. E., Stubbs, E. C., & Taylor, S. N. (2002). Learning cognitive and emotional intelligence competencies through graduate management education. *Academy of Management Journal on Learning and Education, 1*(2), 150–162.

Bray, D. W., Campbell, R. J., & Grant, D. L. (1974). *Formative years in business: A long term AT&T study of managerial lives.* New York: John Wiley.

Campbell, D. T., & Fiske, D. W. (1959). Convergent and discriminant validation by the multitrait–multimethod matrix. *Psychological Bulletin, 56,* 81–105.

Chen, G., Gully, S. M., Whiteman, J. A., & Kilcullen, R. N. (2000). Examination of relationships among trait-like individual differences, state-like individual differences, and learning performance. *Journal of Applied Psychology, 85,* 835–847.

Cherniss, C., & Adler, M. (2000). *Promoting emotional intelligence in organizations: Make training in emotional intelligence effective.* Washington, DC: American Society of Training and Development.

Dreyfus, C. (1990). *The characteristics of high performing managers of scientists and engineers.* Unpublished doctoral dissertation, Case Western Reserve University.

Gardner, H. (1983). *Frames of mind: The theory of multiple intelligences.* New York: Basic Books.

Goleman, D. (1985). *Vital lies, simple truths: The psychology of self-deception*. New York: Simon & Schuster.

Goleman, D. (1995). *Emotional intelligence*. New York: Bantam Books.

Goleman, D. (1998). *Working with emotional intelligence*. New York: Bantam Books.

Goleman, D. (2006). *Social intelligence*. New York: Bantam Books.

Goleman, D., Boyatzis, R. E., & McKee, A. (2002). *Primal leadership: Realizing the power of emotional intelligence*. Boston: Harvard Business School Press.

Howard, A. (2006). Positive and negative emotional attractors and intentional change. *Journal of Management Development, 25*, 657–670.

Jacobs, R., & McClelland, D. C. (1994). Moving up the corporate ladder. *Consulting Psychology Journal, 46*, 32–41.

Kant, I. (1987). *The critique of judgment* (W. Pluhar, Trans.). Indianapolis, IN: Hackett. (Original work published 1790)

Kolb, D. A. (1984). *Experiential learning: Experience as the source of learning and development*. Englewood Cliffs, NJ: Prentice Hall.

Kolb, D. A., & Boyatzis, R. E. (1970). Goal-setting and self-directed behavior change. *Human Relations, 23*, 439–457.

Kotter, J. P. (1982). *The general managers*. New York: Free Press.

Kram, K. E. (1996). A relational approach to careers. In D. T. Hall (Ed.), *The career is dead: Long live the career* (pp. 132–157). San Francisco: Jossey-Bass.

Leonard, D. (1996). *The impact of learning goals on self-directed change in management development and education*. Doctoral dissertation, Case Western Reserve University.

Locke, E. A., & Latham, G. P. (1990). *A theory of goal setting and task performance*. Englewood Cliffs, NJ: Prentice Hall.

Luthans, F., Hodgetts, R. M., & Rosenkrantz, S. A. (1988). *Real managers*. Cambridge, MA: Ballinger.

Mayer, J. D., Salovey, P., & Caruso, D. R. (1999). Emotional intelligence meets traditional standards for an intelligence. *Intelligence, 27*, 267–298.

McClelland, D. C. (1973). Testing for competence rather than intelligence. *American Psychologist, 28*, 1–14.

McClelland, D. C. (1998). Identifying competencies with behavioral event interviews. *Psychological Science, 9*, 331–339.

McClelland, D. C., Baldwin, A. L., Bronfenbrenner, U., & Strodbeck, F. L. (1958). *Talent and society: New perspectives in the identification of talent*. Princeton, NJ: D. Van Nostrand.

Munro, T. (1928). *Scientific method in aesthetics*. New York: Norton.

Munro, T. (1970). *Form and style in the arts*. Cleveland, OH: Press of Case Western Reserve University.

Novak, P. (1994). *The world's wisdom: Sacred texts of the world's religions*. New York: HarperCollins.

Rosier, R. (1994–1997). *Handbook of competency studies*. Boston: Linage Associates.

Salovey, P., & Mayer, J. D. (1990). Emotional intelligence. *Imagination, cognition, and personality, 9*, 185–211.

Santayana, G. (1896). *The sense of beauty*. New York: Scribner.

Seligman, M. (1991). *Learned optimism*. New York: Knopf.

Specht, L., & Sandlin, P. (1991). The differential effects of experiential learning activities and traditional lecture classes in accounting. *Simulations and Gaming, 22*, 196–210.

Spencer, L. M., Jr., & Spencer, S. M. (1993). *Competence at work: Models for superior performance.* New York: John Wiley.

Sternberg, R. (1996). *Successful intelligence.* New York: Simon & Schuster.

Taylor, C. (1991). *The ethics of authenticity.* Cambridge, MA: Harvard University Press.

Thornton, G. C., III, & Byham, W. C. (1982). *Assessment centers and managerial performance.* New York: Academic Press.

Webster's seventh new collegiate dictionary. (1963). Springfield, MA: G & C Merriam.

Wheeler, J. V. (1999). *The impact of social environments on self-directed change and learning.* Doctoral dissertation, Case Western Reserve University.

Wolff, S. (2005). *Emotional Competence Inventory: Technical manual.* Boston: Hay Group.

11

Organizational Aesthetics

Aesthetics and Wisdom in the Practice of Organization Development

W. Warner Burke

A colleague of mine, an art museum junkie, has made me more aware of the distinction between fine art in, say, the Metropolitan Museum of Art (the Met) in New York City and so-called art that hangs on the walls of a motel room. The former is good and tasteful; the latter is bad and tasteless.

When looking at tasteful fine art at the Met, we are often filled with awe and feelings of admiration and perhaps even excitement. Moreover, we are likely to remember certain paintings, sculptures, and the like, whereas in our motel room we may barely look at what is hanging on the walls, much less remember anything once we have paid our bill and checked out. If we remember anything, it may only be how tacky we thought the wall hangings were.

The practice of organization development (OD) can be good and tasteful, yet some practice can be bad and tasteless. The difference between bad "art" in the motel room and bad OD practice is that the latter is likely to be remembered by both the practitioner and the client.

AUTHOR'S NOTE: I thank David Bradford and Debra Noumair for helping me to conceptualize and write this chapter. I also express my gratitude to members of the AAH Pharmaceuticals board of management, in particular Steve Dunn (managing director), Ian Davidson, Mark James, and John Richards, for their support and implementation of wise OD practice, and especially to Simon Day, my internal counterpart and OD colleague, for his significant contribution to crafting the mission statement at AAH.

Why make this comparison? Although the practice of OD is based on the application of the behavioral sciences, much of this practice is an art form. Successful OD is largely a function of how well practitioners use themselves— their listening skills and ability to be empathetic, their influence skills and ability to be persuasive, their oral presentation skills and ability to conceptualize and simplify complex data from a variety of sources, and so on.

Even with an art form and effectiveness being highly dependent on the competence of the practitioner, OD is nevertheless based on sound knowledge and experience, thereby making it possible to realize wisdom in the practice and to feel joy, passion, and aesthetic satisfaction in the work and in the results.

Wisdom in the practice of OD is about (a) having the relevant knowledge from the behavioral sciences and (b) knowing when and how to apply that knowledge. The latter comes from experience, which can be described as follows. First, experience involves learning how to gauge the depth of intervention. By *depth,* Harrison (1970) meant "how deep, value-laden, emotionally charged, and central to the individual's sense of self are the issues and processes about which a consultant attempts directly to obtain information and which he seeks to influence" (p. 181). The deepest type of intervention is intrapersonal analysis, and a less deep type might be change in the organization's structure. Second, experience involves having learned the timing of an intervention. This knowledge is based on diagnosing an organization's readiness for change and can be gauged in terms of degrees and the nature of resistance. See, for example, Hambrick and Cannella (1989) and their distinctions among blind resistance (a knee-jerk reaction and relatively rare), ideological resistance (honest disagreement about what should change), and political resistance (when individuals feel that they will lose something of value to them, such as status, size of the budget, or the corner office). Third, experience involves having learned the criteria for an effective intervention. Argyris (1970) specified three criteria, namely that the intervention must provide (a) valid and useful information ("that which describes the factors plus their interrelationships, that create the problem for the client systems" [p. 17]), (b) free choice (the client is given alternatives for action and the decision rests with the client), and (c) internal commitment (the client owns the choice made and feels responsible for implementing it).

These are illustrative of wisdom in the practice of OD and are not meant to be comprehensive. The point is that OD practice that is wise is grounded in a knowledge base that has been in existence for decades and continues to expand. Examples of the former are Cummings and Worley (2005, now in its eighth edition), French and Bell (1995, now in its fifth edition), Burke (1994), and Gladwell's (2000) *The Tipping Point,* a wise book about change even though it is from the popular press. And an example of the latter is the *Handbook of Organization Development* edited by Cummings (2007).

With respect to the aesthetic quality of OD, it is not unlike love; it is difficult to describe and articulate, but you know it when you experience it. Experiencing a process that contributes to a productive outcome and to needed change is indeed joyful, satisfying, and a work of beauty; if art, it would be worthy of hanging on one of the many walls at the Met. The next section, which describes a case of crafting a corporate mission statement, is an attempt to illustrate wisdom in OD practice with a beautiful outcome.

The purposes of this chapter, then, are to (a) define OD, (b) clarify what good and wise OD is, (c) note what bad and unwise OD is, (d) specify desired outcomes with examples, and (e) provide a case example of OD in action with aesthetic qualities.

What Is OD?

As anyone in the field knows, there are about as many definitions of OD as there are practitioners. Even though the origination of OD was circa 1959, people today still talk about the lack of clarity regarding definition. Is it organization transformation, continuous improvement, or both? In spite of the many definitions and debates, Beckhard's (1969) early definition has stood the test of time, practice, and experience. Building on his definition and modernizing it somewhat, Burke and Bradford (2005) defined the field as follows:

> Based on (1) a set of values largely humanistic, (2) application of the behavioral sciences, and (3) open system theory, organization development is a system-wide process of planned change aimed toward improving overall organization effectiveness by way of enhanced congruence of such key organizational dimensions as external environment, mission, strategy, leadership, culture, structure, information and reward systems, and work policies and procedures. (p. 12)

With this definition, OD can be transformational or transactional, discontinuous or continuous, yet change in either case.

What Is Wise OD?

OD is very much about process, that is, following a set of steps or phases for bringing about change. Central to OD are Lewin's (1958) three steps: unfreeze, change, and refreeze. Lippitt, Watson, and Westley (1958) expanded Lewin's three steps to five steps, adding "establishment of a change relationship" and "terminating the relationship." Later, Schein (1987) elaborated on each of Lewin's original three steps with examples of how to unfreeze, change, and refreeze a social system. But following these steps and phases may or may not result in "wise OD."

Staying with the good/bad art comparison for a moment, the question becomes the following: What does the outcome of OD practice, the "artwork" if you will, look like? That is, is it museum art or motel art? Returning to our definition of OD, the outcome of practice should be a more effective organization. And what does "effective" look like? Again building on Beckhard's (1969) earlier list of characteristics (he referred to them as "operational goals") of an effective organization, years later I doubled his list of 5 to 10 (Burke, 1994, pp. 197–198). The following is a slight expansion of the list:

1. The organization is managed against goals and plans for achieving these goals. This characteristic is based on a rational process and applies to the total system as well as its subparts (e.g., business units). A part of the rational wisdom here is that having clear goals not only provides direction but also enhances motivation.

2. Form (organization design and structure) follows function. An architectural principle, this characteristic means that organization design needs to be based on what the organization is trying to accomplish strategically and not on executives' power needs.

3. Decisions are made at the source of information and expertise. Decision making is a function of where the expertise is located and not according to the hierarchy—unless it is the boss who actually has the information.

4. Rewards are based on performance. Pay for performance is problematic; that is, often it does not work. Nevertheless, attempts should be made to guard against reward systems being perceived as arbitrary and inequitable.

5. Communication is open and undistorted. Organization members tend to interpret any and all messages, and often these interpretations are wrong. Therefore, it is critical that managers err on the side of being too open to prevent misunderstandings.

6. Conflict is confronted and managed. The longer differences are allowed to remain, the greater the resistance to resolution is likely to be. There are wise OD processes to follow that help with resolution.

7. Differences are valued for their potential to enhance innovation. Although the value from differences is difficult to attain, there is considerable evidence and wisdom here to support this admonition.

8. The organization is viewed as, and managed according to, an open system perspective. This characteristic is based on sound theory and research, especially the importance of an organization's dependence on its external environment for survival and required change.

9. Valuing integrity and interdependence is primary. It is likely that the most important value for any organization is the integrity of its leadership, particularly with respect to how customers are treated. The interdependence characteristic concerns the need for and importance

of cooperative behavior among organizational members to prevent the more natural tendency to be competitive and overly differentiated in the way work is carried out in the organization—the so-called "silo effect."

10. The organization is managed and led in an action research way building on data and feedback. Action research is the bedrock of OD and ensures that change is data based rather than overly political and at the whim of some executive.

Good and wise OD work, then, results in an organization that possesses these 10 characteristics of effectiveness.

Another way to consider wise OD is to take an organizational culture perspective. I can recall giving a talk on OD back during the 1960s, and I was essentially arguing that OD was about changing the organization's culture. A professor in the audience asked, "Change to what kind of culture?" I stammered a bit and said something about participation and involvement. To be honest, I was somewhat stymied and embarrassed at my awkwardness and lack of an articulate and brilliant response. This was years before considerable "culture work" had been done. I did not have Schein's (2004) book under my belt, Kotter and Heskett's (1992) research about culture and performance in my head, or access to Martin's (2002) splendid work on "mapping the terrain" of organizational culture. My response to such a question today might not be brilliant, but I would not be stymied. Most likely, I would refer to the work of Kotter and Heskett (1992), in which they showed a relationship between organizational culture and performance. In other words, are some cultures better than others? Are there defining characteristics of culture that are associated with high performance? According to Kotter and Heskett, there are indeed defining characteristics that they labeled an "adaptive culture," one capable of change yet maintaining a core set of values. Thus, what might wise OD look like with respect to culture change? Kotter and Heskett's 11 "striking characteristics," as they called them, could easily serve as a "picture" of wise OD outcomes:

1. *Willingness to make changes in culturally engrained behaviors.* High-performing organizations were much less resistant to change; in fact, they embraced change and saw it as a "way of life." More recent research shows the wisdom of this characteristic, that is, to work hard on changing "locked-in" behaviors to ensure that the organization is dealing effectively with its rapidly changing environment (Foster & Kaplan, 2001).

2. *Emphasis on identifying problems before they can occur and rapidly implementing workable solutions.* I recall a primary value of the chief executive officer (CEO), at the time, of the Dime Bank in New York City: *anticipation.* He believed strongly, and emphasized it with his top team, that trying to anticipate what the competition might be

doing, what could go wrong with some new software package, or what the consequences of some change in the organization might be was a wise form of management and leadership. Wise indeed.

3. *Focus on innovation.* High-performing organizations constantly try to improve, rarely punish failure, and question "tried-and-true" ways of conducting work and business. A prime example in the Kotter and Heskett (1992) research was the 3M Company.

4. *Shared feelings of confidence regarding managing problems and opportunities.* This characteristic is very much a reflection of the "can-do" attitude of the American culture, but not all organizations live by this philosophy. Those that do tend to be high performers.

5. *Emphasis on trust.* It is difficult to prove, of course, but it seems that as a consultant I encounter an issue of trust in practically every organization with which I work. Trust and integrity go together and may be the most important determinants of whether OD will work. High-performing organizations apparently have a stronger foundation of trust than do those that are moderate or poor performers.

6. *Willingness to take risks.* This characteristic correlates positively with the number 3 characteristic on this list. Risk taking is rewarded in high-performing organizations.

7. *Spirit of enthusiasm.* This means doing whatever it takes to achieve organizational success. This characteristic overlaps with the number 4 characteristic on this list and emphasizes the importance of energy and persistence in bringing about successful OD.

8. *Candidness.* This is another overlap, this time with the number 5 characteristic in the Beckhard–Burke list covered earlier. Executives of adaptive cultures are open and tell the truth.

9. *Internal flexibility in response to external demands.* Adaptive cultures are nimble and can respond to problems (e.g., with competitors or changing technology) quickly and effectively.

10. *Consistency in word and action.* My favorite question here is, "Does the audio match the video?" Especially in times of significant organization change, consistency of word and deed is critical to success. Executives of high-performing organizations are better at this critical behavior than are those in low-performing organizations.

11. *Long-term focus.* Unwise organizations are those that focus heavily on quarterly results. Adaptive cultures are characterized as taking a long-term view and perspective.

Kotter and Heskett (1992) emphasized two significant findings associated with their high-performing organizations (i.e., those having adaptive cultures). First, all organizations have multiple constituents, but the three stressed the most among their high-performing organizations were customers, employees, and owners (stockholders). Second, successful organization change is not possible without competent leadership, particularly at the top of the organization.

On a larger and more total system scale, there are case examples of good OD, that is, where the intended changes were realized and the outcomes were more effective organizations. Three examples with which I am personally familiar are (a) the transformation of British Airways from a government-sponsored and financially supported airline to a private corporation (British Airways became the most profitable airline in the world by 1990 [Goodstein & Burke, 1991]), (b) the successful merger of SmithKline Pharmaceuticals in the United States with Beecham Ltd. in the United Kingdom (Bauman, Jackson, & Lawrence, 1997; Carter, Giber, & Goldsmith, 2001), and (c) the successful merger of two banks, Dime and Anchor Savings, in New York City (Burke, 2007, chap. 11). And as long ago as the late 1960s, Beckhard (1969) described five cases of successful OD change efforts, one of which was a culture change. Wise and good OD has existed and still does exist. The pictures in these cases are worthy of display in a museum. But what about motel art OD?

What Is Unwise OD?

We can easily define bad and unwise OD as practice that does not lead to positive change. There have been numerous examples. A case in point is Mirvis and Berg's (1997) book, *Failures in Organization Development and Change,* which they filled with failures in OD. Unwise OD can often be characterized as "much ado about nothing." It is like prints covering the walls in our motel room that ostensibly are there to make the atmosphere feel warm and inviting when in the end we might not experience these feelings at all. Considerable activity may abound in the organization that gives feelings of OD being practiced when actually nothing systemically about the organization is being addressed, much less changed. In other words, root causes of problems and issues are never quite invoked.

When organizational members (clients) initially present problems to an OD practitioner, they typically are symptoms of some deeper system issue that is not readily apparent. It is imperative, however, that the OD practitioner address and attempt to deal with these symptoms. Otherwise, organizational members will feel as if their issues are not worthy and engagement between the practitioner and client will break down. But ultimately the practitioner cannot leave it at that. For real and good OD to occur, causal factors of a systemic nature must be identified and treated, that is, changed. For a case example of OD work that treated symptoms but never reached the stage of dealing with root causes even though they were identified, see Burke (1994, chap. 1). Thus, there was in this case OD practice but not actual OD because nothing about the larger system ever changed fundamentally or culturally.

To add some points and summarize, the following list provides some examples of unwise OD with the potential for ugly outcomes:

- *Not being data based and theory driven in one's practice.* Data come from the client, and what to do with the data by way of conceptualization based on models and theory (the wisdom of OD) comes from the practitioner.
- *Not relating OD process to business issues.* The question that must be answered is how OD will help to solve business (broadly defined) problems. If it is not answered, what is the relevance of OD?
- *Tolerating arbitrary uses of power.* In a report on organizational climate studies from the 1950s up to the 1990s, Hogan, Raskin, and Fazzini (1990) found that 60% to 75% of employees from a variety of organizations, occupational groups, and levels stated that the worst or most stressful aspect of their work lives was their bosses. Tolerating bad boss behavior is a form of unwise OD.
- *Imposing one's values.* Sometimes pushing humanistic values leads to unwise OD, for example, when one's personal values may conflict with what we know should be done based on sound behavioral science research and theory (Beer & Norhia, 2000; Bradford & Burke, 2005) or, in the case of the previous point about the arbitrary use of power, when one's humanism is allowed to supersede the need to confront and deal with unacceptable organizational behavior that may include firing a bad manager.
- *Ignoring issues of organizational power and politics because they are "bad" and cause one to feel anxious and averse to dealing with these "bad" behaviors rather than viewing them as normal.* This example is related to the previous two points.

Wise OD With Beautiful Outcomes

To accentuate the positive and return to the practice of wise OD, let us consider a few examples of potentially lovely outcomes. These examples help to summarize some of the points made earlier regarding effective organizations and adaptive cultures. Following these examples of wise OD is a more detailed case of crafting a corporate mission statement, with the purpose being to illustrate how the processes and subtleties of practice can lead to highly effective outcomes.

Conflict resolution is seeing and facilitating the behavioral movement from anger and antagonism to understanding and acceptance of difference with an outcome that is superior to where the respective parties were at the outset. This can, of course, occur at all levels—interpersonal, intergroup, and interorganizational.

Trusting the process is moving from a comfortable place of knowing what is and what to expect to a new and different place that is unknown and being unclear about what to expect yet willing to believe that working together in an open and trusting manner can lead to innovation, creativity, and a more effective organization.

A possible example of the above is when a group achieves synergy—a beautiful thing to see. However, it might not be beautiful to watch at the time. More than once, I have observed groups that achieved synergy on a decision-making task. The process was anything but smooth—people talking over one another, not listening to one another very well (or so it seemed), talking loudly, physically moving around the room, and occasionally subgrouping rather than staying together as a total group. Yet in the end, their outcome was better than the sum of their parts. Somehow they came together in the end—in part, no doubt, due to their trusting the process they were in and believing that it (consensus) could pay off.

Leader coaching is about the OD practitioner's providing useful suggestions for improving the leader's performance. Highly satisfying for an OD practitioner is to see the outcome of coaching a leader to do something that actually works. A simple example was when I suggested that a CEO tell his top 100 executives a couple of stories from his experience that illustrated the values he wanted to instill in the company. He did so, and it was beautiful to see how inspired his executives became as a result. That episode occurred roughly a decade ago. It would not surprise me at all if most of those executives could relate the CEO's stories today.

Another example of beauty in OD work is when practitioners facilitate an *intervention* that has significant consequences for the *organization as a whole*. An illustration is helping to craft an organizational mission statement that not only clarifies purpose and direction but also reflects deeply held beliefs and values that are owned and lived by organizational members. This final point with a few examples of wise OD and beautiful outcomes is a segue to the next section, which serves as a case example of developing a mission statement.

Case Example

There is beauty in an OD process that helps an organization to change and/or to realize potential that otherwise would be buried. And there is wisdom in an OD process when the activities are grounded in valid theory and applied research. This case example is an attempt to illustrate such a process, namely the OD process of helping organizational members to craft a mission statement. First, however, I offer a few words about mission statements.

Mission Statements

One of the most important initiatives that leaders of organizations need to undertake is the formulation of the organization's mission—its purpose, raison d'être, role in society, and (if a business) its role within a particular market. A well-crafted statement of mission helps organizational members to understand not only the organization's purpose but also how the roles and responsibilities they fill and implement fit with that purpose and mission. In the words of Mary Parker Follett, an early sage in describing and articulating what leadership is all about, "Leaders and followers are both following the invisible leader—the common purpose. The best executives put this common purpose clearly before the group" (Follett, 1996, p. 172).

Crafting a mission statement at the outset for a newly formed organization is, of course, a highly appropriate initiative to take. Consider, however, not only a "start from scratch" situation but also the possibility of, say, a new joint venture between two long-standing and well-established companies.

Yet there are other needs for crafting a mission statement, for example, when two organizations merge. In the case of two New York savings banks, Dime and Anchor, coming together during the mid-1990s (Burke, 2007, chap. 11), with each institution having a mission statement, they were advised to scrap their respective statements and to formulate a new one that would serve as the mission for the newly merged organization. In effect, this new mission served as a superordinate goal for the two banks, that is, as a way of preventing unnecessary competition and conflict.

Another example is when an organization has been in business for quite a number of years but, for one reason or another, never got around to establishing a mission. One such organization, AAH Pharmaceuticals, a distribution company in the United Kingdom, had spent so much time and energy on strategy over the years that senior management had overlooked the need for helping employees to understand the organization's ultimate purpose. Was it just to make money and provide jobs for people? Once confronted about this omission—simply stated as mission being the *what*, which was missing, and strategy being the *how*—senior management got behind a significant effort to craft a mission statement for the company.

Generating a mission statement can be hierarchically a top-down process, a bottom-up process, or something in between. A top-down process can work (with "work" meaning, in this case, acceptance of the statement by organizational members). For example, the mission statement (referred to as "The Promise") for the newly merged SmithKline Pharmaceuticals of Philadelphia and Beecham Ltd. of London was essentially written by the chairman, Henry Wendt. It became widely accepted in the company due in part to his careful wording and asking for feedback all along the way (Bauman et al., 1997; Wendt, 1993).

Generating a mission statement can also be somewhat bottom-up with much more involvement of organizational members. As indicated earlier, what now follows is a detailed description of generating a company mission statement that involves organizational members and reflects what I believe to be some of the beauty and wisdom of OD work. This description is based on conducting essentially the same process in the two different companies just mentioned: one in the United States that was a consequence of a merger between two banks (Burke, 2007, chap. 11) and the other in the United Kingdom with a pharmaceutical distribution company that for many years emphasized strategy but not mission. Both succeeded; that is, there was organization-wide acceptance of the final statement. What follows is a description of how this process can work. It was essentially the same for both organizations.

Crafting a Mission Statement

Once the CEO and senior management give the "okay" to proceed with crafting a mission statement, the external consultant working in tandem with an internal organizational member, usually an OD or human resources (HR) person, provides criteria for forming an organizational mission statement task force. The size of the group should be 16 people representing a cross section of the overall organization, in essence, a diagonal slice of the organization chart. Each function and business unit should have a representative—one from marketing, one from finance, one from operations, one from information technology (IT), one from HR, and so on, as well as one from each key business unit. And all hierarchical levels should be represented—from salesperson, to "back-office" operations, to first-line supervision, all the way up to senior executive (one of the CEO's direct reports).

At the initial meeting of the task force, the consultant provides an overall orientation explaining why the decision was made to craft a mission statement for the organization and then describing the process for going forward. Prior to this initial meeting, all members have been given a copy of the Pearce and David (1987) article on corporate mission statements and asked to read it. The consultant reviews the article with the task force members and suggests that the eight components that Pearce and David found in their study be used as criteria for crafting the mission for their organization. In other words, in the end they should have done the following:

1. Specified the organization's target customers and markets

2. Identified the principal products and services that the organization provides

3. Specified the organization's geographic domain

4. Identified the organization's core technologies

5. Made a statement of commitment to survival, growth, and profitability

6. Specified key elements of the organization's philosophy

7. Identified the organization's self-concept

8. Identified the organization's desired public image

The consultant's internal partner then explains that each member of the task force will work closely with one other member. The task of each of the eight pairs will be to collect data, that is, to gather suggestions for what the answers should be for each of the eight components just summarized. Following this initial meeting of the task force, each pair goes forth to conduct two focus groups: one with the constituents of one of the paired members and the other with the constituents of the other paired member (e.g., a focus group with operations people). In other words, each task force member conducts a focus group with his or her constituents and has the assistance of one other task force member. When meeting with one's constituents, the task force member concentrates on asking eight questions and takes notes (or tape-records the discussion). The other member of the pair serves as a facilitator. When conducting the second focus group with the other member's constituents, the roles are reversed; that is, the task force member for the first focus group now serves as a facilitator. It should be noted that prior to conducting the focus groups, all task force members participate in a 1-day workshop on (a) how to conduct a focus group and (b) how to facilitate a group meeting of 12 to 15 people.

Once all focus groups have been conducted, meaning that more than 200 organizational members have been involved in contributing to the content of the forthcoming mission statement, the task force reconvenes for a meeting lasting 1½ to 2 days, preferably off-site, to consolidate all of its focus group data.

The meeting begins with the CEO, or an executive from the top team, making a presentation that covers the following:

- What they are trying to accomplish overall and how the mission statement contributes
- How mission differs from, yet is related to, strategy
- How this work will establish what needs to follow regarding any gaps between mission and strategy

The consultant then follows with a brief presentation on an organizational model, in this case the Burke-Litwin model of organizational performance and change (Burke & Litwin, 1992), that helps the task force members to understand how mission fits and relates with other organizational dimensions such as the external environment, leadership, structure, systems, and especially culture. After all, embedded in a mission statement are organizational values that are fundamental to culture.

The consultant then explains the work of the task force now, namely to consoidate the data and begin the writing, with the ultimate goal being a mission statement that fits on one page.

The initial work of consolidation is done in the original pairs, with each pair taking all of the data from task force members for one of the eight components and writing a summary statement for that component. A copy of the Pearce and David (1987) article remains available to everyone as a reminder of what each component means and includes examples of statements and phrases for each of the components.

Once all of the pairs' work is complete, the total task force comes together to listen to each pair's report, followed by subgroups of four members working on the larger consolidation effort.

The final session of the meeting is a subgroup of 6 members, with the other 10 members primarily observing yet having the option of briefly adding to the discussion, bringing together all of the consolidated work and crafting a complete draft of the mission statement.

Once the draft is done, the entire task force comes together to edit and perhaps modify some details. With the statement completed to the satisfaction of the task force members, the consultant then reviews the next steps following the meeting.

The final step for the task force is to meet with the senior executive team (CEO and direct reports). The purposes of this meeting are (a) for the task force members to present their statement, (b) to provide the opportunity for the senior executives to edit the draft, and (c) to finalize the statement. (The final mission statement for AAH Pharmaceuticals is shown in Table 11.1.)

With respect to the company in the United States, there was one additional step. The CEO wanted the entire task force to attend the next board of directors meeting and present its statement to the board. At the conclusion of the task force members' presentation of their work, the board of directors gave them a standing ovation.

The process of crafting an organizational mission statement just described and based on two actual company examples represents OD work at its best, that is, (a) getting needed organization change work accomplished, (b) doing so by way of extensive involvement and consequent commitment to and ownership of that accomplishment in the organization, and (c) recognizing organizational members for their participation and achievement in a significant and meaningful way.

This process, as mentioned, may represent OD at its best, but there are "costs." This kind of process takes time—4 to 6 months in both cases. Many senior executives do not want to expend the time required. After all, valuable human resources are necessary to conduct this "off-line" work. Besides, a more efficient way is for one person to write a draft; circulate it to get others' reactions, comments, and suggestions for improvement; and then revise the draft. This iterative process was how it was done by Wendt, the SmithKline Beecham chairman.

This process may represent OD at its best, but maybe not. More than 200 organizational members were involved, but the remainder of the organization, except for the top executive group, was not. Was there really widespread commitment?

With these caveats in mind, we can conclude nevertheless that with the process described here and implemented accordingly—and, yes, with a limited number of people involved—the task force work was made known

Table 11.1   AAH Pharmaceuticals Group Mission Statement

We are the UK's leading distributor of pharmaceutical and healthcare products and services to pharmacies, hospitals, and doctors.

As the essential link in the pharmaceutical supply chain, we are respected within the industry for our knowledge and expertise.

We supply a full range of healthcare products including ethicals, generics, PI's [parallel imports], and OTC's [over-the-counter] delivering a reliable personalized service to our customers in local communities throughout our national network.

We commit to mutually beneficial partnerships with our customers and suppliers providing them with flexible professional support services. As specialists in anticipating and adapting to market trends, we develop innovative solutions to meet their constantly changing needs.

Through our use of state of the art technologies, we provide a process driven quality service. Key to our future success is continued investment in:

- Warehouse management systems
- Supply chain support solutions
- Customer ordering and information systems
- Communication technologies

In order to sustain our long term success and growth, we explore and exploit new business and market opportunities whilst maintaining our cost efficiency and increasing our existing profitable business.

We believe that open communication, honesty and trust breed loyalty and commitment. This together with our continued investment in the training and development of our people leads us to be the employer of choice in our sector.

The dedication of our people and partnerships with customers and suppliers ensure that we will remain the industry leader.

SOURCE: Reprinted with permission from AAH Pharmaceuticals, Ltd.

throughout the respective organizations. Organizational members who participated in the focus group told others about it. Task force members were seen as *representatives* of their constituents. The Coch and French (1948) study showed many years ago that total participation achieved better results than the comparative representative group, yet the latter group significantly outperformed the control group (neither participation nor representation). Benefit was realized from both of the experimental groups (total participation and representation). A similar benefit was probably realized in our cases described here some six decades later.

Critical to motivation and high performance in organizations is for all employees to see the connection between what they do in their daily work and the organization's mission. Although it is difficult to prove, that link in the eyes of organizational members, I believe, contributes significantly to high motivation and subsequent performance. And seeing the process of facilitating such linkage apparently work well is a thing of beauty and indeed provides a deep feeling of satisfaction for an OD consultant.

Regarding an organization's mission statement, one final note is in order. Once a mission statement is in place, it is wise to revisit it every 2 or 3 years. Things change. One of the strengths of Johnson & Johnson's credo is that it is reconsidered about every 3 or so years. In other words, its long-standing use in the company is no doubt due to the credo's currency. A successful organization finds ways to ensure an alignment of its mission with the external environment and with key factors inside the organization. As Crotts, Dickson, and Ford (2005) noted, "Too often there is a gap between what the organization says it seeks to do and what its employees actually do" (p. 54). They provided a useful list of 15 audit items (e.g., alignment of department goals with customer service, whether top management walks the mission talk, whether job descriptions incorporate mission components) to help with this alignment process. This kind of process can be used as a tool to facilitate the revisitation of the organization's mission statement.

A Final Word

The practice of OD is a combination of (a) applying knowledge from the behavioral sciences, (b) reflecting on one's experience and attempting to put into service the learning therefrom in a wise manner, and (c) using oneself in the practitioner role as skillfully as possible. Therefore, OD is applied science and practice, and it is only as wise and useful as the skill and ability of the practitioner.

Wisdom comes from knowledge and experience. The wise OD practitioner, by definition, must be a lifelong learner.

Beauty in OD work comes from realizing positive change—change that is needed and leads to a more effective organization. Beauty is also seeing organizational members and the organization itself realizing more of their potential and experiencing more joy in the workplace. When done wisely, OD and change are likely to be experienced as a work of art.

References

Argyris, C. (1970). *Intervention theory and method.* Reading, MA: Addison-Wesley.

Bauman, R. P., Jackson, P., & Lawrence, J. T. (1997). *From promise to performance: A journey of transformation at SmithKline Beecham.* Boston: Harvard Business School Press.

Beckhard, R. (1969). *Organization development: Strategies and models.* Reading, MA: Addison-Wesley.

Beer, M. E., & Norhia, N. (2000). Cracking the code of change. *Harvard Business Review, 78*(3), 133–141.

Bradford, D. L., & Burke, W. W. (2005). The future of OD? In D. L. Bradford & W. W. Burke (Eds.), *Reinventing organization development: New approaches to change in organizations* (pp. 195–214). San Francisco: Pfeiffer/Wiley.

Burke, W. W. (1994). *Organization development: A process of learning and changing* (2nd ed.). Reading, MA: Addison-Wesley.

Burke, W. W. (2007). *Organization change: Theory and practice* (2nd ed.). Thousand Oaks, CA: Sage.

Burke, W. W., & Bradford, D. L. (2005). The crisis in OD. In D. L. Bradford & W. W. Burke (Eds.), *Reinventing organization development: New approaches to change in organizations* (pp. 7–14). San Francisco: Pfeiffer/Wiley.

Burke, W. W., & Litwin, G. H. (1992). A causal model of organizational performance and change. *Journal of Management, 18,* 532–545.

Carter, L., Giber, D., & Goldsmith, M. (Eds.). (2001). *Best practices in organization development and change.* San Francisco: Jossey-Bass/Pfeiffer.

Coch, L., & French, J. R. P. (1948). Overcoming resistance to change. *Human Relations, 1,* 512–532.

Crotts, J. C., Dickson, D. R., & Ford, R. C. (2005). Aligning organizational processes with mission: The case of service excellence. *Academy of Management Executive, 19*(3), 54–68.

Cummings, T. G. (Ed.). (2007). *Handbook of organization development.* Thousand Oaks, CA: Sage.

Cummings, T. G., & Worley, C. G. (2005). *Organization development and change* (8th ed.). Mason, OH: Thomson South-Western.

Follett, M. P. (1996). The essentials of leadership. In P. Graham (Ed.), *Mary Parker Follett—Prophet of management: A celebration of writings from the 1920s* (pp. 163–181). Boston: Harvard Business School Press.

Foster, R. N., & Kaplan, S. (2001). *Creative destruction: Why companies that are built to last underperform the market—And how to successfully transform them.* New York: Currency.

French, W. L., & Bell, C. H., Jr. (1995). *Organization development: Behavioral science interventions for organization improvement* (5th ed.). Englewood Cliffs, NJ: Prentice Hall.

Gladwell, M. (2000). *The tipping point: How little things can make a big difference.* Boston: Little, Brown.

Goodstein, L. D., & Burke, W. W. (1991). Creating successful organizational change. *Organizational Dynamics, 19*(4), 5–17.

Hambrick, D. C., & Cannella, A. A., Jr. (1989). Strategy implementation as substance and selling. *Academy of Management Executive, 3*(4), 278–285.

Harrison, R. (1970). Choosing the depth of the organizational intervention. *Journal of Applied Behavioral Science, 6,* 181–202.

Hogan, R., Raskin, R., & Fazzini, D. (1990). The dark side of charisma. In K. E. Clark & M. B. Clark (Eds.), *Measures of leadership* (pp. 343–354). West Orange, NJ: Leadership Library of America.

Kotter, J. P., & Heskett, J. L. (1992). *Corporate culture and performance.* New York: Free Press.

Lewin, K. (1958). Group decision and social change. In E. E. Maccoby, T. M. Newcomb, & E. L. Hartley (Eds.), *Readings in social psychology* (pp. 197–211). New York: Holt, Rinehart & Winston.

Lippitt, R., Watson, J., & Westley, B. (1958). *Dynamics of planned change.* New York: Harcourt, Brace.

Martin, J. (2002). *Organizational culture: Mapping the terrain.* Thousand Oaks, CA: Sage.

Mirvis, P. H., & Berg, D. N. (Eds.). (1977). *Failures in organization development and change.* New York: John Wiley.

Pearce, J. A., & David, F. (1987). Corporate mission statements: The bottom line. *Academy of Management Executive, 1*(2), 109–116.

Schein, E. H. (1987). *Process consultation: Vol. 2. Lessons for managers and consultants.* Reading, MA: Addison-Wesley.

Schein, E. H. (2004). *Organizational culture and leadership* (3rd ed.). San Francisco: Jossey-Bass.

Wendt, H. (1993). *Global embrace: Corporate challenges in a transnational world.* New York: Harper Business.

12 Strategic Aesthetics

Wisdom and Human Resource Management

Angelo S. DeNisi
Carrie A. Belsito

There are many definitions of the term *wisdom*. *Webster's Ninth New Collegiate Dictionary* (1988) defines it as follows: "1a. Accumulated philosophic or scientific learning: KNOWLEDGE; 1b. Ability to discern inner qualities and relationships: INSIGHT; 1c. Good sense: JUDGMENT; 2. A wise attitude or course of action" (p. 1354).

Several of these definitions are applicable to the current discussion, but we believe that the notions of good sense and judgment may be the most applicable to our perspective. Essentially, we argue that a "wise" human resource management (HRM) system is one that balances the financial goals of the organization with the individual goals of its employees. We view this balance as representing good sense as well as sound judgment; therefore, it is an approach that can help an organization to meet *all* of its strategic objectives. As such, a balanced and wise approach to strategic HRM represents strategy at its highest level of artistry—the true aesthetics of strategy.

Artistry and *aesthetics* are terms that are not typically associated with HRM, but we believe that these are exactly the right terms for the type of system we are describing here. As we discuss in the next section, the field of HRM grew out of a humanistic concern for people at work and what made them happy. Over the years, this concern was replaced by a need to justify human resource (HR) activities and to show how these activities contributed to a firm's bottom line. It is relatively easy to design HRM systems that emphasize people over firm performance or vice versa, but the true "art" of HRM lies in the design of a system that can satisfy a concern for people and contribute to firm performance, and that is the type of wisdom we are proposing to help guide HR practitioners. Such a system would also be aesthetically pleasing in the true sense of the term. A system that could balance the tastes, preferences, and concerns of both the firm and its employees would satisfy the preferences of both groups and would truly be a "beautiful" thing to behold.

But of course, this is not the way scholars and practitioners typically have approached the issue of strategy. Instead, the concept of *strategy* has been associated with an attempt to gain some type of advantage. Traditionally, treatments of strategy have focused on ways to gain this advantage in warfare, whether on the battlefield (Sun Tzu's *The Art of War*) or in the court of a Renaissance Italian ruler (Machiavelli's *The Prince*). It is easy to see how these treatments could be transferred to a business setting where firms compete against each other in the marketplace. Specifically, in each case, a "strategy" referred to the means by which a competitor sought to gain advantage over others. At the simplest level, a firm could compete by offering products at the lowest price or, alternatively, could compete by offering the "best" products (e.g., finest materials, most advanced technology). In either case, the firm would seek to gain advantage or "beat" its competitors by adopting the strategy that was effective and could actually be executed by the firm.

The resource-based view of the firm made some of these arguments more specific when dealing with business competition. Barney (1991) suggested that all firms had resources but that when a firm possessed resources that were both valuable and difficult to copy or replace, that firm possessed an important source of competitive advantage. The key, then, was for the firm to find a way to leverage those rare and unique resources to gain that competitive advantage. The literature contains many examples of the resource-based view being applied. One of the more interesting examples dealt with the way Hollywood studios used the stars they had under contract to gain advantage over rival studios (Miller & Shamsie, 1996), and another interesting study discussed college basketball coaches and how they developed strategies based on the players they could sign (Wright, Smart, & McMahan, 1995).

Among the most important resources possessed by a firm are its human resources—the people the firm employs. Several scholars have discussed the importance of human resources as a source of competitive advantage (e.g., Pfeffer, 1994), and some have even demonstrated empirically how HRM practices can lead to substantial gains for a firm that understands how to develop those practices in a way that allows the firm to best leverage its human resources (e.g., Huselid, 1995). But the focus of these strategic HRM practices has been on firm performance, generally defined in terms of financial returns (Huselid, 1995), profitability, and shareholder value (e.g., Becker, Huselid, Pickus, & Spratt, 1997). That is not to suggest that these scholars and practitioners do not recognize any other possible advantages to be gained from these practices (cf. Becker, Huselid, & Ulrich, 2001), but the major focus is clearly on firm financial performance.

We believe that this focus is too narrow in its concern for financial outcomes only. Although we recognize that some of the proponents of these approaches do recognize the potential for gain to the individual employee, we suggest that a truly "wise" HRM system would seek a balance between financial outcomes and personal outcomes. Furthermore, we suggest that if there needs to be trade-off, it would be wiser to emphasize the returns to the individual over the returns to the firm because, in the long run, this will actually result in a more profitable and more competitive enterprise.

Some Historical Perspective

Early management theorists and scholars traditionally were focused on ways to increase productivity. The clear underlying assumption was that if a firm could increase productivity without increasing costs, it could sell its products for less and/or at a higher profit margin. Thus, proponents of scientific management (Taylor, 1911) developed specific performance strategies, focusing on physical movement and elemental physical motions that would allow a worker to be more productive. Interestingly, these proponents also suggested that these more productive workers should be paid at a higher rate to reflect their contributions to the company.

But it was the human relations movement that provided the impetus for many of our modern management, and especially HRM, practices. Proponents of this approach (Mayo, 1933) argued that happy workers were productive workers, and so practices that would lead to workers feeling more satisfied with their jobs ultimately would lead to higher levels of productivity. The assumed link between satisfaction and performance, however, was more elusive than the early proponents had believed. In fact, most scholars reported only weak and inconsistent relationships between satisfaction and performance, and some suggested that performance actually led to satisfaction rather than the other way around. Although there are many sound arguments for why the relationship between satisfaction and performance should not be as strong or direct as had originally been suggested, and although some more recent views have proposed alternate ways to examine this relationship, for many years HRM practices focused on ways to improve employee satisfaction without paying as much attention to performance.

This is not to suggest that HR scholars and practitioners were not interested in performance; they were simply more interested in individual performance than in firm performance. Therefore, a great deal of literature emerged with either employee attitudes (e.g., job satisfaction) or individual performance as the dependent variable of interest. Of course, most writers recognized that job satisfaction was also related to absenteeism and turnover and that these outcomes (especially turnover) were related to organizational productivity and performance as well. A focus on employee attitudes did not, therefore, represent an abandonment of concern over firm performance, but firm performance was clearly relegated to a secondary status. Furthermore, most writers also assumed that if the individual-level performance of every employee increased, ultimately firm-level productivity must also increase.

This latter relationship between individual performance and firm-level outcomes has been approached from a variety of perspectives. Tables, such as those of Taylor and Russell (1939), allowed a firm to estimate the increase in productivity that would be gained by using a selection tool with a validity of x and hiring y new employees with a selection ratio of z. Brogden (1949) extended this work further by translating this increase in selection efficiency (also referred to as utility) into a dollar metric. Although Brogden's proposals were available for quite some time, it was left to other scholars, such as Cascio and his associates (e.g., Cascio, 1987; Cascio & Ramos, 1986) and especially Schmidt and his associates (e.g., Schmidt & Hunter, 1983), to develop techniques to estimate the values needed for Brogden's models.

These utility models realized their fullest potential with the strategic HRM approach (also referred to as the "best practices" approach), as demonstrated by Huselid (1995) and others. This approach involves measuring the presence or absence of certain HR practices (best practices or high-performance work practices) in firms and then relating this to measures of firm performance. The fact that the presence of these HR practices is associated with increases in most measures of firm performance suggests that their adoption does have utility for the firm and that this utility can be calculated very specifically.

Thus, with this work, we have come full circle in our focus on different outcomes in designing HRM systems. The emphasis on employee attitudes, such as job satisfaction, coexisted with an emphasis on individual performance, and these emphases eventually gave way to an emphasis on unit or firm performance. But have we lost something by focusing primarily on firm performance and competitive advantage? We believe that this is the case, and so we propose an alternative approach to designing HRM systems that focuses on the individual's well-being (broadly defined) as well as firm performance in the hope that the system we are suggesting will serve both the firm and its employees well in the long run.

Individual Versus Firm Outcomes and HRM Strategy

We do not believe that serving the individual employee must always come at the cost of firm performance and competitiveness or vice versa. Yet there are clearly examples where we can see trade-offs between the two sets of goals.

For example, it is safe to assume that although firms do not want to truly exploit employees, they do desire to minimize their wage bills. As a result, a firm would search for a wage rate (broadly defined) that would keep its employees attached to the organization, and keep the employees motivated to exert effort, but that would not be any higher than it needed to be. A competitor might raise wages to attract better employees and gain some advantage, but this could succeed only in the short term. In the long term, a different firm could raise wages even higher and thus attract the best employees and gain a temporary advantage. This would result in yet another firm raising wages even higher, and so on, until the marginal productivity could not justify any further wage increases.

But organizations employ wage surveys and consultants to ensure that they never approach that equilibrium point. They collect enough information to know what competitors are offering, and it is in no one's long-term best interest to increase wages. It is, of course, in the employees' best interest to receive wage increases up to the point where their marginal cost is equal to their marginal productivity. It is not in the employees' best interest to increase wages beyond that point because the firm would then need to stop hiring and perhaps even lay off employees rather than pay the higher wages.

In other examples, employers desire fairly low selection ratios (i.e., many applicants for each job) so that they can be more selective about who they hire. Employees prefer very high selection ratios because that results in near full employment. Also, employers prefer selection criteria that result in hiring the best people for each job, whereas employees prefer selection criteria that result in hiring everyone who can carry out the job at a reasonable level. Finally, employers prefer specific training for employees because employees cannot transfer this training to another firm, whereas employees prefer generalized training so that they can transfer knowledge gained in one firm to another firm and capture some return for this knowledge.

But not all preferences are so clearly in conflict. Employees desire other outcomes at work as well, and these are not necessarily in conflict with employer goals. In fact, as we will argue, in the long run these goals are consistent with employer goals. In fact, by meeting these employee goals, an employer should be able to leverage its employees to gain some competitive advantage.

For example, research on the meaning of work suggests that people take jobs to achieve a number of goals. Work provides people with a feeling of self-worth; the mere fact of being employed and receiving a salary also leads to increased feelings of worth. Individuals also take jobs to experience feelings of accomplishment and achievement, and they expect their jobs to reinforce those feelings. In addition, work helps to define who people are. That is, people's self-concepts are often tied closely to what they do for a living. Apart from actual earnings, individuals may feel good about saying that they are teachers but may feel less good about saying that they sell used cars. Finally, people work for purely economic reasons. Although some individuals volunteer for different jobs (especially during retirement), very few people would go to work—even at jobs that are prestigious and challenging—if they were not paid for performing the job. Of course, there are exceptions, and some jobs (e.g., museum curator) actually pay far under market value and so are performed only by people wealthy enough to not need the money. But for most people, money is an important reason for working.

None of these goals is in absolute conflict with organizational goals. It may be true that for an organization to maximize certain goals (profits) it would need to do so at the expense of the goals of its employees (to earn a living wage), but there is clearly a great deal of room for both sides of the arrangement to satisfy their goals. This is the primary focus of the remainder of the chapter. We propose a wisdom-based strategic HRM model that can meet the desires and goals of both the organization and the individual employees, and it is the balancing of these two sets of desires that makes such a system aesthetically pleasing. As we noted earlier, we also believe that such an approach will, in the long run, serve the organization's strategic goals better than will the more typical strategic approach to HR.

A Wisdom-Based Strategic Model

Thus, we believe that, from a strategic aesthetic perspective, a wisdom-based approach to strategic HRM is to seek practices and policies that balance the needs of the employees and the employer simultaneously. Typically, strategic HRM models are built around best practices in various aspects of HRM. We follow suit and suggest a set of best practices for a wisdom-based model. In addition, we discuss, in each case, why the practice proposed serves both parties well.

Selection

Several models of strategic HRM (e.g., Huselid, 1995) focus on selection ratios when dealing with best practices in the selection area. That is, these authors assume that if an organization has many applicants for each job opening, it will be possible to select the best applicants and hire effective performers for all job openings. In fact, charts such as the Taylor-Russell Tables (Taylor & Russell, 1939) explicitly consider selection ratios as part of the calculation of how much using a valid selection tool will improve organizational effectiveness. We do not dispute the importance of selection ratios, but we would argue that wisdom-based systems should focus on other aspects of the selection process.

Specifically, most views of the selection process assume that an organization can fashion some type of rank ordering of applicants on the knowledge, skills, and abilities (KSAs) required to carry out the job. Even selection models based on fit (cf. Kristof-Brown, 2000) assume some ranking of candidates from the best fit to the worst fit. Once such a ranking is produced, the organization is assumed to start at the top candidate and work down the list until all jobs are filled. This approach makes sense so long as there are meaningful differences among the candidates on the criteria for selection. That is, if the first candidate is "significantly" better than the second candidate, it is clearly reasonable to select the first candidate before the second one. But ranking does not inform us about the size of the differences between ranked candidates, and some scholars have argued that many of these differences are not very great.

In fact, a number of selection scholars have argued that candidates form clusters around certain levels of whatever criteria are used. Candidates within these clusters do not differ meaningfully from each other; therefore, there is no compelling reason to select one candidate within a cluster or "band" over another one. Although these issues have been pursued primarily relative to test score banding, the logic applies to any selection criterion (for an excellent discussion of the issues involved in test score banding, see the various chapters in Aguinis, 2004).

Once they are liberated from the need to select the top person for each job, organizations can then select people, with equal probabilities of success, according to other criteria. These other criteria can help to meet employee needs, which could include diversity initiatives and affirmative action. Because the logic behind the banding argument is that there are not meaningful differences in the predicted performance of applicants within the band, this approach would allow an organization to help satisfy employee (or societal) needs without sacrificing anything in terms of effectiveness. In fact, using a test or another selection tool in this way would increase organizational effectiveness because it would still identify clusters of applicants who are better than other clusters of applicants. Then if the organization selected from among those employees in the top cluster, this would still result in more qualified applicants being hired than would be the case under some alternative approach.

Compensation

Many strategic HRM models focus on the use of various types of incentives as the key to more effective HRM. Incentive plans are indeed an important part of any effective compensation strategy, but we believe that wisdom-based approaches should focus on other aspects of the compensation system. Specifically, we believe that their focus should be on *what* is compensated rather than on the absolute levels of compensation. Most job evaluation systems that are used to determine compensation rates focus on what a person does on the job as the major determinant of compensation. But advocates of skill- or knowledge-based pay propose that people should be paid for what they know rather than for what they do.

Such an approach makes sense from an organization's perspective because it pays people for the extent to which they contribute valued skills or knowledge to the organization. If these skills or knowledge are truly important, the organization should perform better as the store of knowledge within the organization is increased. In fact, there is evidence that organizations do benefit from these programs (e.g., Murray & Gerhart, 1998), and there is also evidence that employees perceive these programs to be fairer than more traditional compensation programs. Furthermore, not only will employees' compensation increase when they acquire these skills, but their value in the larger marketplace also should increase because of these skills and can have a significant long-term impact on compensation.

Training and Development

Strategic HRM models also focus on forms of training as a means to enhance employees' KSAs (Huselid, 1995). Typically, strategic HRM models assess training as the number of hours that an employee receives in training per year. We believe, however, that the focus of training, and its closely related concept, development, should not be solely on the *number* of training hours that employees receive; rather, the focus should be on the *quality* of those training hours and on what value those training hours can bring to both employees and organizations. For example, if an organization simply calculates the number of hours spent on training per employee per year and equates that figure with whether or not "enough" training is being conducted, the organization is missing out on a rich contextual component that may or may not indicate superior (or even adequate) training programs. With a wisdom-based training approach, however, employees do not just put in time to complete yearly training hours; they actually make use of those training hours to acquire valuable sets of KSAs that they can use to make themselves more appealing both within and outside of the organization.

Thus, the focus in a wisdom-based HRM system would be on the exact content of the training and development activities. For example, organizations often prefer training that focuses on the specific activities that take place within the organization over more general training that might apply to a wide variety of organizations. That is, many organizations would rather train HR employees to maintain a specific compensation system used in those organizations than train them in the theories underlying compensation strategy and how specific decisions fit within this strategy. From a narrow perspective, this approach makes sense for an organization because it precludes employees from going to another firm that would then reap the benefits of the training. But on the other hand, allowing employees to receive more general training may actually help the organization in the long run as situations change the exact skill set needed for job changes. Of course, from the employees' perspective, more general training allows them

to develop themselves more fully and gives them the potential to contribute
to the organization in new ways.

Performance Appraisal Systems

Most models of strategic HRM focus on whether or not regular performance appraisals occur rather than on the specific content of those appraisals.
A wisdom-based approach is more concerned with the content as well as with
the process of performance appraisal. For example, employee input would be
an important part of any appraisal system developed under a wisdom-based
approach. That is, employees (or ratees) should have input concerning what
is to be rated, what standards are to be applied, and how the entire process
will be conducted. Allowing employee input communicates to employees that
their opinions are valued and also draws on the expertise that employees possess concerning their jobs and the standards that should be applied. Thus,
employee input should result in more effective and useful appraisal systems.

But such input, and the opportunity to discuss their performance with a
supervisor, also increases employees' level of perceived procedural justice of
the process (e.g., Folger, Konovsky, & Cropanzano, 1992). Perceptions of
justice are also tied to the actual content of the appraisals such that ratings
of vague traits, which cannot be observed directly and which seem more
prone to bias by a rater, are less likely to be seen as fair. On the other hand,
ratings based on specific goals (especially when employees have input in
determining those goals) are much more likely to be seen as fair and "objective." These perceptions of justice and fairness are critical for employees'
acceptance of the decisions that follow from the appraisals, as well as for
the perceived legitimacy of the entire process, and so are important to both
employees and employers.

Interestingly, during the 1980s and 1990s much of the research in the
area of performance appraisal was focused on rater cognitive processes that
were involved in making appraisal decisions, and several such models of the
appraisal process were proposed (e.g., DeNisi, Cafferty, & Meglino, 1984;
Feldman, 1981). The research that followed from these models investigated
ways in which raters would be better able to provide fair and accurate
ratings. Note that this research did not consider the related problem of
whether raters would *want* to provide fair and accurate ratings. It was concerned only with helping raters to have access to the information they
needed to be accurate. For example, several studies (e.g., DeNisi & Peters,
1996; DeNisi, Robbins, & Cafferty, 1989; Varma, DeNisi, & Peters, 1996)
examined how diary keeping would provide raters with the information
they needed to be accurate and to provide meaningful feedback to employees. Thus, following these recommendations, organizations would benefit
from the accurate evaluation information they would be collecting, and
employees would benefit from the meaningful and useful feedback and also

would be evaluated fairly. Thus, it would seem that organizations adopting the interventions proposed in these studies would be moving toward a wiser and aesthetically pleasing appraisal system.

Union–Management Relations

One last area where a wisdom-based approach can be important is in dealing with unions. We are not suggesting that management should encourage employees to unionize, but there are some insights that can be gained about how a company's management deals with attempts at unionization or the actual relations with a union.

For example, historically textile manufacturers in the Southeast fought off repeated attempts by unions to organize their employees. Several even went so far as to violate the Taft-Hartley Act in trying to keep unions out. But such violent opposition to unionization may be misplaced in some respects. For example, Eli Lilly has never been unionized, nor have there been many attempts to unionize its employees. That is because Eli Lilly has always treated its employees with respect and even managed to retain its entire labor force throughout the Depression. The point is that companies that treat employees well often have less trouble with unions. The time to oppose unionization, then, is before anyone tries to organize employees. Although there are other reasons for employees to join unions, dissatisfaction with management is a major reason (e.g., Youngblood, DeNisi, Molleston, & Mobley, 1984). Therefore, serious organizational efforts indicate that the management has not met the needs of employees, and violent opposition at that point is likely to lead to other problems later and might not even be successful. Thus, a wisdom-based approach would suggest treating employees with dignity at all times. This will result in employees who feel better about themselves and will reduce the effectiveness of union organizing campaigns.

A wisdom-based approach also leads to suggestions about how to deal with an existing union. Some companies (e.g., Phillip Morris) have learned to work with unions as opposed to against them. Some managers have even stated a preference for dealing with unionized employees because there is one voice that speaks for all (or most) employees, making communications simpler. Even automakers have learned that it is easier to deal with unions by working with them to solve problems jointly. Chrysler has actually put a union official on its board, but even without taking such a radical step, General Motors has found that union cooperation has gone a long way toward easing problems at its Saturn facilities.

In these cases, the needs of employees are met because the organizations are responding (positively) to union calls for changes in conditions at work, and there is no need for the high level of conflict that has characterized some more traditional union–management relationships. But organizations also benefit from the absence of conflict and the fact that many unions *do* appreciate the competitive pressures faced by modern organizations and are often willing to work with management to help deal with those pressures.

The "True Wisdom" of This Approach

We have described aspects of a wisdom-based strategic HRM system that can provide benefits to both the organization and its employees. The research linking high-performance work systems with organizational performance has supported a link between the two for the most part. But in fact some scholars have argued for universal best practices, whereas others have suggested that the best practices for a given firm are dependent on that firm's strategy and that, in any case, the HRM systems do not explain very much of the variance in firm performance. Furthermore, there is a great deal of ambiguity concerning *how* HR practices affect firm performance. Many argue that when a firm uses the best HR practices, this builds commitment in the employees and increases their motivation to perform, but others have found that commitment is not important in explaining the link between the two (for a review of these findings, see Becker & Gerhart, 1996).

We believe that the ambiguity and inconsistency comes with the assumption that changes to a more strategic HRM system cause improvements in firm performance. We believe that there are HR practices (some of which are similar to those proposed in strategic systems) that can benefit both the organization and its employees simultaneously. Thus, we suggest that a wisdom-based approach to strategic HRM will result in both a motivated and committed workforce and improved firm performance. Furthermore, we believe that in the long run, our approach will yield even higher returns in firm performance because it will produce efficiencies and develop committed, motivated employees.

Finally, it is worth noting that a wisdom-based approach to HRM, such as the one we have proposed here, may actually have implications for management education and training. Our historical review of the field of HRM also provides information concerning from where the philosophical bases of the field were being drawn. When HRM was most concerned with the welfare of people at work, the perspective of HR managers was being taken primarily from psychology and sociology, with a strong flavoring of counseling. During those times, there were few professional HR managers, and so they were trained in a wide variety of settings but were often exposed to a strong liberal arts educational foundation. As the field became more professionalized, and as the field became more concerned with financial performance, the educational backgrounds of HR managers were more likely to be in business. This background only reinforced the notion that HRM should consider employees as resources that needed to be leveraged for competitive advantage while downplaying the importance of meeting the needs of the employees.

If a more balanced approach, such as ours, is to have an impact on the workplace, it is important that future HR managers be exposed, once again, to the psychological and sociological disciplines that will reinforce the importance of helping employees to grow as people. This is not to suggest that the training of HR managers should move out of the business school; to the contrary, it is critical that HR managers appreciate the business side of managing people. Instead, we propose that this education should also include exposure to the "softer side" of people management, allowing future mangers to develop the balanced approach we are advocating.

In conclusion, we have provided several examples of the kind of HR practices that we believe are dictated by such a wisdom-based approach, but the list is by no means meant to be exhaustive. Just as individuals engaged in negotiations are often urged to seek "win–win" solutions rather than to view negotiations as competition, we are advocating the benefit of approaching the design of HRM systems in the same way. The kinds of suggestions we have made in this chapter are based on practices that have received support in the literature, and so they are not a radical departure from what an organization might have decided on its own. A wisdom-based approach, however, means that an organization would evaluate these alternatives with an eye toward developing systems that help both the organization and its employees. We believe that such an approach will result in HRM systems that are capable of yielding sustainable competitive advantage to the firm because the firm will have committed employees, greater efficiency, and higher profits. Surely it is desirable to find systems under which everyone can win and benefit, and that is the basis for our proposed wisdom-based approach.

References

Aguinis, H. (Ed.). (2004). *Test score banding in human resources selection: Legal, technical, and societal issues.* Westport, CT: Praeger.

Barney, J. B. (1991). Firm resources and sustained competitive advantage. *Journal of Management, 17,* 99–120.

Becker, B. E., & Gerhart, B. G. (1996). The impact of human resource management on organizational performance: Progress and prospects. *Academy of Management Journal, 39,* 779–801.

Becker, B. E., Huselid, M. A., Pickus, P. S., & Spratt, M. F. (1997). HR as a source of shareholder value: Research and recommendations. *Human Resource Management, 36,* 39–47.

Becker, B. E., Huselid, M. A., & Ulrich, D. (2001). *The HR scorecard linking people, strategy, and performance.* Boston: Harvard Business School Press.

Brogden, H. E. (1949). When testing pays off. *Personnel Psychology, 2,* 171–185.

Cascio, W. F. (1987). *Costing human resources: The financial impact of behavior in organizations* (2nd ed.). Boston: PWS-Kent.

Cascio, W. F., & Ramos, R. A. (1986). Development and application of a new method for assessing job performance in behavioral/economic terms. *Journal of Applied Psychology, 71,* 20–28.

DeNisi, A. S., Cafferty, T. P., & Meglino, B. M. (1984). A cognitive view of the performance appraisal process: A model and research propositions. *Organizational Behavior and Human Performance, 33,* 360–396.

DeNisi, A. S., & Peters, L. H. (1996). The organization of information in memory and the performance appraisal process: Evidence from the field. *Journal of Applied Psychology, 81,* 717–737.

DeNisi, A. S., Robbins, T., & Cafferty, T. P. (1989). The organization of information used for performance appraisals: The role of diary-keeping. *Journal of Applied Psychology, 74,* 124–129.

Feldman, J. M. (1981). Beyond attribution theory: Cognitive processes in performance appraisal. *Journal of Applied Psychology, 66,* 127–148.

Folger, R., Konovsky, M. A., & Cropanzano, R. (1992). A due process metaphor for performance appraisal. In I. B. Staw & L. L. Cummings (Eds.), *Research in organizational behavior* (Vol. 14, pp. 129–177). Greenwich, CT: JAI.

Huselid, M. A. (1995). The impact of human resource management practices on turnover, productivity, and corporate financial performance. *Academy of Management Journal, 38,* 635–672.

Kristof-Brown, A. L. (2000). Perceived applicant fit: Distinguishing between recruiters' perceptions of person–job and person–organization fit. *Personnel Psychology, 53,* 643–671.

Mayo, E. (1933). *The human problems of industrial civilization.* New York: Macmillan.

Miller, D., & Shamsie, J. (1996). The resource-based view of the firm in two environments: The Hollywood film studios from 1936 to 1965. *Academy of Management Journal, 39,* 519–543.

Murray, B., & Gerhart, B. (1998). An empirical analysis of a skill-based pay program and plant performance outcomes. *Academy of Management Journal, 41,* 68–78.

Pfeffer, J. (1994). *Competitive advantage through people: Unleashing the power of the workforce.* Boston: Harvard Business School Press.

Schmidt, F. L., & Hunter, J. E. (1983). Individual differences in productivity: An empirical test of estimates derived from studies of selection procedure utility. *Journal of Applied Psychology, 68,* 407–414.

Taylor, F. W. (1911). *The principles of scientific management.* New York: Harper.

Taylor, R. C., & Russell, J. T. (1939). The relationship of validity coefficients to the practical effectiveness of tests in selection. *Journal of Applied Psychology, 23,* 565–578.

Varma, A., DeNisi, A. S., & Peters, L. H. (1996). Interpersonal affect in performance appraisal: A field study. *Personnel Psychology, 49,* 341–360.

Webster's ninth new collegiate dictionary. (1988). Springfield, MA: Merriam-Webster.

Wright, P. M., Smart, D. L., & McMahan, G. C. (1995). Matches between human resources and strategy among NCAA basketball teams. *Academy of Management Journal, 38,* 1052–1074.

Youngblood, S. A., DeNisi, A. S., Molleston, J., & Mobley, W. H. (1984). The impact of worker attachment, instrumentality beliefs, perceived labor union image, and subjective norms on union voting intentions and union membership. *Academy of Management Journal, 27,* 576–590.

PART IV

Epistemology

13

Individual Epistemology

Interpretive Wisdom

Dennis A. Gioia

I f the larger purpose of art is to prompt viewers to see differently, let me begin by asking you to look at the accompanying photo. Let me ask, further, that you not merely look at it but also try to make sense of it. Add another dimension to the cognitive task and try to develop not just one interpretation but rather several interpretations of the ambiguous image before you. Then decide which of your several interpretations is the most plausible to you. Last, rouse your scholarly curiosity and, while you are trying to make sense of the image, reflect on the processes you are engaging to accomplish this little sensemaking challenge. Try it before reading further.

What do you see?

Is it just people climbing a stairway? (If so, why are they surrealistically distorted? It must be more than that.) This image appears in a book on wisdom and organization. Is the artist connecting with that context? Probably. The figures all seem to be a group moving in the same direction. Is it some sort of representation of teamwork? Maybe. But they appear to be on different levels. Might it be a metaphorical study of people climbing up the organizational hierarchy? (So what then is the significance of the halo light?) Could it instead be some dark commentary on the oppressiveness of organizational hierarchies? (Perhaps that explains the dominant black.) Or is the artist asking you to really stretch your interpretive imagination? Possibly the image is meant to be extraorganizational. Maybe it is intended to be an observation on modern society, or maybe its opposite—anarchy. Might it be a symbolic commentary on terrorism? Or nuclear winter? Maybe the intention is more mystical. Might it be a whimsical stairway to heaven? Or maybe it really is serious, even religious—an image of the long day's journey into night, of the soul into the unknown? (Consider, after all, the apparition-like quality of that fourth "person.") Or could the image in conjunction with these previous musings be some sort of sly metacommentary on interpretations? Perhaps it is none of those high-minded notions—only a stark dreamlike image for its own sake. After all, a photograph can be just a photograph. Factually speaking, it is nothing more than exposed silver halide crystals on a sheet of paper or, in the case of the printed image in this book, just half-tone ink on a page—in either case, a chemical representation of an optical representation of . . . what?

Goodness, the interpretive imagination can take flight!

People who see this image want to know, "What is it, really?" If you must know, I shot this image at the Sebring 12-Hour Grand Prix of Endurance race in 1968. In simple descriptive terms, it is a night image of spectators climbing the stairs of a bridge that crosses over the racing circuit. The figures are backlit by the headlights of the onrushing racing cars. Those are the "facts" behind the recording of the image. Yet the image did not come alive meaningfully until I began to work with it in the darkroom. Some simple custom printing techniques produced this surreal version of the original image, including the use of high-contrast photo paper, some judicious "dodging and burning" to accentuate or attenuate features on the negative, and finally some ambiguous distortion achieved by tilting the printing surface to elongate the figures. After all of those manipulations, you have an artistic statement. But a statement of what? Well, that is not for me to decide—especially given that the photo is untitled. The interpretation is up to you. I have done little more than offer a single image that serves as a trigger for your sensemaking. I, and others, have suggested some interpretive possibilities to which you can add those you might have generated. Yet the larger point is that all of those possible interpretations emerge from the same "factual" grounds. This is a centrally important point for the case I would like to make in this chapter and is the root of an approach to a certain kind of wisdom—wisdom that is grounded in an appreciation of the ontology and epistemology of the social and organizational world.

Before we pursue those issues, however, let us develop the entrée notion of artistic interpretation a bit further. Let us lend an additional dimension of vitality to the contextual prompts for sensemaking and make a short transition from the "fine art" form of a static image to the "performing art" form that begins to encompass more dynamism—a key hallmark of the social and organizational experience. Instead of asking for an interpretation of a photo, consider instead a musical example—the Beatles' (1967) *Sergeant Pepper's Lonely Hearts Club Band,* the album that probably has had the most impact on popular music over the past 50 years. More has been read into this music suite and the context surrounding it than into any other album in history.

Various listeners and critics have deemed it to be a profound study in existentialism, perhaps especially because of the final cut, "A Day in the Life" ("I read the news today, oh boy . . . "). Others have found it to be a creative pastiche capturing the British zeitgeist of the 1960s, and still others have pointed to it as a much more universal performance than that. The *New York Times Review of Books* extolled it as "a new and golden Renaissance of song" (cited in Norman, 1981, pp. 292–293). One of England's most famous critics, Kenneth Tynan, went a big step further, hailing the album as "a decisive moment in the history of Western civilization" (p. 293). Timothy Leary went completely over the top in labeling the Beatles as "prototypes of evolutionary agents sent by God with a mysterious power . . . the wisest, holiest, most effective avatars [God incarnations] the human race has ever produced" (p. 293). Impressive, yes?

Other critics have hailed *Sergeant Pepper's* as the closest representation ever recorded of the LSD experience, perhaps most tellingly represented when people noted that one track, "*Lucy* in the *Sky* with *Diamonds*," was a none-too-subtle mnemonic allusion to the drug—a charge that the song's author, John Lennon, vehemently denied, explaining that it was merely his son's literal description of his elementary school drawing. The BBC banned *Sergeant Pepper's* shortly after its release, citing its alleged, if obscure, drug or sexual (but notably not spiritual) references ("I'd love to turn you on"). Others were similarly negative, if no less impassioned, denouncing the music as subversive, both socially and politically.

This was also the first album to include the printed lyrics on the album cover, and the interpretation of these lyrics became a popular pastime— hippies interpreting the lyrics as "commandments" to live by, scholars interpreting them as inspired poetry, moralists interpreting them (alternatively) as either bricks on the path to decadence and decay or bricks on the path to enlightenment and redemption, and members of the John Birch Society seeing them as supplying the guidelines for a Communist conspiracy aimed at undermining democracy itself. Many others saw in the lyrics, the music, and the album cover hidden messages, prophecies, and symbols— perhaps best exemplified by the "Paul Is Dead" hoax, where the album and its cover supposedly contained many hidden clues planted by the Beatles suggesting that Paul McCartney had been killed in a car accident, prompting McCartney not only to deny that the Beatles had planted any clues but also to invoke Mark Twain in noting that reports of his death had been greatly exaggerated.

What were the Beatles intending or attempting to do with this acclaimed masterpiece of rock music? Although the Beatles themselves were aware that *Sergeant Pepper's* was something special even for them, they nonetheless professed innocence of any intended larger (or smaller) messages. They claimed simply to be creating snippet images of British life circa 1966–1967 by putting down words with accompanying music. McCartney is on public record as saying, "We never planned anything! I still don't know what *Sergeant Pepper's* was about" (quoted in Palmer, 1996). Lennon denied any ulterior motive, explaining that "I just shove a lot of sounds together, then shove some words on" (quoted in Norman, 1981, p. 294).

The larger point, of course, is that even if the Beatles intended certain messages or representations, listeners will attribute their own meanings on the basis of their own interpretations given their experiences, motives, predispositions, personal schemas, and the like—as you undoubtedly did in trying to make sense of the introductory photo. It is the interpreter who ascribes meaning and imposes sense on ambiguous presentations. Even if a specific meaning were intended by the performers, it is not the only—or even the most important—meaning associated with the songs in their context.

The leap from making sense of static images or musical lyrics to making sense of social experience is not as great as might first appear. Sensemaking, especially in organizations, occurs in more circumscribed contexts than those posed by open-ended artistic interpretations, but the essence of the experience is surprisingly similar. It is that essence that I would like to take as the centerpiece of this chapter. It is an essence that has grand sweep in social and organizational study, arguably on the order of the most profound observations about the nature of the physical world. That essence is this: When we experience ambiguous presentations—in the form of messages, images, actions, or events—we rely on our sensemaking processes to figure out what we are confronting. When we do that, we create an understanding of the experience that constitutes the reality with which we must then deal. Ours is an interpreted world (Spinelli, 1989; Weick, 1979). What is less evident, and what constitutes the grounds for a form of organizational wisdom, is that the sense we make is the reality we confront.

Let us take one more "pure" example, but this time let us set the sensemaking context in motion. Let us give even more prominence to the dynamism dimension by considering an interpersonal interaction, thereby better representing the kind of cues we deal with in actual social and organizational settings. Including interpersonal dynamism complicates the sensemaking process yet ironically demonstrates that the fundamental principles remain essentially the same, even as the social setting begins to spiral into complexity. Consider the following one-sentence scenario (which I sometimes enact in classes as a demonstration): "Denny strikes Allison on the shoulder." Assume that Denny did indeed physically hit Allison on the shoulder. Nearly all observers of the incident would agree that an event "objectively" occurred. Beyond that point of agreement that Denny struck Allison, we are out of the epistemic world and into an interpreted world.[1]

What did the blow mean? Was it a punch thrown in anger? Was it a "love tap"? Was it some symbol of camaraderie among friends or lovers? Could it be construed as a form of sexual assault? Was it some sort of degrading demonstration of dominance? Was it a joking physically enacted reference to shared inside knowledge? Or, if it occurred in a classroom, was it perhaps a clever intentional demonstration of differences between objective and subjective views about the nature of the social world? It is simply ambiguous unless we appreciate that the meaning is relative to the context and the knowledgeability of players involved. All of the interpretations are potentially viable, depending on the relationship of the actors and the situation in which they find themselves as well as the interpretive framing of the observers. The event itself is epistemically objective; the sense made of it is not. And it is the sense made that constitutes the "reality" with which the observers must cope. Put differently, *the reality we confront is the reality we construe* (Gioia, 2003).

Now, this observation is certainly not new to me. Philosophers have recognized it for millennia (Johnstone, 2006), and psychologists and organizational scholars have written about it for many decades (Merton, 1968). Yet although this view is well acknowledged in many social science literatures, including organization study, it still has an air of being some sort of fringe view. Most organizational scholars are aware of what is commonly termed the *social constructionist* position and view it as one of many (but not necessarily as one of the most important) ways of studying organizations—a position that scholars ostensibly ought to be aware of but need not necessarily account for in their work.

My stance in this chapter is a bit more provocative. I would argue that the social creation of organizational reality is the *only* viable grounds on which we can begin to understand the essential nature of organization. Furthermore, if we define the essence of wisdom as the exercise of informed judgment that leads to sound courses of action, then wisdom itself arises out of recognizing and acting on the constructed (created, invented, fabricated, fictional, illusory, etc.) character of social reality. Constructionism does more than merely infuse the social and organizational world; it *constitutes* the social and organizational world. I will go even further for the sake of acting as an intellectual agent provocateur: Any other way of comprehending the social world can be viewed as a derivative of this pillar of understanding.

Perception Is Reality?

W. I. Thomas is most often credited with the first formal social science statement of the constructionist approach when he famously noted, "If men define situations as real, they are real in their consequences" (Thomas & Thomas, 1928, pp. 571–572).[2] Sexist language aside, there is profundity in this simple observation. Merton (1968) even argued that if the implications of Thomas's assertion were more widely known, people would better understand the workings of our society. Nearly 40 years later, in the modern media and image-laden environment, the statement is more accurate than ever. Modern social and political leaders display an implicit awareness of the phenomenon. For instance, Jesse Jackson, in commenting on changing the impression of African Americans as a basis for racial progress, noted, "We keep struggling to change the definition every day . . . because in a real sense, the struggle is won at the point of definition . . . [and] definition determines winning" (Jackson, 1988, p. 3). Politicians clearly understand the power of perception and image in the construction of influential realities. For better or worse—and such constructions can be used for either virtuous or vicious ends—organizational leaders (and those of us who study them) also need to understand the nature of social reality.

The phrase "perception is reality" has been in the folk lexicon for many years. Jack Valente, in his role in 1967 as adviser to President Lyndon Johnson, used the phrase in commenting on the media presentation of the Vietnam War. But it is important to appreciate that the folk phrase, as apparently astute as it might seem, is itself misconstrued. Perception is akin to apprehension or observation. We must do something with those observations (either cognitively or behaviorally) to make sense of them, so it is not that perception is reality, per se, but that conception is reality—or, if you like, interpretation is reality (or, even more appropriately, sense made is reality). My stance is that there is a nonobvious form of wisdom in recognizing and accepting the created nature of social and organizational reality.

Pillars of the Position

I would like to articulate some of the pillars of this "interpretivist approach," especially those that relate to ontology and epistemology (where ontology has to do with the nature of the phenomenon of interest and epistemology has to do with how we know about the nature of that phenomenon). To accomplish this aim, I sound five major related themes: (a) that the ontology of the social world derives from the construction of reality, (b) that we inhabit an interpreted world largely of our own making, (c) that we collectively construct this created world, (d) that this world is necessarily a relative world, and (e) that we treat this virtual world as if it were objectively real. I take the construction of meaning (sensemaking) as the central issue in the human experience. Although sensemaking processes are not always (or even often) obvious, they dominate life.[3]

Ours Is a Constructed World

First of all, as noted, we interpretivists/constructionists begin with the ontological recognition that social and organizational reality is negotiated via consensual agreement as to the labeling and meaning of features and events. Perhaps the clearest way of distinguishing this stance is to do so by comparison with the ontological assumptions of other domains. I might note, by contrast, that the nature of physical reality is substantive (it is substantively "out there"), that the nature of biological reality is genetic (it is programmed into the genes and, therefore, is substantively "in there"), but that the nature of social reality is created (it resides in our intersubjective interpretations because there is nothing "there" to grasp).[4] So, whereas reality in physical/biological domains can be taken as "located" in objects, genes, structures, facts, and events, social constructionists avoid analogous assertions about the social domain. Reality is instead located in the sense made of facts, events, and the like. That is the reality with which people must deal—that which they invented or enacted themselves. As Weick (1979) put it, "There is not an underlying 'reality' waiting to be discovered. Rather, organizations are viewed as the inventions of people, inventions superimposed on flows of experience and momentarily imposing some order on these streams" (pp. 11–12). The stuff that matters, therefore, is not objective. The paradox here is that the ostensibly fictional "make-believe world" is the "real world" in fact.

There is no hand-waving involved here—just an appreciation for the sensemaking processes brought to bear on the human experience. Yet this notion is difficult for many people to accept because it does not seem to be consistent with our everyday experience. Perhaps the most important point, however, is to see the lay experience as essentially an illusion. I mean "essentially" in its very literal sense; the essence of social reality is illusory. Now, of course, our illusory creations come to be accepted, legitimized, institutionalized, and (over time) treated as though they were objective structures (Berger & Luckmann, 1967). Such structures then serve to both enable and constrain further interpretation and action, so interpretations, actions, and structures form a recursive "structurational" relationship that is defined and accepted as "objective" social reality (Giddens, 1976, 1984). That observation, however, does not obviate the essential character of the social world. It merely tends to disguise it.

I would like to pursue this crucial issue just a bit further, at the risk of boring the members of the choir to whom I might be preaching, with the hope of clarifying this most pivotal point to those who are not (yet) members of the choir. The key to this appreciation is really quite straight-forward. If one believes that reality lies in facts and events, it often leads to a distracting focus on trivial matters (i.e., what happened) rather than on more consequential matters (i.e., the meaning of what happened). Perhaps this is the clearest way to emphasize the importance of understanding ontology and epistemology as a basis for wisdom. In the dynamic world of organizations, it should be clear that people can agree that a given event happened, but the occurrence of the event usually tells us very little (as the example of Denny hitting Allison demonstrates). It is much more important to understand that the sense made of what happened actually constitutes the reality with which people must deal.

Ours Is an Interpreted World

Ours, then, is not a world rendered in objective facts; rather, ours is an interpreted world—a world of sensemaking and sense made as well as sense given to other people. Because of this fairly straightforward recognition, the exasperated expression from so many scholars that there must be an objective referent somewhere comes across as a nostalgic desire for some sort of absolute anchoring in a sea of ongoing ambiguity. There simply is none—not in the world of organizational sensemaking and meaning construction. Let us be clear here. There is no denial of observable facts (e.g., General Motors has more assembly plants than does any other car manufacturer) or events (e.g., BankAmerica acquired MBNA). But neither of those generates social or organizational reality. "Stuff happens to us and because of us. We experience actual economic recession, terrorist attacks that disrupt business, technological innovations that change business practice, etc." (Gioia, 2003, p. 287). It is how we interpret these events and how we act on those interpretations that matters. Traditional organization theorists are fond of making statements implying that multiple interpretations are simply different views attempting to describe one world that is "there" (Meckler & Baillie, 2003). Constructionists see such statements either as naive or as a matter of being seduced by a prior hypothesis bias about the nature of the social world—a phenomenon best described by the colorful phrase, "My mind is made up; do not confuse me with the facts!" The fact is that the facts simply supply the inputs to the sensemaking/reality construction process. Nothing more.

Furthermore, we need to give up the tacit sense that recognizing that there is no substance to social reality is scary. It is not. If anything, it is quite freeing. It allows us to see that we are the enactors of or, at a minimum, the influencers of our realities if we can just get a grip on the processes that produce them. To comprehend and accept this idea is to be on the path to a deeper understanding that sets the stage for organizational wisdom. Now, none of this is to imply that if you do not see the world as interpretivists see it, you do not have wisdom. There are many kinds of wisdom, as is evident from even a quick perusal of this handbook. Yet there is a certain kind of essential fundamental wisdom that derives from recognizing, understanding, and accepting the illusory nature of the social world that confers the potential for more informed ways of working within that world.[5]

Ours Is a Collectively Constructed World

When events occur or a constellation of features presents itself, people in organizations are confronted with occasions for interpretation. How do they accomplish the feat of assembling the data into meaningful patterns? Obviously, they do it on the basis of experience, reasoning, personal schemas, and so on. Yet importantly for understanding organizing, they do it collectively, arriving at some intersubjective mutual consensus about a plausible interpretation that enables the development of workable subsequent courses of action. That is why we refer to the process as social (rather than individual) construction; reality is fashioned via negotiated consensus about plausible practicable sensemaking, sensegiving (Gioia & Chittipeddi, 1991), and action taking.

Even Goldman (1999) missed a basic point when he argued that facts are nothing more than negotiated beliefs. That is a misstatement. It is not that facts are negotiated beliefs; rather, it is that reality is created by negotiating beliefs *about* facts and features in the world. This point seems to me so basic that I have difficulty in understanding why we continue to debate it. I think that the reason is because, despite our disquieting suspicion that there really is something quite ethereal about the nature of the social world, we cling to natural science ways of understanding to try to explain that essential ethereality. It is not that natural science mappings do not explain quite enough, however; it is that they are ontologically and epistemologically inappropriate (and therefore essentially irrelevant) to the task of explaining sensemaking and sensegiving processes.

Ours Is a Relative World

To understand a given event, we need language, as Gorgias pointed out 2,500 years ago (Johnstone, 2006). Epistemologically, language matters. Look at what happens when we entertain different possible linguistic descriptors of the same factual occurrence: Denny hit Allison; Denny tapped Allison; Denny smacked/beat/punched/pummeled/attacked/assaulted/battered Allison. Suddenly the event takes on a whole host of viable interpretations depending on the verbs chosen to describe it, the context in which it occurred, and the particular predispositions of the observers. We now have multiple possible versions of the event, all because of the language used to describe it. This was Wittgenstein's (1967) point of entry into his recognition that the "language game" constituted the reality with which people needed to deal (and also the genesis of his momentous shift from a realist ontology to a constructivist ontology in his understanding of social experience). It also is why public framing of events matters so much in the (post)modern era and why we have seen the rise in prominence of "public relations" offices in corporations over the past generation. Actions matter, but the interpretation of those actions arguably matter more.

There is a profound role for labeling in understanding any event. For that reason, although it might be possible to talk about an unbiased observation (e.g., that an event occurred), it is never possible to talk about unbiased descriptions, judgments, or interpretations. Never. As Mauws and Phillips (1995) noted, "Each language game produces a particular form of life; our participation in a particular language game is fundamentally constitutive of the 'reality' within which we find ourselves" (p. 325). Consequently, language is not the ostensibly neutral medium for communicating facts that it is often cracked up to be; instead, language "determines the epistemological constitution of those facts in the first place" (Astley & Zammuto, 1992, p. 445). From this perspective, there is not one world to be "discovered" but rather as many possible worlds to be invented as there are language games to be used (Astley, 1985; Gergen, 1985; Mauws & Phillips, 1995; Wittgenstein, 1967). Consider your own view of Microsoft Corporation, which undoubtedly has been influenced by years of media coverage. In your view, is Microsoft a predatory giant that wants to take over the global information domain by ruthlessly undermining competitors so that it can rule the world (as its detractors would have it)? Or is Microsoft a marvelously inventive company that uses its capabilities to unite humankind by developing common information technologies that everyone can use (as its boosters would have it)? Your view depends on the language game into which you have bought. The descriptive language is obviously not neutral in either case; rather, it is relative—to values, interests, means, ends, and so on.

Ours Is an "As If" World

It is not necessarily evident to me why the demonstration that the social world is a world invented by its players is subject to such resistance even by scholars. Apparently, the notion that the real world is in some sense (or in any sense) an illusory world is rather spooky even to learned people. Many people who read Weick, Schutz, or Berger and Luckmann are first thrown a bit off balance, but they right themselves, apparently by reasoning that the phenomenal world is a rather narrowly circumscribed world that does not seem to intrude visibly on everyday organizational experience and, therefore, is allowed to lurk in the background undisturbed and largely unmentioned (in a fashion akin to *Harry Potter*'s ominous figure, Voldemort, whose name should not be invoked, lest he come forth and intrude on the world as we would like it to be).

One upshot of interpretivist understanding is the recognition that all structures are human creations. We are veritable masters at reifying those structures and acting toward them "as if" they were objectively there, but they are not—despite the fact that so many otherwise intelligent people seem to be so deep in denial over this recognition. My advice for dealing with this disconcerting awareness is, as I have said before, to accept it. Then ignore it if that gets you through the workday. Act as if. Everybody else does (Gioia, 2003). If we are going to engage this subject at a deep level, however, we need to stop developing convoluted arguments that try to convince us that the stuff that matters is objective. It simply is not. The root fear here seems to be that if we relent and see the social world as interpretivists would have us see it, we would be bereft of grounds for the presumed objectivity that is so cherished by social "science." Correct. Now our charge is to deal with *that* reality. Even Donaldson (1992), a staunch positivist, acknowledged that if we accept interpretive understandings, that does not mean that we cannot treat social facts as if they were objectivities. Virtually all subjectivist scholars accept this point, and that distinguished list includes philosophers, enactment theorists, structurationists, and nearly all other stripes of constructionists, with the notable exception of some radical postmodernists and a few remaining die-hard solipsists.

To many interpretivists, this point is a matter of intellectual honesty. Yes, we acknowledge the practical usefulness of treating social structures as if they were real. Yet as probing scholars, we recognize that they are not. We grant that we can conceive of such a thing as objectivity because we have objectified the conception of the social world and we get along marvelously in this make-believe world—thank you very much—but we insist that we recognize it as the outcome of our collective consensual constructions. Doctoral students often chafe at a requirement to take a course in the philosophy of science. My inveterate response is to ask, "What will your degree say? It will say Ph.D., doctor of philosophy. That title means that you should understand not just theory and methodology but also (and first) ontology and epistemology." And social ontology and epistemology are not quite what they first seem. For that reason, it takes a scholarly sorcerer to grasp the deeper nature of social reality and to point out to the layperson or nonreflective organizational practitioner that what appears to be social fact is not actually the way it first appears. It is profoundly important to recognize these essences.

Revisiting Wisdom

I now view wisdom as *the acquired ability to create viable realities from equivocal circumstances and to use informed judgment to negotiate prudent courses of action through the realities created.* To me, the vital notion in understanding the concept of wisdom is the idea of sound judgment—sound judgment that is based on experience, sound judgment that implies good sense, discretion, diplomacy, and even political sensitivity in choosing workable interpretations and sensible paths of action. And if judgment is indeed the pivotal concept in arriving at wisdom, then informed sensemaking and learned sensegiving are its operative processes. An interesting corollary to this approach to defining wisdom is to note that a wise person is one who is skilled in the "hidden arts, a sorcerer" (*New Webster's Encyclopedic Dictionary,* 1977). In that sense, the person who is wise has tacit or explicit access to the often concealed character of the socially constructed world in which we live. Bradbury (1984) acknowledged as much when he characterized himself as a magician when seeking answers to perennial questions of management and leadership.

Wisdom most often follows from experience—experience that allows the simultaneous expansion of one's repertoire of appropriate schemas for understanding and action and the distillation of that experience into principles that are portable, that is, those that extend to wider domains so that they may inform others' experience. Wisdom often resides in "profound simplicities" (Schutz, 1967) or in the "simple profundities" that allow the development of heuristics for navigating organizational life. Of course, one should constantly retain Whitehead's caution to "seek simplicity, then distrust it" (cited in Bennis, 2003). There is fundamental wisdom, with a small "w," for knowing, understanding, and accepting that social reality is a created reality. Wisdom with a capital "W" comes for *acting* with sound judgment in accordance with that acceptance. Wise judgments lead to informed action (and vice versa). We should be relentlessly attuned to the wisdom in recognizing that wisdom is not just informed judgment; it is judgment that produces knowledgeable and effective action appropriate for a context. Wisdom, then, is actionable knowledge of what works in practice while simultaneously informing knowledgeable action and practice.

Recognizing the recursiveness of knowing and doing is yet another important element of wisdom. As Maslow (1963) noted, a fear of knowing is very much a fear of doing. More to the point, Leonardo da Vinci (an old hero of mine) was inspired by "the urgency of doing! Knowing is not enough. We must act on it. Being willing is not enough. We must do!" A person is wise if he or she knows what to do, not just that he or she understands on some supra level. A person is wise if he or she can extend a principle for understanding and action from a specific instance of personal or vicarious experience to a wider context of practice. A person is wise if he or she can structure understanding for others (give sense) in a way that produces principles for helping those others to cope with problematic constructions created by other people's understandings and enactments.

Wise counsel must be presented in a way that resonates with the recipients' mode of understanding about actionable knowledge. Microsoft founder Bill Gates learned as much in pursuing the charitable work that led to his being named one of the "Persons of the Year" by *Time* magazine in 2005. He noted that Western beliefs about medical practice, as much as Westerners might believe in their scientific basis, might not be workable in another culture. To have actionable knowledge is to account for local beliefs. Wisdom is associated with devising actionable interpretations and constructions of reality that are effective within a specific context.

One upshot of recognizing that interpretations constitute the reality with which we deal, and that these interpretations are negotiated consensually, is the need to develop a willingness to reconsider our own assumptions and interpretations in light of others' viable interpretations. For that reason, multiparadigm sensemaking (cf. Gioia & Pitre, 1990) should prevail. Interpretive wisdom allows one to see and to point out to others that given constructions are illusory and that alternative constructions might better lead to desired outcomes. Interpretive wisdom implies a facile ability to entertain and even adopt markedly different perspectives for understanding—perhaps best illustrated by former Israeli hardliner (and belligerent opponent of compromise) Ariel Sharon, who explained his newly acquired, more receptive stance toward negotiating land deals with the Palestinians after he became prime minister by saying simply, "What you see from here is not what you see from there" (quoted in Derfner, 2006, p. 29). Sharon's constructions of reality had changed as he shifted perspective from being a representative of a narrowly focused point of view to the necessarily broader view of a leader of a nation. The same "portable principle" applies to organizational leaders who are capable of seeing the wisdom in the profoundly simple, but extraordinarily general, notion to "think globally, act locally" in deciding to operate in accordance with sustainable policies in guiding their organizations.

_____ Some Reflection About Writing on Wisdom

When the editors of this volume first asked me to write a chapter on wisdom, I balked on two counts. First, I simply thought it was pretentious of me to write something on wisdom when I was fairly convinced that I had not achieved that august state, even at my advancing age. Second, they wanted me to write, for some unfathomable reason, on the topic of wisdom and epistemology, which struck me as a patently boring subject to tackle. The fact that you are reading this chapter is prima facie evidence that I caved on both counts. Although I still consider it as rather pretentious to presume that I have arrived in the realm of wisdom, I have concluded that wisdom, somehow defined, should be a superordinate goal for any serious scholar—or anybody pursuing Socrates's ideal of the examined life. Similarly, I concluded that talking about ontology and epistemology need not be boring unless I lapse into "academese"—that peculiar form of writing of which we in organization study are so fond. Ontology and epistemology, despite the intimidating labels, are actually rather fascinating subjects to address in trying to understand wisdom.

As a self-described cognitive theorist, I have done my share of self-reflection over the years. I now recognize that I have long been operating under an implicit assumption that there is a developmental progression in the states that precede the arrival at wisdom. That progression looks something like this:

Data → Information → Knowledge → Understanding → Wisdom.

Data are raw facts or basic perceptions, and information is data converted into some coherent form. Both data acquisition and conversion to information are less interesting processes for the purposes of this chapter, so I treat only the latter three in this chain.[6]

I spent my younger years chasing knowledge—usually (mis)conceived as some "thing" to be possessed rather than a dynamic set of interrelationships among concepts. That endeavor was mostly a misguided enterprise because, if for no other reason, it is readily apparent to me that I have forgotten most of the content knowledge I ever learned. I spent my middle years trying to figure out ways of arriving at understanding (i.e., converting essential knowledge into meaningful memorable patterns). Lately, I have been taking tentative steps toward trying to assimilate my distilled knowledge, my direct and vicarious experience, and my synthesized understandings into heuristics that lead to good judgment—good judgment about sound ways of personal and professional being, about sound ways of doing, and about sound ways of counseling others and, thus, imparting wisdom. Nothing has been more helpful to me in these enterprises than recognizing that the reality with which we deal daily is a consensually created reality—and also that as the collective authors of our realities, we are the bearers of the responsibilities and consequences of our own actions. I take to its deepest level Betty Friedan's profound statement, "My version of religion is, 'You are responsible.'" We are responsible—on every level, from individual to organizational to societal—for creating realities for ourselves and others and for assuming the responsibility for dealing with the consequences of those realities. We are the authors of our experience, as organizations are the authors of their experience. The human hand is in the construction of so many events and environments that too often look as if they are produced by higher forces. Of course, the creation of some of these environments can be long-linked, indirect, and circuitous, but we should keep in mind that we are the authors of our contexts, our fates, and our realities (Gioia, 2006). Individually or collectively, we create the realities we confront. Wisdom lies in creating realities that are not only workable but also responsible.

Coda

In 1982, long before I became aware of the writings of Leo Buscaglia, Steven Covey, or Carol Ferrara, I wrote my aging mother a letter because she was despairing that she did not think she had done enough with her life, that she had not gotten it figured out, and that she was not sure whether she was going to leave anything significant behind after she left this world. I felt for her because she really was a smart woman trapped in traditional conceptions (constructions) of what it meant to be a wife and mother. I was not at all sure what to say to her, but I thought a lot about her situation for some time. Then I wrote to her that I had recently had a flash of insight— that for some mysterious reason, I saw life as describable more or less sequentially in terms of "5 Ls":[7]

Living–Loving–Learning–Leaving–Legacy

Living just alludes to entering this world and living in it, albeit subject to social constructions of the person, the group, the organization, and so on. Loving needs no definition or exposition from me. Learning implies moving beyond the acquisition of knowledge to a state of understanding and eventual wisdom about how to be and do. Leaving simply represents my projective belief that exiting gracefully and with acceptance matters. Legacy has to do not only with work but also with remembrance. It revisits wisdom, as well, in the sense that I believe legacy should involve wisdom imparted to others. Now, my mother left a legacy (with her children) of emphasis on achievement and contribution, but she did not recognize it in herself. She did not understand her own role in creating a reality and giving sense to us that carried long beyond her own departure.

My point here is simply that the dynamics and principles underlying the production of reality in the family domain extend in their essence to the organizational domain. Everyone is a sensemaker and a sensegiver. Sensemaking, in its epistemological elements, has to do with how what one knows influences what one can know. Sensegiving has to do with how what one knows influences what others can know (Gioia, 1986). In this way of seeing, organization members engage both processes to create a workable organizational reality, and ideally both should be infused with wisdom. Such wisdom implies the recognition that we are the collective creators of our collective reality. In metaphorical terms, we create a dominant convincing image that seems very real to us—a kind of "great and powerful Oz" image that is so captivating it often distracts us from questioning or exploring the nature of the image itself. If we go looking for the source of that convincing image, however, we find that the wizards behind the curtain, actively working to maintain the image, are none other than ourselves.

Joseph Cardinal Ratzinger, before becoming Pope Benedict XVI, observed, "Pure objectivity is an absurd abstraction. . . . It is not the uninvolved [person] who comes to knowledge. Rather, interest itself is a requirement for the possibility of coming to know" (quoted in Ostling, 1988, p. 41). Your interest in exploring the ontology and epistemology of the organizational world, and my stance that such exploration leads to an understanding that helps to pave a path to at least one form of wisdom, is one of the reasons I asked you to consider your own sensemaking processes as you were looking at the photo introducing this chapter. Contemplative consideration of an ambiguous photograph is merely one of many entrées into a deeper realm of understanding. If it is the artist's job to encourage people to see the world differently—to present images and events that demonstrate how we impose a workable plausibility, a workable clarity, and a workable reality on the essential messiness of life—that is what I have tried to do in this chapter.

In my view, a path through interpretive wisdom is our best hope for understanding the essence of the human organizational experience in human terms. It provides a viable path for accomplishing the great scholarly project of our time—appreciating and acting on the intelligibility of organized human action. We need, above all, to cut loose from our comforting moorings in the ontology and epistemology of the substantive world and to set sail in the sea of ambiguity that is the social and organizational world. If we do that, we at least allow ourselves the opportunity for understanding organization according to its fundamentally subjective ontology—not as we pretend it to be when we fool ourselves into believing it is ontologically objective. And if we can arrive at understanding organizing and organization in this fashion, we set ourselves up for converting common knowledge into some uncommon wisdom.

Notes

1. Of course, we can complicate this little example even further by accounting for Allison's response and further actions and consequences, but my intent is to keep the example at an elemental level. For a much more complete treatment of such "double interacts," see Weick (1979, 1995).

2. Curiously, the earliest published source of this quote is Thomas and Thomas (1928), but W. I. Thomas seems invariably to be given credit for it, probably because he was known to use it frequently in his teaching and lecturing.

3. The following subsections draw heavily from Gioia (2003).

4. Part of my reason for making this point in this way is that some scholars maintain that if one uses the word *nature,* its referent is taken to be physical or (even more often) genetic (cf. the nature vs. nurture debate). It is important to understand, however, that the nature of a phenomenon has to do with its ontological makeup. Because intersubjective interpretation plays such an essential role in sensemaking, social reality actually inheres in consensually created conceptions. That is, the nature of social reality is nonsubstantive—and this seems to contradict the physical/biological definitions of *nature,* both of which are grounded in substantive realities.

5. It is interesting to note that even an understanding of the physical world is susceptible to our imposed attempts to understand it. Consider Burke's (1985) wonderful summation of Heisenberg's delvings into physical uncertainty: "We cannot know if light is a particle or a wave. There is nothing at the fundamental level of existence that you can see as it is, because in seeing it you do something to it. There is no true reality to find, beyond the one you yourself make by looking."

6. Some astute readers might notice that "truth" is missing from this chain. The omission is intentional because truth is itself constructed and, in my view, is subsumed under wisdom. As Lyotard (1984) noted, truth is a human creation.

7. My daughter, Erin, recently noted that I could include a sixth "L," "laughter," as the fourth term in this chain. Seems like pretty good advice.

Appendix

I am an inveterate fan of quotes to express aspects of wisdom. Here are a few for your consideration—ranging from the profound to the whimsical—that relate to my main thesis in this chapter:

> "The real voyage of discovery consists not in seeing new landscapes, but in having new eyes." (Marcel Proust)

"The first responsibility of a leader is to define reality. The last is to say thank you. In between, the leader is a servant." (Max De Pree)

"The best way to predict the future is to invent it." (Alan Kay)

"The optimist proclaims that we live in the best of all possible worlds. The pessimist fears that this is true." (James Branch Cabell)

"He made his Bedlam, let him lie in it." (Anonymous)

"It's now a race between wisdom and senility." (Gerry Susman, on turning 60 years old)

References

Astley, W. G. (1985). Administrative science as socially constructed truth. *Administrative Science Quarterly, 30,* 497–513.

Astley, W. G., & Zammuto, R. G. (1992). Organization science, managers, and language games. *Organization Science, 3,* 443–460.

Beatles. (1967). *Sergeant Pepper's Lonely Hearts Club Band* [music album]. London: EMI Records.

Bennis, W. (2003). *On becoming a leader.* New York: Basic Books.

Berger, P. L., & Luckmann, T. (1967). *The social construction of reality.* Garden City, NY: Doubleday/Anchor Books.

Bradbury, R. (1984). Management from within. *New Management, 1,* 12–15.

Burke, J. (1985). *The day the universe changed* [film documentary]. London: BBC-TV/RKO Pictures.

Derfner, L. (2006, January 16). A warrior's legacy. *U.S. News and World Report,* pp. 27–31.

Donaldson, L. (1992). The Weick stuff: Managing beyond games. *Organization Science, 3,* 461–466.

Gergen, K. J. (1985). Social constructionist inquiry: Context and inquiry. In K. J. Gergen & K. E. Davis (Eds.), *The social construction of the person* (pp. 3–18). New York: Springer-Verlag.

Giddens, A. (1976). *New rules of sociological method.* London: Hutchinson.

Giddens, A. (1984). *The constitution of society.* Berkeley: University of California Press.

Gioia, D. A. (1986). Symbols, scripts, and sensemaking: Creating meaning in the organizational experience. In H. P. Sims, Jr., & D. A. Gioia (Eds.), *The thinking organization* (pp. 49–74). San Francisco: Jossey-Bass.

Gioia, D. A. (2003). Give it up! Reflections on the interpreted world. *Journal of Management Inquiry, 12,* 285–292.

Gioia, D. A. (2006). On Weick: An appreciation. *Organization Studies, 27,* 1709–1721.

Gioia, D. A., & Chittipeddi, K. (1991). Sensemaking and sensegiving in strategic change initiation. *Strategic Management Journal, 12,* 433–448.

Gioia, D. A., & Pitre, E. (1990). Multiparadigm perspectives on theory building. *Academy of Management Review, 15,* 584–602.

Goldman, A. (1999). *Knowledge in a social world.* Oxford, UK: Clarendon.

Jackson, J. (1988, May 4). Making progress on race. *Centre Daily Times* (State College, PA).

Johnstone, C. (2006). Sophistic wisdom: Politike arête and "logosophia." *Philosophy and Rhetoric*.

Lyotard, J. F. (1984). *The postmodern condition: A report on knowledge*. Manchester, UK: Manchester University Press.

Maslow, A. H. (1963). The need to know and the fear of knowing. *Journal of General Psychology, 68*, 111–125.

Mauws, M. K., & Phillips, N. (1995). Understanding language games. *Organization Science, 6*, 322–332.

Meckler, M., & Baillie, J. (2003). The truth about social construction in administrative science. *Journal of Management Inquiry, 12*, 273–284.

Merton, R. K. (1968). *Social theory and social structure* (Enlarged ed.). New York: Free Press.

New Webster's encyclopedic dictionary. (1977). Chicago: Consolidated Book.

Norman, P. (1981). *Shout!* New York: Simon & Schuster.

Ostling, R. N. (1988, August 15). Who was Jesus? *Time*.

Palmer, L. (1996). *All you need is love*. New York: Grossman.

Schutz, A. (1967). *The phenomenology of the social world*. Evanston, IL: Northwestern University Press.

Spinelli, E. (1989). *The interpreted world: An introduction to phenomenological psychology*. London: Sage.

Thomas, W. I., & Thomas, D. S. (1928). *The child in America: Behavior problems and programs*. New York: Knopf.

Weick, K. E. (1979). *The social psychology of organizing* (2nd ed.). Reading, MA: Addison-Wesley.

Weick, K. E. (1995). *Sensemaking in organizations*. Thousand Oaks, CA: Sage.

Wittgenstein, L. (1967). *Philosophical investigations*. Oxford, UK: Blackwell.

14

Interpersonal Epistemology

Wisdom, Culture, and Organizations

P. Christopher Earley
Lynn R. Offermann

The recent spate of corporate scandals, executive denials, and organizational failures may lead people to conclude that many of our modern-day organizations and their leaders are anything but wise. However, rather than viewing organizational wisdom as an oxymoron, organizational scholars such as the chapter authors in this volume are starting to examine issues around the nature of wisdom and how it can be better developed in organizations. Here we join that dialogue by examining wisdom as it is viewed cross-culturally. In contrast to absolutist epistemological views, we argue that wisdom has both universal and more culture-specific aspects.

Wisdom has been defined in many ways and, as we discuss later, is sometimes viewed differently in different locations. At the simplest level, wisdom has been defined as "the power of judging rightly and following the soundest course of action based on knowledge, experience, understanding, etc." (*Webster's New World College Dictionary*, 1997, p. 1533). More recently, Sternberg (2003) defined wisdom as the application of successful intelligence and creativity as mediated by values toward the achievement of common good by balancing intrapersonal, interpersonal, and extrapersonal interests.[1] One of the most prominent and extensive efforts to examine the wisdom construct has been by Paul Baltes and his colleagues at the Max Plank Institute, who, under the heading of the Berlin wisdom paradigm, conceptualize wisdom as both a cognitive and motivational metaheuristic (pragmatic) that serves to orchestrate knowledge toward excellence in mind and virtue on both individual and collective levels (Baltes & Staudinger,

2000). Like Sternberg, the Berlin paradigm scholars describe wisdom as an interplay of intellectual, affective, and motivational components that involves positive intentions for the well-being of self and others.

Research using the Berlin paradigm has shown wisdom to be a unique construct with many predictors, none of which is sufficient alone to fully grasp its breadth. Significant predictors included traditional scales of fluid and crystallized intelligence, personality, life experience, and the interface between personality and intelligence. The personality–intelligence interface included variables such as social intelligence, cognitive style, and creativity, and it contributed the largest share of unique variance in wisdom-related performance (Baltes & Staudinger, 2000). In this chapter, we adopt the definition of wisdom articulated in the Berlin paradigm and suggest that one of the predictors of wisdom-related performance in multicultural contexts is cultural intelligence.

Cultural intelligence is the ability to function effectively in a diverse context where the assumptions, values, and traditions of one's upbringing are not shared uniformly with those with whom one needs to work. If culture is considered as the collective mental programming that distinguishes members of one human group from those of another (Hofstede, 1980), cultural intelligence is the ability to function successfully in environments where individuals have experienced different programming. Earley and Ang (2003) defined cultural intelligence as "a person's capability to adapt effectively to new cultural contexts" (p. 59). This is a form of "intelligence in context," where the "right answers" are dependent on the situation and the people involved. Cultural intelligence typifies an interaction between traditional cognitive intelligence, culturally relevant knowledge and experience, and personality and motivational characteristics that would be required for someone to be perceived as wise in a cross-cultural setting.

We maintain that in organizational life, intelligent action and wise action coincide if the intelligent action is directed in a positive direction. The concept of intelligence typically is defined as successful adaptation to a given situation; as shown in the definitions offered by Sternberg (2003) and Baltes and Staudinger (2000), wisdom goes beyond intelligence as successful adaptation where success is defined by cultural and personal benefit of the community, a sense of moral rightness. This means that there can be intelligent but unwise organizational actions, but when an action is intelligent and directed toward the moral good of society and individuals, it is deemed "wise." As Malan and Kriger (1998) put it, "Managerial wisdom is the ability to detect those fine nuances between what is right and what is not" (p. 249).

What does all of this mean for organizations? First of all, it means that organizations need to recognize that the attribution of wisdom can shift based on cultural context. On some aspects of wisdom, there is little disagreement, but differential emphases and unique aspects across cultures would make "wise" people look different and behave quite differently in different places.

Thus, it is risky for diverse organizations to assume that there would be full agreement in identifying their more "wise" members. Knowledge, experience, and a commitment to group or organization goals beyond what might benefit someone personally are a good universal foundation for identifying the wise. But those who push that knowledge aggressively might well be viewed as intelligent but foolish to some non-Westerners, whereas the modest and discreet presentation of wise non-Westerners might not be listened to as carefully as it should be by Western staff members.

Understanding these nuances and their implications for organizations requires a more careful examination of the nature of culture. In this chapter, we begin by discussing the basic nature of culture as it relates to wisdom and intelligence. We then proceed to examine the constructs of wisdom and intelligence in a cross-cultural context, highlighting commonalities as well as differences. From there, we take a more detailed look at four major areas of organizational concern that have implications for the application of wisdom in cross-cultural contexts within organizations: cross-cultural training, leadership, multinational teams, and multinational organizations.

Basic Nature of Culture

A useful distinction for our chapter is to separate and define culture from related constructs. Kluckhohn (1954) defined culture as patterned ways of thinking, feeling, and reacting to various situations and actions. It is acquired and transmitted mainly by symbols, including their embodiments in artifacts. The essential core of culture consists of historically derived and selected ideas and especially their attached values. Culture can be seen as shaping the nature of social structures as they grow and adapt. Hofstede (1991) provided a commonly cited definition of culture. His view holds that culture is best represented as a set of programs for people within a nation—the "software" of the mind. This approach has the strength of capturing a sense of culture as a psychological variable (Earley & Mosakowski, 2004). Societies shape their collectivities and social aggregates according to the rules implied by culture. Culture is sometimes viewed in terms of antecedents such as time, language, and locality variables as well as historical and ecological commonalities. Culture is a set of imperfectly shared rules for behavior and meanings attached to such behavior (Martin, 1992).

Although this discussion provides a sufficient distinction of culture from related constructs, an additional complication arises in discussing concepts that are unique and idiosyncratic to particular cultures, in contrast to those that are common across cultures. Clearly, this is a critical issue in discussing something such as wisdom and intelligence, and arguments have been made for decades concerning the universality versus particularism of such constructs (Berry, 1990, 2003, 2004; Sternberg & Grigorenko, 2006; Triandis, 1972). Before we tackle the specific differences and similarities of these

constructs across boundaries, a more general discussion of cultural specificity is warranted, and we turn to this in the next subsection.

Emic and Etic Constructs

Another important assumption of wisdom and intelligence is that both
emic and etic constructs and processes exist in a cultural setting (for more
complete discussions of these issues, see Berry, 1990; Earley & Mosakowski,
1996, 2004). Briefly, a construct is considered as emic if it has its basis
within a given culture (or group of cultures), and it is fully appreciated only
within this context. An emic construct gains meaning from its context, and
it cannot be appreciated fully absent a contextual interpretation.

Some constructs are etic or universal (Berry, 1990; Earley & Mosakowski,
1996), existing across cultures. Many constructs are presumed to be etics,
only to find that they are not truly universal. An example of a universal is
that all people have certain cognitive functions such as memory and recall
(with the exception of people suffering from some impairment). Although
people's memories and ability to recall events differ, these cognitive functions are ubiquitous. Some social institutions are etic, including marriage
and mourning of a lost loved one (Berry, 1997; Resaldo, 1989). The existence of a psychological universal is difficult to establish and defend.
Murdock (1945) developed a list of 70 cultural universals that he argued
were exhaustive and could be used to describe differences and similarities
among cultures. These universals included variables such as food taboos,
hospitality, trade, etiquette, and folklore.

There are a number of constructs that only appear to be universals. Berry
(2003) referred to these constructs as imposed-etics (what Triandis, 1972,
referred to as pseudo-etics) or constructs that are derived in a limited
number of cultural systems but that do not really apply beyond the fringes
of these cultures. An etic is imposed if it is developed in one subset of
cultures and applied to others even if it is inappropriate to do so. Earley and
Mosakowski (1996) described a parallel notion of the pseudo-emic, meaning that some constructs are assumed to be idiosyncratic and unique but, in
fact, are not. An imposed-etic captures some generalizability across cultures
while being relatively situation specific.

What about wisdom or intelligence? Are there norms, regardless of the
culture, suggesting an appropriate (and hence wise) direction for problem
solving and adaptation? Not only would identifying such norms border on
the impossible; the results of such a daunting task would not be testable
using traditional statistical methods (for further discussions of this point,
see Earley & Mosakowski, 1996; Leung & Bond, 1989). Most psychological and sociological principles fall into a derived-etic category. These constructs are an attempt at taking emic instances of some entity and building
it into a general principle.

Perhaps a more tenable approach to the study of wisdom and intelligence across cultures may be related to the structure of the constructs as opposed to their content and prescription. That is, the moral or value base of a culture provides guidance concerning the content of what constitutes wisdom, whereas its structure may be predicated on particular universals. In the next subsection, we describe a framework provided by James Q. Wilson in his book *The Moral Sense* (Wilson, 1993).

Moral Foundation of Wisdom

From a strictly structural viewpoint, wisdom might be described as an individual's capacity to inculcate and express the moral imperatives of a society. The specific nature of these morals may be manifested emically (i.e., specifically defined within a culture) even while they transcend cultural boundaries and are etic. For example, all societies have a taboo against the purposeful and wanton killing of other people (Mead, 1934). However, this is not to say that killing other humans is a universal moral value across societies (Mead, 1934; Resaldo, 1989). In a head-hunting tribe of Papua New Guinea, tribesmen consider the killing and consumption of an enemy's flesh as desirable because the enemy is considered as less than human in their eyes.

Some believe that wisdom has a moral underpinning leading to the living of a good and righteous life. Moral wisdom reflects the capacity to judge rightly what should be done in various contexts so that one's life (and the lives of others) is better. Baltes and Kunzmann (2004) argued that wisdom not only is a cognitive process but also requires an integration of cognitive, emotional, and motivational characteristics. Most important in their definition is the existence of a motivational element having a moral basis underlying emotions and values. Tantamount in their discussion of wisdom was creating a generally beneficial environment for all individuals, that is, providing a societally beneficial outcome from one's actions. What, then, constitutes a moral foundation from which a societally beneficial outcome might be defined?

Wilson (1993) argued that there are universal moral imperatives. He argued that there are four general moral anchors across societies and that these moral orientations provide a general perspective of how more specific cultural (and personal) values are formed. Wilson's four universal morals are sympathy, fairness, self-control, and duty, and he argued that these four sentiments constitute a moral sense in all people. Sympathy refers to a capacity for being affected by the experiences of others. Fairness reflects the outcome and procedural standards by which actions are judged as fair or just, a finding well supported in an organizational context (for more general discussions of justice, see Greenberg, 1996; Greenberg & Lind, 2000; Lind & Earley, 1992; Lind & Tyler, 1988; Thibaut & Walker, 1978). The most common allocation of scarce resources is through the application of one of three rules: equity (in relation to input), equality (equal shares regardless), and need (based on a person's needs). Self-control refers to an individual's restraint in the present on behalf of the future, or delayed gratification. An organization that channels its extra profits into research and development rather than issuing extra dividends will ensure a more profitable future for itself and its shareholders. Finally, Wilson's (1993) concept of duty refers to an individual's willingness to be faithful to obligations derived from society, family, and important referent others.

Extending this framework of moral values to the cultural bounded (unbounded) nature of wisdom, it is the content of a desirable (culturally and personally beneficial) course of action that is defined by these four moral parameters. That is, if we refer back to Csikszentmihalyi and Rathunde's (1990, p. 25) criteria of wisdom's meaning—(a) a cognitive process or way of knowing; (b) a virtue in which wisdom became the best guide for the supreme good, providing the most compelling guide to action; and (c) a personal good, meaning that it was an intrinsically rewarding experience that provided some of the highest enjoyment and happiness available—it is clear that a moral underpinning must be used to delineate what is captured in the second and third criteria. For example, Wilson's (1993) view is that all cultural communities have a standard of fairness in exchange relationships, and this point was reiterated by Fiske (1991). Likewise, Wilson's idea of duty and obligation suggest universally that wisdom reflects actions having positive consequences for one's compatriots even as the manifestation of duty may vary from caring for the elderly (e.g., Northern Europe) to voluntary banishment (e.g., some Artic Circle communities).

The very idea of a cultural moral absolute is controversial and not without criticism, but we believe that if such an anchor is lacking, the notion of wisdom reduces to a relativism that is not very useful for managerial application. Now that we have discussed some potential moral structures that underpin wisdom, we are in a position to relate them to the general cultural values that capture variation across the globe.

Comparisons of Wisdom and Intelligence Across Cultures

Evolutionary epistemology suggests that knowledge is constructed by people so as to adapt to their environments. Presumably, then, knowledge may be constructed differently by people living in different environments or cultures. The nature of wisdom and intelligence as they differ across cultural boundaries has been an area of avid attention in the cross-cultural literature for decades, dating back to work on problem solving and learning by anthropologists such as Levi-Strauss (1969). More accurately, attention has been paid to the varying nature of intelligence primarily with secondary attention extended to the idea of wisdom. As attention returned to the concept of intelligence during the late 1960s and early 1970s, Berry and his colleagues renewed the interest and debate concerning intelligence and its potential relativism. In reaction to the reductionist and absolutist perspectives expressed by traditional work on intelligence, a number of critics have voiced alternative definitions of the construct. Probably the most prominent and long-standing critic of research on intelligence is John Berry, who argued that existing work on intelligence fails to capture the essential richness of a cultural context. Berry suggested that the existing definitions of intelligence are largely Western, are overly restrictive, and typically are tested using Western methods having dubious value in non-Western cultures. He suggested that intelligence is best considered to be reflective of a set of cognitive tools that help a group of people to operate in a particular ecological context (Berry, 2003).

The definition of intelligence offered by Berry seems to capture the difficult nature of understanding intelligence in a cross-cultural context. The type of radical cultural relativism (Berry, 2003; Berry & Ward, 2006) that Berry discussed reflects a potential contrast to a universalist view even though his ecocultural framework has absolutist features. An advantage of the ecocultural approach is that it offers a "value-neutral" framework for describing and interpreting similarities and differences in human behavior across cultures (Berry, 2003). According to Berry and Ward (2006),

> As adaptive to context, psychological phenomena can be understood "in their own terms" (as Malinowski insisted), and external evaluations can usually be avoided. This is a critical point since it allows for the conceptualization, assessment, and interpretation of culture and behaviour in non-ethnocentric ways. . . . It explicitly rejects the idea that some cultures or behaviours are more advanced or more developed than others. . . . Any argument about cultural or behavioural differences being ordered hierarchically requires the adoption of some absolute (usually external) standard. But who is so bold, or so wise, to assert and verify such a standard? (p. 68)

Berry and Ward (2006) argued that the sociopolitical context brings about contact among cultures, so that individuals need to adapt to more than one context. When many cultural contexts are involved (as in situations of culture contact and acculturation), psychological phenomena can be viewed as attempts to deal simultaneously with two (sometimes inconsistent and sometimes conflicting) cultural contexts. These attempts at understanding people in their multiple contexts is an important alternative to the totalitarian approach of colonialism reflecting many traditional approaches to expansion.

Many studies confirm differences in the patterns and styles of decision making and thinking of Western and non-Western cultures related to cultural values on social perception (Miller, 1984, 1997; Nisbett, Peng, Choi, & Norenzayan, 2001; Shweder & LeVine, 1984). For example, Chiu (1972) argued,

Chinese are situation-oriented. They are obliged to be sensitive to their environment. Americans are individual-centered. They expect their environment to be sensitive to them. Thus, Chinese tend to assume a passive attitude, while Americans tend to possess an active and conquering attitude in dealing with their environment. (p. 236) . . . [The American] orientation may inhibit the development of a tendency to perceive objects in the environmental context in terms of relationships or interdependence. On the other hand, the Chinese child learns very early to view the world as based on a network of relationships; he is *socio-oriented* or *situation-centered*. (p. 241, italics in original)

This rather well-accepted notion of context sensitivity is well rooted in Hall's (1976) work that we described earlier as well as in Witkin's work on field dependence/independence (Witkin & Goodenough, 1977), among other sources. More recent empirical and conceptual work following in this tradition was presented by Nisbett and his various colleagues (for a review, see Nisbett et al., 2001). For example, Masuda and Nisbett (2001) presented Japanese and American participants with pictures of animated scenes of fish, and they were asked to report what they had seen. As expected, the Americans generally focused on the focal fish in the scene, whereas the Japanese tended to focus on background elements. Furthermore, the Japanese overall tended to make more references to the background scene and relationships among elements within the scene itself.

However, the contrast of Eastern and Western thinking is not so simple as might be assumed based on the arguments of Nisbett and colleagues (2001). For example, in a comparative study between India and the United States, Miller (1984) found that Indian Hindus use more concrete and contextually qualified descriptions of people they know than do Americans. She also found that Americans made attributions according to personal dispositions more often than did Indian Hindus, who tended to attribute behavior to the situation. Yet there were no significant differences between the two groups in tests of abstract thinking. This finding rules out cognitive deficit and strengthens the impact of indigenous cultural meanings. Cultural orientations such as individualism–collectivism may help to explain this result. Americans stress autonomy and self-reliance, whereas Indian Hindus view the person as related to others. Sociocentric cultural premises, rather than a lack of abstract skills, may be related to Indians' focus on interpersonal context and behavior.

In contrasting high-context versus low-context cultures, we see additional evidence of culture's influence on decision making and what might be construed as wise decision making. In conflict situations, members of low-context cultures handle conflicts by using a factual–inductive style or an axiomatic–deductive style more often than do members of high-context cultures. High-context cultures tend to avoid direct confrontation (Erez & Earley, 1993). For example, in China an executive is advised to solve a conflict between two subordinates by meeting separately with the two of them, whereas in the United States the supervisor is advised to meet jointly with the two sides of the conflict (Bond, 1997; Bond, Leung, & Giacalone, 1985). Differences between high- and low-context cultures influence communication between superiors and subordinates as well. This approach can be seen in superior–subordinate relationships. In low-context cultures, superiors directly criticize subordinates for poor-quality work, but in high-context cultures, superiors are very careful not to do so in public (Earley, 1997) or with such directness that subordinates' feelings will be negatively and directly affected.

Yang and Sternberg (1997a) reviewed Chinese philosophical conceptions of intelligence. The Confucian perspective emphasizes the characteristic of benevolence and of doing what is right. As in the Western notion, the intelligent person spends a great deal of effort in learning, enjoys learning, and persists in lifelong learning with a great deal of enthusiasm. The Taoist tradition, in contrast, emphasizes the importance of humility, freedom from conventional standards of judgment, and full knowledge of oneself as well as of external conditions. The difference between Eastern and Western conceptions of intelligence may persist even in the present day (Nisbett, 2003; Yang & Sternberg, 1997a, 1997b). Yang and Sternberg (1997b) studied contemporary Taiwanese Chinese conceptions of intelligence and found five factors underlying these conceptions: (a) a general cognitive factor much like the g factor in conventional Western tests, (b) interpersonal intelligence (i.e., social competence), (c) intrapersonal intelligence (d) intellectual self-assertion, and (e) intellectual self-effacement.

Grigorenko and colleagues (2001) studied conceptions of intelligence in Kenya among various rural communities. They identified four different concepts capturing intelligence—*rieko* (knowledge and skills), *luoro* (respect), *winjo* (comprehension of how to handle real-life problems), and *paro* (initiative)—with only the first referring directly to knowledge-based skills (including, but not limited to, the academic).

There is clearly less cross-cultural information on wisdom than there is on intelligence. Nonetheless, researchers have examined both implicit and explicit perspectives on wisdom in a variety of cultures. Table 14.1 attempts to organize wisdom dimensions found by various researchers into four major categories: cognitive capability (likely the aspect of wisdom most closely related to conceptions of intelligence); the application of cognitive competencies to the issues of life, including judgment, experience, procedural knowledge, and sagacity; interpersonal capacities, including relatedness, compassion, and caring for others; and a more personal dimension of demeanor associated with those deemed most wise. As shown, there are some elements of wisdom conceptions that appear to be shared across the various cultural samples. Most prominent among them is the cognitive/analytical aspect of wisdom that is emphasized in Western definitions. While emphasized by Western definitions, these capabilities are recognized

Table 14.1 Aspects of Wisdom Categorized by Type and Nationality

		Dimension of Wisdom			
Subject Sample	Author(s)	Cognitive Capability	Applied Cognition	Interpersonal Capacity	Personal Demeanor/Attitude
United States and Australia	Takahashi & Bordia (2000)	**Knowledgeable**	• Intuitive • Experienced		
United States	Sternberg (1985, 1990)	• Reasoning ability • Learning from ideas and environment	• Sagacity • Judgment • Expeditious use of information • Perspicacity		
Canada	Holliday & Chandler (1986)	• Exceptional understanding • General competencies	Judgment and communication skills	Interpersonal skills	Social unobtrusiveness
Germany	Baltes & Smith (1990)	• Factual knowledge • Relativism	• Procedural knowledge • Ability to understand and manage uncertainty	Life span contextualism	
U.S. Hispanics	Valdez (1994)			Service/caring in relationships	• Spiritual aspects • Attitude toward learning
Tibetan Buddhist monks	Levitt (1999)	Ability to recognize Buddhist truths about reality		Compassionate	• Being beyond suffering • Being oneself • Treating all creatures as worthy and equal

Table 14.1 (Continued)

Subject Sample	Author(s)	Dimension of Wisdom			
		Cognitive Capability	Applied Cognition	Interpersonal Capacity	Personal Demeanor/Attitude
India	Takahashi & Bordia (2000)	Knowledgeable	Awakened		**Discreet**
Japan	Takahashi & Bordia (2000)	Knowledgeable	Experienced	Awakened	• **Discreet** • Aged
Japan	Takayama (2002)	Knowledge and education	Understanding and judgment	Sociability and interpersonal relationships	Introspective attitude
Taiwan	Yang (2001)	Competencies and knowledge	Openness and profundity	Benevolence and compassion	Modesty and unobtrusiveness

NOTE: Characteristics in bold were viewed as closest to wisdom in multidimensional space.

in most cultural samples as important, albeit not necessarily primary determinants of wisdom. Eastern cultures tend to emphasize more social, interpersonal, spiritual, or affective components of wisdom, stressing discretion, modesty, and unobtrusiveness as key components of wisdom while also incorporating the knowledge and experience components that dominate Western views. Recent Western views, such as Sternberg's (2003) balance theory of wisdom, have begun to offer more extensive views of wisdom that incorporate the traditional Eastern perspective, proposing that wisdom is the application of successful intelligence toward the common good that stems from a balance of intrapersonal, interpersonal, and extrapersonal interests. Similarly, Takahashi and Overton (2005) presented an inclusive developmental model of wisdom that integrates the traditionally Western analytical approach to wisdom with the more traditionally Eastern synthetic/integrative approaches. Thus, the integration of the various capacities becomes important in differentiating the wise from the unwise.

Thematically, it appears that across samples wisdom has two consistent components. Wise people are conceived of broadly as possessing superior knowledge, which they apply to real-world situations. Despite these commonalities, the parameters surrounding these components, the behavioral styles in which they are enacted, and their meaning in everyday life can be substantially different depending on culture. Although most definitions assume that the wise work for the common good, the Japanese word for wise, usually a positive characteristic, can also imply the evil wisdom of a cunning strategist (Takahashi & Overton, 2005). Non-Western cultures add a component that involves the way wise people comport themselves, usually identifying modesty, discretion, and/or social unobtrusiveness as characteristic of the wise—a demeanor unlikely to be associated with wisdom in Western societies. We examine the more emic, culture-specific aspects of wisdom in terms of specific organizational applications in the next section.

Applications of Culturally Based Wisdom and Intelligence to Organizational and Managerial Issues

Cultural Training

The approach we take in this section is to discuss wisdom and intelligence in the context of preparing a manager for a global or expatriate assignment.[2] We draw from work on what is now referred to as "cultural intelligence" (Earley, 2002; Earley & Ang, 2003; Earley & Mosakowski, 2004; Earley & Peterson, 2004; Offermann & Phan, 2002; Thomas & Inkson, 2004). In particular, we draw heavily from Earley and Peterson (2004) in their discussion of cultural intelligence in relation to intercultural training for managers.

According to Earley and Ang (2003), cultural intelligence consists of three aspects: metacognitive/cognitive, motivational, and behavioral elements. The metacognitive/cognitive aspect refers to general cognitive skills that are used to create new specific conceptualizations of how to function and operate within a new culture as well as culture-specific knowledge (both declarative and procedural). The general (or meta-level) skills reflect etic categories of definition (e.g., long-term pairing of mating partners, or the so-called marriage institution) as well as meta-level procedural aspects (e.g., styles of cognizing and discovery).

The second element of cultural intelligence refers to the motivational basis for cultural intelligence. By this, it is meant that for a person to adapt successfully to a new cultural setting, the person must be able to cognize and understand a culture, but he or she also must feel motivated to engage others in the new setting. Without such motivation, adaptation will not occur, and so we argue that this does not reflect cultural intelligence. If an individual is unmotivated and will not engage the world, why would we expect to find evidence of adaptation? In this usage, Earley and Ang (2003) looked at several aspects of motivation, including self-efficacy expectations, goal setting, and self-concept through identity.

The final element of cultural intelligence refers to the capability of an individual to actually engage in behaviors that are adaptive. Earley and Ang (2003) argued that cultural intelligence reflects a person's ability to generate appropriate behaviors in a new cultural setting. Without this aspect of cultural intelligence, a person may be able to cognize what is appropriate in a given culture and feel motivated to move forward, but the person will be unable to do so if the appropriate response is not in his or her repertoire.

There are a wide range of methods and techniques used in intercultural training, but many of these approaches lack a rigorous theoretical underpinning. They tend to be highly piecemeal, throwing all available methods at the training dilemma. A few of the dominant training methods having the best overall efficacy include country- and cultural values–based assimilators, experiential training, self-awareness training, and behavioral training. We then propose the alternative of a cultural intelligence framework to cultural training.

Cultural Values–Based Assimilators

One of the best methods developed for intercultural training (i.e., having the most rigorous conceptual and empirical validation) is referred to as a country-based cultural assimilator. In a cultural assimilator, a wide range of social behaviors key to operating effectively in the culture are identified a priori and are adapted into a programmed instruction form. In this instruction format, a learner is given a scenario (e.g., how to introduce one's boss to a fellow employee) and is provided with multiple-choice alternative actions from which to choose. After making a choice, the individual determines whether his or her choice was appropriate and then proceeds to additional scenarios if the correct answer was given. If not, the learner returns to the item to make another selection and so on until the correct answer is learned.

A variation on a traditional country-based cultural assimilator was presented by Bhawuk, Brislin, and their colleagues (Bhawuk, 1998, 2001; Bhawuk & Brislin, 1992; Brislin & Yoshida, 1994). Rather than focusing on a particular target country, the emphasis is on a target cultural value that can be shared across countries. For example, Bhawuk's (2001) individualism cultural assimilator draws from core culture theory (Triandis's [1995] theory of individualism–collectivism) to create critical incidents that apply across countries rather than emphasizing an observed (i.e., atheoretic) incident. Critical incidents are drawn from individualism–collectivism theory and cover a wide range of social behaviors based on the self, goal prioritization, and motivation factors (Earley & Peterson, 2004).

Experiential Training

In experiential training, the emphasis is on applied training and techniques, including role-plays, field visits, and simulations. Participants are engaged more affectively as they participate in work samples of the actual target culture. For example, participants can be put in social situations with representatives from other cultures in simulated social or work events. The downside of this kind of training, however, is that it typically is emotionally demanding for both the participants and the trainers.

Self-Awareness Training

Self-awareness training involves raising the trainees' awareness of their own culture and of typical reactions that people from other cultures have to them. These programs also focus on the potential loss of self-esteem in these settings. Self-awareness training helps participants to become more aware of their own values, attitudes, and behaviors using methods that contrast with their own culture and the target culture. Trainers behave in sharp contrast to the preferred behavior of the participants (e.g., a culture contrast), explain the reasons for their actions, and highlight the trainees' discomfort with the experience.

Behavior Training

Finally, in behavior training, the emphasis is on observable behavior. Trainees practice displaying behaviors appropriate for the target culture across various scenarios. There is also an emphasis on behavior regulation and monitoring of one's own actions, including nonverbal displays such as body orientation, proxemics, and social distances. This type of training is demanding of its participants and is time-consuming, so it typically is not used in intercultural training programs.

A Cultural Intelligence Framework for Training

Although these various methods have their positive features, an alternative approach is that proposed by Earley and Peterson (2004) in applying a cultural intelligence framework to training. Although the content of country or culture specifics differs by definition, wisdom or intelligence in this context implies that the means of acquiring knowledge and behavioral capability is universal. That is, the facets of cultural intelligence operate across all cultures to aid a person in acquiring culture-specific content. In this sense, cultural intelligence refers to wisdom of a universal nature, whereas the specific content of what is learned for a given culture or setting is idiosyncratic or emic.

Cognitive aspects of cultural intelligence reflect the specific knowledge of content and process concerning a target culture that is acquired through metacognitive mechanisms. That is, cognitive cultural intelligence captures the *what, who, why,* and *how* of intercultural interaction. This aspect of cultural intelligence is well addressed through culture assimilators and other knowledge-based training systems. Interventions focusing on the acquisition of culture-specific knowledge through documentary and experiential methods may help people to understand more about a given culture.

Methods focusing on the motivational facet of intelligence are tied most heavily to the values orientation approach often employed in intercultural training. That is, an emphasis on cultural values not only provides specific knowledge about a target culture but also is intended to develop empathy. This assumption has an obvious shortcoming in that a person may feel highly empathetic and positive toward a host culture but still lack the efficacy to deal with the challenges he or she inevitably faces. Cultural experiences need to be leveraged as a means of building and enhancing efficacy through proximate mastery situations. One possible way of doing this is to expose an uninitiated person through a series of short, simple, and controlled intercultural interactions in a classroom setting. As the trainee builds confidence, greater complexity could be added, progressively graduating to an actual encounter.

Leadership

Another area of organizational application of wisdom and intelligence is in leadership. Examining the implicit theories of leadership that people hold about leader characteristics suggests that people inherently believe that leaders are—or at least should be—intellectually capable, wise individuals. In a study of both students and working adults, Offermann, Kennedy, and Wirtz (1994) examined the content of people's implicit theories about leadership and found support for a cognitive capability factor as one of eight core dimensions of people's leader perceptions. In order of decreasing factor loading, this factor was composed of six items: intelligent, knowledgeable, wise, clever, educated, and intellectual. Thus, respondents naively saw both intelligence and wisdom as being prototypic of leaders, with both concepts clustered with the experientially based characteristics of being knowledgeable and educated as well as intellectual. In contrast, much of the leadership literature has been less positive about the contributions of intelligence to leadership. A recent meta-analysis of 151 independent samples found that the correlation between intelligence and leadership was .21 (uncorrected for range restriction) and .27 (corrected) (Judge, Colbert, & Ilies, 2004). Although this is a modest relationship, industrial/organizational psychologists maintain that even moderate validities can have substantial practical applications (Schmidt & Hunter, 1998). Perceptual measures of intelligence had much stronger correlations with leadership than did paper-and-pencil measures of intelligence, supporting implicit theories of leadership by suggesting that leadership status is given to those who manage to acquire a reputation for intelligence rather than necessarily being the most intelligent. Additional research is needed to determine whether reputedly intelligent leaders with less intelligence than that attributed to them could ever be viewed as wise.

These meta-analytic results also supported cognitive resources theory (Fiedler & Garcia, 1987), which proposes that leader stress level and directiveness moderate the intelligence–leadership relationship. According to this theory, leader stress diverts intellectual capabilities from the task, resulting in lower effectiveness, whereas directive leader behavior enhances effectiveness as the leader's superior intellectual ability is communicated clearly to followers. As would be predicted, Judge and colleagues' (2004) meta-analysis found that intelligence and leadership were more strongly correlated when leader stress was low and when leaders exhibited more directive leadership behaviors.

The modest relationship of leadership and intelligence may occur because it might not be intelligence per se that matters in leadership; instead, it might be the relative intelligence of leaders to their followers (Bass, 1990; Stogdill, 1948). Researchers have suggested that leaders can be most successful when they are slightly more intelligent, but not too much more intelligent, than their followers. As Gibb (1969) put it, "The evidence suggests that every increment of intelligence means wiser government, but that the crowd prefers to be ill-governed by people it can understand" (p. 218). This proposition was supported by Simonton (1985), who proposed a curvilinear relationship between intelligence and a person's influence over other group members (an indication of leadership), such that there would be a high correlation between the group mean IQ and the IQ of its most influential member, with a leader–follower IQ gap of between 8 and 20 points, depending on organizational level, and with smaller leader–follower gaps at more senior levels of an organization's hierarchy. Thus, intelligence may set the stage for leadership, but many other factors are involved in successful leadership as well.

Culturally Intelligent Leadership

One of these factors is the lack of leader training in dealing with cultural diversity. For many leaders, the scope of their intelligence may be limited to settings where they are more familiar. To the extent that wisdom depends on accumulated experiences, leaders faced with increasingly diverse followers may have difficulties. Unfortunately, leadership scholars have not devoted much time to rethinking traditional theories to accommodate the more diverse "followership" that is becoming common in modern organizations around the world (Offermann, 1998). Cultural intelligence, as described earlier, is a life skill in today's pluralistic societies that is particularly relevant to those who seek to lead. Although cultural intelligence is desirable for anyone who functions in multicultural environments, it is particularly important for leaders who are responsible for maximizing the value of a multicultural workforce. We suggest that the ability to engage in the mental processes and adaptive behaviors needed to function effectively as a leader in collective environments where there is a diverse followership is culturally intelligent leadership (Offermann & Phan, 2002). Wise leadership will become increasingly synonymous with culturally intelligent leadership.

Research shows that demographic differences between leaders and followers can affect follower effectiveness and satisfaction. For example, Tsui and O'Reilly (1989) found that increasing difference between superior and subordinate demographic characteristics was associated with lower superior ratings of subordinate effectiveness, less attraction toward subordinates, and the experience of greater subordinate role ambiguity. Work with ethnic groups in New Zealand also found higher levels of follower satisfaction when leaders and followers were ethnically similar (Chong & Thomas, 1997). Leaders clearly face the challenge of finding ways to overcome tendencies to work more effectively with demographically similar staff. Offermann and Phan (2002) suggested a three-pronged approach to developing culturally intelligent leadership, namely to (a) understand the impact of one's own culture and background in terms of values, biases, and expectations for oneself and others; (b) understand others and their comparable values, biases, and expectations; and (c) be able to diagnose and adaptively match appropriate leadership behaviors and expectations to specific cross-cultural situations.

Understanding Oneself. The first step in understanding one's own culture requires self-knowledge. Like people in general, many leaders are unaware of how their own acculturation affects the way they view others. Although leaders might not recognize the impact of their own culture, evidence suggests that followers can see it. Offermann and Hellmann (1997) found that among internationally well-traveled managers, the cultural values associated with a manager's country of origin related to what subordinates saw as their manager's leadership style, with the values of power distance and uncertainty avoidance having significant impacts on leadership ratings. Consistent with the view that high power distance is associated with a greater tendency for a leader to autocratically retain power rather than empower others, managers from higher power distance societies were rated significantly lower than other managers on leader communication, delegation, approachability, and team building. Managers from higher uncertainty avoidance cultures were viewed as significantly more controlling and less likely to use leader styles emphasizing delegation and approachability that produce uncertainty, consistent with cultural values. The managers in this study had been exposed to other views, yet cultural differences in their leadership behaviors closely followed predictions based on cultural background. The danger is that these culturally set values may become the standard of correctness against which all others are judged, setting the stage for in-group bias (Gudykunst & Bond, 1997; Triandis, 1994). Fortunately, it is possible for people to value their own heritage without denigrating that of others (Gudykunst & Bond, 1997).

One element of self-knowledge that is important for leaders is how they make attributions for the causes of the behaviors they observe in others. Research suggests that many people overestimate the contribution of personal dispositional factors, as opposed to situational factors, to observed outcomes (Nisbett & Ross, 1980). Although this is well documented with European American samples, other cultural groups may show different attributional patterns. As noted earlier, Asians may focus more on social roles, obligations, and situational constraints (Markus, Kitayama, & Heiman, 1996). If leaders make erroneous attributions for the performance of culturally different followers, their leader behavior may be unwise. Work by Offermann, Schroyer, and Green (1998) found that leader attributions about the causes of group performance affected how the leader later interacted with group members, with the leader being more behaviorally active in working with groups whose members were perceived as performing poorly due to lack of effort rather than lack of ability. Misattributing unsatisfactory performance of culturally different staff to lack of ability, rather than to lack of clarity about what they were supposed to do, may cause a leader to give up on them and miss the opportunity to coach individuals who could perform well. The leader then may harbor low expectations for those who are different, denying them needed support, and this in turn becomes a self-fulfilling prophecy (Eden, 1990).

Understanding Others. The second step in understanding others builds on self-knowledge and includes understanding, at a practical level, the implications of cultural values for everyday work behavior. There are many intercultural training and education opportunities available for leaders, with the most common forms of cross-cultural training described in detail by Brislin and his colleagues (e.g., Brislin & Horvath, 1997). Training goals typically focus on changing thinking (increasing knowledge of cultural differences and issues), improving affective reactions (how to manage challenges and enjoy diversity rather than merely tolerate it), and changing actual behaviors (Brislin & Horvath, 1997). Evidence suggests that even short-term training is usually beneficial (Triandis, 1994) and is a wise investment for leaders.

However, although leaders can, and (we believe) should, learn about core dimensions of cultural values, they must also take care not to categorize or stereotype individuals based on group membership. Miroshnik (2002) argued that managers are often culture biased and that skills in cross-cultural management must begin by recognizing cultural differences without judging them. Individuals are not cultural categories, and within-culture variation can be as great as, or greater than, between-culture variation. Managers who are wise are able to perceive greater variability within and between organizations, recognize both consistency and outliers, and respond accordingly (Malan & Kriger, 1998).

Adaptive Leadership. Understanding oneself and others in terms of cultural conditioning is the foundation of the third stage of successful leader adaptation. Many leadership models and approaches historically have advocated some tailoring of style to situation, with the core aspects of the situation attended to defined differently by different models. We suggest that one of the bases for tailoring needed is cultural differences.

For leaders to function effectively across cultural boundaries, leaders need to understand that, depending on their cultural background, followers come to work with different patterns of intelligent behavior that may or may not be seen as intelligent in the current setting. Wise leaders must identify the work behaviors that are truly required by the work or the organization. Is "top-of-the-head," quick responding really critical, or would a predistributed agenda allow those with more reflective thinking patterns to participate more fully? Leaders may unduly limit acceptable job behavior to that with which they are culturally familiar and attempt to force others into that mold, experiencing problems in the process. Yet the real value of a multicultural workforce comes from capitalizing on the varied skills and perspectives brought by staff rather than attempting to homogenize them. Miroshnik (2002) called this moving from a parochial "our way is the only way" approach or an ethnocentric "our way is the best way" approach to a more synergistic approach that allows for a combination of ways without a presumption of inherent superiority of any single way.

Based on cultural differences in values, followers' expectations of leaders may also differ significantly. The 61-nation GLOBE study found both commonalities and differences in cultural perceptions of effective leadership, with several characteristics reflecting charismatic/transformational leadership being universally endorsed as contributing to effective leadership (Den Hartog, House, Hanges, Ruiz-Quintanilla, & Dorfman, 1999). However, even where commonalities are found, leadership expectations and preferences may be affected by cultural values in important ways. For example,

Smith, Misumi, Tayeb, Peterson, and Bond (1989) supported the universal relevance of leader consideration but also indicated that a leader who discusses a follower's personal problems with others in the follower's absence was viewed as considerate in Japan but as violating the follower's privacy in the United States. Likewise, Schmidt and Yeh (1992) identified common leader influence strategies across Australian, English, Japanese, and Taiwanese managers but noted that their relative importance and tactical definitions differed by nationality.

Other leadership behaviors are very likely to differ significantly in degree of cross-cultural endorsement. For example, delegation may be viewed by individuals from high power distance countries as weak leadership, whereas other societies may view leader delegation as either positive or mandatory for leaders. Therefore, culturally intelligent leaders must be prepared and able to adapt their ways of interacting to accommodate cultural differences and help their multicultural staff to better adapt to the demands of their organizations.

It is clear that leaders in our global society will increasingly need to become more skilled in developing mature leader–follower relationships with culturally diverse followers (Graen & Wakabayashi, 1994) as well as multinational partners, customers, and suppliers. Results from a recent survey of managers at Fortune 500 companies indicated that 85% did not think they had enough competent global leaders in their organizations and that 65% believed their leaders needed more knowledge and skills to be effective globally (Javidan & House, 2001). We suggest that the three aspects of culturally intelligent leadership just described can increase the cultural competence of leaders and enable them to function more effectively in our multicultural world.

Multinational/Multicultural Teams

In this section, we extend our arguments about the culturally based nature of wisdom and intelligence to focus on some dynamics underlying the development of effective multinational/multicultural teams. Working on a multinational team provides a number of strong challenges for a member. There are at least three internal (to the team) issues confronting multinational teams as they develop and build momentum: establishment of goals and common purpose, clarification of roles played by team members, and delineation of rules for conduct and interaction (Earley & Peterson, 2004).

Working in a highly diverse team consisting of members from a range of cultures and backgrounds makes the establishment of goals, roles, and rules highly problematic because of the additional complexity added due to cultural differences (Earley & Gibson, 2002). Take, for example, the issue concerning rules for interaction within a multinational team. How should members interact and discuss core issues? If disagreements occur, how are they to be resolved? Team members who come from more confrontational cultures might not notice the subtle cues coming from team members who come from cultures where face saving is important and/or conflict tends to be expressed indirectly. Another concern is how resources should be distributed if the team receives limited resources. And how might team members decide individual responsibilities? A team member coming from a strong need-based culture might well expect that scarce resources will be allocated based on need rather than on accomplishment, whereas a fellow team member coming from an equity-based culture might have an opposing view. The unstated assumptions concerning right and wrong, due process, expectations for membership, and so on are tied to cultural background and experience.

Universal aspects of wisdom and cultural intelligence based on metacognition and motivation are of particularly high importance for the multinational team. Functioning in such a team requires that members acknowledge their weak overlapping knowledge and focus on the most basic commonality to create a hybrid or synergistic culture that grows out of something more fundamental than distribution of rewards and decision rules (Adler, 1997; Earley & Mosakowski, 2000). That is, all teams must build momentum from their commonalities, but multinational teams have a special challenge insomuch as their commonalities will be harder to identify. Multinational teams need to resist focusing initially on their differences. Metacognitive thinking is critical for developing and identifying strategies that might be used to determine the bases for a hybrid culture. Although the old adage of goals, roles, and rules is a reasonable starting point for developing a hybrid culture, there are likely to be team-specific elements that must be uncovered by team members as well.

Multinational team building also requires strong motivational discipline because many unstated practices and assumptions may need to be set aside and etiquette violations may need to be overlooked. A common trap for managers participating in a multinational team from a nationally heterogeneous company is to assume that they are cosmopolitan by virtue of their choice of institution for training or past travel experiences. At critical points in time, such as impending deadlines and negative performance feedback, teams lacking a strong sense of trust are likely to experience high relationship or emotional conflict and may self-destruct (Earley & Mosakowski, 2000; Simons & Peterson, 2000). Once a group receives negative feedback, differences that once were easily overlooked can become salient, and what once were quaint eccentricities can become unacceptable irritants resulting in personal disliking (Peterson & Behfar, 2003). Team members having high cultural intelligence and universal wisdom recognize this difficulty and remain motivated to look beyond individual differences toward what might benefit the entire team, even at critical pressure points.

Our point here is that success for multinational teams does not lie with cultural values training or broad orientations to diversity; instead, it requires members of the team to possess the metacognitive skills and long-term foresight to overcome specific and transient challenges rather than become overwhelmed by them. To uncover these various elements requires team members who are able to recognize these features in fellow team members as well as themselves and to generate new ways to do so as new team members are encountered. Metacognitive cultural intelligence addresses these different learning strategies in the way that cognitive knowledge training addresses the content differences. Motivational propensities provide the confidence to persist when trying to determine the basis of experienced differences, and behavioral capabilities guide appropriate ways of interacting with others from different cultures.

Multinational Organizations

Wisdom depends on context, and many organizations now operate in a variety of cultural contexts. A key issue for today's global or multinational corporations (MNCs) is how to socialize staff from many cultures into a single organization that benefits from the culture-specific knowledge and wisdom brought in by diverse staff while maintaining effectiveness and coherence. MNCs that encompass a variety of businesses across many nations have the particular challenge of spanning both national and business cultures. Organizations take various approaches to these issues.

Some organizations espouse common values but, to the extent possible, allow different local practices within dispersed organizational units. In Africa, the actions of the Roman Catholic Church, a clearly multinational organization, illustrate both the problems and potential of this approach. Vatican Council II (1962–1965) encouraged the use of the vernacular rather than the traditional Latin in worship services, and it allowed changes in singing, changes in musical instruments, and (most particularly) the incorporation of drums into traditional Catholic services in Africa. Thus, the church was better able to reach out to local communities in ways that increased comfort while maintaining its core values and beliefs. The limits of this approach could be seen when local customs violated the basic values of the church. Although the church encouraged priests to incorporate the sacramental blessing of the church into traditional African marriage ceremonies, this did not fit well with traditional ceremonies that could last for months and often were not finalized until the wife proved her fertility by the birth of her first child, a practice that was far removed from church doctrine on marriage and childbearing.

A second approach is for organizations to accept that values differ cross-culturally and try to develop common organizational practices to which all organizational staff must adhere. For example, the World Bank Group is composed of individuals from around the world who are accustomed to many different organizational systems. To maintain a collective sense of appropriate behavior, the bank and other internationals or MNCs have found it important to develop a standardized code of professional conduct to guide staff and make behavioral expectations clear to everyone. As Hofstede (1991) noted, people do not need to think, feel, and act in similar ways to agree on practical issues and work cooperatively. He noted that IBM staff around the world have long cooperated toward organizational goals and that they are by no means unique in that respect. Organizational leaders have important roles in developing and communicating shared norms and practices in their diverse communities. Leaders can help their organizations to forge a collective perspective on "how we do things around here" that is an integration of different approaches, known by all, and that diverse people can endorse as their own even if it differs in significant respects from some of their culturally formed values. When different perspectives are integrated into organizational practices, greater comfort with them from a greater proportion of staff can be expected, as opposed to a more autocratic development approach that emphasizes the traditions of only a single national culture.

In addition, organizations can create conditions that make positive intercultural experiences more likely. Triandis (1995) proposed that positive interactions among diverse individuals are more likely to occur in settings that value pluralism, share superordinate goals, are familiar with each other's culture and share some commonalities, perform cooperative tasks with peers of equal status, are rewarded for positive interactions, and have overlapping social networks. MNCs should be able to provide common purposes around organizational goals, and coalescing around organizational requirements and objectives is more likely if the value system advocates and rewards pluralism. In addition, better communication among different people allows an open flow of communication throughout an organization, for although the organization may have wise individuals, "the organization does not become wise unless individuals' wisdom is articulated and transferred to others" (Bierly, Kessler, & Christensen, 2000, p. 609).

Furthermore, Hofstede (1991) suggested that there is a potential for synergy from the combination of cultures with differing values, for example, combining staff from more innovating (low uncertainty avoidance) cultures whose members are more tolerant of new ideas with staff from more implementing cultures (stronger uncertainty avoidance) whose members may have superior skills with detail in making innovative ideas become reality. He cited as evidence that, consistent with the countries' levels of tolerance for uncertainty, the United Kingdom has produced more Nobel Prize winners than has Japan, but Japan has put more new products on the world market. Culture may be one of a number of factors affecting individual job performance, and providing an organizational culture that allows each person to contribute his or her best, combined with others with different strengths, offers the best prospects for optimal organizational achievement.

This perspective is the antithesis of assimilation and homogenization. In the United States and elsewhere, the metaphor of a melting pot has given way to the image of a mosaic or stew that maintains the identity and contribution of different parts in the context of a coherent organizational creation. Leveraging diversity in this manner yields the potential for enhanced creativity and performance in diverse groups as different perspectives are combined (Triandis, Kurowski, & Gelfand, 1994). However, this potential might not be realized if effective communication and cooperation cannot be preserved simultaneously. In practice, multicultural groups can be either highly effective or ineffective, depending on whether diversity is managed successfully (Adler, 1997). If destructive conflict develops, performance will suffer; if different perspectives help to generate and develop new ideas in a mutually supportive and learning-oriented environment, performance can be enhanced. Typically, it falls on organizational leaders to bring out the best from diverse perspectives in a way that maintains positive interpersonal relations and avoids negative conflict. Organizational leaders presumably are also the repository of organizational knowledge and experience, factors that are predictive of wisdom and that can be drawn on to make diverse groups work effectively.

The benefits of diversity appear at many levels. Research has shown that top management teams in MNCs benefit from cultural heterogeneity and can achieve better performance without a loss of cohesion (Elron, 1997). Evidence suggests that companies that implement good diversity management programs are more likely to attract and retain employees as well as to create good corporate reputations. In contrast, poor diversity management can substantially cripple organizations. For example, individuals examining alleged organizational recruiting materials that either did or did not feature a managing diversity program evaluated the organization with the diversity program as significantly more attractive to them (Williams & Bauer, 1994). This suggests that providing support for a diverse workforce may be a potent recruiting tool. As the workforces of MNCs continue to diversify, maintaining a positive environment for diverse staff may differentiate those organizations that are able to attract and keep the best talent from those that are not.

Summary Thoughts

Our emphasis in this chapter was on exploring the nature of wisdom and intelligence in a cursory fashion across cultural boundaries. In so doing, we began with a description of culture itself as an anchor point for understanding how wisdom and intelligence might operate. Thus, our emphasis was on providing the reader with a taste of what differences might exist and the implications that such differences might have for various aspects of organizational and managerial functioning across domains of intercultural training, leadership, multicultural teams, and MNCs. Although a complete review of these topics would constitute a major treatise, our intention was to stimulate a preliminary frame for thinking about this integration of topics.

In terms of epistemology, a key aspect of our discussion is that wisdom itself has a complex foundation with both universal and culture-specific elements. We introduced Wilson's (1993) view of moral values as an illustration of potential universal or etic foundations of wisdom, that is, the direction in which wisdom should guide us for a positive societal influence. In addition, we described a variety of perspectives concerning wisdom and intelligence as they vary across cultural boundaries, that is, the emic or culture-specific aspects. Consistent with evolutionary epistemology, knowledge may be constructed differently by different cultural groups so as to adapt to their respective environments. Nonetheless, some elements of human existence may transcend environment to such an extent that some elements of knowledge construction will be universal, although their expression may differ by location. So, although a concept such as fairness may be universal to societies, the specific definition of fairness (e.g., equity based, equality based, need based) may be idiosyncratic. This suggests that wisdom and intelligence have a variability when examined at a specific level of actions or outcomes. The underlying themes based on values and desirable end states (e.g., fairness) may be universal, but recognizing this requires an acceptance of idiosyncrasy at an outcome level.

In addition, we discussed the overlap of wisdom and intelligence, drawing from the definition provided by Csikszentmihalyi and Rathunde (1990). Intelligent actions that result in a societally beneficial outcome are indistinguishable from wise actions in this usage. Thus, intelligence and wisdom are interchangeable in this context. However, one might argue that the true difference between intelligence and wisdom lies in the culture-specific versus universal nature of action and deed. For example, if we accept that there are certain universal positive values (e.g., procedural fairness), perhaps there are universal actions required to achieve these outcomes. In some Western political thinking, there is an assertion that all people have a right to democracy and a right to self-determine their future. If democracy is the correct and universal form of political practice, this might suggest that wisdom captures a true universal of value and form, whereas intelligence (directed toward a positive value goal) may be idiosyncratic and capture differences within cultures.

Are there differences in wisdom across cultures? Certainly, it appears that wise "action" differs across cultures, just as do intelligent "behaviors." Therefore, scholars pursuing the topic of wisdom are advised to tread carefully in making generalizations about the structure, form, and manifestation of wisdom across cultures. Wisdom ultimately may be subject to the trap of beauty—held not as an absolute but rather as a virtue of an interested party.

Notes

1. Throughout this chapter, we refer to wisdom and intelligence as related in the instance that intelligence has a specific (and morally positive) directionality. Thus, it is possible that a behavior is intelligent but negative (e.g., sneaky, illegal), and this would not reflect wisdom. However, in cases where intelligent action has a target of a socially and personally desirable aim, it is also wise. Indeed, Staudinger, Smith, and Baltes (1992) drew from a dual model of intelligence and defined wisdom as dependent on "practical" intelligence or intelligence seen as factual and procedural depending on context, culture, and experience. Thus, wisdom might be seen as a subset over which intelligence may exist in various forms.

2. By a global assignment, we are referring to a temporary or short-term (less than 1 year) assignment that appears to be more characteristic of the current work environment than was the tradition. In contrast, an expatriate assignment typically involves full-time relocation of a manager and his or her family for more than 1 year.

References

Adler, N. J. (1997). *International dimensions of organizational behavior* (3rd ed.). Cincinnati, OH: South Western.

Baltes, P. B., & Kunzmann, U. (2004). The two faces of wisdom: Wisdom as a general theory of knowledge and judgment about excellence in mind and virtue vs. wisdom as everyday realization in people and products. *Human Development, 47,* 290–299.

Baltes, P. B., & Smith, J. (1990). Toward a psychology of wisdom and its ontogenesis. In R. J. Sternberg (Ed.), *Wisdom: Its nature, origins, and development* (pp. 87–120). New York: Cambridge University Press.

Baltes, P. B., & Staudinger, U. M. (2000). Wisdom: A metaheuristic (pragmatic) to orchestrate mind and virtue toward excellence. *American Psychologist, 55,* 122–136.

Bass, B. M. (1990). *Bass and Stogdill's handbook of leadership.* New York: Free Press.

Berry, J. W. (1990). Imposed etics, emics, and derived-etics: Their conceptual and operational status in cross-cultural psychology. In T. N. Headland, K. I. Pike, & M. Harris (Eds.), *Emics and etics: The insider/outsider debate* (pp. 84–89). Newbury Park, CA: Sage.

Berry, J. W. (1997). An ecocultural approach to the study of cross-cultural I/O psychology. In P. C. Earley & M. Erez (Eds.), *New perspectives on international industrial/organizational psychology* (pp. 130–147). San Francisco: Jossey-Bass.

Berry, J. W. (2003). Fundamental psychological processes in intercultural relations. In D. Landis, J. Bennett, & J. Bennett (Eds.), *Handbook of intercultural training* (3rd ed., pp. 166–184). Newbury Park, CA: Sage.

Berry, J. W. (2004). An ecocultural perspective on the development of competence. In R. J. Sternberg & E. Grigorenko (Eds.), *Culture and competence* (pp. 3–22). Washington, DC: APA Books.

Berry, J. W., & Ward, C. (2006). Commentary on "Redefining Interactions Across Cultures and Organisations." *Group and Organization Management, 31,* 64–77.

Bhawuk, D. P. (1998). The role of culture theory in cross-cultural training: A multi-method study of culture specific, culture general, and culture theory-based assimilators. *Journal of Cross-Cultural Psychology, 29,* 630–655.

Bhawuk, D. P. (2001). Evolution of culture assimilators: Toward theory-based assimilators. *International Journal of Intercultural Relations, 25,* 141–163.

Bhawuk, D. P., & Brislin, R. W. (1992). The measurement of intercultural sensitivity using the concepts of individualism and collectivism. *International Journal of Intercultural Relations, 16,* 413–446.

Bierly, P. E., Kessler, E. H., & Christensen, E. W. (2000). Organizational learning, knowledge, and wisdom. *Journal of Organizational Change, 13,* 595–618.

Bond, M. H. (1997). Two decades of chasing the dragon. In M. H. Bond (Ed.), *Working at the interface of cultures* (pp. 179–190). London: Routledge.

Bond, M. H. K., Leung, W. K., & Giacalone, R. A. (1985). How are responses to verbal insult related to cultural collectivism and power distance? *Journal of Cross-Cultural Psychology, 16,* 111–127.

Brislin, R., & Horvath, A. (1997). Cross-cultural training and multicultural evaluation. In J. W. Berry, M. H. Segall, & C. Kafitgibasi (Eds.), *Handbook of cross-cultural psychology* (Vol. 3, pp. 327–369). Boston: Allyn & Bacon.

Brislin, R. W., & Yoshida, T. (Eds.). (1994). *Improving intercultural interactions: Modules for cross-cultural training.* Thousand Oaks, CA: Sage.

Chiu, L. H. (1972). A cross-cultural comparison of cognitive styles in Chinese and American children. *International Journal of Psychology, 7,* 235–242.

Chong, L. M. A., & Thomas, D. C. (1997). Leadership perceptions in cross-cultural context. *Leadership Quarterly, 8,* 275–293.

Csikszentmihalyi, M., & Rathunde, K. (1990). The psychology of wisdom: An evolutionary interpretation. In R. S. Sternberg (Ed.), *Wisdom: Its nature, origins, and development* (pp. 25–51). New York: Cambridge University Press.

Den Hartog, D. N., House, R. J., Hanges, P. J., Ruiz-Quintanilla, S. A., & Dorfman, P. W. (1999). Culture-specific and cross-culturally generalizable implicit leadership theories: Are attributes of charismatic/transformational leadership universally endorsed? *Leadership Quarterly, 10,* 219–232.

Earley, P. C. (1997). *Face, harmony, and social structure: An analysis of organizational behavior across cultures.* New York: Oxford University Press.

Earley, P. C. (2002). A theory of cultural intelligence in organizations. In B. M. Staw & R. Kramer (Eds.), *Research in organizational behavior* (Vol. 24, pp. 271–299). Greenwich, CT: JAI.

Earley, P. C., & Ang, S. (2003). *Cultural intelligence: An analysis of individual interactions across cultures.* Palo Alto, CA: Stanford University Press.

Earley, P. C., & Gibson, C. B. (2002). *Multinational work teams: A new perspective.* Mahwah, NJ: Lawrence Erlbaum.

Earley, P. C., & Mosakowski, E. (1996). Experimental international management research. In B. J. Punnett & O. Shenkar (Eds.), *Handbook of international management research* (pp. 83–114). London: Blackwell.

Earley, P. C., & Mosakowski, E. (2000). Creating hybrid team cultures: An empirical test of international team functioning. *Academy of Management Journal, 43,* 26–49.

Earley, P. C., & Mosakowski, E. (2004, October). Cultural intelligence. *Harvard Business Review,* pp. 139–146.

Earley, P. C., & Peterson, R. S. (2004). The elusive cultural chameleon: Cultural intelligence as a new approach to intercultural training for the global manager. *Academy of Management Learning and Education, 3,* 100–116.

Eden, D. (1990). *Pygmalion in management: Productivity as a self-fulfilling prophecy.* Lexington, MA: D. C. Heath.

Elron, E. (1997). Top management teams within multinational corporations: Effects of cultural heterogeneity. *Leadership Quarterly, 8,* 393–412.

Erez, M., & Earley, P. C. (1993). *Culture, self-identity, and work.* New York: Oxford University Press.

Fiedler, F. E., & Garcia, J. E. (1987). *New approaches to effective leadership: Cognitive resources and organizational performance.* New York: John Wiley.

Fiske, A. P. (1991). *Structures of social life.* New York: Free Press.

Gibb, C. A. (1969). Leadership. In G. Lindzey & E. Aronson (Eds.), *Handbook of social psychology* (Vol. 4, pp. 205–282). Reading, MA: Addison-Wesley.

Graen, G., & Wakabayashi, M. (1994). Cross-cultural leadership making: Bridging American and Japanese diversity for team advantage. In H. C. Triandis, M. D. Dunnette, & L. M. Hough (Eds.), *Handbook of industrial and organizational psychology* (2nd ed., Vol. 4, pp. 415–446). Palo Alto, CA: Consulting Psychologists.

Greenberg, J. (1996). *The quest for justice on the job: Essays and experiments.* Thousand Oaks, CA: Sage.

Greenberg, J., & Lind, E. A. (2000). The pursuit of organizational justice: From conceptualization to implication to application. In C. L. Cooper & E. A. Locke (Eds.), *Industrial and organizational psychology: Linking theory with practice* (pp. 72–108). Oxford, UK: Blackwell.

Grigorenko, E. L., Geissler, P. W., Prince, R., Okatcha, F., Nokes, C., Kenny, D. A., Bundy, D. A., & Sternberg, R. J. (2001). The organisation of Luo conceptions of intelligence: A study of implicit theories in a Kenyan village. *International Journal of Behavioral Development, 25,* 367–378.

Gudykunst, W. B., & Bond, M. H. (1997). Intergroup relations across cultures. In J. W. Berry, M. H. Segall, & C. Kagitgibasi (Eds.), *Handbook of cross-cultural psychology* (Vol. 3, pp. 119–161). Boston: Allyn & Bacon.

Hall, E. T. (1976). *Beyond culture.* Garden City, NY: Doubleday.

Hofstede, G. (1980). *Culture's consequences: International differences in work-related values.* Beverly Hills, CA: Sage.

Hofstede, G. (1991). *Culture and organizations: Software of the mind.* London: McGraw-Hill.

Holliday, S. G., & Chandler, M. J. (1986). *Wisdom: Explorations in adult competence.* Basel, Switzerland: Karger.

Javidan, M., & House, R. J. (2001). Cultural acumen for the global manager: Lessons from Project GLOBE. *Organizational Dynamics, 29,* 289–305.

Judge, T. A., Colbert, A. E., & Ilies, R. (2004). Intelligence and leadership: A quantitative review and test of theoretical propositions. *Journal of Applied Psychology, 89,* 542–552.

Kluckhohn, C. (1954). *Culture and behavior.* New York: Free Press.

Leung, K., & Bond, M. H. (1989). On the empirical identification of dimensions for cross-cultural comparison. *Journal of Cross-Cultural Psychology, 20,* 613–620.

Levi-Strauss, C. (1969). *The elementary structures of kinship* (Rev. ed.). Boston: Beacon.

Levitt, H. M. (1999). The development of wisdom: An analysis of Tibetan Buddhist experience. *Journal of Humanistic Psychology, 39*(2), 86–106.

Lind, E. A., & Earley, P. C. (1992). Procedural justice and culture. *International Journal of Psychology, 27*, 227–242.

Lind, E. A., & Tyler, T. R. (1988). *The social psychology of procedural justice.* New York: Plenum.

Malan, L. C., & Kriger, M. P. (1998). Making sense of managerial wisdom. *Journal of Management Inquiry, 7*, 242–251.

Markus, H. R., Kitayama, S., & Heiman, R. (1996). Culture and "basic" psychological principles. In E. T. Higgins & A. W. Kruglanski (Eds.), *Social psychology: Handbook of basic principles* (pp. 857–913). New York: Guilford.

Martin, J. (1992). *Culture in organizations: Three perspectives.* New York: Oxford University Press.

Masuda, T., & Nisbett, R. E. (2001). Attending holistically versus analytically: Comparing the context sensitivity of Japanese and Americans. *Journal of Personality and Social Psychology, 81*, 992–934.

Mead, G. H. (1934). *Mind, self, and society.* Chicago: University of Chicago Press.

Miller, J. G. (1984). Culture and the development of everyday social explanation. *Journal of Personality and Social Psychology, 46*, 961–978.

Miller, J. G. (1997). A cultural-psychology perspective on intelligence. In R. J. Sternberg & E. L. Grigorenko (Eds.), *Intelligence, heredity, and environment* (pp. 269–302). Cambridge, UK: Cambridge University Press.

Miroshnik, V. (2002). Culture and international management: A review. *Journal of Management Development, 21*, 521–544.

Murdock, G. P. (1945). The common denominator of cultures. In R. Linton (Ed.), *The science of man in the world of crisis* (pp. 123–142). New York: Columbia University Press.

Nisbett, R. E. (2003). *The geography of thought: Why we think the way we do.* New York: Free Press.

Nisbett, R. E., Peng, K., Choi, I., & Norenzayan, A. (2001). Culture and systems of thought: Holistic versus analytic cognition. *Psychological Review, 108*, 291–310.

Nisbett, R. E., & Ross, L. (1980). *Human inference: Strategies and shortcomings in social judgment.* Englewood Cliffs, NJ: Prentice Hall.

Offermann, L. R. (1998). Leading and empowering diverse followers. In G. Hickman (Ed.), *Leading organizations: Perspectives for a new era* (pp. 397–404). Thousand Oaks, CA: Sage.

Offermann, L. R., & Hellmann, P. S. (1997). Culture's consequences for leadership behavior: National values in action. *Journal of Cross-Cultural Psychology, 28*, 342–351.

Offermann, L. R., Kennedy, J. K., & Wirtz, P. W. (1994). Implicit leadership theories: Content, structure, and generalizability. *Leadership Quarterly, 5*, 43–58.

Offermann, L. R., & Phan, L. U. (2002). Culturally intelligent leadership for a diverse world. In R. E. Riggio, S. E. Murphy, & F. J. Pirozzolo (Eds.), *Multiple intelligences and leadership* (pp. 187–214). Mahwah, NJ: Lawrence Erlbaum.

Offermann, L. R., Schroyer, C. J., & Green, S. K. (1998). Leader attributions for subordinate performance: Consequences for subsequent leader interactive behaviors and ratings. *Journal of Applied Social Psychology, 28*, 1125–1139.

Peterson, R. S., & Behfar, K. J. (2003). The dynamic relationship between performance feedback, trust, and conflict in groups: A longitudinal study. *Organizational Behavior and Human Decision Processes, 92,* 102–112.

Resaldo, R. (1989). *Culture and truth.* Boston: Beacon.

Schmidt, F. L., & Hunter, J. E. (1998). The validity and utility of selection methods in personnel psychology: Practical and theoretical implications of 85 years of research findings. *Psychological Bulletin, 124,* 262–274.

Schmidt, S. M., & Yeh, R. (1992). The structure of leader influence: A cross-national comparison. *Journal of Cross-Cultural Psychology, 23,* 251–264.

Shweder, R. A., & LeVine, R. A. (1984). *Culture theory: Essays on mind, self, and emotion.* New York: Cambridge University Press.

Simons, T. L., & Peterson, R. S. (2000). Task conflict and relationship conflict in top management teams: The pivotal role of intragroup trust. *Journal of Applied Psychology, 85,* 102–111.

Simonton, D. K. (1985). Intelligence and personal influence in groups: Four nonlinear models. *Psychological Review, 92,* 532–547.

Smith, P. B., Misumi, J., Tayeb, M., Peterson, M. F., & Bond, M. (1989). On the generality of leadership style measures across cultures. *Journal of Occupational Psychology, 62,* 97–109.

Staudinger, U. M., Smith, J., & Baltes, P. B. (1992). Wisdom-related knowledge in life review task: Age differences and the role of professional specialization. *Psychology and Aging, 7,* 271–281.

Sternberg, R. J. (1985). *Beyond IQ: A triarchic theory of intelligence.* New York: Cambridge University Press.

Sternberg, R. J. (1990). *Metaphors of mind: Conceptions of the nature of intelligence.* New York: Cambridge University Press.

Sternberg, R. J. (2003). *Wisdom, intelligence, and creativity synthesized.* Cambridge, UK: Cambridge University Press.

Sternberg, R. J., & Grigorenko, E. L. (2006). Cultural intelligence and successful intelligence. *Group and Organization Management, 31,* 27–39.

Stogdill, R. (1948). Personal factors associated with leadership: A survey of the literature. *Journal of Psychology, 25,* 35–71.

Takahashi, M., & Bordia, P. (2000). The concept of wisdom: A cross-cultural comparison. *International Journal of Psychology, 35*(1), 1–9.

Takahashi, M., & Overton, W. F. (2005). Cultural foundations of wisdom: An integrated developmental approach. In R. Sternberg & J. Jordan (Eds.), *A handbook of wisdom: Psychological perspectives* (pp. 32–60). Cambridge, UK: Cambridge University Press.

Takayama, M. (2002). *The concept of wisdom and wise people in Japan.* Unpublished doctoral dissertation, Tokyo University.

Thibaut, J., & Walker, L. (1978). A theory of procedure. *California Law Review, 66,* 541–566.

Thomas, D. C., & Inkson, K. (2004). *Cultural intelligence: People skills for global business.* San Francisco: Berrett-Koehler.

Triandis, H. C. (1972). *The analysis of subjective culture.* New York: John Wiley.

Triandis, H. (1994). *Culture and social behavior.* New York: McGraw-Hill.

Triandis, H. C. (1995). *Individualism and collectivism.* Boulder, CO: Westview.

Triandis, H. C., Kurowski, L. L., & Gelfand, M. J. (1994). Workplace diversity. In H. C. Triandis, M. D. Dunnette, & L. M. Hough (Eds.), *Handbook of industrial and organizational psychology* (2nd ed., Vol. 4, pp. 769–827). Palo Alto, CA: Consulting Psychologists.

Tsui, A. S., & O'Reilly, C. A., III. (1989). Beyond simple demographic effects: The importance of relational demography in superior–subordinate dyads. *Academy of Management Journal, 32,* 402–423.

Valdez, J. M. (1994). Wisdom: A Hispanic perspective. *Dissertation Abstracts International, 54,* 6482-B.

Webster's new world college dictionary (3rd ed.). (1997). New York: Macmillan Reference Books.

Williams, M. L., & Bauer, T. N. (1994). The effect of a managing diversity policy on organizational attractiveness. *Group and Organizational Management, 19,* 295–308.

Wilson, J. Q. (1993). *The moral sense.* New York: Free Press.

Witkin, H. A., & Goodenough, D. R. (1977). Field dependence and interpersonal behavior. *Psychological Bulletin, 84,* 661–690.

Yang, S. (2001). Conceptions of wisdom among Taiwanese Chinese. *Journal of Cross-Cultural Psychology, 32,* 662–680.

Yang, S., & Sternberg, R. J. (1997a). Conceptions of intelligence in ancient Chinese philosophy. *Journal of Theoretical and Philosophical Psychology, 17,* 101–119.

Yang, S., & Sternberg, R. J. (1997b). Taiwanese Chinese people's conceptions of intelligence. *Intelligence, 25,* 21–36.

15

Organizational Epistemology

Interpersonal Relations in Organizations and the Emergence of Wisdom

Peter B. Vaill

You understand something and I don't.
You understand that I don't understand, but
you don't understand what it is that I don't understand.
I understand that I don't understand, but
I don't understand what it is that I don't understand.
Not only do you not understand what it is I don't understand,
you don't understand how you came to understand
what it is that you understand.
You understand that your understanding is more advanced than
mine, but
you don't understand exactly how it is more advanced,
nor do you understand how to make yourself simple again like me.
I understand that your understanding is more advanced than mine,
but
my understanding doesn't feel simple; rather,
it feels chaotic and confused.
I can't begin to explain simply to you
what it is I don't understand
so that you can help me understand it.
You and I have a problem
if I am to come to understand what you understand and
if you are to come to understand what I don't understand.[1]

We live in an age of what might be called the "receding galaxies of specialized knowledge." All of us could write the poem above with respect to other people's expertise, and other people could write it with respect to our expertise. We do indeed have a problem if genuine wisdom is to emerge in organizations from the myriad encounters, not to say collisions, of the various kinds of expertise needed to conduct the organization's affairs.

Implicit in this poem is an idea about epistemology that is not normally found in surveys of the subject.[2] Epistemology is usually discussed in terms of the problem of the logical grounds for knowing what we believe we know. In this chapter, on the other hand, the epistemological problem is of the form, "How can I learn from you, and how can you learn from me?" Epistemological validity is viewed as a two-dimensional affair, in other words. One dimension is the question of the validity of knowledge, and the other is the problem of consensus. Unfortunately, epistemological validity on this first dimension does not force consensual validity—the second dimension. It is this second dimension of knowing as a collective conversation that I am concerned with here on the assumption that wisdom emerges from such conversations—people interacting with each other and learning (or, sadly, not learning) from each other.

This chapter is concerned with the development of wisdom in organizational contexts. There are three premises with which I begin so as to set the stage for my main argument. The first premise is that wisdom is needed in all organizational action, not just in special instances. Second, I treat wisdom as a fundamentally social phenomenon despite the common assumption that wisdom somehow inheres in a single person. These two premises provide a suitable platform from which to discuss wisdom proper—how it arises and is sustained in organizational contexts, what "threats" it has to deal with, what the prospects are for a fuller realization of the need for wisdom, and what the prospects are for its greater expression.

The third premise is in fact the organizing principle for the main argument of this chapter. This is that wisdom seems to result from two interrelated sources: (a) an *external* source of facts, problems, data, and expectations of others and (b) an *internal* source of the actual relationships that exist among the men and women who together create and practice wisdom in some kind of a social grouping.

A fuller definition of wisdom will emerge as I proceed, but for the moment let us think of wisdom in terms of the meaning of a statement or set of statements to two or more organizational actors as they communicate concerning an organization's affairs. True, a professional epistemologist could make a technical assessment of their communication as to the validity of the knowledge they possess and perhaps as to whether or not it qualifies as "wisdom." But in the first instance, it is the involved parties' assessment with which I am concerned. This is, then, a consensual definition of wisdom.

Premise 1: Wisdom Is Needed in All Organizational Action

We tend to think that wisdom is needed only at particular times and places in organizational affairs and that most of the time we can get along with a combination of scientific principles and common sense. Only in particular dilemmas do we need "wisdom" to guide us. With regard to common sense, it is still wisdom—"conventional wisdom," as J. K. Galbraith famously memorialized it in *The Affluent Society* (Galbraith, 1958/1998). Conventional wisdom—common sense—is not particularly reflective (except for the conventional wisdom that it pays to reflect!) and not particularly conscious of itself, and that is its chief defect. But in content, the conventional wisdom is often a useful guide to action.

Scientific principles, on the other hand, are notoriously unspecific despite their use in phrases such as "scientific reasoning," "management science," and "applied behavioral science." Even the sciences that are far more developed than those we use in organizational life have their "fudge factors," "redundancy," "safety nets," and "backup systems." The most fundamental safety net of all is science's ceteris paribus ("other things being equal"), which is to be understood as attached to all scientific findings. If the "other things" are *not* equal, as is so often the case, some scientific idea that purports to be a guide to action may actually be not very useful at all. One can never be sure that available science, no matter how developed, is adequate to the task. Action problems in organizations are usually mixtures of things we know a lot about—have scientific knowledge of—and things we do not know a lot about and do not have scientific knowledge of. This means that the "problem-as-whole" cannot be a scientific one![3] Some problems can be decomposed into scientific pieces and "judgment" pieces, but in the organizational world of mixtures of people, technologies, and markets, decomposition is usually not possible. People, technologies, and markets are the objects of psychology, engineering, and economics, respectively. Of these, engineering is probably the most developed as an applied science, with economics and psychology well behind. Moreover, the three tend not to be sciences of each other! Each makes assumptions about the nature of the other two, and this often gets them into trouble.[4]

In addition, the people toward whom we might take action in an organization are reactive; even if we think we are acting "scientifically," the scientific principle employed would not be about the *reactions* people will have to the use of it. Just because we may be trying to be scientific toward people does not mean that they need to behave as the science predicts they will. Another way of saying this is that science always must make abstractions from the flux of organizational life so as to have some clear-cut things to study scientifically. These abstractions are science's value judgments, although they are often not seen as value judgments. Once findings have been generated, however, they are taken back to the original flux, where they meet people who might not be at all interested in or impressed by the parts of the situation that we chose to study scientifically. Finally, science cannot have the things it studies be constantly changing and evolving, yet this is exactly what humans, singly and in groups, are doing all of the time—coming up with thoughts, feelings, and actions that may have never been seen before. It is hard to be scientific about the never-before-seen.

But for all of these reasons, there will be few organizational situations, if any, that can be handled scientifically. It is better to assume that we will always need to be wise in addition to being scientific when deciding what to do in an organization.

Wisdom sees where it is needed in organizational action, and it sees why. Perhaps most important, wisdom sees how it is needed; that is, it sees what kinds of insights and what kinds of judgments are needed. Significantly, Sir Geoffrey Vickers[5] made his whole "appreciative system" for taking action in organizations a matter of judgment—"reality judgment," that is, the ability to see what is the case; "value judgment," that is, the ability to see what is important in the current case; and "multivalued choice" or "instrumental judgment," that is, the ability to see how to implement the chosen values in relation to the given reality (Vickers, 1968, chaps. 6–7).

As is well known, there are a great many different models for managerial action in organizations. In presenting a model of management action in organizations, it is common to draw boxes containing various important factors and connect them with arrows or to make lists of factors showing, step-by-step, how a course of action should proceed. However, the arrows and the idea of "step-by-step" are misleading metaphors, for the causal relations between the boxes or in the lists of factors are loose at best. It is along these arrows, so to speak, or between the steps that we can find the need for judgment and wisdom. Iron laws do not bind the boxes and lists together.

Premise 2: Wisdom Is a Social Phenomenon _____

The more common assumption is that it is a single person who is "wise." On reflection, however, we see that we experience wisdom only in conversation with another person (or persons)—our own wisdom and/or the other's (or others'). The importance of the idea that wisdom, or "sensemaking" as Weick (1995) called it, emerges from careful communication—both speaking and listening—with others is repeatedly confirmed in the managerial literature (Athos & Gabarro, 1978; Dixon, 1996; Goleman, 1998; Kouzes & Posner, 2002; Senge, Scharmer, Jaworski, & Flowers, 2004; Weick, 1995). Moreover, sometimes talking with people who are purportedly wise does not give the needed insight, and sometimes talking with someone not seen as wise results in insights and understandings we did not expect. In other words, wisdom can sometimes fail to arise where we expect it to arise and can actually appear where we are not expecting it. Finally, wisdom is usually an after-the-fact phenomenon; it is in looking back, after a few hours, days, or years, that we can see that some idea we had or that was communicated to us was in fact an extraordinarily wise notion. Wisdom, in other words, seems to be very situational, very much a function of the relationships of all parties involved, with not everyone deferring to the supposedly wise person.

For all of these reasons, it is best to think that wisdom may emerge as a property of relationships among two or more people.[6] It is still all right to think that there are wise individual persons, but this means only that in talking with them we expect to acquire insights and understandings that would not come so easily if we did not talk with them because that has been our past experience with them.

This chapter is intended to be relevant to all levels of social scale and complexity in an organization: two-person interactions, small groups, intergroup relations, and organization-wide processes and events. However, I am developing a view of wisdom as emerging from concrete interactions. Therefore, it is necessary to keep the focus on what people specifically say and do in relation to each other, and that means that I speak mainly of groupings of people that are small enough for these concrete interactions to be mutually enacted.[7] The content of communications can be just about what concerns the immediate speakers. But it can also be about issues and events far larger and more wide-ranging than the personal concerns of the parties to the interaction. In this latter sense, this chapter's focus is more organizational than it is about the parties working out their personal relationship and exchanging wisdom that is relevant only to them individually.

Premise 3: Wisdom Is Dual-Sourced

In terms of my first two premises, the need for wisdom can arise anywhere and on any subject in an organization, and always in the conversations that individuals and groups are having about the organization's affairs. Am I then saying that wisdom is present in all conversations that occur in an organization? No, only that wisdom is potentially available and probably needed in all conversations that occur in the organization.

Here is the basic argument of this chapter. Potential wisdom becomes actual wisdom for two reasons or from two sources: first, in the choice the parties make of what to talk about; and second, in the quality of the parties' talk itself—the quality of their communication, whether direct, face-to-face, or mediated electronically and/or in written documents. If the parties choose trivial problems, or misframe problems, and/or if the parties engage in forms of talk that block or deny the abilities of one or both, they cannot expect wisdom to arise out of such a relationship. Wisdom is contingent on the choice of problems and the quality of interpersonal communication. Moreover, these two sources—without and within—are interrelated, for it takes a certain quality of communication to choose and frame problems "wisely," and the problems chosen in terms of their interest and challenge affect the parties' ability to sustain the high-quality interaction that energizes them all and stimulates their best thinking.

We now give a sketch of the without/within point of view about wisdom, followed by much more detailed discussion of each of these two sources of wisdom.

The Need From Without for Wisdom

In *Smart Thinking for Crazy Times,* Mitroff (1998) provided a very useful analysis of the problem of "choosing the right problems." Playing off the well-known Type I and Type II errors in statistics, Mitroff formulated the "error of the third kind" (chap. 2), which is the act of "solving the wrong problem precisely." The causes of a third kind error, he stated, are as follows:

1. Picking the wrong stakeholders

2. Selecting too narrow a set of options

3. Phrasing the problem incorrectly

4. Setting the boundaries/scope of a problem too narrowly

5. Failing to think systemically (p. 20)

We have all been in conversations where, sooner or later, we realized we had committed one or more of these mistakes. Put in more colloquial language, mistake number 1 often takes the form of "What does the boss want?" as if the boss were the only stakeholder. Number 2 occurs when we get into either/or, black-or-white thinking and cannot see, or refuse to see, shades of gray. Number 3 often occurs when we mistake symptoms for the real problem or when we commit the so-called "Law of the Hammer": When all you have is a hammer, everything looks like a nail. In number 4, we may state the problem too narrowly or simplistically. Number 4 is seen in reductionist "nothing but" thinking as in, "This problem is nothing but a software problem." Since Senge (1990) if not before (e.g., Katz & Kahn, 1966), we know that systems thinking (number 5) is an important mode of thought for organizational problems. But it is easy to underestimate the complexity of factors that underlie the problem in view. True systems thinking is far more than merely saying that everything is related to everything else. To be really powerful as a mode of thought, we need to be able to say how much of an effect one element is having on another and whether the effect is in a positive or negative direction for the element being affected. Systems thinking is very demanding, in other words, and it is not surprising that we do not adopt it easily. But because we are talking about wisdom, we can say that the ability to think systemically is one of wisdom's most important expressions.

There is a sixth type of error of the third kind implicit in Mitroff's (1998) factors that needs to be highlighted because it is a common form and is becoming more and more intrusive as time goes on. This is that all aspects of the problem are undergoing various forms of change, so that any statement of what the problem is continually runs the risk of being "overtaken by events." The error consists in thinking about problem elements as static rather than dynamic. The technologies present in the problem, whatever it is, are continually changing. The major stakeholders do not have a fixed point of view, nor are they constant as a cast of characters, and one never knows when some entirely new stakeholder will suddenly speak up. If there are legal parameters involved (e.g., government regulations), these are continually being modified. If the organization exists in a competitive environment, competitors are constantly seeking new ways to try to "win." Changing economic facts and trends are continually on organization members' minds. To capture this atmosphere of constant change, I use the metaphor of "permanent white water" (Vaill, 1989a, 1989b, 1996). The world that wisdom confronts is one of surprising, novel, complex, and intrusive events. Wisdom finds that one of its most important expressions during the 21st century is to be "wise about change itself," something I have called "process wisdom" (Vaill, 1989a, 1989b, 1996, 1998, in press). In the next major section, I explore permanent white water and process wisdom further.

The idea that everything is changing, furthermore, is the subject of a rapidly growing modern[8] literature, following a pioneering book by Bennis and Slater (1968/1998) and a landmark article by Emery and Trist (1965) (see, e.g., Beckhard & Harris, 1987; Connor, 1993; Morgan, 1988; Stacey, 1992; Strebel, 1992; see also Vaill, 1989a, 1989b, 1996).

As one last observation for the moment on Mitroff's (1998) error of the third kind, note that from an epistemological point of view, the error is not so much one of the validity of knowledge derived from these five or six sources. Those who commit an error of the third kind still have something positive to talk about. They still have data. They still think they are addressing a real issue. They still come up with an "answer" or interpretation. But it turns out that they have made a judgment error. They misframed the problem in the first place. They have taken themselves and the organization down a wrong road that they discover is a wrong road only as they near the end of it and can see that the problem or condition that originally got their attention is still there and perhaps has even intensified during the time that has been lost working on a wrong definition of the problem.

Mitroff (1998) did not put it this way, but it is apparent that the best defense against an error of the third kind is the quality of communication that exists among the parties. Errors of the third kind are especially likely when the parties do not use all of the talent available to them, or engage in win/lose game playing with each other, or do not take the problem seriously enough. For reasons such as these, the quality of their interaction is of enormous importance.

The Need From Within for Wisdom

From within, wisdom depends on the quality of relationships that arise among the parties and that they are able to sustain through time. Picture a typical cross-functional meeting in an organization, convened perhaps to try to decide how to make better use of the software the organization uses. This would be participants' initial understanding of the issues outside the group that are the reasons for its meeting. There will be some operating people present, the so-called "users." There will be people from the "information services" department, the people who designed or (more likely) bought the package in the first place. A vendor or vendors may be present. There probably will be someone from a marketing or client relations function who presumably knows the needs of the customer the software package is supposed to serve. If there are legal issues regarding the organization's liability, there will be someone from the legal department present. Sometimes a human resources person will be present, particularly if there are questions of job definitions, workforce utilization, and so on. It is unlikely that such a group would just gather spontaneously, although many of the members may think that such a meeting is needed. So there will be a convener, possibly an operating vice president with the concurrence of his or her counterpart in the information services function.

It is important to remember that with a few changes in the names of functions, a meeting like this one could and does occur in any kind of organization—public or private, profit or not-for-profit. Some organizations, such as health systems and institutions of higher education, have long traditions of influencing the relationships that people have with each other. Professional prerogatives, a polite name for jealousies, are ever-present. The reason why all organizations are finding that they need these cross-functional meetings is that the problems they face during the 21st century have outrun the structures and the role definitions that we have inherited. But as we will see, just because these meetings are imperative does not mean that they run smoothly and effectively.

We all participate in these kinds of meetings all of the time on all kinds of different subjects. Everyone knows what the ostensible purpose of a particular meeting is; in this hypothetical case, it is to get more out of the software on behalf of the customer. One would think that it should not be so hard to "solve" the problem of how to use the software more effectively. And indeed, that might be the attitude of most of the participants, each defining the issue from his or her own point of view and considering its resolution as a straightforward matter. It would be relatively rare for a member of this group to see at the outset what a difficult problem of integration or synergy this group faces, and for everyone or a majority in the group to see that, and to know that others see it too, would be extremely unlikely.

From the assumption that the group's problem is not all that hard, members may then move on to the familiar behaviors we find in North American[9] meetings: people coming to and going from the meeting, people sending representatives or being "present" on speakerphone or video hookup, with each member primarily conscious of what he or she has to contribute and very alert at the same time to any implication that his or her own expertise is not taken seriously or is even considered irrelevant to the issue. In many organizations, the members of such a group might not know each other. If that is the case, such a group might take only a minute or two to go around the table with the members introducing themselves[10] when in fact a great deal more familiarity with each other's experience and points of view might be essential to a creative perception of what the task is and what will constitute a satisfactory resolution.

As time goes on, one can note increasing impatience with how long the meeting is taking. In North American organizational cultures, such group meetings are often not seen as the fundamental settings in which the organization functions.[11] Rather, many people assume that their "real work" occurs in their own offices at their own terminals; if so, the meeting becomes an interruption for them, and members' motivation is to get done as quickly as possible. "We're going round and round and getting nowhere" is an attitude we all have felt and perhaps occasionally voiced.

The advent of wireless access to the Internet and other organization networks means that more and more "multitasking" is probably going on in group meetings that are ostensibly focused on one subject. Such divided attention by group members further compounds the challenge to the quality of communication with each other that members are able to sustain.

It is not uncommon for such a group to decide that it needs to meet again. Or perhaps the software utilization issue is an ongoing one, and this group has been constituted as a "utilization task force" with the responsibility of meeting regularly for an indefinite period of time. Under such conditions, it is even more likely that members will become more and more frustrated as they find the group members not paying as much attention to their own expertise as they would like. Given the need to do something, the group is likely to simplify the task by dividing it up into supposedly manageable bites, thereby risking making one or more of Mitroff's (1998) five mistakes as described earlier. Often when members get back to their terminals, they realize that they do not quite understand exactly what their piece of follow-up work is.

Where is wisdom in such a scenario? It might be present in at least two forms. The first form of wisdom, which every organization researcher has encountered many times, is "off-line wisdom," where members individually, outside the context of the meeting itself, can often give extraordinarily perceptive, epistemologically sophisticated descriptions of the technical problem and of the group's relative progress, or lack of progress, in dealing with it. The poem that opened this chapter has been shared with hundreds of managers, who seem to have found it to be an accurate description of the meetings they attend. Sometimes, too, members will give a strikingly sophisticated analysis of the group as a social system, describing the roles people are playing, the interaction patterns in the group, the organizational politics and power dynamics being played out among members, the quality of leadership (or lack of it) the group is getting, and the larger meaning of the group's work for the organization at large.

These insights, however, all are off-line. They rarely get expressed in any detail in the meetings themselves. But sometimes they are expressed, and this is the second form that wisdom can take. From time to time in group meetings, one member or another will say something about the problem that is truly insightful and is recognized as such by some other members of the group. Such a contribution will draw on the speaker's own expertise but be put in such a way that other members can really hear it and learn from it. That does not mean that the group will then use such wisdom, but it does mean that the perspective is in the minutes and maybe will contribute a little to progress.

Such comments, particularly if they are about the group itself, often express the off-line wisdom just described. However, a member's insights about the group itself frequently are not expressed in such a way that the group can deal with them. If a professional facilitator is present, as is sometimes the case, this person might help some of the off-line wisdom to get expressed and worked through in the group. Without a professional facilitator, and even with one, members are usually quite uncomfortable in sharing their perceptions of how the group is working. To many people, it feels like finger-pointing, although it need not be that. It is hard to have such a discussion without the "political agenda" of various members suddenly making itself felt in the things people say. The group sometimes seems to be playing the "blame game." If someone starts talking at a more personal level about how he or she feels in the meetings, there is a good chance that someone else will say it is "touchy-feely" to go much further with such talk. However, after such an event, many members will privately say that "we need to do more of that kind of thing."

So this is wisdom's challenge: from both without and within, to find ways of expressing itself that contribute to the collective understanding of organization members. It is not enough just to be wise about pieces of such an issue as we have sketched. The real need is for wisdom that helps members to integrate their knowledge, their skills, and their energies.

So far, I have not really given a definition of wisdom. Doubtless, there are explicit and implicit definitions throughout this volume. However, there has been a definition of wisdom implicit in the comments heretofore. Wisdom consists of avoiding Mitroff's (1998) five errors of the third kind, supplemented by meeting the sixth challenge of being wise about change itself, and that humans are able to be together such that their collective knowledge and skill can be brought to bear on the organization's challenges and opportunities. Wisdom here is not seen as an abstract concept; rather, it is seen as what resides concretely within these two conditions. And because wisdom resides in the concrete and the particular, the question is not so much one of defining wisdom as an abstract concept as it is one of what it means to be acting "wisely."

Permanent White Water and Process Wisdom

I am choosing to focus on the turbulence and change that organization members confront in the issues they discuss, but not because these characteristics are the only challenges to Mitroff's (1998) "smart thinking." For example, many issues have extreme technical complexity, particularly since the intrusion of the computer and sophisticated software into everyday affairs. Some issues are highly charged culturally, and some have very high costs of being wrong—what master of business administration (MBA) students learn to call "downside risk." Some are beclouded by strong traditions in the organization or culture—powerful norms that may seem to dictate how a problem is to be framed. And so on through what is no doubt a very long list of problem characteristics. But, as noted earlier, virtually all of these issues are permeated with turbulence and change. Moreover, the problem of being wise about change itself—what I have called "process wisdom"—has not received the attention it merits in our world as it is evolving.

The metaphor of "permanent white water" is intended to capture the common yet underdiscussed phenomenon of surprising, novel, ill-structured, and obtrusive events that cannot be planned out of existence. There may well be other metaphors or titles describing these conditions that appeal to the reader, who is encouraged in this regard to use whatever metaphors or analogies best capture the phenomenon.

Occasionally, actual white water rafters and kayakers will observe that they have learned all kinds of techniques for managing to navigate even the wildest "Class 6" rivers and that therefore maybe the white water metaphor is not really adequate. On the contrary, I reply, their experience makes the absolutely crucial point that indeed people do learn to handle surprising, novel, messy, and obtrusive events almost routinely. Hospital emergency rooms are one good example, especially those personnel who perform the "triage" function. Fire departments and emergency rescue squads are excellent examples. Those whose effectiveness depends on being knowledgeable and competent about computer networks and software capabilities, or about any other similarly evolving technologies, certainly know what it is to ride the wild river of technological revolutions.[12] Airline flight crews are trained to deal with a whole range of emergencies, both known and unknown. It goes without saying that most wartime battle conditions meet the criteria perhaps more intensively than does any other walk of life.

The distinctive thing about all such groups is that the situations they deal with are permanent in nature, unlike the actual river runners, who run the rapids voluntarily and who can pull out on a sand bar at the bottom of the rapid, open a cold drink, and relax. For those whose job is to deal with emergencies and revolutions, there is no "sand bar" easily and regularly available.

Increasingly, everyday organizational problems, although not as dangerous and frenzied as war, have these surprising, novel, ill-structured, obtrusive, and permanent characteristics. Maybe after a particular crisis has been dealt with, the organization can prepare itself so that it is ready the next time a particular event occurs. But what is permanent is the continual stream of these kinds of events. The type cannot be planned out of existence.

In this chapter, I have chosen not to give detailed descriptions of these white water events that are surprising, novel, messy, and obtrusive and that cannot be planned out of existence. However, in the original research that was done to formulate the permanent white water idea, the following events are examples of the kinds of things that exemplify the condition:

- Overnight, a sinkhole swallows up the parking lot of a large urban luxury hotel.
- A company in the business of maintaining unlisted telephone numbers inadvertently releases thousands of numbers to telemarketers, thereby incurring very heavy fines from the governmental regulatory authority.
- A leading sports magazine labels a photograph of a national champion team at the delirious moment of victory when in fact it is a photograph from 2 weeks earlier of one of the teams the actual winners had defeated.
- A heart transplant team discovers, after successfully transplanting a heart, that the wrong heart had been taken from the tissue bank and so the operation will need to be undone and redone.
- A high school principal receives complaints from a Parent–Teacher Association (PTA) group about a teacher who is allegedly using voodoo to discipline students in class.
- The company that prints diplomas for the U.S. Naval Academy accidentally spells the word "Navel" on the commencement diplomas.
- When a large office building is renovated, the plumbing is reconnected in such a way that all of the human waste from the building is discharged into the basement of the building next door for 2 days before the error is discovered.

We all can tell stories like these. In every case, the problem lands on the desk of some managerial leader who never thought that he or she would be needing to deal with something like this. Surprising, novel, messy, obtrusive, and recurrent—the real question is whether we can learn to handle such turbulence when it occurs and not in the process commit one of Mitroff's (1998) errors of the third kind. If I ask any group of experienced managers how many of them currently have situations on their desks that they have never dealt with before, and where there is a high degree of risk and confusion, a significant percentage of hands will go up. If the time frame is increased to the past 30 days, virtually all of the managers' hands will go up.

We speak casually about how things are constantly changing; it has nearly become a cliché. But have we reflected on what this really means? When we speak of "continual change," here are the meanings that often go unsaid:

- Change in what is already changing
- Change interacting with, crosscutting, amplifying, or canceling out other changes originating at other points
- Change where the knowledge base for dealing with it is itself changing or is entirely unknown
- Change that is interrupted, evaluated, and redirected in midstream
- Intended change that is unpredictably affected by unintended change
- Change that is not so much initiated to seize opportunity as it is initiated as a defense against serious damage or even extinction
- The "dinosaur problem," where the environment is changing faster than the organization's capacity to adapt, leading to a feeling among members of constantly "playing catch-up" and never succeeding
- Unanticipated and dramatic social changes emerging from what seemed to be needed and reasonable technological changes
- Continual changes in the external infrastructures that we would like to be able to take for granted as predictable and reliable resources such as transportation, banks, water, electricity, mail, and the current political alignment and agendas
- Continual changes in the needs and expectations and skills of the workforce available to organizations

This is just a sketch of what we really are saying when we say casually that "change is a constant." Furthermore, changes of these kinds may create confusions, anxieties, and self-protective behaviors in the very people who are responsible for identifying and dealing with these changes effectively. As the rate of change increases, does the capacity to adapt also increase? I do not know, but I have more to say about these psychological issues in the next major section when I discuss what needs to happen among organization members to improve the chances of wisdom emerging from their interactions.

Consider the interfunctional task force scenario presented earlier. The members of such a group are living in such an environment of continual change, and they know it. What they might not know are the attitudes and skills they need to operate wisely in such a world.[13] After a considerable amount of interviewing and observation of groups in such circumstances, I have formulated the following hypotheses about dealing with problems in a world of permanent white water.

First, *group members need to learn more about how they may be inadvertently disempowering each other and their work associates by the way they use their expertise, their authority, and their power.* Hardly anyone deliberately intends to block other people's thinking and abilities. Disempowerment, however, is built into professional roles in ideas about professional prerogatives, the imperatives of one's expertise, the technical language one learns to employ, and even the legal restrictions governing when one's expertise should hold sway. All of these can operate to trump others, as it were. To participate in the generation of wisdom, group members need to learn to transcend their roles. This does not mean that they throw out their roles. Rather, it means that they should be mindful of how, if one operates only within the boundaries set by one's role, this can block oneself and others from having a wise discussion of the problem.

Kouzes and Posner (2002), in their influential empirical study of the behaviors of effective leaders, found "enabling others to act" to be one of the five most prominent abilities of such leaders (chaps. 9–10). The striking thing about their effective leaders is the consciousness of the danger of disempowerment that these individuals bring to their work. They know that in today's organizations, where fear is pervasive and emotional intimidation is common (Kelly, 1988; LaBier, 1986), a special effort to remove the forces of disempowerment must be made.

Second, *group members need to discover the team possibilities offered by their task force and develop themselves as a team* (Bradford, 2002). It may seem obvious from the outside that such a task force needs to become a team. But from the inside, it is not always apparent (Manz & Sims, 1995). Sadly, each individual may believe that teamwork is needed, but as he or she observes the comments and actions of others, the individual does not see the same commitment to becoming a team. It is a tragic state of affairs; each member may believe that teamwork is needed but cannot see it in some or all of the others. It takes only one or two people acting individualistically to cause others to fall back on their own professional styles and prerogatives and give up on the idea of becoming a team. The end result is a group of people making speeches to each other. Ironically, many times the speeches contain lip service to "we're a team here." The need for teamwork has become a cliché, unfortunately, for it masks the real needs and real possibilities for teamwork.[14]

Third, difficult as it may be, *group members need to learn to step back from all of the turbulence they perceive in the organization and its environment.* As the saying goes, they need to learn to step "out of the box." They need to become aware of the paradigm of problem formulation that they are unconsciously accepting and transcend it. Each of Mitroff's (1998) five ways of committing an error of the third kind can operate to narrow thinking. To avoid committing these errors amounts to enlarging one's view of the total situation faced by the task force, not just the problem it is supposed to solve but also all of the organizational factors bearing on it: the expectations of stakeholders; the talents, energies, and potential that the members bring to the situation; whether this is the right cast of characters in the first place; and contextual factors such as budget, meeting times and places, time lines, deadlines, and secretarial support. All of these contextual factors play a role in whether a group is as wise as it has the potential to be. If ignored, any of these factors can operate to narrow thinking and constrict a group's understanding of the issues it is addressing (Levy, 1986, p. 11).

Fourth and related to the previous hypothesis, it has frequently been said that organizations need to adopt a new paradigm (Adams, 1998). What tends to go unsaid is that *there needs to be something that might be called "paradigm leadership," which may be defined as the kind of leadership that helps group members to think quite differently about their situation.* Such leadership can arise anywhere in a task force of the sort I have described; it need not come only from the most organizationally senior person in the group. Or a group such as the one I have imagined might be meeting to begin carrying out someone else's vision of a broad change that is needed, that is, following someone else's "paradigm leadership." Bolman and Deal (2003) emphasized the leader's ability to look at organizational situations from multiple points of view. Epistemologically speaking, the person is freed from a singular perspective and is able to explore different meanings of a situation from different points of view. Such a person is both able to learn from a wider variety of individuals and able to influence a wider variety of individuals with this flexibility of perspective. Moreover, paradigm leadership is not necessarily a fully worked out strategy for change. More often, it may occur in the form of a whole new way of looking at a situation. Although the term "vision" has been overworked to the point of becoming nearly a cliché, it is nevertheless true that without a new vision of what might be that becomes a powerful motivating and reframing device for organization members, the energy and focus for sustained change is not likely to occur (Kouzes & Posner, 2002; Vaill, 2002). Levy (1986) stated that paradigm shifts are marked by "change in context" and "revolutionary jumps" and that such changes are "seemingly irrational . . . based on different logic" (p. 11). There are many such sketches in the literature; what is not identified as often is the need for some particular person (or persons) to practice this paradigm leadership.

Sometimes, as pressures mount from within and without, such groups can become very sober, even a bit depressive, places. They want control, but they do not have control. Everyone adopts a very task-oriented style. Group members lose the ability to stay upbeat and innovative. Permanent white water drains humor from situations. Murphy's Law, that wonderfully sardonic protest, is that "whatever can go wrong will go wrong." We might imagine that Murphy, who supposedly was a real person at the U.S. Navy's testing facility in China Lake, California (personal conversation with Will McWhinney, University of California, Los Angeles, mid-1960s), was expressing frustration and anger at his recalcitrant project and the organization around it. I see him as a somewhat driven man, trying to get things right while struggling against complexities and contingencies that forever defeated his desire for control. Thinking of such a man at home, and of what he might have been like to live with and have as a husband and father, we might formulate, as a fifth hypothesis, "Ms. Murphy's Law": *Murphy has got to lighten up!* Murphy needs to learn to let go a little and to come to terms with the fact that he cannot control everything. He needs to step back and try to see the humor in the situation and his struggles with it. If "consultants + humor" is entered into the Google search engine, what comes up are pages and pages of companies that can be hired to bring humor into one's organization. It seems that the organizational world has learned the truth of Vaillant's (1977) observation that humor is one of our healthy defenses against stress and confusion; it is "one of mankind's most potent antidotes for the woes of Pandora's box" (p. 116).

Permanent white water can be dispiriting. The sixth hypothesis is that *wisdom entails what may be called a spiritual foundation—a fundamental framework of meanings and values.* What makes wisdom wise is that it connects our awareness to this foundation. People can see that a wise statement is deeper and more insightful than ordinary discourse, which tends to stay on the surface of issues, leaving deeper values and meanings unaddressed. Therefore, group members need not shrink from their perceptions of the deeper significance of the issues they are addressing. Exploring this deeper significance is the very way they can be most valuable in their work.

Finally, and of utmost importance, group members need to realize that *the posture of a learner is the most useful one for their situation.* In organizations, where there is so much pressure to perform, it is often difficult to remember that the continual stream of new problems and new opportunities means opportunities—indeed, the necessity of continual learning. There are important learning opportunities in the way the substantive issues are framed and analyzed. Equally important, there are learning opportunities in working with each other. This latter kind of learning—the opportunity to learn other points of view—is frequently mentioned by people who have been members of such task forces. This is the very kind of learning that is pointed to in the last three lines of the poem that opened this chapter. The learning never stops, either, given that problems are as dynamic as they are and that the rest of the group's environment is undergoing continual change of the kinds described earlier.

These seven hypotheses by no means exhaust the things that a group such as my hypothetical task force needs to work on so as to increase the wisdom it brings to its task and to increase its wisdom as a result of its work. These seven hypotheses, however, certainly constitute a start on the question. The first two hypotheses—reducing disempowerment and team building—are probably the most important in the sense that if a group can make progress on these two, the other five will be a great deal easier; whereas if the first two hypotheses are ignored, the other five will have little chance of emerging in the group's work.

This, then, has been a discussion of how wisdom can emerge from working on the external problem (or problems) a group has been constituted to address. I think that the seven hypotheses described apply to all kinds of organizational work, not just to cross-functional task forces. These same hypotheses can be applied to a group of departmental associates. Notice that all seven of these hypotheses are about processes, not about static conditions. They all involve forms of learning. They all exist as matters of degree, not in clear-cut "present or absent" states. Moreover, they are applied to a dynamic world of continual change in technology, economics, politics, and social relationships. For all of these reasons, these seven hypotheses taken together can be thought of as "process wisdom." These seven hypotheses are the wisdom about change itself that is so urgently needed.

Reference has been made at several points to the actual relationships, which are also processes, that exist among people working on their organization's problems. I now turn to a discussion of the conditions between people that will aid in the emergence of wisdom in their work—the "process wisdom of relationships."

Interpersonal Relationships and the Emergence of Wisdom

In this section, we spend most of our time on the question of how wisdom can emerge from effective relationships among organization members. Before turning to that question, however, there is one preliminary matter to discuss. It may have occurred to the reader that linking the emergence of wisdom to healthy relationships is somewhat debatable. Is there not a "wisdom born of adversity?" one might ask. What if a person spends a few hours sitting in a group where a lot of really unproductive wrangling goes on? Or what about a group where everyone hides behind their expertise and no one seems to care about finding an integrative solution? Could one not walk out of such meetings much wiser, having learned a lot about oneself, the others, and the problem? The answer, of course, is *yes*. But even if one does emerge "sadder but wiser," it will still require a healthier interactional climate for such a person's hard-won wisdom to be put to use in the future.

Alternatively, a wise person may conclude that the chances of a healthier climate are remote, so he or she sets about amassing enough power to be able to enforce his or her wisdom on behalf of others and the organization.

This might be called the "benevolent autocrat" strategy. However, no one in the leadership field is seriously arguing today that the would-be leader's best strategy is to amass enough power to be able to act unilaterally. Of course, it does happen, but it is not something anyone is advocating. Instead, the leadership field seems to be unanimous that the best strategy is to seek to build an organizational climate that is as inclusive of everyone's perspectives as possible (e.g., Collins & Porras, 1997; Harris & Moran, 1996; Kouzes & Posner, 2002; Peters & Waterman, 1982).

I conclude that although there is such a thing as wisdom born of adversity, for wisdom to be of use it still requires interaction patterns among members that recognize the diversity and validity of talents of as many members as possible. So what are these patterns?

Writing at the dawn of formal studies of organizational behavior, Ronken and Lawrence (1952/1972) conducted extensive research on just the sort of cross-functional group we envisioned earlier. In the company they studied, they found an outwardly puzzling case of a technical innovation that seemingly would have required just a few weeks to implement. In fact, it took more than 2 years of work in various groupings within the company. In explaining why the implementation took so long, Ronken and Lawrence offered five general propositions about the communication problems such groups face. I reproduce these findings here because these authors' interpretation of the problem of how wisdom can emerge in these cross-functional groups has rarely, if ever, been stated more aptly:

1. Everyone we saw in the Amicon tube project brought to the situation a picture of himself[15] in relation to the world, a way of interpreting his experiences, a set of feelings, assumptions, and expectations—in short, a frame of reference from which he looked at the world. These factors were prime determinants of what was communicated in any given interaction: what was "said," what was "heard," and what was "done." (p. 294)

2. Communication was impaired when the demands of the job brought together people with frames of reference which were incompatible (i.e., which led them into behavior which seemed to deny the validity of another's feelings, assumptions, and expectations). Under those circumstances, people tended to have no more contact with one another than was strictly necessary; to dislike, discount, resist ideas from, and even resent one another; and to make comparatively little progress on the task at hand. (p. 297)

3. Communication was facilitated when the demands of the job to be done brought together people with complementary frames of reference. Under those circumstances people tended to see more of one another than the necessary minimum, to like and respect one another, and to get more work done. (p. 298)

4. Communication was facilitated when there was in the situation someone who was able to recognize and accept a frame of reference different from his own, who was sufficiently free from preoccupation with the intent of his behavior to be able to see its effect on someone else, [and] who was able to state his point of view in terms that made sense from the listener's frame of reference. (p. 302)

5. Communication was facilitated when there was in the situation someone who had some insight into his own frame of reference, who recognized that his own feelings affected his perceptions, [and] who was aware that he had to be perceived as a source of help before he could be helpful. (p. 305)

Ronken and Lawrence (1952/1972) were not explicitly focused on how wisdom can emerge. Clearly, however, their concern for quality communication and for effectively making use of the talents of everyone involved shows that they were interested in how the best thinking can emerge from the kinds of interpersonal relationships that are needed to do the organization's work. The technical innovation they called "the Amicon tube project"—a disguised name—involved crossing departmental lines and required various professional specialists who had not worked together before. The reason why implementation of the innovation took so long was because of Proposition 2 in the preceding list. Although Proposition 3 states a desirable goal, it is now more the exception than the rule. In the world of permanent white water, we no longer can assume we will be working in groupings where people have "complementary frames of reference." Propositions 4 and 5 are offered as ways in which a group that is not initially in the condition of Proposition 3 can move toward that state. It might be assumed that Propositions 4 and 5 are saying that the group needs an external consultant or facilitator; however, Ronken and Lawrence were not specifically making this recommendation. In any event, in 1952 there were very few, if any, consultants who could do what the authors envisioned.

Although today there are a large number of professional consultant–facilitators who can play the role described by Propositions 4 and 5, it is also true that a group such as the one I have described can perform the functions the propositions describe. In the remainder of this chapter, I discuss in more detail what it is group members need to learn how to do, whether by themselves or with the help of a facilitator.

A few years after the original publication of Ronken and Lawrence's (1952/1972) book, Lawrence and his colleagues at the Harvard Business School crystallized the ideas in the five propositions into a second-year elective course in the MBA program. Research and theory continued to evolve in connection with this course and was published in two textbooks: Turner and Lombard (1969) and Athos and Gabarro (1978). It is the core of ideas in Athos and Gabarro that contains a useful framework for the emergence of wisdom in organizations. These two authors combined two different sets of ideas of the great psychotherapist, Carl Rogers, to envision a process by which healthier interpersonal relationships can evolve.

Rogers (1961a), over a long career, probably did as much as, or more than, any other individual to describe how one person can act such that another person (or persons) is freed to reflect and respond—to learn and to grow. During the 1930s, Rogers discovered that this learning and growth seemed to occur best when he, as a therapist, was able to create a safe environment that allowed the client to explore attitudes and feelings that had been giving him or her trouble. Rogers initially named his approach "nondirective therapy" (Rogers, 1942), but later he renamed it "client-centered therapy." To be client-centered is to be more concerned with letting the client express himself or herself than with giving interpretations and advice to the client. This idea was expressed by Ronken and Lawrence in Proposition 4 in the remarkable phrase "sufficiently free from preoccupation with the intent of his own behavior to see its effect on someone else."

There are three key concepts: acceptance, empathy, and congruence (Athos & Gabarro, 1978, chap. 8). *Acceptance,* although seemingly a straightforward idea, turns out to be extraordinarily difficult for many people. We live in a highly judgmental society. Although we espouse tolerance, "live and let live," "to each his own," and so forth, when face-to-face with a point of view we disagree with, it is hard to be accepting. The more we disagree, the more difficult it is to simply accept another point of view in all its complexity and perhaps uniqueness. In a landmark essay on the basic values of the field of organization development, Tannenbaum and Davis (1969) offered a variety of propositions that they maintained must undergird a healthy organization. At least two of their propositions speak directly to the idea of acceptance: "Away from avoidance or negative evaluation of individuals toward confirming them as human beings" (p. 133) and "Away from resisting and fearing individual differences toward accepting and utilizing them" (p. 135).

Acceptance is something other than agreement or disagreement. It is obvious that disagreement can hardly be called acceptance, but ironically, agreement can be just as nonaccepting as can disagreement. Agreement can be very selective of the speaker's frame of reference rather than accepting it as a whole. Agreement can distract the speaker from digging into aspects of himself or herself that may be troubling or that he or she is unaware of. Having won the agreement of the listener, the person seeks to retain it and refrain from saying things that might jeopardize it.

Acceptance is fundamentally a recognition that the other person and his or her point of view exist. They are real. Acceptance is an act of wisdom in and of itself.

One reason why acceptance is difficult to practice is the question of what is accepting behavior, in contrast to agreeing or disagreeing behavior. How does one communicate to the other that one accepts him or her without seeming to agree or disagree? Often, acceptance is most effectively communicated nonverbally by maintaining eye contact, avoiding gestures that suggest boredom or lack of attention, and continually indicating to the speaker that one is paying attention. But in any case, acceptance may seem relatively passive. By itself, it does not lead us to explore another person's world beyond what the other person offers us. In a highly competitive, fast-paced culture, speakers might not be satisfied with acceptance initially; they want to know whether the others agree or disagree.

This is why Rogers's second core idea of *empathy*, as interpreted by Athos and Gabarro (1978), is so important. Rogers was focused on the therapist empathizing with the client. Athos and Gabarro showed that empathy between superiors and subordinates, and in lateral relationships in organizations and across other boundaries of all kinds, can be just as important as it is in the therapeutic setting. With empathy, we move on from acceptance to an active exploration of the other person's world. The aim is to understand the other person from his or her point of view—to understand, in contemporary jargon, "where the other person is coming from."[16] The key attitudes are curiosity and caring. Empathy is the ability to "walk in the other person's shoes," as the saying goes. It is interest in the other person's frame of reference, including his or her experience, attitudes, skills, and even those areas where the other person, in his or her own eyes, is in need of further learning and development. It is risky to expose the areas in which we know we have a lot to learn. We will tend to do it only when we feel accepted and when others are interested in understanding more about how things are for us.

In terms of epistemology, empathy is the quest not just for our own knowing but also for the knowing—and feeling—of other persons. The poem that began this chapter is a plea by the speaker for the other person to understand "what it is I don't understand." Once again, epistemology becomes not an abstract category but rather a living process among individual "knowers." To know the other's knowing—this is what empathy attempts.

As with acceptance, the question arises as to what empathetic behaviors are. If one is trying to be empathetic, what does one actually do? But unlike acceptance, empathy is more active. What needs to be communicated is that one is trying to understand. Rogers suggested somewhere that a very useful way to communicate empathy is to simply repeat back to the other person what seem to be the key phrases in his or her comments. For example, "You're saying we can't possibly stay on budget and on schedule at the same time, am I right?" might be an attempt to reflect what one has just heard from the other. This gives the other person the opportunity to agree and then continue to say more or to reply, "No that's not quite it. What I really mean is . . ." In either case, the listener has communicated interest and a desire to understand.

Today's organizations often do not seem to be very empathetic places. People get focused on their own schedules and projects and their own standing with others. They can often seem not particularly interested in finding out a lot about others' worlds or frames of reference, as Ronken and Lawrence (1952/1972) called them. However, in my hypothesized cross-functional group that is meeting to improve software utilization, each member presents to the group the tip of a very large iceberg, as it were. One might argue that each member is responsible for expressing as much of his or her frame of reference as possible and for being assertive, and that is true, as I discuss further in a moment. If the assertiveness is done in a climate that lacks acceptance and empathy, however, it may be judged as "hogging the floor," "bidding for power," "talking to hear oneself talk," or some other dismissive cliché. It is in a climate of acceptance and empathy that we can best express the ways we think our own perspective and skills can contribute to understanding the problem the group is addressing.

Relatively late in his career, Rogers (1961b) published an extraordinary book chapter titled "A Tentative Formulation of a General Law of Interpersonal Relationships." In this chapter, Rogers formulated an idea he called *congruence*. To explain congruence, Rogers hypothesized three general regions of experience: (1) what we choose intentionally to communicate openly to other people; (2) all that we are actually aware of out of our total experience as we communicate at any given moment, including ideas, attitudes, and feelings we may intentionally *not* be communicating in a given instance; and (3) the totality of our experience in all its complexity, all about ourselves that we are both aware of and (at the moment) unaware of, including aspects of our experience that may be troubling to us and/or that we may be actively denying. Region 3, for example, includes everything we know about our childhoods, even though it is not in our awareness (i.e., Region 2), each moment as we communicate with others throughout the day. Region 3 is the whole "iceberg" of ourselves—past, present, and future, what we are aware of and what we are not aware of, and what we are not able to become aware of without help. The three regions may be thought of as concentric circles, with Region 3 being the largest and Regions 2 and 1 being contained within it. We refer to these three regions as (1) communication, (2) awareness, and (3) experience.

Congruence in Rogers's terms occurs when there is relative matching among these three regions. Obviously, this does not mean that in our communications (Region 1) we should try to tell the whole story of ourselves (Region 3); rather, what Rogers seemed to be after is for there to be an openness among the three regions and a lack of distortion as we communicate. It is a matter of degree of openness—relatively open versus relatively closed, relatively accurate versus relatively distorted. When there is incongruence between communication and awareness—when communication attempts to give an impression that is inconsistent with what we are really thinking—we may call it "being discreet" or "being diplomatic" but also "being phony," "dissembling," or even "lying." Because it occurs so often, there are many words and metaphors for the situation in which what we say is not matched by what we are thinking. Because we communicate on multiple levels, it is sometimes the case that others can tell whether a person is dissembling by his or her body language—by a "silent language" (Hall, 1973) of nonverbal communication. Flickering eyes are said to be a sure sign that a person is lying. A variety of body movements may communicate (unstated) sexual interest. One's words may express confidence and optimism, but one's tone of voice might communicate fear, uncertainty, and so forth. Rogers realized that the more congruence there is between a person's communication and awareness, the more the listeners are likely to trust what they are hearing from the person. This is particularly important if the intended communication is to convey what we are calling acceptance or empathy. Nothing undercuts each of these two kinds of communication more than if they are incongruent, that is, if they are not backed up by honest and genuine intent in one's awareness.

Congruence between awareness and one's total experience (Region 2 and Region 3) involves relative self-acceptance and a relative willingness to be uncomfortable occasionally as feelings we had not been aware of come bubbling up in us or as we become confused as we speak and need to decide whether or not to admit it. If we do not have self-acceptance and instead are actively holding certain thoughts out of awareness, we call it being in a state of "denial"—of blindness to oneself—or use a variety of more technical terms relating to the Freudian concept of "repression." Denial has fear behind it. If our awareness is infused with fear, it can garble our communication. Moreover, fear has a perniciously contagious quality. If fear infuses our words, it may also make others uncomfortable—either afraid *for* us, afraid *of* us, or afraid of the situation we are talking about. In any case, these "mixed messages" may make it difficult for people to listen to what we are saying.

Because much of experience is not in awareness and not even available to awareness for whatever reason, one may surprise oneself from time to time with ideas and feelings that one did not know were "in there," so to speak. One may want to be communicating as openly as possible; the desire to be open is in awareness, in other words. But for some reason the person cannot understand, it is proving to be difficult, in a given communication, to get that across to others. Instead, what the person may be sensing is confusion or evasiveness, for example. The person cannot see why the listeners are sensing that because he or she is not trying to sound confused or be evasive. Such a situation would be an example of incongruence between awareness and experience; the person does not know why others are picking up what they are picking up in the communication. And to compound the complexity, of course, the listeners might not be communicating what they are hearing very well. For their own reasons, they too may be confused or evasive; they may be responding incongruently, in other words. It is not hard, with Rogers's concepts, to see how miscommunications occur and how groups can lapse into states of frustration and annoyance, with task effectiveness suffering as a result.

If we consider congruence in terms of the communication of wisdom, it is not hard to see how important congruence is. Unfortunately, wisdom qua wisdom does not compel understanding and agreement just because it is wisdom. In content, it may be an order of magnitude more insightful and appropriate than other things being said in the same context, but if it is communicated incongruently it will probably not be heard as wisdom. Truly effective wisdom is valuable as content, and it carries with it the psychological and even spiritual maturity to express itself congruently. This amplifies one of the premises with which we began—that wisdom is a social phenomenon, not a private possession.

After sketching the three regions of behavior—communication, awareness, and experience—Rogers (1961b) then formulated his tentative general law:

> The greater the congruence of experience, awareness, and communication on the part of one individual, the more the ensuing relationship will involve: a tendency toward *reciprocal* communication with a quality of increasing congruence; a tendency toward more *mutually* accurate understanding of the communications; improved psychological adjustment and functioning in *both* parties; [and] *mutual* satisfaction in the relationship. (p. 344, italics added)

In other words, the idea is that congruence begets congruence. And as just noted, wisdom implies congruent communication for the kinds of benefits that Rogers (1961b) postulated to occur. Once again, Rogers was drawing primarily on his knowledge of the therapeutic context. Athos and Gabarro (1978) carried the idea into the organizational world and combined it with the ideas of acceptance and empathy. Without acceptance and empathy, the idea that "congruence begets congruence" by itself could be a shouting match! We need to add the two notions of acceptance and empathy. The parties need to be congruently accepting and congruently empathetic. Rogers tended to take this for granted, but Athos and Gabarro saw that congruence can be problematic without the addition of acceptance and empathy.

Admittedly, it is a tall order for acceptance, empathy, and congruence to come to characterize a group's conduct. There are two reasons, however, for seriously suggesting the importance of these three ideas. First, the question I am pursuing is how wisdom can arise in an organizational context. Perhaps it is possible for an individual to become personally wise without all of these interpersonal conditions. But the question asks how wisdom can be expressed and used in the conduct of an organization's affairs. To achieve that, I am suggesting that an interpersonal climate characterized by some degree of acceptance, empathy, and congruence is needed.

Second, from an empirical point of view, there are data to suggest that very high-performing groups contain communication patterns that are not unlike what Athos and Gabarro (1978), after Rogers (1961b), called acceptance, empathy, and congruence. Over and over, studies of such teams and organizations reveal communication patterns that are affirming and supportive, caring, and interested in others. Over and over, we find studies of effective leadership emphasizing the importance of valuing and empowering organization members and of "straight talk."[17] To put it the other way around, no one talking about organizational effectiveness is suggesting that communications need not be marked by acceptance and empathy and need not be particularly congruent (see, e.g., Collins & Porras, 1997; Kouzes & Posner, 2002; Peters & Waterman, 1982; Quinn, 1996; Vaill, 1978, 1982). What we have in the acceptance/empathy/congruence model is a deeper explanation for what is meant by the phrase "good communications." This deeper level, however, shows us how much more difficult good communication is. It requires a desire and a determination to grow. It is not just a matter of being "clear."

Athos and Gabarro (1978) suggested that acceptance, empathy, and congruence can be practiced in organizational contexts. They considered these three as the keys to effective interpersonal communications. Looking back at the five propositions of Ronken and Lawrence (1952/1972), we can see in their Propositions 4 and 5 that they were envisioning a process very like what Rogers (1961b) formulated as a "general law" of congruence begetting congruence, even though Ronken and Lawrence were writing a decade earlier and basing their ideas on empirical research, not on psychotherapy.

I take the idea that congruence begets congruence one step further in this chapter by suggesting that for wisdom to operate within organizational groupings, and for the products of their work to contain wisdom that can then become available to others, acceptance, empathy, and congruence need to be relatively present. The qualification of "relatively," moreover, is important. These three qualities are matters of degree—matters of intention and improvement—rather than matters of either/or. *Acceptance, empathy, and congruence are matters of learning and development.*

Furthermore, I am suggesting that talk becomes wisdom as acceptance, empathy, and congruence are realized in organizational communications. The body of knowledge that has validity and that can be trusted, the substance of wisdom, was called "episteme" by the Greeks. Epistemology has become the search for the nature and conditions of such knowledge. This chapter has tried to show what the organizational challenges to the emergence of such wisdom are. It has also tried to show how these challenges can be effectively met.

Conclusion

The unquestionable technical expertise and wisdom that members bring to approaching the organization's problems need to be supplemented and infused with the psychological skill and wisdom of acceptance, empathy, and congruence. Ironically, more and more organization members hold advanced degrees in various aspects of the organization's operations. In pursuing these degrees, they have been rewarded for attaining in-depth knowledge at the absolute frontiers of their disciplines. However, they tend not to be educated in the process of explaining this expertise to those who do not have that specialty or in finding the synergy that exists between their expertise and that of others. The synergy will produce integrative solutions that truly will be the "smart thinking" that Mitroff (1998) described, and more than just smart thinking—true wisdom—can then emerge.

Notes

1. This poem by the author, titled "The Layman's Lament," is found in Vaill (1989a, p. 103).

2. For example, it is not found in works such as Edwards (1967), Honderich (1995), and Reese (1999).

3. Interestingly enough, Abraham Maslow reached a similar conclusion in his critique of "means-centering" in science, whereby an excessive concern with neatness, precision, scientific "objectivity," and quantifiable results leads to an oversimplification and sterilization of the problem to be solved (Maslow, 1954, p. 13).

4. A noteworthy exception is the so-called sociotechnical systems approach to organizational change, which was created at the Tavistock Institute of Human Relations in London during the early 1950s and was influential for the next 40 years or so. See Kleiner (1996), Trist (1997), and Weisbord (2004).

5. Vickers is probably better known in Europe and Great Britain than in North America. In the United States, his principal influence has been more among scholars and practitioners in the public sector than in the private sector. In a series of powerfully argued books (Vickers, 1965/1995, 1968, 1973), he propounded a view of the senior executive leader rooted in systems thinking and a detailed understanding of the reciprocal influence of the institution and its environment.

6. Drath and Palus (1994) and Drath (2001), in fact, made the interesting argument that the relationship is all we have. Leadership *is* the relationship, and if the relationship does not work there will be no leadership.

7. Of course, various kinds of communiqués can emerge from these concrete interactions that can then be read and reacted to by thousands or even millions of people, both inside and outside the social systems in which the original concrete interactions occurred. Moreover, now that the age of electronic communication networks is upon us, the concrete interactions themselves can be participated in by much larger groups than could formerly interact easily face-to-face.

8. Of course, the idea that everything is continually changing goes back to Heraclitus and the pre-Socratics. Continual change, moreover, is the second (as "impermanence") of Buddhism's Four Noble Truths (Reese, 1999, p. 97).

9. There are cultures in East Asia, for example, where there are traditions of group harmony. It is more important in these cultures for the group to solve the problem than for any given individual to have his or her way. Accordingly, there is less impatience with long, complex discussions. See Harris and Moran (1996, chaps. 5 and 12).

10. Bennis and Slater (1968/1998), in a prophetic book, envisioned a world of "temporary systems" where no one knows anyone else very well and the whole challenge a group faces is to learn to manage its temporariness well enough so that work can get done and people's talents and energies are developed.

11. Of course, for years people have been bringing material from their in-baskets to meetings and looking through it in their laps while ostensibly paying attention to their meetings. A ridiculous extreme of this phenomenon in my experience was a Saturday afternoon meeting of the board of governors of one of the most prominent and powerful professional associations in America. One member indignantly announced that he was missing the Purdue–Ohio State football game for the meeting, so he hoped that the group would not mind if he watched it on his pocket television receiver during the meeting. No one challenged him, of course, including (I must ruefully admit) myself.

12. "The computer revolution is pushing the definition of what a professor even is," commented a faculty colleague of mine recently. This colleague is a professor of information systems and technology.

13. This point was made emphatically by Bennis and Slater (1968/1998, p. 140).

14. For many years, a continual demonstration of what real teamwork looks like has been taking place in team sports. Year after year in sport after sport, the team that wins the championship is seen to be more effective *as a team* than its competitors. Yet we do not seem to take the next step and ask concretely, "What is it that distinguishes true teamwork from non-team play?"

15. This research was done during the late 1940s and early 1950s, before gender-neutral language had become the norm. Perhaps it is significant, too, that this research and these resulting insights occurred this long ago. We have known for a long time, in other words, what some of the key determinants of a climate of wisdom are.

16. Told to practice "empathy," we might object to being told to act like a therapist. Yet we all can think of situations in which we have been quite willing to explore where another person was "coming from" and quite willing to grant how important this knowledge can be for both parties.

17. Interestingly, Rogers presented a seminar on "a demonstration of student-centered teaching" to faculty members of the Harvard Business School some years before the course using his ideas was created. The seminar itself illustrates his point that "congruence begets congruence" with improved communications resulting. In Rogers's (1961a) words, following his opening remarks, "I did not expect the tumult which followed. Feelings ran high. It seemed I was threatening their jobs, I was obviously saying things I didn't believe, etc., etc. . . . [But] after much storm, members of the group began expressing, more and more frankly, their own significant feelings about teaching" (p. 274).

References

Adams, J. D. (Ed.). (1998). *Transforming work* (2nd ed.). Alexandria, VA: Miles River Press.

Athos, A. G., & Gabarro, J. J. (1978). *Interpersonal behavior: Communication and understanding in relationships.* Englewood Cliffs, NJ: Prentice Hall.

Beckhard, R., & Harris, R. T. (1987). *Organizational transitions: Managing complex change* (2nd ed.). Reading, MA: Addison-Wesley.

Bennis, W. G., & Slater, P. E. (1998). *The temporary society.* San Francisco: Jossey-Bass. (Original work published 1968)

Bolman, L. G., & Deal, T. E. (2003). *Reframing organizations* (3rd ed.). San Francisco: Jossey-Bass.

Bradford, D. L. (2002). The challenge of a team. In A. R. Cohen (Ed.), *The portable MBA in management* (2nd ed., chap. 3). New York: John Wiley.

Collins, J. C., & Porras, J. I. (1997). *Built to last.* New York: HarperCollins.

Connor, D. R. (1993). *Managing at the speed of change.* New York: Villard Books.

Dixon, N. M. (1996). *Perspectives on dialogue: Making talk developmental for individuals and organizations.* Greensboro, NC: Center for Creative Leadership.

Drath, W. H. (2001). *The deep blue sea: Rethinking the source of leadership.* San Francisco: Jossey-Bass.

Drath, W. H., & Palus, C. J. (1994). *Making common sense.* Greensboro, NC: Center for Creative Leadership.

Edwards, P. (Ed.). (1967). *The encyclopedia of philosophy.* New York: Macmillan.

Emery, F., & Trist, E. L. (1965). The causal texture of organizational environments. *Human Relations, 18,* 21–32.

Galbraith, J. K. (1998). *The affluent society.* Boston: Houghton Mifflin. (Original work published 1958)

Goleman, D. (1998). *Working with emotional intelligence.* New York: Bantam Books.

Hall, E. T. (1973). *The silent language.* Garden City, NY: Anchor Books/Doubleday.

Harris, P. R., & Moran, R. T. (1996). *Managing cultural differences: Leadership strategies for a new world of business* (4th ed.). Houston: Gulf Publishing.

Honderich, T. (Ed.). (1995). *The Oxford companion to philosophy.* New York: Oxford University Press.

Katz, D., & Kahn, R. L. (1966). *The social psychology of organizations.* New York: John Wiley.

Kelly, C. M. (1988). *The destructive achiever: Power and ethics in the American corporation.* Reading, MA: Addison-Wesley.

Kleiner, A. (1996). *The age of heretics: Heroes, outlaws, and the forerunners of corporate change.* Garden City, NY: Doubleday.

Kouzes, J. M., & Posner, B. Z. (2002). *The leadership challenge* (3rd ed.). San Francisco: Jossey-Bass.

LaBier, D. (1986). *Modern madness.* Reading, MA: Addison-Wesley.

Levy, A. (1986). Second-order planned change: Definition and conceptualization. *Organizational Dynamics, 15*(1), 5–20.

Manz, C. C., & Sims, H. P. (1995). *Business without bosses.* New York: John Wiley.

Maslow, A. H. (1954). *Motivation and personality.* New York: Harper.

Mitroff, I. I. (1998). *Smart thinking for crazy times.* San Francisco: Berrett-Koehler.

Morgan, G. (1988). *Riding the waves of change: Developing managerial competencies for a turbulent world.* San Francisco: Jossey-Bass.

Peters, T. J., & Waterman, R. H., Jr. (1982). *In search of excellence.* New York: Harper & Row.

Quinn, R. E. (1996). *Deep change.* San Francisco: Jossey-Bass.

Reese, W. L. (1999). *Dictionary of philosophy and religion.* Amherst, NY: Humanity Books.

Rogers, C. R. (1942). *Counseling and psychotherapy*. Boston: Houghton Mifflin.

Rogers, C. R. (1961a). *On becoming a person*. Boston: Houghton Mifflin.

Rogers, C. R. (1961b). A tentative formulation of a general law of interpersonal relationships. In C. R. Rogers (Ed.), *On becoming a person* (pp. 338–346). Boston: Houghton Mifflin.

Ronken, H. O., & Lawrence, P. R. (1972). *Administering changes*. Westport, CT: Greenwood Press. (Original work published by Harvard Business School press, 1952)

Senge, P. M. (1990). *The fifth discipline*. New York: Doubleday/Currency Books.

Senge, P. M., Scharmer, C. O., Jaworski, J., & Flowers, B. S. (2004). *Presence: Human purpose and the field of the future*. Cambridge, MA: Society for Organizational Learning.

Stacey, R. D. (1992). *Managing the unknowable: Strategic boundaries between order and chaos in organizations*. San Francisco: Jossey-Bass.

Strebel, P. (1992). *Breakpoints: How managers exploit radical business change*. Boston: Harvard Business School Press.

Tannenbaum, R., & Davis, S. A. (1969). Values, man, and organizations. *Industrial Management Review, 10*, 67–83. (Reprinted in W. H. Schmidt, Ed., 1970, *Organizational frontiers and human values*, pp. 129–149, Belmont, CA: Wadsworth)

Trist, E. L. (Ed.). (1997). *The social engagement of social science*. Philadelphia: University of Pennsylvania Press.

Turner, A. N., & Lombard, G. F. F. (1969). *Interpersonal behavior and administration*. New York: Free Press.

Vaill, P. B. (1978). Toward a behavioral description of high-performing systems. In M. W. McCall, Jr., & M. M. Lombardo (Eds.), *Leadership: Where else can we go?* (chap. 6). Greensboro, NC: Center for Creative Leadership.

Vaill, P. B. (1982). The purposing of high-performing systems. *Organizational Dynamics, 11*(2), 23–39.

Vaill, P. B. (1989a). *Managing as a performing art*. San Francisco: Jossey-Bass.

Vaill, P. B. (1989b). Seven process frontiers for organization development. In W. Sikes, A. Drexler, & J. Gant (Eds.), *The emerging practice of organization development* (pp. 261–272). Alexandria, VA: NTL Institute for Applied Behavioral Science.

Vaill, P. B. (1996). *Learning as a way of being*. San Francisco: Jossey-Bass.

Vaill, P. B. (1998). *Spirited leading and learning*. San Francisco: Jossey-Bass.

Vaill, P. B. (2002). Visionary leadership. In A. R. Cohen (Ed.), *The portable MBA in management* (2nd ed., pp. 17–47). New York: John Wiley.

Vaill, P. B. (in press). Process wisdom: The heart of O.D. In T. Cummings (Ed.), *The O.D. handbook*. Thousand Oaks, CA: Sage.

Vaillant, G. (1977). *Adaptation to life*. Boston: Little, Brown.

Vickers, G. (1968). *Value systems and social process*. New York: Basic Books.

Vickers, G. (1973). *Making institutions work*. New York: John Wiley.

Vickers, G. (1995). *The art of judgment*. Thousand Oaks, CA: Sage. (Original work published 1965)

Weick, K. E. (1995). *Sensemaking in organizations*. Thousand Oaks, CA: Sage.

Weisbord, M. R. (2004). *Productive workplaces revisited* (2nd ed.). San Francisco: Jossey-Bass.

16

Strategic Epistemology

Innovation and Organizational Wisdom

Arnoud De Meyer

What do innovation and organizational wisdom have to do with each other? What is the nature of the relationship between them? It would be simple to argue that innovation is the direct result of the careful and wise generation of, reflection on, and application of what the organization knows. But I argue in this chapter that the relationship is more complex than such a linear sequence from wisdom to innovative application. To explore this complex relationship, we need to start with an operational definition of both innovation and organizational wisdom.

In this chapter, innovation is defined as the economically successful introduction of a new technology or a new combination of existing technologies to create a drastic change in the value/price relationship offered to a customer or user.

Essential for innovation is that it starts with a customer or user. From our perspective, innovation exists only if a customer or user is convinced that there has been a drastic change in what he or she perceives as value for price. We always mention both a customer and a user because they might not be the same. In the case of an industrial product, for example, the customer is a company, but the user is an employee who might not always have a real influence over the purchasing decision.

Innovation affects the value/price relationship perceived by a customer or user. It can affect both sides of that relationship. This suggests that we consider all forms of innovations: products, services, systems, and processes. Innovation is about drastic changes in the value/price relationship. When there is a small adjustment in the value, we would not call that an innovation. It is perhaps a rejuvenation of the product or a product adaptation. Changing the value offered to the client does not mean increasing the value of what is offered to the customer or user. Kim and Mauborgne (2005) argued in their description of what they call "value innovation" that very often innovation comes from eliminating some obsolete values and replacing them with new values. One of their classic examples is the Canadian company Cirque du Soleil, which renovated the concept of a circus by eliminating all animal shows (thereby reducing the cost considerably) and creating a show that is much more theatrical and attractive to adults.

We are not limiting innovation to technological changes. Innovation and technology are not identical. Innovation can, of course, be the result of a new technology. Some of the innovations in the genetic engineering industry or the telecommunication industry are indeed exploiting new technology. But many examples of innovation are based on a clever redeployment or recombination of existing technologies. Equally important in the success of innovation is the development of an innovative business model. This often requires major innovations in the administrative and managerial systems of the organization.

Finally, a creative breakthrough becomes an innovation when it has led to economic success for the firm. When one innovates, one needs to make the distinction among technical, commercial, and economic success. Technical success means that one is able to translate one's dream or idea into a real product, service, system, or process. This is the step of invention. It does require a lot of hard work and creativity, and it is clearly a necessary condition for success in innovation. But there have been many technically successful products that ended up on the waste dump. One can speak about innovation only when one can transform the technical success into a commercially successful product that has a return on investment that is higher than the return one would have made on a conservative investment in the stock market.

Wisdom of the individual sage is the ability and desire to make the best use of available but incomplete knowledge so as to make choices that can gain approval in a long-term examination by a wide variety of people. It does rely on past experience but at the same time is able to anticipate future likely consequences. An organization benefits from the sum of its individual members' wisdom but also of the accumulation of wisdom built up over the years of the organization's existence and commonly shared by the members of the organization. As we saw earlier, innovation is often based on redeployment and recombination of existing technologies, thereby anchored in the cumulative knowledge of the organization. But innovation is also about entering uncharted terrain. To be successful with innovation, we need to be able to anticipate the future. Thus, wisdom is needed to innovate.

But how does this play out in practice? Where are the concrete interfaces between innovation and wisdom? The exploitation of new technology and the recombination of existing technologies are undoubtedly anchored in the organizational wisdom created by the firm. From the earliest studies on innovation (Myers & Marquis, 1969), the observations have constantly been pointing in the same direction; most of the information used by innovators was personal knowledge rather than personally researched knowledge. Only 8% of innovative information came from experimentation and calculation, and 7% came from printed materials. As such empirical findings, and those of countless studies that followed this first work, suggest, "Science and technology are vital tools that need to be applied effectively and developed selectively. But . . . innovation is more a matter of flexible, productive, and focused employee relations in the workplace than it is the result of technological resources or the impact of science" (Carnegie & Butlin, 1993). This seems to suggest that organizational wisdom, which is embedded in the interactions between the employees of the firm, is indeed an important source for innovation. I have argued elsewhere that applied research, as carried out by firms, is precisely the activity that builds up the organizational knowledge and wisdom that will enable the firm to innovate in the future (De Meyer, 1993b). But we need to go further than to see the stock of wisdom about technology, administration, and management systems as the main source of innovation. My definition of innovation also implies that it must be the result of the interaction between this organizational knowledge and wisdom and the experience and tacit knowledge that the user has about the fulfillment of his or her needs; the collective wisdom of the users recognizes when a new product, process, or system provides the stepwise change in the value/price relationship. And it is this interaction between two types of wisdom that will lead to economic value. Innovation exists only when one can couple the organizational wisdom with the user wisdom. The strategic choices about the creative production function can be wise only if they are made in a way that is consistent with the evolving interests of the firm and the users.

Thus, the managerial challenge for the innovator is to mobilize these two types of wisdom. Such a mobilization requires actions at the level of the organization, at the level of the individual, and at the level of systems. In the next paragraphs, we provide some ideas on how one needs to organize for translating the firm's organizational wisdom and the users' wisdom into actionable ideas. Essential in my view of the innovation process is that it is an information processing activity; creative people take in information and process it creatively and with their wisdom use it to produce product processes, systems, and services. Leveraging the organizational wisdom is, to a large extent, working on the intake of "raw materials" and the improvement of the productivity of the creative transformation function. How can organizational wisdom help us to make the right choices about what kind of information and knowledge accumulated over the past to use to prepare for the future? What in the stock of knowledge is relevant and revealing? And how can organizational wisdom help us to make the most out of incomplete information and conceive a reasonable future situation for the organization that is broadly beneficial to it?

This leads me to how I want to define wisdom in relationship to innovation. In this chapter, organizational wisdom is defined as the cumulative and integrated knowledge that can enable the organization to make the necessary and strategically correct choices to enhance the productivity of the creative transformation function, as well as the proper orienting and executing of that function, in the face of a high level of uncertainty about the likely consequences of the decisions. The link between wisdom and innovation requires these choices to be made in a way that is consistent with the fundamental but evolving interests of the organization, the users, and perhaps a larger collective.

Now that we have clarified the foundations and nature of innovation and wisdom and their relationship, we can address the question of how this can be rolled out in a practical and actionable way. But before we explore this, I must mention an important caveat. Organizational wisdom can also be a hindrance to innovation, in particular when disruptive innovation (Christensen & Overdorf, 2000) is needed, that is, when the innovation is of a nature fundamentally different from, or is in conflict with, the cumulated and integrated knowledge the organization has built up over its existence. Leonard-Barton (1992) argued that the technical, administrative, and system core competencies can easily become core rigidities that stop the firm from innovating. She asserted that when a firm attempts to innovate in the three areas of its competencies at the same time, the innovation is virtually guaranteed to fail. Wisdom can lead to rigidity, and when the innovation is too far away from the wisdom of the firm, it will reject the innovation. True organizational wisdom not only is about making choices about actions to pursue but sometimes also is about knowing when and how to let go of conventional knowledge.

Creating and Mobilizing
the Organizational Wisdom

I argued in earlier publications that one of the roles of the research and development (R&D) function in the firm is to contribute to the creation and maintenance of the organizational knowledge that may lead to organizational wisdom (e.g., De Meyer, 1993a). I called this the organizational technical learning of the firm. The R&D function has, of course, the immediate task of technical problem solving so as to get products out into the market and to do this in close collaboration with the other functions in the organization. In so doing, it also builds knowledge and wisdom about user needs and spurs developments in proprietary technology not only at the firm but also at research institutes and universities as well as with competitors. Thus, the firm learns and prepares itself for future innovations. This organizational learning is a process within the organization by which knowledge, and ultimately wisdom, is developed about the action–outcome relationships about innovation and the effects of these relationships on the environment. The outcome of this learning process is knowledge that needs to be distributed throughout the organization, is communicable among the members of the organization, has consensual validity, and is finally integrated into the working procedures of the organization.

In my own research, I have learned that five managerial areas of action can stimulate the technical learning that leads to organizational wisdom: creating credibility, stimulating diversity among learning units, investing in communication, developing the extended network of the firm, and providing the appropriate tools for communication to build up the knowledge base. In what follows, I provide a few lines of explanation on each of these.

To do so, I model the part of the firm that creates and exploits innovation as a network of individuals or small groups, either colocated or in different parts of the world and either all belonging to the same firm or being parts of different organizations that partner on the innovation project. Individual knowledge is created by individual experimentation and learning. Organizational knowledge is created by the interaction among these individuals or groups, leading to a set of actionable true beliefs for the organization. Organizational wisdom is the ability to make the best use of this accumulated and integrated but inevitably incomplete knowledge so as to cope with an uncertain future in a way that is consistent with the interests of all stakeholders in the innovation process.

It is quite clear from this simple modeling that organizational wisdom often cannot be limited to one organization but rather will be spread out over several groups that partner with each other. Organizational wisdom is often embedded in a network. In fact, I would argue that organizational wisdom is never limited to one organization but rather always crosses the organizational borders. Suppliers, vendors, distributors, and partners in development hold some of the organizational wisdom of the organization and contribute to it. In a vertically integrated firm, the role played by this "external" organizational wisdom may be negligible compared with that played by the internal organizational wisdom. But in today's business environment, where companies tend to focus on their core activities and outsource more and more of their nonessential activities, this part of the organizational wisdom may become very significant and needs careful and proactive management.

Let us now revisit the five areas of action that were mentioned earlier.

Creating Credibility

Learning from each other, and in particular the consensual validation of the individual learning, requires that individuals or small groups believe in each other. Innovation teams are prepared to learn from each other if they have accepted each other's credibility. If not, they will not buy into the results obtained by the other team and might not even notice the other team's results or successes. During the early 1990s, quite a few European and U.S. multinational firms created small laboratories in Japan. After the initial hype about the creation of these small labs (often expressed as, e.g., "we now also have a significant presence in Japan"), many of them became isolated and lost the possibility of contributing to the creation of organizational knowledge. Why? Because of a combination of communication difficulties, an inability to work in cross-border teams, too high initial expectations, and so on, these Japanese labs were often unable to live up quickly to what the rest of the organization had expected to get out of them. As a consequence, they lost their credibility. Without credibility, there was no organizational learning, and quite a few of these labs disappeared silently. I suspect that we will soon see some of the same disappointments with the labs created in China and India today (although I must admit that companies these days have become better at managing cross-border teams).

How does a manager create a sufficient level of credibility? In our studies on international R&D networks, we have observed two particularly important drivers of this credibility: a clear strategic mandate for the different groups that will contribute to the organizational wisdom and an early action agenda for new individuals or groups that enter the network. There may be some overlaps in the strategic mandates, but it needs to be clear what the technological and geographical scopes are for the nodes in the network and to what extent overlap is accepted. Too much overlap will lead to competition between the teams in the network and will be negative for the creation of a clear strategic mandate. It is also of great importance that this strategic mandate evolves over time and adjusts itself to the changes in the environment. Otherwise, the team will lose its credibility and become ineffective in contributing to organizational knowledge. An extreme case of this was a process development laboratory of a large U.S. petrochemicals company with some 50 professionals located in the north of France. Originally, the lab had been created to support a local tar factory. But after approximately 10 years, the factory was closed and its activities were folded into a nearby plant roughly 100 kilometers away. The lab was not moved. The physical distance made it less relevant to the plant, but the mandate of the lab was not adjusted. The lab kept on producing interesting results and published them, but it became less relevant to, if not nearly forgotten by, the organization as a whole. The most painful example of this separation came when the petrochemicals company approached a competitor to take a license on a production process and got to hear something like, "Why do you come to us? The process is based on a paper that was published as a result of work carried out in your laboratory in France." The mandate had become obsolete, and the lab had lost its credibility to its peers within the organization and did not contribute anymore to the organizational knowledge. Having a clear and dynamic mandate is one driver of credibility.

Creating some early and visible successes is a second driver of credibility. If new nodes are entered into the network—that is, when new partners come into the innovation project or new organizational units are created—one can help them to develop the credibility by giving them some early successes. This can be done by providing them with an early project agenda that can lead to quick visibility in the rest of the organization. One possibility is to make them part of a successful project that is already well on its way to completion. Another is to give them some short-term projects that will be well celebrated on completion.

Stimulating Diversity Among Learning Units

Organizational wisdom related to innovation projects comes from the confrontation and combination of different information (i.e., the creative transformation I referred to earlier). Therefore, diversity, or the number of elements within the innovation process that can contribute to innovative solutions to complex problems, needs to be stimulated. Nonaka (1990) was referring to a similar idea when he argued that an innovative organization needs to build up information redundancy, that is, a condition in which some types of excess information are shared in addition to the minimal amounts of requisite information held by every individual, department, group, or organization in pursuing innovation. Bower and Hilgard (1981) argued that the breadth of categories into which prior knowledge is organized, and the linkages that exist across these categories, permit individuals to make sense of and, in turn, acquire new knowledge. In practice, this implies that the components of a network that pursues innovation need to be sufficiently different from each other. R&D labs or marketing groups in different parts of the organization or in different countries need to be different from each other, integrate themselves into local organizational processes and structures, have different innovation management systems, attract different profiles of employees and leaders, and so on. That does not make the management of the network easy. I have often observed innovation teams composed of French and North American experts that struggled to collaborate effectively. In my perception, the main difficulties did not come from the obvious language or cultural differences; rather, they seemed to come much more from fundamentally different scientific methods. Simplifying enormously, one can argue that French scientists have been trained to be Cartesian and deductive, that is, to develop a theory and test the consequences of the theory. Many North American scientists have a more inductive approach and are very good in building knowledge out of a series of experiments. Bringing together scientists with such different (and potentially complementary) approaches can be enormously enriching but, at the same time, also very frustrating, in particular if the two groups do not understand the difference in approach and each group thinks that the other is incapable of doing good R&D. A good understanding of local organizational processes is also very important. Let us stay with the difference between France and the United States. In the United States, there is a long-standing tradition of collaboration between industry and universities. Most of the government-sponsored research is also carried out through universities. The tradition of industry–university cooperation is less extensive in France, where it also used to be that the universities were, to a large extent, academic teaching institutions. Most of the high-quality government-sponsored research was carried out in largely independent laboratories such as those of the CNRS, often having no strong link with universities. A company wanting to link up with the local research networks needs to understand very well these differences in research culture and organization.

This leads to an interesting question: Who should lead the node in a knowledge-generating network? Should the head of a lab be a local manager or an overseas manager. The local manager has the advantage that he or she will be better integrated into the local research culture and organization. But employing a local manager may lead to isolation of the lab and an inability to contribute to the organizational knowledge. Therefore, nearly all observers would suggest that one is best off with a local manager with international experience.

Investing in Communication

The communication network is of great importance to the diffusion, validation, and integration of newly acquired know-how. The organizational prescriptions to stimulate communication and cooperation are well known (and often mentioned as the core elements of how to organize innovation)—to create a flat egalitarian organizational structure that diminishes unequal power, mandate functional integration to minimize conflicts and competition, reeducate or remove prima donnas and autocrats who intimidate the rest of the organization, support development of specialist generalists and discourage development of narrow specializations and domains, tolerate error and risk taking so as to encourage unconventional and creative interpretations and to discourage safe and obvious ones, and recognize and reward supportive cooperation and communication. This all usually works within a colocated organization on the condition that these prescriptions are experienced to be authentic (Steiner, 1995). In an international organization with organizational units spread out over many countries, or in virtual organizations where suppliers, vendors, competitors, and other types of partners collaborate on innovation, there is an additional challenge due to geographical distances and (national and organizational) cultural differences. Information stickiness—that is, the effect that information can be understood only in a particular context of tacit knowledge and is difficult to transfer and be actionable in different contexts (Von Hippel, 1988)—becomes a lot stronger, and communication and cooperation need to be stimulated with even greater emphasis. Three ideas can help the innovators. First, key people who will work explicitly on network building are needed. In international contexts, we have seen the very high effectiveness of "international projects ambassadors" who can play a boundary-spanning role. An international projects ambassador goes and works in a different organizational unit for a significant amount of time (usually 6 months to 2 years) as a sort of ambassador representing his or her home unit and comes back later to the original organizational unit with the network of contacts. These people must understand that enhancing communication and cooperation is an explicit task for them. Second, procedural mechanisms are necessary complementary tools to support communication and cooperation, and formalization of communication processes may help to improve the communication requirements. I have seen, in an automotive organization such as Toyota, simple computer-generated forms that can help to report on the progress of a development project in a very structured way. The interesting part was that the forms required hardly any knowledge of the language because they used drawings and standardized specifications that could easily be shared across different languages and cultures. Third, socialization efforts play a very important role in overcoming the cultural and geographical distances and help in creating goal congruency between different units. A barbecue, a bowling party, or a good meal can work miracles. But one should be aware that some of these socialization efforts are not culturally neutral; for example, a wine-tasting party is common in France but may be quite alien to a large group of Indians.

Developing the Extended Network of the Firm

We have already made it clear that the organizational wisdom related to innovation is seldom limited to one (sub-)organization. We used the model of a network of individuals and small groups exchanging information with each other as a proxy for the innovating organization. But one needs to understand that there are often four types of networks:

1. The local internal network, or the network between the different groups and functions in a local organization (e.g., marketing, development, purchasing)

2. The local external network with suppliers, vendors, research institutes and universities, distributors, and the government

3. The international internal network, or the links that exist between the groups of the same organization that are located in different geographical locations

4. The international external network, or the network that may exist between the international units of the firm's external networks (e.g., vendors, suppliers, outsourced research teams)

The fourth network type just listed may sound a bit more abstract. Think about a supplier that follows a customer in its internationalization and that keeps a good account management system, thereby often being better at tying together information the supplier acquires about its customer in different parts of the world. Or think about faculty members from different universities who work with different units of a multinational firm in different locations and who meet at a conference and compare notes about the research projects they carry out for this multinational firm. There is often a wealth of well-structured knowledge about the firm out there with its partners, and this knowledge should become part of the firm's organizational wisdom. One example I have in mind is that of a large North American automobile producer with development groups throughout Europe. At one point, the firm asked for some technical advice from its roller bearing supplier. Overnight, the firm got the answer to what it thought was a significant technical challenge. Puzzled by the speed of response, it queried the supplier, who answered along the lines of, "Oh, we already solved this for you in the United States." The roller bearing supplier had good account management and kept an international overview of the technical relations with this automobile manufacturer. The external international network worked better than the international communications network in the automobile manufacturer.

The first three network types listed are usually well known and recognized, and management systems are put in place to manage these networks more or less. The fourth one is either not recognized or rarely well managed. This is a pity because it is possible that the stock of organizational wisdom that is available for innovation can be even greater outside the firm—in the external networks—than inside the firm. In particular, during these times of globalization, when firms have become lean, have focused on the core activities, and have outsourced all "nonessential" activities, it becomes highly probable that the stock of organizational wisdom outside the firm will become higher than the inside stock. One cannot leave it to the partners to manage themselves. One needs active management of this external international network.

In these lean companies, where the focus is on the core activities, innovative knowledge diffuses quickly, and all too often these companies find themselves in one of two unpleasant situations. They either see that essential knowledge is spreading to the competition (because their partners work also for them) or realize that they have insufficient control over the organizational wisdom that is needed for their renewal. Imagine, for example, an engine manufacturer that casts the engine block, does the machining, and assembles the engines from different components. What happens if this engine manufacturer decides to outsource the casting of the engine block and the machining to a foundry in China and does only the design and final assembly of the engine itself. In the early situation, this manufacturer probably has close relationships with the suppliers of raw materials (e.g., steel producer, iron producer). It could interact and build up organizational wisdom together with these big suppliers. By focusing and outsourcing, it has lost contact with them, and gradually the wisdom about iron and steel will decay. It may still keep some insight into what machining is. Yet to design good engines, one will need to understand the latest developments in materials, for example, to be able to maker lighter engines. That means that the engine manufacturer needs to get better control over the wisdom that is developed throughout the value chain, not only with first-tier suppliers but probably also with second- and third-tier suppliers. Leaving a free hand to this will not work. The maintenance of the organizational wisdom will require a "visible hand" to target technologies properly, identify partners, and adopt and incorporate innovation successfully. Companies such as Zara (Spain) in the clothes industry and Cisco (United States) in telecommunications equipment do exactly this.

An interesting example of a company that has been able to create a good system to manage the organizational wisdom across the organizational borders is ARM Holdings, the Cambridge (United Kingdom)-based producer of reduced instruction set computer (RISC) processors for applications in mobile phones and the like (Williamson & O'Keefe, 2002). ARM is probably not a household name, but with roughly three quarters of the total market it has become the de facto global standard for the RISC processors in mobile phones. ARM designs the chips but does not produce them. It describes its business model as a licensing partnership. It licenses the chip designs to semiconductor companies, which add their application-specific technology to the ARM enabling technology and sell the chips they produce to original equipment manufacturers (OEMs) such as Nokia and Hewlett-Packard, where they end up in a vast range of consumer and industry products from mobile phones to printers. To ensure that the ARM design became a global standard, ARM also needed to build up partnerships with and influence design companies, tool development producers, operating systems developers, and application software companies. All in all, ARM partnered with more than 100 companies and ensured that these partnerships were reciprocal. ARM not only licensed its Internet provider but also tried to build such a relationship that the technology partner would give ARM insight into the licensee's process technology road map and access to new knowledge about emerging solutions. One of ARM's senior managers described the relationship as one in which the partner saw the ARM personnel almost as their own employees. To manage this complicated network of partners, ARM had developed sophisticated partnership management systems, including specialized partner managers, lots of face-to-face meetings with individual partners or in groups per sector, investment in trust building, stability in the personnel who interacted with the partner, and an annual big partner event. As a consequence, one of the partners described

ARM as having a better picture of what was going on inside the partner than did the two locations of the partner company itself given that the latter seldom communicated with each other internally.

Providing the Appropriate Tools for Communication

For the four previous actions, one can put in place tools and procedures that support them. Communication and cooperation can be enhanced by all sorts of modern telecommunication techniques, software vendors sell sophisticated knowledge management systems, search engines can reveal the existence of hundreds of thousands of references, procedures for reporting can simplify credibility enhancement and cooperation, and integrated enterprise resource planning (ERP) systems and intercompany value-added networks can help an organization to steer the external networks. But all of us know of cases in which the implementation of such systems was close to a disaster or, more commonly, did not live up to the expectations. Knowledge management was probably one of the most used and abused concepts during the past 15 years. The reason was probably that it was reduced to a better word for the deployment of information technology (IT) equipment and databases or that it focused more on knowledge production and diffusion. But the challenge is neither this knowledge production nor its diffusion but rather the integration of knowledge into products, services, processes, and practices. We have barely started to understand how that integration happens, but we did observe (De Meyer, Dutta, & Srivastava, 2001) that it is based on the careful linking of four components:

1. *An appropriate knowledge architecture.* This requires that one answers questions such as who gets access to the knowledge, what is the structure in which knowledge is kept, and who guarantees updates and quality control.

2. *A smart organization that enables the transfer and processing of tacit information.* Creating communities of users who share experiences with each other is one way of doing this, but one can also think of conferences, training sessions, and so on.

3. *A technological system that enables the access to and the efficient transfer of codified knowledge.* Communication, cooperation, and (more important) value are added to the extent that what a firm knows how to do is accessible to the maximum number of participants.

4. *The presence of a knowledge "switchboard" or a system that actively encourages exchange of knowledge.* We use the term *switchboard* as a comparison with telephone operators who in older days would make the physical connection between telephone subscribers.

Often the operator would add value to the connection by indicating that the person one tried to reach was out, would be calling back, and so on. In the same vein, a knowledge switchboard operator remains neutral but facilitates and activates the exchange within and between knowledge communities.

Accessing User Wisdom

We argued earlier that innovation will happen when we can create the interaction between the organizational wisdom of the innovator and the wisdom of the user in how to exploit the value created through the innovation. Innovation without intimate customer or user knowledge is not possible. Von Hippel (1988) made the point that in many cases the source of innovation lies outside of the organization, often with users who have a stake in the development of the innovation because they can reap the benefits of it. His original example was that of scientific instruments. In that case, the user often develops a handcrafted prototype that meets the unique user's specifications. With creativity, the supplier of scientific instruments can probably see the wider applications and transform this prototype into an industrial product. A similar process happened with Internet use. In many cases, it is a frustrated user who develops a software improvement or an additional service, and many Internet-based companies have been successful by exploiting the ideas of the users.

Often we think that this knowledge is available only in sophisticated markets. But that is not the case today. We know that emerging markets in Asia, South Africa, and Latin America are not the most supportive ones for an innovator. Customers tend to be more conservative, markets are heterogeneous, and market data simply are not available. But customers do often have needs that are different from those of users in traditional industrialized countries.

Doz, Santos, and Williamson (2001) developed the concept of the metanational organization or an international organization that is able to take advantage of its global presence to combine information and knowledge from different parts of the world so as to come up with an innovation. Let us take a stylized example to illustrate this. Assume that you want to come up with a new mobile phone that combines the sophisticated use of short message service (SMS) as one finds it in the Philippines (one of the most sophisticated markets for mobile messaging), the patents of Qualcomm in the United States, the fashion trends for electronic gadgets prevalent in Los Angeles (United States), the technology of miniaturization developed in Japan or Korea, and the competitive benchmarking of Nokia in Finland. You need antennas in different parts of the world to capture the knowledge, and you need the ability to combine this knowledge and roll it out. Doz and colleagues called these three activities sensing, melding, and deploying. Sensing is the activity whereby a firm attempts to gather knowledge about user needs all over the world. It is much more than gathering business intelligence or technology scanning. The challenge is often to identify and plug into the complex, messy, and incomplete knowledge of local users, that is, to tap into their wisdom. It is really about getting into "local minds." To gain competitive advantage from sensing that local user wisdom, one needs to find ways of anticipating emerging sources of knowledge and leapfrogging competitors and breaking out of the traditional dogmas about where to look.

In the "melding" (i.e., a combination of melting and welding), one needs to have the entrepreneurial insight to identify an opportunity to create an innovative product, service, or process. To understand the dimensions of the melding problem, one needs to find answers to questions such as the following. Which pieces of knowledge does the firm need to innovate? Where can these pieces be found? How do they fit together? Who needs to be involved? One of the interesting propositions about the metanational firms is that one needs to find a "magnet" or an activity or symbol around which to rally the knowledge that is obtained from all over the world. Examples of such magnets include a sophisticated customer, a common technological platform, and an activity such as the common evaluation of opportunities.

The deployment also requires the cumulated wisdom of the organization. To roll out the innovation and get global leverage as quickly as possible, one needs to be flexible about building the most efficient and rapidly scalable global supply chain. This may involve outsourcing, alliances, and so on. The speed with which this can happen is highly dependent on the stock of knowledge of the organization.

In recent work, we have explored how firms from emerging countries that do not have the capabilities or resources of large multi-metanational firms, and that often suffer from being far away (both culturally and geographically) from leading markets, can overcome their disadvantage to tap into user wisdom (De Meyer & Garg, 2005). Strategies developed by these companies combine the creation of antennas (through alliances with companies in industrialized countries), acquisitions, and/or small wholly owned subsidiaries.

But there is another strategy possible. One can also tap into the vast potential of emerging markets. They may not have the same spending power, but they do have the numbers on their side. The low-income markets also tend to be large. This approach to tap into the user wisdom of large poor markets is somewhat similar to the "bottom of the pyramid" strategy proposed by Prahalad (2004).

One of the challenges of emerging markets is that it may be tough to find early adopters for cultural or other reasons. But one company we studied iRiver, has been able to use the Internet to overcome this cultural problem so as to get access to user wisdom (De Meyer & Garg, 2005). This successful midsized Korean company, which produces MP3 players, has created an uncensored bulletin board on its website where customers can express their opinions, criticisms, praise, and/or suggestions. To keep it fair and transparent, the online bulletin board for customers is not moderated. Keeping it open in this way assures the customers that the company takes them seriously. Through this website, the company has been able to tap into user comments and suggestions from all over the world, in particular from markets where the users are less hesitant to comment on the products they buy.

The Dark Side of Organizational Wisdom

In the introduction to this chapter, we pointed out that organizational wisdom can also become a hindrance to innovation. When the innovation happens to be in a space that is too far away from the wisdom based on the core knowledge of the organization, defense mechanisms will get into place to reject the innovation. In fact, what is probably happening here is that badly leveraged wisdom may lead to inflexibility. Perhaps there is a comparison to be made with aging wise individuals. Although their wisdom is still based on accumulated knowledge and the common sense to use this to propose good decisions, the aging process often makes people less agile and flexible in their thinking. Organizations with strong managerial and organizational wisdom may suffer from a similar lack of agility in their decision making. Real organizational wisdom needs to incorporate the agility to address the choice of whether it makes sense for the organization to innovate and, if so, the domain to which the organization needs to restrict itself in its innovative endeavors.

In the second and third sections of the chapter, we offered a number of prescriptions on how to leverage wisdom so as to innovate. At this stage of the chapter, we also see that organizational wisdom can help one to make the choice of whether the organization should innovate. Kimberly and Evanisko (1981) pointed out more than 20 years ago that organizations have a positive bias toward innovation, and even a cursory examination of the managerial press indicates that innovation always seems to be seen as good and the solution to virtually all managerial and economic challenges. It has become nearly a credo—"when in doubt, innovate." But not all organizations can do all types of innovations. Organizational wisdom should also play an important role in the choice of whether and what to innovate.

Let us explore this a bit more deeply. Organizational wisdom exists in three areas: technology, administration, and systems. In these three areas, an organization builds up organizational knowledge, and all three can lead to a temporary competitive advantage. Technology is probably the most straightforward. The technological process knowledge has been a source of wisdom in deciding on further developments in R&D. But the administrative processes, such as those for good project management for car manufacturers or aircraft builders, can be a source of wisdom on which to build further development of the company (Loch, De Meyer, & Pich, 2006). And some systems (e.g., some of the more successful demand management systems used in the travel industry, the supply chain management by Dell, some of the Japanese manufacturing techniques that were so heavily promoted at the start of the 1990s) can also lead to a competitive advantage. Each of them separately can lead to a virtuous cycle of continuing innovation with the widening and deepening of the knowledge on which they are based. And often the integration of the three domains can lead to a formidable competitive position. But for each of them, there is a decrease in marginal return in further development. And it is agile wisdom that will provide the basis for disrupting the very basis of the success. According to Leonard-Barton's (1992) empirical research, an organization seems to be able to cope with disruptive innovation on the condition that the disruption is on only one of the dimensions. If the disruption happens on several dimensions at the same time, the organization will not be able to handle the innovation and so will isolate or reject it. Integrated and nonagile organizational wisdom then becomes a hindrance to innovation. Agile wisdom will help to limit the disruption that an organization can handle.

There is a second angle to the choice of whether to innovate and, if so, in what domain. Innovation also has an ethical dimension. Organizations can innovate toward the wrong product or process, aim it at the wrong market, or execute it in an unacceptable manner. Products or services may create significant harm if appropriate care is not taken. Was the development of LSD, the artificial drug of the 1970s, good for society? Is milk powder, a product without any negative connotation in principle, good when it is heavily promoted in developing countries? Is it okay to carry out massive field tests with new lifesaving medical drugs in developing countries with paid participants without having sufficient information about the long-term potential negative consequences of the drugs? These are important questions that have no easy answers and for which organizational wisdom should bring guidance in the choices. Innovation in a vacuum is not appropriate. Innovation needs to be contextualized in a set of values. Organizational wisdom can make this connection or prevent one from doing so when the context is too far away from the current experiences of the organization.

How do we combine organizational wisdom with agility? We can find some ideas in Royer's (2003) description of two clinical case studies that illustrate how organizational wisdom can become a killer for successful innovation in a different way. The cases about two large and successful French companies, Essilor and Lafarge, do not describe disruptive innovations; on the contrary, they describe innovations that are in line with the companies' strengths in terms of technology and business models. An objective post factum analysis indicated that the innovation projects went wrong relatively early in their development but that for some reason the companies were not able to stop the projects. What Royer described were not cases of bureaucratic inertia or stifling control. If anything, it appeared that control was actually too lax. Nor were these situations in which misguided product champions kept on pushing their pet projects against the organizations' interests. What seemed to be at work in each case was the desire of the whole organization to continue believing in the project. Royer described this as the "seductive appeal of collective belief." The collective belief may start with an individual but spread as a contagious disease throughout the organization because it fits the organizational wisdom very well. The collective belief "served as an umbrella that sheltered an array of hopes and dreams; those, in turn, worked together to reinforce the collective belief." Royer also proposed a few ideas of how to cope with situations where the collective wisdom and beliefs become a blindfold and hurt the innovation effort of the organization. Some of these include (a) creating caution about cheerleading squads or teams that have a stake in preserving or promoting some parts of the organizational wisdom (in case their power is based on that piece of wisdom), (b) building up early warning systems (i.e., systems that challenge the value of the organizational wisdom continuously), and (c) recognizing the important roles of exit champions (i.e., those people who can help organizations to get out of situations or help to stop projects in cases where the organizational wisdom has become a blindfold).

Conclusion

The argument that I have developed here is simple. Innovation is to only a very small extent the result of scientific and technological research and is to a large extent anchored in the organizational wisdom, and it is the result of the close coupling of this organizational wisdom with the user wisdom. The organizational wisdom is not limited to the firm or organization itself; rather, it is often spread out over partners and collaborating units. To innovate successfully, one needs to mobilize the organizational and user wisdom, and I provided some pointers as to what can be done to do this effectively. Credibility, diversity, communication and cooperation, cleverly deployed knowledge systems, and magnets for capturing the diffused user wisdom are some of these key pointers. But I also warned about the negative impact of organizational wisdom on innovation; it rejects disruptive innovation, and it creates blindfolds for mistakes that sit well with the organizational wisdom.

References

Bower, G. H., & Hilgard, E. R. (1981). *Theories of learning*. Englewood Cliffs, NJ: Prentice Hall.

Carnegie, R., & Butlin, M. (1993). *Managing the innovating enterprise*. Melbourne, Australia: Business Library.

Christensen, C. M., & Overdorf, M. (2000). Meeting the challenge of disruptive change. *Harvard Business Review, 78*(2), 66–76.

De Meyer, A. (1993a). Internationalization of R&D improves a firm's technical learning. *Research Technology Management, 36*(4), 42–49.

De Meyer, A. (1993b). Management of an international network of industrial R&D laboratories. *R&D Management, 23*(2), 109–120.

De Meyer, A., Dutta, S., & Srivastava, S. (2001). *The bright stuff: How innovative people and technology can make the old economy new.* New York: Financial Times/Prentice Hall.

De Meyer, A., & Garg, S. (2005). *Inspire to innovate: Management and innovation in Asia.* London: Palgrave Macmillan.

Doz, Y., Santos, J., & Williamson, P. (2001). *From global to metanational: How companies win in the knowledge economy.* Boston: Harvard Business School Press.

Kim, W. C., & Mauborgne, R. (2005). *Blue ocean strategy: How to create uncontested market space and make competition irrelevant.* Boston: Harvard Business School Press.

Kimberly, J. R., & Evanisko, M. J. (1981). Organizational innovation: The influence of individual, organizational, and contextual factors on hospital adoption of technological and administrative innovations. *Academy of Management Journal, 24,* 689–713.

Leonard-Barton, D. (1992). Core capabilities and core rigidities: A paradox in managing new product development. *Strategic Management Journal, 13,* 111–125.

Loch, C. L., De Meyer, A., & Pich, M. T. (2006). *Managing the unknown: A new approach to managing high uncertainty and risk in projects.* Basingstoke, UK: Wiley.

Myers, S., & Marquis, D. G. (1969). *Successful industrial innovations: A study of factors underlying innovation in selected firms.* Washington, DC: National Science Foundation.

Nonaka, I. (1990). Redundant overlapping organisation: A Japanese approach to managing the innovation process. *California Management Review, 32*(3), 27–38.

Prahalad, C. K. (2004). *The fortune at the bottom of the pyramid: Eradicating poverty through profits.* Philadelphia: Wharton School Publishing.

Royer, I. (2003). Why bad projects are so hard to kill. *Harvard Business Review, 81*(2), 48–56.

Steiner, C. J. (1995). A philosophy for innovation: The role of unconventional individuals in innovation success. *Journal of Product Innovation Management, 12,* 431–440.

Von Hippel, E. (1988). *The sources of innovation.* New York: Oxford University Press.

Williamson, P., & O'Keefe, E. (2002). *ARM Holding PLC.* INSEAD–EAC case study, European Case Clearing House, Bedford, UK.

PART V

Metaphysics

17

Individual Metaphysics

The Getting of Wisdom: Self-Conduct, Personal Identity, and Wisdom Across the Life Span

Nigel Nicholson

Metaphysics is concerned with the nature and origins of existence. This makes it a reflexive human enterprise, invoking questions about the nature of mind, identity, and perception of reality through time and place. These are interesting and deep questions, but what, one may ask, have they got to do with organizations and management?

Two answers form the justification for this chapter and perhaps even for this volume. First, given that wisdom is a valued commodity in business as anywhere else, we need to be assured that we are not chasing shadows, that is, that the concept has some genuine meaning, reference, and substance. Second, if we agree that it does, it behooves us to consider how wisdom is acquired and whether it can be enhanced by any means. My answer to both of these questions is affirmative, from which it is a simple deduction that organizations, their leaders, and their members need wisdom now as much as ever before in their history.

The framework that I invoke in this chapter is the neo-Darwinian view of human nature and social existence (Nicholson, 2000, 2005b). This construes wisdom as a quality conferring fitness advantages on those who possess it or who have the wisdom to be able to draw on the wisdom of others. After defining the concept, I explore its contents, principally in terms of self-identity concepts, before moving on to consider what this implies for how wisdom can be acquired or enhanced. Wisdom is a project that is never completed, so the last part of this chapter puts it in a biographical life span perspective, considering the implications of this analysis for how individuals, such as business leaders, may aspire to live and lead wisely.

The Problem of Wisdom

A perusal of the writings about wisdom reveals common themes to include the use of tacit knowledge and humility about one's fallibility (Sternberg & Lubart, 2001). At the risk of invalidating everything that follows in this chapter, one might say that this should convince us that it is not wise to define wisdom. Because I am not the first or the last to attempt this, I risk the folly of rushing in where angels fear to tread, appealing for support in this endeavor from Socrates, who said, "The beginning of wisdom is the definition of terms." Searching for definitions in philosophy down the ages yields one overarching canopy of agreement: Wisdom is something good to have (Birren & Svensson, 2005). Wise actions are desirable and commendable. Wise people have a gift greater than mere knowledge, skill, or happiness. They are people to be attended to and followed.

But what does it mean to be a wise individual and to lead a wise life? Are these two questions with a single answer, or can they diverge? It is apparent that wisdom is an attribution applied both to individuals and to actions. It is logically conceivable that wise people can engage in foolish acts and that wise actions can be enacted by foolish people. This raises some obvious challenges. How do we spot wise people? Should we always imitate or seek to follow them? When can we trust ourselves to be wise? How do we go about getting wisdom?

These are trickier questions in modern Western economies than they have been in other times and places. For example, casting back to early philosophy, the Aristotelian take on wisdom is fundamentally ethical (Osbeck & Robinson, 2005). This view at its simplest is expressed in the words of Cicero: "The function of wisdom is to discriminate between good and evil." The wise person understands the nature of goodness and acts in ways that are good, and this helps to attune the person and his or her milieu to the propagation and maintenance of an ethical social order. This contrasts with the modern view, as expressed by Thoreau: "A man is wise with the wisdom of his time only." The Aristotelian ethical stance on wisdom is tenable only if there is a unitary consensus about the ethical architecture of the prevailing social order. In contemporary pluralistic society, this is hardly the case, confronted as we are by a startling array of belief systems and ideologies—all competing for our attention. Meanwhile, the climate of modern Western belief is increasingly relativistic, such that one might be minded to judge as self-falsifying any claim that a person of a particular faith or belief was the possessor of an ethically normative wisdom. Yet people do still follow sages, and those who are willing to accept their claims are likely to be perceived by those who do not accept them to be captives of a belief system bounded by time and culture, that is, a sect. Awkwardly, sages tend to be disinclined to relativism and want their wisdom to be generalized across all societies. Therefore, any definition of wisdom likely to pass muster in our times, and for sure in a volume such as this where the unspoken ideology is the stance of nonideological social science, will need to follow Thoreau before Cicero.

Defining Wisdom

Stripped of ethics and unanchored in any unitary view of social values, what can wisdom connote for us today? The neo-Darwinian view, which I outline shortly, denies any metaphysic other than realist empiricism and requires wisdom to have some fitness-enhancing value that can be verified, that is, to have practical value. Wisdom, I therefore assert, consists in the ability to make good judgments. And what are good judgments? They are those that are proven to be correct or are demonstrated to lead to beneficial outcomes in the long term as well as the short term. Philosophical writings on wisdom are at pains to note that this comes not from the mere possession of expert knowledge but rather from the way in which knowledge and understanding are deployed (Sternberg, 1990). This implies, inter alia, knowing when not to act, being a person of judiciously few selected words, and having a developed awareness of the importance of doubt in making judgments plus a corollary awareness of one's own limitations. This makes wisdom a mix of insight, humility, and open-mindedness plus shot selection (to borrow a sports metaphor). An additional stream in the literature is the idea that wisdom is gained by having lived through and learned from experience. However, mere immersion is not sufficient; particular kinds of intelligence need to work on the raw material (Baltes & Smith, 1990). As Aldous Huxley, the novelist and essayist, put it, "Experience is not what happens to a man, it is what he does with what happens to him."

The implication of this analysis is that having lived longer increases one's chances of having obtained wisdom, (but without guaranteeing it) as the age-venerating Confucian tradition maintains, for a mark of wisdom is having done more with less. People can be wise beyond their years. Yet we should not confuse this with the so-called wisdom of the child or idiot savant, an error richly and comically immortalized in the novel and movie *Being There*. The hero, an intellectually challenged and amiable gardener, is mistaken for a political adviser and becomes credited with surpassing political wisdom on the strength of his gnomic, ambiguous, but ultimately vacuous utterances.

In short, wisdom—the ability to make good and farsighted judgments—can be acquired, requires time and experience, and yet is at best only weakly correlated with age (Jordan, 2005).

An operational definition of wisdom, therefore, could be that it is the quality of judgment that someone possesses that leads more experienced and knowledgeable people to seek advice from that person. Managers recognize this quality; it is what leads some individuals to be spotted as leadership material quite early in their careers. It is a sought-after magic that organizations covet yet do not know how to cultivate, for wisdom cannot be readily appropriated. As Michel de Montaigne, the French Renaissance thinker, put it, "We can be knowledgeable with other men's knowledge, but cannot be wise with other men's wisdom."

My aim in this chapter is to help the reader to understand the processes by which individuals acquire, maintain, and use wisdom so defined and how this relates to the leadership and management of organizations.

A Darwinian Perspective

The Darwinian perspective, briefly, holds that we are a species of ape, with a mental apparatus that contains biases and capabilities that evolved, along with our physical morphology, to support our way of life as clan-dwelling hunter–gatherers. The world may have changed in the short span of human civilization over the past 10,000 years since the advent of agriculture and fixed settlements, but our mental design and capabilities have not changed (Barrett, Dunbar, & Lycett, 2002; Buss, 1999). We retain the psychological architecture of our origins (Nicholson, 1998; Pinker, 1997).

A first port of call in the search for the meaning of wisdom in this context, therefore, is to look at undeveloped societies. Wisdom here can be reduced to "the one to be followed." My own experiences in looking at the Maasai in Kenya (Nicholson, 2005a) show that (a) wisdom consists in superior capacity to give service to the community; (b) it is vested more in the elders than in the juniors, although in each age set[1] wise individuals are acknowledged implicitly rather than explicitly; and (c) it is depersonalized in that wisdom is the property either of a group (of elders) who make judgments or of individuals who are able to embody the spirit and intent of the community without any apparent "ego" or personal glorification. Thus, wisdom here has the status of (covert) reputation. This would seem close to the Aristotelian ideal; we follow the wise because the wise follow the spirit of our community. It is a selfless ideal that has value because it does not seek to be valued—something close to a Buddhist concept of wisdom. It is a theme in the literature on tribal leadership—the concept of the "big man" who demonstrates his greatness by skill in acquiring what the tribe most needs and shows his fitness to lead by sharing it selflessly with his people (Harris, 1978). In Darwinian terms, the costliness of this beneficence is a guarantee against false signaling of the giver's worth and, therefore, is a genuine mark of superiority or fitness (Zahavi & Zahavi, 1996). In contemporary times, the concept of "servant leadership" treads the same path (Greenleaf, 1991).

But in modern times, the model we follow is a simpler association of wisdom with fitness. We desire and require wise people we can follow—to help guide us with their superior judgment through the thicket of an ever more complex and ambiguous world. Unique perhaps to contemporary life is also the phenomenon of the person who is imputed with wisdom but is not followed. We live in a world where it is not so easy to follow as it is to desire to emulate, for example, when we find ourselves looking with envy at neighbors making good but inimitable judgments in their personal lives. Thus, wisdom becomes, in neo-Darwinian terms, a mark of people who have learned how to live by decisions and codes that raise their well-being and, ultimately, their "fitness" (Miller, 2000).

The Darwinian perspective points out that in the human community, reputation is one of the most precious commodities and is directly related to the reproductive fitness of the collective and thereby of the individual members of the collective (Wilson, 2002). In contemporary society, we inhabit multiple hierarchies in which people make social comparisons, and the reputation for wisdom, as we have defined it, is one of the highest qualities a person can possess. Although imperfectly related to age, farsighted good judgment is widely perceived to increase with experience. Hence, in tribal societies, the elders are venerated not just for their past contributions to the commonwealth but also for their knowing what to do because they have seen it all before. In corporate life and well-established organizations, it remains largely true that leaders are the equivalent of elders. Notwithstanding the attention that management and popular media tend to pay to the young stars of new organizations, the leadership ranks of most organizations remain firmly gerontocratic in character. One need only look at the age profile of most company boards—whether public or private companies—to see that many have a preponderance of directors in their 50s and, especially in large companies, in their 60s (Segal Company, 2001).

Let us now analyze more precisely the content, status, and ontogenesis of wisdom in human identity.

Wisdom and Self-Identity

Wisdom, in its most basic manifestation—the search for good and farsighted judgments—requires foresight, a uniquely human gift deriving from the capacity for self-consciousness. Thus, we need to analyze the getting of wisdom via the contents and processes of the self.

Following our earlier definition—wisdom as the capacity for farsighted good judgments—we can consider the *contents* of wisdom to be a library of heuristics that may be deployed to solve life's problems and meet its challenges (Gigerenzer, Todd, & ABC Research Group, 1999; Schloss, 2000). This implies that it is possible for people to be wise in specific domains.

For example, people could be astute in their political judgment but foolish in their personal lives.

We can focus our discussion on three broad domains: the world of human affairs, interpersonal relationships, and self-conduct. These have a scalar aspect; folly in relationships impairs capacity for wisdom in human affairs, and failure in self-conduct can undermine the capacity for wisdom in all other domains. This helps to solve the problem of defining a wise person. The more a person's judgment is recognized to generalize across these domains, the more likely the person is to be called wise.

Let us look at the meaning of wisdom across these three domains, focusing most of our discussion on self-conduct.

Wisdom in the first domain, the world of human affairs, is relatively straightforward to analyze. It amounts to an empirically testable capacity to guide and lead the opinions of others. This encompasses all areas of expert knowledge and, in some cases, broader domains of human interest and activity. The heuristics that constitute wisdom in such areas have the character of tacit knowledge (Sternberg, 1990)—hard to communicate and appropriate. It comes from having lived, experienced, and learned—and not just from having had the luxury of time to formulate opinions. As comedian George Burns put it, "Too bad that all the people who really know how to run the country are busy driving taxicabs and cutting hair."

Wisdom in relationships is more complicated. The Darwinian psychologist Nicholas Humphrey theorized that the evolutionary purpose of self-consciousness is to read other minds; it is the essential precondition to the art of empathy, that is, to understand and predict the motives of others (Humphrey, 1980). The Darwinian approach to interpersonal relationships revolves mainly around the mechanisms for achieving and sustaining cooperation, with the essential corollary skills of cheater detection and strategies for dealing with free riders (Boyd, Gintis, Bowles, & Richerson, 2003; Cosmides & Tooby, 1992). One could equate these qualities with elements of emotional intelligence. The abilities to correctly discern emotions and to deal effectively with the emotions of others are clearly implicated in the search for the source of wisdom in relationships (Brackett, Warner, & Bosco, 2005). There is also an analytical element. We all use cues, tacit knowledge, and heuristics when interacting to "read minds" (Whiten, 1991), and some are able to do this more deeply and profoundly than are others (Eisenberg, Fabes, & Miller, 1990). Again, this wisdom is empirically testable via predictions of future actions and assessing the efficacy of interventions. It is the wisdom that psychotherapy and other interventions deploy to help individuals redirect their psychic energies.

The construct of emotional intelligence attempts to tie together elements of wisdom in the self and in relating to others. Even if one does not accept the unity of the construct (Zeidner, Matthews, & Roberts, 2004), it does embody a key point, namely that interpersonal wisdom is hard, if not impossible, to achieve without some mastery of the third domain—self-conduct. People who are at the mercy of impulses, thoughts, and feelings that they do not comprehend will have impaired judgment in relationships, especially where they themselves are directly involved.

Looking more closely at the elements of wisdom in the self and its conduct, first, we may note that the self is both fragile and robust. Its fragility comes from its ability to shift parameters and values, with potentially enormous impacts on the person, for example, the shift to suddenly seeing oneself as unattractive, guilty, or blessed. Numerous psychological experiments have demonstrated how readily people's self-perceptions may be manipulated (Robins & John, 1997). The robustness of the self lies in its persistence. Yogis and mystics must submit to rigorous disciplines to rid themselves of self-consciousness. The capacity for self-deception is also a tribute to the resilience of the self as a vital organ (Trivers, 2000), and again in the psychological laboratory there have been striking demonstrations of how people can easily be led into perceiving their selves to be the origins of actions that were externally caused (Bargh & Chartrand, 1999).

Mark Leary has provided an extended analysis of the dysfunctional consequences that come with self-consciousness (Leary, 2004). He argues that its surpassing value as an instrument for insight, planning, and control comes at some burdensome costs, which escalate the further we depart from the ancestral environment in which the organ of the self evolved. Faced by a burgeoning array of choices, seemingly infinite possibilities for social comparison, and opportunities for different imagined futures, we are beset by anxieties, regrets, jealousies, shame, and myriad disturbances to our peace of mind. The consequences are serious and sometimes fatal as people seek respite or escape from the agonizing extremes of inner preoccupation and its perturbations.

Leary (2004) points out that a universal theme of world religions, and perhaps a root theme for their metaphysics, is a shared recognition that the self is a problem, for all faiths offer solutions that promise either purification or release from the tyranny of the self. The concept of wisdom offered by people of spiritual faith is of this character—advocacy of self-denial or of strategies that will enable one to rise above the clamor of the self and attain states of peace and equanimity. But these do not fit the definition of wisdom I am seeking to discuss here, namely the active ability to grapple with the challenges of this world rather than to seek only to rise above them.

The Wise Self

Leary's (2004) analysis is much concerned with what he calls "self-talk"—our ability to conduct internal dialogues with ourselves over choices, self-perceptions, and judgments. This ability would seem to be a prime candidate for explaining the functionality of wisdom in the domain of self-conduct. It is a necessary process to achieve the following:

- *Self-appraisal.* Wise conduct is likely to emanate from people who are able to use self-talk to maintain positive self-imagery by incorporating a realistic appraisal of their deficiencies, limitations, and conflicts (Erez & Earley, 1993). Related to this is the ability to make appropriate attribution and correctly focus their locus of control (Carver & Scheier, 1998). Faulty attributions are hazardous. At one end of the spectrum is the dysfunction of blithe indifference to evidence of the failure and its causes, an element that makes the recurrence of error more likely (Kernis, Zuckerman, Cohen, & Spadafora, 1982). At the other extreme is the false attribution of taking undue responsibility for events that are beyond one's psychological control, a malady that engenders disabling states of guilt or shame (Tangney, Wagner, & Gramzow, 1992; Turner, 1995). Thus, wisdom here equates with equilibrating self-esteem through well-judged attribution combined with ego strength. It also facilitates self-prediction (Shrauger & Osberg, 1983).

- *Self-regulation.* The self has been analyzed as being capable of switching its focus between promotion and prevention in goal-related decision making (Higgins, 2002), that is, by moving toward or avoiding stimuli so as to orient effectively. In a like manner, theorists have discussed self-regulation as an instrument for controlling mood through the duration of streams of action (John & Gross, 2004; Karoly, 1993). These functions are semiautomatic—occurring mostly below the level of conscious choice—but occasionally they are knowingly engaged. This reflexivity, to be effective, requires insight and willpower. This may be considered wisdom in self-regulation—the capacity to override automaticity with conscious control so as to respond to stimuli proportionately.

- *Perceptual control.* The interplay between goal states and perceptions lies at the heart of judgment and action, and it is especially relevant to risk assessment, probabilistic calculus, and planning. The vast literature on psychological biases documents the hazards that ensnare us all (Piattelli-Palmarini, 1994). Errors occur during all stages of decision making—in what we pay attention to, how we process information, our choices and preferences, and the ex post assessments we make after we have chosen and observed the consequences (Staw, 1980). Much of the time, perceptions are pressed into service to manage the unseen force of goal states (Powers, 1973). Thus, the more we want something, the more likely we are to misperceive dangers by underestimating the risks we run in getting it (Yates, 1992). Effective self-talk should help us to be more vigilant about the games we play to get what we want.

Thus, wisdom is constituted in self-talk—the reflexive capacity to be aware of one's self as a system and to engage the cognitions that will regulate mood, perception, goal modification, and self-evaluation. It will often involve the capacity to reframe perceptions and experiences.

One can elaborate the beneficial consequences of self-talk being done effectively:

- *Quieting.* Equanimity in judgment can come from muting unnecessary internal chatter. This noise clogs the processing of information within a stream of goal-directed action (Baumeister, 1984). Strategies can be developed, for example, those deployed by artists and presenters to calm performance nerves.

- *Decentering.* I have adapted this Piagetian concept to apply to interpersonal relationships in management (Nicholson, 2002) so as to connote the art of imagining how the phenomenal world of others is different from one's own, especially people we find "difficult." It is not easy to counter the instinctive tendency to judge interactions from the perspective of ourselves as the victims or beneficiaries of others' actions, but doing so can yield major benefits, especially in problem solving.

- *Cognitive self-analysis.* This denotes the ability to engage in a critique of the biases affecting one's perceptions, evaluations of events, and estimation of their causes and consequences (Robins & John, 1997). Our recent research on traders in finance highlights the value of this gift (Fenton-O'Creevy, Nicholson, Soane, & Willman, 2005).

- *Detachment.* Achieving cognitive separation from potentially disabling emotions is a key skill in managing many critical events such as strategies for mastering irrational fears, painful longings, jealousy, and excessive guilt and shame (Snyder, 1974).

- *Questioning.* Insight comes from a willingness to challenge and question one's implicit taxonomies. This applies not least to the concepts by which we analyze our own states and those of others, for example, avoiding insidious stereotypes, negative assessments of groups, and attachment to empty concepts.

- *Control.* Effective living requires enabling actions to be effectively selected and executed, avoiding excessive risk taking and self-destructive strategies in the quest for self-management such as substance abuse (Baumann & Kuhl, 2005; Hull, 1981).

- *Skepticism.* It is desirable to question belief systems and ideologies to an appropriate degree. Note that this does not mean the absence of belief systems; rather, it means a heightened sense of the contingencies and relativities to which we are subject, thereby avoiding intolerance, fanaticism, and susceptibility to unproductive conflict.

- *Integrity.* Maintaining the integrity of the self means avoiding surrender to the will of others and also avoiding self-depletion (Baumeister, Bratslavsky, Muraven, & Tice, 1998)—the draining of psychic energy through excessive attempts to regulate the self. In effect, this is the self-talk that regulates all of the other self-talk—what one might call balance and realism in self-conduct.

This analysis illustrates the earlier observation that wisdom in the conduct of the self is a platform for all other kinds of wisdom—optimizing the intrusion of one's personal thoughts and feelings into one's judgments of other people, relationships, and human affairs more generally. Therefore, there is a critical question that remains: How does one cultivate the art of effective self-talk and the wisdom that it may yield?

The Getting of Wisdom

What kind of actions can one engage in to acquire wisdom? Let us first consider key underlying processes.

Trial and Error

I have already noted that a platform of experience is a necessary, but not sufficient, condition for the acquisition of wisdom. Wisdom is as domain specific as are the arenas of a person's experience. Experience needs to be sufficiently varied within a domain for the heuristics to be reliable. It also needs to be active for initiated acts to yield positive consequences. Philosophers are apt to point to the pain of acquiring wisdom resulting from taking risks and making mistakes. Learning from errors is easier said than done (Cannon, 1999; Frese, 1995). It requires a degree of analytical detachment that is hard to achieve, especially when the error is large enough to be branded a "failure." The instinctive response is to minimize the pain and seek to avoid its recurrence. This may include recourse to "magical" and superstitious beliefs about how to escape future failures. Thus, wisdom is constituted partly by an accepting approach to the inevitability of failures and a determination for them not to inhibit the process of seeking and learning.

Observing and Imitating

The tough question here is what or whom to observe and imitate as well as what or whom not to imitate. The Darwinian view of fitness makes this an imperative skill for successful adaptation. The prerequisite for this is twofold: wide experience of a diverse range of people and opinions and some effective mental models for understanding and predicting the behavior of others. This amounts to an injunction to cultivate the awareness of a good "naive" psychologist.

Instruction

It may be true that wisdom cannot be taught, but it can be learned. Self-improvement literature has been a publishing phenomenon since Victorian times, when it offered recipes for living to an increasingly needy readership beset by the challenges of modern life. Today, evangelists, shamans, management gurus, and counselors of every hue are on hand to satisfy the even greater needs of our times. Wisdom may emanate from judicious selection from these and other sources, such as works on psychology, philosophy, and religion, but only if guided by a coherent purpose and a commitment to test ideas before they are assimilated.

Smart Questioning

Agency is central to the getting of wisdom, and the ability to interrogate the world is a key skill in achieving it. Some of the wisest writers on psychology and organization have demonstrated its effectiveness. Karl Weick, writing on sensemaking, portrayed it as a fundamentally active process (Weick, 1995), whereas Chris Argyris used a dialoging methodology to discern the gap between "espoused theory" and "theory-in-use," offering a means to helping organizations get out of defensive routines (Argyris, 1993). This is linked with "double-loop learning"—the ability to understand the overarching and systemic errors in systems, including those that exist to detect errors.

Analyzing and Theorizing

A key element in the learning cycle (Kolb, 1984) is the ability to abstract principles from sense data and reflection. This suggests that some kinds of intelligence are probably threshold conditions for wisdom, that is, the ability to construct and understand representations and chains of reasoning.

Intuiting and Testing

In his best-seller *Blink,* Malcolm Gladwell, drawing on a mix of anecdotes and academic research, celebrates the power and mystery of "thin slicing" intuition (Gladwell, 2005). However magical this facility might appear to be, it clearly requires the possession of a matrix of relevant knowledge and understanding from which insights may be generated; otherwise, intuitions are no better than guesswork. The mental process by which one cultivates insight is more difficult to formulate, but it would seem to involve many of the elements of self-control that we have already reviewed, such as the ability to detach, reframe, and challenge assumptions. Finally, having a frame of mind that insists on testing intuitions and analyzing the causes of their success or failure is also important—as wise traders do in financial markets (Fenton-O'Creevy et al., 2005).

The Biography of Wisdom

Let us now move up to the level of the person. What is the wisdom of living? We have noted that the person attributed to be wise is not without blemish or error—quite the contrary. Rather, what distinguishes the wise person is the ability to assimilate the good and the bad of day-to-day living and extract superior meaning, that is, more penetrating, prudent, and promising heuristics than others might commonly desire. The forgoing analysis of self-identity suggests that wisdom blends heuristics of three main kinds: reflexive, conceptual, and action oriented.

The reflexive heuristics are those that apply by introspection to aspects of self-functioning and relationships in which one is involved. The conceptual are the heuristics for challenging, updating, and exploring new ideas and ways of thinking. The action-oriented heuristics are those that govern risk taking, exploration, spontaneity, and choice in behavior (both verbal and nonverbal).

The question that will occupy us for the remainder of this chapter is why and how people seem to have unequal access to these heuristics. Are people born with the seeds of wisdom? Does it require any particular schedule of experience during early or later life? What does living wisely connote in terms of how people configure their lives? The dangers of this agenda are self-evident—the arrogance of imposing normative prescriptions on the lives of others. I attempt to avoid this, but some normative judgments are inevitable because an empirical science approach will inevitably lead to conclusions about what are the predictors of superior judgment. Let us approach this chronologically with a model of biography.

Figure 17.1 presents a framework for analyzing lives that I use in a biography course I teach at London Business School for a predominantly career-shifting, middle-aged class of professional and executive students on the Sloan Fellowship Masters Program. It is designed to enhance self-determination and, in effect, to help students accelerate the getting of wisdom.

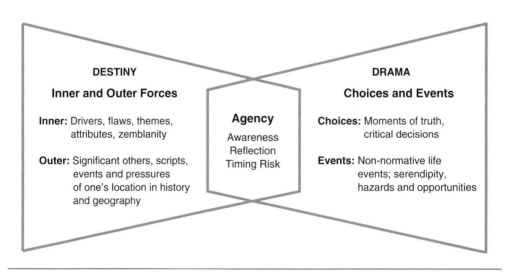

Figure 17.1   Destiny, Drama, and Deliberation: The Crossroads of Biography

The course involves a mix of autobiographical analysis and time spent looking at the lives of leaders and others to help make sense of the forces that shape lives, so that students may achieve greater control over their life course through insight.

Figure 17.1 summarizes the constituents of biographical analysis as a crossroads between destiny and drama. Destiny is a deeply unfashionable concept in an age in which we elevate freedom of choice to the pinnacle of idealized existence, yet none of us is unconstrained in how he or she lives. I define destiny as the "gravitational" forces, both internal and external to us, that pull us toward a limited set of destinations via our preferences and opportunities.

The inner forces of destiny include genetic dispositions, abilities, physical characteristics, vulnerabilities, and susceptibilities—the hand we are dealt to live with (Bouchard, 1997; Plomin, 1994). Figure 17.1 also includes the word "zemblanity." This neologism was coined by the writer William Boyd in his novel *Armadillo*. Boyd (1998) defined it as follows: "Zemblanity, the opposite of serendipity, the faculty of making unhappy, unlucky, and expected discoveries by design. Serendipity and zemblanity: the twin poles of the axis around which we revolve" (pp. 234–235). The concept of zemblanity counters the idea that we make our own good luck with the equal and opposite notion that we make our own misfortune just by being who we are. Zemblanity consists of the traps that we dig for ourselves and, predictably, stumble into.

The outer forces of destiny are the limitations, resources, and opportunities available to us in the milieu of our origins. There is plentiful evidence that careers are as much inherited as they are freely chosen—or, more precisely, that life chances are quite unevenly distributed for each newborn (Ellis, 1993). They are predictable from the status and resources of the family milieu as well as from involuntary factors such as inherited wealth, education, location, ethnicity, and local historical events (Han & Mulligan, 2001; Nicholson & De Waal-Andrews, 2005). Destiny also resides in the "scripts" we carry with us throughout life about who we are, where we are going, and why we are going there (McAdams & Ochberg, 1988; Steiner, 1974). These are constructed during childhood, tested and refined during adolescence, and enacted during adulthood. They are partly self-wrought, that is, definitions of the self that sit comfortably with our self-identity. Others are handed down by parents, siblings, teachers, and others who have an idea of who we are and, more dangerously, what we will or should become (Ibarra, 2003).

It is possible to submit to the forces of destiny—following one's impulses and acting out the script that one finds oneself holding. But even in the most docile life, these can come into conflict; the spirit rebels against what is bequeathed. This is the story of many a failed family business succession, where the next generation is unwilling or unable to take the baton that the senior generation wishes to pass along (Lansberg, 1999).

Such intrusions into the otherwise predictable life course are what I call the drama of biography. Many of them are externally originating events—what are called "non-normative life events" in life span development theory

(Baltes, Reese, & Lipsett, 1980). These are wide-ranging, from choosing a marriage partner to losing a job through retrenchment. Some are happy accidents. Serendipity, the converse of zemblanity, is the good stuff that comes to us unbidden—the good luck that can change the course of one's life without having been wished or willed. Yet Louis Pasteur (wisely) said, "Chance favors the prepared mind."

It is the drama of the life course that is the chief focus of published biographies. The dramatic elements to which we pay most attention are those originating in the person, that is, acts of choice that are internally driven diversions from the path of destiny. Some are moments of truth. These often arise through some external trigger stimulating us to interrogate and sometimes overturn previously unchallenged processes and involvements. These are the Damascene moments in many careers where new paths are chosen after some external shocks (Young & Rodgers, 1997).

In my biography class, quite often I hear the view that our destiny changes with every momentary decision. This idea is captured in the parable "for the sake of a horseshoe nail the kingdom was lost" and the idea in chaos theory that a butterfly wing beat can trigger a causal chain that escalates to culminate in a mountain avalanche. There is an alternative view that the self-correcting compass of destiny—our dispositions, scripts, and restricted menu of opportunities—keeps tugging us back to the same quite circumscribed set of possible destinations. We have many possible selves we can live, but the set is delimited and finite (Yost, Strube, & Bailey, 1992). In systems theory, this is called "equipotentiality," where one can have numerous choice nodes in a network but the end point remains the same.

Many of the choices we make are more algorithmic than we care to think. We agonize about them as if they are life changing, but in actuality (a) each choice is quite predictable from the prevailing conditions and (b) it is not a genuine crossroads so much as a decision about which diversion to indulge before we are drawn back to our mainstream. Thus, wisdom in life choices is the ability to determine which junctures are really crossroads and which are energy-consuming diversions that ultimately come back into the main pathway of one's life course. This choice process is what I call "deliberation." This requires exercise of "agency," the concept that stands at the crossroads of biography in Figure 17.1.

Agentic deliberation means awareness of the forces shaping one's life—the ability to reflect on events to assess whether they should be allowed to trigger far-reaching change or whether they should be stabilized by force of will, the skill and strength to know which risks should be taken and which risks should be left alone, and the art of picking the best time for destiny to be challenged and perhaps changed. Figure 17.2 shows this schematically as metaphorical modalities.

Young people are inclined to think that unless one is sailing—making willed changes—one is not really living life to the fullest. But as exciting as sailing may be, it is also tiring, often lonely, and occasionally fruitless.

	Stable	Changeful
Chosen	A. Moored in harbor	B. Sailing
Not Chosen	C. Shipwrecked	D. Following the river

Figure 17.2   The Life Journey: Metaphorical Modalities

A simpler way to travel is to follow the river—enjoying the landscapes that life presents as one follows the stream of destiny and drama. We often have the luxury of neither sailing nor following the river and instead find ourselves moored in harbor. This can provide the rest and tranquility that we need before we set sail again. Shipwreck may be undesired, but it can be a powerful source of insight and altered perspectives and should not be appraised as wholly negative. Many of the most important triggers for life-transforming choice and change emanate from this region—the area where we have been forced to relinquish control and accept change. Surrendering to chance and chaos is sometimes the wise thing to do—trusting in the integrity of the self to forge creative sensemaking out of what follows.

What does this tell us about the wisdom of living? Perhaps we are putting the old wine of philosophers and sages into new bottles, but that may be necessary for a concept that has become obscured in the complexities of modern living. One major cause of difficulty in conceiving of wisdom in living is that we have become obsessed by the youthful image of sailing through a life of adventurous choices, blinding ourselves to the unseen hand of shaping forces. Wisdom in living means recapturing concepts such as destiny and working with them. Destiny is shaped by will as well as by circumstance, and wisdom consists in knowing when to submit, when to fight, and when to steer. As William James put it, "The art of being wise is knowing what to overlook" (James, 1890).

Individual differences matter. This is easier for some than it is for others. It follows that wisdom is more accessible to those who have the qualities of mind and life to be able to engage in the processes we have analyzed. Early life experience may be critical. Karen Horney, along with other writers on disorders of development, showed how impairments to the development of healthy self-functioning during early life make wisdom nearly inaccessible for those individuals who become locked into neurotic strategies to right wrongs that cannot be undone and to fight demons who lie trapped within the interstices of their minds (Horney, 1950). These are not hopeless cases. Redemption can come from therapeutic intervention through which such lost souls find the wisdom of self-acceptance and the possibility of new growth.

Practical Implications for Leaders and Others

Recalling the three domains in which wisdom has been considered—human affairs, interpersonal relations, and self-conduct—and expanding the latter to a consideration of wise living, a number of implications can be derived. First, wisdom in human affairs requires attention to boundary conditions. The acquisition of tacit knowledge is noted as domain specific, and possession of mere expertise is not enough. Qualities of the individual and their differential ability to assimilate knowledge and distil wisdom are implicated. Wisdom is an unequally distributed form of social capital. The implication, therefore, is that we should seek to recognize the wise as not necessarily those who are designated as the keepers of wisdom or those who are charged with making the most far-reaching judgments. Wise people are located in every walk of life and at all levels of organizations. How do we find them? Ask others. They are known and recognized by their peers.

Second, wisdom in relationships cannot be acquired merely by studying psychology, as any psychologist will tell you. It does require elements of emotional intelligence. It also must be accepted that people have unequal access to these qualities. This is partly a matter of inborn and stable individual differences and partly a product of formative experiences. Yet any person can become more skilled in the practices of reading others, self-insight, and self-control. Formal disciplines can help in this area, as can self-help media and coaching. To this degree, wisdom can be enhanced by disciplines and practice.

Third, wisdom in self-conduct benefits from many of the same inputs, including disciplines and practices. These we have reviewed as residing in the domains of self-appraisal, self-regulation, and perceptual control. They involve feats of imagination, discipline, detachment, and intellectual and emotional courage. How can one assist such processes? Probably the best aids are what Carl Rogers called "psychological space" and "psychological freedom" (Rogers, 1954) plus insight into the processes by which self-knowledge is concealed or revealed by the self's machinations.

Finally, let us return to the whole person perspective that the biographical approach brings into focus. Figure 17.3 contains a tool for autobiographical self-analysis that I offer to my Sloan Fellowship students. In itself, it offers no more than an inventory—a process that, if conducted rigorously, offers the possibility of insight into where on one's life's journey one acquired the goals, styles, flaws, and capabilities that currently constitute one's traveling gear. The last question on the list is the invitation to wisdom—challenge to

- *Origins.* Why were you born? Do you know what was happening to your parents at that time? What life themes come from these origins?
- *Dispositions.* What long-lasting personality traits do you recognize in yourself? Which ones do you see as inborn temperament, and which ones did you acquire as a child?
- *Bonding.* What family relationships were especially formative? What parenting styles, sibling relationships, and other key influences affected you?
- *Role models.* What other critical relationships—peers, teachers, and so on—were important as role models (positive or negative) up to adolescence?
- *Context.* What was the context of your childhood? Was it rich, poor, or full of change? How did this shape your goals?
- *Scripts.* What were the key learning experiences that shaped your early identity? What scripts are you carrying from that time?
- *Choices.* During young adulthood, what choices did you make that turned out to be crucial for you? Which were not really "you"?
- *Reflection.* How might your answers above be biased by rationalization, hindsight, and the stories others tell of you?

Figure 17.3   Journey to Adult Identity: Autobiographical Analysis

question what one is taking for granted and what one might seek to claim greater control over. Socrates put the case in the strongest terms: "The unexamined life is not worth living."

For leaders, this injunction can be troublesome. How much do leaders really want wisdom? We must accept the harsh truth that some leaders might feel as if they are better off without it. By this, I mean that there are leaders who are in positions where they are constrained to act unethically, manage for the short term, obey immovable constraints, and compromise principles for the sake of immediate contingencies. Wisdom will be a source of pain for those on a path to destruction regardless of the other benefits it might bring. We need to acknowledge that many well-meaning leaders do not realize what they are taking on until they are incumbent and then come to apprehend that there is no easy or safe exit route. For these, we may wish that organizations become wiser in how they operate and in what they value, so that they can find and retain leaders who can afford to be wise.

Note

1. Maasai society is structured in age sets of up to 14 years, marking the transitions between male juvenile, warrior, and elder.

References

Argyris, C. (1993). *Knowledge for action.* San Francisco: Jossey-Bass.
Baltes, P. B., Reese, H., & Lipsett, L. (1980). Lifespan developmental psychology. *Annual Review of Psychology, 31,* 65–110.

Baltes, P. B., & Smith, J. (1990). Toward a psychology of wisdom and its ontogenesis. In R. J. Sternberg (Ed.), *Wisdom: Its nature, origin, and development* (pp. 87–120). New York: Cambridge University Press.

Bargh, J. A., & Chartrand, T. L. (1999). The unbearable automaticity of being. *American Psychologist, 54,* 462–479.

Barrett, L., Dunbar, R., & Lycett, J. (2002). *Human evolutionary psychology.* Basingstoke, UK: Palgrave.

Baumann, N., & Kuhl, J. (2005). How to resist temptation: The effects of external control versus autonomy support on self-regulatory dynamics. *Journal of Personality, 73,* 443–470.

Baumeister, R. F. (1984). Choking under pressure: Self-consciousness and paradoxical effects of incentives on performance. *Journal of Personality and Social Psychology, 46,* 610–620.

Baumeister, R. F., Bratslavsky, E., Muraven, M., & Tice, D. M. (1998). Ego depletion: Is the active self a limited resource? *Journal of Personality and Social Psychology, 74,* 1252–1265.

Birren, J. E., & Svensson, C. M. (2005). Wisdom in history. In R. J. Sternberg & J. Jordan (Eds.), *A handbook of wisdom: Psychological perspectives* (pp. 3–31). New York: Cambridge University Press.

Bouchard, T. J. (1997). Genetic influence on mental abilities, personality, vocational interests, and work attitudes. In C. L. Cooper & I. T. Robertson (Eds.), *International review of industrial and organizational psychology: 1997, Vol. 12* (pp. 373–395). Chichester, UK: Wiley.

Boyd, R., Gintis, H., Bowles, S., & Richerson, P. J. (2003). The evolution of altruistic punishment. *Proceedings of the National Academy of Sciences (USA), 100,* 3531–3535.

Boyd, W. (1998). *Armadillo.* London: Hamish Hamilton.

Brackett, M. A., Warner, R. M., & Bosco, J. S. (2005). Emotional intelligence and relationship quality among couples. *Personal Relationships, 12,* 197–212.

Buss, D. M. (1999). *Evolutionary psychology: The new science of the mind.* Boston: Allyn & Bacon.

Cannon, D. R. (1999). Cause or control? The temporal dimension in failure sensemaking. *Journal of Applied Behavioral Science, 35,* 416–438.

Carver, C. S., & Scheier, M. F. (1998). *On the self-regulation of behavior.* Cambridge, UK: Cambridge University Press.

Cosmides, J., & Tooby, J. (1992). Cognitive adaptations for social exchange. In J. H. Barkow, L. Cosmides, & J. Tooby (Eds.), *The adapted mind* (pp. 163–228). New York: Oxford University Press.

Eisenberg, N., Fabes, R. A., & Miller, P. A. (1990). The evolutionary and neurological roots of prosocial behavior. In L. Ellis & H. Hoffman (Eds.), *Crime in biological, social, and moral contexts* (pp. 247–260). New York: Faber.

Ellis, L. (1993). A biosocial theory of social stratification: An alternative to functional theory and conflict theories. In L. Ellis (Ed.), *Social stratification and socioeconomic inequality: Vol. 1. A comparative biosocial analysis* (pp. 159–174). Westport, CT: Praeger.

Erez, M., & Earley, P. C. (1993). *Culture, self-identity, and work.* Oxford, UK: Oxford University Press.

Fenton-O'Creevy, M., Nicholson, N., Soane, E., & Willman, P. (2005). *Traders: Risks, decisions, and management in financial markets.* Oxford, UK: Oxford University Press.

Frese, M. (1995). Error management in training: Conceptual and empirical results. In C. Zucchermaglio, S. Bagnara, & S. U. Stucky (Eds.), *Organizational learning and technological change* (pp. 112–124). Berlin: Springer.

Gigerenzer, G., Todd, P. M., & ABC Research Group. (1999). *Simple heuristics that make us smart*. Oxford, UK: Oxford University Press.

Gladwell, M. (2005). *Blink: The power of thinking without thinking*. Boston: Little, Brown.

Greenleaf, R. K. (1991). *Servant leadership: A journey into the nature of legitimate power and greatness*. New York: Paulist Press.

Han, S., & Mulligan, C. B. (2001). Human capital, heterogeneity, and estimated degrees of intergenerational mobility. *Economic Journal, 111*, 207–243.

Harris, M. (1978). *Cannibals and kings: The origins of cultures*. London: William Collins.

Higgins, E. T. (2002). How self-regulation creates distinctive values: The case of promotion and prevention decision-making. *Journal of Consumer Psychology, 12*, 177–191.

Horney, K. (1950). *Neurosis and human growth*. New York: Norton.

Hull, J. G. (1981). A self-awareness model of the causes and effects of alcohol consumption. *Journal of Abnormal Psychology, 90*, 586–600.

Huxley, A. (1932). *Texts and Pretexts*. London: Chatto & Windus.

Humphrey, N. (1980). Nature's psychologists. In B. D. Josephson & V. S. Ramachandran (Eds.), *Consciousness and the physical world* (pp. 55–75). New York: Pergamon.

Ibarra, H. (2003). *Working identity*. Boston: Harvard Business School Press.

James, W. (1890). *The principles of psychology*. New York: Henry.

John, O. P., & Gross, J. J. (2004). Healthy and unhealthy emotion regulation: Personality processes, individual differences, and life-span development. *Journal of Personality, 72*, 1301–1333.

Jordan, J. (2005). The quest for wisdom in adulthood: A psychological perspective. In R. J. Sternberg & J. Jordan (Eds.), *A handbook of wisdom* (pp. 160–190). New York: Cambridge University Press.

Karoly, P. (1993). Mechanisms of self-regulation: A systems view. *Annual Review of Psychology, 44*, 23–52.

Kernis, M. H., Zuckerman, M., Cohen, A., & Spadafora, S. (1982). Persistence following failure: The interactive role of self-awareness and the attributional basis for negative expectancies. *Journal of Personality and Social Psychology, 43*, 1184–1191.

Kolb, D. A. (1984). *Experiential learning: Experience as a source of learning and development*. Englewood Cliffs, NJ: Prentice Hall.

Lansberg, I. (1999). *Succeeding generations*. Boston: Harvard Business School Press.

Leary, M. R. (2004). *The curse of the self*. New York: Oxford University Press.

McAdams, D., & Ochberg, R. (Eds.). (1988). Psychobiography and life narratives [Special issue]. *Journal of Personality, 56*(1).

Miller, G. (2000). *The mating mind: How sexual choice shaped the evolution of human nature*. London: Heinemann.

Nicholson, N. (1998). How hardwired is human behavior? *Harvard Business Review, 76*(4), 134–147.

Nicholson, N. (2000). *Managing the human animal*. London: Thomson/Texere.

Nicholson, N. (2002). How to motivate your problem people. *Harvard Business Review, 81*(1), 56–67.

Nicholson, N. (2005a). Meeting the Maasai: Messages for management. *Journal of Management Inquiry, 14*, 255–267.

Nicholson, N. (2005b). Objections to evolutionary psychology: Reflections, implications, and the leadership exemplar. *Human Relations, 26,* 137–154.

Nicholson, N., & De Waal-Andrews, W. (2005). Playing to win: Biological imperatives, self-regulation, and trade-offs in the game of career success. *Journal of Organizational Behavior, 26,* 137–154.

Osbeck, L. M., & Robinson, D. N. (2005). Philosophical theories of wisdom. In R. J. Sternberg & J. Jordan (Eds.), *A handbook of wisdom: Psychological perspectives* (pp. 61–83). New York: Cambridge University Press.

Piattelli-Palmarini, M. (1994). *Inevitable illusions.* New York: John Wiley.

Pinker, S. (1997). *How the mind works.* New York: Norton.

Plomin, R. (1994). *Genetics and experience: The interplay between nature and nurture.* Thousand Oaks, CA: Sage.

Powers, W. (1973). *Behavior: The control of perception.* Chicago: Aldine.

Robins, R. W., & John, O. P. (1997). The quest for self-insight: Theory and research on accuracy and bias in self-perception. In R. Hogan, J. Johnson, & S. Briggs (Eds.), *Handbook of personality psychology* (pp. 649–679). San Diego: Academic Press.

Rogers, C. R. (1954). Towards a theory of creativity. *ETC: A Review of General Semantics, 11,* 249–260.

Schloss, J. P. (2000). Wisdom traditions as mechanisms for organismal integration: Evolutionary pressures on homeostatic "laws of life." In W. S. Brown (Ed.), *Understanding wisdom: Sources, science, and society* (pp. 193–213). Philadelphia: Templeton Foundation.

Segal Company. (2001). *Annual survey of small–medium and large sized public company boards.* New York: Author.

Shrauger, J. S., & Osberg, T. M. (1983). Self-awareness: The ability to predict one's subsequent behavior. In G. Underwood (Ed.), *Aspects of consciousness: Vol. 3. Awareness and self-awareness* (pp. 267–314). New York: Academic Press.

Snyder, M. (1974). Self-monitoring of expressive behavior. *Journal of Personality and Social Psychology, 30,* 526–537.

Staw, B. M. (1980). Rationality and justification in organizational life. In B. M. Staw & L. L. Cummings (Eds.), *Research in organizational behavior* (Vol. 2, pp. 45–80). Greenwich, CT: JAI.

Steiner, C. (1974). *Scripts people live by.* New York: Grove.

Sternberg, R. J. (Ed.). (1990). *Wisdom: Its nature, origin, and development.* New York: Cambridge University Press.

Sternberg, R. J., & Lubart, T. (2001). Wisdom and creativity. In J. E. Birren & K. W. Schaie (Eds.), *Handbook of the psychology of aging* (pp. 500–522). San Diego: Academic Press.

Tangney, J. P., Wagner, P., & Gramzow, R. (1992). Proneness to shame, proneness to guilt, and psychopathology. *Journal of Abnormal Psychology, 101,* 469–478.

Trivers, R. (2000). The elements of a scientific theory of self-deception. *Annals of the New York Academy of Sciences, 907,* 114–192.

Turner, F. (1995). Shame, beauty, and the tragic view of history. *American Behavioral Scientist, 38,* 1060–1075.

Weick, K. (1995). *Sensemaking in organizations.* Thousand Oaks, CA: Sage.

Whiten, A. (Ed.). (1991). *Natural theories of mind: Evolution, development, and simulation of everyday mindreading.* Oxford, UK: Blackwell.

Wilson, D. S. (2002). *Darwin's cathedral: Evolution, religion, and the nature of society*. Chicago: University of Chicago Press.

Yates, J. F. (1992). *Risk-taking behavior*. New York: John Wiley.

Yost, J. H., Strube, M. J., & Bailey, J. R. (1992). The construction of self: An evolutionary view. *Current Psychology: Research and Reviews, 11*, 110–121.

Young, J. B., & Rodgers, R. F. (1997). A model of radical career change in the context of psychosocial development. *Journal of Career Assessment, 5*, 167–182.

Zahavi, A., & Zahavi A. (1996). *The handicap principle*. New York: Oxford University Press.

Zeidner, M., Matthews, G., & Roberts, R. D. (2004). Emotional intelligence in the workplace: A critical review. *Applied Psychology: An International Review, 53*, 371–399.

18

Interpersonal
Metaphysics

"We Live in a Political World":
The Paradox of Managerial Wisdom

Tyrone S. Pitsis
Stewart R. Clegg

A fool who knows he is a fool is truly wise. A fool who thinks he is wise is truly a fool.

—Buddhist proverb

Philosophy is the love of wisdom (the *philo* of *sophia*). However, wisdom is not something that people necessarily have or live by. Our perspective of philosophy in this chapter is predominantly concerned with metaphysics—or, more precisely, the experience of being that preoccupied much of the ancient Greek philosophers' thoughts, what Aristotle described as "first philosophy" or the study of "being qua being." Metaphysically, the appropriate question to ask is not so much "what is wisdom?" as it is "what does it mean to ask what is wisdom?"[1] This is the metaphysical question that underpins the chapter. What something is can be defined only within the limits of its knowability, which involves both epistemology and ontology, both how it is known and the nature of how one can claim to know. Metaphysical scholars concern themselves mostly with ontology—the nature of that which is taken to be, as derived from the Greek *ontos* (to be) and *logos* (discourse). The ontology of modern management can be seen in terms of what, epistemologically, contemporary thought has sought to define it as being. Thus, we inquire into the central institutions and practices around which management is organized as well as management as a form of theoretical knowing of these practices.

We argue for the phenomenology of wisdom—that wisdom concerns the pursuit of knowledge about the nature of what is taken to be ultimate reality. Wisdom is socially constructed knowledge, intersubjectively created and shared through relationships between people across time and space. Thus, wisdom is defined not by its possession—that information which is at hand and graspable—but rather by one's natural attitude toward knowing. Metaphysically, the social construction of wisdom entails a public shared knowledge. Wisdom that is not communicated to another person is worthless. For wisdom to mean anything, there must be a reciprocal relationship of understanding, and not because a person is persuaded or obliged to do so; that is, one either influences the other person positively or exercises power over him or her negatively to secure consent. In short, values underpin our approach as social scientists toward any phenomena we investigate or theorize about in management and organizations.

Because all contributors to this volume are management scholars, in this chapter we concern ourselves with the wisdom that such people espouse. We concern ourselves with the ways in which management educators are often blind to the utilitarian biases inherent in their wisdom. What are most powerfully embedded in management as an institution are the hierarchies of everyday life—those control systems and principles of efficiency, performance, and profit maximization through which we live our everyday lives and that are taken for granted as reality. We offer an alternative to hierarchy that we call "heterarchy" and marry this with the fledgling field of positive organizational scholarship as a way of transforming managerial wisdom back toward principles that value humanity. We close by discussing the implications for management education and research. But first we begin with a Socratic notion of wisdom.

Knowing Wisdom

> *We live in a political world, Wisdom is thrown into jail, It rots in a cell, is misguided as hell, Leaving no one to pick up a trail.*
>
> —Bob Dylan, *Political World* (1989)

Wisdom is a social construction, and those who have power are able to imprison it within their values system. Imprisoned wisdom loses any semblance of its original meaning—somewhat like prisoners who are sentenced to life in prison lose their humanity, as Dylan's analogy suggests. If imprisoned wisdom loses something, it is to the loss that we must address ourselves; we borrow from the original metaphysical scholars to define wisdom as acknowledging that we never fully know everything about anything. To be wise in the terms favored by Socrates is to admit the limits of our "knowability." It is not to make the vain assumption that know-how of some practice is equivalent to knowledge of some essential thing.

But management, by its very nature, is immodest because it concerns knowing answers to problems, making decisions, and behaving powerfully even when one is uncertain or knows little about that which is acted on. "Make a decision" and "be decisive" are catch cries synonymous with managers. In essence, despite the volumes of books, lectures, and workshops seeking to enlighten managers, a chasm exists between people's knowledge and their actions. Pfeffer and Sutton (1999) referred to this as the knowledge doing problem—where managers seldom act in accordance with what they know. Rather, we say that often what we know and take for granted determines what we do, whereas what we do not know may be more useful to us. As exemplified in the garbage can model, solutions define the phenomena we encounter as those problems to which we know the solutions (Cohen, March, & Olsen, 1972), even when we may get the designation badly wrong. Managers constantly search for assurances, data, and advice as to which judgments to make, but more often than not they rely on knowledge that reifies that which they know. We define this as know-how. The decision to continue with a course of action or to change it is based on a desire to keep ignorance at bay through mastery of the practices of know-how. Thus, doing management and seeking wisdom exist in a paradoxical relation with each other; management seeks to inscribe metaroutines that reduce the necessity of deciding, thinking, and seeking, whereas wisdom resides precisely in such processes of search, decision, and thought. As Socrates demonstrated, we need to think before we act, and thinking requires knowledge.

Socrates was the wisest man in Athens, not because of what he did or knew but because of what he did not do and admitted he did not know.[2] As such, wisdom was the most important concept for the ancient Greek philosophers. Wisdom for Plato involved the habit and will to always do the right things, tendencies to do good things, and a resolution to live a balanced life. As such, Plato (1955a) saw wisdom as embedded in notions of ethics, and so to be ignorant was analogous to acting unethically. Thus, philosophy, as with the love of wisdom, should underpin the fundamental training of all leaders in society. For Socrates, the cure to ignorance was clear; wisdom comes from knowing the limits to knowledge. Wisdom could be present only when one was constantly reflexive through critical evaluation of the self and of others. The Socratic method of dialogue was oriented precisely to this end—that if we cannot admit our ignorance, and we fail to critically reflect on our own and other people's thoughts and actions, we will never find wisdom.

Given much of management education and training concerns offering students of management answers to questions and problems, rather than teaching them to ask questions of themselves and other managers to make things problematic, Socrates's ideas run counter to much of modern management education and training. Modern management education and training closes down discourse so as to privilege both action and the extant structures of know-how within which that action is embedded. A Socratic conception of management wisdom is rarely sought; traditionally, wise

managers are valued as those who achieve outstanding actions and thus
who embody themselves less in reflection and more in action. It is not
merely that managers are often ignorant, venal, or stupid. (Many are. One
need only read the financial pages daily to see plenty of anecdotal evidence
testifying to stupidity, venality, and ignorance at work. Enron, an organization in which dissent was demonized and so upward criticism was prevented, would be a prime example.) Being biased toward action is inimical
to wisdom. Wisdom comes from a willingness to open up discourses, to
engage in dialogue, and to accept that we ever know only what we know
now and that what we know can and will change in an instant—and so we
can never fully know anything.

The process of acknowledging that we can never fully know anything is
not only daunting but also problematic. Often, showing that one is not
"knowing" or is uncertain in such contexts damns one to hell by those who
make claims to certainty, by those who make claims to knowing, or in the
eyes of those who are secure in their certainty—even though they might not
know in any way that is at all defeasible. Among powerful actors, if people
admit that they do not know or argue against those powerful actors, they
are often seen to be ignorant, at best, and dangerous, at worst, rather than
wise. These powerful agents (be they persons, organizations, or states),
whose power claims are embedded in the exercise of discretionary control
over what is known, what should be known, and what is knowable, necessarily make a claim to wisdom. Notions of wisdom become skewed to mean
the total opposite of "acknowledging our ignorance"; to put it succinctly,
the wise are seen to be those who claim to be able to provide solutions to
problems. It is those people who bring solutions to problems who, increasingly, define what knowledge is taken to be. Knowledge is no longer defined
in terms of thinking, questioning, and interrogating; instead, it has become
positioned as something that can be bought off the shelf—something standardized, routinized, and monetized.

The Phenomenology of Wisdom

Reading each of the chapters in this volume, one might observe each
author's bias in terms of what does and does not constitute wisdom. One
should not be surprised if one accepts that the notion of wisdom is socially
experienced through lifetimes of reflection and social and symbolic interaction. Such an idea was central to the thought of the great Austrian philosopher Alfred Schütz (1899–1959). Schütz's story is similar to the stories of
many outstanding intellectual Jews of his time; he fled Austria for France
after members of his family were interned in concentration camps. For a
while, Schütz used his legal skills to help relocate Jews from Nazi states, but
as Nazism spread in 1939 he fled for the freedom of America.[3] There, he
published one of the greatest philosophical works in the social sciences, *The*

Phenomenology of the Social World (Schütz, 1967). He examined the structure of the social world and how humans within it interact and make sense. Central to Schütz's thought is the idea that knowledge is generated between individuals, and so "intersubjectivity" and the way in which it creates a "life-world" of meaning should be the core subject of investigation. Every individual has a unique stock of knowledge built up through experience and interaction with family, friends, lovers, and work colleagues as well as through books, movies, stories, and symbols. This knowledge becomes taken-for-granted ways of being and of perceiving the world. Borrowing heavily from Heidegger and Husserl, Schütz expanded on the notion of "lived temporally." Time is not measured in seconds and minutes; rather, it is understood and shared as lived events:

> In order to observe a lived experience of my own, I must attend to it reflectively. By no means, however, need I attend reflectively to my lived experience of your lived experience. On the contrary, by merely "looking" I can grasp even those of your lived experiences which you have not yet noticed and which are for you still prephenomenal and undifferentiated. This means that, whereas I can observe my own lived experiences only after they are over and done with, I can observe yours as they actually take place. This in turn implies that you and I are in a specific sense "simultaneous," that we "coexist," that our respective streams of consciousness intersect. (p. 10)

Using Schützian philosophy, we can conceive wisdom as a form of knowing that operates as a way of passing on a sense of tradition and culture. Wisdom is attained and passed on through reflexive interaction with the experience of the "Other." One lives one's life as one's self through the eyes of those others in whom one sees one's self, something that always involves a spatial and temporal way of being in the world.[4] The imparting of wisdom is the process of one's own ego gathering into its cognition others' consciousness in such a way as to ensure the metaphysical survival of that which links oneself and the Other—a shared knowledge and understanding. Wisdom is a process of reciprocal dialogue and mutual influence.

For Schütz, spatiotemporal intersubjective relationships intersect and influence in a number of ways. The relationships of people, as "consociates," require sharing space and time at both the physical and cognitive levels, and then there are "contemporaries" who are connected only by being located in the same time. Contemporaries include work colleagues who are united by "work time"; they share their lives temporally. Finally, there are "predecessors" and "successors" with whom people share neither space nor time. Predecessors and successors have their identity formed through the construction of ideal types based on storytelling, letters, books, history, films, and other documentary methods. For instance, the sage of Kirkcaldy, Adam Smith, is often referred to as the father of capitalism. Smith's ideas are discussed in economics and political economy circles around the world and are taught in leading economics courses—although usually stripped of the theory of moral sentiments. He has long been dead, but successors sell themselves as experts on Smith or build on Smith's work to develop their own work and ideas. Their wisdom is a function of their predecessor (Smith), and Smith's wisdom lives on in his successors. It is likely that many entrepreneurial capitalists have never heard of Smith or his successors. However, introducing one of Smith's successors to a wealthy entrepreneurial capitalist as an expert on capitalism brings Smith's successor into copresence as a contemporary of the capitalist—and, as an expert on capitalism, one who may be expected to have sage advice and knowledge. Imagine that the entrepreneurial capitalist has amassed great wealth and fame and has developed a close friendship with the scholar and that together they write an article for the *Academy of Management Perspectives*. They now become consociates and predecessors, and together they influence a generation of successors in the form of up-and-coming economists and entrepreneurs in what constitutes entrepreneurial wisdom—and so the tradition continues. In simple terms, this is how the knowledge of power and influence is generated and transmitted across time and space, and it is no different in the wisdom of management theory, research, education, training, and practice today.

What Passes for Wisdom in Management Thinking Today?

With respect to current managerial and organization practice, there are many for whom what wisdom is taken to be passes for that privileged knowledge that is bought and sold through the market as master of business administration (MBA) courses, executive development courses, DVDs, and management books. Therefore, we now focus specifically on the gaining of wisdom that occurs overtly and covertly in managerial education. As a person capable of profoundly influencing the course of a person's life, an educator has a privileged and important role in shaping intersubjective experiences and interpretations. Knowing, being the embodiment of knowledge, is often seen as the meaning of what it is to be an educator, with the process of being educated constituted in terms of a straightforward transmission and transfer model. It is assumed that knowers know and students do not know; this is the constitutive basis of power–dependence relations in nearly any classroom. Yet, in Aristotelian terms, many educators will have much theoretical knowledge (*theoria*) but little in the way of experience (*techne*). In contrast, many business students will be wise in the ways of specific, contextual, and limited techne while being quite ignorant of theoria. In such a context, wisdom can reside in neither techne nor theoria; it requires *phronesis,* which is based on practical values-based rationality and deliberation about these values with reference to praxis. Such phronesis can proceed only through interlocution, dialogue, and an opening up of the one to the Other. It cannot be served through a one-way imposition of either theory onto practice (which is how the business student who is experienced in some necessarily limited business ways of the world often sees it) or practice onto theory (whereby theory is assumed to be "wrong" because it does not fit the case that one knows as one's lived experience). Each perspective needs to be open to the other through an acknowledgment of the limits of each.

Conceptualizing wisdom as an acknowledgment that we cannot be certain that we know anything has important implications. How can management educators presume to exercise power if they lack wisdom as defined by Socrates, that is, if they seek to privilege their theory over the other's practice? In Schütz's terms, how can educators prescribe ways in which to act here and now if they have barely reflexively interrogated the limits of their knowledge? Those who fail to acknowledge their limitations in knowledge, and who operate in a mode that circumvents interlocution, will merely be feigning wisdom and ultimately must resort to the use of coercive forms of power and ego defense of their theories and ideas, for they lack the necessary capabilities to influence others in any other way.[5]

It is not just in the classrooms that ignorance is promulgated. Sadly, many institutionalized tendencies in the current organization of management knowledge, especially those that presume it is some kind of utilitarian science in which only the strong survive so that robust theory may be equated with the most rigorous journals' editorial policies, run counter to wisdom. Instead, what is institutionalized is a faith in the scientificity of certain powerful words that are published in certain powerful places— talismans whose power is such that both techne and theoria should bow down and worship them. Those questioning how these words know what is taken to be true are likely to be discounted; acceptable questioning fits the truth of what is already secured. Management as a discipline fetishizes methodological controls premised on models of science that rarely range beyond the most scientistic and philosophically naive. And such scientism, of course, connects with the lived experience of most managers insofar as it both presumes the knowability of most of that which is managed and assumes that a part of this "that which" comprises compliant and controllable individuals. Thus, in principle, the object world is wholly knowable, and the subject world is conceived nearly wholly as if it were a part of the object world. Whatever might be its indeterminate obdurateness is imagined away. The model of management and the model of managing reach a perfect approximation in their relative ignorance; each expunges otherness.

Managing in any epoch will be a particular skill that involves execution; it will involve doing, it will be active, and it will be a practice. Moreover, it will be not only a practice of the self—one does not just learn how to be a manager—but also a practice of the many others who are to be managed; they must learn to be managed just as those who will manage them must learn that which constitutes managing in any given place and time. In this sense, management education that is premised on a scientist model in which the other can be shown to be indubitably wrong already mirrors the world of management that the other will inhabit; that is, it prepares the other for a world of adverse judgments delivered from positions of authority.

The power that is at work in programs of management—a programmatic science of immediate practical consequence shaping the existence of people in their everyday lives—is highly specific in its wisdom. It is not merely a repressive or prohibitory power; it does not involve just the possibility of imposing one's will on the behavior of other persons through prohibiting behavior to which they normally would otherwise be disposed. Rather, it works in a more positive way by shaping the dispositions that define the knowledge that we normally take to be true. The calculations that individuals make about effort, disposition, and demeanor, for instance, are both subject to and resources for the pragmatic wisdom of what management theory constitutes as its science.

Much of what is taught in MBA programs assumes that organizations operate to make profits above all else and that the business world is characterized by survival of the fittest in an individualistic sense rather than a cooperative sense (Clegg, Kornberger, & Pitsis, 2005).The reluctance to move away from tradition is evident in managerial education. Ghoshal (2005) was published posthumously as lamenting the state of play of management education. He drew on the original musings of John Maynard Keynes, who argued that the ideas of economists and political philosophers—irrespective of whether those ideas were right or wrong—powerfully enslave the ideas of those individuals they influenced (Dylan's lyrics resonate here). For Ghoshal, the discipline of management deserves the same critique:

> Our theories and ideas have done much to strengthen the management practices that we are all now so loudly condemning. . . . This is precisely what has happened to management. Obsessed as they are with the "real world" and skeptical as most of them are of all theories, managers are no exception to the intellectual slavery of the "practical men" to which Keynes referred. (p. 75)

Ghoshal (2005) stated the case perfectly, and we see Schützian ideas of consociates, contemporaries, successors, and predecessors reiterated here. The traditions and ideas of the past are thrown forward into the future by way of successors who, perhaps unknowingly, illuminate and interrogate their current realities with the tools they have inherited from the past. As Karl Weick, whose work is also heavily inspired by the ghost of Schütz, argued more than a decade ago, "Drop your tools or you will die" (Weick, 1996, p. 301). For Weick, scholars of organizations occupy perilous positions as they hold on to their heavy tools. Indeed, Weick (2004) went on to argue that the reality that organizational and management scholars construct exerts influence over what is noticed and labeled as significant and what is ignored. And as we argue, what is ignored is always more deadly than that which one thinks one knows.

Ghoshal is not a lone voice lamenting the state of management education, theory, and practice. There has been much debate and discussion, especially in several issues of the journal *Academy of Management Learning and Education*. Related thoughts can be found in Mintzberg and Gosling (2002), Pfeffer and Fong (2002), Pefffer and Sutton (1999), and Pfeffer (2005). Mintzberg (2004) also argued that both management and management education are in serious trouble and that neither can change without changing the other. He focused his sights directly on conventional MBA classrooms, which emphasize the cross-sectional and causal science model and thereby ensure that other approaches are left out. Mintzberg called for another approach to management education, whereby practicing managers learn from their own experiences in an interactive classroom setting. His aim is to bring the art and craft back into managerial practice and education. We take it that he implicitly, if not explicitly, called for a shift from the either/or of theoria and techne while seeking instead to instill phronesis into practice.

Underlying Weick, Mintzberg, Ghoshal, Pfeffer, and their colleagues' views of managerial theory, education, and practice are implicit theories of knowledge and power. All of these authors have implicitly commented on the power and influence of dominant management discourses; metaphysically speaking, they are dealing with the question of "what is it to ask what wisdom is?" and seek to change the nature of "what is." For Ghoshal, wisdom comes from better management theory; for Mintzberg, it comes from managers themselves; and for Weick, it comes from reflective management scholars who should question what they think they and the Other know in a move reminiscent of Socrates's calls for self-reflection. For Pfeffer, wisdom comes from reducing the knowing–doing gap, reflecting on what one knows, and implementing the results of reflection rather than being biased toward immediate application of know-how. For us, wisdom comes from changes in the values underlying power structures and relations. The debate, then, is both ontological and epistemological; whose is the "right" wisdom? For example, is it positivistic science, creationism, or some other knowledge?[6]

Managers are not usually management scientists and are hardly likely to act as if they are. They do not control all of the variables (they do not have any idea what all of the variables are, anyway), they cannot be systematic experimentalists, and they rarely have time for reflection. Managers, above all, are practical people who need to manage extremely difficult and challenging tasks; they are beset by many contingencies on a daily basis—some routine, others not. If Mintzberg (1973) is a reliable guide, managers need to find solutions to new problems every 10 minutes or so. Not surprisingly, they have little time for other than the most local, contextual, and bounded working knowledge that comes through experience. From an academic point of view, managing involves creating an ordered ensemble of relations between past histories and future actions as strategies that construct the present. Managing means creating nexuses of people, materials, and technologies that can act semiautonomously in pursuit of these strategies. Managing enables people, materials, and technologies—bound together through ideas about their interrelations—to traverse spaces and times. Managing makes knowledge work to constitute specific spaces and times into patterned locales and arenas in which people make sense of and transform materials and technologies. Managers in various contexts will have different relevancies guiding their managing and constituting their know-how. In historical and comparative practice, managers draw on many different forms of knowledge—not only university courses but also popular books, training sessions, magazines, websites, the popular press, the arts, sports, and the usual friendship networks. Their knowledge is a function of what they know, who they know, and how they know created in a social context.

In practical terms, if not those that underpin the management scholar's key institutions such as the top-tier refereed journals, university academics increasingly enjoy neither an exclusive nor a privileged role; they are not legislators of management wisdom but rather simply among its many interpreters (Bauman, 1987). Thus, their power is very limited, their knowledge is in no way legislatively mandated, and their wisdom is not necessarily respected except in outlets with which most managers will hardly be familiar and with which the majority of non-research-based management academics will barely be familiar.[7] The legislative science base of management knowledge is largely a myth maintained by and for the few university academics who do continue to practice their craft as if they were powerful and wise legislators rather than particular interpreters. The institutionalized norms of journal production support this myth; "publish or perish" is the cry, and so management scholars are driven by the need to publish so as to be seen as productive. So eventually the worth of academics' knowledge is a measure of their publication statistics rather than their philosophical wisdom. Given the hierarchical nature of the journals, a cannibalistic orthodoxy that feeds off itself is the institutionalized norm, and "innovation" is recognizable only within the existing channels.

How do the various sources of management knowledge relate to the work that management academics do? There is a range of views on this central question. For some colleagues, such as Lex Donaldson, a clear relation exists; it should be "the moral project advocated by Popper . . . for social science: by use of the critical method of theory construction and testing to dispense with bogus ideologies and thereby to ground social discourse in actualities so that policy choices could be made in a clearer light" (Donaldson, 1992, p. 464). Wisdom is clearly aligned with power here. Moral projects are all very good but are not necessarily descriptive of what ordinarily occurs. If they were, they would hardly be considered as necessary. Moreover, as Latour (1993) suggested, Popper did not even capture what scientists actually did when they did science, so one should not easily assume that Popper's representations will prescribe the relation between the hard-pressed 10-minute managers and a body of evidence taught and published elsewhere in rather abstracted conditions.

Astley and Zammuto (1992) saw the relation between managers and academics as metaphorical; sometimes managers and academicians play coincidental metaphorical language games, and sometimes they do not. Presumably, wisdom is contingent on mutual utility. If utility is a criterion, managers should set the terms of trade, Astley and Zammuto suggested. Beyer (1992) struck a midpoint where it is the operationalization of everyday metaphors and testing them against empirical reality that is important. Wisdom dictates that if academicians are serious about trade with managers, they should commit resources to mechanisms designed to maximize the trade on the model of the successful diffusion of innovation by the U.S. agricultural extension service (Rogers, 1995). What may be required is a cadre of academics who specialize in translation into field settings—knowledge out-workers under-laboring and prefabricating scientific knowledge by shaping it to applied purposes.

Each of these accounts seems to characterize managers as what Garfinkel (1967) once referred to as "cultural dopes"—actors unable to write or mouth their own scripts but subject only to those foisted on them by analytic outsiders, in this case organization scholars. What is clear is that whereas Donaldson (1992) and Beyer (1992) saw the role of organization science as something that should be the source of management practice, Astley and Zammuto (1992) saw the possibility of management practice as an autonomous sphere. For the former, organization science stands as a causal grammar underlying what managers do or should do; for the latter, the accounts of managing that managers have available are not causal springs of their actions. Instead, Astley and Zammuto tended to see practical management actions as something that may be discursively legitimated by abstract management knowledge in another version of "elective affinity" where practitioners choose the affinities. No necessary relation exists between the words and the deeds; managing means being discursively creative in justifying situational actions.

For managers, the craft of academia provides, at best, a set of popular recipes and tools that constitute their know-how. These can be useful in trying to find solutions to the problems of managing modern organizations; with such guidelines and tools, managers are able to create order out of potential chaos and are able to be seen to be managing rather than merely coping. In fact, like the general practitioner prescribing the latest drug (whose name the practitioner cannot forget because it is on the free coffee mug on his or her desk and on the pen in his or her hand), most of what is borrowed lacks scientific proof and is often used retrospectively to legitimate decisions made and actions taken on grounds that are more personal or political.

Now, managers might not be scientists, but they do know the value of research, at least in their terms. As any researcher studying organizational behavior knows, the manager of the organization under investigation nearly always asks, "What value does your study have for my organization?" By virtue of the sheer fact of needing to reflect on that question in approaching an organization to do research, one loses any credible claim to noninstrumental objectivity. So to maintain true objectivity, one would need to replicate an organization in a sterile controllable environment. The best management scholars can hope to do is create an artificial organization made up of university students who must complete a survey or an experiment for credit or for a nominal fee. The data are then manipulated, dredged, and orthogonally rotated until they make some sense in relation to the original hypotheses, and then the manager is asked to practice his or her profession informed by such results because they are scientifically proven. Managers essentially use what knowledge is available, or what knowledge can be bought, that fits what they want to hear and know. There has been scientific proof for decades that cigarettes kill people, as does asbestos, as do many of the residual chemicals of manufacturing (pollutants), and as do many of the chemical additives in food. Unless forced by government to declare such things, or unless an occasional brave soul becomes a whistle-blower, the public is kept in the dark. With the fear of falling share prices and risk to profit, managers either seek to suppress or ignore such knowledge or commission their own research to prove otherwise—and, for some reason, it usually does so.

So here is where we come to the crux of the matter. It is the underlying values of people that drive their behavior, reinforced through lifetimes of intersubjective interactions, and so claims of objectivity are very difficult to take seriously. The same goes for management scholars espousing their wisdom in management research and education, and so we call for a rethinking or reorientation away from the obsession with economic rationalist ideals about performance and efficiency. We now address this issue specifically.

The Value(s) of Management Wisdom

How soaked and shot-through life is with values and meanings which we fail to realize because of our external and insensible point of view. The meanings are there for the others, but they are not there for us.

—William James[8]

We believe that the key to reorienting the focus of managerial wisdom away from predominantly economic concerns is by way of addressing the inherent values of wisdom. Management research is value driven. As Ghoshal (2005) and Pfeffer (2005) lamented, current approaches in management theory and education overvalue the perspective that efficiency and profit should be management's key objective. The dominant ideology is one of economic rationalism. Economic rationalism is a term developed by Australian sociologist Michael Pusey and refers to the dogma that markets and money can always do everything better than governments, bureaucracies, and the law (Pusey, 1991). Government should allow prices and market forces to deliver their own economically rational solution. Benefits will accrue as hierarchies through the trickle-down effect; as people seek to maximize profit through self-interest, they will employ and pay for services, which in turn create wealth. The hallmark of the approach is that capitalists' self-interest must prevail to ensure economic growth (Pusey, 1991). Management education is driven by, and drives, such ideas of efficient, free-market, rational, profit-maximizing organizations, where relationships and intersubjective meaning are powered by a dominant discourse of hierarchical power relationships. Management scholars are rarely cognizant that they do so from an ideologically driven basis. As Schütz (1970) wrote,

> Man is born into a world that existed before his birth, and this world is from the outset not merely a physical, but also a sociocultural one. The latter is a pre-constituted and pre-organized world whose particular structure is the result of an historical process and is therefore different for each culture and society. . . . Everywhere we find sex groups and age groups, and some division of labor conditioned by them. . . . Everywhere we also find hierarchies of superordination and subordination, of leader and follower, of those in command and those in submission. (pp. 79–80)

As Schütz argued, everywhere we find organizations we also find hierarchies; indeed, such hierarchies are constitutive of the normalized knowledge of management. At the outset, Frederick W. Taylor explicitly sought to redesign and subjugate the human body in its accommodation to a material and social environment that organizations created (Taylor, 1911/1967). Latter-day functionalists believe, just as strongly, that organization will be as it is because when it is in fit with those contingencies with which it must deal, it will have evolved to the one best way of dealing with them. And an aspect of that being, in any normal organization, will be for hierarchy to divide tasks, set rules, and design structures. All of these divisions, rules, and designs are necessary for organizations to exist; thus, it is extrapolated that hierarchy must be a necessity. Hierarchy is a necessary bulwark against disorder, that is, against lower order members exerting their agency and using power to mess up the rules, task divisions, and structural designs. Hierarchy is the necessary prerequisite for lower order members to know enough about the conditions of their existence as members to hold them submissively in thrall to the necessity of power's devices. Thus, we may say that what power constitutes as wisdom requires power to protect and safeguard it. It thrives on that ignorance it maintains.

It is not just the case that, as Schütz argued, hierarchy is everywhere. It is also the case that, as Fairtlough (2005) argued, most people seem to be strangely addicted to hierarchy. There are good reasons why hierarchies should be addictive. Practically, from our earliest experiences in school, organized by a "principal" or "head teacher," we spend all of our formative years in a hierarchical organization—a training ground for an ordered, organized, hierarchical life of work. For those who attended elite schools, the sense of hierarchy is probably much more pronounced, meaning that, given dominant models of social reproduction whereby elite groups tend to reproduce themselves, the experience of most elites who actually run organizations is imprinted in terms of hierarchy. And if practical experience were not sufficient, the normalcy of hierarchy has been a constituent aspect of nearly all English-language thinking about power in organizations that, revoking domination, placed authority at center stage and deviation from it as power, a resistant and insubordinate property of hierarchical systems (Clegg, Courpasson, & Phillips, 2006).

Now it is difficult for one to propose alternatives to hierarchy without being labeled a "Communist" or some such similar shibboleth. It should be emphasized that Gerard Fairtlough, in thinking about alternatives to hierarchy, is one of the few current organization theorists to have run several multi-million-dollar enterprises, which in his case include Royal Dutch Shell Chemicals U.K. and Celltech, and as Fairtlough explained elsewhere, many of his ideas were worked out while in the job of running these companies (Fairtlough, 1994). As Fairtlough (2005) suggested, "Hierarchies tend to learn slowly, especially because a lot of effort goes into preserving the superior status of those at the top, inevitably an anti-learning activity" (p. 18). In other words, they are inimical to wisdom. Can alternative forms of organizations be offered that break with the tradition of dominant hierarchies without threatening "capitalist" ideas? Is it possible to have workable alternative forms of organization that are not modeled on the premise that authority is good and power is bad? Fairtlough (2005) answered by stating,

> In fact, there are two excellent alternatives—ones that don't lead to chaos. These two are called heterarchy and responsible autonomy. These names will be strange to most people. The strangeness isn't surprising. Because of our addiction to hierarchy we don't, and indeed can't, give serious thought to its alternatives. Whether hierarchy is desirable, or not, in a particular situation, we don't know, because it never gets tested against anything other than anarchy or chaos. (p. 9)

The alternative to hierarchy is not chaos or anarchy; people often equate hierarchy with organization. It is only our powerful addiction to hierarchy, bred in habit, that leads us to believe this is the case. And it is a "powerful" addiction in a double sense; first, it is strong, and second, it is obfuscatory because, where power is concerned, it creates blind spots, absences, and silences where critical reflection should be. In the absence of critical reflection, alternatives are not thinkable; where there is critical reflection, alternatives become visible. Fairtlough (2005) saw responsible autonomy as flourishing best where it is encapsulated within rules that are widely understood, transparent, legitimated, and shared as well as where action is open to critique, such as regular audit, or is being held in some way accountable for the actions taken as a responsibly autonomous subject or unit. We see these as contemporary forms of interlocution. Many forms of audit are increasingly institutionalized to deal with conditions of power at a distance—holding people accountable at a distance—such as the growth of standards (Brunsson, Jacobson, & Associates, 2002). The essence of responsible autonomy is that there is audit and disputed determination by some independent third party that is held in good standing and institutionalized as such. What distinguishes heterarchy from responsible autonomy is that in the former there is a constant and continuous interaction between entities and agents in deciding what and how to do something. In many instances, this means that for heterarchy to be successful, the alliance that is building it needs to develop an identity for instances of it that is separate from whatever organizational bodies comprise and host the constituent parts (Clegg, Pitsis, Rura-Polley, & Marosszeky, 2002). Responsible autonomy means that there can be a lot more distance between agencies. Both differ from hierarchy in not being subject to arbitrary power vested only in relations of domination.

No pure versions of these types are found in reality; they are abstracted "ideal" types in the Weberian sense. Most organizations are composed of different mixes of hierarchy (or direct control), heterarchy, and responsible autonomy. In heterarchy, through rotation of office and reward schemes related to risk and innovation rather than position, tendencies to domination can be reduced. Heterarchy builds democratic skills and capabilities in what has the potential to be a virtuous circle; it encourages more sophisticated general skills for interpersonal processes, dialogical relations, teamwork, mutual respect, and openness (see the "alliance culture" reported in Pitsis, Clegg, Marosszeky, & Rura-Polley, 2003). Admittedly, as Fairtlough (2005) suggested, heterarchies work best when the size of the organizations is small—less than approximately 150 people, he recommended. Heterarchy cannot be extended indefinitely because it is impossible to work in what are highly direct democracies once the number of participants rises beyond the circle of people who can know each other reasonably well. However, responsible autonomy within forms of heterarchical organization enables encapsulated boundedness to be created—with devices and agents for boundary spanning—thereby extending functional capabilities. Of course, the establishment of efficient responsible autonomy means critique must be in place from the start; the rules and accountabilities need to be clear, and a dispute resolution mechanism must be in place.

However, heterarchy is only part of the approach to develop and practice freedom based on shared power. If those who share power do so in collusion to dominate and seek power *over* others rather than to seek power *with* others, this is not heterarchy but rather hierarchy. It may be a new organization form (as are self-managing work teams and alliances), but its aim continues to be power of the few over the many or protection and reinforcement of privileged powerful positions based on economic interests. So there is a missing element to heterarchy that can be found in positive organization scholarship (POS).

Developing Wisdom on Different Values

The notion of heterarchy fits well within the current POS movement. In this section, we consider how POS and the theoretical development and study of heterarchy—through empirical scholarly multidisciplinary and multi-methodological traditions—can offer a truly alternative approach to not only how we conduct research on organization but also how we reflect on the implications of the outcomes of our research on humanity and how we use research to educate and inform future and current managers.

POS is derived from positive psychology (PP), which was the brainchild of Martin E. Seligman (Seligman, 1999; see also Seligman & Csikszentmihalyi, 2000). The principles behind PP are simple; it is a response to psychology's obsession with achieving mental health through investigating negative dysfunction and abnormality. Positive psychologists argue that psychology should concern itself with those things that lead to excellence, resiliency, hope, virtues, and happiness (Seligman & Csikszentmihalyi, 2000). From PP emerged positive organizational behavior (POB) and POS. Fred Luthans and his associates have sought to establish POB as a counter to traditional organization behavior. POB's current work on authentic leadership concentrates on a person's ability to create both social and positive psychological capital that refers to the networks of individuals' strengths, resiliency, optimism, hope, and other positive factors within an organization and the society within which it belongs (see, e.g., Avolio & Luthans, 2005; Luthans, Avolio, Walumbwa, & Li, 2005; Luthans and Youssef, 2004). POS also draws on PP, but from a more macro perspective of organization studies, and also acknowledges, more so than PP, the importance of the humanistic and phenomenological scholars who sought to enrich society. Moreover, for POS and its ideals to succeed requires collaboration among the arts, sciences, and social sciences and among members of groups, organizations, communities, and nations.

Peter Frost,[9] a leading figure in POS prior to his untimely death in 2004, highlighted the need for managers and leaders to be better able to deal with issues in a compassionate and caring way. Through inclusiveness rather than exclusiveness, POS has the potential to change the world of management research, education, and practice:

Imagine another world in which almost all organizations are typified by appreciation, collaboration, virtuousness, vitality, and meaningfulness. Creating abundance and human well-being are key indicators of success. Imagine that members of such organizations are characterized by trustworthiness, resilience, wisdom, humility, and high levels of positive energy. Social relationships and interactions are characterized by compassion, loyalty, honesty, respect, and forgiveness. Significant attention is given to what makes life worth living. Imagine that scholarly researchers emphasize theories of excellence, transcendence, positive deviance, extraordinary performance, and positive spirals of flourishing. (Cameron, Dutton, & Quinn, 2003, p. 3)

As POS grows as a serious alternative, it is at risk of reverting to the power of hierarchy that seeks to exert its truth over others. POS must find room for critical reflexivity that invites the kind of questioning we have discussed in this chapter. An ability to question itself, to allow voices for critique and descent and not ignore or avoid voices such as those of fringe-dwelling lunatics (albeit as avenues of exploration), is what will ensure the growth and survival of POS as a significant movement (Pitsis, 2007).

If most organizations exile positivity because of the formal deference of their members to hierarchy and its rights, dues, and entitlements (irrespective of what might happen most often informally), it is worth looking at cases where organizations and their managers have consciously sought to expand heterarchy and suppress hierarchy. Are they wiser in consequence? Clegg and colleagues (2002) presented a case study of a heterarchy in the form of an alliance in which private and public organizations, customers and contractors, and the community worked together to achieve extraordinary outcomes through key performance indicators that sought to meet not only typical business objectives such as schedule and budget but also community, environment, and safety objectives. At the core of the project was a dialogic commitment to exploring wisdom mutually—to discover new ways of doing and being. So when the AU$400,000,000+ project was completed, its managers needed to ensure that it left the community and environment better off than they were when they went into the project. The project did so with no industrial action, a construction site that had input from the community in its design, and extraordinary levels of commitment. However, it was also emotionally exhausting and required exceptional effort and commitment, beginning with the alliance leadership team and continuing all the way through to the subcontractors. It also needed to do so with resistance from government departments that were also accustomed to hierarchical traditional forms of organizing, often based on adversarial contracts. For Clegg and colleagues, such commitment was gained through a specific mode of governmentality, best thought of as a form of consensual subjugation in pursuit of extraordinary outcomes. Indeed, according to Pitsis and colleagues (2003), organizations can achieve extraordinary outcomes in social, economic, and environmental areas by seeking to achieve a perfect future through the empowerment of all people involved. However, such endeavors are complex, demanding, and rare because they require people to act in ways with which they are not familiar.

What makes this an instance of a more practical wisdom? First, the project was not scoped and managed in advance; its action was not merely the rolling out of something that was already predesigned with predesignated routines. Thus, its managers did not know in advance what they already knew and did not need to know. The leadership team began each meeting with the assumption of the "unknowability" of things. Second, it was not a project where the analytic head told the literal body what to do; the project was premised on dialogic encounters internally as well as with external stakeholders. These were arranged internally on the basis of organizing constant opportunities for interlocution from "toolbox talks" to board meetings with constantly revolving champions for different areas of the project and a revolving chair, where people from different organizations involved in the alliance would take turns in leading the agenda. Thus, it built dialogic encounters and shifting positions of interest into its daily routines. Third, the project rewarded creativity and innovation where it was achieved through virtuous cycles, but not where it was premised on vicious cycles where one goal was achieved through the sacrifice of another. Thus, it enabled space for all to learn, but not at a cost to the Other; it instilled respect for those Others with whom the project dealt, including coworkers, community members, and the ecology. In essence, this is reflective of Avolio and Luthans's (2005) authentic leadership introduced earlier.

It should be evident that an organization premised on these practices would be much closer to Socratic wisdom than would one run on the basis of tightly prescribed routines, for example, a typically exploitative McDonald's-type organization. The latter is programmed not to learn—to remain ignorant and do only what it knows to do. A wise organization is exploratory, in March's (1995/2002) terms, rather than exploitative. It thrives on chaos, accident, randomness, dialogic encounters, and the possibility of being surprised by what it does not already know.

Concluding Remarks: The Challenge of Developing and Applying Wisdom

Society grows great when old men plant trees whose shade they know they shall never sit in.

—Ancient Greek proverb

In this chapter, we began with the view that wisdom admits its limits and, as a social construction always in process, is never actually achieved. Rather than conceiving of managerial wisdom as big business based on the provision of answers, we envisage it as a way of being. Based on continued questioning, wisdom unsettles power relations. Management scholars must drop their tools (answers), as Weick (1996) maintained, and reflect on how they have come to know what they know and what they may be ignoring (questioning). The wisdom that informs management educators and many managers is biased toward an overly rationalized economic view of people and life at work. Similarly, wise managers need to relax their grip on some of the tools that they take for granted (Schütz, 1967, 1970; Weick, 1996). Wise managers will appreciate that the single biggest tool restricting their creativity is the existence of a singular hierarchy in which they strive and struggle for position based on unique individual qualities. Rather than create conformance among others through claims of managerial prerogative in discussions and debate, they encourage discord from which creativity will flow. Ignorance thrives on order; wisdom thrives on chaos.[10]

The "moral" project of management should, we believe, always concern a conception of humanity that is based on a questioning of what is taken to be wisdom. This is a difficult challenge for those who believe that wisdom is based on power—on how things have always been done, should be done, and will be done. From such a position, the natural attitude is to resist and ridicule such ideals. Adapting words from Charles Dubois, the important thing is to remember that we are always, in principle and in practice, able at any moment to sacrifice what we are for what we could become. What is required is a letting go of being that which we are to become that which we might be as we learn *with* those others we encounter. And the presuppositions of hierarchy are the biggest obstacle to such learning, as Fairtlough suggested.

Wisdom, as a social construction created through intersubjective relationships, requires discourse rather than obedience, creativity rather than routine. The calling of management academics might instead encourage them to practice transgression; to read and engage with philosophers, social theorists, and arts and humanities scholars; and to explore limits. To develop wisdom, management education should engage with the classics of philosophy, with Socrates as well as Simon, with Wittgenstein as well as Weick, with strange ideas as well as those with which it feels at home. It should be as prepared to find its ideas about professional practice in architecture, aesthetics, or art as in engineering.

To develop wisdom, interrogating the limits of their own and others' knowledge is a must for all students of management—be they academics, researchers, or practitioners. A manager raised on textbook order, primed to presume a singular hierarchy of command and control, is likely to see organizational stability as a desired end to be achieved by controllability and predictability in which change seems only to be a necessary act of superordinate will. Above all, such a manager will want to keep control and see everything running smoothly; if something develops not according to plan, it should be eradicated, simplified, and arrested. All that is required is a little order. From such order can flow all of those things desired—more hierarchy, more control, and less chaos. With more order, the hierarchs can plan what should be and design it so that it becomes so. They can impose rule and order on the organization without understanding the complex interrelation between these rules, the order they impression manage, and the necessary violations they constantly evoke.

Management education can be thought of as a process of shared inter-subjective experiences based on heterarchical power relations rather than on the traditional hierarchical expert–novice relationships based on the "one best way" so endemic in management education today. Rather than help managers to seek solutions to the problems that their current state of knowledge creates, educators should instead try to facilitate their discovery of new problems of which they are ignorant. At the same time, we (as educators) might learn a lot from the very people we educate. It is only when we confront what we do not know that we will stand any chance of finding some small moments of wisdom. In other words, good interlocutors should aid further exploration of knowledge rather than exploitation of knowledge. We should have a bias for action in research—for getting involved in the agora and engaging, without fear, favor, or prejudice, in the most robust interlocution possible. We need brighter, more philosophically robust and enlightened managers if we are to help build a better world; leaders are philosopher kings as originally envisaged by Plato (1955b).

Academic research in management should be unremittingly oriented to critique. That is, rather than being something that is conducted in a small ghetto for "critical management scholars," the practices of critique should be the institutionalized norm for research and scholarly practice. Managers have no need for orthodox academics dispensing orthodox knowledge other than in management training kindergarten. If management thinkers make a part of their own lives a critical practice that orients toward interlocution in the everyday organizational lives and practices of others, there is some possibility of usefulness. What is useful is to disrupt, unsettle, question, and disturb. Unfortunately, such actions are also least desired in organizations and institutions today; questioning can be an uncomfortable process.

Developing and applying managerial and organizational wisdom needs to revalue the ideals of positive organizational scholarship; however, this assertion comes with a caveat. The economic concerns of an organization, such as production, cost minimization, efficiency, and managerial control, still seem to be a driving feature in POS works. Just because POS scholars use terms such as "shared leadership" and "empowerment" does not mean that such concepts differ from existing knowledge. One person's experience of empowerment may be another person's experience of subjugation. More important, we believe that POS will never be accepted as a scientific approach to gaining management knowledge because from the very beginning of the research process it is biased toward positive outcomes and assumes that these positive outcomes improve organizational performance. POS scholars argue that researchers should be unashamedly biased toward those factors or phenomena that help us to foster, make sense of, and create a positive society based on humanity, growth, relationships, and human and ecological sustainability. Of course, these are not extras; rather, they are integral to wisdom per se. However, as scholars, we should acknowledge that how we define and conceptualize the objects of our research is always contextual and intersubjectively experienced and constructed; it is always biased. Concepts are always underscored by power structures. The world is more complex than dualist notions of good and evil—of positive and negative—and other such concepts that we use to frame our research, yet when we utter a word such as *performance*, we do so with preconceived ideas of what the word *performance* means. This issue is applicable to all social science research that informs management scholarship; no matter how objective it pretends or believes itself to be, it is always underscored by systems of hierarchies.

Wise scholars should seek to be complexity enhancers, not complexity reducers. Managers can do the latter job only too well. Most management remains obsessed with order and control when in fact it needs more disorder. Organization is threatened equally by chaos and order; leave order to the managers and help to foster chaotic ideas. Managing, when creative, lives between chaos and order, encouraging people to make differences where before there was homogeneity. Obsession with order does not protect organization from likely disasters; it merely manages impressions. Innovative managers should lose any pretensions of control that orthodox textbook accounts (and their radical opponents) encourage. Creative problem solving in innovative organizations demands a technology of foolishness (March, 1988), improvisation, and playfulness rather than an iron will to power. Wisdom means trouble for what is; wisdom is oriented to what is not but may yet become. For ignorance, wisdom is error. Wise persons know that they know less and, in knowing less, know better.

Finally, the application and developing of wisdom is an interactive and simultaneous process. Practice and collaboration among management scholars, management researchers, and management practitioners from interdisciplinary and multidisciplinary spaces will prepare the way forward. Especially, there is much promise in the possible collaboration between positive organizational scholars and critical management studies in moving management research, theory, education, and training forward to achieve the aims outlined in this chapter. Moreover, there is room for collaboration in teaching across disciplines, where medical students or fine arts students learn with MBAs and bring their ethical and aesthetic sense of values to bear. The overcompartmentalization of knowledge acts against wisdom because it restricts trade and cross-fertilization in ideas. Becoming wise means letting go of certainty and embracing the unknown; being wise is a state of not being closed, of being open, of knowing that one should and must always be a seeker and that what one seeks should, even when oriented toward its pursuit, be a calling nobler than merely making a profit. Any fool can make a profit,[11] but who knows what the wise can achieve as they do so?[12]

Notes

1. That is, we need to inquire into that which we study, its subject matter (being), and the manner in which the subject matter is studied (qua being).

2. At the time, Athenians placed great importance on consultations through the oracle at Delphi, and the oracle claimed Socrates to be the wisest. For a good discussion on the oracle, see Bowden (2005). *Classical Athens and the Delphic Oracle Divination and Democracy.* Cambridge: Cambridge University Press.

3. In America, Schütz established himself as an independent and innovative thinker who also had an exceptional business sense, amassing great wealth from his day job on Wall Street.

4. We capitalize the "Other" following Emmanuel Levinas's lead in his treatise, *Totality and Infinity* (Levinas, 1961). The Other is one who is close enough for his or her sense of being to be disclosed to a person—someone whose ontological constitution as another is evident to the person.

5. There may be some MBA programs that encourage Socratic dialogue as the medium of education and facilitate interlocution, and it may well be our misfortune not to have encountered these programs, but it would seem reasonable to note that the whole ethos of the MBA, from its solutions-oriented cases to the lionization of the management guru, is more inimical to systematic ignorance in a Socratic mode than to wisdom.

6. See the special issue of the *Academy of Management Review* (Vol. 24, No. 14, 1999) and more recent issues of *Academy of Management Learning and Education.*

7. As a result of empirical inspection that resulted in our deciding to try to do some things differently, we can predict that the references of many popular introductory management texts will cite *Fortune* rather than Foucault, the *Wall Street Journal* rather than Weick, and magazine columnists rather than March.

8. From William James's student lecture series, "What Makes a Life Significant," available for download at www.des.emory.edu/mfp/jsignificant.html.

9. The reader can see the last interview to be given by Frost when he visited the first author of this chapter in Sydney, Australia, during his lectures on toxic emotions in 2004. See www.ckmanagement.net/ and click on "resources" and then "interviews." Moreover, to witness the impact that a person who conducts himself or herself with honor, love, compassion, and integrity has on the world of work, see http://isr.sauder.ubc.ca/peterfrost/peter.asp.

10. We should point out that when we say "chaos," we do not mean the disorder of no organization; rather, we use it as the term is used in chaos theory—order that appears disordered to people because it does not fit what they know and expect in terms of order, and so it must be chaotic.

11. A fool is, by definition, one who does not seek wisdom; in fact, we think that it is probably easier in the short term to be a profitable fool than to be profitably wise.

12. By way of clarification, it should be evident that we think that not much of what is taught at universities as management or is practiced in the "real world" as management is particularly wise. In fact, much of it is not so difficult to master. The risk is that, as in all things, the routine drives out the nonroutine—or, in other words, the ignorant overwhelms the wise.

References

Astley, W. G., & Zammuto, R. F. (1992). Organization science, managers, and language games. *Organization Science, 3,* 443–460.

Avolio, B., & Luthans, F. (2005). *The high impact leader: Moments matter in accelerating authentic leadership development.* New York: McGraw-Hill.

Bauman, Z. (1987). *Legislators and interpreters: On modernity, post-modernity, and intellectuals.* Cambridge, UK: Polity Press.

Beyer, J. M. (1992). Metaphors, misunderstandings, and mischief: A commentary. *Organization Science, 3,* 467–500.

Bowden, H. (2005). *Classical Athens and the Delphic oracle divination and democracy.* Cambridge, UK: Cambridge University Press.

Brunsson, N., Jacobson, B., & Associates. (2002). *World of standards.* Oxford, UK: Oxford University Press.

Cameron, K. S., Dutton, J. E., & Quinn, R. E. (2003). Foundations of positive organizational scholarship. In K. S. Cameron, J. E. Dutton, & R. E. Quinn (Eds.), *Positive organizational scholarship* (pp. 3–13). San Francisco: Berrett-Koehler.

Clegg, S. R., Courpasson, D., & Phillips, N. (2006). *Power and organizations.* Thousand Oaks, CA: Sage.

Clegg, S. R., Kornberger, M., & Pitsis, T. S. (2005). *Managing and organizations: An introduction to theory and practice.* London: Sage.

Clegg, S. R., Pitsis, T. S., Rura-Polley, T., & Marosszeky, M. (2002). Governmentality matters: Designing an alliance culture of interorganizational collaboration for managing projects. *Organization Studies, 23,* 317–339.

Cohen, M. D., March, J. G., & Olsen, J. P. (1972). A garbage can model of organizational choice. *Administrative Science Quarterly, 17,* 1–25.

Donaldson, L. (1992). The Weick stuff: Managing beyond games. *Organization Science, 3,* 461–466.

Fairtlough, G. (1994). *Creative compartments: A design for future organization.* London: Greenwood.

Fairtlough, G. (2005). *The three ways of getting things done.* Dorset, UK: Triarchy Press.

Garfinkel, H. (1967). *Studies in ethnomethodology.* Englewood Cliffs, NJ: Prentice Hall.

Ghoshal, S. (2005). Bad management theories are destroying good management practices. *Academy of Management Learning and Education, 4*(5), 75–91.

Latour, B. (1993). *We have never been modern* (C. Porter, Trans.). Cambridge, MA: Harvard University Press.

Levinas, E. (1961). *Totality and infinity: An essay on exteriority* (A. Lingis, Trans.). Pittsburgh, PA: Duquesne University Press.

Luthans, F., Avolio, B. J., Walumbwa, F. O., & Li, W. (2005). The psychological capital of Chinese workers: Exploring the relationship with performance. *Management and Organization Review, 1,* 249–271.

Luthans, F., & Youssef, C. (2004). Human, social, and now positive psychological capital management: Investing in people for competitive advantage. *Organizational Dynamics, 33,* 143–160.

March, J. (1988). The technology of foolishness. In J. March (Ed.), *Decisions and organizations* (pp. 253–265). Oxford, UK: Blackwell.

March, J. G. (2002). The future, disposable organizations, and the rigidities of imagination. In S. R. Clegg (Ed.), *Central currents in organization studies II: Contemporary trends* (Vol. 8, pp. 266–277). London: Sage. (Original work published 1995)

Mintzberg, H. (1973). *The nature of managerial work.* New York: Harper & Row.

Mintzberg, H. (2004). *Managers not MBAs: A hard look at the soft practice of managing and management development.* San Francisco: Berrett-Koehler.

Mintzberg, H., & Gosling, J. (2002). Educating managers beyond borders. *Academy of Management Learning and Education, 1*(1), 64–76.

Pfeffer, J. (2005). Why do bad management theories persist? A comment on Ghoshal. *Academy of Management Learning and Education, 4*(1), 96–100.

Pfeffer, J., & Fong, C. T. (2002). The end of business schools? Less success than meets the eyes. *Academy of Management Learning and Education, 1*(1), 78–95.

Pfeffer, J., & Sutton, R. I. (1999). *The knowing–doing gap: How smart companies turn knowledge into action.* Boston: Harvard Business School Press.

Pitsis, T. S. (2007). Positive psychology. In S. R. Clegg & J. Bailey (Eds.), *International encyclopedia of organization studies.* Thousand Oaks, CA: Sage.

Pitsis, T. S., Clegg, S. R., Marosszeky, M., & Rura-Polley, T. (2003). Constructing the Olympic Dream: A future perfect strategy of project management. *Organization Science, 14,* 574–590.

Plato. (1955a). *The last days of Socrates* (H. Tredennick, Trans.). Middlesex, UK: Penguin Classics.

Plato. (1955b). *The republic* (H. D. P. Lee, Trans.). Middlesex, UK: Penguin Classics.

Pusey, M. (1991). *Economic rationalism in Canberra: A nation-building state changes its mind.* Cambridge, UK: Cambridge University Press.

Rogers, E. (1995). *Diffusion of innovations* (4th ed.). New York: Free Press.

Schütz, A. (1967). *The phenomenology of the social world.* Evanston, IL: Northwestern University Press.

Schütz, A. (1970). *On phenomenology and social relations: Selected writings* (H. Wagner, Ed.). Chicago: University of Chicago Press.

Seligman, M. E. P. (1999). The president's address. *American Psychologist, 54,* 559–562.

Seligman, M., & Csikszentmihalyi, M. (2000). Positive psychology. *American Psychologist, 55,* 5–14.

Taylor, F. W. (1967). *Principles of scientific management.* New York: Harper. (Original work published 1911)

Weick, K. E. (1996). Drop your tools: An allegory for organizational studies. *Administrative Science Quarterly, 41,* 301–313.

Weick, K. E. (2004). Mundane poetics: Searching for wisdom in organizational studies. *Organization Studies, 25,* 653–668.

19

Organizational Metaphysics

Global Wisdom and the Audacity of Hope

Nancy J. Adler

The 21st century confronts society with challenges that will determine the future of humanity and the planet. Such challenges defy traditional analysis. Paralyzed by the inadequacy of our standard logic, we search for meaningful and effective understandings that can guide us— understandings that seem inherently true, right, and just. Wisdom, as the dictionary defines it, is that which "is true and right coupled with just judgment as to action."[1] Few of us question the need for wisdom, yet to date academic scholarship has failed to address the role that wisdom plays in supporting organizational processes capable of addressing the world's most demanding societal challenges.

This chapter explores the nature of pragmatic wisdom—wisdom that includes both profound understanding and action. Philosophically, therefore, it fits within the tradition of pragmatic metaphysics.[2] The approach is classically metaphysical in that it attempts to understand the complexity of reality while at the same time not being satisfied with simply understanding. The overarching focus is on action, that is, on those understandings that can be used to make a positive difference in the world.

This chapter uses the founding of a new international development initiative, Uniterra, to highlight the need for and influence of wisdom in organizational processes and outcomes. It follows the step-by-step process that Uniterra employed in designing and conducting its inaugural global meeting in Gaborone, Botswana. Uniterra exemplifies the role that multicultural wisdom can play in conceptualizing and forming novel organizational structures and processes that embody the qualities needed for successful change efforts when confronting extremely challenging and complex issues. Uniterra's core structure and central process involve partnering—forming networks of nonhierarchical relationships. The chapter therefore investigates the wisdom needed to create and maintain various aspects of global partnering. Because the chapter focuses on pragmatic wisdom, it also explores the concepts of hope and courage, for without hope and courage, wisdom could never move beyond conceptualization to action.

The chapter is purposely organized and written in a style that differs from that of most scholarly articles. Beyond discussing wisdom in the context of a specific situation—that of the founding of Uniterra—the chapter attempts to offer possibilities to experience wisdom via a series of indigenous wisdom sayings (proverbs) from many of the world's more pragmatic wisdom traditions. So as not to interrupt the reader's appreciation of the wisdom sayings or reduce the meaning of such sayings strictly to their underlying logical constructs, the chapter uses endnotes rather than more traditional text references. Given the wide range of potentially unfamiliar cultural traditions included in the chapter, the endnotes offer more extensive background information than is generally included in more familiar data-focused articles.

The study of wisdom within scholarly management traditions is in its infancy. The issues addressed in this chapter have, as yet, few academic roots within organizational literature. It is hoped, therefore, that the chapter will lead to research into some of the more important wisdom-based organizational issues, including the following:

1. How do societal leaders obtain the wisdom and courage needed to address the world's gravest challenges?

2. How can global wisdom traditions support organizational actors and action that are true, just, and right?

3. How can multicultural wisdom traditions be used in complementary ways to support just organizational action?

4. In what ways can global partnering support wise action?

5. How can managers and leaders learn to combine their more traditional analytical approaches with wisdom?

Global Wisdom and the Audacity of Hope

Our children may learn about the heroes of the past.
Our task is to make ourselves architects of the future.

—Jomo Kenyatta, first president of Kenya[3]

> *In Pakistan, . . . members of a high-status tribe sexually abused one of Ms. Mukhtaran's brothers and then covered up the crime by falsely accusing him of having an affair with a high-status woman. The village's tribal council determined that the suitable punishment for the supposed affair was for high-status men to rape one of the boy's sisters, so the council sentenced Ms. Mukhtaran to be gang-raped.*
>
> *As members of the high-status tribe danced in joy, four men stripped her naked and took turns raping her. Then they forced her to walk home naked in front of 300 villagers.*
>
> *In Pakistan's conservative . . . society, Ms. Mukhtaran's duty was now clear: She was supposed to commit suicide. . . . Her older brother . . . explained, "A girl who has been raped has no honorable place in the village. Nobody respects the girl or her parents. There's a stigma, and the only way out is suicide."[4]*

Does society need to change? Absolutely. Is the enormity of the task seemingly overwhelming? Absolutely. Is there reason for hope? Perhaps, but only when delivered with frame-breaking courage.[5]

> *Instead of killing herself, Ms. Mukhtaran testified against her attackers and propounded the shocking idea that the shame lies in raping rather than in being raped. The rapists are now on death row, and [Pakistan's] President . . . presented Ms. Mukhtaran with the equivalent of $8,300 and ordered round-the-clock police protection.[6]*

Is change possible? Absolutely. Is it probable? No. Moments of profound humanity, wisdom, and courage do occur yet often remain strangely invisible within the broader society, hidden beneath the negative barrage of more-of-the-same journalism and practiced cynicism. The very moments that keep hope alive often become clear only to those privileged few who are able to learn about the stories and to the fewer still who are able to transcend the world's all-too-common cynical appellations of naïveté and to see within each story its latent potential for transformative change.

> *Ms. Mukhtaran, who had never gone to school herself, used the money to build one school in the village for girls and another for boys because, she said, education is the best way to achieve social change. . . . She is now studying in its fourth-grade class. "Why should I have spent the money on myself?" she asked, adding, "This way the money is helping . . . all the children."[7]*

Unquestionably, Ms. Mukhtaran's is a story of wisdom, generosity, and courage. Will the broader society change? Not necessarily. In Ms. Mukhtaran's case, the government has unfortunately chosen not to keep its promises.

[Ms. Mukhtaran] . . . has had to buy food for the police who protect her as well as pay the school's operating expenses. . . . [Now she admits], "I've run out of money." Unless the schools can raise new funds, they may have to close.[8]

Even with the wisest courageous action, is societal change ever easy or certain? No, never.

Meanwhile, villagers say the relatives of the rapists are waiting for the police to leave and then will put Ms. Mukhtaran in her place by slaughtering her and her entire family.[9]

Ms. Mukhtaran personifies the audacity of hope.[10] Although life has not given her reasons to be hopeful, Ms. Mukhtaran's personal wisdom and courage have supported her in bringing hope to a seemingly hopeless situation. From Ms. Mukhtaran, we do not merely learn about a new elementary school and a potentially changed legal statute; we also learn about the power of wisdom, courage, and the audacity of hope to bring about profound societal change.

Global Wisdom and Societal Change

Wisdom begins in wonder.

—Socrates[11]

Wisdom, according to the dictionary definition, is "knowledge of what is true and right coupled with just judgment as to action."[12] Courage transforms wisdom—knowledge of what is true and right—into meaningful action. Hope inspires people to aspire toward dreams that others judge to be unrealistic—dreams that others are no longer capable of dreaming. Dee Hock, founder and chief executive officer (CEO) emeritus of VISA International, reminds us, "It is no failure to fall short of realizing all that we might dream—the failure is to fall short of dreaming all that we might realize."[13]

Can society do better than it has done in the past? History, of course, would suggest that the answer is either *no* or, at best, *very unlikely*. Yet a multitude of global crises challenge us every day to transcend the confines of pessimistic precedent. Speaking on a much more prominent world stage than that of Ms. Mukhtaran, former U.S. Secretary of State Madeleine Albright reminds us, "We have a responsibility in our time, as others have had in theirs, not to be prisoners of history, but to shape history."[14] We have a responsibility to reclaim the audacity of hope. How do we proceed?

Shaping History: The Audacity of Hope

Only a life lived for others is worth living.

—Albert Einstein[15]

"What you do in response to the ocean of suffering may seem insignificant, but it is very important you do it."[16] How do we find the wisdom, courage, and hope needed to respond to what India's Mahatma Gandhi described so accurately as "the ocean of suffering"? What supports us in acting wisely and courageously when the odds we are given by rational analysis consistently demand that we quit—that we turn away from situations that are, or appear to be, beyond the reach of repair? Although there are many potential answers, one that is currently being tried is to create "a structure of hope" that systematically draws on the collective wisdom, courage, humanity, and dreams of people from throughout the world. To date, we have only the beginning of the story, but nonetheless, its beginning offers a noteworthy approach. The story, not altogether dissimilar from that of other international development efforts, tells of the birth of a global initiative that is committed to making a difference in the world. In this particular case, however, the founding organizations are consciously attempting to design a structure that can support the audacity of hope. In addition to supporting what they seek to achieve in the world, the structure is being designed to support individual members' ability to partner with and support each other while working for the greater good.

Uniterra: Creating a Structure of Hope

Man is the remedy to man.

—Proverb of Mali[17]

Heralded as the first major social innovation among international development efforts in more than 30 years, Canadian-based Uniterra was founded as a new type of global initiative.[18] With a 5-year, $75-million mandate, Uniterra's strategic mission is to contribute to achieving the United Nations' Millennium Development Goals while supporting individual countries' national poverty reduction strategies. The Millennium Development Goals include eradicating extreme poverty and hunger; achieving universal primary education; promoting gender equality and empowering women; reducing child mortality; improving maternal health; combating HIV/AIDS, malaria, and other diseases; ensuring environmental sustainability; and developing a global partnership for development—all by the year 2015.[19] American economist Jeffrey Sachs, arguably the most influential—and perhaps the most controversial—voice in international development today, asserts unequivocally, "To the extent that there are any international goals, they are the Millennium Development Goals."[20]

Uniterra was founded by two Canadian-based nongovernmental organizations: World University Service of Canada (WUSC) and the Canadian Centre for International Studies and Cooperation (CECI).[21] WUSC's mission is to foster human development and global understanding through education and training, whereas CECI's mission is to fight poverty and exclusion by strengthening the development capacity of disadvantaged communities.[22] Between the two organizations, they have worked in more than 50 of the world's neediest countries. The creation of the Uniterra partnership is the first time in Canadian history that an Anglophone organization (WUSC) and a Francophone organization (CECI) have chosen to form a joint venture designed to implement a major international development initiative.[23]

The founding organizations do not plan to rely on a headquarters-dominated hierarchy. Such a "traditional model for social and organizational change doesn't work [and] . . . never has. . . . The problem is that you can't . . . bring permanent solutions in from outside."[24] Uniterra's operational vision is, therefore, to create a field-driven process of international development that draws primarily on the wisdom, experience, and expertise of local people in its network of 14 partner countries.

Although excitement about Uniterra within Canada and in the broader international development community is palpable, the leaders are well aware of the dismal record of failure that pervades international joint ventures. Historically, three quarters of all international joint ventures fail.[25] The inability of global organizations to work successfully across cultures remains humbling. However, with an unswerving conviction in the importance of its mission, combined with an equally strong belief that new approaches must be tried, Uniterra has chosen to focus not on the question of *if* the joint venture should proceed but rather on the question of *how* to support its success—and thus beat the statistically predictable prognosis of failure.

Prior to committing to delivering new programs in the field, Uniterra is intentionally developing an internal organizational structure and processes that can support the hope-defined courageous action that it sees as necessary for achieving meaningful change in the world. From the beginning, Uniterra understood that such processes cannot come from a single country but rather must draw on the combined wisdom of all cultures involved.

The Inaugural Global Meeting: Creating the Right Beginning

If you understand the beginning well, the end will not trouble you.

—Ashanti proverb, Ghana[26]

To inaugurate the new partnership, Uniterra chose to bring together its representatives from Asia, Africa, and the Americas to meet in Gaborone, Botswana, in the fall of 2004. The purpose of this first global meeting was to weave together a network of relationships that would be strong enough to put Uniterra's mission into action and sustain it when faced with the enormity of the task facing organizations attempting to improve the quality of life on the planet. To develop such a network, the inaugural meeting attempted to draw on the richest possible range of available wisdom. As an American proverb counsels, "Only trees with deep roots continue to stand in a storm."

Most dictionary definitions recognize that wisdom includes both contemporary "scholarly knowledge" and traditional "wise sayings."[27] From the beginning, it was clear that creating an effective partnership network would require drawing on both historic wisdom traditions and contemporary scholarly expertise, on both subjective and objective experience, and on both modern and ancient traditions of insight. Given the desire to create something new (rather than simply replicating the structure of an existing organization), Uniterra drew particularly heavily on personal insight and relied much less on the objective experience of other international organizations. Drawing explicitly on the wisdom traditions of each country, the members of Uniterra selected proverbs and wisdom sayings from their respective cultures to support each aspect of their venture.

Partnering With Each Other: Developing Generative Relationships

> *Sticks in a bundle are unbreakable.*
>
> —Bondei proverb, Tanzania[28]

The 50 Uniterra representatives arrived from Bolivia, Botswana, Burkina Faso, Canada, Ghana, Guatemala, Guinea, Malawi, Mali, Nepal, Niger, Senegal, Sri Lanka, and Vietnam as strangers to each other.[29] To begin building the strongest possible network of relationships—a web that would hold in the face of the world's greatest challenges—Uniterra relied on two sources of wisdom: scholarly knowledge and insight from personal experience. In the realm of scholarly knowledge, one of the most promising recent developments in individual and organizational psychology is the move away from deficit-based models (which focus on fixing what is not working) to strength-based models (which accentuate and leverage what is working).[30] On the opening morning of the global meeting, the members of Uniterra were invited to use appreciative inquiry—a strength-based approach—to interview their colleagues about what allowed their most extraordinary relationships to flourish. In cross-cultural and cross-continental pairings, the interviews elicited colleagues' most personal relationship memories and wisdom.[31]

Remember a particularly great relationship that you have had? What made it so great? So satisfying? What did you and your partner do that allowed the relationship to be so great? Which aspects of the surrounding environment supported the extraordinary quality of your relationship?

Following the interviews, participants gathered in multicultural teams to collectively make sense of their memories.

What would you say are the global "secrets" to relationship success? What wisdom have we gathered that could support Uniterra in creating a network of global relationships of this extremely high quality?

Armed with a deeper appreciation of what leads to extraordinary relationships among individuals, the appreciative inquiry process was repeated to identify the success factors supporting extraordinary inter-team and inter-organizational partnerships.[32] For the first (but not last) time during the global meeting, the 50 colleagues—who even this early on the first day were already dropping their identities as strangers—were involved in wisdom creation (in combining "knowledge of what is true" with personal "insight").[33]

Although the relationship building continued informally throughout the global meeting, it was also formally supported each morning during a session designed to build trust and deepen relationships across projects, sectors, countries, and continents. During the first "morning connections,"[34] colleagues worked on strengthening their relationships by giving each other feedback on which of their contributions from the prior day had been most helpful.[35] The following day, they created a web of morning connections involving multiple brief meetings with colleagues from other parts of the world. Participants selected each encounter for its potential to help advance a current domestic project or future multinational initiative. To reduce the traditional reliance on headquarters and strengthen direct relationships among field-driven operations, the headquarters-based Canadians did not participate in that morning's series of morning connections meetings. Each conversation deepened a particular personal relationship and increased the probability of successful non-headquarters-based cross-cultural, cross-sectorial, and cross-continental alliances.

To further develop the ability of network members to trust each other, each participant shared with colleagues an artifact that symbolized his or her most profound personal commitment to Uniterra's goal of creating a better and more equitable world.[36] As the trust among colleagues deepened, generative relationships formed that were capable of producing new value for the organization—value that could not have been foreseen or created by any individual acting alone.[37] Thus, morning connections became essential in strengthening the generative capacity of the emerging network. Watching the process, one of the Vietnamese members of Uniterra captured the strength he saw emerging in the network with a proverb from his culture: "A tree cannot make a small rock; however, three trees together form a big mountain."[38]

Partnering With Oneself: Developing Insight

Some doors open only from the inside.

—Ancient Sufi saying

British poet David Whyte observes,

We are a busy people in a busy . . . culture. But even the busiest person wants wisdom and sense in busyness. . . . All of us want to work smarter rather than harder. Yet all of us are familiar with frantic busyness as a state that continually precludes us from opening to the quiet and contemplation it takes to be smart.[39]

Confirming the experience of most profound wisdom traditions, Harvard University professor Howard Gardner's research identified reflection as one of the three competencies (along with leveraging and framing) that distinguishes extraordinary leaders from their more ordinary counterparts.[40] According to Gardner, "Reflection means spending a lot of time thinking about what it is that you are trying to achieve, seeing how you are doing, continuing if things are going well, [and] correcting course if not, that is, being in a constant dialectic with your work, your project, or your set of projects and not just going on blind faith [for extended periods] without stepping back and reflecting."[41] Leaders who make extraordinary contributions to society take time every day to step back from the busyness of their work in the world to consider the broader meanings behind what they are doing and why and how they are doing it. In contrast, and to the detriment of the quality of their contributions, most people focus primarily (and in all too many cases exclusively) on action rather than on reflection.[42]

To support the members of Uniterra in gaining access to their personal wisdom, and thus to their ability to make more significant contributions, reflective practices were integrated into the daily rhythm of the inaugural meeting. Rituals of quiet reflection and contemplation opened and closed each day, starting with individual reflection and journal writing and followed by small- and large-group discussions on relevant issues that the personal reflection had raised.[43] Although not limited to the suggested questions, individuals considered questions for reflection such as the following:

What have been the most meaningful moments for you at the meeting thus far? What questions has the discussion raised for you? What have you learned that might be of most help back home? Based on what you've learned, what experiments might you want to try? Who will be most interested in what you have learned? What questions do you need to ask, and of whom, to clarify your learning? What have you done so far at the meeting that has most contributed to your colleagues' learning and future success?[44]

The actual questions are not as important as the practice of setting aside daily time for silent reflection. Perhaps Arthur Frank best summarizes the value of reflection for people as committed to contributing to the world as those who gathered in Botswana for Uniterra's inaugural global meeting:

To live is to write one's credo, every day in every act. I pray for a world that offers us each the gift of reflective space, the Sabbath quiet, to recollect the fragments of our days and acts. In those recollections we may see a little of how our lives affect others, and then imagine in the days ahead, how we might do small and specific acts that create a world we believe every person has a right to deserve.[45]

Without the wisdom that comes from personal reflection, other forms of wisdom become less relevant if not altogether meaningless.

Partnering With Generosity: Giving Gifts

Giving does not impoverish the giver.

—Proverb of Guinea[46]

In the broadest sense, the nature of Uniterra's work, along with that of most international development agencies, involves gift giving—giving the world the gift of a more civil, compassionate, sustainable, and economically vibrant society. At the global meeting, Uniterra explored the nature and rituals of giving gifts across cultures. While presenting the group with gifts from their respective cultures, representatives from each country explained their culture's gift-giving rituals. Who gives a gift to whom? When? Why? Is gift giving always reciprocal? How is respect communicated? Is the gift received in public or in private? Is it opened in front of the gift giver? How does the recipient show appreciation? How does the giving and receiving of gifts help to create and strengthen relationships and partnerships?

From the exchange of gifts came a more profound understanding of the reciprocal nature of generosity. Both givers and receivers gain; both receive meaning. Unless there is mutuality, the exchange strips recipients of both their respect and their personal power. International development, at its best, is founded on a mutuality of generosity. As is wisely said in Burkina Faso, "The father guides his son, and the son guides his father."[47] Living on a different continent and in a completely different culture, Ms. Mukhtaran similarly understood the wisdom and power of partnering with generosity:

> *Ms. Mukhtaran, who had never gone to school herself, used the [$8,300 the Pakistani government had given her] . . . to build one school in the village for girls and another for boys. . . . "Why should I have spent the money on myself?" she asked, adding, "This way the money is helping . . . all the children."*
>
> *[Ms. Mukhtaran] is now studying in . . . [the new school's] fourth-grade class.*[48]

As the Reverend Martin Luther King, Jr., recognized years ago, "Whatever affects one directly, affects all indirectly. I can never be what I ought to be until you are what you ought to be. This is the interrelated structure of reality."[49] Mutuality underlies the interrelated structure of today's world and encompasses the very meaning of generosity in international development.

Partnering With Expertise: Developing Understanding and Competencies

> *With the aid of the tree, a tree-climber makes contact with the sky.*
>
> —Ashanti proverb, Ghana[50]

One definition of wisdom, although not the most common, is "knowledge."[51] Although knowledge is necessary, everyone within Uniterra's network knows that knowledge alone is not sufficient for success. To increase basic understanding, various briefing sessions were held during the global meeting to update everyone on organizational policies and practices in areas such as finance, human resources, programs and partnerships, public engagement, and advocacy skills.

In addition, to facilitate the transition from delivering primarily local projects to involving themselves with local, regional, and global initiatives simultaneously, the members of Uniterra drew on their extensive expertise to update each other in a series of briefings on current social, cultural, political, and economic conditions throughout Asia, Africa, and the Americas. To further augment their country-specific knowledge, these factually based regional and country briefings were complemented with sessions designed to develop individuals' interpersonal cross-cultural skills.[52] As part of the inaugural meeting, Uniterra held its first Global Cultural Festival at which members invited their colleagues to participate in the music, dance, storytelling, film, drama, and other cultural rituals that are unique to their respective countries.

Similarly, over lunch each day, participants joined in animated not-so-trivial cross-cultural pursuit collaborations in which they attempted to deepen their culture-specific knowledge by discovering which of a series of seemingly incongruous facts described each country. They sought, for example, to discover for which countries the following facts are true:

An elderly man, more than 70 years old, was elected president of this country primarily by the nation's youth.[53]

This country went from being unable to produce enough rice to feed its own people to becoming one of the world's largest rice exporters.[54]

Beyond identifying the correct country, participants sought to discover the conditions that allowed particular "facts" to become reality in each country.

While explicitly adding to everyone's knowledge about the world, the not-so-trivial cross-cultural pursuit collaborations also increased Uniterra's understanding of the dynamics of possibility. How do seemingly impossible paradoxical events occur? What can a network, such as that of Uniterra, do to create more ostensibly unbelievable positive "facts" in the world? For more examples of the cultural facts that Uniterra explored, see Box 19.1.

Years ago, American essayist and poet Ralph Waldo Emerson remarked, "The invariable mark of wisdom is to see the miraculous in the common."[55] Unfortunately today, with more than half of the world's children living in poverty, extreme deprivation has become "the common."[56] It takes the ability to see miracles to be able to imagine how all of the world's children could have access to basics such as clean water, enough to eat, and primary education. The ability to see possibilities for positive change, even in situations where others cannot or will not, is one of the most valuable competencies that people in international development can bring to their work. If we assess the global situation honestly, is not the ability to imagine possibility a prerequisite for all potentially effective international development efforts? Positive change—reuniting reality with possibility—has a chance of happening only if the world reclaims its ability to imagine positive possibilities.

Strangely, most international development efforts have focused primarily on the process of change. Although change management is certainly important, the core international development skill is not change management but rather the ability to discern seemingly unimaginable possibility, that is, the ability to dream of outcomes so positive that they are worthy of the world's—and our own personal—best efforts. Thus, the members of Uniterra began reclaiming their collective right to dream—their innate ability to imagine and to believe in miracles.

Box 19.1   Global Complexity: How Well Do You Know the World?

A Game of Not-So-Trivial Cross-Cultural Pursuit

Bolivia, Botswana, Burkina Faso, Canada, Ghana, Guatemala, Guinea, Malawi, Mali, Nepal, Niger, Senegal, Sri Lanka, and Vietnam all have unique characteristics. From your knowledge of the world, decide which country best fits each description. Collaboration is encouraged. (Answers are in endnotes 112 through 123.)

- Women in this country do not change their name to their husband's family name when they get married. However, they are rarely referred to by their own name; rather, they are referred to as the wife of their husband or the mother of their first child.[112]

- Although the United Nations Development Program (UNDP) lists it as the third poorest country in the world, it is known as the "country of honest people."[113]

- With the biggest lake in the region, this country is rich in natural resources, but unfortunately, the people remain extremely poor.[114]

- This extremely hot country has a huge expanse of sand. Its rural population is very resilient, and these people continue to fight for their survival in an environment hostile to economic development.[115]

- This country produces more than 30% of the world's diamonds, yet it has a rapidly decreasing life expectancy.[116]

- This country, with the largest man-made lake in the world, was the first sub-Saharan country to gain independence.[117]

- In terms of geography, it is the second largest country in the world.[118]

- Among countries in the region, this country has ratified the most treaties and international documents supporting human rights, including those of women and children.[119]

- *Sinankounya,* or "cousins joking," is a traditional social pact deeply rooted in this country that supports the use of jokes by members of all communities in all circumstances, even in the midst of major conflict. The pact forbids rivalry and hostility among members of the community.[120]

- The country's civilization is more than 2,200 years old. It had a successful history of irrigation and of trading with the Greeks and Romans already 1,500 years ago. Unfortunately, in 1995 the country earned dubious world recognition for having had the largest number of combatants killed in a single battle since World War II; between 5,000 and 7,000 people were killed overnight.[121]

- With more than 100 ethnic and linguistic groups, this country has still been able to maintain its independence. It has never been ruled by outsiders.[122]

- Living in one of the most beautiful countries in the world, with a wide variety of microclimates, this country's 23 distinct ethnic groups strive hard each day to reach peace and live dignified lives.[123]

In seeking to broaden their global perspective while deepening their cross-cultural skills and understanding, the members of Uniterra demonstrated their courage to engage with the challenges set forth for the world by Vaclav Havel, the former president of the Czech Republic:

There are good reasons for suggesting that the modern age has ended. Many things indicate that we are going through a transitional period, when it seems that something is on the way out and something else is painfully being born. It is as if something were crumbling, decaying, and exhausting itself, while something else, still indistinct, were arising from the rubble. . . .

This state of affairs has its social and political consequences. The planetary civilization to which we all belong confronts us with global challenges. We stand helpless before them because our civilization has essentially globalized only the surface of our lives. . . .

[Leaders] are rightly worried by the problems of finding the key to ensure the survival of a civilization that is global and multicultural. . . . The central . . . task of . . . [the 21st century] . . . is the creation of a new model of co-existence among the various cultures, peoples, races, and religious spheres within a single interconnected civilization.[57]

At its inaugural meeting and, more important, in its work around the world, Uniterra is attempting to learn to be both global and local—to respect the common humanity of all people while honoring each culture's characteristic uniqueness—and to recognize the depth of tragedy in the world while continuing to believe in the power of creating miracles. As Nobel Laureate Albert Einstein understood, "There are only two ways to live your life. One is as though nothing is a miracle. The other is as though everything is a miracle."[58]

Partnering With the Unknown: A Parking Lot for Questions

For every problem there is one solution which is simple, neat, and wrong.

—H. L. Mencken, American political commentator[59]

Honoring Confucius's dictum that "real knowledge is to know the extent of one's ignorance," questions that could not be answered immediately during the conference briefings and discussions were sent to a "parking lot for questions."[60] The parking lot for questions was a highly visible place where an unanswered question could stay posted until someone within the group, not necessarily the presenter, found an answer.[61] Questions that could not be answered remained indefinitely in the parking lot—a testament to the fact that, in the type of ambiguous, rapidly changing environment faced by all development organizations today, many of the most important questions will remain unanswerable.

The parking lot for questions visibly contradicted the leftover, 400-year-old Newtonian worldview that gave us the illusion that everything in life is either "known" or currently "unknown-but-ultimately-knowable." It is not—and certainly not in the complex world of international development. With the help of chaos theory and the complexity sciences, Uniterra, and all the rest of us, have been helped to understand that beyond the known and the unknown-but-knowable is the unknowable.[62] We therefore accept that in today's turbulent environment, good questions often guide us much more powerfully than do their hoped-for answers. The essence of wisdom is to know that we do not know.[63]

Partnering With the World: Engaging the Public

> It requires wisdom to understand wisdom;
> the music is nothing if the audience is deaf.
>
> —Walter Lippmann, political commentator[64]

Some of the fact-, technique-, and knowledge-oriented briefings led to discussions about broader underlying issues. The presentation on public engagement, for example, could not help but raise questions about the reasons for the public's general lack of awareness, and similar lack of concern, about global issues and global crises.

Is it that the public doesn't know about Ms. Mukhtaran? Or is it that they don't care?

How could they not know? How could they not care?

Using knowledge alone, such questions cannot be addressed. For even minimally appropriate levels of understanding, we must recombine knowledge with more classical wisdom-based approaches to understanding—those of insight and sensemaking.

How could they not know? How could they not care? Marianne Williamson thoughtfully reflects on why the public seemingly neither knows nor cares: "The fact that we go about our lives as though the survival of the world is not at stake is not the sign of a stiff upper lip. It is the sign, rather, of a society not yet able or willing to hold a conversation about its deepest pain."[65] How does Uniterra engage that public? A public that is "not yet able or willing to hold a conversation about its deepest pain"?

In the same global conversation, South Africa's Archbishop Desmond Tutu quietly offers his own succinct wisdom: "My humanity is bound up in yours, for we can only be human together."[66] Decades earlier, German-born Albert Einstein foreshadowed Tutu's words: "A human being is part of a whole, the universe. Our task must be to free ourselves from the delusion of separateness."[67] Because Uniterra is a partnership organization, is that public engagement role? To remind the world that "we can only be human together"? To help the world free itself of its delusion of separateness? And if so, how does Uniterra do it? The questions, although crucially important and unequivocally needing the best of both our knowledge and our wisdom, may in fact remain unanswerable. For now, they remain prominently in the parking lot of all our minds.

Partnering With Structure:
Designing a Field-Driven Process

When the moon is not full, the stars shine more brightly.

—Proverb of the Buganda people, Uganda[68]

Unlike many international development efforts, Uniterra's operational goal is to create a field-driven process that draws primarily on the wisdom, experience, and expertise of local people.[69] Rather than relying on a traditional headquarters-dominated hierarchy, as is still the case in many international development efforts, Uniterra seeks to design a web of partnerships within the organization as well as with businesses, government agencies, and civil sector organizations external to Uniterra. To benefit from the partnerships, Uniterra plans to develop its ability to leverage the synergies inherent in working across organizations, cultures, countries, and continents.[70]

Using the vocabulary of international business, Uniterra seeks to operate more in the fluid, flattened, and networked structure of 21st-century transnational organizations than in the more centralized traditional hierarchies of 20th-century multinational and multidomestic organizations.[71] Given the complex turbulent environment facing all international development efforts, the proposed partnership structure offers flexibility and responsiveness, and therefore more hope for success, than does any centralized hierarchical structure in which a single Northern Hemisphere donor country attempts to impose solutions, however well intended, on the peoples of the Southern Hemisphere. Not surprisingly, the organizations that founded Uniterra are already taking the lead in creating and using decentralized and networked structures. Thus, the current operational challenge facing Uniterra is to extend and expand the structures of the founding organizations, based on historical experience and new opportunities, into a flattened network of partnerships.[72] That no one knows exactly how to create and effectively use such a network for international development in the 21st century is evident to everyone; that it needs to be tried is even more evident. As an ancient Chinese proverb advises, "Better to light a candle than to curse the darkness."[73]

From Traditional Mechanistic Organization Charts to More Fluid Organic Structures

The Talmud tells us, "We don't see things as they are. We see things as we are."[74] Philosopher and scholar Thomas Kuhn, in explaining how thought systems change, counseled that it is impossible to see something new until one has a metaphor that will let one perceive it.[75] So to be able to invent a new structure, the members of Uniterra first need to change themselves and their thinking. Prior to changing their thinking, they must change the metaphor through which they see the world and their organization. Not surprisingly, in the process of becoming open to new metaphors and new thinking, individuals themselves change.

What allows individuals and organizations to let go of prior worldviews and approaches that seemingly worked in the past but might no longer be appropriate? To even ask the right questions requires a profound commitment to what the organization is seeking to accomplish and a deep trust in the individuals involved. Otherwise, the completely human response is "why bother?" Canadian Ian Wilson wisely observes, "No amount of sophistication is going to allay the fact that all your knowledge is about the past and all your decisions are about the future."[76] To move ahead in spite of not knowing, which is where profound hope and commitment lead people, is to embrace the unknown while not yet knowing whether it ultimately will become knowable or continue to remain beyond the grasp of our understanding.[77]

Following the advice of chaos and complexity theorists, Uniterra chose to experiment with envisioning its emerging organizational structure as organic rather than continuing to perceive it through the lens of a traditional mechanistic organization chart. Following Kuhn's advice to change metaphors in order to change thinking patterns, Uniterra selected the metaphor of a spider plant to catalyze its ability to see the new possibilities inherent in a more organic organizational structure.[78] Using this biological metaphor, the members of Uniterra began questioning the role, or lack thereof, of all forms of centralized leadership, authority, and control. If *Uniterra was to be like a spider plant, what role would the central pot play? How small could the central pot become? What would be the best ways to connect the offshoots to the pot?*[79] Similarly, they questioned the relationship of the worldwide country operations to Canada. How should Uniterra define its stems—its "umbilical cords"? *How could it best use its stems to support the autonomy of each decentralized region and project (each offshoot) while still ensuring the network's overall integration and accountability?*[80] They also questioned how Uniterra as a whole could best support the individual country and sector operations in working more directly with one another. *How could Uniterra encourage its network of offshoots to work more closely with each other without directly involving the pot? How could the spider plant metaphor help Uniterra's network to manage its multiple internal and external partnerships in a generative and effective, yet decentralized, fashion?*[81]

Management scholar Gareth Morgan suggests that, when using the spider plant metaphor for organizational design, a number of insights are particularly relevant. From Morgan's perspective, Uniterra needs to do the following:[82]

- *Break the constraint of a large pot.* Uniterra's overall network can increase its effectiveness and grow larger in a decentralized fashion while reducing the size of its headquarters.
- *Integrate operations without exerting direct control.* The success of Uniterra's decentralization depends on creating good stems, not on instituting traditional control mechanisms.
- *Avoid getting caught in the uniformity syndrome.* Uniterra needs to avoid cloning. It needs to adapt each partnership (each hybrid offshoot) to its particular local environment and situation.
- *Encourage bumblebees.* To benefit from potential synergies and field-driven coordination, Uniterra needs to encourage the offshoots to work directly with each other without involving the central pot.

Shifting from a more centralized hierarchy to a flatter, more inclusive organizational structure is often most difficult for the people in the center. Giving away power, even for the best reasons, is never easy. One of Uniterra's Asian-based Canadian directors struggled with how to empower his local colleagues so that they could take more responsibility for making decisions. He did not want to continue the culturally expected hierarchical pattern in which he, as "the boss," made all of the decisions, nor did he want to violate fundamental cultural norms by suddenly seemingly abdicating his decision-making responsibilities. His innovative decision was to request that his Asian colleagues offer him a "suggested course of action" whenever they brought him problems to resolve. He could then role-model the more empowering and inclusive behavior he desired in the network by simply accepting and then publicly implementing his colleagues' best suggestions. In cases where their initial suggestions were less than what the situations called for, he could coach his colleagues (primarily by asking questions) on ways to improve their suggestions. In both cases, he would be augmenting the capacity of the network as a whole to assess situations appropriately and to develop effective courses of action. The resulting dynamic would be a subtle, culturally appropriate transfer of power from the center to the network.

As the members of Uniterra worked with the spider plant metaphor, they quickly came to realize that the type of structure they were seeking to design was less centralized and yet more integrated than their image of a spider plant. In recognizing the need to stretch their thinking, and the metaphor, even further, they began letting the image of the spider plant evolve into a new equally organic but less centralized metaphor.

The spider plant metaphor evolved into the metaphor of a web. Yet the web metaphor also raised concerns. Isn't the image of a web too fragile to support the network of strong partnerships that Uniterra seeks to foster? From the perspective of organizational design, the most optimistic answer to the "Isn't a web too fragile?" question is a cautious "Probably, although we hope not." From the perspective of ancient cultural wisdom, however, the answer to the same question is a resounding "No, it's absolutely not too fragile!" As an Ethiopian proverb asserts, "When spider webs unite, they can tie up a lion."[83] "Yes," the ancient wisdom declares, "a web is certainly strong enough to support the most ambitious aspirations."

From Maximizing Rules to Minimizing Specifications

How do complex adaptive systems, such as the web of innovative, self-organizing initiatives that make up Uniterra, simultaneously support the network's overall success, leverage its multicultural relationships, and give as much freedom as possible to each individual partnership? For organic web-like networks in complex environments, such as those faced in international development, rules do not work. Rules, in acting like control mechanisms, attempt to force people and systems to act in uniform and predictable ways. In attempting to assert maximum control, rules constrict behavior and thereby impede needed flexibility and innovation.[84] In contrast to rules, minimum specifications—referred to as "min-specs"—do work.[85] Min-specs are the minimum critical success factors an organization needs to succeed. To operate effectively, Uniterra needs to avoid creating rules and to limit itself to using the minimum number of specifications needed to guide the overall network toward success.

Selecting the fewest and best min-specs is not easy. To make certain that Uniterra chooses min-specs based on its current and future strengths, its search must rely on strength-based questions. As Uniterra engages in the process of identifying the best min-specs, it will need to use appreciative questions such as the following:[86]

1. *Think about a moment when you and your partners performed at their absolute best, a moment when you were particularly and rightfully proud of the team. Describe the moment to your colleagues.*

2. *What are the min-specs that supported those moments of extremely high performance—those moments when your partnership achieved outstanding success? What were the conditions without which it would have been impossible to reach that level of outstanding success?*

Following engagement with these first appreciative questions, which help to identify a broad list of possible min-specs, the second step is to limit the number of specifications to the smallest set needed for the global network's overall success:

3. *What are the min-specs for extremely high network performance that appear to be necessary in all situations worldwide?*

4. *Is there any circumstance in which you can imagine extremely high performance without one of the min-specs you have identified? If so, drop it. It is not a min-spec.*

In minimizing the number of specifications guiding it, an organization maximizes its freedom to respond appropriately and effectively to whatever combination of challenges currently confront it or will face it in the future. However, the additional freedom afforded by min-specs cannot be realized if those participating in the network have not developed a high level of trust in their own thinking and wisdom as well as that of their colleagues.

Partnering With Challenges: Asking Wicked Questions

[Wisdom is] the ability to offer useful advice to others about the pragmatics of everyday life.

—C. Peterson and M. Seligman, psychologists[87]

The Nepalese are caught in a vicious cycle of poverty and backwardness.[88] Nearly 50% of Nepalese live in absolute poverty, lacking even basic amenities.[89] Poverty in Nepal continues to increase while the gap between the rich and the poor widens.[90] At the same time, the ability of both the economic and social sectors to provide services is decreasing. This deteriorating situation is exacerbated by decades of political conflict and a dearth of functional public institutions. Unfortunately, according to concerned Nepalese, development experts over the years have succeeded in bringing to the table more issues than solutions.

Given the government's lack of accountability, should Uniterra focus on developing the capacity of Nepalese organizations to govern effectively and provide adequate services? Which other countries in the world (Ghana? Guatemala? Sri Lanka?) have addressed similar challenges successfully? How might the Nepalese draw on this global expertise? How should Uniterra proceed if it wants to avoid joining the cluster of well-intentioned, but ultimately ineffective, development efforts?[91]

Challenges faced in international development are complex, and complex challenges never have easy answers. Complex challenges are sometimes referred to as wicked problems because many of their characteristics are not reducible to their constituent parts.[92] When trying to understand complex challenges, neither simple nor complicated cause-and-effect relationships explain the current situation or predict future scenarios accurately. Descriptively, whereas the solutions to simple and complicated problems tend to follow rules, and thus appear to act in a more predictable machine-like manner, complex problems do not follow rules, and thus seem to behave in more unpredictable lifelike ways. As Uniterra and the Nepalese are well aware, if the situation was merely simple or complicated, rather than complex, the problem of poverty in Nepal, and in other countries, would have been solved years ago.

Making the challenges even more difficult for Uniterra is its awareness that, even when resolved successfully, a solution to a complex problem in one situation rarely functions as a recipe that can be applied to other seemingly similar situations. Success in reducing the HIV/AIDS rate in one country—Brazil, for example—fails to act as a template for reducing the infection and mortality rates in other countries.[93] Therefore, complex challenges call for a combination of wisdom and more traditional analytic approaches combined with seemingly infinite creativity, persistence, and patience.

Representatives from Uniterra's 14 countries brought their most daunting operational challenges—all of which are complex—to the global meeting and asked their colleagues for help in addressing them. To make the best use of the assembled network of wisdom, experience, expertise, and alternative perspectives, Uniterra formed cross-cultural and cross-continental coaching teams to work on each challenge. While their colleagues from around the world listened, country representatives described, from their own points of view, what made each challenge so difficult and frustrating. In response, the coaches resisted the temptation to immediately suggest possible solutions. Rather, they initially endeavored to deepen each team's understanding of its particular challenge by exposing underlying assumptions. The coaches asked questions, often referred to as wicked questions, intended to reveal contradictory assumptions that the team might be holding about the challenge itself, its history, the context, the organizations involved, and possible outcomes.[94] Such wicked questions, which never have obvious answers, often reveal paradoxical assumptions that the team has allowed to subconsciously shape, and therefore constrain, its actions and choices. Because such assumptions—even when completely inaccurate—are often implicitly accepted as true based on popular beliefs, they are rarely questioned and are particularly difficult to expose. "Articulating these assumptions provides an opportunity to see patterns of thought and surface differences. . . . [Such] patterns and differences can then be used . . . to find creative alternatives for stubborn problems."[95]

Using wicked questions, along with other appreciative techniques, nominally slows down the process of addressing challenges, including in situations whose severity begs for immediate action. Such slowed-down processes, however, are much more likely to produce options that work in complex situations than are any of the more commonly used, and seemingly more efficient, analytic approaches. Underscoring the trap of apparent, but false, efficiency, the Shona people in Zimbabwe remind us, "Running is not getting there!"[96] The wisdom of the people of Niger reinforces the same warning: "Going slowly does not keep one from reaching the destination."[97]

Partnering With Success: Designing Reality Based on Commitment to a Dream

Hope doesn't kill; it's rushing that kills.

—Proverb of the Ndebele people, Zimbabwe

Actuary and consultant Taddy Blecher joined the members of Uniterra for an evening of intense discussions on the power of courage, tenacity, partnering, and believing in self-created miracles to turn seemingly impossible dreams into reality. Lauded by South Africa's President Mbeki as one of the country's pioneers of change, Blecher officially launched CIDA University in Johannesburg in 2002.[98] Blecher's dream "is to mould motivated students from the country's poorest and most marginalized communities into a new generation of business leaders and high-powered entrepreneurs who will spread knowledge and prosperity across the continent."[99] CIDA operates on a fraction of the cost of other universities. To keep expenses down, "from the outset, the campus harnessed multimedia technology in its lecture rooms, got students involved in the day-to-day running of the university, and set up partnerships with a range of companies and other institutions which enabled CIDA to secure 'donations in kind,' study and other materials, and the teaching services of private-sector professionals."[100] Not surprisingly, the now-accredited university received more than 19,000 applications for its 1,600 places.[101] Living its motto, "It takes a child to raise a village," students partner with their home communities to pass on their learning. In just one month, for example, "CIDA students taught 300,000 young people about AIDS and money management in communities throughout South Africa."[102] Thus, CIDA operationalizes the wisdom of the Ouambo people of the Central African Republic: "The sun does not rise for one person alone."[103]

CIDA University developed its innovative education model and recruits students based on an appreciative approach aimed at amplifying positive deviance.[104] As some observers describe it, CIDA's business model aims at leveraging self-created miracles. CIDA looks for "learners who, despite severe disadvantages, have [excelled] . . . academically and who [also] found time to . . . contribute to their communities."[105] In other words, CIDA looks for positive deviants, that is, students who have succeeded in environments where most other kids could not. Before opening the university, Blecher and his colleagues studied these surprisingly successful students (these self-created miracles) to understand what allowed them to deviate in such positive ways from the more common patterns of failure experienced by most of their friends. They then built CIDA's curriculum and selection criteria based on the distinguishing characteristics that allowed these outstanding young people to achieve so much more than their similarly disadvantaged peers.

In the space of just a few years, CIDA University's graduates have begun winning top performance awards and attracting Africa's most forward-looking employers.[106] The corporate partnerships, however, are not motivated simply by altruism on the part of business. As one Africaans mining executive explained, "CIDA University is the next Silicon Valley. Any African company that doesn't recognize that will not succeed in the twenty-first century."[107] Galia Durbach, an executive with First National Bank of South Africa, agrees: "We see it as sort of an incubator for the talented leaders of the future."[108] CIDA identifies and brilliantly educates the best of the best. No company can succeed in the 21st century by hiring the second or third tier. No society can succeed without broadly educating its population, including the best of the best.

The members of Uniterra have begun experimenting with appreciative approaches to help them recognize, and ultimately use, positive deviance to bring about extraordinary organizational performance and outcomes. As a first step, they reviewed their performance over the prior year and selected photographs highlighting their most spectacular moments of achievement. At the meeting, they shared the pictures with colleagues in what came to be known as Uniterra's First Annual Photo Exhibition. The group began seeing global patterns in what led to spectacular performance—positive deviance—and looking for ways to create such conditions more consistently.

In viewing the gallery of photographs, the members of Uniterra also became aware of which pictures captured most people's attention and which, in contrast, were most easily ignored. They came to recognize the power of extraordinary images (those that deviate visually in a positive way) to capture the group's visual, emotional, and intellectual attention. In our visually over-crowded world, capturing people's attention and interest—whether in engaging the public or in obtaining the commitment of colleagues—is critically important yet never easy. Amid the cacophony of visual stimuli bombarding each of us every day, the competition for our attention to notice specific images, and the messages they embed, is intense. Yet if we fail to capture people's attention, the process of engagement will not even begin.

Partnering With Hope:
Designing the Architecture of the Future

We judge a person's wisdom by his hope.

—Ralph Waldo Emerson, American poet[109]

"Whenever we try to speak up in an organization, we reveal the precarious balance of innocence and experience in our voice. Too much innocence and we are sensed as 'dangerous idealists,' too much experience and we may sabotage everything we touch with a practiced cynicism."[110] The challenge facing Uniterra, along with every other organization that is committed to helping create a better and more equitable world, is how to remarry wisdom with hope—experience with idealism. Wisdom and hope are what organizations and individuals bring to challenging situations; they are never simply the outcome of an objective assessment of reality. In Pakistan, there was neither wisdom nor hope in the rape and threatened murder of Ms. Mukhtaran. If she had allowed circumstances, or an objective assessment of her situation, to define her reality, she would have succumbed to historical precedent long ago and accepted suicide as her preordained fate. She did not, and we—the rest of the world—look on in awe at her wisdom, courage, and unrealistic (naive) optimism.

The struggle for the members of Uniterra, and ultimately their choice, is to find the courage to approach a world that is sadly lacking in wisdom and hope and to bring both qualities more fully back into their work and the world. No matter how admirable, Ms. Mukhtaran's efforts, as one woman alone, cannot change the world. A global network of Ms. Mukhtarans, however, could change the world. It is for that reason that Uniterra was launched and that many people support it. With palpable yearning, we wait and hope that Uniterra's partnership network of wisdom, experience, and commitment will make a difference in the quality of our lives and those of our children and our children's children.

We do not inherit the earth from our ancestors;
we borrow it from our children.

—Kenyan proverb[111]

AUTHOR'S NOTE: I acknowledge the committed and forward-thinking leadership of Michel Chaurette and Paul Davidson, the executive directors of the two founding organizations, CECI and WUSC, respectively, as well as that of Claude Perras, the executive director of Uniterra, the new joint venture initiative. Equally important, I recognize the members of Uniterra's network, without whose courage, commitment, creativity, and humanity no idea of this magnitude would be imaginable.

Notes

1. Definition from *Random House Dictionary of the English Language* (1969, p. 1639).

2. "Metaphysics refers to the branch of philosophy that attempts to understand the fundamental nature of all reality, whether visible or invisible" (http://websyte.com/alan/metamul.htm).

3. Jomo Kenyatta, founding father and undisputed leader of Kenya, came to be known as *Mzee,* which is Swahili for "respected elder." In Swahili, he was also referred to as *Taa ya Kenya* (the "Light of Kenya") for having brought the light of independence to his country. For a more in-depth background of Kenyatta, see http://kenya.rcbowen.com/government/kenyatta.html. The quote attributed to Kenyatta is found at www.aap.org/advocacy/archives/jun70.htm.

4. Story excerpted from Kristof (2004). Kristof is a *New York Times* op-ed columnist who invites contributions to help Ms. Mukhtaran and her schools. Send checks to Mukhtaran Bibi, c/o Nicholas Kristof, The New York Times, 229 West 43rd Street, New York, NY 10036. Copyright © 2004 by The New York Times Co. Reprinted with permission.

5. *Webster's New World Dictionary* (1982) defines courage as the "willingness to confront risk to do what one thinks is right." Quinn (1996) stated that courage requires "walking naked into the land of uncertainty" (p. 3). By anyone's definition, Ms. Mukhtaran certainly demonstrated courage. For a discussion of courageous principled action, see Worline and Quinn (2003).

6. See Kristof (2004).

7. Ibid.

8. Ibid.

9. Ibid.

10. Barack Obama included the phrase "the audacity of hope" in his July 2004 speech at the Democratic National Convention in Boston ("Everyone Loves Obama," 2004). Hawaiian-born Obama is the Harvard University–educated son of Kansas and Kenyan parents and at the time was a newly elected member of the U.S. Congress. Perhaps the reason why hope is considered as audacious within the fields of leadership and organizational studies is that it has been ignored so consistently (Luthans & Avolio, 2003, p. 253). Only now, in the 21st century, is there initial research on hope and leadership, including Peterson and Luthans's (2003) particularly interesting study suggesting that "high-hope leaders have higher performing business units and more satisfied associates with lower levels of turnover" (as cited in Luthans & Avolio, 2003, p. 254) than do their lower hope colleagues.

11. Quote attributed to Socrates, a Greek philosopher; as cited on the Quote DB website (www.quotedb.com/quotes/1499).

12. Definition from *Random House Dictionary of the English Language* (1969, p. 1639). For alternative definitions of wisdom, see Peterson and Seligman (2004), who included definitions such as "the ability to judge correctly in matters relating to life and conduct; . . . understanding what was true, meaningful, or lasting. An emphasis on scholarly learning, . . . on good judgment in the service of effective living, . . . and an emphasis on one's insight into transcendent ends rather than practical means" (p. 183). For a review of psychological perspectives on wisdom, see Sternberg (1998).

13. As stated by Hock (1997) and cited on the Paradigm Shift International website (www.parshift.com/Speakers/Speak010.htm). Hock, one of 30 living laureates of the Business Hall of Fame, designed the "chaordic" organizational structure of VISA that led to its becoming the world's largest credit card company.

14. Quote from Albright's Harvard University commencement address on June 5, 1997, as cited in "Albright's Words" (1997).

15. Albert Einstein (1879–1955), one of the world's noted physicists, received the Nobel Prize for his theory of relativity. Born in Germany, Einstein immigrated to

the United States in 1933. The quote is cited on the Motivational and Inspirational Corner of the American System for Success website (www.motivational-inspirational-corner.com/getquote.html?authorid=23).

16. Quote from Mahatma Gandhi, as cited in Franck, Roze, and Connolly (1998, p. 93). Note that the more common version of this quote, attributed to Gandhi is "Whatever you do will be insignificant, but it is very important that you do it."

17. This proverb was shared by the members of Uniterra from Mali who attended the global meeting in Botswana. Although the traditional proverb is "Man is the remedy to man," the sense of the proverb is non–gender specific: "People are the remedy to people."

18. For a detailed description of the stages leading up to the initial formation of Uniterra, see Aarup and Raufflet (2004).

19. For more details on the United Nations' Millennium Development Goals, see the United Nations website (www.un.org/millenniumgoals).

20. Quote from Jeffrey Sachs of Columbia University, as cited in Eviatar (2004).

21. Although the majority of international business literature has focused on the private sector and multinational enterprises, there is a growing interest in understanding the role, dynamics, and contribution of nongovernmental organizations to value creation. For a review, see Teegen, Doh, and Vachani (2004).

22. World University Service of Canada (WUSC) is a leading Canadian development organization that has been active since 1939. WUSC is committed to fostering human development and global understanding through education and training and is devoted to the concept that all peoples are entitled to the knowledge and skills necessary to contribute to a more equitable world. WUSC's development work is supported by the Canadian International Development Agency, AusAid (Australia), NORAD (Norway), HIVOS (The Netherlands), the Asian Development Bank, and individual donors.

23. Anglophone organizations are those working primarily in English, whereas Francophone organizations are those working primarily in French. The linguistic diversity reflects the constitutionally supported multicultural nature of Canada.

24. Quote from Jerry Sternin, as cited in Dorsey (2000, p. 284). Sternin is a highly respected international development expert whose radical and successful approach to child nutrition was first implemented with starving children in Vietnam and later served as a model for rehabilitating tens of thousands of children in more than 20 countries worldwide. His approach is based on amplifying positive deviance. For a description of the process, see Dorsey (2000).

25. Most joint venture research has been conducted on the merger of companies; a comparable literature on international joint ventures among international development organizations does not exist. The three-quarters failure rate is as reported in the A. T. Kearney study cited in Haebeck, Kroger, and Trum (2000) and in Schuler and Jackson (2001). The same study, as cited by Schuler and Jackson, concludes that "only 15 percent of mergers and acquisitions in the U.S. achieve their objectives, as measured by share value, return on investment, and post-combination profitability." For research on the instability of international joint ventures, see the summary by Yan and Zeng (1999). Although the definitions (complete termination vs. significant change of ownership) and overall results vary, numerous studies have reported substantial international joint venture instability, including 55% termination reported by Harrigan

(1988), 49% termination reported by Barkema and Vermeulen (1997), and 68% instability through termination or acquisition reported by Park and Russo (1996). See also Hammel's (1991) classic article, "Competition for Competence and Inter-partner Learning Within International Strategic Alliances."

26. Ashanti proverb, as drawn from Burton (1865) and found on the Daily African Proverbs website (www.afriprov.org/resources/dailyproverbs.htm).

27. Wisdom, as defined in the *Random House Dictionary of the English Language* (1969, p. 1639).

28. Bondei proverb, as found on the Afritopic website (www.afritopic.com/afritopic-proverbs-a.htm).

29. Most participants at the meeting knew only the other people from their own country or region. Only a few had traveled worldwide and met all of those involved previous to this meeting.

30. Positive organizational behavior focuses on "that which is extraordinarily positive in organizations—the very best of the human condition and the most ennobling organizational behaviors and outcomes" (Cameron, Dutton, & Quinn, 2003, p. 207). Focusing on "the virtuous or excellent," it is the "positive cousin" of the traditional negative focus in psychology and organizational behavior (Dodge, 1985). For a discussion of the newly emerging field of positive organizational scholarship, see Cameron and colleagues (2003). For a discussion of appreciative inquiry, see Cooperrider, Whitney, and Stavros (2003) and Fry, Barrett, Seiling, and Whitney (2002).

31. Interview questions were designed with the help of David Cooperrider of Case Western Reserve University (personal communication, September 2004) based on his appreciative inquiry approach. See also the current research of Peterson and Seligman (2003) documenting the nature of people's most positive relationships.

32. Later in the global meeting, the members of Uniterra analyzed more systematically the quality of the inter-organizational partnerships they were currently in and were considering forming using the "STAR" analytic process designed by Zimmerman and Hayday (1999, 2003).

33. Definition from *Random House Dictionary of the English Language* (1969, p. 1639).

34. The idea for morning connections came from management professors Henry Mintzberg (McGill University, Canada) and Jonathan Gosseling (Lancaster University, United Kingdom). Adler first introduced it in their Advanced Leadership Program. Morning connections build on the practice in Mintzberg's International Program for Practicing Managers in which each day starts with morning reflections. Theoretically, morning connections are based on research on the importance and power of high-quality connections in organizations and work-related settings (Dutton & Heaphy, 2003).

35. Underlying this morning connections exercise were the concepts of generosity and gratitude. Gratitude, considered as a virtue in all philosophical traditions, is defined as "positive recognition of benefits received" (Emmons, 2003, p. 82). In the exercise, the only allowed response to receiving positive personal feedback was "thank you"—a clear expression of gratitude. Expressing gratitude is a form of appreciation. According to Kaczmarski and Cooperrider (1997), to appreciate is to "deliberately notice, anticipate, and heighten positive potential." Thus, the exercise was used to develop the appreciative capacity of participants. As described in the chapter, other forms of appreciative inquiry were used throughout the meeting, with

each being based on the premise that "mutual valuing and affirmation is necessary for collaborative learning and social transformation" (Tenkasi, 2000, as cited in Emmons, 2003, p. 88). Although not yet well developed in practice or in research, it has been recommended that management and leadership programs incorporate modules on gratitude (Cherniss & Goleman, 2001; Emmons, 2003).

36. The exercise using an artifact to symbolize profound commitment was designed by Frances Westley as part of the opening sessions for the McGill–McConnell Program for Leaders in the Voluntary Sector. For Uniterra, the question of profound commitment, as symbolized by the selected artifacts, was focused specifically on each individual's commitment to Uniterra's mission and hoped-for outcomes. Whereas other organizations often focus on how to create meaning in the workplace, the meaningfulness of Uniterra's goals and hoped-for outcomes—creating a better and more equitable world—makes such a pursuit irrelevant. Working for Uniterra is perceived by all parties involved to be extremely meaningful and significant. Note that in Uniterra's case, as well as in the case of other similar organizations, "meaningfulness is not necessarily dependent on the goals actually being realized; the pursuit of valued goals . . . may by itself foster a sense of purpose" (Baumeister, 1991, and Emmons, 1991, as cited in Pratt & Ashford, 2003, p. 311). For a review of the recent literature on fostering meaningfulness, see Pratt and Ashford (2003).

37. For a discussion of the importance of generative relationships in chaotic and complex organizational environments, see Zimmerman, Lindberg, and Plsek (1998).

38. Proverb contributed by Duong Hoang, agriculture and rural development sectorial specialist from Vietnam.

39. Quote from Whyte (1994, p. 98).

40. Gardner, as cited in the Howard Gardner Creativity and Leadership Video Guide (p. 20). See Gardner (1995).

41. See Gardner (1995).

42. For other authors strongly supporting reflective practice for leaders and managers, see Drucker (1999), Loehr and Schwartz (2001), and Palmer (2000).

43. The pattern of opening each seminar day with individual refection, followed by small- and large-group reflection, was initiated by Henry Mintzberg in his innovative International Management for Practicing Managers global executive program. The pattern has since been used in other McGill University–based programs, such as Mintzberg's Advanced Leadership Program and the McGill–McConnell Program for Leaders in the Voluntary Sector.

44. The emphasis on being a contribution is supported by Zander and Zander's (2000) discussion on moving from success to significance. The Zanders view leaders' and managers' primary role as "being a contribution."

45. Quote from Arthur Frank, as cited in Franck and colleagues (1998, p. 280). Note that a new first edition of Franck and colleagues' book was published in 2000 by St. Martin's Press.

46. Proverb shared at the global meeting by the Uniterra representatives from Guinea.

47. Proverb shared at the global meeting by Uniterra representatives from Burkina Faso. The wisdom it offered Uniterra on how to approach international development was inescapable. Although stated here as it is said in Burkina Faso, the meaning is non–gender specific: "The parent guides the child, and the child guides the parent."

48. See Kristof (2004).

49. Quote from King (1963), as cited on the U.S. Department of State's, International Programs website (http://usinfo.state.gov/products/pubs/civilrts/ excerpts.htm).

50. Ashanti proverb, as cited on the Heritage Classic website (www .eachoneteachone.com/heritagetennis).

51. Definition of wisdom, as found in *Webster's Seventh New Collegiate Dictionary* (1963, p. 1025).

52. For a discussion of the cross-cultural management skills and competencies needed for global success, see Adler (2007).

53. The country is Senegal, and the president referred to here is Abdoulaye Wade. According to former U.S. Secretary of State Madeleine Albright, Senegal is a "beacon of light for other African countries. Senegal is 'a beacon' that can 'show the way' to free elections and a democratic way of life in other sub-Saharan countries. . . . Much of Senegal's success . . . could be attributed to its president Abdoulaye Wade . . . , a modern version of a Renaissance man, trained in law and economics, literature, and math. Today he is leading a country that is helping to lead a continent." Albright was speaking at the National Democratic Institute's ceremony on December 6, 2004, at which Wade was awarded the W. Averell Harriman Democracy Award, as reported in Ellis (2004) and as cited on the AllAfrica.com website.

54. Vietnam.

55. Ralph Waldo Emerson (1803–1883) was an influential American poet and essayist. This quote is found in Emerson (1992, p. 38).

56. The United Nations Children's Fund (UNICEF) report released on December 9, 2004, stated, "More than a billion children—over half the children in the world—suffer extreme deprivation because of war, HIV/AIDS, or poverty . . . . The report said that nearly half the estimated 3.6 million people killed in wars since 1990 were children, reflecting the fact that civilians increasingly have become the victims in contemporary conflicts" (Dugger, 2004).

57. Quoted from the speech given by Vaclav Havel in accepting the Liberty Award (Havel, 1994).

58. Quote from Einstein, as cited on the Quote DB website (www.quotedb .com/quotes/12).

59. Henry Louis Mencken (1880–1956) was the most prominent political commentator, newspaperman, and book reviewer of his time. See www.goucher.edu/ library/mencken/mencken_homepage.htm.

60. Confucius was a Chinese philosopher (551 to 479 BCE). This quote is found on the Quotations Page website (www.quotationspage.com/quote/4316.html).

61. E. Raufflet of Montreal's Hautes Etudes Commerciales recommended creating a space at the global meeting for a parking lot for questions.

62. Brenda Zimmerman, a York University management professor, presented the framework based on complexity theory, diagramming the continuum of the known, to the unknown-but-knowable, to the unknowable. For further discussion, see Zimmerman and colleagues (1998).

63. According to Meacham (1990), "the essence of wisdom . . . lies not in what is known but rather in the manner in which that knowledge is held and in how that knowledge is put to use. To be wise is not to know particular facts but to know without excessive confidence or excessive cautiousness. . . . To both accumulate

knowledge while remaining suspicious of it, and recognizing that much remains unknown, is to be wise" (pp. 185, 187). Thus, "the essence of wisdom is in knowing that one does not know, in the appreciation that knowledge is fallible" (p. 210) (as cited in Weick, 2003, p. 71). "To act with wisdom is to accept ignorance, to be wary of simplification" (Weick & Sutcliffe, 2001, pp. 11–12, 59–62).

64. American Walter Lippmann won a Pulitzer prize for his literary work. This quote is found on the WorldofQuotes.com website (www.worldofquotes.com/author/Walter-Lippman/1).

65. Williamson is an American author and lecturer. This quote is from the introduction to her latest book (Williamson, 2004).

66. Desmond Tutu is a Nobel Peace Prize laureate. This quote is his attempt to take the meaning of umbuntu or botho into English. The quote is found on the Schipul website (www.schipul.com/en/quotes/display.asp?). See also Tutu's latest book (Tutu, 2004).

67. Quote from Albert Einstein is found on the DesigningLife.com website (http://designinglife.com/index.php/Main/CollaborationMints).

68. This Buganda proverb is found in the African Proverbs section on the Oneproverb.net website (http://oneproverb.net/bwfolder/africanbw.html).

69. Note that whereas the World Bank, for example, still tends to use a more centralized approach, many of the initiatives of the Scandinavian countries employ more decentralized efforts that support local autonomy.

70. For a discussion of the advantages of cultural synergy and the process for achieving synergy, see Adler (2002).

71. For a conceptualization and discussion of transnational corporations, see Bartlett and Ghoshal (1998). For further discussion on the contrasting organizational cultures among domestic, multidomestic, multinational, and transnational organizations, see Adler (2002).

72. CECI, one of the two founding organizations, is a leader in having developed, experimented with, and used a more localized decentralized structure. CECI has drawn from the experience of decentralized international development initiatives worldwide such as the Women's Rights in Africa initiative. The question is not simply one of centralization versus decentralization but rather one of continuing to learn from and invent structures that will work best in the 21st century.

73. This Chinese proverb is found on the Chinese Culture website (http://chineseculture.about.com/library/literature/blsproverb-ad.htm).

74. In addition to their written scriptures, the Torah, Jewish people have an "Oral Torah"—a tradition explaining what the Torah means and how to interpret it. This tradition was maintained in oral form only until roughly the 2nd century CE, when the oral law was compiled and written down in a document called the Mishnah. Over the next few centuries, additional commentaries elaborating on the Mishnah were written down in Jerusalem and Babylon. These additional commentaries are known as the Gemara. The Gemara and Mishnah together are known as the Talmud, which was completed during the 5th century CE. For a more in-depth explanation, see the Judaism 101 website (www.jewfaq.org/torah.htm).

75. Thomas Kuhn (1922–1996) was a professor of linguistics and philosophy at the Massachusetts Institute of Technology. This quote is from Kuhn (1962).

76. Ian E. Wilson is the National Archivist of Canada, appointed in 1999. This quote is found on the Best Signatures website (http://home.bi.no/fg188001/sigs.htm).

77. In their discussion of authentic leadership, Luthans and Avolio (2003) identified confidence, or self-efficacy, as critical. Confidence is defined as "one's belief about his or her ability to mobilize the motivation, cognitive resources, and courses of action necessary to execute a specific task within a given context" (Strajkovic & Luthans, 1998, p. 66). The challenge for people such as the members of Uniterra is that they face situations of such complexity that no one can realistically have confidence in their efficacy or success. Choosing to engage with the situation is based on the profound belief that something must be done, combined with optimism (as opposed to confidence) that one's approach will work and confidence that oneself and others will bring to the situation the best of their skills and abilities. If people refrained from acting except in those situations where they had confidence that they could successfully "execute the specific task within the given context," they would not act at all. Confidence in successful outcomes is beyond reasonable expectations in the complex situations faced in international development.

78. See Morgan (1993a).

79. Based on York University management professor Gareth Morgan's use of the spider plant metaphor (Morgan, 1993b).

80. See Morgan (1993b).

81. Ibid.

82. Ibid.

83. The Ethiopian adage "Der biaber Anbessa Yaser" translates as "When spider webs unite, they can tie up a lion." The translation is found on the Engender Health website (www.engenderhealth.org/ia/cbc/ethiopia-2.html) as well as on the African Proverbs website (http://oneproverb.net/bwfolder/africanbw.html).

84. A major challenge for Uniterra, as it identifies the internal minimum specifications that will guide it, is to continue to adapt to the rules of the Canadian International Development Agency (CIDA), the current primary funder of the initiative. In Canada, as in other countries, receiving public funding means following a lot of rules. CIDA is no exception. A current, perhaps transitional, challenge for Uniterra is to reconcile the rule-based requirements involved in accepting funding from CIDA with the more flexible framework of minimum specifications (min-specs).

85. For a discussion of min-specs and their uses in complex organizations, see Zimmerman and colleagues (1998).

86. These questions are based on appreciative inquiry and were constructed with the advice of David Cooperrider (personal communication, September 2004).

87. See Peterson and Seligman (2004, p. 181).

88. See "Vicious Poverty" (2001).

89. Ibid.

90. Ibid.

91. The situation in Nepal is as described by Kabita Bhattarai, the Harvard University–educated Nepalese Uniterra representative to the global meeting.

92. The discussion of wicked problems and wicked questions is based on the work of Brenda Zimmerman. See Zimmerman and colleagues (1998).

93. For a discussion of the uses of complexity theory for addressing the HIV/AIDS situation in Brazil, see Glouberman and Zimmerman (2002). Also see Begun, Zimmerman, and Dooley (2003).

94. For a summary by Zimmerman describing the use of wicked questions, see www.plexusinstitute.org/edgeware/archive/think/main_aides5.html.

95. Based on Zimmerman's conceptualization of wicked questions; see Zimmerman and colleagues (1998) and web page on wicked questions (www .plexusinstitute.org/edgeware/archive/think/main_aides5.html).

96. Shona proverb from Zimbabwe, as cited on the Bulawayo website (www .bulawayo1872.com/aw/shona.htm).

97. Proverb of the people of Niger contributed by the Uniterra representatives to the global meeting from Niger.

98. CIDA here stands for Community and Individual Development Association. For further information, see the CIDA University City Campus website (www.cida .co.za). For background on Taddy Blecher, see Aarup and Raufflet (2003).

99. See Friedman (2002).

100. See "'Ubuntu' University Lifts Off" (2002).

101. See the CIDA University City Campus website (www.cida.co.za).

102. See " 'Ubuntu' University Lifts Off" (2002). The month referred to is October 2001.

103. The exact saying, "The sun does not rise for one man alone," has been altered to render it inclusive of both women and men in today's vernacular.

104. "Within organizational behavior, scholars define deviance as intentional behavior that significantly departs from norms (i.e., shared understandings or expected ways of doing things)," stated Robinson and Bennett (1995). Historically, most discussions of deviance have focused on negative behavior (Warren, 2003). However, positive deviance exists and was recently defined as "intentional behaviors that depart from the norms of a referent group in honorable ways" (Spreitzer & Sonenshein, 2003, p. 209). For in-depth discussions of positive deviance and its use in creating extraordinary organizations and outcomes, see Spreitzer and Sonenshein (2003) and Dorsey (2000).

105. See Davie (2001).

106. Private conversation with Taddy Blecher in Gaborone, Botswana, October 7, 2004.

107. Private conversation with a South African executive in New York City, October 21, 2004.

108. See Lindow (2004).

109. The original Emerson quote, "We judge a man's wisdom by his hope," has been altered to render it non–gender specific. The original wisdom saying is found on the World of Inspiration website (www.worldofinspiration.com/Quotes.aspx? pg=1&category=5).

110. Quote from poet David Whyte. See Whyte (1994, p. 147).

111. Proverb of the people of Kenya, as found in Duncan (1994).

112. Vietnam.

113. Burkina Faso.

114. Malawi.

115. Niger.

116. Botswana. ("In many ways, Botswana symbolizes the tremendous challenge that HIV/AIDS poses to African development in the 21st century. It is blessed with sizable diamond reserves that have fueled rapid economic growth since independence and have raised incomes for tens of thousands of its 1.7 million citizens to world-class standards. Indeed, it is estimated that the average life expectancy of Botswana's citizens would be 74 years in the absence of HIV/AIDS, or nearly as high as the average life expectancy in the U.S. Yet the impact of HIV/AIDS, which contributes to the death of more than 25,000 Batswana every year, will likely reduce the nation's average life expectance to 27 [years] by 2010; ("Giving Women Economic Tools," 2004).

117. Ghana.
118. Canada.
119. Guinea.
120. Mali.
121. Sri Lanka.
122. Nepal.
123. Guatemala.

References

Aarup, K., & Raufflet, E. (2003). *Social entrepreneurship and leadership: Taddy Blecher and CIDA City Centre University, South Africa.* Montreal, Canada: HEC Centre for Case Studies.

Aarup, K., & Raufflet, E. (2004). *Uniterra, the joint volunteer initiative between CECI and WUSC: Social innovation in the Canadian non-governmental sector.* Montreal, Canada: HEC Centre for Case Studies.

Adler, N. J. (2002). *From Boston to Beijing: Managing with a worldview.* Cincinnati, OH: Thomson Learning.

Adler, N. J. (2007). *International dimensions of organizational behavior* (5th ed.). Cincinnati, OH: South-Western.

Albright's words: Global task for U.S. (1997, June 6). *New York Times.*

Barkema, H., & Vermeulen, F. (1997). What differences in the cultural backgrounds of partners are detrimental for international joint ventures? *Journal of International Business Studies, 28,* 845–864.

Bartlett, C., & Ghoshal, S. (1998). *Managing across borders: The transnational solution* (2nd ed.). Boston: Harvard Business School Press.

Baumeister, R. F. (1991). *Meanings of life.* New York: Guilford.

Begun, W. J., Zimmerman, B., & Dooley, K. (2003). Health care organizations as complex adaptive systems. In S. M. Mick & M. Wyttenbach (Eds.), *Advances in health care organization theory* (pp. 253–288). San Francisco: Jossey-Bass.

Burton, R. F. (Comp.). (1865). *Wit and wisdom from West Africa: A book of proverbial philosophy, idioms, enigmas, and laconisms.* London: Tinsley Brothers.

Cameron, K. S., Dutton, J. E., & Quinn, R. E. (Eds.). (2003). *Positive organizational scholarship.* San Francisco: Berrett-Koehler.

Cherniss, C., & Goleman, D. (Eds.). (2001). *The emotionally intelligent workplace: How to select for, measure, and improve emotional intelligence in individuals.* San Francisco: Jossey-Bass.

Cooperrider, D. L., Whitney, D., & Stavros, J. M. (2003). *Appreciative inquiry handbook.* Bedford Heights, OH: Lakeshore.

Davie, L. (2001). *South Africa's first ubuntu university* [Online]. Available: www.joburg.org.za/december/university.stm

Dodge, D. (1985). The over-negativized conceptualization of deviance: A programmatic exploration. *Deviant Behavior, 6,* 17–37.

Dorsey, D. (2000, December). Positive deviant. *Fast Company,* p. 284.

Drucker, P. (1999). Managing oneself. *Harvard Business Review, 77*(2), 65–74.

Dugger, C. W. (2004, December 10). UNICEF report says children in deprivation reach a billion. *New York Times.*

Duncan, K. (1994). *Vision of hope: Children of the world*. Wamberal, Australia: HarperCollins Australia.

Dutton, J. E., & Heaphy, E. D. (2003). The power of high-quality connections. In K. S. Cameron, J. E. Dutton, & R. E. Quinn (Eds.), *Positive organizational scholarship* (pp. 263–278). San Francisco: Berrett-Koehler.

Ellis, S. (2004, December 8). President Wade of Senegal honored with democracy award. *United States Department of State News* (Washington, DC).

Emerson, R. W. (1992). *The selected writings of Ralph Waldo Emerson* (*Nature*, Vol. 8: *Prospects*). New York: Random House (Modern Library ed.).

Emmons, R. A. (1991). *The psychology of ultimate concerns: Motivation and spirituality in personality*. New York: Guilford.

Emmons, R. A. (2003). Acts of gratitude in organizations. In K. S. Cameron, J. E. Dutton, & R. E. Quinn (Eds.), *Positive organizational scholarship* (pp. 81–93). San Francisco: Berrett-Koehler.

Everyone loves Obama. (2004, August 23). *New York Times*.

Eviatar, D. (2004, November 7). Spend $150 billion per year to cure world poverty. *New York Times*.

Franck, F., Roze, J., & Connolly, R. (Eds.). (1998). *What does it mean to be human?* Nyack, NY: Circumstantial Productions.

Friedman, H. (2002, November 14). City's university of hope. *Daily Mail and Guardian* (South Africa) [Online]. Available: www.teacher.co.za/cms/article_2002_11_14_4058.html

Fry, R., Barrett, F., Seiling, J., & Whitney, D. (2002). *Appreciative inquiry and organizational transformation*. Westport, CT: Quorum Books.

Gardner, H. (1995). *Leading minds: An anatomy of leadership*. New York: Basic Books.

Giving women economic tools to fight HIV/AIDS in northern Botswana. (2004). *ADF E-News, 1*(1). Available: www.adf.gov/enews0504war.htm

Glouberman, S., & Zimmerman, B. (2002). *Complicated and complex systems: What would successful reform of Medicare look like?* Discussion Paper No. 8, Commission on the Future of Health Care in Canada. Available: www.change ability.ca

Haebeck, M. H., Kroger, F., & Trum, M. R. (2000). *After the mergers: Seven rules for successful post-merger integration*. New York: Prentice Hall/FT.

Hammel, G. (1991). Competition for competence and inter-partner learning within international strategic alliances. *Strategic Management Journal, 12*, 83–103.

Harrigan, K. R. (1988). Strategic alliances and partner asymmetries. In F. Contractor & P. Lorange (Eds.), *Cooperative strategies in international business* (pp. 205–226). Lexington, MA: Lexington Books.

Havel, V. (1994, July 8). The new measure of man. *New York Times*, p. A27.

Hock, D. (1997). *The birth of the chaordic century: Out of control and into order* (part 2) [Online]. Available: www.parshift.com/Speakers/Speak010.htm

Kaczmarski, K. M., & Cooperrider, D. L. (1997). Constructionist leadership in the global relational age. *Organization and Environment, 10*, 235–258.

King, M. L., Jr. (1963). *Letter from a Birmingham jail, April 16, 1963* [Online]. Available: http://usinfo.state.gov/products/pubs/civilrts/excerpts.htm#14

Kristof, N. (2004, September 29). Sentenced to be raped. *New York Times*.

Kuhn, T. (1962). *The structure of scientific revolutions*. Chicago: University of Chicago Press.

Lindow, M. (2004, January 6). Stepping into Africa's future. *Christian Science Monitor*. Available: www.csmonitor.com/2004/0106/p14s01-legn.htm

Loehr, J., & Schwartz, T. (2001). The making of a corporate athlete. *Harvard Business Review, 79*(1), 120–128.

Luthans, F., & Avolio, B. (2003). Authentic leadership development. In K. S. Cameron, J. E. Dutton, & R. E. Quinn (Eds.), *Positive organizational scholarship* (pp. 241–258). San Francisco: Berrett-Koehler.

Meacham, J. A. (1990). The loss of wisdom. In R. J. Sternberg (Ed.), *Wisdom: Its nature, origins, and development* (pp. 181–211). New York: Cambridge University Press.

Morgan, G. (1993a). *Imagination: The art of creative management.* Newbury Park, CA: Sage.

Morgan, G. (1993b). On spider plants. In G. Morgan (Ed.), *Imagination: The art of creative management* (pp. 63–89). Newbury Park, CA: Sage.

Palmer, P. (2000). Leading from within. In P. Palmer (Ed.), *Let your life speak: Listening for the voice of vocation* (pp. 73–94). San Francisco: Jossey-Bass.

Park, S. H., & Russo, M. V. (1996). When competition eclipses cooperation: An event history analysis of joint venture failure. *Management Science, 42,* 875–890.

Peterson, C., & Seligman, M. E. P. (2003). Positive organizational studies: Lessons from positive psychology. In K. S. Cameron, J. E. Dutton, & R. E. Quinn (Eds.), *Positive organizational scholarship* (pp. 14–31). San Francisco: Berrett-Koehler.

Peterson, C., & Seligman, M. E. P. (2004). Perspective [wisdom]. In C. Peterson & M. E. P. Seligman (Eds.), *Character strengths and virtues: A handbook and classification* (pp. 181–196). New York: Oxford University Press.

Peterson, S. J., & Luthans, F. (2003). Does the manager's level of hope matter? *Leadership and Organizational Development Journal, 24*(6), 26–31.

Pratt, M. G., & Ashford, B. E. (2003). Fostering meaningfulness in working and at work. In K. S. Cameron, J. E. Dutton, & R. E. Quinn (Eds.), *Positive organizational scholarship* (pp. 309–327). San Francisco: Berrett-Koehler.

Quinn, R. E. (1996). *Deep change: Discovering the leader within.* San Francisco: Jossey-Bass.

Random House dictionary of the English language: The unabridged edition. (1969). New York: Random House.

Robinson, S. L., & Bennett, R. J. (1995). A typology of workplace behaviors: A multidimensional scaling study. *Academy of Management Journal, 38,* 555–572.

Schuler, R. S., & Jackson, S. E. (2001, October 22). Seeking an edge in mergers and acquisitions. *Financial Times.*

Spreitzer, G., & Sonenshein, S. (2003). Positive deviance and extraordinary organizing. In K. S. Cameron, J. E. Dutton, & R. E. Quinn (Eds.), *Positive organizational scholarship* (pp. 207–224). San Francisco: Berrett-Koehler.

Sternberg, R. J. (1998). A balance theory of wisdom. *Review of General Psychology, 2,* 347–365.

Strajkovic, A. D., & Luthans, F. (1998). Social cognitive theory and self-efficacy: Going beyond traditional motivational and behavioral approaches. *Organizational Dynamics, 26,* 62–74.

Teegen, H., Doh, J. P., & Vachani, S. (2004). The importance of nongovernmental organizations (NGOs) in global governance and value creation: An international business research agenda. *Journal of International Business Studies, 35,* 461–483.

Tenkasi, R. V. (2000). The dynamics of cultural knowledge and learning in creating viable theories of global change and action. *Organization Development Journal, 18,* 74–90.

Tutu, D. (2004). *God has a dream: A vision of hope for our time.* Garden City, NY: Doubleday.

"Ubuntu" university lifts off. (2002, November 18). [Online]. Available: www.safrica.info/essinfo/sa_glance/education/ubuntu.htm

Vicious poverty. (2001, May 26). *Rising Nepal–National Daily* [Online]. Available: www.nepalnews.com.np/contents/englishdaily/trn/2001/may/may 26/editoria11.htm

Warren, D. (2003). Constructive and destructive deviance in organizations. *Academy of Management Review, 28,* 622–632.

Webster's new world dictionary (2nd concise ed.). (1982). New York: Webster's New World.

Webster's seventh new collegiate dictionary. (1963). Springfield, MA: G. C. Merriam.

Weick, K. E. (2003). Positive organizing and organizational tragedy. In K. S. Cameron, J. E. Dutton, & R. E. Quinn (Eds.), *Positive organizational scholarship* (pp. 66–80). San Francisco: Berrett-Koehler.

Weick, K. E., & Sutcliffe, K. M. (2001). *Managing the unexpected.* San Francisco: Jossey-Bass.

Whyte, D. (1994). *The heart aroused.* New York: Currency Doubleday.

Williamson, M. (2004). *The gift of change: Spiritual guidance for a radically new life.* San Francisco: Harper San Francisco.

Worline, M., & Quinn, R. W. (2003). Courageous principles action. In K. S. Cameron, J. E. Dutton, & R. E. Quinn (Eds.), *Positive organizational scholarship* (pp. 138–157). San Francisco: Berrett-Koehler.

Yan, A., & Zeng, M. (1999). International joint venture instability: A critique of previous research, a reconceptualization, and directions for future research. *Journal of International Business Studies, 30,* 397–414.

Zander, R., & Zander, B. (2000). *The art of possibility: Transforming professional and personal life.* Boston: Harvard Business School Press.

Zimmerman, B. J., & Hayday, B. C. (1999). A board's journey into complexity science: Lessons from (and for) staff and board members. *Group Decision Making and Negotiation, 8,* 281–303.

Zimmerman, B. J., & Hayday, B. C. (2003). Generative relationships STAR. In G. Eoyang (Ed.), *Voices from the field* (pp. 197–214). Minneapolis, MN: HSDI Press.

Zimmerman, B., Lindberg, C., & Plsek, P. (1998). *Edgeware: Insights from complexity science for health care leaders.* Irving, TX: VHA Inc.

20

Strategic Metaphysics

Can Wisdom Be Taught?

Cynthia V. Fukami

There is clearly an opportunity to better address wisdom within the context of management education. On a seemingly daily basis, we are bombarded with examples of the lack of managerial wisdom. From WorldCom to Katrina, we observe and wonder how smart people can make such stupid decisions. Among other things, this suggests to me that although we might be effective in filling our students' heads with knowledge, facts, and data, we are much less effective in developing graduates who use this knowledge wisely. Wisdom in management education, in my opinion, is achieved through teachers who are willing and able to act as role models so that students are better able to link theory and practice. In addition, wisdom is more likely to be developed when scholarly teachers make appropriate pedagogical choices. In this chapter, I start by defining wisdom as the linkage between theory and practice. Next, I explore the barriers we face in developing wise students. Finally, I offer suggestions on best practices for developing wise leaders for the future benefit of organizations.

The Gap Between Knowing and Doing

In our current educational systems, excellence is often defined as intellectual performance (Martin & Martinez de Pisón, 2005). Knowledge is a quantity of data to be possessed, and an educator is the means to obtaining these data. Thus, our classrooms become places where educators dispense knowledge and our students soak it up, to varying degrees on either side. The student's performance in the class is evaluated on the basis of how much of this knowledge can be recalled in short-run, 10- to 16-week assignments, and the educator's performance is evaluated at least in part by how effectively he or she has conveyed this knowledge. What to do with this knowledge, however, is often left out of the picture. A symptom of this situation is captured by the comment sometimes heard from those who employ our graduates, that is, that they know much but cannot do anything. Many excellent companies, such as Southwest Airlines, do not recruit at leading business schools and do not show a preference for hiring master of business administration program graduates (MBAs) (Pfeffer & Sutton, 1999a).

In a rather eye-opening essay, Pfeffer and Fong (2002) found that (a) there has been little assessment of the impact of business schools either on their graduates or on the profession, (b) what assessments do exist suggest that business schools are not particularly effective, and (c) there is little evidence that business schools have influenced management practice. Others have reported similar findings. One such study reported that 73% of the surveyed MBA program graduates indicated that they made little use of what they had learned in the classroom on their first assignments as managers (McCall, Lombardo, & Morrison, 1988). Students who graduate successfully from an MBA program must earn a minimum grade point average to do so, implying that they have gained a "passing" level of knowledge. Yet the results mentioned earlier imply that these students were unable or unwilling to put their knowledge into practice.

The concept of wisdom may be useful in addressing this gap. Wisdom implies the integration and transformation of knowledge (Eastham, 1992), such that knowledge is interpreted and applied appropriately within a context. The difference between knowledge and wisdom, then, is that wisdom embodies and transforms knowledge into human experience (Martin & Martinez de Pisón, 2005) and, thus, may help to close the gap between knowing and doing (Pfeffer and Sutton, 2000a).

Wisdom has been contemplated since the ancient Greeks first coined the term and also linked wisdom with knowledge. Aristotle (1941) posited that there were three kinds of knowledge associated with wisdom. The first is *episteme,* which is theoretical knowledge or what I have described here as that typically dispensed in the classroom. The second is *techne,* or the knowledge of making, which is the knowledge a craftsperson would have. The third kind of knowledge associated with wisdom is *phronesis,* or what is thought of as "practical wisdom," that is, the ability to interpret and adapt knowledge to a particular context, situation, or problem. In addition, Aristotle introduced the concept of "virtue ethics" to indicate that intellectual virtues and practical virtues are applied in a context. Over the years, we have come to associate wisdom with strong judgment and being prudent or astute like King Solomon (Small, 2004). In other words, practical wisdom can be thought of as the ability to link the other two forms of wisdom: knowledge and practice.

In this vein, some interesting research has indicated that situation recognition is a key difference between expert and novice leaders (Halverson,

2004). Virtuoso performers recognize when rules apply, which rules to select, and when to discard or reform the rules based on emergent circumstances (Dreyfus & Dreyfus, 1986). In studies of practitioners in action, Schön (1991) found that effective problem solvers are adaptable and have developed "honed intuition" based on practice. Finally, Kolb (1984) argued that learning is a continuous process grounded in, and tested by, experience. Thus, the mere possession of a quantity of knowledge does not create leaders who make good judgments. In higher education in general, and in business schools in particular, we have focused on disseminating information and knowledge and have neglected the development of wisdom. The following section outlines a number of potential explanations for why this neglect may have occurred.

The Neglect of Wisdom in Management Education

The (Low) Status of Teaching

A primary cause of the neglect of wisdom in education, in my opinion, can be traced to the overall sense that teaching is not scholarly work but rather the price faculty members must pay to do their scholarly work. As others have noted, this belief is conveyed symbolically in our language about teaching. For example, faculty members can be heard to comment about their teaching "loads" (Martin & Martinez de Pisón, 2005), and when they are fortunate, faculty members are granted "release" time. The inference is obvious, namely that teaching is a burden to bear and certainly not the road to glory.

As Steven Kerr noted many years ago in his classic article, "On the Folly of Rewarding A While Hoping for B," the typical university "*hopes* that professors will not neglect their teaching responsibilities but *rewards* them almost entirely for research and publications" (Kerr, 1975, p. 773, italics in original). This hope is often played out in what universities tell prospective students and their parents—that teaching matters at their institutions. An examination of their performance and reward systems would likely expose the opposite, namely that there are few significant consequences associated with excellent teaching. In fact, I know of at least one institution where the "reward" given to the annual "best teacher" is a year of "release" time!

Professors are faced with allocating scarce time among teaching, research, and other obligations. Because rewards for good teaching—and, conversely, punishments for poor teaching—are rare, it follows that professors would place a lower priority on teaching. Alternatively, rewards for research—and punishments for failure to publish—are common in the academy. As Kerr (1975) concluded, "It is rational for university professors to concentrate on research, even to the detriment of teaching and at the expense of their students" (p. 773).

Focus on Teaching, Not Learning

Perhaps related to the lack of status accorded to teaching, there has also been more attention paid to "teaching" students than to their "learning." The difference between the two is one key to our neglect of wisdom. The teaching model reminds me of a (very) old film on effective communication that I used to show. The film depicted a model of communication called "the conveyor belt." In the conveyor belt model, one person would pluck out an idea from his or her head and deliver it into the head of the other person. This was essentially a one-way model in which it was assumed that the sender had encoded the message appropriately, that there was no noise in the surrounding area, and that the receiver had decoded the message exactly as the sender had intended it. As most of us know, this is a wildly unrealistic model of communication. The parallel here is that many of us teach with this one-way model. We have a body of knowledge stored away in the file cabinets in our brain, and when we teach we pull out the folder and disseminate the information to our students. Of course, we assume that they "get it" and that we have conveyed it in a way that ensures their understanding, much like the conveyor belt model. In addition, this model puts all emphasis on the teacher in the learning process. The educator is the only agent that matters in the traditional classroom; thus, the teacher takes patriarchal or matriarchal control of the learning process (Martin & Martinez de Pisón, 2005).

An educator attempting to develop wise students cannot ignore the need for students to develop deep understanding of the concepts the educator is attempting to convey. Knowledge is made explicit by practice as it both sharpens understanding and clarifies misunderstanding. Like Aristotle's notion of phronesis, deep understanding requires the ability to link knowledge with action given the contextual limitations and opportunities. Simply put, there is much room for improvement in student understanding and a need to focus on students and their learning rather than on educators and their teaching.

The Harvard–Smithsonian Center for Astrophysics, in conjunction with the Annenberg School of Communication at the University of Pennsylvania, has produced a thought-provoking video called *A Private Universe* that demonstrates this point (Schneps & Sadler, 1987). The video begins with a group of students and faculty members at Harvard University's commencement exercises being quizzed about a basic concept of astronomy: Why are there seasons of the year? Virtually all graduates interviewed fail to answer the question correctly. The video moves to a high school classroom where the teacher experiences great difficulty in getting bright students to move beyond their misconceptions and myths about the planets and the sun and to have an accurate understanding of the concepts. Instead, students rely on their private universe of knowledge—what they already believe they know. This video reminds us that we need to consider what is happening in the minds of our students and to focus not only on our teaching but also on their learning.

Focus on Quantity, Not Quality

Another related issue is the emphasis on the quantity of knowledge conveyed rather than on the quality of our students' learning. How much knowledge do we disseminate during the course of a term? How many pounds are on our conveyor belts? How much depth do we sacrifice to gain breadth? As a Pew Scholar in the Carnegie Foundation's Academy for the Scholarship of Teaching and Learning, I met a fellow scholar who taught a course on Shakespeare. At the beginning of our tenure as Pew Scholars, he lamented the fact that he could teach only five plays during his 10-week quarter. At the end of our 2-year tenure as Pew Scholars, he was down to teaching three plays during the term and was happier with the results. Rather than quickly memorizing facts that were just as easily forgotten after the class moved to the next play, his students were able to gain a deeper understanding of fewer works. He assessed this change by staying in contact with his students after the term was over and having them fill out surveys about what they had learned during the previous quarter. His results indicated that students had retained understanding of the plays following the end of the term. I have observed this same phenomenon in my own classes. I used to struggle to get at least six different theories of motivation on the table. Then I would assess "learning" by having students compare and contrast the different theories. Although I never conducted a formal assessment of the changes, I am much more satisfied by the learning I observe by covering fewer theories and spending more class time reflecting on what can be done about motivation by managers or to self-manage. Perhaps if we concentrated more on learning, we could close the gap between theory and practice and could develop wiser leaders.

Competitive Classrooms

A climate of competitiveness in the classroom is also a barrier to developing wisdom. Pfeffer and Sutton (2000b) argued that "trying new things means having the confidence to learn from mistakes, and this requires driving fear out of organizations" (p. 13). Unfortunately, a competitive classroom environment can breed fear and, thus, dampen the willingness of students to take chances. A competitive classroom environment has several potential sources, including grading for participation, emphasizing brutal criticism, and using pedagogy that encourages competition.

Grading for Participation

One of the ways in which we introduce competition is by basing a substantial part of students' grades on how much they say and how smart they sound in class (Pfeffer & Sutton, 1999b). To be sure, there are valid reasons for grading students on class participation. Participation develops their skills for thinking on their feet and expressing themselves effectively, and it rewards them for preparing materials in advance of class discussion. On the other hand, students learn that they need to "sound smart" (Pfeffer & Sutton, 1999b) to gain good grades from their professors and to earn the respect of their peers. Unlike the protagonists in the cases they are discussing, or the abstract concepts they are debating, students do not need to prove the soundness of their statements by actually doing something.

Emphasizing Brutal Criticism

In addition, and perhaps more unfortunately, we learn early on in our higher education experiences that we can earn "points" in the classroom by criticizing others, sometimes quite callously. This may be because, as part of our doctoral training, professors have been rewarded for being critical. I recall vividly (although it occurred many years ago) preparing for my presentations to potential employers while I was a doctoral student. My peer doctoral students were much more critical of me than were the potential employers. This is exactly why we developed a norm of presenting to each other before making our first campus visits. I also recall preparing to be a session discussant at the Academy of Management annual meeting for the first time as a new assistant professor. I sought the counsel of a senior colleague, who told me that my reputation would depend on how critical I was of the papers I was discussing. In other words, I would earn professional credibility for being brutal, and the more brutal I was, the better. And he was right. After the session, I received much praise for my critique.

Of course, being critical in and of itself is not the problem. There are good outcomes to be gained from being critical and being free in expressing criticism. The problem here is the fear. A competitive classroom climate may inhibit the asking of questions that expose students to criticism. If students are afraid to make mistakes or to express controversial opinions, either because they will lose participation points or because they will suffer the pain of peer disapproval, they will be less likely to link theory and practice and, thus, to develop practical wisdom.

Using Pedagogy That Encourages Competition

The last way in which I have observed competition in the classroom is through pedagogy that encourages competition to flourish and discourages collaboration. In general, collaboration has not been cultivated in the traditional classroom. In fact, teachers typically get concerned about collaboration and call it "cheating" (Harvey, 1984). Examples of this include using individual assignments exclusively, not using team assignments to their best advantage, and using fixed grading distributions.

Team assignments can cause headaches for the professor because team dynamics are not always smooth and pleasant. Has any professor avoided the visits of students who are disgruntled with the free rider behavior of teammates? As I have heard my colleagues lament, and as I have lamented myself, we are not relationship counselors or group therapists. If we stick to individual assignments, we are less likely to be pressed into service as such. Of course, students will miss an opportunity to learn how to put their knowledge about team dynamics to work in an actual team, and teachers will miss an opportunity to coach their students. If we as teachers take the risk and expose ourselves to the activity of coaching students through the very real problems of team dynamics, we and the students learn together how to apply knowledge to real-world situations.

On the other hand, some of us stick our big toes into the water of team assignments but do not manage the team assignments to their fullest advantage. Sometimes, we do not place enough of a stake in the grades of the team assignments, so there is not enough compensation for the amount of effort that goes into teamwork. Sometimes, we do not teach or support effective team process in the classroom because we believe that it is not part of the facts and data we dispense. Sometimes, we do not hold all team members accountable for contributions and deliverables. There is an extensive literature on using teams effectively in the classroom, and it is not my intention to cover it here. Suffice it to say that there is ample room for improvement in the way many of us approach this issue. For the purposes of this discussion, I suggest that it is worth looking into doing this better because of the opportunity it presents to link knowledge and practice and, hence, to develop wisdom.

Finally, there is the issue of grading "on the curve" or using a fixed distribution. In this practice, the professor limits the number of As, Bs, and so on to a predetermined percentage of the class. As in other fixed-pie, zero-sum games, the key to maximizing one's outcome is to be competitive. Why should one student help another student to get an A when doing so lessens the first student's own chances of getting one? Competitive classroom behavior reinforces and develops competitive organizational behavior. Unfortunately, competitive classroom behavior also contributes to the fear of making mistakes.

Ignoring the "Whole Student"

If wisdom is an integrative aspect of human life, it is a way of knowing rather than knowledge itself (Small, 2004). As such, unlike episteme and techne, phronesis cannot be separated from the person (Halverson, 2004). Thus, another barrier to the development of wisdom is our reluctance to address and develop the whole person. Traditionally, higher education takes a tabula rasa approach to our students; that is, we consider them to be "blank slates" on which we write. This is debatable in any student, but more so in higher education where we work with adults. Students enter our classrooms as fairly well-formed mature individuals with thoughts, opinions, values, attitudes, and beliefs. Yet we often avoid those situations that bring their individuality into the classroom. We simply do not define this as part of our agenda, much as we do not want to provide "group therapy" as discussed earlier. Personally, this reluctance has come from my fear that I have left the bounds of my expertise. In other words, I have a Ph.D. in organizational behavior, but I am not an expert in psychotherapy. Perhaps this is a convenient excuse or even a way of simplifying my life. On the other hand, it may be my way of doubting my own wisdom. Nonetheless, as we attempt to be politically correct, we may be avoiding opportunities to bring the whole person into the classroom and to provide the possibility of linking knowledge and practice. The recent work of my dear colleague Peter Frost and his associates (cf. Dutton, Frost, Worline, Lilius, & Kanov, 2002) on factors such as compassion in leadership is a notable exception to this barrier.

Ignoring Tacit Knowledge

In a review of the knowledge management literature, Pfeffer and Sutton (1999a) concluded that most knowledge management efforts focus on codified knowledge and information while ignoring tacit knowledge. Tacit knowledge is not easily codified but is essential for doing work. This knowledge is transferred informally by workers to tell each other about their trials and errors and by inexperienced people being coached by experienced people. Pfeffer and Sutton concluded, "Knowledge management systems seem to work best when the people who generate the knowledge are also those who store it, explain it to others, and coach them as they try to implement the knowledge" (p. 88).

The Role of Professional Schools

So far, I have discussed a number of barriers to developing wisdom that occur because of actions taken by individual professors. In my opinion, there are at least a few barriers that can be traced to business schools themselves. In the past, business school faculties were composed largely of enlightened practitioners. These were individuals who did not have terminal degrees but rather had many years of experience in the classroom from which they drew. For example, when my father earned his MBA in 1957, the vast majority of his teachers were either retired businesspeople or part-time faculty members who worked in business during the day and taught MBA classes at night. Over time, as schools started producing more Ph.D. graduates in business, enlightened practitioners became less common and faculty members became more "scholarly" in the traditional sense of the word. The growth in the power of the Association to Advance Collegiate Schools of Business (AACSB) as our accrediting body also contributed to this shift away from practitioners to researchers as the acceptable number of non-terminally "qualified" faculty was capped and the number of refereed journal publications was counted. It is interesting to note that, as often happens, the pendulum is now swinging in the other direction as the AACSB has begun to relax its quotas on each.

I do think that part of the trend toward research among business school faculty members can also be attributed to the uneasy relationship between professional schools and traditional departments in a university setting. In my experience as a professor, I have observed a "love–hate" relationship between business schools and other parts of universities. Our research is minimized as "applied," and we are thought to make lots of money, as compared with other faculty members, both from our inequitable salaries and from our robust consulting practices. In addition, students enroll in our programs in large numbers, making us even more suspect. In short, although we may have more students, and although we may produce more revenue for our universities, we do not enjoy more status. I believe that, at least in part, our push for research has been fueled by our quest to be taken seriously in the academy. Nonetheless, if wisdom is the marriage of knowing and doing, experienced teachers must play an important role in the classroom.

In other words, can wisdom be taught by those who are not wise themselves? As the old adage goes, "Those who can, do; those who can't, teach." Would our students be wiser if they were taught by lifelong practitioners instead of by lifelong scholars? Perhaps, but the end product may merely be a shift from the wisdom of episteme to the wisdom of techne. Phronesis, or practical wisdom, would still be missing. So, what can be done about this? Is there any hope for the future? I now turn to a discussion of some avenues with the potential to enable the pursuit of wisdom.

The Pursuit of Wisdom in Managerial Education

The Scholarship of Teaching and Learning

There are some reasons for optimism in the pursuit of developing wise graduates. In my opinion, the most notable of these is the concept of the scholarship of teaching and learning (SOTL). Simply put, SOTL recognizes that teaching is an integral part of faculty scholarship. In other words, rather than thinking about teaching as the price to be paid to do research,

SOTL considers teaching to be an important part of the job of the professor. SOTL was introduced largely through the work of Ernest Boyer, then president of the Carnegie Foundation for the Advancement of Teaching, in his book *Scholarship Reconsidered* (Boyer, 1990). Boyer argued that the role of the university professor was broader than the traditional tripartite model of research, teaching, and service. He proposed an alternative model that identified four separate but overlapping functions: the scholarship of discovery, the scholarship of integration, the scholarship of application, and the scholarship of teaching.

Through this model, Boyer (1990) elevated the status of teaching by recognizing that there is a set of problems inherent in teaching that are worth pursuing as an ongoing intellectual quest. And because this is an intellectual quest, we can use the same intellectual process we follow in our disciplinary work to improve our teaching and our students' learning. In other words, to apply the term *scholarship* to our teaching implies that we apply the same scientific process, and standards for evaluating our work in teaching, as we apply in our disciplinary research.

I believe that business schools are particularly suited to SOTL because of the fundamental synergy between the substance of our disciplines and the substance of teaching. Using my disciplinary field of management as an example, we are a discipline in which *how* we teach, and the tools we use, most closely mirrors important aspects of *what* we teach (Frost & Fukami, 1997). In short, the field of management is about understanding human behavior in organizations as well as about understanding the organizations themselves. Our classrooms can be thought of as organizations and, as such, provide real-time laboratories in which to illustrate, experiment with, and (more important) model most of our important disciplinary concepts. This observation is not lost on our students, who often recognize the parallels between the content we are delivering on effective management and the process we use to manage our classrooms and departments, interact with peers, and conduct our personal lives (Bilimoria & Fukami, 2002). Not being sensitive to this connection would be a lost opportunity to develop, and to model, wisdom.

Pedagogical Choices Supporting Wisdom

Once we start to pay more attention to our teaching, and to our students' learning, there is a plethora of research on pedagogy that can be drawn on to link "knowing" and "doing." This pedagogy includes, but is not limited to, cooperative learning, experiential learning, problem-based learning, internships, and the case method. Based on the work of pioneers such as Kolb (1984), these approaches share the expectation that real knowledge requires personal engagement in the process of knowing (Zundel, 1947). Because wisdom is thought to be obtained only through extensive life experience (Small, 2004), these methods are critical to the development of wise graduates.

Cooperative Learning

Cooperative (sometimes called collaborative) learning (Johnson, Johnson, & Smith, 1991) is an especially promising pedagogical approach in the pursuit of developing wisdom because it directly addresses several of the barriers outlined earlier. Cooperative learning is a structured, systematic instructional strategy in which students are organized into small groups to work together in the classroom (Cooper, Robinson, & McKinney, 1994). For one, the creation of a collaborative climate in the classroom counters the competitiveness, and the resulting fear of failure, that might stifle the level of engagement required for developing wisdom. Individuals are more likely to adopt a mastery orientation if learning occurs in cooperative learning contexts rather than in competitive ones (Martin & Martinez de Pisón, 2005). In addition, collaborative learning requires students to work in teams, a requirement that both provides extensive experience in critical organizational behavior and demands action. A student cannot be a passive observer successfully in a collaborative learning community.

A collaborative learning community is based on five attributes, the use of which is less likely to produce the barrier of brutal criticism that can be found in a competitive classroom. The five attributes are (a) positive interdependence (i.e., the members of the group perceive that they sink or swim together), (b) promotive interaction (i.e., the members of the group have face-to-face interactions where help, assistance, encouragement, and support are provided), (c) individual accountability (i.e., each member is assessed on his or her individual contributions to the group), (d) social skills (i.e., the need to develop leadership, decision making, trust building, communication, and conflict management skills in the group members), and (e) group process (i.e., the requirement that the group members must process how they are achieving their goals and how they are maintaining effective working relationships) (Johnson et al., 1991). In essence, the use of collaborative learning pedagogy should create a classroom that is perceived by the students as a safe haven for learning by doing.

Measurement of Learning Outcomes

We can also foster the development of wisdom by carefully designing the assignments we require of our students. Exam questions can be crafted such that the answers require a link between theory and practice. Written assignments can ask students to analyze experiences they have had with concepts in the class. Schön's (1991) work concluded that framing is at the core of professional problem solving. Rather than finding the answer to problems, the wise practitioner actually poses the right questions.

Expanding the Classroom

Activities that take students out of the classroom may also prove to be fruitful avenues for developing wisdom. Internships, for example, have long been a staple of higher education in general and in business schools in particular. An internship experience allows students to work in an actual organization while earning credit toward their degrees, a clear example of learning by doing. At a number of business schools, we have been taking our MBA students out of the classroom for extended learning opportunities such as outdoor leadership training. Through high-ropes and low-ropes exercises, students confront problem-solving situations, challenge themselves, and have the opportunity for introspection and reflection of these experiences. The development of wisdom may be facilitated by leaving the classroom itself; sailing in calm waters does not teach (Talbot, 2004).

Practical Experience

The use of pedagogical approaches such as these, which rely on the marriage of theory and practice, is supported by research in both cognitive science and artificial intelligence, suggesting that learning is best undertaken in a milieu of slow incubation, frequent practice, and recognition of the private language of the learner (Talbot, 2004). Schön (1991) found that solving problems and learning to solve problems involve complex processes that ultimately bind one to the other. Essentially, the development of wisdom requires book learning but also practical experience.

Pfeffer and Sutton (1999b) drew a parallel to the training that is undergone by members of some life-or-death professions such as soldiers, pilots, and surgeons. Each of these professions involves theoretical knowledge, but eventually members of these professions learn by doing before they graduate from the classroom. To be sure, pilots can train in a simulator and surgeons can practice techniques on a cadaver, but only for so long. How long is enough? Cognitive science tells us that the change from naive understanding to seasoned performer occurs in small, gradual, almost leisurely steps using "slow modes" of thought, most likely during periods of long immersion (Talbot, 2004). Schön (1991) found that the more practice that occurs, the better the performance. The improvement in performance does not follow a linear progression; rather, it is something like the wave of an ocean and is termed "water logic" (de Bono, 1991). There is forward and backward flow with eddies and tributaries. This process has been discussed in the context of artificial intelligence, where even computers develop better problem-solving capabilities through practice without additional programming (Copeland, 1993). To be sure, expert work has knowledge as its foundation but has preparation and incubation as its cornerstones (Talbot, 2004). Over time, students may develop a propensity for identifying situations worthy of action and of developing action plans (Halverson, 2004).

Integrated Curricula and Team Teaching

My own college, the Daniels College of Business, has experimented successfully with two approaches that may be fruitful in developing wisdom in our students: an integrated curriculum and the use of team teaching (Fukami et al., 1996). Our integrated curriculum created classes that were "transdisciplinary"; that is, they included different disciplinary foci within one course. In addition, they were taught by faculty teams representing different disciplinary backgrounds. We felt that this approach provided much more realistic preparation for the world of doing and helped our students to make the link between theory and practice. In addition, the practice of team teaching allowed us to create synergistic combinations of "researchers" and "practitioners" in the same classroom, thereby addressing the problem of the inexperienced faculty member, the unscholarly practitioner, or the unpracticed scholar as the teacher.

Practicing What We Preach

This leads me to one of the mantras that have played in my head throughout my career, namely that faculty members, in general, need to embrace their responsibilities as role models, in other words, to practice what we preach. I have argued that this approach is critical in the management classroom (Bilimoria & Fukami, 2002), but the literature suggests that it may also be critical to the development of practical wisdom. The relationship between students and educators changes when the focus is on developing wisdom. Wisdom is communicated by example, so the professor is the medium of learning, not the means for acquisition of factual knowledge (Martin & Martinez de Pisón, 2005). So, educators must be wise themselves. Whether they have developed this wisdom by gaining personal experience in organizations, or whether they are capable of facilitating and coaching the journey for others, their students will be better prepared for life's challenges if the educators accept the responsibility for fostering these relationships.

The pursuit of wisdom requires a close, nearly apprenticeship-type relationship between the learner and the expert (Talbot, 2004). But we must recognize the barriers to such a significant relationship between faculty members and students, not the least of which is time. Thus, developing wisdom will be more difficult in environments that contain large classrooms and/or do not provide significant rewards for teaching excellence.

Values and Wisdom

I have identified a number of potential avenues to enhance the development of wisdom in our students. However, none of these will be effective without recognizing that if knowledge is to be put into action, it must have a foundation of values. As Pfeffer and Sutton (1999a) stated,

Although specific practices are obviously important, such practices evolve and make sense only as part of some system that is often organized according to some philosophy or meta-theory of performance. As such, there is a knowing–doing gap in part because firms have misconstrued what they should be knowing or seeking to know in the first place. (p. 89)

Part of what makes an individual wise is not *what* he or she does but *why* he or she does it. Thus, a classroom that only conveys facts and data without venturing into the values that underlie our choices will be missing the point of wisdom. We can teach all of the skills we want to our students, but that will not make them wise in their use of these skills. A strong and clear sense of value has been associated with the success of many companies, including Starbucks, Southwest Airlines, and Whole Foods. Our classrooms should aspire to develop the foundation that will allow our students to link knowledge and action.

This chapter started with a question: Can wisdom be taught? After reviewing the barriers and identifying the possibilities, I conclude that wisdom itself cannot be taught. To be sure, the barriers on this path present real and significant challenges for even the most well-intentioned professor. Nonetheless, avenues leading to wisdom do exist and lead me to be optimistic about the classroom of the future. In short, I believe that wisdom can be developed, and I trust that we will not miss our opportunity to develop it.

References

Aristotle. (1941). *The basic works of Aristotle* (R. McKeon, Ed.). New York: Random House.

Bilimoria, D., & Fukami, C. (2002). The scholarship of teaching and learning in the management sciences. In M. T. Huber & S. P. Morreale (Eds.), *Disciplinary styles in the scholarship of teaching and learning: Exploring common ground* (pp. 125–142). Washington, DC: American Association for Higher Education.

Boyer, E. L. (1990). *Scholarship reconsidered: Priorities of the professoriate.* Princeton, NJ: Carnegie Foundation for the Advancement of Teaching.

Cooper, J. L., Robinson, P., & McKinney, M. (1994). Cooperative learning in the classroom. In D. Halpern & Associates (Eds.), *Changing college classrooms* (pp. 74–92). San Francisco: Jossey-Bass.

Copeland, J. (1993). *Artificial intelligence: A philosophical introduction.* Oxford, UK: Blackwell.

De Bono, E. (1991). *I am right—You are wrong: From this to the New Renaissance—From rock logic to water logic.* London: Penguin.

Dreyfus, H., & Dreyfus, S. (1986). *Mind over machine: The power of human intuition and expertise in the era of the computer.* Oxford, UK: Blackwell.

Dutton, J. E., Frost, P., Worline, M. C., Lilius, J. M., & Kanov, J. M. (2002). Leading in times of trauma. *Harvard Business Review, 80*(1), 54–61.

Eastham, S. (1992). How is wisdom communicated? Prologue to peace studies. *Interculture, 25,* 1–33.

Frost, P. J., & Fukami, C. V. (1997). Teaching effectiveness in the organizational sciences: Recognizing and enhancing the scholarship of teaching. *Academy of Management Journal, 40,* 1271–1281.

Fukami, C. V., Clouse, M. L., Howard, C. T., McGowan, R. P., Mullins, J. W., Silver, W. S., Sorensen, J. E., Watkins, T. L., & Wittmer, D. P. (1996). The road less traveled: The joys and sorrows of transdisciplinary team teaching. *Journal of Management Education, 20,* 409–410.

Halverson, R. (2004). Accessing, documenting, and communicating practical wisdom: The phronesis of school leadership practice. *American Journal of Education, 111,* 90–121.

Harvey, J. B. (1984). Encouraging students to cheat: One thought on the difference between teaching ethics and teaching ethically. *Organizational Behavior Teaching Review, 9,* 1–13.

Johnson, D. W., Johnson, R. T., & Smith, K. A. (1991). *Active learning: Cooperation in the college classroom.* Edina, MN: Interaction Books.

Kerr, S. (1975). On the folly of rewarding A while hoping for B. *Academy of Management Journal, 18,* 769–783.

Kolb, D. (1984). *Experiential learning.* Englewood Cliffs, NJ: Prentice Hall.

Martin, M. K., & Martinez de Pisón, R. (2005). From knowledge to wisdom: A new challenge to the educational milieu with implications for religious education. *Religious Education, 100,* 157–173.

McCall, M. W., Jr., Lombardo, M. M., & Morrison, A. M. (1988). *The lessons of experience: How successful executives develop on the job.* Lexington, MA: Lexington Books.

Pfeffer, J., & Fong, C. T. (2002). The end of business schools? Less success than meets the eye. *Academy of Management Learning and Education, 1,* 78–95.

Pfeffer, J., & Sutton, R. I. (1999a). Knowing "what" to do is not enough: Turning knowledge into action. *California Management Review, 42,* 83–108.

Pfeffer, J., & Sutton, R. I. (1999b). The smart-talk trap. *Harvard Business Review, 77*(3), 134–144.

Pfeffer, J., & Sutton, R. I. (2000a). *The knowing–doing gap.* Boston: Harvard Business School Press.

Pfeffer, J., & Sutton, R. I. (2000b). Overcoming the "knowing–doing" gap. *Corporate University Review, 8,* 12–15.

Schneps, M. H., & Sadler, P. M. (1987). *A private universe* [Videotape]. Washington, DC: Pyramid Film and Video. (Annenberg/CPB project)

Schön, D. A. (1991). *The reflective practitioner.* Aldershot, UK: Arena Books, 1991.

Small, M. W. (2004). Wisdom and now managerial wisdom: Do they have a place in management development programs? *Journal of Management Development, 23,* 751–764.

Talbot, M. (2004). Good wine may need to mature: A critique of accelerated higher specialist training—Evidence from cognitive neuroscience. *Medical Education, 38,* 399–408.

Zundel, M. (1947). *Itinéraire.* Paris: La Colombe.

PART VI

Synthesizing
Commentary

21

Wisdom

Objectivism as the Proper Philosophy for Living on Earth

Edwin A. Locke

The term *wisdom* means "understanding of what is true, right, or lasting" (*American Heritage Dictionary of the English Language,* 1992). Wisdom begins with philosophy. Why? To quote Ayn Rand,

> Philosophy studies the *fundamental* nature of existence, of man, and of man's relationship to existence. As against the special sciences, which deal only with particular aspects, philosophy deals with those aspects of the universe which pertain to everything that exists. In the realm of cognition, the special sciences are the trees, but philosophy is the soil that makes the forest possible. (Rand, 1982, p. 2, italics in original)

Philosophy provides answers to the following questions. What is the nature of existence and of man? (*metaphysics*). How do I know it? (*epistemology*). How should I act? (*ethics*). How should men live together in society? (*politics,* including economics). And what is the nature and function of art? (*aesthetics*). These are the five branches of philosophy.

Without some type of philosophy, one would be unable to function rationally. For example,

> Are you in a universe which is ruled by natural laws and, therefore, is stable, firm, absolute—and knowable? Or are you in an incomprehensible chaos, a realm of inexplicable miracles, an unpredictable,

AUTHOR'S NOTE: The author is greatly indebted to Onkar Ghate of the Ayn Rand Institute for his many helpful editorial suggestions on this chapter.

unknowable flux, which your mind is impotent to grasp? Are the things you see around you real—or are they only an illusion? Do they exist independent of any observer—or are they created by the observer? Are they the object or subject of man's consciousness? Are they *what they are*—or can they be changed by a mere act of your consciousness, such as a wish? (Rand, 1982, p. 3)

Most people do have some sort of conscious or subconscious philosophy, but for most it is a mishmash of emotions, empty slogans, half-digested concepts, conventions, fuzzy approximations, and contradictions. This explains, in large part, why so many people make such a mess of their lives—why they are so unhappy and so unable to function effectively and consistently.

Rand, with some debt to Aristotle, developed a startlingly original philosophy—making unique insights in each of its five branches. It is her wisdom that I present in this chapter. Because this volume is focused on business, I focus most heavily on ethics and politics. However, because her philosophy was totally integrated, it is necessary to present an overview of all the branches.

I must make three important philosophical points before I begin. First, Rand is not a conservative. Conservatives defend their views on the basis of religion, whereas objectivism eschews faith and advocates reason as an absolute. Conservatives also hold most of the same moral–political premises as does the left regarding ethics and capitalism; the conservatives are pro-altruist (an ethical issue I discuss later) and want only slightly fewer controls than do the leftists.

Second, Rand is not a libertarian. Libertarians view "freedom" as a kind of free-floating emotion ("I wanna do what I want") not backed by any serious or consistent philosophical thinking (although some libertarians quote out of context snatches of Rand's philosophy from time to time). Some even advocate anarchy. Rand scornfully called libertarians "hippies of the right." Objectivism does not fall into any other philosophical or political category; it is simply objectivism.

Third, although objectivism is hierarchical (each branch building on the one below) as noted above, it is not primarily deductive but rather inductive. It is based on looking at the outside world, the evidence gained from introspection, and the integration of that knowledge.

The most systematic presentation of Rand's philosophy can be found in Peikoff (1991; see also Ghate & Locke, 2003; Rand, 1964a, 1991, 1957/1992). Consistent with the way in which Rand presented her ideas, I use the male pronoun throughout to refer to all humans.

Metaphysics

The key to any philosophy lies in its starting premises. If these are invalid or arbitrary, the rest of the philosophy is built on sand and soon collapses (e.g., on Kant's philosophy, see Ghate, 2003). A valid philosophical system must rest on unshakable axioms. Following Aristotle, Rand held that valid philosophical axioms cannot be proved (deduced from prior knowledge) because they are the basis for—the precondition of—all proof. A valid philosophical axiom forms the base of all subsequent knowledge. How, then, does one know that a philosophical axiom is true, that one's starting point is correct? An axiom is self-evident to perception (meaning that it is implicit in one's first perception of reality, whether one conceptually identifies this fact or not). Because an axiom forms the foundation of all further knowledge and thought, it cannot be rejected without accepting it in the process.

Rand has identified three basic philosophical axioms: existence, identity, and consciousness. The self-evident axiom of existence means that what is, is; whatever exists, exists; existence exists. The axiom of identity means that whatever exists has a specific nature (to exist is to be something, to possess specific attributes and characteristics). In other words, everything is something. To use her own words, "existence is identity." That which has no specific nature is nothing in particular, and nothing does not exist. (Incidentally, this is why the universe [existence] cannot have been created and cannot have an age. Nothing is *no thing,* not another type of thing, which can magically become an actual thing.) The nature of an entity determines its capacity for action and the actions it will take under specific circumstances. This means that every action in the universe (including the actions of man and those of elementary particles) is caused. (Causality is a derivative axiom, a corollary of the axiom of identity.)

The third axiom, consciousness, means that consciousness is conscious of existence; one's mind is aware of reality; consciousness is the faculty of awareness, the faculty of perceiving reality. To quote Rand (1961), "If nothing exists, there can be no consciousness; a consciousness with nothing to be conscious of is a contradiction in terms. A consciousness conscious of nothing but itself is a contradiction in terms; before it could identify itself as consciousness, it had to be conscious of something" (p. 124). Consciousness does not create reality, as the postmodernists claim, but rather perceives and identifies it. Reality, not consciousness, comes first. A key tenet of objectivism is *the primacy of existence (reality).*

Objectivism differentiates between the metaphysical (e.g., the laws of nature) and the man-made (e.g., houses). Through volitional thought, one can create new objects by rearranging the materials of nature, such as for the purpose of building houses, but the houses will not stand unless one has obeyed the nature (identity) of the materials that are used and the proper methods of integrating the parts into a functioning whole. If one uses pieces of cardboard connected with transparent tape, because one feels like it, instead of wood connected with nails, based on the principles of engineering and construction, the houses will collapse regardless of one's wishes. (The issue of free will vs. determinism is technically metaphysical, but I discuss it in the next section because of its inherent connection to reason.)

Epistemology

The science of epistemology deals with the question of how one acquires knowledge. The postmodern skeptics, reaching the dead end of Kant's philosophy that divorced consciousness from reality (Ghate, 2003), claim that one cannot acquire knowledge at all (Locke, 2003). Kant claimed that the real or "noumenal" world was unknowable (if so, how did he know this?) and that we can know only the "phenomenal world," a world of appearances (appearances of what?). Why did Kant claim this? Because, he said, we have a specific means of awareness, a consciousness with a specific identity; this means, he argued, that our consciousness must distort rather than perceive existence. For example, causality is not a phenomenon of the real world but rather part of the way in which our consciousness creates the phenomenal world. In short, because we have a definite means of awareness of reality, we cannot be aware of reality. Rand (1961) was the first to identify the absurdity of Kant's fundamental approach:

> His argument, in essence, ran as follows: man is *limited* to a consciousness of a specific nature, which perceives by specific means and no others, therefore, his consciousness is not valid; man is blind because he has eyes—deaf, because he has ears—deluded, because he has a mind—and the things he perceives do not exist, *because* he perceives them. (p. 32, italics in original)

(For a detailed refutation of Kant's approach to epistemology, see Rand, 1991; see also Ghate, 2003.)

Objectivism holds, in contrast to Kant, that a foundation of all knowledge is the capacity of consciousness to grasp reality. Consciousness is conscious of existence; this is an axiom. (To deny this axiom is to reaffirm it; to assert that consciousness is not conscious, as Kant in effect does, is to assert that one is conscious of the fact that reality is such that man's consciousness is not aware of reality—an obvious contradiction.) In regard to sensory perception, it is a contradiction to deny the validity of the senses. One cannot logically claim that the senses give us false or distorted information about the world while relying on sensory information to identify the alleged distortion. To claim something is an error presupposes that one knows the truth.

Each sense organ responds to a particular type of physical energy (e.g., the eyes detect electromagnetic radiation within a certain range, the ears detect sound pressure levels within a certain range). We experience each aspect of the outside world in a specific *form* (e.g., we experience electromagnetic radiation as light within a certain range, we experience specific wavelengths of light as different colors). The fact that we experience reality in certain forms by means of specific types of sense organs does not invalidate perception. On the contrary, the fact that sense organs have a specific nature is precisely what makes knowledge of the world possible. All aware-ness requires a specific means of awareness; there can be no such thing as awareness by no means (Rand, 1991; see also Ghate, 2003).

Man's distinctive form of cognition, although based on sense perception, is conceptual. Man has the power of reason. This means that he can inte-grate sensory material to form concepts. The conventional view of concepts (which goes back past Kant all the way to Plato) is that concepts are not connected to reality as perceived by the senses. Today, it is generally believed that concepts are a subjective product of the human mind, mean-ing that concepts are not, and cannot be, objective. If this claim is true, it invalidates reason.

It is undeniable, of course, that at the conceptual level man is fallible, but fallibility is not to be equated with subjectivity. An idea that a man holds is not automatically correct. He can make errors. A science of epistemology is needed precisely to help man gain objective knowledge. Given sensory information as the starting point, a nonskeptical epistemology must provide a valid theory of concept formation. As the issue has traditionally been for-mulated, what exactly is the "one in the many"? Is there actually a meta-physical essence of "man-ness" in man or of "chair-ness" in chairs? If not, what does the concept of man or of chair actually refer to?

Rand's (1991) revolutionary approach shows that, using the proper method, one can form reality-based concepts. Concept formation starts with the perceptual observations of similarity and difference between objects. One can observe directly that chairs are similar to one another and are different from tables. Most philosophers would not deny this (even though Kantian skeptics would claim that we cannot see actual chairs but only our "perceptions of chairs"). The heretofore unresolved problem has always been the following: What is it specifically that a concept such as chair refers to? There is, in fact, no metaphysical essence in chairs. Every chair is different in every concrete respect from every other chair, so what is it we do when we form a (valid) concept such as chair?

Rand's resolution to the problem of concept formation lies in her discov-ery of the (subconscious) process of measurement omission (for details, see Rand, 1991). One integrates the similar entities into a single mental unit by differentiating them from other entities and then specifying, for example, that chairs must be of a certain shape (e.g., with legs or a base supporting a seat with a backrest) but *omitting the actual measurements;* the chair must be of some specific shape, but it may be of any length, width, height, and so on *within* certain ranges. When integrating chairs into a mental unit, one ignores or omits the specific measurements but takes it as a given that they exist.

The next step in concept formation is to choose a word to designate the concept. This transforms one's conceptual grasp of a group of similar objects into a single mental unit.

The final step is to objectively define the word (concept). The definition accomplishes two things: It ties the concept to reality and differentiates this concept from other concepts. The genus ties the concept to a wider category of knowledge (e.g., a chair is a piece of furniture), and the differentia distinguishes it from other members of that category (e.g., chairs differ from tables, sofas, and beds based on their distinctive shape and purpose). Thus, a chair is a piece of furniture with a seat, legs (support), and back to accommodate one person. Observe that words, which stand for concepts, are not just arbitrary sounds, as the postmodernists claim, but rather actual mental units based on observations of reality.

It must be stressed that the definition is *not* the same as the concept. The definition only identifies the essential distinguishing characteristics of the concept based on the knowledge available. The *concept* of chair refers to any and all attributes of any chair that exists, has existed, or will exist in the future. In this respect, concepts are open-ended. New discoveries can add to our knowledge and lead to improved definitions, but the concept is what it is. For example, when gold (a type of soft yellow metal) was first discovered, people knew nothing about atomic numbers, atomic weights, specific gravity, and the like. But gold was still gold even when a more advanced definition was formulated.

The cognitive function of concepts is to expand the range of one's consciousness; an unlimited number of concretes (of a certain kind) can be treated cognitively as a single mental unit. This gives man cognitive powers far beyond those of the lower animals. For example, an animal might be able to group certain chairs together very roughly based simply on perceptual similarity, but the animal could not abstract out the differences and hold the concept of chair as a single mental unit. Nor could it form the next higher level concept of furniture because the different types of furniture do not even look alike, even though the elements of furniture fulfill a similar function (i.e., they are man-made movable articles that make a room fit for living).

Consider another example, namely the concept *ten*. To form the concept, number (quantity) is separated from any particular set of entities by abstraction. *Ten* can refer to an unlimited number of different types of entities, can be used in mathematical equations, and can be subdivided into smaller units (e.g., one, one tenth) or combined into larger units (e.g., a million, a trillion). Armed with a grasp of numbers, man can trace history back billions of years and can measure speeds and distance (and much more) far beyond his capacity to directly visualize.

For objectivism, concepts are neither "out there" (as hidden essences inside things) nor "in here" (as subjective constructions of the mind). They are mental integrations of things in reality. They are the *form* in which a rational or conceptual consciousness grasps reality. If formed by the correct method, as noted earlier, they are objective. (Concepts pertaining to consciousness, such as emotion, and to the products of consciousness, such as knowledge, are formed by introspection using the same basic processes as those pertaining to the outside word [Rand, 1991].)

Higher level or more abstract concepts are formed by integrating lower level ones, for example, integrating chairs, beds, tables, and sofas into furniture. All valid concepts ultimately are reducible to the perceptual level. This ensures that concepts are not "floating" in space, detached from the real world as they were with Plato. "Floating abstractions" (combined with arbitrary or no definitions) are, unfortunately, one of the most widespread of contemporary academic diseases.

The method of achieving objectivity in thought, as Aristotle first discovered, is logic. Logic for objectivism is not primarily deductive but rather inductive—gaining knowledge from observing reality and integrating one's percepts into concepts, one's concepts into propositions, and all of one's knowledge into a noncontradictory whole. Logic is not separate from reality but rather is based on reality. The law of contradiction must be obeyed in thought because *in reality* a thing cannot be A and non-A at the same time and in the same respect. Logic includes reducing all conceptual knowledge to the perceptual level, as noted earlier.

Objectivism rejects both traditional approaches to epistemology: rationalism, which entails reason divorced from sensory data, and empiricism, which entails sensory observation divorced from integration (concepts). For objectivism, knowledge results from reason applied to sensory experience. Rand's metaphysics and epistemology refute philosophical skepticism (Ghate, 2003; Peikoff, 1991). (For a discussion of the nature and meaning of certainty in objectivist epistemology, see Peikoff, 1991.)

As noted, the conceptual level of knowledge, unlike the perceptual level of knowledge, is fallible; this is because the former, but not the latter, is volitional. Sense perception (given a normal brain state) is valid (a corollary of the existence of consciousness); thinking is not. Rand's original theory of volition or free will asserts that it consists of the fundamental choice of whether to use one's rational (conceptual) faculty or not or, as Rand put it, "the choice to think or not to think" (cited in Peikoff, 1991, p. 55). One can observe the validity of this claim by direct introspection. One has the power to actively focus one's mind and conceptually integrate one's observations or to let the mind drift passively at the subconceptual level (or to evade facts that one does not wish to acknowledge). The choice to act is a derivative choice and depends on one's prior thinking, one's knowledge and values, and the decision to keep one's premises in mind when acting. Consciousness, in this view, has causal efficacy.

All human knowledge presupposes volition. It is a corollary of the axiom of (human) consciousness. To deny volition is a contradiction in terms. The determinist must assert that although everything he believes or says is forced on him by his heredity and/or environment, nevertheless what he says is true. But one cannot make a claim to truth if one is a robot—a preprogrammed object that is unable to look at the facts, evaluate and integrate them, and come to a logical conclusion. A determinist can only say, "I was programmed to emit these word sounds." And he cannot even *know* that!

Volition is not a violation of the law of causality but rather a form of causality—the form that applies to a conceptual consciousness. The choice to think is not random and is not forced on one. The cause of one's choice to think is oneself. Thinking is a *self-caused* action (Binswanger, 1991), a causal primary. According to objectivism, although consciousness depends on a physical brain for its existence, it is not reducible to brain activity (Peikoff, 1991). The motion of a neuron is obviously not the same thing as a logical thought. In terms of the traditional categories pertaining to the relation of body and mind, objectivism is neither materialistic (only matter exists), idealistic (only ideas exist), nor dualistic (man is composed of separate conflicting parts, as postulated by Plato and Descartes). It is simply objectivism (Peikoff, 1991). Mind and body are attributes of a single integrated entity.

Ethics, of course, presupposes volition. There would be no point in offering a moral code to beings who were incapable of free choice.

Ethics

During recent years, the American business world has been rocked by scandals (e.g., Adelphia Communications, Enron, HealthSouth, MCI, the mutual fund industry, Marsh & McLennan, Tyco). The common element in these scandals was that management apparently committed fraud on its customers and/or stockholders.

The government's response to these scandals, aside from the proper response of prosecuting companies where fraud existed, was to pass new draconian legislation allegedly to "prevent" future fraud. For example, chief executive officers (CEOs) now need to personally guarantee the accuracy of quarterly and annual financial statements (thereby demanding omniscience) and are told who they can and cannot put on their boards of directors (as though the government knows more about business than they do).

In addition to violating the rights of businessmen, preventive legislation that does not directly relate to punishing actual fraudulent activity is hopelessly impractical. The very passage of the Sarbanes-Oxley Act of 2002 (SOX) cost stockholders $1.4 trillion in lost market value (Zhang, 2005). Consider also the costs of compliance. I asked the CEO of a totally scandal-free Fortune 500 company what it cost his company to comply with SOX. He said that it cost the company $20 million in the first year (he said 95% of the money was completely wasted) and will cost $10 to $15 million each year thereafter. Zhang (2005) estimated total first-year costs to American business to be $21 billion. Note that all of this is money that could have been put to productive use; thus, compliance actually undermines the economy. There are also more indirect effects. SOX has generated so much fear among CEOs that it is widely accepted it will make them less willing to take creative risks. Some companies have delisted from, or refused to be listed on, U.S. stock exchanges as a result of this legislation. Many small entrepreneurial firms have chosen not to go public because of the costs and risks of SOX, a choice that greatly diminishes their opportunities for growth (Mount, 2005). Such laws also divert managerial thinking, time, and attention from "How can I grow the business?" to "How can I be sure I am not breaking one or more of the draconian regulations controlling business?" Finally, preventive laws cannot ensure honest business dealings because devious businessmen can always find a way around them. If every business leader or manager were dishonest, our entire (semi)capitalist system would collapse overnight. The truth is that capitalism depends on, encourages, and rewards the essential honesty of business owners and managers.

Nevertheless, it is clear that some dishonest business leaders and managers exist. In fact, given the ethical philosophy that is most prevalent in business (and among many people in society at large) today, it is surprising that dishonesty is not more widespread than it is. The prevalent philosophy practiced by business leaders today is pragmatism. This philosophy was popularized by John Dewey and William James near the beginning of the 20th century. What is pragmatism? Rand (1961) described its essence as follows:

> [The pragmatists] declared that philosophy must be *practical* and that practicality consists of dispensing with all absolute principles and standards—that there is no such thing as objective reality or permanent truth—that *truth is that which works,* and its validity can be judged only by its consequences—that no fact can be known with certainty in advance, and anything may be tried by rule-of-thumb—that reality is not firm, but fluid and "indeterminate," that there is no such thing as a distinction between an external world and a consciousness (between the perceived and the perceiver), that there is only an undifferentiated package-deal labeled "experience," and whatever one wishes to be true, *is* true, whatever one wishes to exist, *does* exist, provided that it works or makes one feel better. (p. 34, italics in original)

Under pragmatism, there can be no firm grasp of reality and no firm moral principles. Doing "whatever works" readily translates into "Doing whatever I can get away with" or "Doing whatever makes me feel good today." Fortunately, not all business leaders and managers are pragmatists, and those who advocate pragmatism do not practice it consistently. A business based on the premise that wishes control reality would not survive very long. Nevertheless, pragmatism has infected, both consciously and subconsciously, not only the business community but also the culture as a whole. It is an early version of philosophical skepticism (the denial that we can know anything with certainty). By the late 20th century, skepticism had become the dominant philosophy, and it is now known as postmodernism (Locke, 2003).

Today, the only major opposition to skepticism in ethics is religious dogmatism. There are moral absolutes, say the religionists. These absolutes, however, come through revelations from God and are beyond reason and proof. They must be taken on faith. But when obeyed consistently, religion, like pragmatism, works in opposition to business (and life) success. According to religion, whereas faith is an important virtue, reason is not. In the Bible, for instance, reason is never promoted or recommended as a virtue, and it has been attacked by many leading Christian theologians on the grounds that, as compared with faith, it is "limited" (which really means limited by logic and reality). Furthermore, wealth—as many New Testament parables assert—is immoral and prevents the salvation of one's soul. The highest moral virtue is not making a selfish profit but rather sacrificing oneself to God and/or society. Christianity does advocate honesty, but as a commandment; no practical worldly reason to be honest is given.

Both pragmatism (postmodernism) and religion agree on one key premise: You cannot derive knowledge of an absolute moral code through reason. Either you act as an amoral pragmatist, making decisions based on your feelings of the moment, or you obey the Bible (e.g., the Ten Commandments) on faith, replace thinking with prayer, and seek a life of poverty. (You might be permitted to make a temporary, and guilty, profit so long as you "give back" to society that which you had no moral right to in the first place.) Neither philosophy offers any rational, principled moral guidance for the business leader or owner. Is it any wonder, then, that many business managers are cynically amoral and that even honest ones are unable to defend themselves against attack or even to take pride in their real achievements? Both philosophies divorce business success from moral virtue.

To give moral guidance to those in business (and to people in general), we need an absolute moral code based on reason. Only objectivism provides such a code. The attempt to develop a rational moral code through reason was stymied for centuries by two things: (a) the progressive assault on the validity of reason itself (specifically the validity of the senses and/or the validity of concepts) starting with Plato and followed later by Hume and Kant and (b) Hume's famous assertion to the effect that "You can't get an *ought* from an *is*"—meaning that you cannot derive a moral code from facts. Let us see how Rand's philosophy resolves these problems.

Before I start, I must stress once again that Rand's theory of ethics does not stand alone, divorced from a wider philosophical system. For example, a theory of ethics depends on whether there is a real world out there and whether it obeys causal laws. Otherwise, all is whim and chaos. A theory of ethics also depends on man's nature. If all of man's choices are determined by heredity and/or environment, then telling man what he should do is pointless. If man is born evil (with original sin), then advocating a code of ethics is hopeless. All of these issues fall within the field of metaphysics.

A theory of ethics also depends on whether and how man gains knowledge. If no knowledge is possible, then there can be no science of ethics. If knowledge comes from revelation, then reading the Bible is all one needs (although one cannot validate one's dogma). If reason is invalid, then one must rely on faith (which ultimately means feelings). All of these issues fall within the realm of epistemology. The objectivist ethics is based on the fact that there is a real world out there, that man is competent to know it, and that man possesses free will.

It is commonly held that the purpose of ethics is purely social—that one needs moral values only because one lives in a society. But the need for ethics goes much deeper. You would need a code of ethics even on a desert island. There is no "instinct" (inborn knowledge or goal) of self-preservation. On a desert island, you would still need to make choices about how to act (e.g., "Should I kneel on the beach and pray to God for deliverance?," "Should I flagellate myself to cleanse myself of original sin?," "Should I passively accept my fate because it is God's will that I am here?," "Should I act on my feelings of the moment and scream, cry, and curse my situation?," "Should I eat any plant or flower I stumble across?," "Should I fantasize that I am living in a luxurious beach resort and hope it comes true?," "Should I sit on the sand and wait for the waves to wash up boxes of food and water?," "Should I examine my surroundings, think about what to do, and take positive actions to ensure my survival?").

Many people, as noted earlier, consider ethics to be a monopoly of religion. However, religious arguments will not appeal to those who do not accept faith (which reduces to emotion) as a source of knowledge. Religious arguments demand that you switch off your mind and simply obey. They are explicitly anti-reason. Objectivism, of course, rejects all nonrational arguments.

However, rejecting faith does not in itself provide one with an alternative. One of the reasons why previous, seemingly pro-reason, philosophers such as Hume have been baffled by the problem of how to validate an objective code of ethics is that they did not start with the right question. Rand showed that the first question to ask in ethics is not "What is the good?" but rather "Why does man need a code of moral values at all?" (Rand, 1964a).

Her answer is that because man's life is conditional (as is that of all living organisms), he needs to achieve the values that will sustain his life. However, knowledge of the values he must pursue is not inborn. With respect to mental *content*, man is born tabula rasa—without any knowledge or values. He does possess an innate pleasure–pain mechanism that signals him at the sensory level as to whether states or actions are harmful or beneficial (e.g., putting one's hand on a hot stove causes pain). But these range-of-the-moment sensations do not enable one to act long range. Man cannot survive, like the lower animals, acting just on the basis of sensations and perceptual knowledge. To survive, man needs to formulate and practice a moral code, a set of moral principles.

The critical question that previous philosophers have been unable to answer is the following: If man needs a moral code, then what is the ultimate *standard* of morality? The conventional answer is that there is no objective standard—hence the reliance in most moral systems on religious dogma or subjective feelings. Typically, moral philosophers replace individual subjective feelings with the standard of collective subjective feelings (e.g., group consensus). An example is utilitarianism (the greatest good or pleasure for the greatest number), developed by Bentham and Mill. But the subjective feelings of a group are still subjective feelings and, incidentally, gain no superior moral status simply because more than one person is involved.

For Rand, the identification of an ultimate standard is implied by the identification of why man needs a moral code. The key to her solution was to pose this question: What is the root of the concept of value? Man's life, like that of other living organisms, is conditional; man faces the alternative of life or death and must achieve certain goals to remain alive. Rand observed that it is *only* to a living organism that something can be of value (or disvalue). Only this kind of entity has values; only to this kind of entity can things be good or bad. The ultimate objective standard of value is, therefore, life. To quote Rand (1964a), "It is only the concept of 'Life' that makes the concept of 'Value' possible" (p. 17). To use her example, an immortal robot would not have any values because nothing could make a difference to it. The meaning of the observation that life is the standard of value, when applied to man (the rational being), is the following: "Since reason is man's basic means of survival, that which is proper to the life of a rational being is the good; that which negates, opposes, or destroys it is the evil" (p. 23).

This answers Hume's is–ought dilemma. What man is (a living being possessing the power of reason whose life is conditional) determines what he ought to do—if he chooses to live. (There are circumstances in which a rational man might not choose to live. For example, a man may choose to end his life due to unbearable suffering caused by a painful incurable illness because no form of happiness is any longer possible. A man may also choose to risk his life for a loved one because life would no longer be meaningful without that partner. Observe that both of these examples, however, are pro-life in the wider sense; it is because a happy life is no longer possible or is threatened that he chooses to end it or to risk ending it.) To reject life as such, however, is to reject one's own nature and, therefore, to reject reality. This puts man outside the sphere of morality and, soon, outside of existence. The options are life or nothing.

Among the lower animals, the standard of life is built-in, and they act (guided by the pleasure–pain mechanisms sense perception, and memory) to further their lives and well-being (within the range of their knowledge). The lower animals have neither the capacity to understand moral principles nor any volitional choice about how to act. Man, however, cannot survive as an animal. As noted, he needs the guidance of pro-life moral principles. Given that life is the standard of morality, what moral principles should man follow to sustain his life?

This brings us to the realm of virtue: What are the key pro-life virtues? The primary virtue, as implied earlier, is rationality—the consistent use of one's conceptual faculty. Why? Because reason is man's main means of survival;

that is, it is the tool man uses to gain the conceptual knowledge that is required to live (e.g., he needs to use his mind to grow, store, transport, and prepare food; to ensure physical and mental health; to create clothing and shelter; to make discoveries and inventions; and to form viable societies). "The virtue of *Rationality* means the recognition and acceptance of reason as one's only source of knowledge, one's only judge of values, and one's only guide to action" (Rand, 1964a, p. 25, italics in original). To refuse to think or to pursue the irrational is to act against one's life. The businessman who chooses the irrational is rejecting reality and dooms himself to failure.

Rand identified six key derivative virtues (for details, see Peikoff, 1991), applications of rationality to fundamental aspects of human life. The virtue of honesty is the refusal to fake reality (lying is one example). Faking reality destroys the essential function of consciousness, which is to perceive reality. It places one's wishes or desires above the truth. Thus, it destroys one's thinking process at root and leads one to take actions that are self-sabotaging. For example, a businessman who commits fraud loses the trust of his employees and customers, and he often ends up with his career in ruins and himself possibly in jail (for a detailed discussion of the virtue of honesty in business, see Locke & Woiceshyn, 1995).

A second derivative virtue is integrity—loyalty to one's rational convictions in action. It is important to stress the term *rational*. Acting on one's feelings (e.g., like the Ku Klux Klan) does not represent integrity; rather, it represents emotionalism (and, in the Ku Klux Klan's case, flagrant irrationality). The failure to act on one's convictions, when such action is possible, is another means of sabotaging reason. The man without integrity says, in effect, "My judgment declares that A is the right choice, but nevertheless I will choose B." Like dishonesty, this disconnects his mind from reality. In many cases, a lack of integrity is due to moral compromise—giving in to the evil at the expense of the good. Rand showed that in any compromise between good and evil, it is only evil that can win. The evil is the irrational—the anti-life—and can "win" (temporarily) only with the help of the good (e.g., when honest men initially do not speak up when they encounter company fraud or help to cover it up, the defrauders are left free to function).

A third derivative virtue is independence. This means, first, using one's own judgment. Only individual minds exist, and each individual faces the responsibility of gaining the knowledge needed to live. If he blindly obeys the dictates of others, he renounces his mind and is at the mercy of those he follows (secretly hoping they will know what to do). No matter how much advice a business leader gets, in the end he still should rely on his own judgment. (Even a follower should decide for himself whether to follow orders or not.) Independence also means being responsible for earning one's own living. Businessmen should not be asking for special handouts from the government.

A fourth derivative virtue is productiveness—creating, directly or indirectly, the material values that one's life requires. Production is the special province of businessmen; they are, above all, creators of wealth (Rand,

1957/1992)—the goods and services that make survival and comfort possible (Locke, 2000). Contrary to popular belief (especially as propagated by Marxists), the creation (as opposed to the stealing or looting) of wealth is not the product of some lower faculty (e.g., "unprincipled materialistic greed"). Nor is it the product of mindless "labor." Rather, it is the product of man's highest moral virtue—rationality (plus intelligence and creativity). To create wealth requires thinking (Locke, 2000), which means making hundreds or thousands of rational decisions, including what products or services to create, how to finance the company, whom to hire, what code of values the company will stand for, how to structure the organization, where to locate it, how to control costs, how to generate cash flow, how to deal with legal issues, how to gain a competitive advantage, and how to develop the needed technology. Labor has value only if it is directed to a rationally productive end. If man's mind is his spirit, then the creation of wealth is a profoundly spiritual achievement (Rand, 1957/ 1992).

A fifth derivative virtue is justice—the only strictly social virtue in objectivism—which means rationality in the evaluation of other men. This means judging men based on one's best judgment of the facts of their character and accomplishments and treating them accordingly. In business, this would mean, for example, giving promotions and raises based on merit. In hiring, it would mean hiring on the basis of the individual qualities that the organization needs for each particular job. Universal qualities (those relevant to virtually every job) would include moral character, motivation to work, and knowledge or skill (or the ability to learn). Special qualities could include factors such as special technical expertise, language skills, sales skills, managerial experience, and the ability to work on a team.

The sixth derivative virtue is pride, specifically ambition in the creation of one's own moral character and of the practical results attained as a result (e.g., the creation of a successful business, the doing of a competent job). Objectivism holds that a man can be morally perfect and should strive to be so—not because virtue is its own reward (it is not) but rather because life and happiness are the reward of virtue, and the more virtuous one is, the better one's prospects are.

The final ethical question that must be addressed is the following: Who should be the beneficiary of one's moral code? The conventional answer is anyone but oneself; in short, egoism is evil and altruism is good. Altruism literally means otherism and asserts that one should sacrifice oneself—meaning one's time, one's judgment, one's goods, one's productive efforts, one's money, and even one's life—for the sake of others (others whom one does not selfishly value and even one's enemies). The good, according to altruism, means renouncing what one values for the sake of someone else, especially someone who "needs" what one has.

Objectivism holds that altruism, by its very essence, is an anti-life, and therefore evil, moral code. Objectivism also rejects (as should be clear from the preceding discussion) amoralism and mindless hedonism; it advocates rational egoism, a rational concern for one's own interests, as the moral ideal. Rational egoism is the pro-life moral code. According to Rand, *one's highest moral purpose is the achievement of one's own happiness*. Rational egoism is implicit in the answer to the question, noted earlier, of why man needs a moral code. He needs it to live and be happy. Embracing altruism, a code that demands self-immolation, in response to the fact that man needs a moral code to sustain his life is a flagrant contradiction. Altruism is literally the code of death. It does not mean benevolence, generosity, or goodwill; rather, it means the giving up of one's life and happiness to others.

Objectivism advocates benevolence toward others (unless they prove to be unworthy of it) because it values human life. (Human life means the life of real people. Thus, valuing human life does not apply to a potential life, such as sperm, eggs, or protoplasm, which may later become a fetus and then an independent being.) Objectivism considers it proper to give help to people you value who are in trouble (or to give to causes that you selfishly value), but not as a duty and not at the expense of your own well-being (Rand, 1963; see also Smith, 2006, chap. 10).

As to love, objectivism considers it to be profoundly egoistic. To love someone means that that person is important in your value hierarchy, that he or she is critical to your happiness, and that his or her well-being is of vital importance to you. (This view is anathema to altruism, which views love as a sacrifice, and to narcissism, which views others as a means of bolstering one's illusory sense of self-esteem.)

Turning to business, according to objectivism, the businessman who selfishly seeks to make an honest profit, through the use of reason and voluntary trade, is engaging in a profoundly *moral* activity. He does not need to "give back" anything to "society" because he has not taken anything that he did not earn through voluntary trade; his wealth belongs to him to use as he wishes. He should feel pride in his achievements (i.e., his creation of wealth) rather than guilt. In this view, businessmen may properly make donations to people and organizations out of self-interest (e.g., to help a cause they believe in, to create goodwill in the community).

In objectivism, there is no conflict between the moral and the practical. Because objectivist morality holds man's life as the standard of moral value, its principles are formulated to achieve life and happiness (i.e., to be practical). In business, for example, it pays to be rational—to look at the facts, integrate them, and reach a conclusion consistent with the evidence rather than acting on emotion. It pays to be honest—to see reality as real rather than trying to fake the facts (Locke & Woiceshyn, 1995) (e.g., by "cooking the books"). It pays to have integrity—to act on the basis of one's best judgment rather than blanking out what one knows, compromising one's business principles, and losing the trust of others. It pays to be independent rather than to follow the crowd because the crowd (e.g., competitors) might not be doing the right thing. It pays to be productive because that is the way to make profits; if a businessman does not produce, he needs to mooch off of those who do. It pays to be just because that is the way one retains good employees and loyal customers. It pays to take pride in one's own character because it is an incentive to build and sustain that pro-life character.

A businessman may get away with immorality in the short run, but in the long run the usual outcome is failure; the destruction of one's self-respect, career, and reputation; and possibly fines and jail. To defy morality is to defy reality; it is to act against what makes happiness and success possible in this world.

Politics

Politics rests on the foundation provided by metaphysics, epistemology, and ethics and most specifically on the concepts of reason and egoism. Politics is concerned with the question of what principles should govern how men live together in a society. Because reason is man's main means of survival, the key principle is that in society an individual must remain free to exercise his rational faculty. Socially, it is the initiation of physical force by other men (including governments) that negates reason. As Rand said, force and mind are opposites. In a proper society, the initiation of force by individuals or the government against other individuals (in contrast to force used in retaliation or in legitimate self-defense) is banned.

The principle that preserves man's freedom to follow reason and prohibits the initiation of force by others is the concept of individual rights. To quote Rand (1964a),

> "Rights" are a moral concept—the concept that provides a logical transition from the principles guiding an individual's actions to the principles guiding his relationship with others—the concept that preserves and protects individual morality in a social context—the link between the moral code of a man and the legal code of a society, between ethics and politics. (p. 92)

Every political system is based on some code of morality. Before the founding of the United States, virtually all previous systems of government were based on the altruistic–collectivistic principle that men must live (and die) for the state (or tribe, religious authority, party, or aristocracy). Society and its leaders were, in effect, outside moral law and could compel individual citizens to do anything they demanded. The individual existed only to serve the collective; he had duties but no rights. "The most profoundly revolutionary achievement of the United States was *the subordination of society to moral law*" (Rand, 1964a, p. 93, italics in original).

John Locke was the first to offer a systematic presentation of the concept of individual rights (Locke, 1986), and the United States was founded under the guidance of his ideas. However, there were errors in his philosophy (including in his epistemology and ethics) that left the concepts of rights vulnerable to attack. Bentham called Locke's view of inalienable rights "nonsense on stilts," although a more correct description would be "correctness (in essentials) on stilts."

Rand replaced the stilts with girders of philosophical steel. She demonstrated that the source of rights was neither divine revelation nor group agreement but rather man's nature as a rational being whose life was conditional. However, her philosophy came too late to prevent a major perversion of the concept of rights. Due to the influence of altruism, which had never been fully rejected by the Founding Fathers, there was a gradual switch in the meaning of rights as originally formulated—from rights as freedoms of action to rights as entitlements to the products of others' actions. The original and proper meaning of rights was that they sanction one's freedom of action; they define a sphere in which each individual is free to act and in which others are prohibited from using force against you. Rights leave you free to pursue your own happiness but do not guarantee that you will achieve it and do not force others to provide you with what you want. The switch to "rights" as entitlements means that you have a "right" to actually get what you want (e.g., housing, medical care, retirement income, education) at someone else's expense. "Rights" as entitlements imply that you will be forced to provide others with goods and services (and vice versa). *Observe that "rights" as entitlements negate actual rights. They represent a total inversion of the meaning of the concept of rights.* Morally, rights to freedom of action are based on egoism; "rights" as entitlements are based on altruism. If you are forced to serve others, then you are not free to pursue your own values.

For objectivism, the proper functions of government are the police, the courts, and the armed forces. (Welfare would be strictly private.) Observe that all of these serve solely to protect rights, including the use of force, guided by objective law, in retaliation to those who initiate it. (For a discussion of how to finance government in a free society, see Rand, 1964b.)

The application of the concept of individual rights to economics is straightforward. Objectivism advocates laissez-faire capitalism. *"Capitalism is the social system based on the recognition of individual rights, including property rights, in which all property is privately owned"* (Rand, 1967, p. 19, italics in original). The justification for capitalism is not the conventional one, used especially by conservatives, that capitalism is good because it benefits society as a whole or serves the "public good" (although, if that term has any intelligible meaning, that is its consequence). This is an argument from altruism and collectivism (used, unfortunately, by alleged defenders of capitalism such as Adam Smith and Herbert Spencer) and implies that businessmen can be allowed to function only by permission and only on the terms set by those in "need." Objectivism stands for individualism—metaphysically (only individuals exist, and groups are collections of individuals), epistemologically (only individual minds exist), ethically (one's own life is one's highest mortal purpose), and politically (each individual has inalienable rights).

The objectivist advocacy of capitalism is a moral one based on man's right to his own life—meaning the right to trade freely with others.

> In a capitalist society, all human relationships are *voluntary*. Men are free to cooperate or not, to deal with one another or not, as their own individual judgments, convictions, and interests dictate. They can deal with one another only in terms of and by means of reason, i.e., by means of discussion, persuasion, and *contractual* agreement, by voluntary choice to mutual benefit. (Rand, 1967, p. 19, italics in original)

Objectivism advocates only laws pertaining to prohibiting the use of physical force or the threat of force. (Fraud is an indirect initiation of force; for example, if you do work for Mr. X and he gives you a phony check in payment, it means you worked for Mr. X without your consent, as if he had forced you.) Capitalism is the only system consistent with egoism and man's rational faculty (Rand, 1967). Because capitalism is moral, given the objectivist ethics, it is of course also practical. All socialist regimes have ended in failure because production and innovation require freedom of the mind and the freedom to be self-interested. (Observe the specter of North Korea, the most militantly socialist country on the earth, where people are literally starving to death.)

Objectivism makes a critical distinction between economic and political power (Binswanger, 1983). Political power is the power of physical force. Economic power is the power of trade, in other words, my money for your goods or services. Not everyone is equal in their economic power; this would be impossible except in an egalitarian dictatorship. But economic trade is still voluntary. Even a lone worker who is offered a job at the multinational Titan Inc. has the power to refuse the offer (or to quit after he is hired); he retains the power to follow his own judgment. In contrast, if a gun is put to his head, he does not retain the power to follow his own judgment. In a fully capitalist economy, the government would not forcibly seize its productive citizens' money and give it to those who did not earn it. Economic growth would be much higher than it is today, and there would be no shortage of jobs (Rand, 1967).

Our current economy, of course, is a mixed economy, a Rube Goldberg combination of freedom and controls. It is the result of a mixed philosophy—individualism (including egoism) and collectivism (including altruism). The clear trend is toward statism (Peikoff, 1982). Politics is a consequence of philosophy, and neither liberals nor conservatives want to, or are able to, defend capitalism on moral grounds. If the trend is not reversed, it is only a matter of time before the economy is destroyed.

Applications of
Objectivism to the Business World

In this section, I briefly identify how laissez-faire capitalism, as advocated by objectivism, would differ from our mixed economy. I deal with 10 commonly discussed business issues in alphabetical order.

1. Affirmative Action and Racism

Affirmative action is a flagrantly racist policy based on collectivism. To make up for past discrimination, people who were not themselves necessarily victims of governmental racism get special benefits because they are members of the protected collective (as if all of the members were interchangeable), and those who are not members are harmed (by losing jobs and promotions) even though they had no role in causing harm to others. Nothing could be more unjust than such a policy.

Objectivism morally opposes racism as "the lowest, most crudely primitive form of collectivism. . . . Racism is a doctrine of, by, and for brutes. . . . Racism negates two aspects of man's life: reason and choice, or mind and morality, replacing them with chemical predestination" (Rand, 1964a, p. 126). Nevertheless, a property owner should have the freedom to hire whomever he wants (as he possesses the freedom to engage in many other irrational actions so long as he does not violate anyone's rights). The way to protest private racist practices would include boycotts and social ostracism; furthermore, a company that has racist practices harms itself and, other things being equal, will be out-competed by failing to hire many competent people. The government, as a representative of all the people, must prohibit racism in its own operations.

2. Antitrust

Under laissez-faire capitalism, there would be no antitrust laws. A company could grow as large as it is able to grow through free trade. A company would be free to charge whatever prices it wanted. (There are no objective meanings to the terms *unfair prices* and *excess profits*.) The way a company gets to be dominant is by offering better prices and/or a better value than its competitors. The best way to get rich is to offer a good value at a competitive price (cf. Henry Ford). If a dominant company decided to, say, double prices, two things would happen. First, people would cut back their spending on that company's products. Second, competitors (including those from abroad) would sense a great opportunity and start underselling the dominant company. The result would eventually be lower profits. If the company lowered prices to below cost to crush upstart companies, its own profits would be harmed, giving more encouragement to potential competitors. If a dominant company stopped innovating, that would also provide opportunities to competitors. (For a further discussion of monopolies, see Rand, 1967. For a detailed discussion of the economic fallacies that underlie antitrust laws and the immorality of such laws, see Hull, 2005.)

3. Diversity

Diversity literally means difference. The value of diversifying depends on what is being diversified. In a normal business context, there is no value in diversifying across race or gender (as against, say, a ballroom dance club, which will seek diversity in gender).

Most companies, as noted earlier, will want to know, at a minimum, three things about individual applicants. First, do they have moral character (e.g., can they be trusted)? Second, are they motivated to work (e.g., show up regularly, put in effort, get projects completed on time, show initiative)? Third, do they have the knowledge and skills needed for the job or the ability to learn them in a reasonable time? None of these characteristics is a monopoly of any one race or gender or any other demographic group. Diversity of experience and ideas, as opposed to race and gender, may be of value to companies to create productive conflict, but these are attributes of the individual.

4. Environmentalism

Objectivism holds that reshaping the earth to fulfill man's needs is morally good. It rejects the notion that nature has "intrinsic value"; the concept of intrinsic value is invalid because the concept of value presupposes an answer to the question of to whom and for what. Clearing mosquito-infested swamps to build houses is good—for man. This does not imply that there should be no environmental laws. There should be laws that protect man from physical harm. For example, releasing poisonous gases into the air or poisonous chemicals into the water supply obviously would be prohibited because they represent an initiation of force against others. However, because "poison is in the dose," and because individuals differ in their responses to virtually everything in the environment, it would be irrational to demand that every factory be totally pristine in its emissions. This would put all factories out of business and violate all people's rights to their own lives by forcing us back into the Dark Ages. Rational standards, based on honest, objective scientific knowledge and available technology, would need to apply if and when polluting factories or the like were taken to court.

However, in terms of its *philosophical* leadership, the environmental movement is actually not concerned with discovering what is true and what is objectively beneficial and harmful to human life. Consider, for example, global warming. Today, there is probably no scientific issue that has been more politi-cized (other than perhaps nuclear power) than this one. For example, climate models are based partly on science but rely heavily on unproven assumptions and projections that involve guesswork. Early models predicted sea level rises of 25 feet, totally divorced from scientific proof. Some models have looked only at recent trends without looking carefully at unexplained historical vari-ations in climate over millennia that had nothing to do with man-made activ-ities. Although some warming seems to have occurred during recent decades, it is not fully clear exactly how much has actually occurred and, of that, how much is due to man-made actions. One top scientist has refused to release his global warming data and methods of analysis to other scientists. It is even less clear how much warming will occur in the future. Predictions of temperature change proportionate to the rise in levels of carbon dioxide have proven to be wrong repeatedly. The role of sunspots, which evidence suggests can affect cli-mate change substantially, has typically been ignored. The alleged harm of global warming has been publicized repeatedly, but its benefits have hardly been discussed at all. The Kyoto Protocol, even according to its (most honest) proponents, may have only a minimal effect, if any, on global warming, even if it is enacted by all nations. The costs of fully implementing it, on the other hand, could be astronomical. And so on.

The philosophical motivation behind much of this movement is self-professed hatred of human civilization, capitalism, and human progress. In virtually every controversy, it is man who is to be sacrificed to nature (Rand, 1999, especially chap. 13). In other cases, alarmist predictions are a good means of getting government grants. Who would give research money to someone who says that the danger is not all that great? Such a person could even have his or her academic career ruined. Expert climatologists who disagree with the "consensus" are mocked, silenced, or ignored. Businessmen, with the heroic exception of the former CEO of Exxon, feel helpless to resist the environmental onslaught.

There is no way to deal successfully with the issue of global warming, or any other issue, without an objective philosophical base—a base that stresses not only man's right to his own life and the pursuit of happiness but also objectivity, the primacy of facts, looking at the totality of the evidence, integrating it objectively, and distinguishing what is known from what is not known regardless of politics, biases, vested interests, or the desire to go along with the crowd.

5. Ethics Programs

I would strongly endorse the need for all companies to have clear ethical standards. However, posting "value" statements on the wall is not sufficient. The ethical values must be acted on (the virtue of integrity), and adher-ence must be monitored. Corporate values must be set by top management, starting with the CEO, to prevent anarchy. Managers and employees should be selected, in part, based on their moral character, as noted earlier. Training programs for new employees must publicize and explain the importance of the company ethics code. Moral integrity should be built into the performance appraisal process. People who do not adhere to the code not only should not be rewarded but also should be fired, no matter what their job level. Ethical compliance should be monitored, including through employee and customer surveys. A successful ethics program must be totally embedded into the company culture. Of course, it matters greatly *which* code of ethics is promoted. Obviously, I favor objectivism. BB&T, a very successful and scandal-free banking company serving the mid-Atlantic region and currently the 87th most profitable company in the world, in terms of shareholder return, is governed explicitly by the objectivist virtues noted earlier.

6. Government Favors

Objectivism is opposed to any and all special government favors or handouts for business—or any other group. This list would include the rejection of special tax incentives for chosen companies (of course, I am opposed to corporate taxation in principle, as implied earlier), subsidies (including agricultural subsidies), import duties (tariffs) to "protect" certain industries from foreign competitors, government-granted monopolies that forcibly prevent competition, government grants to develop "new" technologies, and government loans for any private purpose (e.g., housing, education).

People complain constantly about business lobbyists descending on Washington in droves and begging for favors. But this is inevitable in a mixed economy. The government has virtually unlimited power to destroy any company through new regulations (or even by strictly enforcing old ones given that no one could obey every regulation on the books) and the granting of special favors to competitors. Thus, even companies with the best of motives need to lobby, if only in self-defense. The only way to stop all of this is to get the government out of the economy altogether, other than enforcing laws against the initiation of force. Lobbyists will stop coming to Washington only when politicians have no favors to sell and no power to harm honest businesses.

7. Minimum Wages

Under a free economy, the government would have no power to set wages (except among its own employees). Such power would violate the rights of employers to offer what they choose. In a free market, wages ultimately are set by the market (supply and demand). The Marxist doctrine that, under capitalism, company owners will reduce wages to the level of starvation is simply nonsense and flies in the face of history. If control over wages could abolish poverty, then why doesn't the government set them, say, at a minimum of $30,000 a year for unskilled labor—way above the market price? The answer is obvious—because it would cause massive unemployment. In contrast, if the minimum wage is set below the market price, it would have no effect. Under capitalism, wages are dynamic and cannot be set rationally (or morally) by a state bureaucrat.

8. Money Supply

Under capitalism, there would be no Federal Reserve. The government would be out of the money business. Thus, it would not have the power to manipulate interest rates or the money supply. Banking would be completely private. The most reputable banks would issue notes backed by gold, and those that circulated unbacked paper money would not be able to compete. Each bank would make its own decision about what interest rates to charge. Private banks could not issue paper money on a whim and, therefore, could not cause inflation.

9. Social Justice

"Social justice" is a Marxist term meaning egalitarianism (i.e., equality of outcomes). According to this doctrine, the rich get rich by exploiting the poor; therefore, money should be forcibly taken from the rich and "redistributed." Social justice is the Robin Hood principle—steal from the rich and give to the poor. This might have been just during the Middle Ages because the poor were in forcible bondage to noblemen and the king, but this is not the Middle Ages. *Redistributing honestly earned wealth is social injustice.* People who earn wealth by voluntary trade own that wealth and have the right to use it in any (legal) way they wish. They do not have a duty to "give back" anything because they did not take anything that did not belong to them. *The true meaning of social justice is that people keep what they earn.* A millionaire, of course, may choose to give or leave his money to any person or charity he wishes based on his own personal interests and values.

10. Social Responsibility and Stakeholder Capitalism

I would argue that the only true stakeholders in a company are its owners (i.e., the stockholders). Thus, the only "social" (i.e., moral) responsibility a company has is to make money for those stockholders (i.e., to maximize profits).

The meaning of maximizing profits must be put in context, however, because it is associated in many people's minds with two things: short-range thinking and dishonesty. I strongly oppose both. Short-range-only thinking in a business (and in life) is flagrantly irrational; it usually leads to disaster, including the possible destruction of the company in the long run. Rational

CEOs must always balance short- and long-term considerations. A company needs to survive in the short term or else there will be no long term, but it cannot survive long term unless it plans ahead. Causal thinking is critical here; in other words, what will be the consequences if you do X? As for ethics, making money unethically is not making money at all but rather stealing it. As we have seen, being unethical is not practical.

What about employees? They, of course, have a stake in the company, but if they are not stockholders the word "stake" has a different meaning than it does for an owner. The employees' stake is that it is in their self-interest for the company to succeed because they get to keep their jobs. On the other side of this coin, it is very important for the company to hire good people and treat them justly because if they do not, their best people will be the first to leave.

What about helping the community? Private companies are not in the welfare business, but it may be in their self-interest to invest some money in their local communities. For example, they may get more customers by showing goodwill through donations to local projects. Community betterment may also make the city or town where companies are located a better place for employees to live, thereby making recruiting easier and decreasing turnover. Donations to, say, the engineering department of a local university may help companies to recruit engineering graduates. Observe that the principle here is the long-term self-interest of the companies, not altruistic duty.

Aesthetics

Rand's theory of art is presented in Rand (1971) and summarized in Peikoff (1991). Her theory is quite complex, so I present only the essentials here. Rand (1971) defined art as "*a selective re-creation of reality according to an artist's metaphysical value judgments*" (p. 19, italics in original). She continued, "By a selective re-creation, art isolates and integrates those aspects of reality which represent man's fundamental view of himself and of existence. . . . Art is a concretization of metaphysics. *Art brings man's concepts to the perceptual level of his consciousness and allows him to grasp them directly, as if they were percepts*" (pp. 19–20, italics in original).

Observe the two key elements here. First, art is concerned with metaphysical value judgments, which are the artist's deepest, most fundamental premises about himself and the world. In other words,

> Is the universe intelligible to man, or unintelligible and unknowable? Can man find happiness on earth, or is he doomed to frustration and despair? Does man have the power of *choice*, the power to choose his goals and to achieve them, the power to direct the course of his life— or is he the helpless plaything of forces beyond his control, which determine his fate? Is man, by nature, to be valued as good, or to be despised as evil? (Rand, 1971, p. 19, italics in original)

Rand holds that such metaphysical judgments underlie every choice that man makes, every emotion he experiences, and every action that he takes. Metaphysical value judgments involve man's broadest, most abstract principles. However, the sum of these basic, complex abstract judgments cannot be held in mind as a unit. This brings us to the second point, that an artwork concretizes these metaphysical judgments in the form of something directly perceivable: "For instance, consider two statues of man: one as a Greek god, the other as a deformed medieval monstrosity. Both are metaphysical estimates of man; both are concretized representations of the philosophy of their respective cultures" (Rand, 1971, p. 20).

Peikoff (1991) wrote,

> Guided by his own metaphysical value-judgments (explicit or otherwise), an artist selects, out of the bewildering chaos of human experience, those aspects he regards as indicative of the nature of the universe. Then he embodies them in a sensory-perceptual concrete such as a statue, a painting, or a story (this last is perceptual in that the writer must make certain characters and events real by conveying their visual appearance, sounds, textures, etc.). The result is a universe in microcosm. To be exact, the result is a view of the universe in the form of a deliberately slanted concrete, one shorn of all irrelevancies and thus broadcasting unmistakably to the viewer or reader: "This is what counts in life—as I, the artist, see life." (p. 417)

What is the function of art in man's life? According to Rand, it serves a philosophical need—more specifically, a need of man's consciousness. As noted earlier, the main form of awareness is conceptual. Man's conceptual faculty holds an enormous number of abstractions, including philosophical abstractions. But abstractions, as such, do not exist in reality; they are man's form of grasping reality. It is impossible to hold all of one's fundamental abstractions as a single sum. Thus, man has a need to see the reality of his deepest values in external concrete form (e.g., a statue, a painting, a character in a novel). Art serves to objectify metaphysics. Art communicates metaphysical values to man in a way that an abstract discussion could not. Instead of trying to grasp a set of broad abstractions inside one's own consciousness, art makes these abstractions fully real by externalizing them in the form of something one can perceive directly. The purpose of art is not didactic; its function is to show, not to teach.

What determines how a person will respond to artwork? This depends, of course, on the nature of the artwork and also on the metaphysical values of the viewer. Men hold their metaphysical value judgments in a form that Rand (1971) calls "sense of life," which she defined as "a pre-conceptual equivalent of metaphysics, an emotional, subconsciously integrated appraisal of man and of existence. It sets the nature of a man's emotional responses" (p. 25).

Sense of life, of course, also directs what the artist strives to project. Thus, if the artist projects man as a heroic being who can achieve values and happiness on the earth, based on his sense of life, then a person with a similar sense of life will respond positively and a person with an opposite sense of life will not. This response will be in the form of an emotion (based on one's subconscious premises) that one may or may not be able to identify consciously.

The experience of contemplating artwork that expresses his sense of life (assuming that it is pro-life) gives man pleasure as an end in itself—the pleasure of contemplating the reality of his deepest values. Furthermore, this experience provides emotional fuel for his existence, an incentive to keep acting to attain his values despite discouragements and difficulties. Art motivates man at the metaphysical level.

To quote Rand (1971),

> It is not journalistic information or scientific education or moral guidance that man seeks from a work of art . . . but the fulfillment of a more profound need: a confirmation of his view of existence . . . in the sense of permitting him to contemplate his abstractions. . . . Art gives him . . . fuel: the pleasure of contemplating the objectified reality of one's own sense of life is the pleasure of feeling what it would be like to live in one's ideal world. . . . The importance of that experience is not *what* man learns from it but *that* he experiences it . . . the life-giving fact of experiencing a moment of *metaphysical* joy—a moment of love for existence. [This assumes that the individual is rational.] (pp. 38–39, italics in original)

Those who have read Rand's (1957/1992) perennially best-selling novel, *Atlas Shrugged,* can see her theory in practice here. Observe that the main characters, nearly all of whom were people in the business world, are essentialized based on their most fundamental premises (in this case pro-life or pro-death). Thus, the reader can "see" how virtuous men would act and the consequences of their actions in their own lives. (On the negative side, one can also view evil people and the consequences of their anti-life premises.) Rand's own basic premise (her sense of life) was that man was a heroic being and that the universe was a "benevolent" place where man, if he uses reason, has the power to achieve his own success and happiness. Thus, although the heroes endure a terrible struggle, they win in the end and save the world from destruction. Readers who share her sense of life experience a strong positive emotional reaction to the book.

Conclusion

Philosophy is fundamental to attaining wisdom. If the philosophy is rational, it not only is wisdom itself but also enables man to acquire further wisdom about all aspects of the world that concern him, that is, to acquire further knowledge and to be guided by a code of values that preserves his life and promotes his happiness. Businessmen today—not to mention the man in the street—desperately need a philosophy to guide their choices and actions and to defend themselves from attack. But so far they have not been offered anything but pragmatism, mysticism, or contradictory mishmashes of flawed ethical doctrines in business ethics textbooks (Locke, 2006). This has led to widespread moral cynicism, not only within business but also within society at large.

Throughout history, only Plato, Aristotle, Kant, and Rand have offered complete philosophies (i.e., original systems that encompass metaphysics, epistemology, ethics, politics, and aesthetics). Rand (1961) presented her critique of previous philosophers. Although she acknowledged a great debt to Aristotle, even he made errors. The question is as follows: Does Rand do what no previous philosopher has done, that is, successfully answer all of the fundamental questions of philosophy, including the question of how to validate a rational theory of ethics? I believe that she does. But because independence is a key virtue in objectivism, readers should decide this issue for themselves. Because Rand has been widely and, in many cases, deliberately misrepresented by the press and by postmodern philosophers, I urge readers to make up their own minds after reading Rand's work (as well as Peikoff, 1991) firsthand.

References

American Heritage dictionary of the English language (3rd ed.). (1992). Boston: Houghton Mifflin.

Binswanger, H. (1983, June). The dollar and the gun. *The Objectivist Forum.*

Binswanger, H. (1991). Volition as cognitive self-regulation. *Organizational Behavior and Human Decision Processes, 50,* 154–178.

Ghate, O. (2003). Postmodernism's Kantian roots. In E. Locke (Ed.), *Postmodernism and management: Pros, cons, and the alternative.* New York: JAI.

Ghate, O., & Locke, E. A. (2003). Objectivism: The proper alternative to postmodernism. In E. Locke (Ed.), *Postmodernism and management: Pros, cons, and the alternative.* New York: JAI.

Hull, G. (2005). *The abolition of antitrust.* New Brunswick, NJ: Transaction Publishers.

Locke, E. (2000). *The prime movers: Traits of the great wealth creators.* New York: AMACOM.

Locke, E. (Ed.). (2003). *Postmodernism and management: Pros, cons, and the alternative.* New York: JAI.

Locke, E. A. (2006). Business ethics: A way out of the morass. *Academy of Management Learning & Education, 5,* 324–332.

Locke, E., & Woiceshyn, J. (1995). Why businessmen should be honest: The argument from rational egoism. *Journal of Organizational Behavior, 16,* 405–414.

Locke, J. (1986). *The second treatise on civil government.* Buffalo, NY: Prometheus Books.

Mount, I. (2005, May 2). Death of the IOP dream. *Fortune,* pp. 120C–D.

Peikoff, L. (1982). *The ominous parallels: The end of freedom in America.* New York: Stein & Day.

Peikoff, L. (1991). *Objectivism: The philosophy of Ayn Rand.* New York: J. P. Dutton.

Rand, A. (1961). *For the new intellectual.* New York: Signet.

Rand, A. (1963, February). The ethics of emergencies. *The Objectivist Newsletter,* p. 5.

Rand, A. (1964a). *The virtue of selfishness.* New York: Signet.

Rand, A. (1964b, February). What would be the proper method of financing the government in a fully free society? *The Objectivist Newsletter,* pp. 7–9.

Rand, A. (1967). *Capitalism: The unknown ideal.* New York: Signet.

Rand, A. (1971). *The romantic manifesto.* New York: Signet.

Rand, A. (1982). *Philosophy: Who needs it?* New York: Bobbs-Merrill.

Rand, A. (1991). *Introduction to objectivist epistemology.* New York: NAL Books.

Rand, A. (1992). *Atlas shrugged.* New York: Signet. (Original work published 1957)

Rand, A. (1999). *Return of the primitive: The anti-industrial revolution* (Expanded ed.; P. Schwartz, Ed.). New York: Meridian.

Smith, T. (2006). *Ayn Rand's normative ethics: The virtuous egoist.* Cambridge, UK: Cambridge University Press.

Zhang, I. X. (2005). *Economic consequences of the Sarbanes-Oxley Act of 2002.* Unpublished manuscript, Simon Graduate School of Business, University of Rochester.

22 Wisdom as Learned Ignorance

Integrating East–West Perspectives

Robert Chia
Robin Holt

Wisdom (which all men seek with such great mental longing) is . . . higher than all knowledge and is unknowable and inexpressible by any speech, incomprehensible by any intellect, unmeasurable by any measure . . .

—Nicholas of Cusa, *Idiota de Sapienta*

A wise man has no extensive knowledge. He who has extensive knowledge is not a wise man.

—Lao Tzu, *Tao Te Ching*

Wisdom is an ancient, enigmatic, and intractable notion whose abiding influence in professional practice in general, and in management practice in particular, remains ever elusive. In this chapter, we develop the idea of wisdom as a form of *learned ignorance*—a cultivated humility, meekness of demeanor, and openness of mind that is distinct from the aggressive and relentless pursuit, acquisition, and exploitation of knowledge. Rather than associate wisdom with learning, we argue that it is ironically *unlearning* that is the path toward genuine wisdom and insight. The inability to attain wisdom arises, paradoxically, from a contemporary obsession with knowledge and information. Wisdom is not about having more information or constructing irrefutable propositions. True wisdom exceeds these quantifiable elements. It takes its cue from vagueness and ambiguity. There is something necessarily strange and foreign about wisdom, although not so foreign as to be entirely alien. Wisdom is rarely to be found in formal learning or knowledge. Rather, it "cries out in the streets" in the hurly-burly of everyday goings-on. It begins, as Socrates discovered, with the knowledge of our ignorance.

Learning to Unlearn

In the East, a story is often told of an eminent scholar who was determined to learn about the ancient Tea Ceremony avidly practiced by Zen masters and to show that this was nothing more than an empty, superfluous, and meaningless ritual. Arriving at the residence of the Zen master, the scholar was duly invited in, both host and guest sat cross-legged on a mat, and then the Zen master proceeded to pour tea first into his own teacup and then into the visitor's teacup. The Zen master, a frail man in his early 90s with unsteady hands, continued to fill the visitor's cup even after it was clearly full. The tea began to overspill onto the mat, and the visitor—thinking that his host had difficulty in coordinating his movements because of his advanced age—determined politely to ignore the spillage. More tea continued to be poured, so much so that the overspill now began to spread over the floor. At this point, the visitor, unable to restrain himself any further, exclaimed, "Zen master, stop! Can't you see? No more tea can go into the cup. It is already too full." The Zen master looked at him and said, "You . . . are exactly like this cup of tea. You are already so full of knowledge. How can I fill you with any more knowledge about this Tea Ceremony? Unless you empty the cup of knowledge you already possess, you will not begin to truly appreciate the subtleties and profound lessons contained in this ancient ritual."

This short vignette vividly illustrates how knowledge often gets in the way of genuine insight and how difficult it is for the clever and the learned to attain wisdom. It also elevates the role of *unlearning* in the quest for wisdom. That wisdom is not to be found in books or formal learning but rather in practical experiences is also emphasized by Nicholas of Cusa (1996, pp. 497–503), the 15th-century German cleric, in the following dialogue between a poor layman and a very wealthy orator (scholar) in the Roman Forum:

Layman: I am amazed at your pride because although in perusing countless books you tire yourself with continual reading, you have not yet been brought to a state of humility. . . . True knowledge makes one humble. . . .

Orator: [Oh] poor, utterly unschooled Layman, what is this presumption of yours [that leads] you thus to make light of the study of written learning, without which study no one makes progress?

Layman: [Oh] Great Orator, it is not presumption, but love, that does not allow me to keep silent. . . . The opinion of authority has held you back, so that you are as a horse that by nature is free but that by contrivance is tied with a halter to a stall, where it eats nothing but what is served to it. For your intellect, restricted to the authority of writings, is fed by strange and unnatural food.

Orator: If the nourishment that comes from wisdom is not present in the books of the wise, then where is it present?

Layman: . . . I maintain that no *natural* nourishment is to be found there. For those who first devoted themselves to writing about wisdom did not derive their growth from the nourishment of books, which did not yet exist; rather by means of natural foods they were brought unto the state of being grown men. And by far they excel in wisdom those others who suppose that they have learned from books.

The dialogue eventually ends with the scholar suitably persuaded of the wisdom of the layman:

Orator: You relate such beautiful things. Explain now, I ask, how can I be elevated into some kind of tasting of Eternal Wisdom?

The basic point that seems to be made repeatedly is that knowledge, information, and symbolic representations, rather than help us to grasp pristine reality, often distract and distort our understanding of the latter. Despite the wonderful achievements of modern science and formal knowledge, we remain at a loss to explain the bases for human hope, resilience, bravery, authenticity, happiness, and tragedy. Wisdom eludes us. Despite all of our material achievements, we remain perpetually in want—always seeking that which is bigger, better, newer, faster, and fuller. "Man," wrote the existential humanist Eric Fromm (1976, p. 27), is an "eternal suckling" with a voracious and insatiable appetite. Because we ordinarily think of our lack in terms of a "gap" in knowledge or possessions, our instinctive tendency is to seek to fill this unfillable void at the core of our being. In that very process, we lose our grip on that which is most near and dear to us—the very richness of life itself. The poet T. S. Eliot lamented this loss poignantly in *The Rock*: "Where is the Life we have lost in living? Where is the Wisdom we have lost in knowledge? Where is the Knowledge we have lost in information?" (Eliot, 1934, Chorus 1). Living debases life, knowledge debases wisdom, and information debases knowledge. Rather than lead us on the path toward greater wisdom and fulfillment, more knowledge and possessions actually distances us from what is fundamental to life.

The French psychoanalyst Jacques Lacan maintained that this unfillable existential void is one initiated through our very entry into the symbolic world of language (Lacan, 1977, pp. 20–29). The desire to know is our attempt to recover this primordial loss—to "plug" this emptiness at the very core of our being that is the root of our ignorance and our very condition for knowledge. Knowledge, therefore, lies on a bed of ignorance; to know is also to "owe," to incur a debt to what one does not know. To know that one does not know, as Socrates concluded, is to begin to acknowledge the inherent *owing* in kn*owing*—the ignorance of knowledge. Puzzling on a pronouncement of a priestess at Delphi that he, Socrates, was the wisest of men, Socrates realized that his own preeminence came from his refusal to claim knowledge that he did not have. Socrates was wise because he was acutely aware of his ignorance and of how much it took to confront this ignorance. The literary critic Barbara Johnson echoed this insight when she wrote, "Ignorance, far more than knowledge, is what can never be taken for granted. If I perceive my ignorance as a gap in knowledge instead of an imperative that changes the very nature of what I think I know, then I do not truly experience my ignorance" (Johnson, 1989, p. 16). Only when we become painfully aware that it is *ignorance of our ignorance,* and not a simple gap in knowledge, that prevents profound insights do we then begin to glimpse that illusive realm called wisdom. It is this Socratic idea of a state of heightened awareness of ignorance that is implied by the term *learned ignorance.*

In this final chapter of the volume, we maintain that the substantive concerns of philosophical inquiry—metaphysics, epistemology, logic, ethics, and aesthetics—are essentially metaphors, intermediary vehicles of transport (*metaphorikos*), that carry us toward that which is ultimately unnameable but knowable, in other words, wisdom. True wisdom cannot be attained by an overreliance on these knowledge categories. To grasp the Socratic view of wisdom, we must learn to transcend words, disciplinary boundaries, and substantive knowledge by "purifying" thought and cleansing ourselves of the overwhelming dependence on such conceptual categories. Only then can we attain that state of awareness that Nicholas of Cusa called "learned ignorance." Wisdom-in-practice is exemplified by what we call here *performative extravagance*—a sudden spontaneous outpouring of offerings that produces outstanding achievements that withstand the test of time. Individual and organizational wisdom is exemplified by the internalized capacity to *resist* surface appearances, quantification, and knowledge representations and to rediscover the true *measure of things* (Bohm, 1980, pp. 20–21) so that wise decisions may be made. This is the real challenge for organizational leaders, managers, and policymakers.

Knowledge, Understanding, and Wisdom Through the Ages

Socrates's wisdom—his awareness of the ignorance underlying all forms of knowing—reflects his wider concern with ethical and moral development.

For him, this love of wisdom (*philosophia*) not provide prescriptive doctrines but rather is a way of life characterized by the method of refutation. Living a good life implies always being prepared to cross-examine knowledge claims wherever they are made. Through such persistent inquiry and refutation (dialectic), we realize that what is most valuable above all things are not proofs or possession of facts but rather the personal ethical development arising from putting ideas and activities to a test. For his pupil Plato, however, philosophy ought to be able to say something more about our experiences of the world and its foundations than merely exposing us to constant irony, paradox, and refutation. Socrates occupies a watershed, looking back to an ancient, poetic, and nearly intuitive struggle with meaning while also suggesting ways forward through an advocacy of philosophical dialectic method by which we can expand and enrich human awareness. Plato, frustrated with the former Socrates, took his cue from the latter, suggesting that rather than simply being about individual ethical development, the love of wisdom ought to become a formalized discipline with specific branches: *metaphysics* (the investigation of the ultimate questions of being and existence), *epistemology* (the extent and accrual of human knowledge), *dialectic* (the concern with correct modes of reasoning), *ethics* (the consideration of principles of right and wrong), and *aesthetics* (the appreciation of what stimulates our imagination and senses). These five cognate areas (with dialectic developing into logic) have become the widely accepted frameworks for Western philosophical inquiry and, as exemplified in this volume, the conventional basis for discussing issues such as managerial and organizational wisdom. In this sense, Platonic systematizing concerns have tended to override the Socratic emphasis on the love of wisdom through personal development. Our purpose in this chapter is to reverse the priority.

Whereas Socrates gestured to the acceptance of ignorance as a condition of personal growth and development, Plato tended to emphasize the value of philosophy as the vehicle for fully articulating our human condition—for revealing our rational selves and their foundation in the essential and unchanging furniture of existence. This aspiration for philosophy is played out in Plato's *The Republic* (509–511), where he made a distinction between the *visible* world and the *intelligible* world (Plato, 1875). The visible world is a world of *appearances* and manifest *forms* that reflect, albeit imperfectly, an underlying realm of perfect unchanging forms (e.g., pure justice, goodness, truth, beauty, equality). All reality is derived from this ultimate realm of unchanging forms, resembling it in some way or another and ultimately returning to it. The task of the various branches of philosophy is to take us from our half-formed *opinions* to a proper *knowledge* of relations using methods of dialectic. Through dialectic, we are able to reach the unchanging forms and hence a state of wisdom (*sophia*) in which we become aware of the harmonious unity of all things—the soul, the state, and the universe (Robinson, 1990, p. 15). Whereas Socrates's use of argumentation pushes at limits and limitations, Plato's use of argumentation identifies unshakable foundations. Whereas Socrates advocated *learned ignorance* as the basis of wisdom, Plato advocated systematic inquiry as the route to *sophia*.

Plato's successor, Aristotle, offered a far less stringent view of wisdom. Wisdom is something accrued through living a life informed by the actions of one's personal and social history rather than the degree of perfection of one's ahistorical dialogue with the realm of ultimate forms. Whereas for Plato correct reasoning concerned the use of dialectic to penetrate the intelligible world, Aristotle was more sanguine, accepting that what can be said to be essential about a thing is to be found within that thing itself rather than in its aping a separate transcendent realm. With this focus on things as they are experienced, Aristotle argued that one thing (p) is made distinct from another (not p) by virtue of its basic substance and the links made between this and other substances. Here it is *logic*, as much as metaphysics, that leads to insight, where correct reasoning involves the coherent progression from more general premises to a more particular conclusion (*deduction*) or from specific premises to more general conclusions (*induction*). Through such proper reasoning, knowledge becomes understood as "justified belief" rather than as the more lofty attainment of foundationless foundations implied by the notion of ultimate forms.

Defining correct reasoning as the analysis of how meaning is attained through logical relations afforded Aristotle scope to begin to separate *knowledge* from wisdom. Knowledge concerns true statements about what exists, whereas with the dilution of metaphysical speculation, wisdom is less a concern with the nature of ultimate reality than with the disposition (*hexis*) to determine when specific uses of reason (informed by emotion and logic) are appropriate (when to be resolute and when to be cautious or whose happiness to favor) (Robinson, 1990, p. 19). This practical wisdom, or *phronesis*, consists of the sensitivity, imagination, and perceptiveness that come from, first, having lived and matured sufficiently to understand how people act and, second, the ability to discern which features of any given state of affairs count for more than others (MacIntyre, 1982). Whereas for Plato the wise are all-encompassing, would-be deities in epistemological communion with the metaphysical foundations governing life, for Aristotle they are people intent on acting well by learning which actions are appropriate, when and where, and for what reasons (Clark, 2003).

This pragmatic view paves the way for the gradual rise of an instrumentalized understanding of wisdom exemplified by social realist thinkers like Machiavelli for whom *phronesis* became nothing more than the ability to act and aver from action according to dictates of circumstance (Machiavelli, 1532/1989, pp. 38–39). Wisdom was a tactical activity of organizing oneself and others so as to bring about a more secure and harmonious human condition. So, for example, Machiavelli's (1989) "wise" prince recognized the following:

Injuries are to be done all together, so that, being savored less, they will anger less; benefits are to be conferred little by little, so they will be savored more. And above all, a wise prince lives with his subjects in such a way that no unforeseen event, either for bad or for good, makes him change; because when, in adverse times, emergencies arise, you are too late for harshness, and the good you do does not help you, because it is considered forced and you get for it no thanks whatever. (pp. 38–39)

Here wisdom is being set up almost in contradistinction to virtue. Machiavelli's *Discourses* recognizes the value of republican virtue but also recognizes its being too idealistic for the human stock inhabiting the city states of Renaissance Europe. Wise rulers prefer social realpolitik to the slavish adoption of fixed principles.

Consigning wisdom to a political level meant a more focused concern within the discipline of philosophy for establishing the foundations of knowledge from within a technical epistemology. This increasing emphasis on rigor and formalism described by the term *natural science* culminated with the 18th-century *empiricists,* for whom questions of metaphysics, ethics, and aesthetics have unnecessarily impinged on the proper investigation of human ideas and knowledge. The wider questions of being, beauty, and good judgment are "cut away" from the technical pursuit of truth. Metaphysics, aesthetics, and ethics deal in intractable problems of spirit, taste, and edict, whereas epistemology (and logic) deals in the unalloyed experience of nature using the methods of verification and proof. The evaluative framing of spiritual, imaginative, and moral statements means that they are consigned to the status of intractable value judgments; they become factually insignificant (Grayling, 2004, p. 217). What remains significant is simply our experience of nature—direct. Yet appeals to direct or unmediated experience (what Francis Bacon evocatively called "standing naked like a child before nature") are no guarantee of truthful knowledge claims. The empiricists still need to respond to the criticism that reliance on our senses to yield accurate mental impressions by which ideas might be built is itself empirically unverifiable. We cannot stand outside of our senses to judge their veracity, and so simply relying on sensory experience to ground our knowledge exposes the entire empirical enterprise to skepticism. It is not so easy to dispense with the background values inherent in questions of metaphysics, ethics, and aesthetics.

Modern Notions of Wisdom and Knowledge

Despite the persistence of such skepticism regarding empiricism, it was not until perhaps the writings of Nietzsche that the dominance of this form of empirical knowledge was seriously challenged. For Nietzsche, Western versions of natural science and the triumph of empirical knowledge were, he argued, so intoxicated with a desire for fact and fear-averting logic that they failed to realize their artificiality. Knowledge was imprisoned by its own objectifying epistemology, what Nietzsche called an Apollonian logical order whose rigidity and stiffness served to absolve us of the very thing that made us human, namely *the responsibility of making choices from an awareness of our own historical complicity with the empirical events of which we seek knowledge*. We must "dare" to choose what it is we know and how to act while knowing that there is no ultimate rationality or reality that can justify our choices other than our need to act authentically.

The philosopher Alfred North Whitehead maintained that the impulse toward an objectifying epistemology issues from what he called a "fallacy of misplaced concreteness" (Whitehead, 1926/1985, p. 64)—the tendency to believe that the world was basically a material set of discrete objects and relations and that the pursuit of knowledge was the accurate and formal representation of such through language, concepts, and symbols. For Whitehead, the problem with this *epistemological representationalism* was simple: Its force depended entirely on what was to count as evidence, a question the empiricists had failed to ask themselves. What so exercizes Whitehead is that in the empiricist attempt to expunge metaphysics, ethics, and aesthetics from the search for truth, a new abstracting shibboleth has emerged—the methodological logic of representationalism itself. It is only when people learned to resist such abstraction and to realize the importance of asserting themselves *against* these epistemological claims (e.g., truths, principles, controls, musts, dogmas) that the fallacy became recognized as such.

Emphasizing our complicity with and responsibility for the creation of knowledge meant that Nietzsche and Whitehead were beginning to revisit the capacity for *phronetic* wisdom because of its inherent acceptance that, unlike empirical knowledge and logical thought, contradiction was not a signal of defeat but rather the very lifeblood of human life (Whitehead, 1926/1985, p. 279). Both Nietzsche and Whitehead emphasized a *phronesis* characterized by personal virtue (Greco, 2004), but where Nietzsche emphasized instinctive "Dionysian" virtues of courage and creative will, Whitehead was less trenchant and advocated the need for both boldness *and* humility. For both of them, however, it is by recognizing the paucity of logical knowledge produced by reason alone that we can begin to grow wise once more. Wisdom involves our abandoning a priori visions of perfection in favor of our own direct creative evolution. Hence, we arrive back at Socrates, but with a twist (as is embodied in Nietzsche's own ambivalent relationship with Socrates's work). Where Socrates's wisdom lay with his defiant insistence that knowledge carries its own risks if unaccompanied by awareness of one's own ignorance, Nietzsche and Whitehead suggested that wisdom is something more than simply a recognition of the inevitable limits of knowledge; rather, it is an ability to bring knowledge into harmonious balance with instinct, emotion, and unconscious will as the sources of our personal creativity and growth.

The American philosopher William James termed this wisdom a metaphysics of last things rather than of first things—an acceptance that *what exists is simply what we experience as the inherently ambiguous and unfurling force of life* (James, 1907, pp. 45–55). For James, Whitehead, and Nietzsche, wisdom comes from recognizing how we as individuals are complicit with each and every event in our lives, recognizing how authentic being is in fact a state of *everyday becoming* without end, and recognizing that our own uniqueness as persons comes from lending experience the hue of personal involvement (Ansell-Pearson, 1999, pp. 127–128). With characteristic brio, Nietzsche called this sense of personal involvement—and hence responsibility—a "defiance of oneself."

Such a view of wisdom as direct personal involvement in fashioning a life refines Sternberg's (1990, p. 153) distinction between wisdom, intelligence, and creativity.

Sternberg argued that if we assume that existing knowledge acts as a constraint on what we say and do, then the intelligent person works to exploit the constraints to the fullest extent, the creative person wishes to break free from the constraints and create alternatives, and the wise person seeks to understand the nature of the constraints. What distinguishes the wise from the intelligent and the simply intuitively creative is the awareness that our constraints of knowledge are human constraints and, hence, ours to change. The wise recognize that it is we who give value to our lives because it is we who divide the world into things, relations, and meanings, and we can do so differently (Searle, 2005). So at its most basic level, wisdom is an awareness of how people, often unwittingly, create and re-create the constraints of knowledge—how people often ignore or avoid the responsibilities of power associated with this complicity with knowledge, masked as it is by an intellectualizing logic of neutrality and objectivity.

This avoidance of taking responsibility for one's actions is well exemplified when organizational leaders, for example, look to justify their actions by appealing to the "demands of the market," or to the logic of cost calculus, as though they themselves were acting outside of these irrefutable facts. From Nietzsche's perspective, this tendency to appeal to "external" reality is both idle and weak—a refusal to take personal responsibility for actions. To be wise involves submitting to and wrestling with reality in all its intended and unintended interdependencies without regret and with a sense of personal responsibility. Wise people embrace doubt, ambiguities, consequences, and experiences—the *effects of decisions* that they need to live with and not just the decisions themselves. Within this "earthy" metaphysics, the concerns of wisdom turn from a question of adding to or expanding knowledge to one of being in close intimacy with our lived experiences. It is to appreciate that an apparent lack of explicit formal knowledge or external justification is not necessarily a situation to be avoided or associated with impotence. Rather, it is to accept that intellectual naïveté and learned ignorance are the very conditions of possibility for an authentic existence.

Wisdom as Learned Ignorance:
A View From the East

> *The idea of "being" is the Archimedean point of Western thought. . . . The whole tradition of Western civilization [has] turned around this point. All is different in Eastern thought. . . . The central notion from which Oriental . . . belief as well as philosophical thought have been developed is the idea of "nothingness."*
>
> —(Takeuchi, 1959, p. 292)

Something akin to this awareness of the virtue of naïveté and ignorance has existed in the East since time immemorial, and comparisons with Western views have occupied some of the most outstanding East–West scholars of our time (Chang, 1963; Graham, 1989; Needham, 1962; Nishitani, 1982). The Sinologist Joseph Needham, for instance, argued that whereas for the dominant Western worldview "what mattered was an ideal world of static form which remained when the world of crude reality was dissolved away," for the Chinese "the real world was dynamic and ultimate, an organism made of an infinity of organisms, a rhythm harmonizing an infinity of lesser rhythms" (Needham, 1962, p. 292). The tendency to keep faith with language, logic, and reason, and hence to linguistically reduce the hurly-burly of life experiences to foundational book categories, is what we have seen characterizes the dominant Western epistemological attitude exemplified by the scholar in Nicholas of Cusa's (1996) dialogue earlier. Like the layman, however, Eastern thought has always been skeptical or suspicious of the capacity of rational analysis in particular, and of language in general, to convey the essence of the human condition. As the Sinologist A. C. Graham observed in his study of Chinese thought and practice, "Reason is for questions of means; for your ends in life listen to aphorism, examples, parable, and poetry" (Graham, 1989, p. 7). This deep suspicion of logic, language, and formal knowledge claims in important matters of life is well captured in the work of the contemporary Japanese philosopher Keiji Nishitani, who observed, "There is a deep-seated awareness of the incompetence of utterance as the mode of man's being" in Eastern thought (Nishitani, 1982, p. 31). For the Eastern mind, ultimate reality cannot be captured or represented linguistically; it is essentially "nameless" or "unnameable" and can be alluded to obliquely only through paradoxical utterances. Thus, the very first lines of the *Tao Te Ching*, arguably the most influential ancient Chinese text, read, "The Tao that can be named is not the eternal *Tao*, the name that can be named is not the eternal name" (cited in Chan, 1963, p. 139). For this reason, communication of thought in the East is often indirect, suggestive, and symbolic; words are used loosely and treated as mere pointers to what lies beyond the realms of intellection. As the Buddhist monk Kao-seng Chuan put it, "Symbols are to express ideas. When ideas have been understood, symbols should be forgotten. Words are to interpret thoughts. When thoughts have been absorbed, words stop. . . . Only those who can take the fish and forget the net are worthy to seek the truth" (cited in Chang, 1963, p. 43).

In matters of deep comprehension, one must be able to grasp the absolute not through words or language but rather by an unmediated act of pure intuition. The idealist philosopher Georg Hegel noted that for the Chinese this absolute "origin of things is nothingness, emptiness, the altogether undetermined, the abstract universal, and this is also called *Tao*" (Hegel, 1825/1955, Vol. 1, p. 125). What unites and underpins the forms of knowledge in Western thinking is the belief in the primacy of "being"—form, substance, essence, fullness, completeness, coherence, and finality. For the East, however, it is *nothingness, emptiness, and the undetermined that are the fecund progenerative origin—the source of potentiality for all things*. Herein lies the fundamental difference between the East and the modern West and, hence, the differently nuanced appreciation of what wisdom entails.

Eastern philosophies advocate the negation and "removal of the immediate and overpowering face of reality," considering this to be "a necessary condition for what is really real to appear" (van Bragt, 1982, pp. xxv–xxvi). Whereas the West emphasizes "filling in" the "gaps," whether they be the cup of knowledge, the empty pages of a book, the blank spaces on a canvas (in the case of painting), the aural void created by silence, the relations between people, or the unwieldy chaos residing between or surrounding instructions, the East is incessantly preoccupied with "emptying out" thought and purifying experience; the search for wisdom is the search for *absolute nothingness*— that ultimate reality unmediated by the intellect. The East seeks to attain what the Japanese industrialist Konosuke Matsushita called a *sunao* mind:

> A person with this mind looks at things as they are at that moment and colors them with no special bias, emotionalism, or preconception. . . . He is open to experience them as they are. . . . Zen training, with its austere life-style and stress on meditation, seeks to free the mind from material concerns and personal prejudices, and in this sense the Zen mind bears a certain resemblance to the *sunao* mind. (Matsushita, 1978, pp. 63–65)

The Japanese term *sunao*, properly translated, means simplicity, humility, and docility in the face of truth; it is a disciplined objectivity that is radically different from the objectivist epistemology of empiricism.

James (1912/1996) attempted to formulate just such a methodological principle in his program of *radical empiricism*, where he insisted on the foundational importance of "pure experience" as the cornerstone of his philosophy. What Zen Buddhism strives toward and what Matsushita called a *sunao* mind, James called "pure experience"—that aboriginal concrete flow of sensations appearing in all its "much-at-onceness." Similarly, the Victorian art critic John Ruskin coined the phrase "innocence of the eye" (Ruskin, 1927, Vol. 4, p. 27) to refer to the attainment of this pure preconceptual apprehension of phenomena (Chia, 2003). Yet, for the most part, the dominant tendency in the contemporary West remains to "fill in" and "complete" through learning rather than to "empty out" or unlearn. For the East, however, *absolute nothingness* is the final ground out of which issues something and nothing, existence and essence. It is the "lining of the kimono, known only by the very way in which the kimono hangs and holds its shape. One sees the lining by not seeing it. . . . This is the form of the formless" (Carter, 1990, p. 98).

The common tenet uniting what we might loosely call the "East," therefore, is an unequivocal rejection of the competency of logic, language, and utterance for expressing the dominant mode of man's being. For this reason, all arenas of life in the East, including the arts, sports, pastimes, and business, are viewed as avenues for purifying thought and for attaining that ultimate experience of reality. As the Zen master D. T. Suzuki observed,

> One of the most significant features we notice in the arts as they are studied in Japan, and probably also all other Far Eastern countries, is that they are not intended for utilitarian purposes only or pure aesthetic enjoyment, but are meant to train the mind . . . to bring it into contact with the ultimate reality. (cited in Herrigel, 1953/1985, p. 5)

The rigorous, disciplined, and nearly obsessive perfecting of action in all aspects of artistic performance, whether it be calligraphy, martial arts, flower arrangement, origami, the tea pouring ceremony, or indeed even practical activities such as sports and business (e.g., the Japanese and Koreans are obsessed with golf even though most of their actual golfing takes place at driving ranges and hardly ever on golf courses!), is viewed as a potential avenue that leads to attainment of that ever-elusive singular moment of pure spontaneous and flawless action. In archery, for example, it is that moment of perfection when "bow, arrow, goal, and ego all melt into one another, so that I can no longer separate them. And even the need to separate has gone. For, as soon as I take the bow and shoot, everything becomes so clear and straightforward and so ridiculously simple" (Herrigel, 1953/1985, p. 86). This pure and spontaneous unfolding of action describes that magical moment when great works of art, flawless performances, and accomplishments—as well as timeless events—take place, when all mediation of words and knowledge is rendered irrelevant, and when the immersion of the self into a seamless flow of action is all there is (Csikszentmihalyi, 1997). The existential urge to grasp this ultimate "form of the formless and hear the sound of the soundless" (Shimomura, 1960, p. 211) lies at the heart of all Eastern culture.

In summary, whereas the dominant Western representationalist worldview seeks to attain the ultimate fullness of "form," "being," "substance," "presence," "perfection," "mastery," "distinctiveness," and "control," and hence to orient itself toward learning and mastery of circumstance, Chinese thought in particular, and Eastern thought in general, finds solace in absolute emptiness, stillness, silence, nothingness, undifferentiatedness, and formlessness. In short, the importance of "unlearning" and "emptying out" traditionally have been associated with insight and wisdom in the East since time immemorial.

Wisdom and Performative Extravagance in Organizations

Much of this talk of absolute nothingness, emptiness, unlearning, and Zen-like naïveté might be viewed somewhat askance by the world of business in which managerial and organizational performance is comprehended in familiar terms such as assets, profits, and increased shareholder value and is evaluated by market judgments on the basis of economic exchange and deliberate rational calculation. According to this dominant "free market" scheme of things, goods and services are produced with a view to achieving a maximum exchange value that is necessarily determined by its reception in the market. The market acts as arbiter and ensures a kind of "allocative efficiency" for the product or service being provided. Such a *restricted* conception of economic exchange, however, does not exhaust the possibilities for explaining the underlying motivation behind outstanding individual and organizational performances. It overlooks a deeper and more fundamental human urge driving performative action—the need for self-transformation and self-realization. An organizationally "wise" viewpoint appreciates the existence of another more fundamental logic of commerce at work—an "X-efficiency" (Wada, 1997) or "immaculate commerce" (Derrida, 1981, p. 9) that accounts for the genuine achievements and outstanding breakthroughs taking place within organizational contexts. Such spontaneous and uncalculated outpourings of offerings that we are occasionally privileged to witness and savor surprise and astound us, filling us with pleasurable experiences.

In art, drama, musical performances, and even sports and business, for instance, there is at times an inexplicable level of productivity and performance attained that goes far beyond that justifiable by any form of restricted economic explanation in that what is actually given, displayed, or offered far exceeds what is anticipated, expected, or even hoped for. These are experiences, events, and performances that literally take our breath away. Such rare moments of *performative extravagance* (what we more trivially in common parlance call "delighting the customer")—truly pathbreaking spectacular displays—are what we really mean by the now overused rhetoric of "excellence." In sports, it may come in the form of a world record–breaking Bob Beamon long jump, a miraculous Tiger Woods escape shot, or an audacious goal attempt by the Brazilian soccer-playing genius Ronaldinho. In art and music, it produces those masterpieces to which we return again and again in awe and appreciation. In business, we talk about the legendary "miraculous" corporate turnarounds achieved against overwhelming odds, those new product innovations in which dreams and ideas predominate and become nearly an obsession rather than a commercial venture, inspired performances by otherwise "mediocre employees," and the critical breakthroughs achieved in terms of novel forms of engagement. All of these exemplify what we mean by personally developing wisdom in practice—a performative extravagance that reflects the continual and relentless search for perfection in action *for its own sake*.

One area in which this performative extravagance is readily displayed is genuine entrepreneurial ventures where the primary object of entrepreneurial activity is not so much to make a profit as it is to disclose new possibilities and transform our lifeworlds in some significant way (Spinosa, Flores, & Dreyfus, 1997, p. 51). The entrepreneur adopts a "strange poise" (Lichtenberg, 1800/2000, p. D30) offering unconditionally and without any anticipation of reward or return some novel insight, service, or implement that radically reconfigures settled patterns of social activity or lifestyle. This is the argument made by the political economist George Gilder, who maintained that, contrary to commonly held views, contemporary capitalism is no less animated by the spirit of the "gift" than are the primitive tribes studied by Marcel Mauss. For Gilder, the capitalistic enterprise is a more elaborate form of *potlatch*—the primitive practice of giving *extravagantly* without the utilitarian expectation of exact, materially equivalent return. The expectation is open-ended in that the would-be entrepreneur needs to invest in and supply goods and services without ever being sure whether he or she will achieve any adequate return for the effort. Here the circulation of exchange is governed less by an invisible hand than by what Mauss called a generous and conspicuous hand of demonstration where reciprocity is wrapped within a complex system of symbolic status and deferred expectations and where what is traded is not simply goods and services but also identities, trust, and relationships (Mauss, 1950/2002, p. 93). Whereas Mauss studied tribes and historical texts (including the Vedic fragments of the Brahmins with their "Eastern" eschewal of simple egoism), Gilder studied entrepreneurs, arguing, "The unending offerings of entrepreneurs, investing jobs, accumulating inventories—all long before any return is received, all without any assurance that the enterprise will not fail—constitute a pattern of giving that *dwarfs in extent and in essential generosity any primitive rite of exchange*" (Gilder, 1981, p. 30, italics added). It is precisely because capitalism is grounded in this irrational attitude of "giving without prior assurance," and of giving more than is expected by the extensive knowledge of market-based exchange, that it can be said to be truly wealth creating and, hence, invaluable to the commonwealth.

This idea of performative extravagance more aptly describes how the inventor James Dyson designed the bagless vacuum cleaner (Muranka &

Rootes, 1996). Frustrated by the bag clogging in his own traditional vacuum cleaner, his response was not to get a new bag, or to search for a replacement, but rather to consider possible alternatives to the fundamental design. He immersed himself for 5 years not only with more than 5,000 prototypes but also with the practices of manufacturing and house-cleaning (e.g., sensory relationships [sight, touch, and sound] with floor care tools). Moreover, he learned from, and was inspired by, other designs and designers who constantly questioned things—whose disposition and orientation meant that they were always looking to relate themselves to objects differently. (Examples include Alex Moulton's bicycle, which pioneered using small wheels [quick acceleration] and a cruciform frame [lighter and less obtrusive], and Buckminster Fuller's geodesic domes, which were built as alternate forms of shelter using light, readily available material held in tension rather than depleting heavy materials held under compression.) What inspired these alternate designs was the ability to *unlearn* standard constraints—to become naive and *ignorant of orthodoxy* and so to redesign the fundamentals of what is considered a typical bike, building, or (in Dyson's case) vacuum cleaner. The machine Dyson finally developed still cleaned floors, but it also became an aesthetic object (various models are housed in places such as the San Francisco Museum of Modern Art and the Pompidou Centre in Paris) and one that delivered health benefits (the suction system filtered microparticles linked to respiratory illnesses such as asthma). It was no longer simply about keeping a house spick-and-span. The final designed output exceeded its pure functional role because it exemplified an *extravagant* outpouring of effort—a dogged expression at pushing at the bounds of what is possible.

Explaining the underlying motivation for this spontaneous outpouring of performative extravagance requires a different logical take from that of the restricted economics of exchange. Derrida (1981) argued that all such outstanding achievements constitute a "pure productivity of the inexchangeable" (p. 9). They issue from a nearly obsessive compulsion to seek that ultimate "formless" form unreached and unreachable by the restricted logic of economic calculation. Like the relentless pursuit of the art of archery, calligraphy, tea making, or origami, genuine entrepreneurial endeavors pursue that Quixotic "impossible dream" for absolute perfection. Such a Quixotic imperative was well understood by Ruskin (1927), who put it forcefully and without compromise:

> The first and absolute condition of the thing's ever becoming saleable is, that we shall make it without wanting to sell it; nay, rather with a determination not to sell it at any price, if once we get hold of it. Try making your Art popular, cheap—a fair article for your foreign trade; and the foreign market will always show something better. But make it only to please yourselves, and ever be resolved that you won't let

anybody else have it; and forthwith you will find everybody else wants it. . . . Art has only been produced by nations who rejoiced in it; fed themselves with it, as if it were bread; basked in it, as if it were sunshine; shouted at the sight of it; danced with the delight of it; quarrelled for it; fought for it; starved for it; did, in fact precisely the opposite with it of what we want to do with it. (Vol. 16, p. 184)

In other words, paradoxically, the more we act in terms of anticipated outcomes according to what James March called a "consequentialist theology" (March, 1996), the more likely we are to produce conformity and mediocrity in performance. The more we crave public acceptance, recognition, and material achievement, the less we are able to produce great works that withstand the test of time. This is the paradox of performance.

This idea of a performative extravagance uncorrupted by exchange valuations constitutes a wisdom-of-practice that remains prevalent in many outstanding Western corporations whose reputations and brands reflect their uncompromising search for achieving perfection in their respective sectors. They ooze quality, distinction, and style. This very same attitude persists in the traditional East, and it was this awareness that prompted Matsushita to insist on the importance of attaining that *sunao* mind in business matters. The interminable search for perfection provides the existential impetus for ceaseless innovation, entrepreneurialism, and the attitude of "continuous improvement" (*kaizen*, which actually means relentless *self-criticism*) with which the Japanese are often credited. This attitude is well exemplified by Sony Corporation, one of the world's most successful companies with worldwide sales in excess of U.S. $64 billion; more important, Sony is globally admired for its record of creativity and innovation. Like those values espoused by Matsushita, who insisted that providing a valuable public service (not making a profit) is the foundational aim of a business, Sony adopts a *potlatch* attitude toward product innovation—as a spontaneous "gift" or offering to the public that cannot be predetermined in terms of its reception in the market. It is not a rational target to which a company can aspire. What is emphasized is the need for offering "lavishly"—for a certain kind of extravagance toward the public. For Sony, as Paul Kunkel observed in *Digital Dreams* (Kunkel, 2000), innovation is the first nonnegotiable goal, with the second being to lead and never follow. Sony's strategy has always been to stay one step ahead of the public's imagination. The greatest successes, such as the Walkman, have come from products for which there was no initially proven demand. This uncompromising attitude echoes Ruskin's insistence on "selfishly" seeking perfection regardless of popular public opinion. This is what helps to account for the remarkable achievements of Sony over the years—pocket radios, Sony Betamax, the Trinitron, the Walkman, and the Mavica camera, to name just a few. Yet underpinning all of this is the importance of *ignorance of orthodoxy* and the unlearning necessarily associated with it. We return once again to the profound notion of wisdom as *learned ignorance*—a deeply sensitized, yet intellectually naive and open-minded, state of being.

Practical Implications:
On Not Eating the Menu

The Tao that can be named is not *the TAO.*

—Lao Tzu, *Tao Te Ching*

In the world of business, the busy management practitioner is bombarded with catchwords, management fads, and the jargon of business academics— just-in-time, business process reengineering, best practice, benchmarking, balanced scorecards, intellectual harvesting, knowledge mapping, virtual teams, leveraging, supply chains, and the like. These serve only to mesmerize the "humble" lay practitioner who is preoccupied primarily with delivering a quality product or service, a reasonable return on investment, and the security of jobs for his or her employees. There is an insidious process in operation in which more and more catchwords and glib phrases (what the postmodernists call endless "regimes of signifiers") come to dominate management discourse and to colonize thought processes, so much so that it becomes nearly impossible to distinguish between what is real and what is fleeting imagery or illusion. To recall one of Rene Magritte's surrealist provocations, we forget to recognize the difference between a pipe and an image of a pipe. Hence, today we all are more prone to "eat the menu" rather than the dish and to "mistake the map for the territory," making our decisions on the basis of circulating opinions, sound bites, and "authoritative" representations rather than on assiduously immersing ourselves and dwelling in the totality of the experience itself. In a telling critique of this modern situation of images and impressions, Mitroff and Bennis (1993) wrote some years ago of what they called the "Unreality Industry" and what it was doing to our modern lives. Nor is the problem simply restricted to these management fads and fashion and business-speak that often overwhelm the lay practitioner. The root problem remains the "fallacy of misplaced concreteness"—that overwhelming modern tendency to mistake abstract representation for concrete reality. In the contemporary global situation of geographical dispersion, cultural diversity, Internet communication, and decontextualized information sharing, this reliance on representations of reality for decisional purposes is even more pervasive and acute in organizations. More and more, abstract representations—e-mails, reports, computer-generated statistics, remote-monitoring processes, performance indicators, charts, and trend analyses—provide the essential basis for important decision making. Swamped with such informational overload, invaded by the jargon of business-speak, piled with analyses upon analyses, advised by advisers who are increasingly concerned with protecting themselves against the consequences of their own advice and who are often culturally unaware of local customs, and pressured by shareholders and other influential constituencies, it is hard for the organizational leader not to adopt such abstracted and opinionated responses to emerging problem situations.

If it becomes nearly impossible to sort out facts from opinions, and if multiple perspectives are all that we have, how can organizational leaders be confident of the "rightness" of their decisions? The answer may perhaps lie in striving to attain that *sunao* mind—to penetrate these representational abstractions and achieve that pristine *seeing* that apprehends the world without the need for *thematizing* it. This "pure seeing" is a cultivated capacity to simply bear mute witness to happenings in the pristine world in all its "blooming, buzzing confusion," soaking in happenings without the "haste of wanting to act." Possession of this "innocence of the eye" entails the long and arduous cultivation of a deep sensitivity and empathetic appreciation of the totality of a phenomenon in all its interrelated complexity. This is what then allows long-reaching quality decisions to be made. The importance of this pure seeing is well encapsulated in Ruskin's (1860/1985) prophetic words that captured the imagination of a young Mahatma Gandhi and inspired him in his quest for humanity: "Hundreds of people can talk for one who can think, but thousands can think for one who can see. . . . To see clearly is poetry, prophecy, and religion" (p. 12).

What are the implications of this importance of pure seeing for organizational leadership in a world awash with representational distractions? For one, it demands of organizational leaders the constant need to be genuinely immersed and "in touch" with the mundane practical goings-on within their own organizational ranks. Given the enormous demand for attention on the part of organizational leaders, it is easy to be seduced by impressive statistics, glossy reports, media coverage, pie charts, and other forms of representational abstractions. The shock comes when organizational leaders begin to immerse themselves in the "underbelly" of everyday organizational life—in trying to understand what Goffee and Jones (2004) called the importance of a relational nonhierarchical *engagement* with others. In Britain recently, the British Broadcasting Corporation (BBC) ran a very successful documentary program titled *Back to the Shop Floor*. In this program, chief executive officers (CEOs) of large organizations were invited to spend a week working alongside their own employees. For example, the chairman of a hotel chain spent a week working as a bellhop, alongside the chambermaid, and as a waiter. In nearly all instances, the shock and disbelief of what went on within their own organizations, contrary to the representations fed to them by their reports, forced a radical rethinking of their organizational policies. They were confronted with *ignorance of their ignorance*. In nearly all of the cases, dramatic policy changes were initiated once these CEOs returned to their boardrooms after the trauma of their "hands-on" experience. If there is one simple message, what the management guru Tom Peters once advocated—"management by wandering around" (MBWA)—remains even more urgent today. Only by wandering around, with intellectual naïveté and *learned ignorance,* can organizational leaders truly *see* for themselves what their priorities are or ought to be in decisional terms. It is this seeing more clearly that equates with what Jim Collins called the seed of Level 5 leadership—the ability to subjugate the ego to the totality of the organization, that is, to recognize the vital importance of humility in transforming a company from good to great (Collins, 2005). Leadership is not just about resolve, confidence, and clear vision brought about through knowledge; it is also about having the calm modesty to recognize the limits of one's own knowledge and, from such learned ignorance, to channel the endeavor for the enduring achievement of the organization as a whole.

Conclusion

We have argued that wisdom is best attained in practice and not in book learning—as a form of *learned ignorance,* where unlearning takes priority over learning and where "purifying" and "weaning" ourselves off of codified knowledge and symbolic representations is a vital step toward genuine enlightened practice and performance. Socrates never wrote, as some have rightly observed, yet he remains a powerful invisible force in our modern consciousness. Socrates's acknowledgment of his ignorance paradoxically reveals a profound wisdom. Such subliminal understanding, and consequently suspicion of formal book learning, creates a deep tension and paradox for a "handbook" such as this that purports to provide valuable insights into organizational and managerial wisdom. More specifically, it creates an internal contradiction regarding the status of the claims about wisdom made here in this chapter! Like the paradox of the Cretan liar, here we are writing in book form about wisdom when what we claim is that wisdom is to be found not in learned books such as this but rather in practice in the hurly-burly of life. What is to be made of this tension of opposites that is well encapsulated in the *written* text of the *Tao Te Ching:* "He who knows does not speak; he who speaks does not know" (cited in Chan, 1963, p. 166)? The answer might be to take words in general, and written words in particular, more lightly—to treat explanations, theories, and concepts not as strong truth-telling claims but rather as usable but disposable notions to be thrown away once they have outworn their use, much like the philosopher Ludwig Wittgenstein's ladder. In his earlier writings, Wittgenstein attempted to articulate and defend a picture theory of truth (i.e., epistemological representationalism), but he soon came to realize the patent impossibility of justifying just such a claim. He therefore suggested that we consider such theoretical attempts as "ladders" that we use to get us up to a higher level of understanding, after which we could discard them because we no longer need them. In so doing, we begin to loosen the hold that representationalism has on us; we begin to question theories, concepts, and categories not in terms of their method or robustness but rather in terms of our reliance on theories per se as the only way of understanding our experiences. That way, we can take the fish, throw away the net, and move on. The problem is not that theories, concepts, and ideas are themselves problematic per se; rather, the problem is our tendency to cling to them rigidly and uncritically. When we begin to realize that wisdom is that elusive fish and not the net/work of words/writings/theories we rely on, we become more willing to *unlearn* and to *relearn* and to realize that this process is an interminable one—yet one that sets us on the path to wisdom. We are then more prepared to embrace ignorance as an ally than as a foe to be defeated. This is something that comes more instinctively to the untutored and "unschooled" layman.

Attaining this wisdom-in-practice is what enables entrepreneurs, designers, and business leaders to offer the kind of *performative extravagance* that opens up new avenues for self-expression, thereby adding real value and richness to our lives. Entrepreneurs and astute organizational leaders are often acutely aware of the limits and constraints of representational knowledge, and it is this deep awareness of an inherent ambiguity—an emptiness—that prompts the entrepreneur or organizational leader to look to disclosing new relations with others and things. Without this sense of ambiguity there is no doubt, and without doubt there is no willingness to unlearn and, hence, no capacity for learning. To differentiate wisdom from knowledge, understanding, or vision is to recognize it as that form of human awareness to which the wise are particularly attuned—how indecisiveness can arise from within established patterns of meaning, how different meanings can arise from similar statements or states of affairs, and how efforts at establishing certainty in meaning are precariously legitimized. Whereas knowledge deals in material finitude and belief in immaterial infinity, wisdom occupies what we might call the fertile hinterland between spirit and matter, mind and body, and heaven and Earth. It slips easily between them, retaining that "strange poise"—an echo, a reminder of a basic wonder/wander that drives human endeavors and that itself can be lost in the habitual urge to intellectually define performance in terms of known goals. What we suggest is that without wisdom we end up simply with tallies and scores and little appreciation for the struggles, the creativity, the meaning, and the sheer human endeavors that have brought about our current worldly possibilities.

References

Ansell-Pearson, K. (1999). *Germinal life*. London: Routledge.

Bohm, D. (1980). *Wholeness and the implicate order*. London: Routledge & Kegan Paul.

Carter, R. E. (1990). *The nothingness beyond God.* New York: Paragon House.

Chan, W. T. (1963). *A source book of Chinese philosophy.* Princeton, NJ: Princeton University Press.

Chang, C. Y. (1963). *Creativity and Taoism.* New York: Harper & Row.

Chia, R. (2003). From knowledge-creation to the perfecting of action: Tao, Basho, and pure experience as the ultimate ground of knowing. *Human Relations, 56,* 953–981.

Clark, S. (2003). The wisdom of Aristotle. *Mind, 112,* 777–780.

Collins, J. (2005). Level 5 leadership: The triumph of humility and fierce resolve. *Harvard Business Review, 83*(7), 136–146.

Csikszentmihalyi, M. (1997). *Finding flow: The psychology of engagement with everyday life.* New York: Basic Books.

Derrida, J. (1981). Economimesis. *Diacritics, 11,* 3–25.

Eliot, T. S. (1934). *The rock: A pageant play.* London: Faber & Faber.

Gilder, G. (1981). *Wealth and poverty.* New York: Bantam Books.

Goffee, R., & Jones, G. (2004). What makes a leader? *Business Strategy Review, 15*(2), 46–50.

Graham, A. C. (1989). *Disputers of the Tao.* La Salle, IL: Open Court.

Grayling, A. (2004). *An introduction to philosophical logic* (3rd ed.). Oxford, UK: Blackwell.

Greco, J. (2004). Virtue epistemology. In E. N. Zalta (Ed.), *The Stanford encyclopedia of philosophy* [Online]. Available: http://plato.stanford.edu/archives/win2004/entries/epistemology-virtue

Hegel, G. W. F. (1955). *Lectures on the history of philosophy* (E. S. Haldane, Trans.). London: Routledge and Kegan Paul. (Original work published 1825)

Herrigel, E. (1985). *Zen in the art of archery.* London: Arkana. (Original work published 1953)

James, W. (1907). *What is pragmatism?* London: Longman, Green.

James, W. (1996). *Essays in radical empiricism.* Lincoln: University of Nebraska Press. (Original work published 1912)

Johnson, B. (1989). *A world of difference.* Baltimore, MD: Johns Hopkins University Press.

Kunkel, P. (2000). *Digital dreams: The work of the Sony Design Centre.* New York: Universe.

Lacan, J. (1977). *The four fundamental concepts of psycho-analysis* (A. Sheridan, Trans.). New York: Penguin Books.

Lichtenberg, G. (2000). *The waste books* (R. Hollingdale, Trans.). New York: New York Review of Books. (Original work published 1800)

Machiavelli, N. (1989). *The prince.* In A. Gilbert (Ed. & Trans.), *Machiavelli: The chief works and others.* Durham, NC: Duke University Press. (Original work published 1532)

MacIntyre, A. (1982). *After virtue.* London: Duckworth.

March, J. (1996, June). A scholar's quest. *Stanford Business School Magazine,* pp. 11–13.

Matsushita, K. (1978). *My management philosophy* (National Productivity Board, Singapore, Trans.). Tokyo: PHP Institute.

Mauss, M. (2002). *The gift.* London: Routledge. (Original work published 1950)

Mitroff, I. I., & Bennis, W. (1993). *The unreality industry: The deliberate manufacture of falsehood and what it is doing to our lives.* New York: Oxford University Press.

Muranka, T., & Rootes, N. (1996). *Doing a Dyson*. Malmsbury, UK: Dyson Appliances.

Needham, J. (1962). *Science and civilisation in China* (Vol. 2). Cambridge, UK: Cambridge University Press.

Nicholas of Cusa. (1996). *Idiota de sapienta* (The layman on wisdom and knowledge) (J. Hopkins, Trans.). Minneapolis, MN: Arthur J. Banning.

Nishitani, K. (1982). *Religion and nothingness* (J. Van Bragt, Trans.). Berkeley: University of California Press.

Plato. (1875). *The dialogues of Plato* (Vols. 1–5, B. Jowett, Trans.). Oxford, UK: Clarendon.

Robinson, D. (1990). Wisdom through the ages. In R. Sternberg (Ed.), *Wisdom: Its nature, origins, and development* (pp. 12–24). Cambridge, UK: Cambridge University Press.

Ruskin, J. (1927). *The complete works*. London: Nicholson & Weidenfeld.

Ruskin, J. (1985). *Unto This Last and other writings*. London: Penguin. (Original work published 1860)

Searle, J. (2005). What is an institution? *Journal of Institutional Economics, 1*(1), 1–22.

Shimomura, T. (1960). Nishida. In *Nishida: A study of good*. Tokyo: Japanese Government Printing Press.

Spinosa, C., Flores, F., & Dreyfus, H. (1997). *Disclosing new worlds: Entrepreneurship, democratic action, and the cultivation of solidarity*. Cambridge: MIT Press.

Sternberg, R. (1990). Wisdom: Relations to intelligence and creativity. In R. Sternberg (Ed.), *Wisdom: Its nature, origins, and development* (pp. 142–159). Cambridge, UK: Cambridge University Press.

Takeuchi, Y. (1959). Buddhism and existentialism: The dialogue between Oriental and Occidental thought. In W. Leibrecht (Ed.), *Religion and culture: Essays in honor of Paul Tillich* (pp. 291–318). New York: Harper.

Van Bragt, J. (1982). Translator's introduction. In K. Nishitani, *Religion and nothingness* (J. Van Bragt, Trans.). Berkeley: University of California Press.

Wada, S. (1997, April). Paternalism as the major corporate culture and stratification principle in Japanese society. *Time and Value*.

Whitehead, A. N. (1985). *Science and the modern world*. London: Free Association Books. (Original work published 1926)

Name Index _____

Subject Index _____

About the Editors _____

Eric H. Kessler is Professor of Management and Founding Director of the Lubin Leaders and Scholars Program at Pace University. He is also a past president of the Eastern Academy of Management where he developed a conference themed around organizational wisdom and launched what has become an ongoing initiative to better apply management theory to business practice. He serves, or has served, on several editorial boards and as the guest editor for a number of professional journals as well as on review panels with the U.S. National Security Education Program. He is widely published in leading academic and technical journals and professional book series in areas related to decision making, innovation, organization, and leadership. He has won numerous outstanding research awards, and is the author or editor of several books, including *Cultural Mythology and Leadership* (in press). He is a member of Phi Beta Kappa has been inducted into national and international honor societies in business, economics, forensics, and psychology. His professional travels have taken him across the Americas, Europe, Australia, Asia, and Africa. He instructs courses on the doctoral, master's, and bachelor's levels; has led several international field studies; and has worked as an executive educator, policy analyst, and business consultant for public and private organizations. He is an avid reader of history and philosophy, a sports and puzzle junkie, and the spinner of many a bad pun. He lives with his best friend/wife, two terrific sons, and faithful Black Labrador.

James R. Bailey is Tucker Professorial Fellow of Leadership and Director of Executive Development Programs at the George Washington University School of Business (GWSB) and is a fellow in the Center for Management Development at the London Business School. He has held, or holds, distinguished or visiting professorships at New York University, the University of Michigan, the Institute of Management Development (Switzerland), the Helsinki School of Economics and Business Administration (Finland), Adelaide University (Australia), and the American College of Greece. He has been the recipient of many teaching distinctions, including the Professor of the Year award from the B.B.A. and E.M.B.A. programs at GWSB. He has published more than 50 academic articles and case studies and is the author of several books, including *The International Encyclopedia of Organizational Studies* (in press). He has designed and delivered hundreds of executive programs for firms such as Nestle, United Bank of Switzerland, Morgan Stanley, and Lucent Technologies. He is a frequent keynote speaker who has appeared on broadcast programs for the BBC and Fox News Network and whose work has been cited in outlets such as *Fortune, Forbes,* and *Business 2.0.* He currently serves as editor in chief of *Academy of Management Learning and Education.* He lives across from the National Zoo in Washington DC with his splendid wife; the couple is expecting their first child in August.

About the Contributors _____

Nancy J. Adler is Professor of International Management at McGill University in Montreal, Canada. She conducts research and consults on global leadership, cross-cultural management, and women as global leaders and managers. She has authored more than 100 articles and published four books: *International Dimensions of Organizational Behavior* (now in its fifth edition, with more than a half million copies in print in multiple languages), *Women in Management Worldwide, Competitive Frontiers: Women Managers in a Global Economy*, and *From Boston to Beijing: Managing With a Worldview*. She consults with global companies and government organizations on projects worldwide. Among numerous other awards, she has been honored as a fellow of the Academy of Management, the Academy of International Business, and the Royal Society of Canada. She has been honored as one of Canada's top university teachers. She is also an artist working primarily in watercolor and ink.

Jean M. Bartunek is Robert A. and Evelyn J. Ferris Chair and Professor of Organization Studies at Boston College. Her doctorate in social and organizational psychology is from the University of Illinois at Chicago. She is a fellow and a past president of the Academy of Management and is an associate editor of the *Journal of Applied Behavioral Science*. She has published more than 90 articles and book chapters and has authored or edited five books. Her most recent book (coedited with Mary Ann Hinsdale and James Keenan) is *Church Ethics and Its Organizational Context: Learning From the Sex Abuse Scandal in the Catholic Church* (2006).

Carrie A. Belsito is a doctoral candidate in the Department of Management of the Mays Business School at Texas A&M University. She received her B.S. (business administration/management) from California State University, Fresno. She currently teaches human resource management, and her research interests include the areas of strategic human resource management, discretion theory, organizational stigma, and business ethics.

Paul E. Bierly, III is Zane Showker Professor of Entrepreneurship and Director of the Center for Entrepreneurship at James Madison University.

His degrees include a B.S. and B.A.S. (University of Pennsylvania) and an M.B.A. and Ph.D. (Rutgers University). His primary research areas are management of technology, innovation, knowledge management, and strategic alliances. He has published more than 25 articles in *Strategic Management Journal, Academy of Management Executive, Journal of Management, IEEE Transactions on Engineering Management, Journal of Engineering and Technology Management, R&D Management, Journal of Organizational Change Management*, and numerous other management journals and books. He is on the executive committee of the Academy of Management, Technology and Innovation Management division, and is on the editorial board of *IEEE Transactions on Engineering Management* and *International Journal of Learning and Intellectual Capital*. Previously, he was an officer on a fast-attack nuclear submarine in the U.S. Navy's Nuclear Power Program, a manager at Johnson & Johnson, and a consultant for Princeton Economic Research.

Richard E. Boyatzis is Professor in the Departments of Organizational Behavior and Psychology at Case Western Reserve University and Adjunct Professor in Human Resources at ESADE in Barcelona, Spain. He was chief executive officer of McBer and Company for 11 years and chief operating officer of Yankelovich, Skelly, & White for 2 years. He is the author of more than 100 articles on behavior change, leadership, competencies, and emotional intelligence. His books include *The Competent Manager; Tansforming Qualitative Information* (in 2 languages); *Innovations in Professional Education: Steps on a Journey From Teaching to Learning* (with Scott Cowen and David Kolb); *Primal Leadership: Realizing the Power of Emotional Intelligence* (with Daniel Goleman and Annie McKee in 28 languages); and *Resonant Leadership: Renewing Yourself and Connecting With Others Through Mindfulness, Hope, and Compassion* (with Annie McKee in 16 languages). He has a B.S. in aeronautics and astronautics from the Massachusetts Institute of Technology (MIT) and an M.S. and Ph.D. in social psychology from Harvard University.

W. Warner Burke is Edward Lee Thorndike Professor of Psychology and Education and Coordinator of the Graduate Program in Social–Organizational Psychology in the Department of Organization and Leadership at Teachers College, Columbia University, and is Codirector of the Eisenhower Leadership Development Program in the U.S. Military Academy at West Point. He was the first executive director of the Organization Development (OD) Network. His consulting experience has been with a variety of organizations in business and industry, education, government, religion, and medical systems. A diplomat in industrial/organizational (I/O) psychology from the American Board of Professional Psychology, he is also a fellow of the Academy of Management, the Association of Psychological Science, and the Society of Industrial and Organizational Psychology as well as a past editor of both *Organizational*

Dynamics and *Academy of Management Executive*. His publications number more than 150, and his most recent book is *Organization Change: Theory and Practice*, 2nd Ed. (2007).

Robert Chia is Professor of Management at the University of Aberdeen Business School. He received his Ph.D. in organization studies from Lancaster University and publishes regularly in the leading international journals in organization and management studies. Prior to entering academia, he worked for 16 years in aircraft engineering and manufacturing management and was the group human resource manager, Asia Pacific, for a large U.K.-based multinational corporation. His research since entering academia after a successful career in industry has been focused on the enhancement of life chances through the systematic analysis and understanding of the guiding principles underlying the general economy of effort involved in wealth creation.

Stewart R. Clegg is Professor of Management at the University of Technology in Sydney, Australia, and is Director of ICAN (Innovative Collaborations, Alliances, and Networks) Research, a Key University Research Center. He completed his first degree at Aston University (1971) and completed his doctorate at the University of Bradford (1974). He holds chairs at Aston University, the University of Maastricht, and Vrije Universiteit. He has published extensively in many journals and is recipient of a number of best paper awards including the Academy of Management's George R. Terry Book Award. His most recent book is *Power and Organizations* (2007 with David Courpasson and Nelson Phillips) and *Managing and Organizations: An Introduction to Theory and Practice* (2008, with Martin Kornberger and Tyrone Pitsis).

Jay Conger holds the Henry Kravis Research Chair Professorship of Leadership at Claremont McKenna College. He is also a visiting professor of organizational behavior at the London Business School and a senior research scientist in the Center for Effective Organizations at the University of Southern California. The author of more than 90 articles and book chapters and of 12 books, he researches leadership, executive derailment, organizational change, boards of directors, and the training and development of leaders and managers. His more recent books include *The Practice of Leadership* (2006), *Growing Your Company's Leaders: How Organizations Use Succession Management for Competitive Advantage* (2003), *Shared Leadership* (2002), *Corporate Boards: New Strategies for Adding Value at the Top* (2001), *The Leader's Change Handbook* (1999), *Building Leaders* (1999), *Winning 'Em Over: A New Model for Management in the Age of Persuasion* (1998), and *Charismatic Leadership in Organizations* (1998). He received his B.A. from Dartmouth College, his M.B.A. from the University of Virginia, and his D.B.A. from the Harvard Business School.

Russell Cropanzano is Brien Lesk Professor of Organizational Behavior at the University of Arizona's Eller College of Management. His primary research areas include perceptions of organizational justice and the experience and impact of workplace emotion. He has edited four books, presented more than 60 papers, and published roughly 80 scholarly articles and chapters. In addition, he is a coauthor (with Robert Folger) of the book *Organizational Justice and Human Resources Management,* which won the 1998 Book Award from the International Association of Conflict Management. He was also a winner of the 2000 Outstanding Paper Award from *Consulting Psychology Journal.* He is currently editor of the *Journal of Management,* a fellow in the Society for Industrial/Organizational Psychology, and a representative-at-large for the Organizational Behavior division of the Academy of Management.

Arnoud De Meyer is Professor of Management Studies at Cambridge University (United Kingdom) and Director of the Judge Business School. He is also a fellow of Jesus College, Cambridge. Until August 2006, he was Akzo Nobel Fellow in Strategic Management and a professor of technology management at INSEAD, where he also assumed several management positions, including that of founding dean of INSEAD's Asia Campus in Singapore. His main research interests are in manufacturing and technology strategy, the implementation of new manufacturing technologies, and the management of research and development, and he has published widely in these areas. Recently, he has coauthored four books, on management and innovation in Asia, on the globalization of Asian firms, on management of novel projects, and on E-readiness in Europe. While serving as an academic, he has also acted as a consultant for a number of medium-sized and large companies throughout Europe and Asia.

Angelo S. DeNisi is Dean of the A. B. Freeman School of Business at Tulane University. After receiving his Ph.D. in industrial/organizational psychology from Purdue University, he taught at Kent State, the University of South Carolina, and Rutgers University before moving to Texas A&M University, where he was head of the Department of Management. He served as the editor of the *Academy of Management Journal* and as chair of both the Organizational Behavior and Human Resources divisions of the Academy of Management, and he is now vice president and program chair for the academy. He also served as president of the Society for Industrial and Organizational Psychology (SIOP). He has published in a wide variety of journals on topics that include performance appraisal and managing expatriates. He has served, or currently serves, on more than a dozen editorial boards and was the winner of the 2005 Distinguished Scientific Contribution Award from SIOP.

Laura Dunham is Assistant Professor of Entrepreneurship in the College of Business at the University of St. Thomas in St. Paul, Minnesota. Her research is in the area of entrepreneurship and ethics, with a specific focus on the ethical issues that arise during the start-up of new ventures and the role of entrepreneurial values in resource acquisition processes and outcomes. She received her Ph.D. from the Darden School of Business at the University of Virginia.

P. Christopher Earley is Dean of the National University of Singapore Business School and is Cycle and Carriage Professor of Management at the London Business School, where he is a former chair and professor of organizational behavior. His research interests include cross-cultural and international aspects of organizational behavior. His recent publications include *Cultural Intelligence: Individual Interactions Across Cultures* (with Soon Ang); *Face, Harmony, and Social Structure: An Analysis of Behavior in Organizations; Multinational Work Teams: A New Perspective* (with Cristina Gibson); and "Cultural Intelligence" (with Elaine Mosakowski) in *Harvard Business Review*.

Amy C. Edmondson, Novartis Professor of Leadership and Management and Chair of Doctoral Programs, joined the Harvard Business School faculty in 1996. Her research investigates leadership influences on learning and change in teams and organizations. In 2003, she received the Cummings Award from the Academy of Management, Organizational Behavior division, for outstanding achievement in early midcareer. Her recent article, "Why Hospitals Don't Learn From Failures: Organizational and Psychological Dynamics That Inhibit System Change" (with Anita Tucker), received the 2004 Accenture Award for a significant contribution to management practice. Before her academic career, she worked as the chief engineer for architect/inventor Buckminster Fuller during the early 1980s, and her book, *A Fuller Explanation*, clarifies Fuller's mathematical contributions for a nonscientific audience. She received her Ph.D. in organizational behavior, A.M. in psychology, and A.B. in engineering and design from Harvard University.

R. Edward Freeman is Elis and Signe Olsson Professor of Business Administration and Codirector of the Olsson Center for Applied Ethics in the Darden Graduate School of Business at the University of Virginia. He is an internationally recognized authority on stakeholder management—how to understand and manage the multiple changes and challenges in today's business environment—and on the connection between business ethics and corporate strategy. He has received numerous awards in recognition of outstanding teaching at the Wharton, Minnesota, and Darden business schools. In 2001, he was recognized with a Pioneer Lifetime Achievement Award by the World Resources Institute and the Aspen Institute Project on Corporate Responsibility.

Cynthia V. Fukami is Professor of Management in the Daniels College of Business at the University of Denver. She has conducted research and published articles on employee commitment, union attitudes, turnover, absenteeism, employee discipline, and total quality management. She was awarded the 1992 Willemssen Distinguished Research Professorship and was presented with the University of Denver's 1992 Distinguished Teaching Award. From 2000 to 2002, she was the Evelyn and Jay G. Piccinati Endowed Professor for Teaching Excellence. She has served on the board of directors (2 years as chair) of the Organizational Behavior Teaching Society and has been a member of the editorial boards of *Journal of Management Education* and *Academy of Management Learning and Education*. From 1998 to 1999, she was appointed as a scholar in the Carnegie Foundation's Academy for the Scholarship of Teaching and Learning and was named a fellow of the Carnegie Foundation for the Advancement of Teaching.

Dennis A. Gioia is Professor of Organizational Behavior, Department of Management and Organization, Smeal College of Business, Pennsylvania State University. Previously, he worked as an engineer for Boeing Aerospace at Cape Kennedy during the Apollo lunar program and for Ford Motor Company as corporate recall coordinator. His current research and writing interests focus on the ways in which identity, image, learning, and knowledge are involved in sensemaking, sensegiving, and organizational change. His work has appeared in *Academy of Management Executive, Academy of Management Journal, Academy of Management Review, Administrative Science Quarterly, Human Relations, Journal of Applied Behavioral Science, Journal of Business Ethics, Organizational Behavior and Human Decision Processes, Organizational Dynamics, Organization Science, Organization Studies,* and *Strategic Management Journal,* among other journals, as well as in numerous book chapters and proceedings. He also has edited two books of original contributions: *The Thinking Organization* and *Creative Action in Organizations.*

Barry M. Goldman is Associate Professor of Management and Policy in the Eller College of Management at the University of Arizona. His primary area of research involves dispute resolution and justice at work, particularly legal claiming. His current focus is on mediation of work-related disputes. He has published in *Academy of Management Journal, Journal of Applied Psychology, Personnel Psychology, Journal of Management,* and *Journal of Organizational Behavior,* among other outlets. He is on the editorial boards of *Journal of Applied Psychology, Journal of Management,* and *Negotiations and Conflict Management Research.* He teaches M.B.A. courses on negotiations and human resource management and doctoral seminars on those same subjects.

Robin Holt is a reader in strategy and ethics at the University of Liverpool Management School. He received his Ph.D. in Government from the London School of Economics. He has worked with both public and private sector organizations, and he has published in a range of social science journals. He has an abiding interest in bringing philosophical perspectives to bear on the prevailing and emerging questions and concerns of business life.

Robert Hooijberg is Professor of Organizational Behavior at the International Institute for Management Development (IMD) in Lausanne, Switzerland. His research, teaching, and consulting focus on leadership and

360-degree feedback, negotiations, team building, and organizational cul-
ture. His research has appeared in journals such as *Leadership Quarterly,
Journal of Management, Human Relations, Organization Science, Human
Resource Management, Hospital and Health Services Administration,
Journal of Applied Social Psychology, Journal of Management Education,
Administration & Society, International Journal of Organizational Analysis,*
and *Journal of Organizational Behavior.* He received his B.A. and M.A.
from the University of Nijmegen in the Netherlands and received his Ph.D.
from the University of Michigan.

Jennifer Jordan is Postdoctoral Research Fellow in the Tuck School of
Business at Dartmouth College. She received her doctorate in social psychology from Yale University. Her research interests include moral leadership, awareness, and decision making within the business domain. She
coedited (with Robert Sternberg) *A Handbook of Wisdom: Psychological
Perspectives.* She is also a 2004 recipient of the Yale University John F.
Enders Research Grant, a 2004 American Psychological Association
Dissertation Award, and the 2005 Academy of Management, Social Issues
in Management division, Best Dissertation Award.

Robert W. Kolodinsky is Assistant Professor of Management at James
Madison University. He did his doctoral work in organizational behavior
and human resources management at Florida State University. His primary
research interests include wisdom in organizations, ethics, leadership, spiritual issues in the workplace, social effectiveness and social influence
processes in organizations, and organizational politics. He has published
several book chapters and articles in journals such as *Journal of Management* and *Journal of Vocational Behavior,* and papers on which he was the
primary author have won best paper awards at two conferences. He also is
one of the primary instructors in the United Nations Demining Program's
Senior Managers Course, a 5-week program that enriches the management
skills of senior managers from countries struggling with the problems associated with land mine removal and civil unrest. He is a three-time small
business owner and a small business founder.

Paul R. Lawrence is Wallace Brett Donham Professor of Organizational
Behavior Emeritus at the Harvard Business School. He did undergraduate
work in sociology and economics at Albion College and did M.B.A. and doctoral training at Harvard. His research, published in 25 books and numerous articles, has dealt with the human aspects of management. His book,
Organization and Environment: Managing Differentiation and Integration
(coauthored with Jay Lorsch), added "contingency theory" to the vocabulary of students of organizational behavior. In 2002, he published *Driven:
How Human Nature Shapes Our Choices* (coauthored with Nitin Nohria),
a book that proposes a four-drive theory of human motivation based on the
biology of the brain.

Roy J. Lewicki is Dean's Distinguished Teaching Professor and Professor of Management and Human Resources in the Max M. Fisher College of Business at The Ohio State University. His research interests are in the areas of trust development, negotiation, and conflict management, and he is the author of numerous research articles and book chapters in these fields. He is probably best known for editing seven volumes of *Research on Negotiation in Organizations* and for his textbooks (*Negotiation, Essentials of Negotiation*, and *Negotiation: Readings, Exercises, and Cases*). He has authored or edited other books on intractable environmental disputes, organizational justice, and organizational change. He is the winner of the Academy of Management's Distinguished Educator Award and was the first winner of the David Bradford Award from the Organizational Behavior Teaching Society. He was the founding editor of *Academy of Management Learning and Education.*

Edwin A. Locke is Dean's Professor of Leadership and Motivation Emeritus in the R. H. Smith School of Business at the University of Maryland. He is a fellow of the Association for Psychological Science, the American Psychological Association, and the Academy of Management. He has been the recipient of the Distinguished Scientific Contribution Award (Society for Industrial/Organizational Psychology), the Career Achievement Award from the Academy of Management (Organizational Behavior division), the J. M. Cattell Award (American Psychological Society), and the Distinguished Scientific Contribution Award from the Academy of Management. He (with Gary Latham) has spent the past 40 years developing goal-setting theory, recently ranked No. 1 in importance among 73 management theories. He has published more than 275 books, chapters, articles, and notes and is internationally known for his research on motivation, job satisfaction, leadership, and other topics.

John McVea is Assistant Professor of Entrepreneurship in the College of Business at the University of St. Thomas in St. Paul, Minnesota. His research is in the areas of entrepreneurial strategy, managerial decision making, and entrepreneurial ethics. Currently, he is completing research in the area of decision making in ethically pioneering situations and is developing a number of entrepreneurial case studies from the Twin Cities area. He received his Ph.D. from the Darden School of Business at the University of Virginia.

Nigel Nicholson is Professor at London Business School, where he has held the positions of Chairman of the Department of Organizational Behavior, Research Dean, member of Governing Body, and Deputy Dean of the school. He is widely known for pioneering the introduction of the new science of evolutionary psychology to business. His current major research interests include the psychology of family business, personality and leadership, and people skills in management. In these fields, as well as in others such as innovation, organizational change, and executive career development, he has published more than 15 books and 200 articles. He has been a guest professor at German, American, and Australian universities and has been honored by the Academy of Management for his contribution to theory and research. He consults, coaches, and advises in all areas of his wide-ranging interests.

Tjai M. Nielsen is Assistant Professor of Management in the School of Business at The George Washington University (GWSB). He teaches in the full-time, part-time, and executive MBA programs and teaches research methods to GWSB doctoral students. His research primarily focuses on work team effectiveness, leadership development, and organizational citizenship. He recently received a *Best Reviewer Award* from the *Academy of Management* at its 2004 annual meeting. Currently, he serves on editorial boards for the *Journal of Organizational Behavior* and the journal, *Group & Organization Management*. Prior to joining GWSB, he spent more than three years working as a consultant for RHR International Company. In this role he provided consulting services in the areas of executive selection and development, succession planning, team development, and executive coaching. He has worked with a variety of organizations within the retail, financial, pharmaceutical, and utility industries in North America, Europe, and the Middle East.

Lynn R. Offermann is Professor of Industrial and Organizational Psychology at the George Washington University. Her research focuses on leadership and followership, teams, organizational processes and influence, and diversity issues. She is a fellow of the Society for Industrial and Organizational Psychology, the American Psychological Association, and the Association for Psychological Science. Her work has appeared in *Harvard Business Review, Journal of Applied Psychology, American Psychologist,* and *Academy of Management Journal,* among other outlets. She has worked with numerous public, private, multinational, and international organizations on executive development and coaching, team development, change management, and organizational development. She has trained and coached hundreds of managers from all over the world to improve their leadership effectiveness in multicultural contexts. She holds a Ph.D. in psychology from Syracuse University and is currently associate editor of *Academy of Management Learning and Education.*

Tyrone S. Pitsis is Senior Research Associate at the ICAN (Innovative Collaborations, Alliances, and Networks) Research Center (University of Technology, Sydney [UTS], Australia). His area of research interest is in the phenomenology of project-based interorganizational collaboration, pragmatic philosophy, and positive organizational scholarship. His work has appeared in both academic and industry journals such as *Organization Science, Organization Studies, Leadership Excellence,* and *Management* amongst others. He has also been recipient of best paper awards at international conferences. He lectures in executive leadership and in organizational behavior in the M.B.A. program within the School of Management at UTS, and also delivers leadership training and development programs to major corporations in Australia and Europe. He attained an honors degree in social science (psychology) from the University of New South Wales and attained his Ph.D. from UTS in 2006. He is member of the American Academy of Management and is a founding member of the Alliance Association of Australasia. In a previous life, he was an executive chef specializing in South-East Asian cuisine.

Jordan Stein is a doctoral candidate in the Department of Management and Organizations at the University of Arizona in Tucson. She previously received her master's in human resources and industrial relations from the University of Illinois at Urbana–Champaign. She has published in *Journal of Management*. Her current research focuses on organizational justice and conflict.

Robert J. Sternberg is Dean of Arts and Sciences at Tufts University. Prior to that, he was the IBM Professor of Psychology and Education in the Department of Psychology, a professor of management in the School of Management, and director of the Center for the Psychology of Abilities, Competencies, and Expertise at Yale University. He also was the 2003 president of the American Psychological Association. Sternberg is the author of more than 1,000 journal articles, book chapters, and books. The central focus of his research is on intelligence, creativity, and wisdom, and he also has studied love and close relationships as well as hate. He has been listed in *APA Monitor on Psychology* as one of the top 100 psychologists of the 20th century and is listed by the ISI as one of its most highly cited authors (top 0.5%) in psychology and psychiatry.

Eric Sundstrom is Professor at the University of Tennessee, Evaluator for the National Science Foundation, and an independent consultant. His research on the effectiveness of work environments, teams, and organizations has generated more than 70 professional publications, including two books (*Work Places* [1986] and *Supporting Work Team Effectiveness* [1999]) and articles in *Academy of Management Journal, Journal of Applied Psychology,* and more than a dozen other refereed journals. He has supervised more than 20 doctoral dissertations to completion and has served on another 80 or more doctoral and master's committees. He has provided consultation to private companies, such as AT&T, ALCOA, Chrysler Corporation, Exxon USA, Lockheed-Martin, M&M/Mars, Maraven (Venezuela), Nortel, PepsiCo, Rhône-Poulenc, United Technologies Corporation, and Weyerhaeuser, as well as to government organizations, such as the Tennessee Department of Human Services, National Institutes of Health, and U.S. Department of Energy.

Jordi Trullen is Assistant Professor in the Human Resource Management Department at ESADE Business School (Universitat Ramon Lull, Barcelona,

Spain). He holds an M.S. and Ph.D. in Organization Studies from the Wallace E. Carroll School of Management at Boston College and an M.B.A. from ESADE. His dissertation explored the role of faculty perceptions in mediating responses to quality evaluations at universities. His research interests include practical wisdom in management, organizational change and cognition, and design research as an approach to accomplishing change.

Peter B. Vaill is Professor of Management in Antioch University's Ph.D. program in Leadership and Change. He has served on the business school faculties at the University of California, Los Angeles (UCLA), the University of Connecticut, Stanford University, the University of St. Thomas, and George Washington University, where he also was dean of the School of Business and Public Management. His doctorate is from the Harvard Business School. He has been a consultant to many corporations, colleges and universities, health systems, and departments of the U.S. government. He is the author of *Managing as a Performing Art* (1989), *Learning as a Way of Being* (1996), *Spirited Leading and Learning* (1998), and many scholarly articles in the fields of managerial leadership and organization change and development. He is a member of the Academy of Management, the Organizational Behavior Teaching Society, and the Organization Development Network, which gave him its Lifetime Achievement Award in 2003.

Karl E. Weick is Rensis Likert Distinguished University Professor of Organizational Behavior and Psychology and Professor of Psychology at the University of Michigan. He joined the Michigan faculty in 1988 after previous faculty positions at the University of Texas, Cornell University, the University of Minnesota, and Purdue University. His B.A. is from Wittenberg University, and his M.A. and Ph.D. in social and organizational psychology are from the Ohio State University. He is a former editor of the journal *Administrative Science Quarterly* (1977–1985), a former associate editor of the journal *Organizational Behavior and Human Performance* (1971–1977), and a former topic editor for human factors at the journal *Wildfire*. His research interests include collective sensemaking under pressure, medical errors, handoffs and transitions in dynamic events, high-reliability performance, improvisation, and continuous change.